DATE DUE

SEP 3 0 1988	RETURNED FEB 02 1992 JAN 03 1992
RETURNED OCT 2 9 1988 OCT 15 1988	RETURNED MAY 1 1 1992 APR 0 9 1992
NOV 1 6 1988 RETURNED DEC 0 9 1988 NOV 2 2 1988	RETURNED JUL 2 3 1993 JUN 2 8 1993
RETURNED JAN 1 1 1989 JAN 0 7 1989	RETURNED DEC 1 9 1996 JAN 2 1 1997
RETURNED JAN 1 5 1990 JAN 0 9 1990	DEC 0 3 1997
RETURNED SEP 0 9 1990 AUG 1 4 1990	JAN 2 6 1998 SEP 2 1 1999
RETURNED DEC 2 4 1990 DEC 2 8 1990	RETURNED SEP 1 1 2000 RETURNED OCT 0 2 2001

Parallel Program Design

A Foundation

K. Mani Chandy

Jayadev Misra

University of Texas at Austin

ADDISON-WESLEY PUBLISHING COMPANY

Reading, Massachusetts • Menlo Park, California • New York
Don Mills, Ontario • Wokingham, England • Amsterdam
Bonn • Sydney • Singapore • Tokyo • Madrid • San Juan

Library of Congress Cataloging-in-Publication Data

Chandy, K. Mani.
    Parallel program design : a foundation / by K. Mani Chandy and
Jayadev Misra.
        p.   cm.
    ISBN 0-201-05866-9   :
    1. Parallel programming (Computer science)   I. Misra, Jayadev.
II. Title.
QA76.6.C42818 1988   87-26124
004'.35--dc19   CIP

ABCDEFGHIJ-HA-898

To our families

Jean	Mamata
Christa	Amitav
Mani	Anuj
Chandy	Sashibhusan
Rebecca	Shanty

"The most general definition of beauty. . .
Multeity in Unity."

Samuel Taylor Coleridge
On the Principles of Genial Criticism (1814)

Foreword

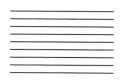

A complete theory of programming includes

1. A method for specification of programs which permits individual requirements to be clearly stated and combined.

2. A method of reasoning about specifications, which aids in elucidation and evaluation of alternative designs.

3. A method of developing programs together with a proof that they meet their specification.

4. A method of transforming programs to achieve high efficiency on the machines available for their execution.

It is not often that we can welcome the advent of a new theory of programming. Twelve years ago, E.W. Dijkstra published his *Discipline of Programming*, which is still a definitive source-book on the development of sequential algorithms. And now Chandy and Misra have shown how Dijkstra's methods, and other more recent developments, can be generalized to distributed and concurrent algorithms. Their work deserves the warmest welcome.

This book treats all essential aspects of the theory of programming. The underlying logic is developed with elegance and rigour. It is illustrated by clear exposition of many simple examples. It is then applied, with matching elegance and simplicity, to a range of examples which have hitherto justified a reputation of baffling complexity. The authors' technique and style are worthy of imitation by all who publish descriptions of distributed algorithms.

The book will be studied with enjoyment and profit by many classes of computing scientists. Teachers will welcome it as a text for an advanced class on programming. Software engineers will use it as a handbook of methods and algorithms for the design of distributed systems. And theoreticians will find a rich source of research ideas that promise to be of relevance in the professional activity of programming.

C. A. R. Hoare

Our Prejudices about Programs, Architectures, and Applications

Goal

The thesis of this book is that the unity of the programming task transcends differences between the architectures on which programs can be executed and the application domains from which problems are drawn. Our goal is to show how programs can be developed systematically for a variety of architectures and applications. The foundation, on which program development is based, is a simple theory: a model of computation and an associated proof system.

Architectures

The architectures considered cover a wide spectrum, including sequential machines, synchronous and asynchronous shared-memory multiprocessor systems, and message-based distributed systems. We propose that there is a continuum from the design of programs to the design of electronic circuits. We also derive programs for fault-tolerant systems in the same way we derive programs for fault-free systems.

Application Areas

We develop programs in a uniform manner for a variety of application areas. Many of the problems considered here appeared initially as operating systems problems, including termination detection of asynchronous programs, garbage collection, and conflict resolution in parallel systems. However, programmers who write so-called "application" programs for execution on parallel architectures are also concerned with these problems—for instance, detecting the termination of a distributed application program is not always a trivial task. We also develop programs for combinatorial problems (shortest path, sorting, combinatorial search, etc.), matrix problems, and communication protocols.

Program Development

This book is based on a small theoretical foundation that is applied to all problems. The theory, which uses elementary mathematics, is described in the first few chapters. A continuum of solutions is developed for each problem, starting with simple programs, i.e., programs with relatively simple proofs. The specifications and proofs are refined to obtain efficient programs for various classes of target architectures.

A small number of heuristics is suggested to refine specifications and programs. Methods to compose larger programs from smaller ones are also suggested. The theory and the heuristics are the unifying framework for the book.

There are many ways to develop programs and even more ways to write books about them. When we began working on this book we were faced with several alternatives. The choices we made, and our reasons for doing so, are described next. Each alternative had some merit. Ultimately our choices were made on the basis of personal preference. By describing the alternatives and our choices, we hope to give the reader an idea of what sort of book this is—and equally important, what sort of book this is not.

Choices in a Study of Programming

Design versus Coding

A conventional view of programming is that given a specification, a programmer produces code and then proves that the code meets the specification. A book based on this view emphasizes programming languages and proofs of program texts. This book, by contrast, is about the *design* of programs. A design consists of a series of small decisions, each dealing with a manageable set of concerns. The larger part of program design is concerned with the stepwise refinement of specifications; the production of code is postponed until the final stages. Therefore the emphasis here is on a model of computation, a notation for specifications, and a theory for proving the correctness of specifications. Much of this book deals with the notation and proofs of *designs*; programming languages and proofs of program texts are accorded only secondary importance. The derivation of a program (in any programming language) from the final specification should be the most mechanical and least creative part of programming.

Taxonomy versus Foundation

There are several paradigms for the development of science. On the one hand, theoretical physics attempts to find the fundamental laws that explain all physical phenomena; the smaller the number of laws, the better. On the other hand, much of experimental botany is concerned with observing, classifying, and describing what exists. In writing this book we were faced with the choice either of attempting to propose a foundation for parallel programming and then applying it to a variety of problems, or of observing, classifying, and describing programs and architectures. Certainly, there is a great deal of interest in program and machine taxonomy. There are categories of machines (sequential machines, single-instruction-multiple-data machines, multiple-instruction-multiple-data machines, etc.), categories of systems (message-based, shared-variable-based, synchronous, asynchronous, etc.), categories of programming styles (functional, logic, imperative, object-oriented, etc.) and categories of applications (operating systems, communication protocols, expert systems, etc.). The advantage of the observation-classification-description paradigm is that it gives the reader a comprehensive description of what exists; very little is left out. Furthermore, it suggests a solution strategy: Given a problem, one looks for the categories that the problem falls into and uses solutions that have proved successful. Finally, a careful taxonomy is guaranteed to be useful. Nevertheless, we have chosen the riskier option of proposing a small foundation and basing our book on it. Our reason is subjective. Today programming appears to be fragmented into increasingly esoteric subdisciplines, each with its priests, acolytes, and incantations. We believe that there is a unity underlying all programming; we hope to contribute to its appreciation.

Choice of Foundation

There seems to be some consensus in physics as to which laws are fundamental: The fundamental laws are those from which all others are derived. In programming, the choice of a foundation—the computational model and proof system—is less clear-cut. The Turing Machine is not our model of choice, though it is a basic model, because it is inappropriate for our purposes—the development of programs. We have a strong personal preference, however, for making do with less (when it comes to computational models). Therefore we have attempted to design a computational model and associated theory with the smallest number of concepts adequate for our purposes.

There are alternatives to our approach of applying a small theory to a wide range of problems. A notation (and an associated theory) rich in expressive power can be used, or many theories can be proposed—an appropriate one for each problem area. Employing rich notations and several theories has advantages, the most obvious of which is that a skillful choice of theory in solving a problem may result in an elegant solution. Our choice of a small theory is based on our desire to explore the unity of all program development. We are willing to pay the price of less elegant solutions for the advantage of a unified framework.

Formal versus Informal Descriptions of Programs

Programs, especially parallel programs, are often described informally. Problems, such as that of the dining philosophers, are posed and solved without using a formal notation. There are advantages to informal descriptions. A problem can be studied without the baggage of a formal notation and proof system. Also, word pictures such as philosophers sitting around a table sending forks to one another are vivid and helpful. We have attempted to take advantage of the benefits that informal reasoning has to offer, but we have chosen to employ a formal notation.

In our choice of programming notation, we limited ourselves to one that *we* could handle mathematically. We limited our expressive power in this way because we are fallible as programmers, and we hope that the use of mathematics will make us less so. We have been amazed at the errors we have made in informal arguments. Programs that seemed so obviously correct at one time are, in retrospect, so obviously wrong. It is humility as programmers that drives us to seek formalism and mathematics. We are fallible as mathematicians as well, of course, but the discipline helps.

Our desire for a simple unifying framework has led to a restricted notation. Restricting concepts to a small, mathematically manageable set has resulted in our not exploring some interesting avenues of research. For instance, we are afraid of self-modifying rule-based systems—in which new rules are added as computation proceeds—because we do not know how to construct proofs for such systems.

Operational versus Nonoperational Reasoning about Programs

One can reason about the unfolding computations of a program (this is called operational reasoning) or one can focus, as much as possible, on static aspects (such as invariants) of the program. We favor the static view here for three reasons. First, we made more mistakes when we used operational reasoning— for example, a common mistake is forgetting to consider certain sequences of events that could occur. Second, we have found it hard to convince skeptics about the correctness of our programs by using operational arguments. (We speak from our experience in teaching distributed systems to many students who are, quite properly, skeptics. Inevitably, a student asks, "But, you don't seem to have considered the case where B follows C which follows D which...?" Operational arguments have reduced us to saying, after fielding several such questions, "Check it out for yourself and you'll see that it is okay.") Third, our operational arguments tend to be longer.

Operational reasoning has value. Again, being very subjective, we have found that the flash of insight that sparks the creation of an algorithm is often based on operational, and even anthropomorphic, reasoning. Operational reasoning by itself, however, has gotten us into trouble often enough that we are afraid of relying on it exclusively. Therefore we reason formally about properties of a program, using predicates about *all* states that may occur during execution of the program.

The Medium versus the Message

The message of this book is that a small theory—a computation model and its associated proof system—is adequate for program design in a variety of application areas and for a variety of architectures. The medium in which this message is couched is a (small amount of) notation to express the programs and their properties. We found that we could not express our ideas without introducing some notation. However, *this book is not about a programming language*. We have paid no attention to several important aspects of programming languages (such as data structures) and little attention to others (such as abstraction mechanisms). We wish to emphasize the message; that is, the theory. We have attempted to write a book that is useful to programmers no matter what programming language they employ. It is our hope that programmers will benefit from our theory for developing programs written in languages of their choice.

Choice of Material

The grandeur of our vision is constrained by the limitation of our ability (and also by the practical necessity of having to finish this book). We have not done everything we wanted to do. In our choice of architectures and applications we have attempted to demonstrate the unity of the programming task. However, we have not given some architectures the space they deserve, and we have omitted some application areas altogether—a situation we hope to remedy in future editions. For instance, designs of electronic circuits and fault-tolerant systems do not receive the attention they deserve. A significant omission is real-time systems. Other significant omissions include the study of complexity models such as NC and different modal logics appropriate for reasoning about parallel programs.

The Bibliography at the end of the book is far from exhaustive. Many of the references are books and survey papers that point to large lists of references and the original sources.

Reading this Book

Who Should Read It?

This book is for those interested in program design and computer architecture. The ideas have been used, and are being used, to teach an introductory (i.e., first-semester) graduate course, and a more advanced, second-semester course in computer science. However, the reader should be warned that the view of program design taken here is somewhat idiosyncratic; the contents do not exactly match the subject matter of a standard course in a standard curriculum. We hope that this preface gives readers some idea of our prejudices, which should help them decide whether to continue reading.

Few prerequisites are needed to read the book. It is based on a small theory that is described in Chapters 3 and 7. The theory employs elementary mathematics including the predicate calculus.

The sources of the example problems are not described in detail. For instance, in describing garbage collection, the origins of the problem in memory management are described with more brevity than in most programming textbooks. Problems are specified formally, so there is little likelihood that the reader will misunderstand them; however, the reader who is not aware of the problems may not appreciate their practical significance. Thus readers should have some maturity in programming or should believe the authors that the problems studied here are genuine.

How to Read It

Read this preface! Here we confess our prejudices, and readers whose prejudices don't match ours are best forewarned.

Most of the sections in this book contain both informal and formal parts. The informal part is an English description with little formal notation. The formal part contains the specifications, programs, and proofs employing the notation presented in Chapters 2, 3, and 7. A reader can learn the main ideas of a chapter by reading all the informal parts and skipping the formal ones. A reader who wishes to obtain all the ideas in a chapter should read it in sequence: The informal part describes what is coming in the next formal part. There are a couple of other ways of reading this book that have proved helpful, depending on the reader's facility with formalisms. One is to read all the informal parts before reading the entire chapter in sequence. The other is to read the informal part and then carry out the derivation in the formal parts oneself, treating each formal section as a worked-out exercise; this is the best way to read the book because it requires the active participation of the reader.

We recommend that the first five chapters be read sequentially; these chapters present the theory and apply it to one example in detail. Chapter 6— "Toy Examples"—illustrates the theory; the reader can pick and choose among these examples. Chapter 7 presents a theory for constructing large programs by composing small ones. Chapter 8 considers a special case of this theory, for the construction of process networks. Chapters 9 through 16 describe operating systems problems; the later chapters in this sequence are based on earlier ones. Chapters 17 and 18 deal with fault-tolerant systems. The next two chapters deal with combinatorial problems—sorting and combinatorial-search strategies. Chapter 21 deals with algorithms for systolic arrays. In Chapter 22, different programming styles—sequential, functional, logical—are contrasted with the style adopted in this book; the chapter also includes the rationale for some of the design decisions of our theory. In the epilog, we give some random thoughts on programming. The initial four chapters and Chapter 7 are necessary for understanding the later ones; the remaining chapters are largely independent and may be read in any order.

A first-level graduate course can be designed around the first five chapters plus one chapter each on combinatorics, operating systems, fault tolerance, and systolic arrays.

Acknowledgments

Our ideas about programming have been deeply influenced by arguments and discussions over a period of years with Edsger W. Dijkstra. Detailed and generous criticism by C. A. R. Hoare helped us understand some of the implications of our work; we are especially indebted to him for his insistence on the importance of designing as opposed to coding, and of proofs of specifications as opposed to proofs of programs. We are thankful to our graduate students, in many sections of CS380D and CS390D at The University of Texas at Austin and in CS131 at Caltech, and the members of the reading course 6.893 at MIT, who have suggested valuable technical and editorial improvements; special thanks go to Alan Fekete, Edgar Knapp, and Mark Staskauskas. Interactions with various individuals in the Concurrent Programming Institute (held under the auspices of The University of Texas Year of Programming, March 2–6, 1987, Austin, Texas) clarified several cloudy issues. We are grateful to the following individuals and groups, who have commented on our work and the earlier drafts of this book: K. R. Apt, the Austin Tuesday Afternoon Club, Manfred Broy, The Eindhoven Tuesday Afternoon Club, Allen Emerson, He Ji Feng, Ira Forman, A. J. M. van Gasteren, M. Gouda, David Gries, Rick Hehner, Ted Herman, Hank Korth, Ben Kuipers, Simon Lam, Chris Lengauer, M. D. McIlroy, Al Mok, Ben Moszkowski, Avi Silberschatz, and Chuck Seitz. We are especially indebted to Nissim Francez, Leslie Lamport, Amir Pnueli, and Jan L. A. van de Snepscheut, for their constructive criticisms. We are grateful to the following reviewers for their detailed comments: Bruce Arden, University of Rochester; Stephen Garland, MIT Laboratory for Computer Science; Maurice Herlihy, Carnegie-Mellon University; Nancy Lynch, Massachusetts Institute of Technology; Alain Martin, California Institute of Technology; Fred B. Schneider, Cornell University; Ken Sevcik, University of Toronto; and William Weihl, MIT Laboratory for Computer Science. Thanks also to Bob Comer for his implementation of our notation on an IBM PC.

Over the years we have received generous research grants for this work from the Air Force Office of Scientific Research and the Office of Naval Research; we are thankful for their continuing confidence. IBM supported the early work in this area and we are especially grateful to Fred May of the Austin Division for his help.

Special thanks go to Nancy Lawler for her outstanding editorial and production skills; this book would not have been possible without her assistance. We are also thankful to Debra Davis, Julie Barrow, and Mary Ghaleb, who typed various portions of the manuscript.

It is a particular pleasure to acknowledge the help of the editorial staff at Addison-Wesley.

Austin, Texas   K. M. C.
                                                                          J. M.

Contents

3. A Programming Logic   39

4. Architectures and Mappings   81

5. The First Case Study: Shortest Path   97

6. Toy Examples   117

7. Program Structuring   153

8. Communicating Processes   173

9. Termination Detection   205

10. Global Snapshots   253

11. Stability Detection   269

12. Dining Philosophers   289

13. Drinking Philosophers   313

14. Committee Coordination   333

15. Mutual Exclusion   359

CHAPTER 1

Parallelism and Programming: A Perspective

1.1   The Unity of the Programming Task

This book is about parallel programs; it is primarily about programs and secondarily about parallelism. The diversity of architectures and consequent programming constructs (such as send and receive, await, fork and join) must be placed in the proper perspective with respect to the unity of the programming task. By emphasizing the differences, we are in danger of losing sight of the similarities. The central thesis here is that the unity of the programming task is of primary importance; the diversity is secondary.

The basic problem in programming is the management of complexity. We cannot address that problem as long as we lump together concerns about the core problem to be solved, the language in which the program is to be written, and the hardware on which the program is to execute. Program development should begin by focusing attention on the problem to be solved, postponing considerations of architecture and language constructs.

Some argue that in cases where language and hardware are specified as part of a problem, concerns about the core problem, language, and hardware are inseparable. For instance, programs executing on a distributed network of computers must employ some form of message passing; in such cases concerns about message passing appear inseparable from concerns about the core problem. Similarly, since the presence or absence of primitives for process creation and termination in the programming language influences the program, it appears that language is inseparable from other issues. Despite such arguments, we maintain that it is not only possible but important to separate these concerns; indeed it is especially important to do so for parallel programs because they are less well understood than sequential programs.

Twenty-five years ago, many programs were designed to make optimum use of some specific feature of the hardware. Programs were written to exploit a particular machine-language command or the number of bits in a computer word. Now we know that such optimizations are best left to the last stages of program design, or best left out altogether. Parallel programs today are designed much as sequential programs were designed in the 1950s: to exploit the message-passing primitives of a language or the network-interconnection structure of an architecture. A quarter-century of experience tells us that it is best to postpone such optimizations until the very end of program development. We now know that a physicist who wishes to use the computer to study some phenomenon in plasma physics, for instance, should not begin by asking whether communicating sequential processes or shared memory is to be used, any more than whether the word size is 32 or 60 bits. Such questions have their place, but concerns must be separated. The first concern is to design a solution to the problem; a later one is to implement the solution in a given language on a particular architecture. Issues of performance on a specific architecture should be considered, but only at the appropriate time.

Programs outlive the architectures for which they were designed initially. A program designed for one machine will be called upon to execute efficiently on quite dissimilar architectures. If program designs are tightly coupled to the machines of today, program modifications for future architectures will be expensive. Experience suggests that we should anticipate requests to modify our programs to keep pace with modifications in architecture—witness attempts to parallelize sequential programs. It is prudent to design a program for a flexible abstract model of a computer with the intent of tailoring the program to suit future architectures.

An approach to exploiting new architectural features is to add features to the computational model. A baroque abstract model of a computer, however, only adds to the complexity of programming. On the other hand, simple models such as the Turing Machine do not provide the expressive power needed for program development. What we desire is a model that both is simple and has the expressive power necessary to permit the refinement of specifications and programs to suit target architectures.

Our emphasis on the unity of the programming task departs from the current view of programming. Currently programming is fragmented into subdisciplines, one for each architectural form. Asynchronous distributed computing, in which component processes interact by messages, is considered irrelevant to synchronous parallel computing. Systolic arrays are viewed as hardware devices, and hence traditional ideas of program development are deemed inapplicable to their design.

The goal of this book is to show how programs can be developed systematically for a variety of architectures and applications. A possible criticism is that this fundamental premise is wrong because programmers should not be concerned with architecture—compilers should. Some styles of programming (e.g., functional and logic programming) are preferred precisely because architecture is not their concern. Our response to this criticism is twofold. First, programmers who are not concerned with architecture should not have to concern themselves with it: They should stop early in the program-development process with a program that may or may not map efficiently to the target architecture. Second, some problems require programmers to be concerned with architecture either because the problem specifies the architecture (e.g., the design of a distributed command and control system) or because performance is critical. For these problems the refinement process is continued until efficient programs for the target architectures are obtained.

1.2   A Search for a Foundation of Parallel Programming

We seek a simple theory that applies to programming for a wide range of architectures and applications. The issues that we consider central to such a theory are nondeterminism, absence of control flow, synchrony/asynchrony, states and assignments, proof systems that support program development by stepwise refinement of specifications, and the decoupling of correctness from complexity, i.e., of programs from architectures. Each of these issues is elaborated on next.

1.2.1 Nondeterminism

How can we develop programs for a variety of architectures through a series of refinements? *By specifying program execution at an appropriate level of detail: Specify little in the early stages of design, and specify enough in the final stages to ensure efficient executions on target architectures.* Specifying little about program execution means that our programs may be nondeterministic. Different runs of the same program may execute statements in different orders, consume different amounts of resources, and even produce different results.

Nondeterminism is useful in two ways. First, it is employed to derive simple programs, where simplicity is achieved by avoiding unnecessary determinism; such programs can be optimized by limiting the nondeterminism, i.e., by disallowing executions unsuitable for a given architecture. Second, some systems (e.g., operating systems and delay-insensitive circuits) are inherently nondeterministic; programs that represent such systems have to employ some nondeterministic constructs.

1.2.2 Absence of Control Flow

The notion of sequential control flow is pervasive in computing. Turing Machines and von Neumann computers are examples of sequential devices. Flow charts and early programming languages were based on the sequential flow of control. Structured programming retained sequential control flow and advocated problem decomposition based on the sequencing of tasks. The prominence of sequential control flow is partly due to historical reasons. Early computing devices and programs were understood by simulating their executions sequentially. Many of the things we use daily, such as recipes and instructions for filling out forms, are sequential; this may have influenced programming languages and the abstractions used in program design.

The introduction of co-routines was an indication that some programs are better understood through abstractions unrelated to control flow. A program structured as a set of processes is a further refinement: It admits multiple sequential flows of control. However, processes are viewed as *sequential* entities— note the titles of two classic papers in this area, "Cooperating Sequential

Processes" in Dijkstra [1968] and "Communicating Sequential Processes" in Hoare [1978]. This suggests that sequential programming is the norm, and parallelism, the exception.

Control flow is not a unifying concept. Programs for different architectures employ different forms of control flow. Program design at early stages should not be based on considerations of control flow, which is a later concern. It is easier to restrict the flow of control in a program having few restrictions than to remove unnecessary restrictions from a program having too many.

The issue of control flow has clouded several other issues. Let us review one. Modularity is generally accepted as a good thing. What is a module? It implements a set of related concerns, it has a clean, narrow interface, and the states of a system when control flows into and out of the module are specified succinctly. Now a clean, narrow interface is one issue and control flow into and out of a module is another. Why not separate them? In our program model, we retain the concept of a module as a part of a program that implements a set of related concerns. Yet we have no notion of control flow into and out of a module. Divorcing control flow from module construction results in an unconventional view of modules and programming—though a useful one, we believe, for the development of parallel programs.

1.2.3 Synchrony and Asynchrony

Synchronous and asynchronous events are at the core of any unified theory of parallel programming. For instance, all events in a systolic array are synchronous: At each clock tick all processors in the array carry out a computational step. On the other hand, a data network spanning the globe has no common clock; processes at different nodes of the network execute steps asynchronously. Some systems have synchronous components interconnected by asynchronous channels; an example of such a system is an electronic circuit consisting of synchronous subcircuits interconnected by wires with arbitrary delays. Partitioning systems into synchronous and asynchronous varieties is artificial; a theory should include synchrony and asynchrony as fundamental concepts.

1.2.4 States and Assignments

A formal model employed by computing scientists, control theorists, communication engineers, circuit designers, and operations researchers, among others, is the state-transition system. Computing scientists use state-transition models in studying formal languages. Control theorists represent the systems they study as continuous or discrete state-transition models; a typical control problem is to determine an optimal trajectory in a state space. Markov processes, employed by communication engineers and operations researchers, are state-transition systems. Communication engineers represent communication protocols as state-transition systems. Physical systems are often described in terms of state transitions. Therefore it appears reasonable to us to propose a unifying theory of parallel programming based on state-transition systems; indeed, we hope that the theory will be helpful to engineers and natural scientists as well as programmers. However, treating a program as a state-transition system—a set of states, an initial state, and a state-transition function—offers little for a methodology of program development. Too much of the semantics of a problem is lost when the problem is represented as a set of states and transitions. Therefore we wish to employ the theory of state-transition systems while enjoying the representational advantages of programming languages. One way to do so is to employ variables and assignments in the notation.

A starting point for the study of assignments is the following quotation from Backus [1978][†]

> The assignment statement splits programming into two worlds. The first world comprises the right sides of assignment statements. This is an orderly world of expressions, a world that has useful algebraic properties (except that those properties are often destroyed by side effects). It is the world in which most useful computation takes place.
>
> The second world of conventional programming languages is the world of statements. The primary statement in that world is the assignment statement itself. All the other statements of the language exist in order to make it possible to perform a computation that must be based on this primitive construct: the assignment statement.
>
> This world of statements is a disorderly one, with few useful mathematical properties. Structured programming can be seen as a modest effort to introduce some order into this chaotic world, but it accomplishes little in attacking the fundamental problems created by the word-at-a-time von Neumann style of programming, with its primitive use of loops, subscripts, and branching flow of control.

One cannot but agree that disorderly programming constructs are harmful. But there *is* an orderly world of assignments. The problems of imperative programming can be avoided while retaining assignments.

Word-at-a-time Bottleneck

Multiple assignments allow assignments to several variables simultaneously; these variables may themselves be complex structures.

[†]Reprinted by permission of the publisher, Copyright 1978, Association for Computing Machinery, Inc.

Control Flow

Assignment can be divorced from control flow. We propose a program model that has assignments but no control flow.

Mathematical Properties

A program model based on assignments and without control flow has remarkably nice properties.

1.2.5 Extricating Proofs from Program Texts

One way to prove the correctness of a sequential program is to annotate its text with predicates; the proof consists of demonstrating that a predicate holds whenever program control is at the corresponding point in the program text—thus the proof is inextricably intertwined with the program text. We seek a proof system that allows the proof to be extricated from the program text, allowing us to develop and study a proof in its own right.

Much of program development in our methodology consists of refining specifications, i.e., adding detail to specifications. Given a problem specification, we begin by proposing a general solution strategy. Usually the strategy is broad, admitting many solutions. Next we give a specification of the solution strategy and prove that this strategy (as specified) solves the problem (as specified). When we consider a specific set of target architectures, we may choose to narrow the solution strategy, which means refining the specification further. At each stage of strategy refinement, the programmer is obliged to prove that the specification proposed indeed refines a specification proposed at an earlier step. The construction of a program is begun only after the program has been specified in extensive detail. Usually the proof that a program fits the detailed specification is straightforward because much of the work associated with proofs is carried out in earlier stages of stepwise refinement. We seek methods of specification and proof that do not require a skeleton of the program text to be proposed until the final stages of design. This differs from conventional sequential-program development, where it is quite common to propose a skeleton of the program text early in the design, and where refinement of a specification proceeds hand in hand with the addition of flesh to the program skeleton.

1.2.6 Separation of Concerns: Correctness and Complexity

A point of departure of our work from the conventional view of programming is this: We attempt to decouple a program from its implementation. A program can be implemented in many different ways: For example, a program may be implemented on different architectures; even for a given computer, it may be executed according to different schedules. The correctness of a program is independent of the target architecture and the manner in which the program is executed; by contrast, the efficiency of a program execution depends on the architecture and manner of execution. Therefore we do not associate complexity measures with a program but rather with a program *and a mapping* to a target computer. A mapping is a description of how programs are to be executed on the target machine and a set of rules for computing complexity measures for programs when executed on the given target machine. Given a specification and a target architecture, a programmer's task is to derive a program with its proof, select a mapping that maps programs to the given target architecture, and then evaluate complexity measures.

The operational model of a program (how a computer executes a program) is straightforward for programs written in conventional sequential-imperative languages, such as PASCAL, executing on conventional sequential machines. Indeed, many sequential-imperative languages (so-called von Neumann languages) have been designed so that the manner in which von Neumann machines execute programs, written in these languages, is self-evident. The complexity measures (i.e., metrics of efficiency) of a program written in such a language are the amounts of resources, such as time and memory, required to execute the program on a von Neumann architecture. Usually, when computing scientists refer to complexity measures of a program, they implicitly assume a specific operational model of a specific architecture; in most cases the architecture is the traditional, sequential architecture, and its abstract model is the Random Access Machine (RAM).

The tradition of tightly coupling programming notation to architecture, inherited from von Neumann languages and architectures, has been adopted in parallel programming as well. For instance, programmers writing in Communicating Sequential Processes (CSP) notation usually have a specific architecture in mind, such as an architecture that consists of a set of von Neumann computers that communicate by means of message passing.

In this book, the correctness of programs (see Chapter 3) is treated as a topic separate from architectures and mappings (see Chapter 4). A brief discussion of mappings is included in Section 1.3.

1.3   Introduction to the Theory

We introduce a theory—a computational model and a proof system—called UNITY, after the way in which we choose to view our programs: Unbounded Nondeterministic Iterative Transformations. In the interest of brevity, the phrase "a UNITY program" is preferred to "a program in unbounded non-deterministic iterative transformation notation." We are not proposing a programming language, but do adopt the minimum notational machinery to illustrate our ideas about programming. This section is incomplete, even as introductions go. A thorough description of notation and proof rules appears in the next two chapters.

1.3.1 UNITY Programs

A program consists of a declaration of variables, a specification of their initial values, and a set of multiple-assignment statements. A program execution starts from any state satisfying the initial condition and goes on forever; in each step of execution some assignment statement is selected nondeterministically and executed. Nondeterministic selection is constrained by the following "fairness" rule: Every statement is selected infinitely often.

Our model of programs is simple, and in fact may appear too simple for effective programming. We show that the model is adequate for the development of programs in general and parallel programs in particular. We now give an informal and very incomplete description of how this model addresses some of the issues described in Section 1.2.

1.3.2 Separating Concerns: Programs and Implementations

A UNITY program describes *what* should be done in the sense that it specifies the initial state and the state transformations (i.e., the assignments). A UNITY program does not specify precisely *when* an assignment should be executed—the only restriction is a rather weak fairness constraint: Every assignment is executed infinitely often. Neither does a UNITY program specify *where* (i.e., on which processor in a multiprocessor system) an assignment is to be executed, nor to which process an assignment belongs. Also, a UNITY program does not specify *how* assignments are to be executed or *how* an implementation may halt a program execution.

UNITY separates concerns between *what* on the one hand, and *when*, *where*, and *how* on the other. The *what* is specified in a program, whereas the *when*, *where*, and *how* are specified in a mapping. By separating concerns in this way, a simple programming notation is obtained that is appropriate for a wide variety of architectures. Of course, this simplicity is achieved at the expense of making mappings immensely more important and more complex than they are in traditional programs.

1.3.3 Mapping Programs to Architectures

In this section, we give a brief outline of mappings of UNITY programs to several architectures. We consider the von Neumann architecture, synchronous shared-memory multiprocessors, and asynchronous shared-memory multiprocessors. The description given here is sufficient for understanding how the example programs of Section 1.4 are executed on various architectures. The subject of mapping is treated in more detail in Chapter 4. Though we describe mappings from UNITY programs to architectures, UNITY programs can also be mapped to programs in conventional programming languages.

A mapping to a von Neumann machine specifies the schedule for executing assignments and the manner in which a program execution terminates. The implementation of multiple assignments on sequential machines is straightforward and is not discussed here. We propose a mapping in which an execution schedule is represented by a finite sequential list of assignments in which each assignment in the program appears at least once. The computer repeatedly executes this list of assignments forever (but see the discussion later in this section). We are obliged to prove that the schedule is fair, i.e., that every assignment in the program is executed infinitely often. Since every assignment appears at least once in the list, and since the list is executed forever, it follows that every assignment is executed infinitely often.

Given that a UNITY program execution does not terminate, how do we represent traditional programs whose executions do terminate (in the traditional sense)? We regard termination as a feature of an implementation. A cleaner theory is obtained by distinguishing program execution—an infinite sequence of statement executions—from implementation—a finite prefix of the sequence.

A state of a program is called a *fixed point* if and only if execution of any statement of the program, in this state, leaves the state unchanged. A predicate, called *FP* (for fixed point), characterizes the fixed points of a program. *FP* is the conjunction of the equations that are obtained by replacing the assignment operator by equality in each statement in the program. Therefore *FP* holds if and only if values on the left and right sides of each assignment in the program are identical. Once *FP* holds, continued execution leaves values of all variables unchanged, and therefore it makes no difference whether the execution continues or terminates. One way to implement a program is to halt it after it reaches a fixed point.

A *stable predicate* or *stable property* of a program is a predicate that continues to hold, once it holds. Thus *FP* is a stable property. The detection of fixed points is treated in Chapter 9, and the detection of general stable properties, in Chapter 11.

In a synchronous shared-memory system, a fixed number of identical processors share a common memory that can be read and written by any processor. There is a common clock; at each clock tick, every processor carries out precisely one step of computation. The synchrony inherent in a multiple-assignment statement makes it convenient to map such a statement to this architecture: Each processor computes the expression on the right side of the assignment corresponding to one variable and then assigns the computed value to this variable. This architecture is also useful for computing the value of an expression that is defined by an associative operator, such as sum, minimum, or maximum, applied to a sequence of data items.

An asynchronous shared-memory multiprocessor consists of a fixed set of processors and a common memory, but no common clock. If two processors access the same memory location simultaneously, then their accesses are made in some arbitrary order. A UNITY program can be mapped to such an architecture by partitioning the statements of the program among the processors. In addition, a schedule of execution for each processor should be specified that guarantees a fair execution for each partition. Observe that if execution for every partition is fair, then any fair interleaving of these executions determines a fair execution of the entire program. Our suggested mapping assumes a coarse grain of atomicity in the architecture: Two statements are not executed concurrently if one modifies a variable that the other uses. Hence the effect of multiple-processor execution is the same as a fair interleaving of their individual executions. Mappings under finer grains of atomicity are considered in Chapter 4. In that chapter we also show that an asynchronous multiprocessor can simulate a synchronous multiprocessor by simulating the common clock; thus programs for the latter can be executed on the former.

To evaluate the efficiency of a program executed according to a given mapping, it is necessary to describe the mapping—the partitions and the schedules of executions—in detail. Descriptions of architectures and mappings can be extremely detailed: Memory caches, input/output devices, and controllers can be described if it is necessary to evaluate efficiency at that level of detail. We shall not do so here, however, because we merely wish to emphasize the separation of concerns: Programs are concerned with *what* is to be done, whereas mappings are concerned with the implementation details of *where*, *when*, and *how*.

1.3.4 Modeling Conventional Programming Language Constructs and Architectures

In this section we show that conventional programming-language constructs that exploit different kinds of parallelism have simple counterparts in UNITY. This situation is not too surprising because the UNITY model incorporates both synchrony—a multiple-assignment statement assigns to several variables synchronously—and asynchrony—nondeterministic selection leaves unspecified the order in which statements are executed.

A statement of the form **await** B **do** S in an asynchronous shared-variable program is encoded in our model as a statement that does not change the value of any variable if B is *false* and otherwise has the same effect as S. A Petri net, another form of asynchronous system, can be represented by a program in which a variable corresponds to a *place*, the value of a variable is the number of *markers* in the corresponding place, and a statement corresponds to a *transition*. The execution of a statement decreases values of variables corresponding to its input places by 1 (provided they are all positive) and increases values of variables corresponding to its output places by 1, in one multiple assignment.

Asynchronous message-passing systems with first-in-first-out, error-free channels can be represented by encoding each channel as a variable whose value is a sequence of messages (representing the sequence of messages in transit along the channel). Sending a message is equivalent to appending it to the end of the sequence; receiving a message, to removing the head of the sequence.

We cannot control the sequence in which statements are executed. By using variables appropriately in conditional expressions, however, we can ensure that the execution of a statement has no effect (i.e., does not change the program state) unless the statement execution occurs in a desired sequence.

1.4   An Example: Scheduling a Meeting

The goal of this example is to give the reader *some* idea of how we propose to develop programs. Since the theory is presented only in later chapters, the discussion here is incomplete. The thesis of this book is unusual and the computational model even more so. Thus skeptical readers may want to get a rough idea of how we propose to design programs before investing more time; this example provides that rough idea.

1.4.1 The Problem Statement

The problem is to find the earliest meeting time acceptable to every member of a group of people. Time is integer valued and nonnegative. To keep notation simple, assume that the group consists of three people, F, G, and H. Associated with persons F, G, H are functions f, g, h (respectively), which map times to times. The meaning of f is as follows (and the meanings of g, h follow by analogy). For any t, $f(t) \geq t$; person F can meet at time $f(t)$ and cannot meet at any time u where $t \leq u < f(t)$. Thus $f(t)$ is the earliest time at or after t at which person F can meet. (Note: From the problem description, f is a monotone nondecreasing function of its argument, and $f(f(t)) = f(t)$. Also, $t = f(t)$ means that F can meet at t.) Assume that there exists some common meeting time z. In the interest of brevity we introduce a boolean function *com* (for *com*mon meeting time) over nonnegative integers defined as follows:

$$com(t) \quad \equiv \quad [t = f(t) = g(t) = h(t)]$$

Problem Specification

Note: All variables r, t, z, referred to in the specification, are nonnegative integers. ∇

Given monotone nondecreasing integer-valued functions f, g, h, where for all t

$$f(t) \geq t \ \wedge \ g(t) \geq t \ \wedge \ h(t) \geq t \ \wedge$$

$$f(f(t)) = f(t) \ \wedge \ g(g(t)) = g(t) \ \wedge \ h(h(t)) = h(t) \ ,$$

and given a z such that $com(z)$ holds, design a program that has the following as a stable predicate:

$$r = \min\{t \mid com(t)\}.$$

Furthermore, the program must establish this stable predicate within a finite number of steps of execution.

Discussion

There are many ways of attacking this problem. One approach is to structure the solution around a set of processes, one process corresponding to each person; people's behavior provides guidelines for programming these processes. We propose an alternative approach based on our theory. We describe both methods as applied to this problem, starting with the operational view.

1.4.2 Operational, Process-Oriented Viewpoint

We describe only the behavior of person F; the behaviors of G and H follow by analogy. Consider persons seated at a round table and a letter containing a proposed meeting time (initially 0), passed around among them. Upon receiving the letter with time t, person F sets the proposed time to $f(t)$ and passes the letter to the next person. If the letter makes one complete round without a change in the proposed meeting time, then this time is the solution.

Another strategy is to use a central coordinator to whom each person reports the next time at which he or she can meet. The coordinator broadcasts t, the maximum of these times, to all persons, and F then sends $f(t)$ back to the coordinator. These steps are repeated until the coordinator receives identical values from all persons.

Yet another solution is to divide the persons into two groups and recursively find meeting times for each group. Then the maximum of these times is used as the next estimate for repeating these steps, unless the two values are equal.

Another approach is to use a bidding scheme in which an auctioneer calls out a proposed meeting time t, starting at $t = 0$; F can raise the bid to $f(t)$ (provided this value exceeds t). The common meeting time is the final bid value, i.e., a value that can be raised no further. The reader can develop many other solutions by casting the problem in a real-world context. Different solutions are appropriate for different architectures.

1.4.3 The UNITY Viewpoint

Here we take the specification as the starting point for program design. A number of heuristics are given in later chapters for constructing programs from specifications. For this example, we merely propose programs and argue that they meet their specifications. Our next concern, after designing a program, is to refine it further so that it can be mapped to a target architecture for efficient execution. We may have to consider alternative refinements of the same program, or even alternative programs, if we cannot find a mapping with the desired efficiency.

A Simple Program

The problem specification immediately suggests the following program. The syntax is as follows: The assignment statements are given under **assign**. Declarations of variables have been omitted.

Program *P1*

    assign $r := \min\{u \mid (0 \le u \le z) \wedge (com(u))\}$

end $\{P1\}$

This program's correctness needs no argument. Now we consider how best to implement program *P1* on different architectures.

    For a von Neumann machine, computation of the right side of the assignment, i.e., finding the first u for which $com(u)$ holds, can proceed by checking the various values of u, from 0 to z, successively. The execution strategy for this program is entirely straightforward. The number of steps of execution is proportional to the value of r; in the worst case, it is $O(z)$.

    For a parallel synchronous machine (see Chapter 4) the minimum over a set of size z can be computed in $O(\log z)$ steps by $O(z)$ processors and, in general, in $O(z/k + \log k)$ steps by $O(k)$ processors.

    For parallel asynchronous shared-memory systems, a similar strategy can be employed to compute the minimum.

Discussion   We showed a very simple program, the correctness of which is obvious from the specification. We described informally how the program could be mapped to different architectures. It is possible to refine this program so that the mappings correspond more directly to the statements and variables. For instance, to describe the mapping to an asynchronous message-passing system, we can introduce variables to represent communication channels and statements to simulate sending and receiving from these channels; then we can describe the mapping by specifying which statements are to be executed by which processors and which channels connect which pairs of processors.

We make some general observations about program *P1* independent of the architecture on which it is to be implemented. We note that $com(u)$ has to be evaluated for *every* u, $0 \leq u \leq r$. This may be wasteful because from the problem statement we can deduce that no u can be a common meeting time—i.e., $com(u)$ does not hold—if $t \leq u < f(t)$. Therefore it is not necessary to evaluate $com(u)$ for any u in this interval. Such an approach is taken in the next program.

Another Program

In the following program, the symbol ▯ is used to separate the assignment statements; the initial condition is specified under **initially**.

Program $P2$

    initially $r = 0$

    assign $r := f(r)$ ▯ $r := g(r)$ ▯ $r := h(r)$

end $\{P2\}$

The program has three assignments: $r := f(r)$, $r := g(r)$, and $r := h(r)$. Computation proceeds by executing any one of the assignments, selected nondeterministically. The selection obeys the fairness rule: Every assignment is executed infinitely often.

This program can be understood as follows. Initially the proposed meeting time is zero. Any one of the participants—F, G, or H—increases the value of the proposed meeting time, if he or she cannot meet at that time, to the next possible time; in this sense, this program is similar to the bidding scheme outlined in Section 1.4.2. At fixed point, r is a common meeting time.

Proof of Correctness   In the absence of a proof theory (which is developed in Chapter 3), the best we can do is to sketch an informal proof. The proof, given next, can be made more concise by employing the formalisms given later in the book. We divide the argument into three parts.

1. We claim that the following predicate is *true* at all points during program execution; such a predicate is called an *invariant*.

     invariant $(0 \leq r) \wedge \langle$for all u where $0 \leq u < r$ :: $\neg com(u)\rangle$

In words, the invariant says that r is nonnegative and that there is no common meeting time earlier than r. Using the specification and this invariant, it is seen that $r \leq z$ is always *true* because there is a common meeting time at z.

To prove the invariant, we show that it is *true* initially and that execution of any statement preserves its truth. Initially $r = 0$. Hence the first conjunct in the invariant is *true* and the second conjunct holds, vacuously. Now consider execution of the statement $r := f(r)$. We know before execution of this statement, by definition, that F cannot meet at any u, $r \leq u < f(r)$. Hence $\neg com(u)$ holds for all u, $r \leq u < f(r)$. Also, from the invariant, we may assume that $\neg com(u)$ holds for all u, $0 \leq u < r$. Trivially, $0 \leq f(r)$. Therefore

$$(0 \leq f(r)) \wedge \langle \text{for all } u \text{ where } 0 \leq u < f(r) \ :: \ \neg com(u)\rangle$$

holds prior to execution of $r := f(r)$. The effect of execution of this statement is to set r to $f(r)$. Replacing $f(r)$ with r in the predicate, we see that the invariant continues to hold after execution of this statement.

Due to symmetry among the statements, similar arguments show that the invariant is preserved by executing any statement.

2. From the definition, *FP* for this program (the conjunction of the equations obtained by replacing := by = in every statement) is

$$FP \ \equiv \ r = f(r) \ \wedge \ r = g(r) \ \wedge \ r = h(r).$$

From the definition of $com(r)$ it follows that $FP \equiv com(r)$.

Combining the results proved in parts (1) and (2), we claim that if the execution of program *P2* reaches a fixed point, then the value of r is the earliest meeting time. Our remaining task is to show that every execution of program *P2* does indeed reach a fixed point; this is shown next.

3. We show that if $\neg FP \ \wedge \ r = k$ holds at any point during computation, then $r > k$ holds at some later point. Thus r keeps on increasing as long as $\neg FP$ holds. We showed in part (1) that r cannot increase beyond z. Therefore, eventually *FP* holds. The proof of the claim that r increases if $\neg FP$ holds is as follows. From the *FP* given in part (2),

$$\neg FP \ \wedge \ (r = k) \ \equiv \ k < f(k) \ \vee \ k < g(k) \ \vee \ k < h(k).$$

Suppose that $k < f(k)$ (similar reasoning applies for the other cases). From the fairness requirement, the statement $r := f(r)$ is executed some time later. Since the value of r never decreases, just prior to execution of this statement, $r \geq k$ (r may have increased in the meantime), and hence

$$f(r) \geq f(k) > k.$$

The effect of the execution of the statement is to set r to $f(r)$, and hence r increases beyond k.

This completes the proof.

Mapping Program *P2* to Various Architectures

We propose a mapping from program *P2* to a von Neumann machine. The mapping is described by a list of assignments (see Section 1.3.3). The following list is proposed:

$$r := f(r) \ , \ r := g(r) \ , \ r := h(r).$$

This list of assignments is executed repeatedly until a fixed point is detected, i.e., when three consecutive assignments do not change the value of r. This program corresponds to a letter, containing r, being passed in a circular fashion from F to G to H and then back to F, with each person setting r to the next time at or after r at which he or she can meet. When the letter is passed by all three persons without being modified, the program terminates.

Now suppose that the functions f, g, h are such that it is more efficient to apply f twice as often as g or h. Therefore we wish to repeatedly execute the following cycle: Apply f, then g, then f again, and then h. So we employ a different mapping from *P1*, with the execution schedule represented by the following list of assignments:

$$r := f(r) \ , \ r := g(r) \ , \ r := f(r) \ , \ r := h(r) \ .$$

The point of showing two different mappings is to emphasize that *P2* describes a family of programs, each corresponding to a different schedule. By proving *P2*, we have proved the correctness of all members in the family. Observe that each member of the family can also be represented as a UNITY program. For instance, the first schedule corresponds to a program with a single assignment statement:

$$r := h(g(f(r))),$$

and the second one to a program with the assignment statement

$$r := h(f(g(f(r)))).$$

Program *P2* can be implemented on asynchronous multiprocessors by partitioning its statements among the processors. For instance, we can employ three processors, each executing one statement, and the value of r resides in the common memory.

We show yet another program whose correctness can be established in the same manner as for *P2*.

Program *P3*

   initially $r = 0$

   assign $r := \max(f(r), g(r), h(r))$

end $\{P3\}$

This program is similar in spirit to the central-coordinator scheme outlined in Section 1.4.4. It is a suitable starting point for programming parallel synchronous multiprocessors. If the number of persons is N ($N = 3$ in this case), the maximum on the right side of the assignment statement can be computed in $O(\log N)$ steps using $O(N)$ processors.

Discussion

It is possible to develop yet other programs and show alternative schedules and mappings to various architectures. We have attempted to illustrate only that certain concerns, particularly dealing with architectures, can be ignored at higher levels of design, and introduced at lower levels based on considerations of efficiency.

Summary

This book proposes a unifying theory for the development of programs for a variety of architectures and applications. The computational model is unbounded nondeterministic iterative transformations of the program state. Transformations of the program state are represented by multiple-assignment statements. The theory attempts to decouple the programmer's thinking about a program and its implementation on an architecture, i.e., to separate the concerns of *what* from those of *where, when,* and *how.* Details about implementations are considered in mapping programs to architectures. We hope to demonstrate that we can develop, specify, and refine solution strategies independent of architectures.

The utility of any new approach is suspect, especially when the approach departs radically from the conventional. Therefore we have made a conscientious effort to apply our ideas to a number of architectures and application domains. Our experience is encouraging.

Bibliographic Notes

UNITY was first discussed in August 1984 at the Conference on the Principles of Distributed Computing in Vancouver, British Columbia, Chandy [1984]. The basic idea has not changed since then. Applications of UNITY in the literature include termination-detection algorithms, Chandy and Misra [1986a], systolic programs, Chandy and Misra [1986b] and van de Snepscheut and Swenker [1987], and self-stabilizing programs, Brown [1987].

The idea of modeling programs as state-transition systems is not new. Works of Pnueli [1981], Manna and Pnueli [1983], and Lamport and Schneider [1984] on using transition systems to model distributed systems are particularly relevant. Lynch and Tuttle [1987] use transition systems to develop distributed programs by stepwise refinement. A state-based model of distributed dynamic programming is in Bertsekas [1982]. A stimulus-response-based approach for program specification is proposed in Parker et al. [1980].

The idea of using mappings to implement programs on different architectures also is not new. Since the 1960s work has been carried out to recognize parallelism in sequential programs—an instance of employing mappings to parallel architectures. The point of departure of UNITY is to offer a different computational model from which to map. Formal complexity models of architectures are in Goldschlager [1977], Pippenger [1979], Aho, Hopcraft, and Ullman [1983], and Cook [1983]. A survey of concurrent programming constructs is in Andrews and Schneider [1983].

The importance of nondeterminism was stressed in Dijkstra [1976], in which he also proposed the nondeterministic construct—the guarded command. The guarded command is used extensively in Hoare [1984], which contains a definitive treatment of program structuring using Communicating Sequential Processes. Milner [1983] contains a general theory of synchrony and asynchrony. A comprehensive treatment of fairness is in Francez [1986]. In its use of nondeterminism, UNITY is similar to expert-system languages such as OPS5, Brownston et al. [1985].

Finally, we wish to point out that some of the initial motivation for UNITY came from difficulties encountered in using spreadsheets, a notation that has not received much attention from the computing-sciences community.

CHAPTER 2

A Programming
Notation

2.1   Introduction

In this chapter we introduce the notation used for the programs in this book. The goal is modest; no attempt has been made to define a complete programming language. The chapter is organized as follows. In Section 2.2, we describe the structure of a UNITY program. Because assignment statements are central to our work, we devote Section 2.3 to describing the notations for assignment statements; the usual notation is augmented to allow for conditional assignments and assignments to an array of variables. In Sections 2.4, 2.5, and 2.7, we describe the notations employed for some of the remaining parts of a program. Section 2.6 contains a few small examples. Section 2.8 contains some additional notation.

The notation is described using BNF. All nonterminal symbols are in italics, and all terminal symbols are in plain or boldface type. A syntactic unit enclosed between "{" and "}" may be instantiated zero or more times.

2.2   UNITY Program Structure

$$
\begin{array}{rll}
program & \longrightarrow & \textbf{Program} \quad program\text{-}name \\
& & \textbf{declare} \quad declare\text{-}section \\
& & \textbf{always} \quad always\text{-}section \\
& & \textbf{initially} \quad initially\text{-}section \\
& & \textbf{assign} \quad assign\text{-}section \\
& & \textbf{end}
\end{array}
$$

A *program-name* is any string of text. The keyword for a section may be omitted if its body is empty.

The *declare-section* names the variables used in the program and their types. The syntax is similar to that used in PASCAL and hence is not described here. For the most part, we use integers and booleans as the basic types. Arrays, sets, and sequences of these basic types are also used.

Families of programs are derived for most problems in this book. Since most programs in a family have the same declare-section, it is sometimes omitted for brevity from the program text, but is described in the accompanying explanation.

We give a quick overview of the remaining sections of a program. The *always-section* (described in Section 2.7) is used to define certain variables as functions of others. This section is not necessary for writing UNITY programs, but it is convenient. The *initially-section* (described in Section 2.5) is used to define initial values of some of the variables; uninitialized variables have arbitrary initial values. The *assign-section* (described in Section 2.4) contains a set of assignment statements.

The program execution starts in a state where the values of variables are as specified in the initially-section. The description of the manner in which programs execute (see Section 1.3.1) is repeated here. In each step, any one statement is executed. Statements are selected arbitrarily for execution, though in an infinite execution of the program each statement is executed infinitely often. A state of a program is called a *fixed point* if and only if execution of any statement of the program, in this state, leaves the state unchanged.

Our programs have no input/output statements. We assume that all I/O is performed by appending items to or removing items from appropriate sequences in a first-in-first-out manner. The description in this chapter does not allow for hierarchical program structure, which is treated in Chapter 7.

2.3   Assignment Statement

Assigning to a single subscripted or unsubscripted variable is well understood. We introduce notation to extend this concept.

We allow a number of variables to be assigned simultaneously in a multiple assignment, as in

$$x, y, z \; := \; 0, 1, 2$$

Such an assignment can also be written as a set of assignment-components separated by $\|$, as in

$$x, y \; := \; 0, 1 \; \| \; z \; := \; 2$$

or

$$x \; := \; 0 \; \| \; y \; := \; 1 \; \| \; z \; := \; 2$$

The variables to be assigned and the values to be assigned to them may be described using quantification rather than enumeration. Thus

$$\langle \| \; i \; : \; 0 \leq i \leq N \; :: \; A[i] \; := \; B[i] \rangle$$

denotes the assignment

$$A[0] \; := \; B[0] \; \| \; A[1] \; := \; B[1] \; \| \ldots \| \; A[N] \; := \; B[N]$$

The following notation is common in mathematics for defining variable values by case analysis:

$$x = \begin{cases} -1 & \text{if} \quad y < 0 \\ 0 & \text{if} \quad y = 0 \\ 1 & \text{if} \quad y > 0 \end{cases}$$

We adopt this notation for assignments, separating the cases by the symbol $\sim$:

$$x := -1 \quad \text{if} \quad y < 0 \quad \sim$$
$$0 \quad \text{if} \quad y = 0 \quad \sim$$
$$1 \quad \text{if} \quad y > 0$$

We now describe formally the syntax of an assignment-statement.

2.3.1 Structure of Assignment-statement

$$\text{assignment-statement} \quad \longrightarrow \quad \text{assignment-component}$$
$$\{ \parallel \text{assignment-component} \}$$

$$\text{assignment-component} \quad \longrightarrow \quad \text{enumerated-assignment}$$
$$\mid \text{quantified-assignment}$$

An *assignment-statement* consists of one or more *assignment-components* separated by $\parallel$. There are two kinds of assignment-components: In an *enumerated-assignment*, the variables to be assigned and the expressions to be assigned to them are enumerated; in a *quantified-assignment*, the variables to be assigned and the expressions to be assigned to them are obtained by instantiating a generic assignment with all possible values of certain quantified variables.

A variable may appear more than once in the left side of an assignment-statement. It is the programmer's responsibility to ensure for any such variable that all possible values that may be assigned to it in a statement are identical.

An operational view of an assignment-statement execution is that each assignment-component is executed independently and simultaneously. Next, we describe the syntax and semantics of each type of assignment-component.

2.3.2 Enumerated-assignment

$$\text{enumerated-assignment} \quad \longrightarrow \quad \text{variable-list} := \text{expr-list}$$

$$\text{variable-list} \quad \longrightarrow \quad \text{variable} \{,\text{variable}\}$$

$$\text{expr-list} \quad \longrightarrow \quad \text{simple-expr-list} \mid \text{conditional-expr-list}$$

$$\text{simple-expr-list} \quad \longrightarrow \quad \text{expr} \{,\text{expr}\}$$

$$\text{conditional-expr-list} \quad \longrightarrow \quad \text{simple-expr-list} \quad \text{if} \quad \text{boolean-expr}$$
$$\{\sim \text{simple-expr-list} \quad \text{if} \quad \text{boolean-expr}\}$$

The syntactic units *expr* and *boolean-expr* denote a PASCAL-style expression and a boolean expression, respectively. An enumerated-assignment assigns the values of expressions on the right of := to corresponding variables listed on the left of :=. This assignment is the same as the traditional multiple assignment: First evaluate all expressions in the right side and any subscripts on the left side of :=, and then assign the values of expressions to the corresponding variables. The assignment succeeds only if the numbers and types of variables match the corresponding expressions.

An assignment with a *conditional-expr-list* causes assignment of values from any constituent *simple-expr-list* whose associated boolean expression is *true*. If none of the boolean expressions is *true*, the corresponding variable values are left unchanged. If more than one boolean expression is *true*, then all the corresponding *simple-expr-lists* must have the same value; hence any one of them can be used for assignment. This guarantees that every assignment statement is *deterministic*: A unique program state results from executing an assignment statement in a given state.

Example 2.1   Examples of Enumerated-assignments

1. Exchange x, y.

$$x, y := y, x$$

2. Set x to the absolute value of y.

$$x := y \quad \text{if} \quad y \geq 0 \quad \sim \quad -y \quad \text{if} \quad y \leq 0$$

Note that for $y = 0$, either expression, y or $-y$, can be used for assignment to x.

3. Add $A[i]$ into *sum* and increment i, provided i is less than N.

$$sum, i := sum + A[i], i + 1 \quad \text{if} \quad i < N$$

4. Assign the smaller of $A[i]$ and $B[j]$ to $C[k]$ and increment k by 1; also increment i if $A[i] \leq B[j]$ and increment j if $B[j] \leq A[i]$.

$$C[k] := \min(A[i], B[j])$$
$$\| \quad k := k + 1$$
$$\| \quad i := i + 1 \quad \text{if} \quad A[i] \leq B[j]$$
$$\| \quad j := j + 1 \quad \text{if} \quad B[j] \leq A[i]$$

or

$$
\begin{array}{llllll}
C[k] & , i & , j & , k & := & \\
A[i] & , i+1 & , j & , k+1 & \text{if} & A[i] < B[j] \quad \sim \\
B[j] & , i & , j+1 & , k+1 & \text{if} & A[i] > B[j] \quad \sim \\
A[i] & , i+1 & , j+1 & , k+1 & \text{if} & A[i] = B[j]
\end{array}
$$

$\triangledown$

Exercise 2.1 Write a statement that orders two variables x, y in increasing order of their values. Extend the solution to order three variables x, y, z.

$\triangledown$

2.3.3 Quantified-assignment

quantified-assignment $\longrightarrow$ $\langle \|$ *quantification assignment-statement* $\rangle$

quantification $\longrightarrow$ *variable-list* : *boolean-expr* ::

The variables in the variable-list of the quantification are called *quantified* or *bound* variables. A quantification has a scope delineated by the brackets "$\langle$" and "$\rangle$". The boolean expression in the quantification may name variables declared in the program, as well as constants and bound variables from this or any outer scope (i.e., a scope within which this scope is contained). An *instance* of a quantification is a set of values of bound variables that satisfies the boolean expression in the quantification.

A quantified-assignment denotes zero or more assignment-components that are obtained from the assignment-statement by replacing bound variables by their instances; one assignment-component is obtained for each instance. It must be ensured that only a finite number of instances exist. If there is no instance, the corresponding quantified-assignment-statement denotes an empty statement.

Notational Convention

We use $x < y < z$ as shorthand for $(x < y) \wedge (y < z)$. Obvious extensions apply to more variables and to transitive relations other than $<$. For an array A, $A[M..N]$ denotes the subarray consisting of the elements $A[i]$, $M \le i \le N$.

Example 2.2 Examples of Quantified-assignments

1. Given arrays $A[0..N]$ and $B[0..N]$ of integers, assign $\max(A[i], B[i])$ to $A[i]$, for all i, $0 \le i \le N$.

   $$\langle \| \; i \; : \; 0 \le i \le N \quad :: \quad A[i] \; := \; \max(A[i], B[i]) \rangle$$

   or

$$\langle \| \; i \; : \; 0 \leq i \leq N \quad :: \quad A[i] \; := \; B[i] \quad \text{if} \quad A[i] < B[i] \rangle$$

or

$$\langle \| \; i \; : \; 0 \leq i \leq N \; \wedge \; A[i] < B[i] \quad :: \quad A[i] \; := \; B[i] \rangle$$

2. Assign an identity matrix to $U[0..N, \; 0..N]$.

$$\langle \| \; i,j \; : \; 0 \leq i \leq N \; \wedge \; 0 \leq j \leq N \quad ::$$
$$U[i,j] \; := \; 0 \quad \text{if} \quad i \neq j \; \sim \; 1 \quad \text{if} \quad i = j$$
$$\rangle$$

or

$$\langle \| \; i,j \; : \; 0 \leq i \leq N \; \wedge \; 0 \leq j \leq N \; \wedge \; i \neq j \quad :: \quad U[i,j] \; := \; 0 \rangle$$
$$\| \; \langle \| \; i \; : \; 0 \leq i \leq N \qquad\qquad\qquad\qquad :: \quad U[i,i] \; := \; 1 \rangle$$

or

$$\langle \| \; i \; : \; 0 \leq i \leq N \quad :: \quad U[i,i] \; := \; 1$$
$$\| \; \langle \| j \; : \; 0 \leq j \leq N \; \wedge \; i \neq j \quad :: \quad U[i,j] \; := \; 0 \rangle$$
$$\rangle \qquad\qquad\qquad\qquad\qquad\qquad\qquad\qquad\qquad\qquad \triangledown$$

Exercise 2.2 Given an array $A[0..N]$, compute a matrix $R[0..N, \; 0..N]$, where row k of R is obtained by a circular shift of A to the right by k positions, for all k, $0 \leq k \leq N$. $\qquad\qquad \triangledown$

2.3.4 Summary of Assignment Statement

An assignment-statement consists of one or more assignment components separated by $\|$. An assignment-component is either an enumerated-assignment or a quantified-assignment. An enumerated-assignment has a variable list on the left and an expression list—simple or conditional—on the right. For a conditional-expression list, all component simple-expression lists whose associated boolean expressions are *true* are equal in value, and hence any one of them can be chosen for assignment; if no boolean expression is *true* the variable values are left unchanged. A quantified-assignment specifies a quantification and an assignment-statement that is to be instantiated with the given quantification. A quantification names a set of bound variables and a boolean expression satisfied by the instances of the bound variables. An assignment-statement is executed by first evaluating all expressions on the right side and any subscripts on the left side and then assigning the values of the evaluated expressions to the appropriate variables.

2.4   Assign-section

assign-section	$\longrightarrow$	*statement-list*
statement-list	$\longrightarrow$	*statement* {⫿ *statement*}
statement	$\longrightarrow$	*assignment-statement* |
		quantified-statement-list
quantified-statement-list	$\longrightarrow$	⟨⫿ *quantification statement-list*⟩

The assign-section specifies the statements of the program. The symbol ⫿ acts as a separator between the statements.

A *quantified-statement-list* denotes a set of statements obtained by instantiating the *statement-list* with the appropriate instances of bound variables; if there is no instance, *quantified-statement-list* denotes an empty set of statements. As before, we require that the number of instances be finite. Furthermore, we place an important restriction on the boolean expression in the quantification for a quantified statement list: It should not name program variables whose values may change during program execution. This restriction guarantees that the set of statements of a program is fixed at all times; statements are not created or deleted during program execution. The rationale for this restriction is given in Chapter 22.

Example 2.3   Examples of Assign-sections

Write a program in which $U[0..N,\ 0..N]$ is an identity matrix at fixed point and in which a fixed point is always reached.

The solutions given for this problem in Example 2.2 are still applicable. Furthermore, replacing any ‖ in any solution by ⫿ (provided the replacement is syntactically legal) also solves the problem (such a replacement is not correct for all programs). We show some of these solutions:

$$\langle ⫿\ i,j\ :\ 0 \leq i \leq N\ \wedge\ 0 \leq j \leq N\ ::$$
$$U[i,j]\ :=\ 0\quad \text{if}\quad i \neq j\ \sim\ 1\quad \text{if}\quad i = j$$
$$\rangle$$

or

$$\langle ‖\ i,j\ :\ 0 \leq i \leq N\ \wedge\ 0 \leq j \leq N\ \wedge\ i \neq j\ ::\ U[i,j]\ :=\ 0\rangle$$
$$⫿\ \langle ‖\ i\ :\ 0 \leq i \leq N\ ::\ U[i,i]\ :=\ 1\rangle$$

or

$$\langle \| \ i \ : \ 0 \leq i \leq N \ \ :: \ \ U[i,i] \ := \ 1$$

$$\| \ \langle \| \ j \ : \ 0 \leq j \leq N \ \wedge \ i \neq j \ \ :: \ \ U[i,j] \ := \ 0 \rangle$$

$$\rangle$$

The first solution has $(N+1)^2$ statements, one for each element of the matrix. The second solution has two statements, one for assignment to the off-diagonal elements and the other for assignment to the diagonal elements. The last solution has $(N+1)$ statement lists, each list corresponding to one value of i, $0 \leq i \leq N$. Each list, in turn, has two statements: one for assigning to a diagonal element and the other for assigning to all off-diagonal elements in that row. ▽

Exercise 2.3 Write an assign-section to guarantee that the value of variable x is 0, 1, or 2 at any fixed point. Your program should admit of all three possibilities. Assume that initially x has a value different from 0, 1, or 2. ▽

Exercise 2.4 Let $A[0..N]$ be an array of integers and *sorted* be a boolean variable whose initial value is *true*. Write an assign-section such that the value of *sorted* is *true* at a fixed point if and only if A is in ascending order. ▽

2.5   Initially-section

The syntax of this section is the same as that of the assign-section except that in assignments := is replaced by =. The initially-section defines initial values of some variables; the initial value of a variable is given as a function of initial values of other variables (and constants). The equations defining the initial values should not be circular. To this end, we define a set of equations to be *proper* if and only if it satisfies the following constraints: (1) a variable appears at most once on the left side of an equation, (2) there exists an ordering of the equations such that any variable in a quantification is either a bound variable or a variable that appears on the left side of an equation earlier in the ordering (ensuring that the program can be "compiled"), and (3) there exists an ordering of all equations after quantified equations have been expanded such that any variable appearing on the right side of an equation, or in a subscript, appears on the left side of an equation earlier in the ordering (ensuring that the initial values are well defined). The initially-section is a proper set of equations.

Example 2.4   Examples of Initially-sections

1. initially

$$N = 3$$
$$\llbracket \; \langle \parallel k \; : \; 0 \leq k < N \; :: \; A[N - k] = k \rangle$$

Note that replacing $\llbracket$ by $\parallel$ in this *initially*-section is illegal: N would then appear in the quantification and it does not appear in any previous equation.

2. initially

$$B[0] = 0 \; \parallel \; N = 2$$
$$\llbracket \; \langle \llbracket i \; : \; 0 < i \leq N \; :: \; A[i] = B[i - 1]$$
$$\llbracket \; B[i] = A[i]$$
$$\rangle$$

The equations denoted by the quantification can be expanded as follows:

$$A[1] = B[0], \; B[1] = A[1], \; A[2] = B[1], \; B[2] = A[2].$$

3. An equation of the form

$$x = 0 \quad \text{if} \quad y \geq 0$$

is illegal because it is equivalent to

$$x = 0 \quad \text{if} \quad y \geq 0 \; \sim \; x \quad \text{if} \quad y < 0.$$

Here x appears on the right side without being defined previously. Therefore, if the right side of an equation contains conditional expressions, at least one of the associated boolean expressions must hold. $\triangledown$

The initially-section of the program defines the *initial condition*, the strongest predicate that holds initially. This predicate is obtained from the initializations, as follows: $\parallel$ and $\llbracket$ are to be treated as $\wedge$, and an initialization with a conditional expression of the form

$$x = e_0 \quad \text{if} \quad b_0 \; \sim \; \ldots \; \sim \; e_n \quad \text{if} \quad b_n$$

is to be treated as $(b_0 \; \Rightarrow \; (x = e_0)) \; \wedge \; \ldots \; \wedge \; (b_n \; \Rightarrow \; (x = e_n)).$

Example 2.5

Given the following initially-section:

$$\langle \| \; i,j \; : 0 \leq i \leq N \; \wedge \; 0 \leq j \leq N \; ::$$
$$U[i,j] = 0 \quad \text{if} \quad i \neq j \; \sim \; 1 \quad \text{if} \quad i = j$$
$$\rangle$$

we obtain the initial condition (the meaning of this quantified expression is defined in Section 2.8.1):

$$\langle \wedge \; i,j \; : \; 0 \leq i \leq N \; \wedge \; 0 \leq j \leq N \; ::$$
$$(i \neq j \; \Rightarrow \; U[i,j] = 0) \; \wedge \; (i = j \; \Rightarrow \; U[i,j] = 1)$$
$$\rangle \qquad\qquad\qquad \triangledown$$

Exercise 2.5   Matrix $T[0..N, \; 0..N]$ is a *Toeplitz* matrix if for all i,j, $0 < i,j \leq N$, $T[i,j] = T[i-1, j-1]$. Write an initially-section that initializes matrix T to a Toeplitz matrix in which the topmost row of T is the same as $A[0..N]$, and the leftmost column of T is the same as $B[0..N]$, for given A, B.

$$\triangledown$$

2.6   Some Small Examples

We present a few UNITY programs for some simple programming tasks. No attempt is made to develop the programs from their specifications, nor is any correctness proof given. The goal of this section is to familiarize the reader with UNITY syntax.

2.6.1   Scheduling a Common Meeting Time

We rewrite program $P2$ of Chapter 1 for N persons. We assume that $i.f$ is the function associated with the ith person, $0 \leq i < N$.

Program $P2$

> **declare** r : integer
> **initially** $r = 0$
> **assign** $\langle \| \; i \; : \; 0 \leq i < N \; :: \; r := i.f(r) \rangle$
> **end** $\{P2\}$

2.6.2 Sorting

Sort integer array $A[0..N]$, $N \geq 0$, in ascending order, i.e., write a program that reaches a fixed point; at any fixed point, A is a permutation of its original values and A is in ascending order. In the following program, pairs of adjacent elements are swapped if they are out of order.

Program *sort1*

    assign

$$\langle \parallel i \; : \; 0 \leq i < N \; :: \; A[i], A[i+1] \; := \; A[i+1], A[i] \quad \text{if} \quad A[i] > A[i+1] \rangle$$

end $\{sort1\}$

A useful heuristic is to combine assignments that name different variables into a single assignment. Using this heuristic for all even i and all odd i, we obtain the following program from the previous one. This program can be shown to be correct in the same manner as program *sort1*.

Program *sort2*

    assign

$$\langle \parallel i \; : \; 0 \leq i < N \wedge \text{even}(i) \; ::$$
$$A[i], A[i+1] \; := \; A[i+1], A[i] \quad \text{if} \quad A[i] > A[i+1] \rangle$$

$$\parallel \langle \parallel i \; : \; 0 \leq i < N \wedge \text{odd}(i) \; ::$$
$$A[i], A[i+1] \; := \; A[i+1], A[i] \quad \text{if} \quad A[i] > A[i+1] \rangle$$

end $\{sort2\}$

Observing the similarities between the two assignment-statements in program *sort2*, we can rewrite them as follows:

Program *sort3*

  assign

  $\langle \| \; j \; : \; 0 \le j \le 1 \; :: $

     $\langle \| \; i \; : \; 0 \le i < N \; \wedge \; j = i \bmod 2 \; :: $

        $A[i], A[i+1] \; := \; A[i+1], A[i] \quad \text{if} \quad A[i] > A[i+1] \rangle$

  $\rangle$

end $\{sort3\}$

2.6.3 Semaphore

This is the first example in which we describe only a portion of a program; the text of the other portion of the program is not shown, though its specification is given informally. Chapter **7** contains a formal treatment of program composition.

   This example shows how to implement a semaphore, g, which is shared between N processes. The ith process, $0 \le i < N$, requests a p-operation on the semaphore by setting a boolean variable $p[i]$ to *true*. This p-operation can be executed only if $g > 0$; the result of its execution is that $p[i]$ becomes *false* and g is decremented by 1. Similarly, the ith process requests a v-operation on the semaphore by setting a boolean variable $v[i]$ to *true*; $v[i]$ is to be set *false* and g incremented by 1 upon completion of this operation. Let the initial value of g be 1. The declarations of $p[i]$s and $v[i]$s, and their settings to *true*, are done external to the *semaphore* program.

Program *semaphore*

  declare g : integer

  initially $g = 1$

  assign

  $\langle \| \; i \; : \; 0 \le i < N \; :: $

     $g, p[i] \; := \; g - 1, \textit{false} \quad \text{if} \quad g > 0 \wedge p[i]$

     $\| \; g, v[i] \; := \; g + 1, \textit{false} \quad \text{if} \qquad \quad v[i]$

  $\rangle$

end $\{semaphore\}$

Exercise 2.6   Argue that this program implements a *weak* semaphore: If $g > 0$, then some request for a p-operation will be eventually honored. Note, though, that a specific request for a p-operation may never be honored, i.e., a $p[i]$ may remain *true* forever.   ▽

This is our first example of a "reactive" program, one that shares certain variables—in this case $p[i]$s and $v[i]$s—with an environment (the set of processes, which are not shown), and one that carries out computations in response to changes in the values of these variables. The following protocol is observed in setting the shared variable values: $p[i]$s and $v[i]$s are set *true* only by the environment and set *false* only by the *semaphore* program. Usually reactive programs do not reach fixed points.

2.6.4 Binomial Coefficients

The following program computes the binomial coefficients, $\binom{n}{k}$, in an array element $c[n, k]$, for all k, $0 \leq k \leq n$ and all n, $0 \leq n < N$, for some given N. We use the fact that $\binom{n}{0} = \binom{n}{n} = 1$, for all n. Also, $\binom{n}{k} = \binom{n-1}{k-1} + \binom{n-1}{k}$, for all $n > 0$ and $0 < k < n$. Assume that c and N have been declared outside this program.

Program *binomial*

  assign

    $\langle\!\![\; n \; : \; 0 \leq n < N \;\; :: $

        $c[n, 0] \; := \; 1 \;\|\; c[n, n] \; := \; 1$

    $[\; \langle\| \; k \; : \; 0 < k < n \;\; :: \;\; c[n, k] \; := \; c[n-1, k-1] + c[n-1, k]\rangle$

    $\rangle$

end {*binomial*}

Notes

1. The order of executions of statements in a UNITY program is arbitrary. Hence some $c[n, k]$ may be assigned a value even when $c[n-1, k-1]$ or $c[n-1, k]$ has not been computed. Eventually, however, every $c[n, k]$ is assigned the correct value.

2. Any $\|$ in this program may be replaced by $[$. (Such a replacement is not correct for all programs.)

3. Observe that, for $n = 0$, $c[0, 0]$ appears twice on the left of an assignment, though the value assigned to it is, uniquely, 1.   ▽

Exercise 2.7   Modify program *binomial* so that $c[n, k]$ is not assigned a value until after both $c[n-1, k-1]$ and $c[n-1, k]$ have received their final values. ▽

2.7   Always-section

An always-section is used to define certain program variables as functions of other variables. The syntax used in the always-section is the same as in the initially-section. A variable appearing on the left side of an equation is called a *transparent* variable. A transparent variable is a function of nontransparent variables and hence does not appear on the left side of any initialization or assignment, though it may appear on the right. A transparent variable may also appear on the right side of an equation. To ensure that each transparent variable is a well-defined function of nontransparent variables, we place the same restrictions on the transparent variables in equations as we did for all variables in the initially-section.

Example 2.6

Let the program variables nf, nm, ne denote the number of female employees, male employees, and employees, respectively. We have the relationship

$$ne = nf + nm$$

at all points during program execution. We can preserve this relationship by modifying ne appropriately whenever nf or nm is changed. Another possibility is to define a function $ne(x, y)$, whose value equals $x + y$ and whose arguments, x, y, are always bound to nf, nm, respectively. A new option, provided by the introduction of the always-section, is to define ne in that section as $ne = nf + nm$. Of course, ne is not assigned a value in any assignment-statement, nor is it initialized. However, ne may appear on the right sides of assignments, and each occurrence of ne may be replaced by its definition, i.e., $nf + nm$, without altering the semantics of the program. $\triangledown$

It should be obvious that the always-section is not necessary for writing programs; every transparent variable can be regarded as a nontransparent one, which can be appropriately initialized and assigned a value in each assignment-statement. However, there are several advantages to using the always-section. First, it is simpler to reason with an always-section because it defines a set of invariants of the program (see Chapter 3 for a discussion of invariants). These invariants are in a particularly nice form, a set of equations. If a program contains only transparent variables, it can be regarded purely as a set of equations, and it is usually easier to understand such programs. Second, it is convenient to regard a transparent variable merely as a macro whose definition can be substituted for its occurrence anywhere in the program. The term transparent comes from this property of *referential transparency*. Third, efficient implementations of transparent variables are possible: Evaluation of a transparent variable can be deferred until it is accessed or until some of the variables in its definition change value.

Exercise 2.8   Can the program *binomial* (Section 2.6.4) be rewritten using only an always-section, with = replacing := in the assignments? ∇

2.8   Additional Notation

2.8.1   Quantified Expression

We allow the use of quantification in writing expressions:

  expr $\longrightarrow$ $\langle op \; quantification \; expr \rangle$.

The syntactic units *expr* and *op* denote expression and operator, respectively. The value of the expression defined this way is the result of applying the operator, *op*, to the set of expressions obtained by substituting the instances of the bound variables in the inner expression. We require that *op* be a binary, associative, commutative operator, and hence the order of application of this operator is immaterial. If there is no instance of the quantification, then the expression value is the unit element of operator *op*; the unit elements of $\min, \max, +, \times, \wedge, \vee, \equiv$ (the only operators used in this book) are ∞, $-\infty$, 0, 1, *true*, *false*, *true*, respectively.

Example 2.7

In the following examples, $N \geq 0$.

  $\langle \vee \; i \; : \; 0 \leq i \leq N \; :: \; b[i] \rangle$ {*true* if some element of $b[0..N]$ is *true*}

  $\langle \min \; i \; : \; 0 \leq i \leq N \; :: \; A[i] \rangle$ {smallest element in $A[0..N]$}

  $\langle + \; i \; : \; 0 \leq i \leq N \; \wedge \; A[i] < A[j] \; :: \; 1 \rangle$ {number of items smaller than $A[j]$ in $A[0..N]$} ∇

Exercise 2.9   Define the *rank* of an element $A[j]$ in an integer array $A[0..N]$ as the number of items smaller than $A[j]$ plus the number of items equal to $A[j]$ with subscripts smaller than j. Write an expression whose value is the rank of $A[j]$. ∇

2.8.2 Notational Conventions

In quantified boolean expressions, we often use the existential quantifier symbol ($\exists$) and the universal quantifier symbol ($\forall$) in place of $\lor$ and $\land$, respectively.

We often omit the boolean expressions in quantifications. In such cases, the bound variables range over all of their possible values.

For a nonnull sequence x, head(x) and tail(x) denote the first element and the sequence remaining after deletion of the first element, respectively.

Comments in a program are enclosed between "{" and "}". The same pair of braces is also used to enclose the items of a set. We expect no confusion because the two usages can be distinguished by the context.

We use "$\times$" to denote the multiplication operator. However, it is often convenient, particularly in subscripts for arrays, to use "." as the multiplication operator, as in $A[2.i]$. The period (.) is also used in expressions such as $y.val$, which denotes the val component of variable y; these two usages are easy to distinguish because only the former is of the form "constant.variable".

We use standard functions—min, max, odd, even, mod, etc.—with their usual meanings. (We have already used some of these functions in the examples in this chapter.)

Summary

We have described a notation primarily to explain the programs in this book, highlighting the essential ideas about unbounded nondeterministic iterative transformations. A notation does not a language make! A design of a programming language requires far more attention to a number of issues ranging from the choice of character set and mnemonics to the choice of appropriate abstraction mechanisms. We have paid little attention to these issues.

Bibliographic Notes

A description of PASCAL appears in Wirth [1971]. Our notation for quantified expressions is influenced by van Gasteren and Dijkstra [1985]. The concept of weak semaphore is from Dijkstra [1968]. The notion of reactive programs is from Pnueli [1987].

CHAPTER 3

A Programming Logic

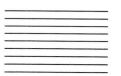

3.1   Introduction

In this chapter we introduce a logic for the specification, design, and verification of UNITY programs. The logic is based on assertions of the form $\{p\}\ s\ \{q\}$, denoting that an execution of statement s in any state that satisfies predicate p results in a state that satisfies predicate q, if execution of s terminates. This notation was introduced originally for proofs of sequential imperative programs. However, our proof system differs considerably from traditional proof systems for such programs. We next list some of these differences.

First, an annotation of a sequential program consists of associating predicates with specific points in a program text; a predicate holds when control reaches the corresponding point in the program text. UNITY does not have the notion of program control. Therefore it is meaningless to attach predicates to points in a program text. Instead, we associate *properties*—such as "predicate I is always *true*" and "if predicate p ever becomes *true* then predicate q will be *true* eventually"—with an entire program. These properties are stated and proved outside the program text. This separation of proofs and programs is particularly valuable in modular system design: Often some program text (such as an operating system) is not available, but if its relevant properties are specified, then other programs (application programs, for instance) can be designed for concurrent execution with the former program.

Second, an execution of a UNITY program is an infinite sequence of statement executions. For nonterminating programs such as operating systems and process-control systems, the traditional precondition-postcondition semantics is inadequate. Instead the program properties should characterize the states of the program during its execution. Therefore we develop a logic for reasoning about infinite sequences of program states.

Induction is one of the most fundamental tools in reasoning about infinite sequences. For instance, if $\{p\}\ s\ \{p\}$ holds for all statements s of a program then we can claim, using induction on the number of statement executions, that p remains *true* once it becomes *true*. Unfortunately, induction is of little help in directly proving properties related to fairness; it is seldom possible to prove a property of a fair (infinite) sequence by asserting that some property holds for every finite prefix of the sequence. In our model, however, fairness is amenable to inductive reasoning. As a simple example, suppose that a program has a statement t for which $\{true\}\ t\ \{p\}$ holds. Then we can claim at any point during program execution that p will eventually hold. This is because statement t will be executed eventually—from our fairness rule—and thereby establish p (execution of every UNITY statement terminates). This fact is asserted without using induction. Once we establish such elementary properties, we can apply induction—not on the number of statement executions, but on the proof structure—to establish more complex properties of programs.

Most properties of a UNITY program are expressed using assertions of the form $\{p\}$ s $\{q\}$, where s is universally or existentially quantified over the statements of the program. Properties that hold for all program states during execution are defined using only universal quantification. Properties that hold eventually are defined using existential quantification as well. Our fairness rule is described operationally in terms of statement executions of a program. Yet we capture its effect nonoperationally using quantifications over program statements.

Traditionally, a program property is regarded as either a *safety* or a *progress* property. Examples of safety properties are that variable x is always nonnegative; that two processes are never in their critical sections simultaneously (Chapter 15); that a message is received only if it has been sent; that a philosopher remains hungry until it eats (Chapter 12). Examples of progress properties are that x will become positive; that a message that is sent will be received; that a hungry philosopher will eat. We will not define the terms safety and progress formally. But we note that existential quantification over program statements seems to be essential in stating progress properties, whereas safety properties can be stated using only universal quantifications over statements (and using the initial condition).

All properties of a program can be expressed directly using assertions. However, it is cumbersome to do so all the time. Certain kinds of properties arise so often in practice that it is useful to give them names and derive theorems about them independent of any specific program. In this chapter, we introduce a few additional terms—*unless, stable, invariant, ensures, leads-to, fixed point*—for describing properties of programs.

This chapter deals with properties of a *single* program; properties of ensembles of programs are treated in Chapter 7.

3.1.1 Structure of the Chapter

In Sections 3.2 and 3.3 we review the well-known ideas about assertions, assignments, and program-execution sequences. In Section 3.4, we introduce the fundamental concepts of our logic—*unless* and its special cases (*stable, invariant*), *ensures, leads-to,* and *fixed point*. A complete example that illustrates these concepts is given in Section 3.5. Section 3.6 contains a number of theorems about the fundamental concepts; these are used throughout the book. Section 3.7 gives a technique for proving bounds on the number of "useful" computation steps, and Section 3.8 illustrates how other logical relations can be defined in terms of the fundamental ones.

3.2   Basic Concepts

We use the symbols $p, p', q, q', r, r', b, b'$ to denote arbitrary predicates and s, t to denote statements of a program. In this chapter we consider a single generic program, without reference to its name. We adopt the convention that every program has at least one statement. This requirement can be met by adding a statement that does not change the program semantics, such as $x := x$, to a program. (We will be quantifying over all statements in a program, and the presence of at least one statement is helpful in defining terms with existential quantification.)

The assertion $\{p\}\ s\ \{q\}$ denotes that execution of statement s in any state that satisfies predicate p results in a state that satisfies predicate q, if execution of s terminates. For our purposes, s is a UNITY statement. We assume that execution of every statement terminates. This is certainly true if the evaluation of each expression in a statement terminates. We use standard terminating functions in this book, and hence termination of every statement is guaranteed.

Here are some useful facts about assertions (an inference rule with hypothesis h and conclusion c is written as $\frac{h}{c}$):

$$\{p\}\quad s\quad \{true\}$$

$$\{false\}\quad s\quad \{q\}$$

$$\frac{\{p\}\ s\ \{false\}}{\neg p}$$

$$\frac{\{p\}\ s\ \{q\}\ ,\ \{p'\}\ s\ \{q'\}}{\{p\ \vee\ p'\}\ s\ \{q\ \vee\ q'\}\ ,\ \{p\ \wedge\ p'\}\ s\ \{q\ \wedge\ q'\}}$$

$$\frac{p'\ \Rightarrow\ p\ ,\ \{p\}\ s\ \{q\}\ ,\ q\ \Rightarrow\ q'}{\{p'\}\ s\ \{q'\}}$$

3.2.1 Proving Assertions about Assignment Statements

The proof of $\{p\}\ s\ \{q\}$, where s assigns to a single variable, is well understood. For instance, to prove

$$\{p\}\quad x\ :=\ E\ \{q\},$$

first substitute E for all occurrences of x in q—call this predicate q_E^x—and show that $p\ \Rightarrow\ q_E^x$. This is because for q to hold after execution of $x := E$, q_E^x has to hold prior to execution of this statement. If E is a conditional expression of the form

$$e_0\quad \text{if}\quad b_0\quad \sim\quad \ldots\quad \sim\quad e_n\quad \text{if}\quad b_n,$$

then q_E^x is

$$(b_0 \Rightarrow q_{e_0}^x) \wedge \ldots \wedge (b_n \Rightarrow q_{e_n}^x) \wedge ((\neg b_0 \wedge \ldots \wedge \neg b_n) \Rightarrow q).$$

Often it is convenient to rewrite an assertion of the form

$$\{p\}\, x \, := \, e_0 \quad \text{if} \quad b_0 \; \sim \; \ldots \; \sim \; e_n \quad \text{if} \quad b_n \; \{q\}$$

as the following set of assertions:

$$\{p \wedge b_0\}\, x \, := \, e_0 \; \{q\},$$

.

.

.

$$\{p \wedge b_n\}\, x \, := \, e_n \; \{q\},$$

$$p \wedge (\neg b_0 \wedge \ldots \wedge \neg b_n) \Rightarrow q.$$

The proof rule for multiple assignment statements has been treated in the literature. Therefore we do not discuss it in detail here; we merely point out how that proof rule is to be modified for UNITY assignment statements.

The precondition of an assignment is obtained from a given postcondition by simultaneously substituting for left-hand-side variables the corresponding expressions on the right-hand side. A quantified assignment in UNITY may assign to an array of variables. To understand how the precondition is obtained from a postcondition in this case, we first review the treatment of assignment to subscripted variables. Any assignment to a subscripted variable is regarded as an assignment to the whole array. Hence, to compute the precondition, the array name in the postcondition is replaced by an expression that denotes the array obtained as a result of the assignment. The notation $(A; i \, : \, u)$ denotes an array whose i^{th} element is u; the remaining elements are the same as the corresponding elements of A. We extend this notation by allowing quantification over array subscripts, as illustrated in the following example.

Example 3.1

Consider the following quantified-assignment statement and its postcondition:

$$\langle \| \, i \, : \, 0 \leq i \leq N \quad :: \quad A[i] \, := \, A[N - i] \rangle$$
$$\{\langle \wedge \, j \, : \, 0 \leq j < N \quad :: \quad A[j] < A[j + 1] \rangle\}.$$

The precondition is obtained by substituting $(A; \, i \, : \, 0 \leq i \leq N \, :: \, A[N - i])$ for all occurrences of A in the postcondition. Thus we obtain

$$\langle \wedge \, j : \, 0 \leq j < N \quad ::$$

$$(A; \, i \, : \, 0 \leq i \leq N \quad :: \quad A[N - i])[j]$$
$$< (A; \, i \, : \, 0 \leq i \leq N \quad :: \quad A[N - i])[j + 1]$$

$$\rangle.$$

This simplifies to

$$\langle \wedge\, j \;:\; 0 \leq j < N \;\;::\;\; A[N-j] < A[N-(j+1)]\rangle$$
$$\equiv\; \langle \wedge\, j \;:\; 0 < j \leq N \;\;::\;\; A[j] < A[j-1]\rangle. \hspace{2cm} \triangledown$$

Exercise 3.1 Derive preconditions from the following statements and post-conditions:

1. $x, y \;:=\; y, x$ if $x > y$ $\{x > 3\}$

2. $A[i], i \;:=\; A[i-1], i+1$ if $1 \leq i < N$ $\{A[2] = 3\ \wedge\ i = 2\}$ $\hspace{1cm}\triangledown$

3.2.2 Quantified Assertions

For a given program F, we write the quantified assertions

$$\langle \forall\, s \;:\; s \text{ in } F \;\;::\;\; \{p\}\, s\, \{q\}\rangle$$

and

$$\langle \exists\, s \;:\; s \text{ in } F \;\;::\;\; \{p\}\, s\, \{q\}\rangle$$

to denote that $\{p\}\ s\ \{q\}$ holds for all statements and some statement in F, respectively. (When the program, F, is understood from the context, we will omit its name from the quantification.) If the program contains a quantified statement list, the quantification over statements is applied to each individual statement in that statement list. Thus

$$\langle \forall\, s \;:\; s \text{ in } \langle\| \, i \;:\; b(i) \;\;::\;\; t(i)\rangle \;\;::\;\; \{p\}\, s\, \{q\}\rangle$$

is proven by showing that $\{p\ \wedge\ b(i)\}\ t(i)\ \{q\}$. Similarly,

$$\langle \exists\, s \;:\; s \text{ in } \langle\| \, i \;:\; b(i) \;\;::\;\; t(i)\rangle \;\;::\;\; \{p\}\, s\, \{q\}\rangle$$

is proven by demonstrating a j such that $b(j)$ and $\{p\ \wedge\ b(j)\}\ t(j)\ \{q\}$ hold.

Example 3.2

We give some examples of program properties and then propose equivalent assertions.

1. The value of x is nondecreasing.

In the following, the assertion is universally quantified over all integer values of k.

$$\langle \forall\, s \;\;::\;\; \{x = k\}\ s\ \{x \geq k\}\rangle$$

2. A message stays in the channel as long as it is not received.

Let the predicate *inch* denote that a (particular) message is in the channel, and *rcvd* denote that this message has been received.

$$\langle \forall\ s\ ::\ \{inch\}\ s\ \{inch\ \lor\ rcvd\}\rangle$$

3. Same as above, with the additional requirement that a received message is removed from the channel.

$$\langle \forall\ s\ ::\ \{inch\ \land\ \neg rcvd\}\ s\ \{(inch\ \land\ \neg rcvd)\ \lor\ (\neg inch\ \land\ rcvd)\}\rangle$$

4. The value of x is nondecreasing and it will increase.

One way to prove this is by proving the following two assertions. An explanation of why these two assertions are sufficient is given in Section 3.4.4. In the following, each assertion is universally quantified over all integer values of k.

$$\langle \forall\ s\ ::\ \{x = k\}\ s\ \{x \geq k\}\rangle$$

$$\langle \exists\ t\ ::\ \{x = k\}\ t\ \{x > k\}\rangle \qquad \triangledown$$

Exercise 3.2   Express the following properties in terms of assertions. In the following, x, y are integer-valued variables.

1. Once x becomes positive, its value is unchanged thereafter.

2. If x is negative, it remains negative or it exceeds 5.

3. The value of x does not change as long as the value of y does not change (x, y may change simultaneously). $\qquad \triangledown$

3.2.3 Conventions about Priorities of Logical Relations

To avoid extensive use of parentheses we adopt the following conventions about the priorities (binding powers) of logical relations. We group the relations having the same priority (enclosing a group within parentheses) and list different groups in increasing order of priority: (*unless, ensures, leads-to*), ($\equiv$), ($\Rightarrow$), ($\land, \lor$), ($=, \neq$), ($\neg$). Other relations and functions have higher priorities. For predicates p, q, $p \equiv q$ and $p = q$ have identical meanings. However, since their binding powers are different, we can unambiguously write an expression such as $p = p' \equiv q \neq q'$.

3.3   A Model of Program Execution

In this section, we formalize our operational view of program execution. With each program, we associate a set of *execution sequences*, which are infinite sequences, each denoting one possible execution of the program. Let R denote any one of these sequences, and R_i, $i \geq 0$ denote the ith element of the sequence. Each R_i is a tuple: $R_i.state$ and $R_i.label$, where $R_i.label$ is the name of the statement selected for execution on the ith step (steps are numbered from 0) and $R_i.state$ is the state of the program, i.e., the values of all its variables, in this particular execution before the ith step. Thus $R_0.state$ is the initial state; the initial state may not be same for all sequences if the initial values of *all* variables are not specified in the program. Observe that for any R and i, $i \geq 0$, $R_{i+1}.state$ is uniquely determined by $R_i.state$ and $R_i.label$ because execution of a statement in a UNITY program leads to a unique next state from a given state. Thus $R_0.state$ and $R_j.label$, for all j, $0 \leq j < i$, determine $R_i.state$.

The requirement of fair selection gives rise to the following condition: For any R and any statement s, $R_i.label = s$, for an infinite number of indices i.

We use $p[R_i]$ to denote that predicate p holds in the state $R_i.state$.

The assertion $\{p\}$ s $\{q\}$ means that, for all R and i,

$$(p[R_i] \quad \wedge \quad R_i.label = s) \quad \Rightarrow \quad q[R_{i+1}].$$

We use the program-execution model to formalize our operational understanding of program execution. However, we never use this formalism to reason about the properties of a program; all such reasoning is carried out using assertions rather than execution sequences.

One consequence of our program-execution model is that the number of machines among which a UNITY program is partitioned for execution is irrelevant for the development of a proof theory. We adopt the convention that executions of different machines are *fairly interleaved*, i.e., the effect of (a pair of machines) executing statements simultaneously is the same as executing the two statements in some arbitrary order; furthermore no machine is prevented forever from executing a statement. It is easy to see that the set of possible execution sequences for a program is the same no matter how many machines are employed. Therefore properties of a UNITY program remain unchanged if its statements are partitioned for executions on multiple processors. This is why there are no notions of "contention," "race condition," "overtaking," etc. in reasoning about a UNITY program.

3.4   Fundamental Concepts

In this section we define three fundamental logical relations: *unless* (and its special cases, **stable** and **invariant**), *ensures*, and *leads-to*. The notion of a *fixed point* of a program is also introduced; this notion is useful for reasoning about "terminating" programs, i.e., programs in which, eventually, there is no state change.

A *property* of a program is of the following form:

p *unless* q or,

p is stable (also written as **stable** p)   or,

p is invariant (also written as **invariant** p)   or,

p *ensures* q or,

p $\longmapsto$ q

where p, q are predicates on program states. (Note that fixed-point predicates are not properties.) The first three properties are often called *safety* properties, and the latter two, *progress* properties.

3.4.1 A Note on Quantification

In this book, properties and inference rules are often written without explicit quantifications; these are universally quantified over all values of the free variables occurring in them. For example,

$x = k$ *unless* $x > k$,

where x is a program variable and k is a free variable, should be understood as

$\langle \forall\, k \;::\; x = k \;\; unless \;\; x > k \rangle.$

(The set over which k is quantified is understood from the context.) Similarly, the following instance of an inference rule, where x, y are program variables and m, n are free,

$$\frac{\begin{array}{c} x = m \;\; unless \;\; x > m\ , \\ y = n \;\; unless \;\; y < n \end{array}}{x = m \;\lor\; y = n \;\; unless \;\; x > m \;\lor\; y < n}$$

is to be understood as

$\langle \forall\, m, n \;::$

$$\frac{\begin{array}{c} x = m \;\; unless \;\; x > m\ , \\ y = n \;\; unless \;\; y < n \end{array}}{x = m \;\lor\; y = n \;\; unless \;\; x > m \;\lor\; y < n}$$

$\rangle.$

3.4.2 Unless

For a given program F, p *unless* q is defined as follows:

$$p \ \ unless \ \ q \ \equiv \ \langle \forall \ s \ : \ s \ \text{in} \ F \ \ :: \ \ \{p \wedge \neg q\} \ s \ \{p \vee q\} \rangle.$$

Thus if p is *true* at some point in the computation and q is not, in the next step (i.e., after execution of a statement) p remains *true* or q becomes *true*. Hence if p holds at any point during the execution of F, then either

- q never holds and p continues to hold forever, or

- q holds eventually (it may hold initially when p holds) and p continues to hold at least until q holds.

This can be formalized using the program-execution model. From the definition of p *unless* q we deduce

$$(p \wedge \neg q)[R_i] \ \ \Rightarrow \ \ (p \vee q)[R_{i+1}].$$

Then it is easy to deduce that

$$p[R_i] \ \ \Rightarrow$$

$$\langle \forall \ j \ : \ j \geq i \ \ :: \ \ (p \wedge \neg q)[R_j] \rangle \ \ \text{(i.e., } p \wedge \neg q \text{ holds forever)} \ \vee$$

$$[\langle \exists \ k \ : \ k \geq i \ \ :: \ \ q[R_k] \ \ \text{(i.e., } q \text{ holds eventually)} \ \wedge$$

$$\langle \forall \ j \ : \ i \leq j < k \ \ :: \ \ (p \wedge \neg q)[R_j] \rangle \ \text{(i.e., until then } p \wedge \neg q \text{ holds)} \rangle$$

$$\rangle].$$

Example 3.3

We write some of the assertions from Example 3.2 using *unless*.

1. The value of x never decreases.

$$x = k \ \ unless \ \ x > k$$

or

$$x \geq k \ \ unless \ \ x > k$$

or

$$x \geq k \ \ unless \ \ false$$

2. A message stays in the channel as long as it is not received and a received message is removed from the channel.

Let the predicates *inch*, *rcvd* denote that a message is in the channel and that the message has been received, respectively.

$$inch \; \wedge \; \neg rcvd \;\; unless \;\; \neg inch \; \wedge \; rcvd \qquad \triangledown$$

Exercise 3.3   Express the properties in Exercise 3.2 using *unless*. $\triangledown$

3.4.3 Special Cases of Unless

Now we define two fundamental notions of our proof theory: *stable* and *invariant*. For a given program,

p is stable $\; \equiv \;$ p *unless false*

q is invariant $\; \equiv \;$ (initial condition $\; \Rightarrow \;$ q) $\; \wedge \;$ q is stable

A stable predicate remains *true* once it becomes *true* (though it may never become *true*). An invariant is always *true*: All states of the program that arise during any execution of the program satisfy all invariants. These two concepts are crucial in all aspects of program design and proof; they occur throughout this book.

Observe that p is stable is equivalent to $\langle \forall \; s \; :: \; \{p\} \; s \; \{p\} \rangle$. Therefore, if p is stable, we say that p is *preserved* by every statement of the program.

Observation: If I, J are stable predicates of a given program, then $I \wedge J$ and $I \vee J$ are also stable predicates of that program. The same observation applies to invariants. $\triangledown$

Notational Convention: We write

constant p

to denote that p and $\neg p$ are both stable. $\triangledown$

Substitution Axiom

If $x = y$ is an invariant of a program F, x can replace y in all properties of F. This is a generalization of Leibniz's rule for substitution of equals. A particularly useful form of this axiom is to replace *true* by any invariant I, and vice versa. This is because $I = true$ is an invariant, for any invariant I. Therefore when the program context is understood, we sometimes write merely I in place of "I is an invariant." In this sense, invariants resemble the way in which theorems are written in mathematics because an invariant is a theorem within the restrictive context of a given program.

We illustrate a consequence of this axiom. We show that

$$\frac{p \;\; unless \;\; q \; , \;\; \neg q \text{ is invariant}}{p \text{ is stable}}$$

Proof:

$\neg q \;\equiv\; true$	, because $\neg q$ is invariant
$p \;\;unless\;\; q$	, from the premise
$p \;\;unless\;\; false$	, substitution axiom on the above two
p is stable	, from the definition of stable $\triangledown$

Equating an invariant with *true* also means that for any invariant I we can replace a predicate p in a property by $I \wedge p$ or $\neg I \vee p$; a term $I \wedge q$ can be replaced by q. Therefore we can prove, for instance, that p is stable by showing that $I \wedge p$ is stable, even though p alone cannot be proven to be stable using the definition.

Treatment of the Always-Section

The always-section of a program can be regarded as defining an invariant. This invariant is obtained from the equations in the always-section in exactly the same manner as the initial condition is obtained from the initially-section. It is helpful to construct this invariant first, and then construct proofs of additional program properties based on this invariant.

3.4.4 Ensures

The *ensures* relation (over predicates) is used to define the most basic progress properties of programs. For a given program, F, p *ensures* q is defined as follows:

$$p \;\;ensures\;\; q \;\;\equiv\;\; (p \;\;unless\;\; q \;\wedge\; \langle \exists\, s \,:\, s \text{ in } F \;::\; \{p \,\wedge\, \neg q\}\, s\, \{q\}\rangle).$$

Thus if p is *true* at some point in the computation, p remains *true* as long as q is *false* (from p *unless* q), and eventually q becomes *true*. The claim that q becomes *true* can be justified as follows. From the second conjunct in the definition of *ensures*, there is a statement s in F whose execution in a state satisfying $p \wedge \neg q$ establishes q. From the fairness rule in statement execution, statement s is executed sometime after p becomes *true*. If q has not been established in the meantime (i.e., at or after p becomes *true* and before the execution of s), then $\neg q$ holds before execution of s and from p *unless* q, p also holds. Execution of s in this state (satisfying $p \wedge \neg q$) establishes q.

From p *ensures* q we can deduce, in terms of the program execution model, that

$$p[R_i] \;\;\Rightarrow\;\; \langle \exists\, j \,:\, j \geq i \;::\; q[R_j] \;\wedge\; \langle \forall\, k \,:\, i \leq k < j \;::\; p[R_k]\rangle\rangle.$$

Example 3.4

To prove that the value of x is nondecreasing and that x will increase (see Example 3.2), it suffices to show that

$x = k$ *ensures* $x > k$.

Note: From the convention about quantification, we interpret

$x = k$ *ensures* $x > k$

to mean

$\langle \forall\ k\ \ ::\ \ x = k\ \ unless\ \ x > k \rangle,$

$\langle \forall\ k\ \ ::\ \ \langle \exists\ s\ \ ::\ \ \{x = k\}\ \ s\ \ \{x > k\} \rangle \rangle.$

Therefore, for different values of k, different statements may increase x. $\triangledown$

The definition of p *ensures* q refers to the existence of *one* statement that establishes q starting from a state in which $p\ \wedge\ \neg q$ holds. For example, if there are two statements, one establishing q for some of the states satisfying $p\ \wedge\ \neg q$ and the other establishing q for the remaining states, then we cannot claim that p *ensures* q. This point is illustrated in Example 3.5. (We owe the example to Roland Backhouse.)

Example 3.5

The assign-section of a program consists of two statements:

$x\ :=\ 0$ if $x > 0$

$[\![\ x\ :=\ 0$ if $x < 0$

It is trivially true that once $x \neq 0$ holds it continues to hold until $x = 0$ holds; also, $x = 0$ is guaranteed to hold eventually in the above program. However, $x \neq 0$ *ensures* $x = 0$ is not a property of the above program, because there is no statement s in this program such that $\{x \neq 0\}\ s\ \{x = 0\}$. $\triangledown$

Exercise 3.4   For the following program, *alt*, show that $0 \leq x - y \leq 1$ is an invariant. Also show that

$x = k$ *ensures* $y = k$,

$y = k$ *ensures* $x = k + 1$.

Program *alt*

   declare x, y : integer

   initially $x, y = 0, 0$

   assign

      $x := y + 1$

   ▮ $y := x$

end $\{alt\}$ ▽

3.4.5 Leads-to

In this book, almost àll progress properties of programs are stated using *leads-to* ($\mapsto$). A given program has the property $p \mapsto q$ if and only if this property can be derived by a finite number of applications of the following inference rules:

-                                  $$\frac{p \ ensures \ q}{p \ \mapsto \ q}$$

- (transitivity) $$\frac{p \ \mapsto \ q \ , \ q \ \mapsto \ r}{p \ \mapsto r}$$

- (disjunction) For any set W, $$\frac{\langle \forall \ m \ : \ m \ \in \ W \ :: \ p(m) \ \mapsto \ q \rangle}{\langle \exists \ m \ : \ m \ \in \ W \ :: \ p(m) \rangle \ \mapsto \ q} .$$

      Given that $p \ \mapsto \ q$ in a program, we can assert that once p becomes *true* q is or will be *true*. However, we cannot assert that p will remain *true* as long as q is not. This is a major difference between *ensures* and *leads-to*. In terms of the program-execution model, from $p \ \mapsto \ q$, we can deduce that

$$p[R_i] \ \Rightarrow \ \langle \exists \ j \ : \ j \geq i \ :: \ q[R_j] \rangle.$$

Notation: As for other transitive relations, we use $p \ \mapsto \ q \ \mapsto \ r$ to stand for $p \ \mapsto \ q$ and $q \ \mapsto \ r$.   ▽

Note: The transitivity rule can be written equivalently as (see Exercise 3.11)

$$\frac{p \ ensures \ q \ , \ q \ \mapsto \ r}{p \ \mapsto \ r} \qquad ▽$$

Note: From the disjunction rule,

$$\frac{p \ \mapsto \ q \ , \ p' \ \mapsto \ q}{p \ \vee \ p' \ \mapsto \ q} \qquad ▽$$

Example 3.6

For the program in Example 3.5, we prove that

$x \neq 0 \;\longmapsto\; x = 0.$

The proof is as follows:

$x \neq 0 \;\; ensures \;\; x \geq 0$, from the program text

$x \neq 0 \;\;\longmapsto\;\; x \geq 0$, from the above

$x \geq 0 \;\; ensures \;\; x = 0$, from the program text

$x \geq 0 \;\;\longmapsto\;\; x = 0$, from the above

$x \neq 0 \;\;\longmapsto\;\; x = 0$, using transitivity on the two *leads-tos*   ▽

Exercise 3.5 Using the properties proven for program *alt* in Exercise 3.4, show that $x = k \;\longmapsto\; y = k + 1$.   ▽

3.4.6 Fixed Point

A *fixed point* of a program, if it exists, is a program state such that execution of any statement in that state leaves the state unchanged. Hence if a fixed point is reached during program execution, further execution of the program does not change its state. If the program state can be changed by some statement outside the program—as is normally the case for a program that runs concurrently with other programs and shares certain variables with them— then a fixed point is a state that can be changed only by other programs. If a program is executing alone, reaching a fixed point is equivalent to termination in standard sequential-programming terminology. An implementation may choose to terminate the program execution in this case.

Define a predicate *FP* for a program G as follows: For each assignment in G, the left and right sides of the assignment are equal in value, i.e.,

$FP \;\equiv\; \langle \forall \text{ statements } s \;:\; s \text{ in } G \wedge s \text{ is } X := E \;::\; X = E \rangle.$

Observe that only fixed points and all fixed points satisfy *FP*. In terms of the program-execution model, for all R and i,

$FP[R_i] \;\equiv\; \langle \forall j \;:\; j \geq i \;::\; R_i.state = R_j.state \rangle.$

Every state "reachable" during a program execution also satisfies any invariant I, and hence every reachable fixed point satisfies $I \wedge FP$.

Example 3.7

We show assign-sections of several programs and their *FP*s.

1. $k := k + 1$

$$FP \quad \equiv \quad k = k + 1$$
$$\equiv \quad false$$

2. $k := k + 1 \quad$ if $\quad k < N$

$$FP \quad \equiv \quad [k < N \quad \Rightarrow \quad k = k + 1]$$
$$\equiv \quad k \geq N$$

3. $\langle \| \, i \, : \, 0 \leq i < N \quad :: \quad m := \max(m, A[i]) \rangle$

$$FP \quad \equiv \quad \langle \wedge \, i \, : \, 0 \leq i < N \quad :: \quad m = \max(m, A[i]) \rangle$$
$$\equiv \quad \langle \wedge \, i \, : \, 0 \leq i < N \quad :: \quad m \geq A[i] \rangle$$
$$\equiv \quad m \geq \langle \max \, i \, : \, 0 \leq i < N \quad :: \quad A[i] \rangle$$

Suppose that $m \leq \langle \max \, i \, : \, 0 \leq i < N \quad :: \quad A[i] \rangle$ holds initially for this program. Then it is easy to see that $m \leq \langle \max \, i \, : \, 0 \leq i < N \quad :: \quad A[i] \rangle$ is an invariant of this program. Therefore every reachable fixed point satisfies $m = \langle \max \, i \, : \, 0 \leq i < N \quad :: \quad A[i] \rangle$. $\qquad \triangledown$

A useful strategy for showing that a program always reaches a fixed point is the following: Display a function, mapping program states to elements of a well-founded set, such that every state change decreases the function value. Of course, any other proof of initial condition $\mapsto$ FP also suffices.

Exercise 3.6 Modify program alt of Exercise 3.4 by adding conditional expressions to the assignment statements, such that the program always reaches a fixed point and, at any fixed point, $x = 10$ and $y = 9$. $\qquad \triangledown$

3.5 A Complete Example

We use one program to illustrate the major concepts of this chapter. The goal of the program is to divide M by N, where M, N are integers, $M \geq 0$, $N > 0$; the quotient is stored in x, and the remainder in y. The specification of the program is that the predicate

$$x \times N + y = M \quad \wedge \quad 0 \leq y < N$$

holds at any fixed point, and that a fixed point is reached eventually.

Program *division*

    declare $\quad x, y, z, k \,$: integer

    initially $\quad x, y, z, k = 0, M, N, 1$

assign

$$z,k := 2 \times z, 2 \times k \qquad \text{if} \quad y \geq 2 \times z \quad \sim$$
$$N \quad, 1 \qquad \text{if} \quad y < 2 \times z$$
$$\| \quad x,y := x+k, y-z \qquad \text{if} \quad y \geq z$$

end {*division*}

This is not an efficient program for division, but it is chosen mainly for purposes of illustration.

3.5.1 Proofs of Some Unless Relations

We show that y does not increase as long as $y \geq z \geq N$. Also, y does not change value, nor does z increase, as long as $y < z$ and $z > N$. Formally, we claim that, for all m, n,

$$y \geq z \geq N \quad \wedge \quad y = m \quad unless \quad y < m$$

$$(y,z) = (m,n) \quad \wedge \quad y < z \quad \wedge \quad z > N \quad unless \quad y = m \quad \wedge \quad z < n.$$

We show the assertions only to prove the first property, leaving the remaining work to the reader. We must prove the following assertion for the first statement of the program:

$$\{y \geq z \geq N \quad \wedge \quad y = m \quad \wedge \quad y \geq m\}$$
$$z,k := 2 \times z, 2 \times k \qquad \text{if} \quad y \geq 2 \times z \quad \sim$$
$$N, 1 \qquad \text{if} \quad y < 2 \times z$$
$$\{(y \geq z \geq N \quad \wedge \quad y = m) \quad \vee \quad y < m\}.$$

This assertion can be seen from the following two, which are proven by straightforward application of the proof rule for assignment:

$$\{y \geq 2 \times z \wedge z \geq N \wedge y = m\} \, z,k := 2 \times z, 2 \times k \, \{y \geq z \geq N \wedge y = m\}$$

and

$$\{y \geq z \geq N \wedge y = m\} \ z,k := N, 1 \ \{y \geq z \geq N \wedge y = m\}.$$

To complete the proof of the first property, we prove the following assertion for the second statement:

$$\{y \geq z \geq N \wedge y = m\} \, x,y := x+k, y-z \, \{y < m\}.$$

Note that the missing alternative—$y < z$, for the second statement— need not be considered in proving an *unless* relation, because execution of the statement under this condition does not change the program state and hence preserves the precondition.

3.5.2 Proof of an Invariant

We prove that I is invariant, where

$$I \;\equiv\; y \geq 0 \;\wedge\; k \geq 1 \;\wedge\; z = N \times k \;\wedge\; x \times N + y = M.$$

First, we show that I is stable, i.e.,

$$\{I\}\; z, k \;:=\; 2 \times z,\; 2 \times k \quad \text{if} \quad y \geq 2 \times z \quad \sim \quad N, 1 \qquad \text{if} \quad y < 2 \times z \; \{I\}$$

$$\{I\}\; x, y \;:=\; x + k,\, y - z \quad \text{if} \quad y \geq z \qquad \{I\}.$$

These reduce to the following assertions.

$$\{I \;\wedge\; y \geq 2 \times z\}\; z, k \;:=\; 2 \times z,\; 2 \times k \; \{I\}$$

$$\{I \;\wedge\; y < 2 \times z\}\; z, k \;:=\; N,\, 1 \; \{I\}$$

$$\{I \;\wedge\; y \geq z\}\; x, y \;:=\; x + k,\, y - z \; \{I\}$$

These assertions are proven by straightforward application of the proof rule for assignment. To complete the proof, we have to show that the initial condition implies I. The initial condition of this program is $(x, y, z, k) = (0, M, N, 1) \wedge M \geq 0 \wedge N > 0$, which satisfies I.

3.5.3 Proofs of Some Ensures Relations

We show that

$$y \geq z \;\wedge\; y = m \quad ensures \quad y < m$$

$$(y, z) = (m, n) \;\wedge\; y < z \;\wedge\; z > N \quad ensures \quad y = m \;\wedge\; z < n.$$

These properties, with *ensures* replaced by *unless*, were shown in Section 3.5.1 ($z \geq N$ was shown to be an invariant in Section 3.5.2 and hence is dropped from the first property). To complete the proof, we observe that

$$\{y \geq z \;\wedge\; y = m\}\; x, y \;:=\; x + k,\, y - z \qquad \text{if} \quad y \geq z \; \{y < m\}$$

and

$$\{(y, z) = (m, n) \;\wedge\; y < z \;\wedge\; z > N\}\; z, k := 2 \times z, 2 \times k \quad \text{if} \quad y \geq 2 \times z \; \sim$$

$$N, 1 \qquad \text{if} \quad y < 2 \times z$$

$$\{y = m \;\wedge\; z < n\}.$$

The first assertion is easy to see. In the second assertion, $y < z$ in the precondition implies $y < 2 \times z$. Thus that assertion can be simplified to

$$\{(y, z) = (m, n) \;\wedge\; z > N\}\; z, k \;:=\; N, 1 \; \{y = m \;\wedge\; z < n\}.$$

3.5.4 Proofs of Some Leads-to Relations

We show that

$$(y, z) = (m, n) \;\wedge\; (y \geq z \;\vee\; z > N) \;\mapsto\; (y, z) \;\prec\; (m, n),$$

where $\prec$ is the lexicographic ordering among pairs of integers. From Section 3.5.3, we have

$$y \geq z \;\wedge\; y = m \;\mapsto\; y < m$$

and

$$(y, z) = (m, n) \;\wedge\; y < z \;\wedge\; z > N \;\mapsto\; y = m \;\wedge\; z < n.$$

Using the general disjunction theorem for *leads-to* (see section 3.6.3), the disjunction of the left sides of the previous two properties *leads-to* the disjunctions of their right sides:

$$(y, z) = (m, n) \;\wedge\; (y \geq z \;\vee\; z > N) \;\mapsto\; (y < m \;\vee\; (y = m \;\wedge\; z < n)).$$

Since $(y < m \;\vee\; (y = m \;\wedge\; z < n))$ means $(y, z) \;\prec\; (m, n)$, we have the desired result.

Next, we show that

$$true \;\mapsto\; y < z \leq N.$$

From the invariant (Section 3.5.2), both y, z are nonnegative. The set of pairs of nonnegative integers is well founded under the lexicographic ordering relation, $\prec$. Hence induction can be applied on

$$(y, z) = (m, n) \;\wedge\; (y \geq z \;\vee\; z > N) \;\mapsto\; (y, z) \;\prec\; (m, n)$$

to deduce that $(y \geq z \;\vee\; z > N)$ cannot hold forever, i.e.,

$$true \;\mapsto\; y < z \leq N.$$

A formal statement of the induction principle for *leads-to* is given in Section 3.6.3.

3.5.5 Proofs Relating to Fixed Point

For the given program,

$$
\begin{aligned}
FP \;\equiv\; & (y < 2 \times z \;\vee\; (z = 2 \times z \;\wedge\; k = 2 \times k)) \;\wedge \\
& (y \geq 2 \times z \;\vee\; (z = N \;\wedge\; k = 1)) \qquad\qquad \wedge \\
& (y < z \;\vee\; (x = x + k \;\wedge\; y = y - z)).
\end{aligned}
$$

From the invariant I (proven in Section 3.5.2), where $I \equiv y \geq 0 \;\wedge\; k \geq 1 \;\wedge\; z = N \times k \;\wedge\; x \times N + y = M$, and the above FP, the following predicate holds at every (reachable) fixed point:

$$x \times N + y = M \ \wedge \ 0 \leq y < N.$$

This completes one part of the proof of the division program. The other part is that the program eventually reaches a fixed point, i.e.,

$$true \ \mapsto \ FP.$$

From $true \ \mapsto \ y < z \leq N$, proven in Section 3.5.4, and the fact that $I \ \wedge \ y < z \leq N \ \Rightarrow \ FP$, we have

$$true \ \mapsto \ I \ \wedge \ y < z \leq N \ \Rightarrow \ FP.$$

For any p, q, from $p \Rightarrow q$, we trivially get p *ensures* q, and hence $p \mapsto q$. Therefore $true \ \mapsto \ FP$.

3.6   Theorems about the Fundamental Concepts

In this section we derive a number of useful theorems about *unless* (and *stable* and *invariant*), *ensures*, *leads-to*, and fixed-point predicates. To prove the programs in this book, we rarely resort to the definitions of these concepts (given in Section 3.4); instead we apply the results of this section for almost all such proofs.

3.6.1 Theorems about Unless

The following theorems are used a great deal in this book.

Statements of Theorems

1. Reflexivity and Antireflexivity

$$p \ unless \ p,$$
$$p \ unless \ \neg p$$

2. Consequence Weakening

$$\frac{p \ unless \ q \ , \ q \ \Rightarrow \ r}{p \ unless \ r}$$

3. Conjunction and Disjunction

$$\frac{p \ unless \ q,}{p' \ unless \ q'}$$
$$(p \wedge p') \ unless \ (p \wedge q') \vee (p' \wedge q) \vee (q \wedge q'), \quad \{\text{conjunction}\}$$
$$(p \vee p') \ unless \ (\neg p \wedge q') \vee (\neg p' \wedge q) \vee (q \wedge q') \ \{\text{disjunction}\}$$

4. Simple Conjunction and Simple Disjunction

$$p \ \ unless \ \ q \ ,$$
$$\underline{p' \ \ unless \ \ q'}$$
$$p \wedge p' \ \ unless \ \ q \vee q', \quad \{\text{simple conjunction}\}$$
$$p \vee p' \ \ unless \ \ q \vee q' \quad \{\text{simple disjunction}\}$$

5. Cancellation

$$p \ \ unless \ \ q \ ,$$
$$\underline{q \ \ unless \ \ r}$$
$$p \vee q \ \ unless \ \ r$$

Proofs of Theorems

1. Reflexivity and Antireflexivity

For any statement s, we have

$$\{false\} \ \ s \ \ \{p\},$$

$$\{p\} \ \ s \ \ \{true\}.$$

The results follow by applying the definition of *unless*.   ▽

2. Consequence Weakening

From p *unless* q, for all statements s in the program,

$$\{p \wedge \neg q\} \ \ s \ \ \{p \vee q\}.$$

From $q \Rightarrow r, \ \ \neg r \Rightarrow \neg q$. Hence

$$p \wedge \neg r \Rightarrow p \wedge \neg q, \quad \text{and} \quad p \vee q \Rightarrow p \vee r.$$

Therefore $\{p \wedge \neg r\} \ \ s \ \ \{p \vee r\}$, from which the result follows.   ▽

3. Conjunction and Disjunction

These results are derived from the fact that conjunction, and disjunction, may be applied to the pre- and postconditions of two assertions to yield a valid assertion. Given that for any statement s,

$$\{p \wedge \neg q\} \ \ s \ \ \{p \vee q\}$$

$$\{p' \wedge \neg q'\} \ \ s \ \ \{p' \vee q'\},$$

We have

$$\{p \ \wedge \ \neg q \ \wedge \ p' \ \wedge \ \neg q'\} \ \ s \ \ \{(p \ \vee \ q) \ \wedge \ (p' \ \vee \ q')\} \tag{1}$$

$$\{(p \ \wedge \ \neg q) \ \vee \ (p' \ \wedge \ \neg q')\} \ \ s \ \ \{p \ \vee \ q \ \vee \ p' \ \vee \ q'\}. \tag{2}$$

To prove the conjunction part, we convert the property to an assertion over all statements, and show that the precondition of the assertion implies the precondition of (1) and also show that the postcondition is implied by the postcondition of (1). Similarly, to prove the disjunction rule we apply the same technique with (2).   ▽

4. Simple Conjunction and Simple Disjunction

Use the result of conjunction and disjunction and weaken the consequence in each case.   ▽

5. Cancellation

Apply disjunction and then weaken the consequence.   ▽

Corollaries

1.
$$\frac{p \ \Rightarrow \ q}{p \ unless \ q}$$

Proof: We have $p \ unless \ p$ and $p \ \Rightarrow \ q$. The result follows from consequence weakening.   ▽

2.
$$\frac{\neg p \ \Rightarrow \ q}{p \ unless \ q}$$

Proof: Similar to the above proof.   ▽

3. $[p \ unless \ q \ \vee \ r] \ \equiv \ [p \ \wedge \ \neg q \ unless \ q \ \vee \ r]$

Proof:

(i) $p \ unless \ q \ \vee \ r$, assume

   $\neg q \ unless \ q$, from antireflexivity

   $p \ \wedge \ \neg q \ unless \ q \ \vee \ r$, using simple conjunction
                              on the above two

(ii) $p \ \wedge \ \neg q \ unless \ q \ \vee \ r$, assume

   $p \ \wedge \ q \ unless \ q$, from corollary (1)

   $p \ unless \ q \ \vee \ r$, using simple disjunction on
                              the above two   ▽

4.
$$\frac{p \ \vee \ q \ \ unless \ \ r}{p \ \ unless \ \ q \ \vee \ r}$$

Proof:

$p \ \vee \ q \ \ unless \ \ r$	, given
$\neg q \ \ unless \ \ q$	, from antireflexivity
$p \ \wedge \ \neg q \ \ unless \ \ q \ \vee \ r$	, using simple conjunction on the above two
$p \ \ unless \ \ q \ \vee \ r$	, using corollary (3) $\qquad \triangledown$

5. For any finite set of predicates p_i, q_i, $0 \leq i < N$,

$$\frac{\langle \forall \ i \ :: \ p_i \ \ unless \ \ p_i \ \wedge \ q_i \rangle}{\langle \forall \ i \ :: \ p_i \rangle \ \ unless \ \ \langle \forall \ i \ :: \ p_i \rangle \ \wedge \ \langle \exists \ i \ :: \ q_i \rangle}$$

Proof: The result is trivial for $N \leq 1$. Use conjunction for $N = 2$. Apply induction over N. $\qquad \triangledown$

Exercise 3.7 Prove the following.

1. $p \ \ unless \ \ true,$

$true \ \ unless \ \ p,$

$false \ \ unless \ \ p$

2. (due to He Ji Feng) Given that $p \ \wedge \ \neg q \ \Rightarrow \ p' \ \Rightarrow \ p \ \vee \ q$, show that

$p \ \ unless \ \ q \ \equiv \ p' \ \ unless \ \ q.$

Hint: From $p \ \wedge \ \neg q \ \Rightarrow \ p' \ \Rightarrow \ p \ \vee \ q$, we get

$p \ \wedge \ \neg q \ \equiv \ p' \ \wedge \ \neg q$. Hence

$p \ \wedge \ \neg q \ \ unless \ \ q \ \equiv \ p' \ \wedge \ \neg q \ \ unless \ \ q.$

3.
$$\frac{p \ \vee \ p' \ \ unless \ \ q \ \vee \ r \ , \quad q \ \vee \ q' \ \ unless \ \ p \ \vee \ r'}{p \ \vee \ p' \ \vee \ q \ \vee \ q' \ \ unless \ \ (p \ \wedge \ q) \ \vee \ r \ \vee \ r'}$$

Note: This is a generalization of cancellation.

4.
$$\frac{p \ \vee \ q \ \text{is stable}}{p \ \ unless \ \ q}$$

5.
$$\frac{p \ \ unless \ \ q \ , \ q \ \ unless \ \ p \ , \ \neg(p \ \wedge \ q)}{p \ \vee \ q \ \text{is stable}} \qquad \triangledown$$

Exercise 3.8 This exercise provides useful information for converting a quantified assertion of the form

$$\langle \forall s \; : \; s \text{ in } F \quad :: \quad \{p'\} \; s \; \{q'\} \rangle$$

to *p unless q*, for program *F*.

Let p', q' be two given predicates and p, q be unknowns in the following equations:

$$p' = p \land \neg q, \; q' = p \lor q.$$

When is there a solution to these equations in p, q? Characterize all solutions. $\triangledown$

3.6.2 Theorems about Ensures

The following theorems are seldom used in program proofs in this book; they are mainly used for proving theorems about *leads-to*.

Statements of Theorems

1. Reflexivity

$$p \;\; ensures \;\; p$$

2. Consequence Weakening

$$\frac{p \;\; ensures \;\; q \; , \; q \;\Rightarrow\; r}{p \;\; ensures \;\; r}$$

3. Impossibility

$$\frac{p \;\; ensures \;\; false}{\neg p}$$

4. Conjunction

$$\frac{\begin{array}{c} p \;\; unless \;\; q \; , \\ p' \;\; ensures \;\; q' \end{array}}{p \land p' \;\; ensures \;\; (p \land q') \lor (p' \land q) \lor (q \land q')}$$

5. Disjunction

$$\frac{p \;\; ensures \;\; q}{p \lor r \;\; ensures \;\; q \lor r}$$

Proofs of Theorems

1. Reflexivity

We have p *unless* p. Also, for any statement s,

$$\{p \wedge \neg p\} \quad s \quad \{p\}.$$

Since we assume that every program has at least one statement, the result follows.

$\triangledown$

2. Consequence Weakening

We know from the corresponding theorem for *unless* that the result holds with *ensures* replaced by *unless*. Therefore it is sufficient to show that if there is a statement s such that

$$\{p \wedge \neg q\} \quad s \quad \{q\},$$

then

$$\{p \wedge \neg r\} \quad s \quad \{r\}.$$

The proof follows from

$p \wedge \neg r \;\Rightarrow\; p \wedge \neg q \qquad$, because $\neg r \;\Rightarrow\; \neg q$

$q \;\Rightarrow\; r \qquad\qquad\qquad$, given

$\triangledown$

3. Impossibility

From p *ensures false*, there is a statement s such that

$$\{p\} \quad s \quad \{false\}.$$

The only predicate p for which the above holds is *false*.

$\triangledown$

4. Conjunction

Similar to the proof of the corresponding result for *unless*.

$\triangledown$

5. Disjunction

Prove using the definition of *ensures*.

$\triangledown$

Corollaries

1.
$$\frac{p \;\Rightarrow\; q}{p \;\; ensures \;\; q}$$

Proof: Use p *ensures* p and then weaken the consequence to q.

$\triangledown$

2.
$$\frac{p \ \vee \ q \ \ ensures \ \ r}{p \ \ ensures \ \ q \ \vee \ r}$$

Proof:

$p \ \vee \ q \ \ unless \ \ r$, from $p \ \vee \ q \ \ ensures \ \ r$

$p \ \ unless \ \ q \ \vee \ r$, from the above, using a corollary for *unless*

Applying conjunction to $p \ \vee \ q \ ensures \ r$ and $p \ unless \ q \ \vee \ r$, and then weakening the consequence, we obtain the desired result.   ▽

3.
$$\frac{p \ \ ensures \ \ q \ \vee \ r}{p \ \wedge \ \neg q \ \ ensures \ \ q \ \vee \ r}$$

Proof:

$p \ \ ensures \ \ q \ \vee \ r$, given

$(p \ \wedge \ q) \ \vee \ (p \ \wedge \ \neg q) \ \ ensures \ \ q \ \vee \ r$, trivially from the above

$(p \ \wedge \ \neg q) \ \ ensures \ \ (p \ \wedge \ q) \ \vee \ q \ \vee \ r$, from the above using
                                                                  corollary (2).

$(p \ \wedge \ \neg q) \ \ ensures \ \ q \ \vee \ r$, from the above.   ▽

Exercise 3.9   Show a counterexample to the following claim:
$$\frac{p \ \ ensures \ \ q \ , \ p' \ \ ensures \ \ q'}{p \ \vee \ p' \ \ ensures \ \ q \ \vee \ q'}$$ ▽

3.6.3 Theorems about Leads-to

These theorems are used a great deal in this book.

Statements of Theorems

1. Implication Theorem
$$\frac{p \ \Rightarrow \ q}{p \ \longmapsto \ q}$$

2. Impossibility Theorem
$$\frac{p \ \longmapsto \ false}{\neg p}$$

3. Disjunction Theorem (general)

For any set W:

$$\frac{\langle \forall\ m\ :\ m\ \in\ W\ ::\ p(m)\ \mapsto\ q(m)\rangle}{\langle \exists\ m\ :\ m\ \in\ W\ ::\ p(m)\rangle\ \mapsto\ \langle \exists\ m\ :\ m\ \in\ W\ ::\ q(m)\rangle}$$

4. Cancellation Theorem

$$\frac{p\ \mapsto\ q\ \vee\ b\ ,\ b\ \mapsto\ r}{p\ \mapsto\ q\ \vee\ r}$$

5. PSP (Progress-Safety-Progress) Theorem

$$\frac{p\ \mapsto\ q\ ,\ r\ \textit{unless}\ b}{p\ \wedge\ r\ \mapsto\ (q\ \wedge\ r)\ \vee\ b}$$

6. Completion Theorem

For any finite set of predicates p_i, q_i, $0 \leq i < N$:

$$\frac{\begin{array}{c}\langle \forall\ i\ ::\ p_i\ \mapsto\ q_i\ \vee\ b\rangle,\\ \langle \forall\ i\ ::\ q_i\ \textit{unless}\ b\rangle\end{array}}{\langle \wedge\ i\ ::\ p_i\rangle\ \mapsto\ \langle \wedge\ i\ ::\ q_i\rangle\ \vee\ b}$$

Proofs of Theorems

Many theorems about *leads-to* can be proven using induction on the *structure of the proof*, as follows. If $p \mapsto q$ appears in the premise of a theorem, we may apply induction on the *length* of this proof, i.e., the number of inference rules for *leads-to* that have been applied in constructing the proof of $p \mapsto q$. Thus the strategy is:

- Base case (the length of the proof of $p \mapsto q$ is 1). Prove the theorem for

  $p\ ensures\ q.$

- Inductive step (the length of the proof of $p \mapsto q$ exceeds 1).

  (transitivity)   Assume that the last step in the proof of $p \mapsto q$ is to apply transitivity to $p \mapsto r$ and $r \mapsto q$, for some r. Proofs of $p \mapsto r$ and $r \mapsto q$ have smaller lengths than $p \mapsto q$. As induction hypothesis, assume that the desired theorem holds with each of $p \mapsto r$, $r \mapsto q$ in the premise, and then prove the theorem for $p \mapsto q$. (In some cases, it is more convenient to use $p\ ensures\ r$ instead of $p \mapsto r$, above.)

(disjunction)   Assume that the last step in the proof of $p \mapsto q$ is to apply disjunction to $\langle \forall\, m\ :\ m \in W\ ::\ p(m) \mapsto q \rangle$ where $p = \langle \exists\, m\ :\ m \in W\ ::\ p(m) \rangle$. Clearly, each of the proofs $p(m) \mapsto q$ has smaller length than $p \mapsto q$. As induction hypothesis, assume that the desired theorem holds for each $p(m) \mapsto q$, and then prove the theorem for $p \mapsto q$.

In those cases where more than one *leads-to* appears in the premise, as in the completion theorem, we will use some combination of individual proof lengths to carry out the induction.

We use this strategy in proving some of the theorems about *leads-to*.

1. Implication Theorem

$p\ \Rightarrow\ q$, premise

$p\ \ ensures\ \ q$, from the above

$p\ \ \mapsto\ \ q$, from the above   ▽

2. Impossibility Theorem

Base case:

$p\ \ ensures\ \ false$, assume

$\neg p$, from impossibility result of *ensures*

Inductive step:

(transitivity)   Given as the induction hypothesis,

$p\ \ \mapsto\ \ r\ ,\ r\ \ \mapsto\ \ q,$

$\dfrac{p\ \ \mapsto\ \ false}{\neg p}$,

$\dfrac{r\ \ \mapsto\ \ false}{\neg r}$,

show $\neg p$, using the premise.

Proof:

$\neg q$, premise

$\neg r$, from $r \mapsto q$, $\neg q$ and the induction hypothesis

$\neg p$, from $p \mapsto r$, $\neg r$ and the induction hypothesis

(disjunction)   Given as the induction hypothesis,

$$\langle \forall\ m\ :\ m\ \in\ W\ \ ::\ \ p'(m)\ \mapsto\ q \rangle$$

$$p = \langle \exists\ m\ :\ m\ \in\ W\ \ ::\ \ p'(m) \rangle$$

$$\langle \forall\ m\ :\ m\ \in\ W\ \ ::$$

$$\frac{p'(m)\ \ \mapsto\ \ \mathit{false}}{\neg p'(m)}$$

$$\rangle$$

show $\neg p$, using the premise.

Proof:

$\neg q$, premise

$\langle \forall\ m\ :\ m\ \in\ W\ ::\ \neg p'(m) \rangle$, from the induction hypothesis

$\neg \langle \exists\ m\ :\ m\ \in\ W\ ::\ p'(m) \rangle$, from the above

$\neg p$, from the above using the definition of p. $\triangledown$

3. Disjunction Theorem (general)

$\langle \forall\ m\ :\ m\ \in\ W\ \ ::\ \ q(m)\ \Rightarrow\ \langle \exists\ n\ :\ n\ \in\ W\ \ ::\ \ q(n) \rangle \rangle$
    , predicate calculus

$\langle \forall\ m\ :\ m\ \in\ W\ \ ::\ \ q(m)\ \mapsto\ \langle \exists\ n\ :\ n\ \in\ W\ \ ::\ \ q(n) \rangle \rangle$
    , using implication theorem on the above

$\langle \forall\ m\ :\ m\ \in\ W\ \ ::\ \ p(m)\ \mapsto\ q(m) \rangle$
    , premise of the theorem

$\langle \forall\ m\ :\ m\ \in\ W\ \ ::\ \ p(m)\ \mapsto\ \langle \exists\ n\ :\ n\ \in\ W\ \ ::\ \ q(n) \rangle \rangle$
    , using transitivity on the above two

$\langle \exists\ m\ :\ m\ \in\ W\ \ ::\ \ p(m) \rangle\ \mapsto\ \langle \exists\ n\ :\ n\ \in\ W\ \ ::\ \ q(n) \rangle$
    , disjunction on the above $\triangledown$

4. Cancellation Theorem

$b\ \mapsto\ r$, given

$q\ \mapsto\ q$, trivially

$q\ \vee\ b\ \mapsto\ q\ \vee\ r$, using disjunction on the above two

$p\ \mapsto\ q\ \vee\ r$, from $p\ \mapsto\ q\ \vee\ b$ and the above. $\triangledown$

5. PSP Theorem

Base case:

Given p *ensures* q,
         r *unless* b

Show $p \land r \longmapsto (q \land r) \lor b.$

The result follows by using the conjunction result for *ensures* and then weakening the right side.

Inductive step:.

(transitivity)   Given as the induction hypothesis,
$p \longmapsto q'$, $q' \longmapsto q$,
r *unless* b,
$p \land r \longmapsto (q' \land r) \lor b$,
$q' \land r \longmapsto (q \land r) \lor b$,
show
$p \land r \longmapsto (q \land r) \lor b.$

Proof: The result follows by applying cancellation to the last two properties in the induction hypothesis.

(disjunction)   Given as the induction hypothesis,
$\langle \forall m : m \in W :: p'(m) \longmapsto q \rangle$,
$p = \langle \exists m : m \in W :: p'(m) \rangle$,
r *unless* b,
$\langle \forall m : m \in W :: p'(m) \land r \longmapsto (q \land r) \lor b \rangle$,
show
$p \land r \longmapsto (q \land r) \lor b.$

Proof:

$\langle \exists m : m \in W :: p'(m) \land r \rangle \longmapsto (q \land r) \lor b$
        , disjunction on the last property in the induction hypothesis
$\langle \exists m : m \in W :: p'(m) \rangle \land r \longmapsto (q \land r) \lor b$
        , from the above
$p \land r \longmapsto (q \land r) \lor b$
        , from the above using the definition of p. $\triangledown$

6. Completion Theorem

First, we assume a simpler result that is proven later.

$$p \mapsto q \, , \, p' \mapsto q' \, ,$$
$$\frac{q \ \ unless \ \ r \, , \ q' \ \ unless \ \ r}{p \wedge p' \mapsto (q \wedge q') \vee r} \tag{1}$$

From this result we derive

$$p \mapsto q \vee r \, , \, p' \mapsto q' \vee r \, ,$$
$$\frac{q \ \ unless \ \ r \, , \ q' \ \ unless \ \ r}{p \wedge p' \mapsto (q \wedge q') \vee r} \tag{2}$$

Proof of (2) from (1):

$q \ \ unless \ \ r \, , \ q' \ \ unless \ \ r$
      , from the premise of (2)
$q \vee r \ \ unless \ \ r \, , \ q' \vee r \ \ unless \ \ r$
      , applying disjunction on the above and $r \ unless \ r$
$p \wedge p' \ \mapsto \ ((q \vee r) \wedge (q' \vee r)) \vee r$
      , substituting $q \vee r, q' \vee r$ for q, q', in (1)
$p \wedge p' \ \mapsto \ (q \wedge q') \vee r$
      , trivially from the above

The result in (2) is a special case of the completion theorem with $N = 2$. The general case follows by applying induction on N.

Now, we prove (1). We apply induction on pairs (m, n) where m, n are the lengths of the proofs of $p \mapsto q$ and $p' \mapsto q'$, respectively. Define,

$$(m, n) < (m', n') \ \ \equiv \ \ m \leq m' \ \wedge \ n \leq n' \ \wedge \ m + n < m' + n'$$

Base case ($m = 1$ or $n = 1$):

Given

$p \ ensures \ q \, , \ p' \ \mapsto \ q',$
$q \ \ unless \ \ r \, , \ q' \ \ unless \ \ r,$
show
$p \wedge p' \ \mapsto \ (q \wedge q') \vee r,$

Proof:

$p \vee q \ \ unless \ \ r$
          , from $p \ unless \ q$ and $q \ unless \ r$
$(p \vee q) \wedge p' \ \mapsto \ ((p \vee q) \wedge q') \vee r$
          , PSP theorem on the above and $p' \mapsto q'$

$$p \wedge p' \;\mapsto\; (p \wedge q') \vee (q \wedge q') \vee r$$
$\quad$, strengthening left side of the above

$$p \wedge q' \;\mapsto\; (q \wedge q') \vee r$$
$\quad$, PSP theorem on $p \mapsto q$, q' *unless* r

$$p \wedge p' \;\mapsto\; (q \wedge q') \vee r$$
$\quad$, cancellation on the above two.

Inductive step ($m > 1$ and $n > 1$):

(disjunction)   Given as the induction hypothesis,

$$\langle \forall\, m \;:\; m \in W \;\; :: \;\; b(m) \;\mapsto\; q \rangle,\; p' \;\mapsto\; q',$$

$$q \;\textit{unless}\; r,\; q' \;\textit{unless}\; r,$$

$$p = \langle \exists\, m \;:\; m \in W \;\; :: \;\; b(m) \rangle,$$

$$\langle \forall\, m \;:\; m \in W \;\; :: \;\; b(m) \wedge p' \;\mapsto\; (q \wedge q') \vee r \rangle,$$

show

$$p \wedge p' \;\mapsto\; (q \wedge q') \vee r.$$

Proof: Similar to the proof of the corresponding case for the PSP theorem.

(transitivity)   From the symmetry between $p \mapsto q$, $p' \mapsto q'$, a proof similar to the base case can be constructed when p' *ensures* q', and a proof similar to the above disjunction can be constructed when p' is a disjunction of some set of predicates. Therefore given as the induction hypothesis,

$$p \;\textit{ensures}\; b\,,\; b \;\mapsto\; q,$$

$$p' \;\textit{ensures}\; b'\,,\; b' \;\mapsto\; q',$$

$$q \;\textit{unless}\; r\,,\; q' \;\textit{unless}\; r,$$

$$p \wedge b' \;\mapsto\; (q \wedge q') \vee r,$$

$$p' \wedge b \;\mapsto\; (q \wedge q') \vee r,$$

$$b \wedge b' \;\mapsto\; (q \wedge q') \vee r,$$

show

$$p \wedge p' \;\mapsto\; (q \wedge q') \vee r.$$

Note that $(m', n') < (m, n)$, where m', n' are the lengths of the proofs of $p \mapsto q$, $b' \mapsto q'$, respectively. That is why we have $p \wedge b' \mapsto (q \wedge q') \vee r$ as an induction hypothesis. Similar remarks apply to $p' \wedge b \mapsto (q \wedge q') \vee r$ and $b \wedge b' \mapsto (q \wedge q') \vee r$.

Proof:

$$(p \wedge b') \vee (p' \wedge b) \vee (b \wedge b') \;\mapsto\; (q \wedge q') \vee r$$
$\quad$, simple disjunction on the last three properties given

$p \wedge p'$ $ensures$ $(p \wedge b') \vee (p' \wedge b) \vee (b \wedge b')$
         , from p $ensures$ b and p' $ensures$ b', using conjunction

The result follows by applying transitivity on the above two.   ▽

Corollaries

1. (finite disjunction)

$$\frac{p \;\mapsto\; q \,,\, p' \;\mapsto\; q'}{p \vee p' \;\mapsto\; q \vee q'}$$

Proof: This is a special case of general disjunction.   ▽

2. $\dfrac{p \wedge b \mapsto q \,,\, p \wedge \neg b \mapsto q}{p \mapsto q}$

Proof: Follows from corollary (1).   ▽

3. $\dfrac{p \;\mapsto\; q \,,\, r \text{ is stable}}{p \wedge r \mapsto q \wedge r}$

Proof: Follows from the PSP theorem.   ▽

Exercise 3.10   Prove the following:

- $$(p \;\mapsto\; q) \;\equiv\; (p \wedge \neg q \;\mapsto\; q)$$

- $$\frac{p \wedge b \mapsto q \,,\, p \wedge \neg b \;\mapsto\; (p \wedge b) \vee q}{p \;\mapsto\; q}$$

- $$\frac{p \wedge q \;\mapsto\; r}{p \;\mapsto\; \neg q \vee r}$$

- $$\frac{p \;\mapsto\; q \,,\, r \;\; unless \;\; (q \wedge r)}{p \wedge r \;\mapsto\; q \wedge r}$$

- $$\frac{p \;\mapsto\; q \,,\, (r \wedge \neg q) \text{ is stable}}{p \wedge r \;\Rightarrow\; q}$$

- (generalization of the completion theorem)
For any finite set of predicates p_i, q_i, r_i, b_i, where $0 \leq i < N$:

$$\frac{\langle \forall i \;::\; p_i \;\mapsto\; q_i \vee r_i \rangle \,,\; \langle \forall i \;::\; q_i \;\; unless \;\; b_i \rangle}{\langle \wedge i \;::\; p_i \rangle \;\mapsto\; \langle \wedge i \;::\; q_i \rangle \vee \langle \vee i \;::\; r_i \vee b_i \rangle}$$ ▽

Exercise 3.11   Show that if the transitivity rule in the definition of *leads-to* is replaced by

$$\frac{p \; ensures \; q \;, \; q \;\mapsto\; r}{p \;\mapsto\; r}$$

then

$$\frac{p \;\mapsto\; q \;,\; q \;\mapsto\; r}{p \;\mapsto\; r}$$

can be derived as a theorem. Observe that the converse of this result is trivially true.   ▽

Exercise 3.12   (due to Jan L. A. van de Snepscheut)   Given only that

$$\frac{p \; ensures \; q}{p \;\mapsto\; q}$$

and that (transitivity)

$$\frac{p \;\mapsto\; q \;,\; q \;\mapsto\; r}{p \;\mapsto\; r}$$

show that

$$\frac{p \;\mapsto\; q \;,\; p' \;\mapsto\; q'}{p \lor p' \;\mapsto\; q \lor q'}$$

Hint: First prove, using induction, that

$$\frac{p \;\mapsto\; q}{p \lor r \;\mapsto\; q \lor r}$$ ▽

An Induction Principle for Leads-to

The transitivity of *leads-to* can be used to formulate proofs using induction over well-founded sets. Let W be a set well-founded under the relation $\prec$. Let M be a function, also called a *metric*, from program states to W; we write simply M, without its argument, to denote the function value when the program state is understood from the context.

The hypothesis of the following induction rule is that from any program state in which p holds, the program execution eventually reaches a state in which q holds, or it reaches a state in which p holds and the value of metric M is lower. Since the metric value cannot decrease indefinitely (from the well-foundedness of W), eventually a state is reached in which q holds.

$$\textbf{induction} \qquad \frac{\langle \forall \, m \; : \; m \in W \; :: \; p \land M = m \;\mapsto\; (p \land M \prec m) \lor q \rangle}{p \;\mapsto\; q}$$

Proof: In the following proof, we use $p(m)$ to denote $p \land M = m$. The following principle of complete mathematical induction, i.e., induction on well-founded sets, is employed in the proof:

$$
\langle \forall\, m \quad :: \\
\dfrac{\langle \forall\, n \,:\, n \prec m \,::\, A(n)\rangle}{A(m)} \\
\rangle \\
\overline{\qquad\qquad \langle \forall\, m \quad :: \quad A(m)\rangle \qquad\qquad}
$$

where m, n are quantified over any well-founded set $(W, \prec)$, and A is any formula over elements of W.

We choose $A(m)$ to be $p(m) \mapsto q$. Then, from the above:

$$
\langle \forall\, m \quad :: \\
\dfrac{\langle \forall\, n \,:\, n \prec m \,::\, p(n) \mapsto q\rangle}{p(m) \mapsto q} \\
\rangle \\
\overline{\qquad\qquad \langle \forall\, m \quad :: \quad p(m) \mapsto q\rangle \qquad\qquad}
\tag{3}
$$

The outline of the proof is as follows. For any m, from the premise of our induction rule and $\langle \forall\, n \,:\, n \prec m \,::\, p(n) \mapsto q\rangle$ we will establish that $p(m) \mapsto q$. Hence, using (3), we can deduce $\langle \forall\, m \,::\, p(m) \mapsto q\rangle$. Next we deduce $p \mapsto q$ from this fact.

For any m:

$\langle \forall\, n \,:\, n \prec m \,::\, p(n) \mapsto q\rangle$, assume

$\langle \exists\, n \,:\, n \prec m \,::\, p(n)\rangle \mapsto q$, disjunction on the above

$q \mapsto q$, trivially

$\langle \exists\, n \,:\, n \prec m \,::\, p(n)\rangle \lor q \mapsto q$, disjunction on the above two

$p(m) \mapsto \langle \exists\, n \,:\, n \prec m \,::\, p(n)\rangle \lor q$, rewriting the premise of
our induction rule

$p(m) \mapsto q$, transitivity on the above two.

Hence, using (3), we have

$$\langle \forall\ m\ ::\ p(m)\ \longmapsto\ q \rangle$$
$$\langle \exists\ m\ ::\ p(m) \rangle\ \longmapsto\ q \qquad\qquad \text{, disjunction on the above}$$
$$\langle \exists\ m\ ::\ p \wedge M = m \rangle\ \longmapsto\ q \qquad \text{, expanding } p(m)$$
$$p \wedge \langle \exists\ m\ ::\ M = m \rangle\ \longmapsto\ q \qquad \text{, } m \text{ does not occur in } p$$

Now we derive $p \longmapsto q$ by using the substitution axiom to replace $\langle \exists\ m\ ::\ M = m \rangle$ by $true$ because the former is an invariant (every program state maps to some value m). $\qquad\qquad \triangledown$

Exercise 3.13 Show that

$$\frac{\langle \forall\ m\ ::\ p \wedge M = m\ \longmapsto\ M \prec m \rangle}{true\ \longmapsto\ \neg p} \qquad \triangledown$$

Note: In applying the induction rule, the set of program states on which the metric M is defined may be limited to those satisfying $p \wedge \neg q$. $\qquad \triangledown$

3.6.4 Theorems about Fixed Point

From the definition of FP, we can show that $(FP \wedge p)$ is stable for *any* predicate p: Since FP holds whenever $FP \wedge p$ holds, execution of a statement does not change the state, thus preserving $FP \wedge p$. The proof of the following theorem is left to the reader.

Theorem (Stability at fixed point.) For any predicate p, $(FP \wedge p)$ is stable.
$$\triangledown$$

Corollary:

$$\frac{p\ \longmapsto\ q}{FP\ \Rightarrow\ (p\ \Rightarrow\ q)}$$

Proof:

$FP \wedge \neg q$ is stable	, from stability at fixed point
$p \longmapsto q$	, from the premise
$p \wedge FP \wedge \neg q \longmapsto false$	, using the PSP Theorem on the above two
$\neg(p \wedge FP \wedge \neg q)$	, from the Impossibility Theorem for *leads-to*
$FP \Rightarrow (p \Rightarrow q)$	, trivially from the above. $\triangledown$

Exercise 3.14 Show that

$$\frac{p\ \longmapsto\ \neg p,\ \neg p\ \longmapsto\ p}{\neg FP} \qquad \triangledown$$

3.7   Proving Bounds on Progress

A proof of $p \mapsto q$ is a proof that q will hold given that p holds. The amount of computation (in a loose sense) between the establishment of p and the establishment of q is not specified. For instance, in the division program of Section 3.5, we have proved that $true \mapsto y < z \leq N$. However, an arbitrarily long computation may take place before $y < z \leq N$ holds. This is because the first statement of that program can be executed repeatedly in such a fashion that the program state remains the same as the initial state. (To see this, consider an initial state that satisfies $2 \times z \leq y < 4 \times z$: Since $y \geq 2 \times z$, statement execution doubles z and hence establishes $y < 2 \times z$; in the next execution of the statement, z is set back to N, which is the same as the initial state.)

Often we wish to guarantee that the amount of computation between the establishment of p and the establishment of q, is bounded. There are several reasonable measures for the amount of computation—for example, the number of statements executed or the number of state changes. Other measures, such as the number of messages communicated or the number of accesses to a common memory, may be appropriate for certain architectures. Counting the number of executed statements is not usually meaningful. For instance, the second statement of the division program can be executed any number of times without causing a state change after y becomes smaller than z. Therefore we regard the number of state changes as more meaningful.

To show that $p \mapsto q$ within at most n state changes, $n > 0$, it is sufficient to display a function (metric) M mapping program states to natural numbers smaller than n such that, starting in a state in which p holds, any state change establishes q, or preserves p and decreases M's value. Since M can take on at most n different values, at most $n - 1$ state changes are possible before M equals 0; then, q will hold within one more state change.

Exercise 3.15   Consider the following two variations, *division1* and *division2*, of the *division* program of Section 3.5. For each of these programs show that the invariant I of Section 3.5.2 holds and that

$$true \mapsto y < z \leq N$$

is achieved within a bounded number of state changes. Propose tight bounds on the number of state changes, as functions of M, N, in each case.

Program *division1*
   declare   {as in *division*}
   initially   {as in *division*}
   assign
        $x, y, z, k := x + k, y - z, 2 \times z, 2 \times k$ **if** $y \geq z$
   $[\!]$ $z, k := N, 1$

end {*division1*}

Program *division2*
   declare   {as in *division*}
   initially   {as in *division*}
   assign
      $z, k := 2 \times z, 2 \times k$ **if** $y \geq 2 \times z$
   $[\!]$ $z, k := z \div 2, k \div 2$ **if** $y < z \ \wedge \ k > 1$
   $[\!]$ $x, y := x + k, y - z$ **if** $z \leq y < 2 \times z$

end {*division2*} $\triangledown$

Exercise 3.16 The following program is proposed for computing the greatest common divisor of three positive integers, X, Y, Z.

Program *gcd*
   declare x, y, z : integer
   initially $x, y, z = X, Y, Z$
   assign
      $x, y := x - y, y$ **if** $x > y$ $\sim$ $x, y - x$ **if** $y > x$
   $[\!]$ $y, z := y - z, z$ **if** $y > z$ $\sim$ $y, z - y$ **if** $z > y$
   $[\!]$ $z, x := z - x, x$ **if** $z > x$ $\sim$ $z, x - z$ **if** $x > z$

end {*gcd*}

Derive the *FP* of program *gcd*. Determine a suitable invariant to establish that whenever a fixed point is reached, $x = y = z$, and that each of these is the greatest common divisor of X, Y, Z. Show that a fixed point is reached in this program. Propose a bound on the number of state changes, as a function of X, Y, Z, before a fixed point is reached (obtaining a tight bound is not trivial).

Generalize the program to compute the greatest common divisor of N, $N \geq 2$, numbers; prove your program. $\triangledown$

3.8   Additional Properties

The fundamental concepts introduced in Section 3.4 are adequate for the problems treated in this book. For some problems it may be convenient to introduce new kinds of properties and derive theorems about them. For instance, detection algorithms (Chapters 9 and 11) can be specified succinctly by introducing a binary relation *detects* over predicates. The relations we have proposed in this chapter are basic; other relations can be defined in terms of them. To illustrate, we define two relations—*detects* and *until*—in terms of the basic ones and derive some theorems about them.

detects

For a given program, we define p *detects* q as follows:

$$p \ detects \ q \quad \equiv \quad (p \ \Rightarrow \ q) \ \wedge \ (q \ \mapsto \ p).$$

That is, p *detects* q for a program F means that $p \ \Rightarrow \ q$ is an invariant of F, and that if q holds then p holds eventually, in F. It is easy to see that *detects* defines a partial order (i.e., a reflexive, antisymmetric, and transitive relation) over predicates. Also, we have

$$\frac{p \ detects \ q}{FP \ \Rightarrow \ (p \ \equiv \ q)}$$

This result can be proven from the definition of *detects* and the corollary given in Section 3.6.4.

until

We define p *until* q as follows:

$$p \ until \ q \quad \equiv \quad (p \ unless \ q) \ \wedge \ (p \ \mapsto \ q).$$

That is, p *until* q means that p holds at least as long as q does not and that eventually q holds. Note that p *until* q differs from p *ensures* q; in the latter case, there is the additional constraint that exactly one statement of the program establishes q as the postcondition given $p \ \wedge \ \neg q$ as the precondition. Thus in Example 3.5, $x \neq 0$ *until* $x = 0$ is a property of the program, though $x \neq 0$ *ensures* $x = 0$ is not a property. We state a few facts about *until* that the reader can verify:

$$\frac{p \ \ ensures \ \ q}{p \ until \ q}$$

$$\frac{p \ until \ q \ , \ \ q \ \Rightarrow \ r}{p \ until \ r}$$

$$\frac{p \ until \ false}{\neg p}$$

$$\frac{p \ until \ q \ , \quad p' \ until \ q'}{p \ \vee \ p' \ until \ q \ \vee \ q'}$$

Summary

In this chapter, we have proposed a logic for UNITY. The basic idea is to use familiar assertions of the form $\{p\} \ s \ \{q\}$. A UNITY program has a set of statements, which naturally leads to quantifying the assertions over the statements of a program. We found that the two kinds of quantification, universal and existential, are appropriate for reasoning about two kinds of program properties, safety and progress, respectively. It is interesting to note that the essence of the fairness rule is captured using existential quantification in the definition of *ensures*. We defined *leads-to* inductively, using *ensures*. This combination gives us the power of induction to reason about progress properties while admitting fairness in program execution.

We have defined *unless*, *ensures*, and *leads-to* for describing properties of programs, not their individual execution sequences. Reasoning about a program never refers to its execution model; only the program text or program specification is used in such reasoning.

The theorems in this chapter refer to a single program. The theory of program composition, introduced in Chapter 7, deals with properties of ensembles of programs.

Bibliographic Notes

The notation for assertions, $\{p\} \ s \ \{q\}$, was introduced in Hoare [1969]. The proof rule for multiple assignment statements is in Gries [1981]. The use of temporal logic in proving programs was proposed in Pnueli [1981]. Our proof theory has been deeply influenced by temporal logic. The notions of safety and progress are from Lamport [1977]; formal definitions of these notions may be found in Alpern and Schneider [1985]. Many of our ideas in proving progress properties, using *leads-to*, have been influenced by Lamport [1977] and Owicki and Lamport [1982]; we have adopted an axiomatic approach instead of using operational models, such as execution sequences, for our progress proofs. The notion of *ensures* is inspired by the "helpful directions" introduced in Lehmann, Pnueli, and Stavi [1981]. Mechanical verifications of temporal-logic formulas are treated in Clarke, Emerson, and Sistla [1986].

CHAPTER 4

Architectures and Mappings

4.1   Introduction

Descriptions of program designs in UNITY have two complementary parts:

- A formal part containing the UNITY programs and proofs.

- An informal part containing descriptions of architectures, mappings of programs to architectures, and motivations for design steps.

The formal part is independent of architecture and therefore does not use terms such as processor, memory, channel, message, and control flow. This chapter considers the informal part, describing how UNITY programs can be executed on different architectures.

There are many ways to execute a UNITY program on an architecture. Therefore, in addition to a program, a programmer also prescribes a particular implementation, called a *mapping*. Mappings are described informally in this book. (We expect, however, that a formal notation for mappings can be developed.) Mappings are not necessary for von Neumann programs executing on von Neumann architectures because the programming notations are so close to the architecture.

In Section 4.2, we suggest the forms that mappings might take for different architectures. Later in this chapter we describe implementations of UNITY programs on a few architectures. To facilitate this description, the concept of *program schema* is introduced in Section 4.3. A program schema is a class of UNITY programs and associated mappings. In Section 4.3 we also propose different implementation strategies for different program schemas. Implementations of UNITY programs as electronic circuits are described briefly in Section 4.4.

4.2   Mappings

This section suggests mappings to asynchronous shared-memory architectures, distributed systems, and synchronous architectures.

4.2.1 Mappings to Asynchronous Shared-Memory Architectures

An asynchronous shared-memory computer consists of a fixed set of processors and a fixed set of memories. Associated with each memory is the set of processors that can read from it and the set of processors that can write into it. A mapping of a UNITY program to an asynchronous shared-memory computer (1) allocates each statement in the program to a processor, (2) allocates each variable to a memory, and (3) specifies the control flow for each processor (i.e., the mapping specifies the sequence in which each processor executes the statements assigned to it). The mapping must satisfy the following constraints:

- All variables on the left side of each statement allocated to a processor (except subscripts of arrays) are in memories that can be written by the processor, and all variables on the right side (and all array subscripts) are in memories that can be read by the processor.

- The flow of control for each processor is such that every statement allocated to the processor is executed infinitely often.

4.2.2 **Mappings to Distributed Systems**

A distributed system consists of a fixed set of processors, a fixed set of channels, and a local memory for each processor. A local memory of a processor is a memory that only that processor can read or write. Channels are error free and deliver messages in the order sent. For each channel, there is exactly one processor that sends messages along that channel, and exactly one processor that receives messages along that channel. Associated with each channel is a buffer. For each channel, the only action that can be taken by the sending processor is to send a message if the buffer is not full, and the only action that can be taken by the receiving processor is to receive a message if the buffer is not empty.

Mapping a UNITY program to a distributed system is the same as in the asynchronous shared-memory case, except that each variable is allocated either to (the local memory of) a processor or to a channel. In addition to the constraints of the shared-memory case, the mapping must satisfy the following constraints:

1. At most one variable is allocated to each channel, and this variable is of type sequence. (The variable allocated to a channel represents the sequence of messages in transit along it.)

2. A variable allocated to a channel is named in statements of exactly two processors, and these statements are of the following form: The statements in one of the processors modify the variable by appending an item of data (the message) to the rear of the sequence, if the size of the sequence does not exceed a constant (the buffer size); statements in the other processor modify the variable by deleting the item at the head of the sequence, if the sequence is not null. The variable is not accessed in any other way.

4.2.3 Mappings to Synchronous Architectures

A parallel synchronous computer has the same processor-memory structure as an asynchronous shared-memory computer. In addition, processors in a synchronous architecture have a common clock. At each step (i.e., at each clock tick) each processor executes an instruction. More than one processor may write into the same memory cell, at the same step, provided that all of them write the same value. An arbitrary number of processors may read a memory cell at the same step. Concurrent reading and writing of the same memory cell is not permitted.

An arbitrary number of processors may cooperate in executing a statement concurrently. For example, in a UNITY program, the multiple assignment $x := x + 1 \parallel y := x + 2$ can be executed concurrently by two processors: Both processors read the value of x, then one computes $x + 1$ while the other computes $x + 2$, then one assigns $x + 1$ to x while the other assigns $x + 2$ to y. In the same vein, the statement

$$\langle \parallel i \; : \; 1 \le i \le N \quad :: \quad x[i] \; := \; y[i] + z[i] \rangle$$

can be executed in constant time using N processors. Consider another example: Two processors can compute the expression $w+x+y+z$ concurrently; one processor computes $w + x$ while the other computes $y + z$, and then the sum of $w + x$ and $y + z$ is determined.

In general, mappings from UNITY programs to synchronous architectures are complex. We shall restrict attention, however, to a particularly simple mapping. In the mapping employed in this book, *exactly one statement of the program is executed at a time*, regardless of the number of processors available. In executing each statement, the operations to be carried out are partitioned among the processors. Only after all processors complete execution of one statement is the execution of another statement begun. For example, the operations to be carried out in executing the multiple-assignment $x := x+1 \parallel y := x+2$ can be partitioned among three processors A, B, C as follows: Processor A is responsible for executing $x := x + 1$, processor B for $y := x + 2$, and processor C is idle. Even though processor C could be profitably employed in executing another statement, our simple mapping does not permit it. Our mapping consists of the following:

- A description of how the operations in each statement are to be executed by the processors,

- An allocation of each variable of the program to a memory, and

- A specification of the *single* flow of control, common to all processors.

The mapping must satisfy the constraint that the manner in which processors execute a statement is consistent with the allocation of variables to memories—that is, if a processor modifies a variable, the variable must be allocated to a memory that the processor can write (a similar constraint holds for reading). Also, the flow of control must be such that each statement is executed infinitely often.

Applying an associative operator—such as $\min, \max, +, \times, \wedge, \vee$—to a sequence of data elements can be carried out efficiently in this architecture. Let *op* be an associative operator. Then the expression

$$\langle op\ i\ :\ 1 \leq i \leq N\ \ ::\ \ x[i] \rangle$$

can be computed in $O(\log N)$ time by $O(N)$ processors; on each step, each processor computes *op* applied to two elements, thus halving the number of elements. The expression can be computed in $O(N/k+ \log (k))$ steps by k processors, where $1 \leq k \leq N$: The N elements are divided into segments of N/k elements each. Each processor applies *op* sequentially to N/k elements in $O(N/k)$ time, and then the k processors compute *op* applied to the resulting k elements in $O(\log (k))$ time. More surprisingly, the computation of *op* applied to all prefixes (i.e., $\langle op\ i\ :\ 1 \leq i \leq j\ ::\ x[i] \rangle$, for all j in the range, $1 \leq j \leq N$) can also be accomplished in $O(\log N)$ time by $O(N)$ processors. (See Ladner and Fischer [1980].)

Systolic arrays and other forms of synchronous process arrays are special cases of synchronous architectures.

4.3   Program Schemas

A program schema is a resticted class of UNITY programs and associated mappings. In this section, detailed execution strategies are presented for some schemas. Throughout the book, architectural considerations are limited to designing programs to fit appropriate schemas.

4.3.1 Read-only Schema

A UNITY program and its mapping to an asynchronous shared-memory computer is in the read-only schema if each variable in the program is modified by (statements in) at most one processor (i.e., each variable appears on the left sides of statements in at most one processor). Programs in the read-only schema can be executed on architectures in which each memory is written into by at most one processor.

We distinguish two categories of read-only schema based on the granularity of atomicity in statements:

- Fine-Grain Atomicity. The right side of an assignment in a processor names at most one variable that is modified by other processors. This maps directly to an architecture in which, in each atomic action, a processor accesses at most one memory cell that is written into by other processors.

- Coarse-Grain Atomicity. The right side of an assignment in a processor may name an arbitrary number of variables that are modified by other processors. This maps to an architecture in which, in each atomic action, a processor can access an arbitrary number of memory cells that can be written into by other processors.

These two forms of granularity have been identified because they define the two extremes. Other, intermediate granularities can be similarly characterized by syntactic constraints on program statements. In many cases it is convenient to develop a coarse-grain program and then refine it to a finer-grain program.

4.3.2 Shared-Variable Schema

Given a program and a mapping, a variable is said to be *local* to a processor if the variable is named only in statements allocated to that processor. A program and mapping fit the shared-variable schema if each statement (allocated to a processor) names *at most one* nonlocal variable. The nonlocal variable may appear on the left or the right side of the statement.

Next we propose an implementation of a program, in the shared-variable schema, on a distributed architecture. This implementation employs *locks* on shared variables. At most one processor holds a lock on a shared variable at any time. A processor executes a statement only if it holds a lock on the shared variable (if any) named in that statement. Locks are implemented as follows. There is a set of processors with the sole task of managing locks on shared variables, and each shared variable is allocated to (the local memory of) one of these processors. Let shared-variable x be allocated to processor A. To execute a statement that names x, a processor B takes the following actions:

- Processor B sends a message to processor A requesting a lock on x.

- After receiving a "request-granted" message from processor A, processor B executes the statement, then sends an "unlock x" message to processor A, and then continues with its execution.

Processor A processes requests for locks on each variable in the order received. If there is a lock request outstanding on an unlocked variable, then the variable is locked and a "request-granted" message is sent to the requestor. On receiving an "unlock x" message, processor A unlocks x, and then processes the next request (if any) for x. Deadlock does not arise because a process waits for at most one lock.

A program in the shared-variable schema can be implemented on an asynchronous shared-memory architecture in a similar way. A statement naming a shared variable is implemented by locking the shared variable, executing the assignment, and then unlocking the variable.

A more general version of the shared-variable schema is one in which a statement may name an arbitrary number of shared variables. To guarantee the absence of deadlock, the shared variables are ordered in some (arbitrary) order. To execute a statement, the shared variables named in the statement are locked in the prescribed order, then the assignment is carried out, and then the variables are unlocked.

4.3.3 Equational Schema

A program in the equational schema is a *proper* set of equations, consisting of only the declare-section and the always-sections. (See Chapter 2 for a definition of *proper*.) All the mappings given in Section 4.2 are admissible in this schema.

We propose an implementation of the equational schema on an asynchronous shared-memory computer. Order the equations in a sequence, such that each variable on the right side of an equation is on the left side of an equation that appears earlier in the sequence. Such a sequence exists because the equations are proper. Now transform the sequence of equations into a sequence, G, of assignments by replacing = in each equation by :=. Obviously the values of variables, after executing the sequence of assignments, satisfy the set of equations. The mapping allocates each assignment in G to a processor, and specifies the control flow of each processor so that the assignments are executed in an order consistent with the sequence G.

Next we propose an implementation of G on a distributed architecture. Each variable appears on the left side of exactly one assignment in G because we started with a set of proper equations. Let variable x appear on the left side of an assignment in processor A. We then propose that variable x be stored in the local memory of processor A; for all other processors B, we introduce a local copy $B.x$ of x. After the value of x has been determined, processor A sends the value of x to each processor B, which stores the value in $B.x$. All occurrences of x in statements allocated to processor B are replaced by $B.x$, and such a statement is executed only after $B.x$ is assigned the value of x. Thus statements in B name *only* variables local to processor B. This implementation can be modified for implementation on a shared-memory architecture, in the obvious manner.

Finally we suggest a way to implement a program that is in the equational schema, on a synchronous architecture. Transform the set of equations into a sequence G of assignments, as described earlier. All processors execute the sequence of assignments G, one assignment at a time. The mapping to the synchronous architecture specifies how the processors cooperate in executing each assignment in G.

4.3.4 Single-Statement Schema

A program is in the single-statement schema if the assign-section of the program consists of a single statement (which may be a multiple assignment). For example, a program with the following assign-section is in the single-statement schema:

Program SSS

    assign $x := f(x, y) \ \| \ y := g(x, y)$

end $\{SSS\}$

    Programs in the single-statement schema are appropriate for synchronous architectures, where each clock tick (or a fixed number of clock ticks) corresponds to an execution of the statement. For instance, program SSS can be executed on a two-processor synchronous computer, where in every computational step, one of the processors executes $x := f(x, y)$, and the other processor concurrently executes $y := g(x, y)$.

    Programs in the single-statement schema can be transformed into a form appropriate for distributed systems in which there are channels between all pairs of processors. We propose such a transformation, using program SSS as an example. Let $X[i], Y[i]$ be the values of x, y, respectively, after the single statement of the program has been executed exactly i times, $i \geq 0$. Assume that one processor, say processor A, determines the values of x, while another processor, say processor B, determines the values of y. Variable x is local to processor A, and y is local to processor B. The operations of the two processors are similar; therefore we only describe the operation of processor A. The initial value of x is $X[0]$, and after step i of processor A, $i > 0$, the value of x is $X[i]$. The sequence of messages sent on the channel from processor A to processor B is the sequence $X[k], k \geq 0$, and initially the channel contains $X[0]$. The processors execute asynchronously. Step i of processor A, for $i > 0$, is as follows. Immediately before step i, the value of x is $X[i-1]$. Processor A waits to receive a message from processor B—this message is $Y[i-1]$. After receiving the message processor A computes $X[i]$ using $X[i] = f(X[i-1], Y[i-1])$. The value of $X[i]$ is stored in x; the value is also sent to processor B.

    In this solution there is at most one message in transit along each channel. Therefore a one-message buffer is sufficient for each channel.

    The distributed solution can be implemented on a shared-memory system by implementing each buffer in shared memory. A buffer is modified both by the process adding messages to the buffer and by the one removing messages from the buffer. However, the distributed solution can also be transformed to execute on an asynchronous shared-memory computer in which each variable is modified by at most one processor. We sketch an outline of an implementation. The description is given in terms of implementing the buffer on the channel from processor A to processor B.

In our implementation, the buffer is written only by processor A, and read only by processor B. The buffer contains the pair $(X[i], i)$ for some i, $i \geq 0$. Let ack be the index of the last element of X read by processor B. Variable ack is written only by processor B, and it is read only by processor A. Initially $ack = -1$, and the buffer contains $(X[0], 0)$. If $i = ack + 1$, processor B reads $X[i]$ from the buffer into its local memory and increments ack, after which $i = ack$. If $i = ack$, processor A writes $(X[i + 1], i + 1)$ into the buffer, after which $i = ack + 1$.

It can be shown that in place of unbounded integers i and ack, a single bit will do for each variable, with i mod 2 in place of i, and ack mod 2 in place of ack (see the discussion of the alternating-bit protocol in Chapter 17).

4.4 Electronic Circuits

In this section we suggest that UNITY can be employed in the design of certain kinds of hardware systems. The hardware systems considered here are electronic circuits. Circuits are synchronous—i.e., they employ a common clock—or delay insensitive, in which case no clock is employed. There are also circuits consisting of synchronous components coupled via delay-insensitive circuitry. Synchronous circuits can be modeled as synchronous programs. Therefore the emphasis in this section is on delay-insensitive electronic circuits. We show how such circuits are modeled in UNITY. We also study the question of atomicity of actions in hardware, and propose methods to model concurrent nonatomic actions in UNITY.

4.4.1 Models of Delay-Insensitive Circuits

An electronic circuit (hereafter referred to as a circuit) consists of combinational logic gates, memory elements, and wires. A combinational logic gate with (a vector of) inputs y, and (a vector of) outputs z, that is computing function f, is represented by the UNITY statement

$$z := f(y).$$

Example 4.1 Combinational Logic-Gate Representation

1. And-gate with inputs x, y and output z:

$$z := x \wedge y.$$

2. Or-gate with inputs w, x, y and output z:

$$z := w \lor x \lor y.$$

3. Exclusive-or-gate with inputs x, y and output z:

$$z := x \not\equiv y.$$

4. Full adder-gate with inputs a, b, c and outputs *carry*, *sum*:

$$carry := (a \land b) \lor (b \land c) \lor (c \land a) \parallel sum := a \equiv b \equiv c,$$

where *true* represents 1 and *false* represents 0.

Remark: The expression $a \equiv b \equiv c$ can be read as $(a \equiv b) \equiv c$ or as $a \equiv (b \equiv c)$, since $\equiv$ is associative. The value of $a \equiv b \equiv c$ is *true* if an even number of terms in it are *false*. $\triangledown$

A memory element with input y and output z is represented by the UNITY statement

$$z := f(y) \qquad \text{if} \quad b(y),$$

where f, b are functions that characterize the memory element.

It should be observed that for a memory element the output variables z appear implicitly on the right side of the assignment:

$$z := f(y) \qquad \text{if} \quad b(y) \quad \sim \quad z \qquad \text{if} \quad \neg b(y).$$

Therefore the output of a memory element is a function of both its input and its previous output; that is, a memory element may be represented by the statement $z := g(y, z)$. By contrast, the output variables of a combinational logic gate do not appear on the right side of the statement representing this gate.

Example 4.2   Memory-Element Representation

1. Muller's C-element has a single boolean output and more than one boolean input. The C-element "fires" (infinitely often) at arbitrary times. If the C-element fires when all its inputs have the same value, the output acquires that value; otherwise the output retains its previous value. A C-element with inputs x, y and output z is represented by

$$z := maj(x, y, z),$$

where the function *maj* returns the majority value of its arguments.

2. The set-reset flip-flop has two inputs s, r and two outputs $z0, z1$. The following is given as an invariant:

invariant $\neg(s \land r)$

That is, the inputs s, r are never set *true* simultaneously by the circuit external to the flip-flop. The outputs of the flip-flop are required to satisfy the invariant

invariant $z0 \not\equiv z1$

If s holds when the flip-flop fires, then $z1$ is set *true*; if r holds, then $z1$ is set *false*; and if neither holds, then $z1$ is unchanged. The flip-flop is modeled by

$$z0, z1 \; := \; r, s \qquad \text{if} \quad r \lor s. \qquad\qquad \triangledown$$

Hereafter we use "gates" to mean both combinational logic gates and memory elements.

A *wire* connects the output of a gate to the input of a gate; its direction is from the former to the latter. A wire connecting the output variable y of a gate to the input variable z of a gate is represented by the UNITY statement

$$z \; := \; y.$$

We do not design electronic circuits in this book. Within the context of exploring the representation of computer architectures in UNITY, however, we study relationships between delay-insensitive circuits and the UNITY programs that represent them. First we characterize delay-insensitive circuits by a (safety) property of the corresponding UNITY program. Next we justify our characterization in qualitative terms.

A circuit is delay-insensitive if its corresponding UNITY program satisfies the following safety property (which we call the DI property, for Delay Insensitivity):

The DI Property

For any assignment in the program, say $y := e$, the value of e does not change as long as $y \neq e$. Formally, for all statements s in the program and all possible values E of e,

$$\{y \neq e \; \land \; e = E\} \;\; s \;\; \{e = E\}.$$

Equivalently, the DI property is

$$(e = E) \;\; unless \;\; (y = e) \; \land \; (e = E).$$

A program with the DI property is called a delay-insensitive program. Indeed, delay-insensitive programs are interesting in themselves, apart from their use in circuit design. We next look at some implications of the DI property.

Let $y := e$ and $x := d$ be two statements in a UNITY program with the DI property. Suppose that e names x. From the DI property,

$$\{y \neq e \ \wedge \ e = E\} \quad x \ := \ d \ \{e = E\},$$

i.e.,

$$y \neq e \ \Rightarrow \ e = e_d^x,$$

where e_d^x is obtained from e by replacing all occurrences of x by d in e.

This condition can be satisfied if the assignment to x is of the form

$$x \ := \ d' \qquad \text{if} \quad b,$$

where

$$b \ \Rightarrow \ y = e.$$

That is, x is modified only if $y = e$. The implementation of this statement requires a feedback from the circuit element with output y (represented by the statement $y := e$) to the circuit element with output x, ensuring that x changes value only if $y = e$. The statement

$$x \ := \ d' \qquad \text{if} \quad b$$

represents a memory element (not a combinational logic gate or wire), suggesting that one of the circuit elements in the feedback loop should be a memory element.

We now give some qualitative reasons for the DI property. A circuit element, i.e., a gate, memory element, or wire, takes an arbitrary finite time to change its output value in response to new input values (it is possible that some circuit elements remain in metastable state forever, but we ignore this possibility when discussing circuit design. If the input values of a circuit element change while the circuit element is in transition, its behavior is unspecified. Therefore we require that our circuits (or, more accurately, the corresponding UNITY programs) satisfy the DI property that guarantees that the values of a gate's inputs remain constant while it is in transition.

We have described three types of circuit elements: combinational logic gates, memory elements, and wires. Other types of elements—arbiters, for instance—are not described here because we have the limited goal of giving the flavor of this topic rather than a comprehensive description.

4.4.2 Modeling Hardware by Programs: The Problem of Atomicity

The execution of a UNITY program proceeds in discrete steps: Each statement execution is an atomic action. It can be argued that hardware is continuous rather than discrete; electrons flow back and forth along wires continuously, voltages change continuously at points on a chip that is itself a continuous piece of semiconductor, and so on. Is it possible to model hardware by programs? We believe that constructs in UNITY—nondeterminism, the interleaving of atomic actions, and the use of program states—allow us to represent hardware at a level of detail that is adequate for initial logic design, even though we cannot model many important aspects of circuit design such as layout, heat dissipation, and the continuous passage of time.

We present an example to illustrate the issue of atomicity in hardware. What happens when two processes attempt to write into a register simultaneously? Can such a situation be modeled? (The design constraint of delay-insensitive circuits requires that circuits be designed so that concurrent writes to a flip-flop, which is a one-bit register, do not occur. However, we may need to model such situations.) The problem is that a write takes nonzero time, so one write may begin before another finishes. If a write is not an atomic action, we propose atomic actions *begin-write* and *end-write*, defining the write operation to take place in the interval between them. Of course, we have merely pushed the problem of atomicity one level further: Can simultaneous begin-writes be modeled? Our answer is that we postulate every operation to have a sharp (rather than fuzzy) boundary in time, and we employ interleaving of atomic actions (i.e., interleaving of boundaries) to model overlapped operations.

Consider the following problem of modeling overlapped write operations. Each write operation is demarcated by instantaneous begin-write and end-write events. To keep notation simple, we consider a time interval in which each process writes the register at most once. Let $y[i]$ be the value written by process i, if it writes at all. We introduce boolean variables $beg[i]$ and $end[i]$ with the following meanings:

$beg[i]$: holds from the point at which process i begins its write operation, and does not hold before that point.

$end[i]$: holds from the point at which process i ends its write operation, and does not hold before that point.

Define a relation *precedes* between processes as follows: i *precedes* j means process i ends writing before process j begins writing. Let x denote the register value. It is given that $x = y[i]$ for some i, which has begun writing and which does not precede any j that has ended writing. This is to model the requirement that upon the end of a write operation, the value written overwrites any earlier value; furthermore, the register always holds a value written by a write operation that has begun. Formally,

invariant $\langle \exists\, i\, :\, beg[i]\quad ::\quad x = y[i]\, \wedge\, \langle \forall\, j\, :\, end[j]\quad ::\quad \neg(i\ precedes\ j)\rangle\rangle$

To satisfy the invariant initially, assume that the following holds initially:

$beg[0]\, \wedge\, x = y[0]\, \wedge\, \langle \wedge\, j\quad ::\quad \neg end[j]\rangle.$

We now model this situation by a UNITY program. We introduce a boolean variable $written[i]$, which holds after process i has set the value of the register to $y[i]$, and does not hold before that. There are certain unspecified external conditions, external-condition1 and external-condition2, under which process i begins and ends its write operation.

$\langle\![\![$ i :: {process i begins writing the register}

$\qquad beg[i]$:= $true$ $\qquad\qquad$ if external-condition1

$\qquad$ {process i sets the value of the register to $y[i]$}

$\qquad[\![$ x, $written[i]$:= $y[i]$, $true$ if $beg[i] \wedge \neg end[i]$

$\qquad$ {process i ends the write operation}

$\qquad[\![$ $end[i]$:= $true$ $\qquad\qquad$ if $written[i] \wedge$ external-condition2

$\rangle$

By defining the read operation in the same way, i.e., as an interval between a begin-read and end-read atomic action, and defining the value read in terms of the state of the register, a variety of physical situations can be modeled.

Summary

Most programming notations are designed for one specific architecture, and no mapping is necessary from a notation to the one architecture for which it was designed. By contrast, the UNITY notation can be implemented on many architectures, and a mapping is necessary to tailor the execution of a UNITY program to a target architecture. The goal of this chapter is to suggest that such mappings are feasible. We have not described mappings to all available architectures because there are too many of them. We have, however, illustrated the basic idea of a mapping: Partition the set of statements of a program among processors, partition the set of variables among memories and channels, and specify the control flow for each processor. Mappings, down to the level of electronic circuitry, are more detailed: Each statement represents a gate or a wire, and each variable represents an input signal or an output signal of a gate. These basic ideas about mappings apply to a variety of computing devices.

One way to provide a unifying framework for programming a variety of architectures is to employ an abstraction for each architecture. The abstraction employed in UNITY is simple; it is the program schema.

In the design of systems, the boundary between software and hardware is fuzzy. Increasingly, systems are being designed for dedicated applications. Our investigations suggest that a unifying theory, such as UNITY, may help bridge the gap between hardware and software, and aid in designing applications all the way down to electronics.

Bibliographic Notes

One of the earliest theoretical studies of a model of parallel computation is in
Karp and Miller [1969]. Discussions of the complexity of parallel synchronous
algorithms are found in Goldschlager [1977], Pippenger [1979], Ladner and
Fischer [1980], Chandra, Stockmeyer, and Vishkin [1982], and Cook [1983].
Descriptions of synchronous processor arrays appear in Kung and Leiserson
[1978] and IEEE [1987b]. A survey of interconnection networks appears
in IEEE [1987a]. Comprehensive studies of programming for asynchronous
shared-memory and distributed architectures are in Brinch-Hansen [1977],
Hoare [1978] and [1984], Tannenbaum [1981], Andrews and Schneider [1983],
and Peterson and Silberschatz [1983]. Delay-insensitive circuits are described
in Seitz [1980] and Martin [1986]; the material in this chapter is based on
their work. Issues of atomicity in hardware are studied in Lamport [1983a],
Misra [1986], and Singh, Anderson, and Gouda [1987]. Several concurrent
architectures are described in Schwartz [1980], Agerwala and Arvind [1982],
Seitz [1984] and [1985], and Hillis [1985].

CHAPTER 5

The First
Case Study:
Shortest Path

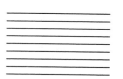

5.1   Introduction

This chapter describes the first nontrivial application of UNITY: the development of programs for the all-points shortest-path problem. The goal of this chapter is to illustrate the systematic development of programs for different architectures. The programs in this chapter are not new, but are chosen for purposes of illustration.

5.1.1 Organization of the Chapter

The remainder of Section 5.1 describes the shortest-path problem. A general solution strategy is proposed in Section 5.2. The strategy is described informally and then formally in terms of an invariant, a stable predicate, and a progress property. The strategy is proved correct; therefore any program with the specified invariant, stable predicate, and progress property solves the shortest-path problem. We do not expect all program developments to fit this strategy, but we do anticipate that a general strategy will be helpful in guiding program development.

Programs for sequential architectures are developed in Section 5.3. Three programs are presented. The first, the Floyd-Warshall algorithm, is a mapping of the simple solution given in Section 5.2. The second is a program in the equational schema, while the third shows explicit sequencing of assignments. Section 5.4 contains programs for parallel synchronous architectures. Simple heuristics are employed to derive parallel synchronous programs from the general strategy and the solutions derived earlier. In Section 5.5 programs for asynchronous shared-memory multiprocessors with various degrees of atomicity are derived. Distributed programs are developed in Section 5.6. Many of the programs developed in earlier sections can be mapped efficiently on to distributed architectures, and therefore it is unnecessary to derive programs specifically for distributed architectures. Section 5.7 consists of a discussion of a program suitable for implementation on processor arrays; this program is derived from the Floyd-Warshall algorithm.

5.1.2 The All-Points Shortest-Path Problem

A directed graph $G = (V, E)$ is a nonempty set V of vertices and a set E of edges. An edge is represented by an ordered pair of vertices. An edge (i, j) is directed from vertex i to vertex j. A path from vertex i to vertex j is a nonnull sequence of edges such that the first edge in the sequence is directed away from i, and the last edge in the sequence is directed toward j, and for every successive pair (u, v), (w, x) of edges in the sequence $v = w$. A *cycle* is a path starting and ending at the same vertex.

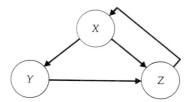

Figure 5.1 Example of a directed graph.

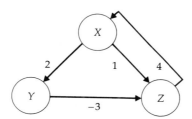

Figure 5.2 Example of a weighted graph.

Example 5.1

Figure 5.1 shows a graph with three vertices—X, Y, Z—and four edges—(X, Y), (X, Z), (Y, Z), (Z, X). One path from vertex X to vertex Z consists of edges $(X, Y), (Y, Z)$. Another path from vertex X to vertex Z has the edge (X, Z) only. A cycle in the graph of Fig. 5.1 is $(X, Z), (Z, X)$.   ▽

A *weighted graph* is one with a *weight*—a number—associated with each edge. In this book all weights are integers. The *length* of a path is the sum of weights of the edges in the path. Figure 5.2 shows a weighted graph. The length of the path consisting of edges $(X, Y), (Y, Z)$ is -1 in this example. An edge-weight matrix of a directed graph with N vertices is an $N \times N$ matrix where $W[i, j]$ is the weight of edge (i, j) if edge (i, j) exists, and is ∞ otherwise. We assume that, for all vertices j, $W[j, j] = 0$.

The all-points shortest-path problem is as follows. Given an edge-weight matrix W of a weighted directed graph that has no cycles of negative length, determine matrix D, where

for all i, j :: $D[i, j] =$ length of a minimum-length path from vertex i to vertex j.

We refer to $D[i, j]$ as the *distance* from i to j.

Note: If there is no path from vertex i to vertex j, then $D[i, j] = \infty$.   ▽

For the graph shown in Fig. 5.2, the distances D are given in Fig. 5.3.

	X	Y	Z
X	0	2	-1
Y	1	0	-3
Z	4	6	0

Figure 5.3 Distance matrix for the graph in Fig. 5.2.

Problem Specification

Our goal is to design a program that computes the distances. More specifically, the program should be designed to compute matrix d, where

invariant FP $\Rightarrow$ $(d = D)$

$true$ $\mapsto$ FP

FP denotes the fixed point of the program.

Notational Convention: Assume that the graph has N vertices indexed $0..N - 1$. The symbols i, j, k are quantified over all vertices; the quantifications will not be shown explicitly.

5.2   A Solution Strategy

5.2.1 Informal Description of the Strategy

We propose a strategy in which $d[i, j]$ is (always) the length of some path from vertex i to vertex j. If a path from i to j with length ℓ is found where $\ell < d[i, j]$, then $d[i, j]$ is reduced to ℓ. We propose the following way to find better paths. There is a path from i to j via k with length $d[i, k] + d[k, j]$. Therefore if $d[i, j]$ exceeds $d[i, k] + d[k, j]$, reduce $d[i, j]$ to $d[i, k] + d[k, j]$; in other words, execute the assignment

   $d[i, j]$:= $\min(d[i, j], \ d[i, k] + d[k, j])$.

This assignment is the basic operation of the solution strategy. The solution strategy is broad—it does not specify how the i, j, k are chosen. Neither does it specify when the operations should be carried out, nor the processor that should carry out the operation.

5.2.2 Formal Description of the Strategy

Now we describe the strategy more formally. Initially $d[i, j]$ may be set to $W[i, j]$. Since $d[i, j]$ is not increased as a result of the assignment proposed earlier, $d[i, j]$ never exceeds $W[i, j]$. Also, in this strategy, $d[i, j]$ is the length of some path from i to j. This is because initially $d[i, j]$ is $W[i, j]$, and hence

$d[i,j]$ is the length of the single-edge path (i,j); $d[i,j]$ remains unchanged or becomes the length of some path when $d[i,j]$ is set to $\min(d[i,j], d[i,k]+d[k,j])$, since $d[i,k] + d[k,j]$ is the length of a path from i to j via k. Therefore this strategy has the following invariant:

invariant

$$d[i,j] \text{ is the length of some path from } i \text{ to } j \wedge d[i,j] \leq W[i,j]. \tag{1}$$

The fixed point of this strategy holds when all the $d[i,j]$ remain unchanged, i.e.,

$$FP \equiv \langle \wedge\, i,j,k \quad :: \quad d[i,j] = \min(d[i,j], d[i,k] + d[k,j]) \rangle. \tag{2}$$

To guarantee that a fixed point is always reached, we show that if the state is not a fixed point then at least one of the $d[i,j]$ decreases. The metric we employ is the sum of the $d[i,j]$ over all i,j; however, since some of the $d[i,j]$ may be ∞, we define the metric to be a pair (num, sum), where comparisons between pairs are made lexicographically, and

$num =$ number of pairs (i,j) for which $d[i,j] = \infty$.

$sum = \langle +\, i,j : d[i,j] \text{ is finite } :: \ d[i,j] \rangle.$

The metric is bounded from below because there are no cycles of negative length and there is no edge with weight $-\infty$. The progress condition is that the metric decreases if the state is not a fixed point: For all integers m, n

$$\neg FP \ \wedge \ (num, sum) = (m, n) \quad \longmapsto \quad (num, sum) < (m, n). \tag{3}$$

The strategy we propose to employ for the shortest path problem is defined by (1), (2), and (3). Now we shall prove that this strategy is correct.

5.2.3 Proof of Correctness of the Strategy

We prove that the invariant and the progress condition given in the problem specification (in Section 5.1) are met by any strategy that satisfies conditions (1), (2), and (3) of Section 5.2.2.

Proof

Since the metric is bounded from below and decreases if the state is not a fixed point, we conclude that a fixed point is eventually reached. At any fixed point reached in a program execution, both the invariant and FP hold. Therefore it is sufficient to show that any matrix d that satisfies both (1) and (2) is a solution to the shortest-path problem; we do so next.

Since there are no cycles of negative length, for every pair of vertices (i,j) there exists a shortest path from i to j that has at most $(N-1)$ edges. Consider all pairs of vertices (x, y) such that there is a shortest path from x

to y that has at most m edges, $m \geq 1$; we shall prove by induction on m that, at fixed point, $d[x, y]$ is the distance from x to y.

Base case ($m = 1$). Consider a pair of vertices x, y such that there exists a shortest path from x to y consisting of a single edge. The distance from x to y is $W[x, y]$. From invariant (1) it follows that $d[x, y] = W[x, y]$.

Induction step. Consider a pair of vertices x, y such that the minimum number of edges on a shortest path from x to y is $m + 1$; let z be the prefinal vertex on this path. The number of edges on the path from x to z is m, and the number of edges on the path from z to y is 1. Also, the path from x to z is a shortest path from x to z, and the path from z to y is a shortest path from z to y. Using the induction hypothesis, the length of the path from x to z is $d[x, z]$, and the length of the path from z to y is $d[z, y]$. From the fixed-point condition (2):

$$d[x, y] \leq d[x, z] + d[z, y].$$

From invariant (1), $d[x, y]$ is the length of some path from x to y. Hence $d[x, y]$ is the distance from x to y. This completes the proof of the correctness of the overall strategy.

5.2.4 A Simple Program

We write the program described informally in Section 5.2.1.

Program *P1*

    initially $\langle \| \ i, j \quad :: \quad d[i, j] = W[i, j] \rangle$

    assign $\langle \| \ i, j, k \quad :: \quad d[i, j] \ := \ \min(d[i, j], d[i, k] + d[k, j]) \rangle$

end {*P1*}

This program consists of N^3 assignments, one for each i, j, k. The proof that the program satisfies the solution strategy, i.e., (1), (2), and (3), was shown earlier.

5.3   Sequential Architectures

We present several solutions to demonstrate different ways of solving the problem for the same architecture.

5.3.1 Map the Simple Solution to a Sequential Machine

An obvious schedule for executing the N^3 assignments of program $P1$ is to loop through all i, then all j, then all k. If the assignments are executed in this order—i.e., with indices i and j varying faster than index k—a fixed point is reached after each assignment is executed *once*. This is a pleasant surprise; this scheme results in $O(N^3)$ running time for the program. The proof of the claim just made is postponed to the end of this section.

5.3.2 A Program in the Equational Schema

We propose a program that is a set of equations. The program is an equational representation of the mapping given in Section 5.3.1.

Consider paths from i to j in which indices of intermediate vertices are smaller than k. Let $H[i, j, k]$ be the minimum length over all such paths.

Theorem 5.1   The $H[i, j, k]$'s satisfy the following equations:

$$\langle \wedge\, i, j \quad :: \quad H[i, j, 0] = W[i, j] \qquad\qquad\qquad \rangle\, \wedge$$

$$\langle \wedge\, i, j, k \quad :: \quad H[i, j, k + 1] = \min(H[i, j, k], H[i, k, k] + H[k, j, k]) \rangle. \qquad (4)$$

Proof: By definition, $H[i, j, 0]$ is the minimum length of paths from i to j that have no intermediate vertex. Therefore $H[i, j, 0] = W[i, j]$.

By definition, $H[i, j, k + 1]$ is the minimum length of paths from i to j whose intermediate vertex numbers are smaller than $k + 1$. Consider any such cycle-free minimum length path. If vertex k is not an intermediate vertex in this path, then

$$H[i, j, k + 1] = H[i, j, k].$$

If vertex k is an intermediate vertex in this path, the path from i to k is the shortest path consisting of intermediate vertices smaller than k, and similarly for the path from k to j. Therefore

$$H[i, j, k + 1] = H[i, k, k] + H[k, j, k].$$

Hence the result.   ▽

By definition, $H[i, j, N]$ is the distance from i to j because there is no vertex in the graph with index exceeding $N - 1$. Hence $d[i, j] = H[i, j, N]$.

Theorem 5.2   The set of equations (4) is proper. (See Chapter 2 for definitions of proper sets of equations.)

Proof: Each $H[i, j, k]$ appears exactly once on the left sides of the equations. Order the equations such that the last index (i.e., k) is nondecreasing. Then the variables named in the right side of any equation appear on the left sides of equations earlier in the ordering. $\triangledown$

The following program, in the equational schema, is a rewriting of (4).

Program {in the equational schema} $P2$

  declare $H : \text{array}[0..N - 1, 0..N - 1, 0..N]$

  always

   $\langle \| \ i, j \ : \ H[i, j, 0] = W[i, j]$ $\rangle$

  $[\!]\ \langle [\!]\ k \ :: \ \langle \| \ i, j \ :: \ H[i, j, k + 1] = \min(H[i, j, k], H[i, k, k] + H[k, j, k]) \rangle \rangle$

  $[\!]\ \langle \| \ i, j \ :: \ d[i, j] = H[i, j, N]$ $\rangle$

end $\{P2\}$

Efficiency of Program $P2$

There are $O(N^3)$ equations in $P2$. Each equation has a constant number of terms on the right side. Therefore the time complexity on a sequential architecture is $O(N^3)$. The program requires $O(N^3)$ words to store H, and hence its memory requirement is $O(N^3)$.

5.3.3 A Program with Explicit Sequencing

The sequencing employed in the mapping of program $P1$ to a sequential architecture, as described in Section 5.3.1, is made explicit in the next program, $P3$. Program $P3$ is equivalent to the following PASCAL program fragment:

```
for x := 0 to N − 1 do
    for u := 0 to N − 1 do
        for v := 0 to N − 1 do
            d[u, v] := min(d[u, v], d[u, x] + d[x, v])
```

The manner in which indices x, u, v are modified in the PASCAL program is captured by the assignment

$$(x, u, v) := (x, u, v) + 1,$$

where (x, u, v) is treated as a single three-digit number in base N, and $+$ denotes addition in base N.

Program {Floyd-Warshall} P3

> **declare** x, u, v : integer;
>
> **initially**
>
> > $\langle \| \ i, j \ :: \ d[i, j] = W[i, j] \rangle$
> >
> > $\| \ x, u, v = 0, 0, 0$
>
> **assign**
>
> > $d[u, v] := \min(d[u, v], d[u, x] + d[x, v])$
> >
> > $\| \quad (x, u, v) := (x, u, v) + 1 \quad$ **if** $\ (x, u, v) \neq (N - 1, N - 1, N - 1)$
>
> **end** {P3}

We leave it to the reader to prove the program based on the following invariant, where H is as defined in Section 5.3.2. (In the following, pairs of indices are compared lexicographically.)

invariant $d[i, j]$ is the length of some path from i to j $\qquad \wedge$

$\qquad\qquad \langle \wedge \ i, j \ : \ (i, j) < (u, v) \ :: \ d[i, j] \leq H[i, j, x + 1] \rangle \qquad \wedge$

$\qquad\qquad \langle \wedge \ i, j \ : \ (i, j) \geq (u, v) \ :: \ d[i, j] \leq H[i, j, x] \qquad \ \rangle$

5.3.4 Summary of Sequential Programs

By far the simplest solution (Section 5.3.1) was a mapping from *P1* because no proof of correctness is required. The evaluation of complexity, however, does require a proof. The next program we derived was a set of equations (Section 5.3.2); it has the nice feature of being declarative. The third program (Section 5.3.3) is an explicit representation of the mapping from *P1*: It makes the sequencing and the detection of fixed points explicit. The choice of a program is a matter of taste and of concern for efficiency.

5.4   Parallel Synchronous Architectures

5.4.1 $O(N)$ Steps with N^2 Processors

We employ the following heuristic: Transform a program by collecting assignments that can be executed concurrently, into a single statement. There are N^3 assignments in $P1$. We observe that the N^3 assignments can be grouped into N sets of N^2 assignments, where, in each set, values are assigned to distinct elements of d; therefore all assignments in a set can be executed concurrently. This heuristic suggests the following program, obtained by transforming $P1$.

Program $P1'$

    initially $\langle \| \; i, j \;\; :: \;\; d[i, j] = W[i, j] \rangle$

    assign $\langle \| \; k \;\; :: \;\; \langle \| \; i, j \;\; :: \;\; d[i, j] \;\; := \;\; \min(d[i, j], d[i, k] + d[k, j]) \rangle \rangle$

end $\{P1'\}$

This program has N statements, each of which assigns values to all N^2 elements of array d. The proof that the program fits the general solution strategy—i.e., that it has properties (1), (2), (3)—is straightforward.

Evaluation of Efficiency

Consider a parallel synchronous architecture with N^2 processors. Each multiple assignment can be executed in constant time by N^2 processors, with all elements of d assigned values concurrently. An obvious schedule for executing the N multiple assignments is to execute them in, say, increasing order of k. From the arguments given for program $P3$, a fixed point is reached after each of the N multiple assignments is executed once. Therefore with N^2 processors the program requires $O(N)$ steps. The sequencing employed in the mapping and the fixed point are made explicit in the following program:

Program $\{$parallel Floyd-Warshall$\}$ $P4$

    declare k : integer

    initially

        $\langle \| \; i, j \;\; :: \;\; d[i, j] = W[i, j] \rangle$

        $\| \;\; k = 0$

    assign

        $\langle \| \; i, j \;\; :: \;\; d[i, j] \;\; := \;\; \min(d[i, j], d[i, k] + d[k, j]) \quad$ if $\;\; k < N \rangle$

        $\| \;\; k \;\; := \;\; k + 1 \qquad\qquad\qquad\qquad\qquad\quad$ if $\;\; k < N$

   end $\{P4\}$

The program in the equational schema, *P2*, is also suitable for parallel processing: It can be executed in $O(N)$ time by N^2 processors.

5.4.2 $O(log^2 N)$ Steps with N^3 Processors

Consider an architecture with N^3 processors. Program *P4* is not efficient for such an architecture because it allows only N^2 processors to be used concurrently. Therefore we employ another heuristic. We attempt to employ constructs that are particularly efficient on parallel architectures, such as associative operations on sequences of elements; an example is computing the minimum. This heuristic suggests the following program, again obtained from *P1*:

Program *P5*

> **initially** $\langle \| \ i, j \ :: \ d[i,j] = W[i,j] \rangle$
>
> **assign** $\langle \| \ i, j \ :: \ d[i,j] \ := \ \langle \min \ k \ :: \ d[i,k] + d[k,j] \rangle \rangle$

end {*P5*}

This program consists of a single statement, which assigns values to all N^2 elements of array *d*. Element $d[i,j]$ is assigned the minimum, over all vertices *k*, of $d[i,k] + d[k,j]$. (Observe that an invariant of program *P5* is $d[i,i] = 0$, for all *i*.)

The proof that this program satisfies (1), (2), and (3) is straightforward.

Evaluation of Efficiency

The following invariant can be proved for program *P5*. After the mth execution of the assignment in *P5* (where *m* is treated as an auxiliary variable that is initially 0 and is incremented by 1 with each execution of the assignment):

invariant $d[i,j]$ is the length of the shortest path from *i* to *j* with at most $2^m - 1$ intermediate vertices.

Hence a fixed point is reached after $O(\log N)$ executions of the assignment statement. To evaluate the complexity of a step, observe that the sums $d[i,k] + d[k,j]$ can be computed in constant time by $O(N^3)$ processors, one for each i, j, k. For given i, j, the minimum over *k* can be computed in $O(\log N)$ time by $O(N)$ processors. Hence each step can be completed in $O(\log N)$ time using $O(N^3)$ processors. Since computation terminates after $O(\log N)$ steps, the execution time of the program is $O(\log^2 N)$ on $O(N^3)$ processors. This is also an efficient synchronous parallel program.

Program *P5* is more efficient than *P4* if at least $O(N^3)$ processors are available, and is less efficient if there are at most $O(N^2)$ processors.

Summary of Synchronous Parallel Programs

For the most part, the heuristics we employ for the development of synchronous parallel programs are very simple: Gather assignment statements that can be executed concurrently into multiple assignments and attempt to employ operations that are efficient on the architecture. These heuristics result in efficient programs for the shortest-path problem. All the programs presented here fit a common solution strategy for this problem, given by conditions (1), (2), and (3).

5.5   Asynchronous Shared-Memory Architectures

5.5.1 A Program in the Equational Schema

Program $P2$ can be mapped to an asynchronous multiprocessor architecture using the strategy described in Chapter 4. For instance, given an architecture with N^2 processors, each processor is made responsible for computing $H[i, j, k]$ for some fixed i, j and for all k.

5.5.2 A Program in the Read-only Schema: A Fine-Grain Solution

Our next asynchronous program exploits a crucial property of $H[i, j, k]$:

$$H[i, j, k + 1] \leq H[i, j, k].$$

As a consequence, it is permissible to have one process race ahead of another because we can use $H[i, j, k+m]$ instead of $H[i, j, k]$, for any nonnegative integer m, in the program. To understand the next program, we first state an invariant of program $P4$:

$$d[i, j] = H[i, j, k] \ \land \ d[i, j] \text{ is the length of some path from } i \text{ to } j \ \land \ k \leq N$$

Synchrony is essential in program $P4$ because the variable k is used in computations for all $d[i, j]$. Now we propose an asynchronous solution in which $d[i, j]$ is written by the $(i, j)^{th}$ processor alone, and k is replaced by a variable $k[i, j]$ local to this processor. We weaken the preceding invariant to

invariant $d[i, j] \leq H[i, j, k[i, j]]$ $\qquad\qquad\qquad\qquad$ $\land$

$\qquad\qquad$ $d[i, j]$ is the length of some path from i to j $\quad$ $\land$

$\qquad\qquad$ $k[i, j] \leq N$

The basis of our next program is the following observation. Let r be a shorthand for $k[i, j]$ in the following discussion.

Theorem 5.3   Given the preceding invariant,

$(k[i,r] \geq r \ \wedge \ k[r,j] \geq r) \ \Rightarrow$

$\min(d[i,j], d[i,r] + d[r,j]) \leq H[i,j,r+1]$.

Proof: Using theorem 5.1 we replace $H[i,j,r+1]$, and then we are required to show that

$(k[i,r] \geq r \ \wedge \ k[r,j] \geq r) \ \Rightarrow$

$\min(d[i,j], d[i,r] + d[r,j]) \leq \min(H[i,j,r], H[i,r,r] + H[r,j,r])$.

We show that each term of the form $d[u,v]$ in the consequent is less than or equal to $H[u,v,r]$.

$d[i,j]$	$\leq H[i,j,r]$	, from the invariant
$d[i,r]$	$\leq H[i,r,k[i,r]]$	, from the invariant
$H[i,r,k[i,r]]$	$\leq H[i,r,r]$	, since $k[i,r] \geq r$ and for all i,j,t, $H[i,j,t+1] \leq H[i,j,t]$
$d[i,r]$	$\leq H[i,r,r]$	, from the above two inequalities

Similarly,

$d[r,j] \leq H[r,j,r]$.

Therefore, the inequality in the consequent is proven. $\triangledown$

Program *P6*, given next, incorporates the result of this observation: $d[i,j]$ is set to $\min(d[i,j], d[i,r]+d[r,j])$, and r to $r+1$ provided $k[i,r] \geq r \wedge k[r,j] \geq r$. The correctness of *P6* follows from the invariant and from the following:

$FP \ \Rightarrow \ \langle \wedge \ i,j \ :: \ k[i,j] \geq N \rangle$.

(See also Exercise 5.1.)

A fixed point is reached in *P6* because the metric, $\langle + \ i,j \ :: \ k[i,j] \rangle$, increases with each state change and because this metric is bounded from above.

Program {asynchronous shortest paths} *P6*

    declare k : array$[0..N-1, 0..N-1]$ of integer,

    initially

        $\langle \| \ i,j \ :: \ d[i,j], k[i,j] = W[i,j], 0 \ \ \rangle$

    assign {r is a shorthand for $k[i,j]$}

        $\langle \| \ i,j \ :: \ d[i,j], r \ := \ \min(d[i,j], d[i,r] + d[r,j]), r+1$

                if $r < N \ \wedge \ k[i,r] \geq r \ \wedge \ k[r,j] \geq r$

    $\rangle$

end {*P6*}

Exercise 5.1   Show that for *P6*

$$FP \implies \langle \wedge \ i,j \ :: \ k[i,j] \geq N \rangle.$$

Hint: Let $k[u,v]$ be a smallest $k[i,j]$ at fixed point. The fixed-point condition for $i = u$ and $j = v$ alone shows that $k[u,v] \geq N$. $\triangledown$

It is instructive to compare the execution sequences of *P4* and *P6*. In *P6*, it can happen during the computation that $k[0,N-2] = N-2 \wedge k[1,N-1] = 0$. In *P4*, computations of all elements of d proceed in lock step, i.e., there is a single k.

Program *P6* cannot be implemented directly on an asynchronous machine with N^2 processors in the read-only model in which the $(i,j)^{th}$ processor assigns values to $d[i,j], k[i,j]$. This is because a statement in one processor names several variables in other processors. It is straightforward to transform *P6* so that a statement in one processor names at most one variable in another. We now carry out this transformation in some detail.

In *P6*, the $(i,j)^{th}$ processor reads $d[i,r]$ only after it determines that $k[i,r]$ is at least r; this sequencing is made explicit in the next program. Sequencing is made explicit in UNITY by the introduction of additional variables. We introduce arrays, ls, lt, lf, rs, rt, rf where the letters l, r refer to the left and right terms respectively in $d[i,r] + d[r,j]$ in *P6*. The $[i,j]^{th}$ terms of these arrays are local to the $(i,j)^{th}$ processor. Boolean variable $ls[i,j]$ holds only if $k[i,r]$ is at least r; $lt[i,j]$ is used to store the value of $d[i,r]$ read by the $(i,j)^{th}$ processor; $lf[i,j]$ indicates that $d[i,r]$ has been read by the $(i,j)^{th}$ processor.

invariant $(ls[i,j] \quad \implies \quad k[i,r] \geq r) \quad \wedge$
$(lf[i,j] \quad \implies \quad ls[i,j] \ \wedge \ lt[i,j] \leq H[i,r,r])$

Similar invariants hold for rs, rt and rf. Initially all the boolean variables are *false*—this guarantees that the above invariants hold initially—and lt, rt are arbitrary. The program is given below.

Program {asynchronous shortest paths; variation of *P6*} *P7*

declare

k : array$[0..N-1, 0..N-1]$ of integer,

ls, lf, rs, rf : array$[0..N-1, 0..N-1]$ of boolean,

lt, rt : array$[0..N-1, 0..N-1]$ of integer

initially

$\langle \| \ i,j \ :: \ d[i,j], k[i,j] = W[i,j], 0$

$\| \ ls[i,j], lf[i,j], rs[i,j], rf[i,j] = \textit{false, false, false, false}$

$\rangle$

assign $\{r$ is a shorthand for $k[i,j]\}$

$\langle \| \ i,j \ ::$

$\quad ls[i,j] \ := \ k[i,r] \geq r$

$\| \ rs[i,j] \ := \ k[r,j] \geq r$

$\| \ lt[i,j], lf[i,j] \ := \ d[i,r], true \qquad \text{if} \quad ls[i,j]$

$\| \ rt[i,j], rf[i,j] \ := \ d[r,j], true \qquad \text{if} \quad rs[i,j]$

$\| \ d[i,j], r, ls[i,j], rs[i,j], lf[i,j], rf[i,j]$

$\qquad :=$

$\quad \min(d[i,j], lt[i,j] + rt[i,j]), r + 1, false, false, false, false$

$\qquad\qquad\qquad \text{if} \quad r < N \ \wedge \ lf[i,j] \ \wedge \ rf[i,j]$

$\rangle$

end $\{P7\}$

5.5.3 A Program in the Single-Statement Schema

Program $P5$ consists of a single statement. Hence it can be implemented on a set of asynchronous processors using the mapping described in Chapter 4. If $O(N^3)$ processors are available, $O(N)$ processors can be employed to compute $d[i,j]$, using a tree of processors to compute the minimum of N terms. If $O(N^2)$ processors are available, computation of each $d[i,j]$ is allocated to a single processor. The heuristic used to obtain $P6$ from $P4$ can be used to obtain a more asynchronous program from $P5$, in which some processors are allowed to race ahead of others.

5.5.4 Summary of Asynchronous Shared-Memory Multiprocessors

Programs in different schemas—equational, read-only, and single statement schemas—were mapped to different architectures. Several refinements were used to obtain solutions with fine-grain atomicity. Program $P7$ illustrates how variables are introduced to simulate sequencing—executing statements "out of order" does not change the program state.

5.6   Distributed Architectures

It is not necessary to derive programs for distributed architectures because the programs derived earlier in the equational schema (*P2*), the shared-variable schema (*P6* and *P7*), and the single-statement schema (*P5*) can be mapped for efficient execution on distributed architectures. This is one of the advantages of separating concerns between programs and implementations.

5.7   Synchronous Processor Arrays

5.7.1 A Processor-Array Implementation of Floyd-Warshall Algorithm

We use the following two-step method to develop programs for processor arrays. Start with a synchronous parallel program, ignoring the requirement that the program is to be run on a processor array. Then, propose a directed graph structure to execute the program. Of course, the separation of concerns between these two steps is not always clear; the program proposed in the first step may not be suitable for any network, in which case the two steps are repeated. We illustrate this strategy for the shortest-path problem.

We begin with program *P2*, consisting of a set of equations that is repeated here for convenience. For all i, j, k,

$$H[i, j, 0] = W[i, j]$$

$$H[i, j, k + 1] = \min(H[i, j, k], H[i, k, k] + H[k, j, k])$$

Now we propose a network of processes to implement these equations. In deriving a network it helps to separate two concerns: communication and processing. Communication is concerned with the flow of data items between the vertices of the network. Processing is concerned with the functions applied to compute the contents of each vertex at each step. To derive the topology of the network we concentrate on communication. To this end we observe that computing of $H[i, j, k + 1]$ requires the values of $H[i, j, k], H[i, k, k], H[k, j, k]$. Therefore we propose a network that is a two-dimensional array of vertices indexed (i, j), where $0 \leq i, j < N$, and we propose that $H[i, j, k]$ be computed at vertex (i, j), for all k. The kind of communication needed to implement this proposal is shown in Fig. 5.4.

We are done except for specifying the times, i.e., the steps at which data flows from one vertex to another. If the storage capacity of a vertex is of no concern, then the solution is trivial. Deriving timing strategies to

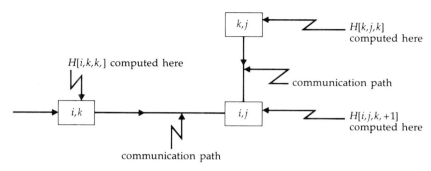

Figure 5.4 Implementing Floyd-Warshall Algorithm on a synchronous array.

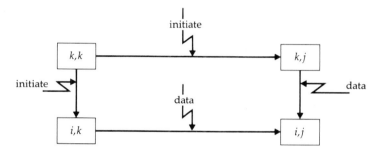

Figure 5.5 Flow of signals and data in the synchronous array.

reduce storage capacity is a tricky problem. In our example we would like to have $H[i, k, k]$ and $H[k, j, k]$ arrive at vertex (i, j) at the same time—otherwise, the data item that got there earlier would have to be stored until the other appeared. A simple technique can be employed to ensure that the required data items arrive simultaneously. The diagonal vertex (k, k) sends an *initiate* signal along the kth row and column; vertices (i, k) and (k, j), upon receiving this signal, send their values, $H[i, k, k]$ and $H[k, j, k]$, respectively, along their row and column, respectively. The diagonal vertex (k, k) and the target vertex (i, j) may be thought of as being on opposite corners of a rectangle. The signal and data travel along the edges of the rectangle (Fig. 5.5). Since opposite sides of a rectangle are of equal length, the desired data items arrive simultaneously at (i, j). The *initiate* signal sent by (k, k) is used for computing $H[i, j, k + 1]$, for *all* i, j; also, a computation can be initiated by $(k + 1, k + 1)$ while the computation initiated by (k, k) is still in progress. We refer the reader to Van Scoy [1980] and van de Snepscheut [1986].

5.7.2 Summary of the Derivation of Programs for Processor Arrays

A heuristic for processor arrays is to separate the concerns of computation and communication. We derive a program in two steps, the first of which deals with computation, and the second with communication. In the first step we derive a synchronous parallel program, ignoring issues dealing with network topology. The program defines a set of values to be computed, i.e., the values taken on by the variables of the program. In the second step we propose a network onto which the computation can be mapped efficiently. It is helpful to break the second step into two parts. First, we identify the vertices at which each value is computed, and which vertices need which values; at this stage we may also prescribe paths from vertices computing the values to vertices needing them. In the second part we propose times—i.e., step numbers—at which a value is computed at a vertex. The purpose of the second step is to minimize memory requirements at each vertex. Timing to optimize memory requirements is often the most difficult part in deriving a solution for a synchronous array. Determining the computation at each vertex is usually trivial. The design of programs for processor arrays is treated at length in Chapter 21, and therefore we treat it only lightly in this chapter.

At each point in the derivation of the processor array, the UNITY program consists of a single statement.

Exercise 5.2   Consider a weighted directed graph G that consists of two subgraphs G', G'', with a single edge between the two subgraphs. There are no negative-weight cycles in G. Explore solutions to the all-points shortest path problem for this graph on various architectures.

Extend your solutions to the case in which there is exactly one edge from G' to G'', and one from G'' to G'.   ▽

Exercise 5.3   Extend the solutions given in this chapter to allow negative-weight cycles in the graph. Define $d[u, v] = -\infty$ if there is a directed path from u to v that includes a vertex on a negative-weight cycle.   ▽

Exercise 5.4   Consider a graph whose edge weights may decrease with time. Therefore D may vary with time, though the graph never has a negative-weight cycle. Propose a program with the following properties:

invariant $d[i,j] \geq D[i,j]$

$(D[i,j] \leq m) \mapsto (d[i,j] \leq m)$

Hint: Consider adding the following statements to program *P1*:

$\langle \| \ i,j \ :: \ d[i,j] \ := \ \min(d[i,j], W[i,j]) \rangle.$ ▽

Summary

We have attempted to show, by means of the all-points shortest-path problem, that there is a unified approach to the development of programs for a variety of architectures. We proposed and proved a solution strategy that is independent of architecture. The solution strategy was described by invariant, progress, and fixed-point conditions. Then we derived programs for different architectures from the solution strategy. A small number of heuristics were employed in deriving solutions and in transforming programs into forms appropriate for different target architectures.

Bibliographic Notes

The Floyd-Warshall algorithm is discussed in Warshall [1962] and Floyd [1962]. The processor-array solution is in Van Scoy [1980] and is described very clearly in van de Snepscheut [1986]. An assertional correctness proof of a distributed shortest-path algorithm is given in Lamport [1982].

CHAPTER 6

Toy Examples

6.1   Introduction

This chapter consists of a number of short examples drawn from a variety of areas: business applications (computation of an amortization schedule), combinatorial computing (prime number generation and other applications), operating systems (the readers-writers problem), and scientific computing (Gauss-Jordan elimination and fast Fourier transform). The title of the chapter is not meant to suggest that the problems are unimportant; indeed, the fast Fourier transform is one of the most important algorithms ever devised. What we have done is to choose problems that can be specified and solved in a few pages of text.

The problems are arranged in a sequence of increasing difficulty within each application area as we perceive it. We provide the necessary background for understanding each problem, though the explanation is often terse.

6.2   Computing an Amortization Schedule

A typical business application, often solved using a spreadsheet, is to compute an amortization schedule for a loan of L units, $L \geq 0$, that is to be paid off in equal amounts over N time periods, $N > 0$; the interest rate is r per period per unit of loan. The purpose of this exercise is to show how to express computation of the amortization schedule as a proper set of equations. We suggest two different solutions, appropriate for sequential and parallel computations, respectively, each expressed as a proper set of equations.

Let pay denote the (constant) amount to be paid per period; this is given by

$$pay = L \times r \times q^N / (q^N - 1),$$

where $q = 1 + r$.

The amortization schedule gives the values of the following for every period i: the amount of interest paid in the ith payment ($int[i]$), the amount paid toward the principal in the ith payment ($pri[i]$), and the remaining loan balance after the ith payment ($bal[i]$). For all i, $0 < i \leq N$,

$$bal[i] = bal[i - 1] - pri[i]$$
$$int[i] = bal[i - 1] \times r$$
$$pri[i] = pay - int[i].$$

Also we have

$$bal[0] = L.$$

These equations are proper. To see this, order the equations as follows, for all i, $i > 0$: the equation defining $bal[i-1]$, followed by the one defining $int[i]$, followed by the one defining $pri[i]$, followed by the one defining $bal[i]$. These equations can be transcribed directly to the following UNITY program.

Program *Amortization-Schedule*

> **always**
>
> $\quad\quad q = 1 + r$
>
> $\quad\llbracket\quad pay = L \times r \times q^N/(q^N - 1)$
>
> $\quad\llbracket\quad bal[0] = L$
>
> $\quad\llbracket\quad \langle\llbracket\ i\ \ :\ \ 0 < i \leq N\ \ ::$
>
> $\quad\quad\quad\quad\quad\quad\quad bal[i]\ \ =\ \ bal[i-1] - pri[i]$
>
> $\quad\quad\quad\quad\llbracket\quad int[i]\ \ =\ \ bal[i-1] \times r$
>
> $\quad\quad\quad\quad\llbracket\quad pri[i]\ \ =\ \ pay - int[i]$
>
> $\quad\quad\rangle$

end *{Amortization-Schedule}*

This program is essentially sequential: $bal[i]$ cannot be computed until $bal[i-1]$ has been computed. A parallel version of this program is obtained by using a different set of equations, in which we express $bal[i]$ in terms of L, q, N only. It can be shown that for all i, $0 \leq i \leq N$,

$$bal[i] = L \times (q^N - q^i)/(q^N - 1).$$

Using this equation for $bal[i]$ in place of the previous one, we obtain the following program.

Program *Amortization-Schedule* {**parallel version**}

> **always**
>
> $\quad\quad q = 1 + r$
>
> $\quad\llbracket\quad pay = L \times r \times q^N/(q^N - 1)$
>
> $\quad\llbracket\quad \langle\|\ i : 0 \leq i \leq N\ \ ::\ \ bal[i] = L \times (q^N - q^i)/(q^N - 1)\rangle$
>
> $\quad\llbracket\quad \langle\|\ i : 0 < i \leq N\ \ ::\ \ int[i] = bal[i-1] \times r \quad\quad\quad\quad\quad\rangle$
>
> $\quad\llbracket\quad \langle\|\ i : 0 < i \leq N\ \ ::\ \ pri[i] = pay - int[i] \quad\quad\quad\quad\quad\rangle$

end *{Amortization-Schedule}*

All variables in this program can be computed in $O(1)$ time using $O(N)$ processors (assuming that the right side of each equation can be evaluated in constant time) by assigning the ith processor to compute $bal[i-1]$, $int[i]$, and $pri[i]$ in sequence.

6.3   Saddle Point of a Matrix

Let $A[0..N-1, 0..N-1]$ be a matrix of integers. An element $A[u,v]$ of this matrix is a *saddle point* if and only if $A[u,v]$ is the smallest element in its column and the largest element in its row, i.e.,

$A[u,v] = \langle \min \ i \ : 0 \leq i < N \ :: \ A[i,v] \rangle \ \wedge$

$A[u,v] = \langle \max \ j : 0 \leq j < N \ :: \ A[u,j] \rangle$

It is required to determine whether the given matrix has a saddle point— that is, to compute the value of a boolean variable, sp, given by

$sp = \langle \exists \ u,v \ : \ 0 \leq u < N \ \wedge \ 0 \leq v < N \ ::$

$\qquad A[u,v] = \langle \min \ i \ : 0 \leq i < N \ :: \ A[i,v] \rangle \ \wedge$

$\qquad A[u,v] = \langle \max \ j : 0 \leq j < N \ :: \ A[u,j] \rangle$

$\rangle .$

We have not specified whether this problem is to be solved by a single processor or multiple processors. In the latter case, the initial distribution of elements of A among the processors, as well as their communication topology, must be specified. As usual, our strategy is to start from the problem and not the architecture. In this example we illustrate the effectiveness of manipulating specifications.

Henceforth all indices i, j, u, v are quantified over the range $0..N-1$; the quantification is not shown explicitly.

Observe that for any u, v,

$\langle \min \ i \ :: \ A[i,v] \rangle \ \leq \ A[u,v] \ \leq \ \langle \max \ j \ :: \ A[u,j] \rangle .$

Therefore $A[u,v]$ is a saddle point if and only if

$\langle \min \ i \ :: \ A[i,v] \rangle \geq \langle \max \ j \ :: \ A[u,j] \rangle .$

Hence

$sp = \langle \exists \ u, \ v \ :: \ \langle \min \ i \ :: \ A[i,v] \rangle \geq \langle \max \ j \ :: \ A[u,j] \rangle \rangle .$

Let $X[v]$ denote $\langle \min \ i \ :: \ A[i,v] \rangle$ and $Y[u]$ denote $\langle \max \ j \ :: \ A[u,j] \rangle$.

Then

$sp = \langle \exists \ u,v \ :: \ X[v] \geq Y[u] \rangle$

$\ = (\langle \max \ v \ :: \ X[v] \rangle \geq \langle \min \ u \ :: \ Y[u] \rangle).$

These equations give us the following program for computing *sp*.

Program *Saddle-Point*

> **declare** X, Y : array $[0..N-1]$ of integer
>
> **always**
>
> $$\langle \| \; v \quad :: \quad X[v] = \langle \min \; i \quad :: \quad A[i,v] \rangle \; \rangle$$
> $$\| \; \langle \| \; u \quad :: \quad Y[u] = \langle \max \; j \quad :: \quad A[u,j] \rangle \rangle$$
> $$[\hspace{-0.3em}] \quad sp = (\langle \max \; v \quad :: \quad X[v] \rangle \geq \langle \min \; u \quad :: \quad Y[u] \rangle)$$
>
> **end** {*Saddle-Point*}

The equations in this program are proper. (Implementations of programs in the equational schema for various architectures were treated in Chapter 4.) Note that the program can be executed in $O(N^2)$ steps on a sequential processor, or in $O(\log N)$ steps on a parallel synchronous machine with $O(N^2)$ processors.

6.4   Reachability in Directed Graphs

Let $G = (V, E)$ be a directed graph with vertex set V and edge set E; an edge directed from vertex u to vertex v is denoted by the ordered pair (u, v). It is required to identify all vertices *reachable* from a specified vertex *init*; henceforth we denote a vertex *reachable* if it is reachable from *init*. Specifically,

1. Vertex *init* is reachable.

2. Given that u is reachable and (u, v) is in E, v is reachable.

3. No other vertex is reachable.

Our goal is to design a solution which guarantees that $r[v]$—where r is a boolean array indexed by the vertices—is *true* at fixed point if and only if v is reachable. (See Chapters 11, 16, and 20 for some other algorithms for this problem and its variations.)

This example illustrates the use of nondeterminism in constructing a program directly from its specification. The specification is to design a program that reaches a fixed point, and at any fixed point

$$\langle \wedge \, v \; : \; v \in V \quad :: \quad r[v] \quad \equiv \quad v \text{ is } reachable \rangle.$$

This condition is satisfied by a program that has the following invariant and *FP*.

invariant $\langle \wedge\, v\, :\, v \in V\, ::\, r[v]\, \Rightarrow\, v$ is reachable$\rangle \wedge r[init]$

   $FP\ \equiv\ \langle \wedge\, u, v\, :\, (u, v) \in E\, ::\, r[u]\, \Rightarrow\, r[v]\rangle$

The expression $r[u]\, \Rightarrow\, r[v]$ is equivalent to

   $r[v] = (r[u]\ \vee\ r[v])$.

Therefore

   $FP\ \equiv\ \langle \wedge\, u, v\, :\, (u, v) \in E\, ::\, r[v] = (r[u]\ \vee\ r[v])\rangle$.

The invariant can be established initially by setting $r[v]$ to *false*, for all v other than *init*. The definition of FP suggests that $r[v]$ be assigned $r[u]\ \vee\ r[v]$, where (u, v) is in E. This gives the following program:

Program *Reachability*

   declare $r\ :$ array [vertex] of boolean

   initially $\langle \|\, v\, :\, v \in V\, ::\, r[v] = (v = init)\rangle$

   assign $\langle \|\, u, v\, :\, (u, v) \in E\, ::\, r[v]\ :=\ r[u]\ \vee\ r[v]\rangle$

end {*Reachability*}

It is easy to see that the proposed invariant holds for this program. To show that this program reaches a fixed point we use metric M, which is the size of the set

   $\{v \mid \neg r[v]\}$.

   Clearly $M \geq 0$, and M decreases with each state change. This argument shows that the number of state changes in the program *Reachability* is bounded by $|V|$. However, the best execution strategy on a sequential computer may require $O(|E|)$ statement executions: Execute the statement $r[v]\ :=\ r[u]\ \vee\ r[v]$ only after $r[u]$ becomes *true* and execute it at most once; since any $r[u]$ becomes *true* at most once, every statement is executed at most once.

Exercise 6.1 Define the *distance* of a reachable vertex v to be the minimum number of edges in a path from *init* to v. Modify program *Reachability* to compute distances of all reachable vertices. $\triangledown$

6.5   Prime Number Generation by Sieving

It is required to obtain an array $X[1..N]$ consisting of the first N primes, $N \geq 1$. A solution appropriate for pipeline architectures is proposed, as an exercise, in Chapter 8. Here we propose a solution better suited for sequential architectures.

We have $X[1] = 2$. The $(n+1)^{th}$ prime, $n \geq 1$, is the smallest integer larger than the nth prime that is not divisible by any of the first n primes. This can be stated as a set of equations, where u div v denotes that u divides v.

$$X[1] = 2$$
$$[\!] \ \langle [\!] \ n \ : \ 1 \leq n < N \quad :: \quad X[n+1] =$$
$$\langle \min p \ : \ p > X[n] \ \wedge \ \langle \forall k \ : \ 1 \leq k \leq n \quad :: \quad \neg X[k] \text{ div } p \rangle \quad :: \quad p \rangle$$
$$\rangle$$

These equations cannot be used directly in a UNITY program because an infinite number of values of p satisfy the condition in the quantification. We implement these equations in a program with assignments. We introduce variables n, p, i where n is the number of primes computed so far, p is a candidate for the next, i.e., $(n+1)^{th}$, prime, and p is not divisible by the first $(i-1)$ primes. Formally we have the following invariant:

invariant I ::

$$p > X[n] \ \wedge \ 1 < i \leq n+1 \ \wedge \ 1 \leq n \leq N \qquad \wedge$$
$$\langle \wedge \ k \ : \ 1 \leq k \leq n \quad :: \quad X[k] \text{ is the } k^{th} \text{ prime} \rangle \ \wedge$$
$$\langle \wedge \ q \ : \ X[n] < q < p \quad :: \quad q \text{ is a nonprime} \rangle \qquad \wedge$$
$$\langle \wedge \ k \ : \ 1 \leq k < i \quad :: \quad \neg X[k] \text{ div } p \rangle$$

Note from invariant I that $\neg X[1]$ div p, and hence p is odd.

Program *Sieve*

    declare n, p, i : integer

    initially $n, p, i = 1, 3, 2 \ \| \ X[1] = 2$

    assign

$X[i]$	,	i	,	p	,	n	$:=$	
$X[i]$	,	2	,	$p+2$	,	n	if $i \leq n \ \wedge \ X[i]$ div $p \sim$	
$X[i]$	,	$i+1$	,	p	,	n	if $i \leq n \ \wedge \ \neg X[i]$ div $p \sim$	
p	,	2	,	$p+2$	,	$n+1$	if $i > n \ \wedge \ n < N$	

end {*Sieve*}

The proof of invariant I for this program is left to the reader. We note that

$$FP \quad \equiv \quad (i > n \ \vee \ \neg X[i] \text{ div } p) \ \wedge \ (i > n \ \vee \ X[i] \text{ div } p) \ \wedge \ (i \leq n \ \vee \ n \geq N)$$
$$FP \quad \equiv \quad (i > n \geq N) \qquad \qquad \text{, from predicate calculus}$$

$$FP \wedge I \;\Rightarrow\; n = N \wedge \langle \wedge k \;:\; 1 \le k \le N \;::\; X[k] = \text{the } k^{th} \text{ prime}\rangle$$

To show that a fixed point is reached, observe that the triple (n, p, i) increases lexicographically in each step. From the invariant, n, p, i are bounded from above by N, the $(N+1)^{th}$ prime, and $N+1$, respectively. Hence a fixed point is reached.

Exercise 6.2   What are the values of p and i at fixed point?   ▽

Exercise 6.3   Observe that $n = N$ does not imply that program *Sieve* is at a fixed point. Modify the program to achieve this.   ▽

6.6   Comparing Two Ascending Sequences

Let $f[0..N]$, $g[0..N]$ be two ascending arrays of integers, i.e.,

$$\langle \wedge i \;:\; 0 \le i < N \;::\; f[i] \le f[i+1]\rangle \;\wedge$$
$$\langle \wedge i \;:\; 0 \le i < N \;::\; g[i] \le g[i+1]\rangle$$

It is required to determine whether f, g have the same set of integers, i.e., whether

$$\{f[i] \mid 0 \le i \le N\} = \{g[i] \mid 0 \le i \le N\}.$$

This example illustrates yet again the virtues of nondeterminism and the effectiveness of manipulating specifications. We present two programs, one for a sequential and the other for a parallel architecture. Another program suitable for a parallel architecture is suggested in an exercise. To avoid case analysis, we assume that $f[0] = g[0]$, $f[N] = g[N]$, and $f[N], g[N]$ are strictly larger than all other elements of f and g, respectively. These conditions can be satisfied by adding $-\infty$ and $+\infty$ to the left and right ends of f, g.

6.6.1 Sequential Architectures

A well-known heuristic for constructing an invariant from a specification is to replace constants by variables. We do so with the given specification. Introducing variables u, v, we postulate an invariant, I, as follows.

invariant I ::

$$0 \le u \le N \;\wedge\; 0 \le v \le N \;\wedge\; \{f[i] \mid 0 \le i \le u\} = \{g[i] \mid 0 \le i \le v\}$$

From the assumption that $f[0] = g[0]$, this invariant can be established initially by setting $u, v = 0, 0$. The following program is immediate; proof of invariant I is left to the reader.

Program *Compare*

    declare u, v : integer

    initially $u, v\ =\ 0, 0$

    assign

        u $:= u + 1$ if $u < N \ \wedge \ f[u] = f[u+1]$

      $[\!]$ v $:= v + 1$ if $v < N \ \wedge \ g[v] = g[v+1]$

      $[\!]$ $u, v := u + 1, v + 1$ if $u < N \ \wedge \ v < N \ \wedge \ f[u+1] = g[v+1]$

end {*Compare*}

For this program,

$$FP \ \equiv \ (u \geq N \ \vee \ f[u] \neq f[u+1]) \ \wedge \ (v \geq N \ \vee \ g[v] \neq g[v+1]) \ \wedge$$
$$(u \geq N \ \vee \ v \geq N \ \vee \ f[u+1] \neq g[v+1]).$$

From invariant I, and the facts that $f[N] = g[N]$ and that $f[N]$ and $g[N]$ are greater than all other values in f and g, we derive

    invariant $u = N \ \equiv \ v = N$

We use this invariant to simplify FP. There are two cases.

1. $u = N \ \wedge \ v = N$

    From invariant I,

    $$\{f[i] \mid 0 \leq i \leq N\} = \{g[i] \mid 0 \leq i \leq N\}.$$

    That is, f, g have the same set of elements.

2. $u < N \ \wedge \ v < N$

    $$FP \ \Rightarrow \ (f[u] \neq f[u+1] \ \wedge \ g[v] \neq g[v+1] \ \wedge \ f[u+1] \neq g[v+1]).$$

    Suppose that $f[u+1] < g[v+1]$. (Similar reasoning applies when $f[u+1] > g[v+1]$.)

    Then

$g[v] = f[u]$	, from invariant I
$f[u] < f[u+1]$	, from FP and the fact that f is ascending
$f[u+1] < g[v+1]$	, from the above assumption

$$g[v] < f[u+1] < g[v+1] \qquad \text{, from the above three facts}$$
$$f[u+1] \text{ is not in } g \qquad \text{, because } g \text{ is ascending}$$
$$\{f[i] \mid 0 \le i \le N\} \neq \{g[i] \mid 0 \le i \le N\}, \text{ trivially from the above}$$

That is, f, g do not have the same set of elements.

From these two cases,

$$FP \wedge I \Rightarrow$$

$$[u = N \equiv v = N] \wedge$$
$$[u = N \equiv (\{f[i] \mid 0 \le i \le N\} = \{g[i] \mid 0 \le i \le N\})].$$

We leave it to the reader to show that a fixed point is reached in program *Compare*.

Exercise 6.4   Show that $(u0, v0)$, the values of (u, v) at any fixed point of program *Compare*, are the largest values up to which f, g match. That is, for any r, s, if

$$\{f[i] \mid 0 \le i \le r\} = \{g[i] \mid 0 \le i \le s\}$$

then

$$r \le u0 \wedge s \le v0. \qquad \triangledown$$

Exercise 6.5   Investigate the possibility of implementing program *Compare* as a system of three asynchronous processes by partitioning the set of statements, one per process. $\triangledown$

6.6.2 Parallel Architectures

Our goal is to compute the predicate

$$\{f[i] \mid 0 \le i \le N\} = \{g[i] \mid 0 \le i \le N\}.$$

We rewrite this predicate by observing that since the two boundaries of f, g are equal in value, an element of f is in g if and only if it does not fall in value between any two consecutive elements of g. That is, for any u, $0 < u < N$,

$$f[u] \in \{g[i] \mid 0 \le i \le N\} \equiv$$
$$\langle \wedge v : 0 \le v < N :: \neg(g[v] < f[u] < g[v+1]) \rangle.$$

We have to compute the predicate that for all u, $0 < u < N$, $f[u]$ is in g and for all v, $0 < v < N$, $g[v]$ is in f:

$$\langle \wedge u, v : 0 < u < N \wedge 0 \le v < N :: \neg(g[v] < f[u] < g[v+1]) \rangle \wedge$$

$\langle \wedge\ u, v\ :\ 0 \leq u < N\ \wedge\ 0 < v < N\ ::\ \neg(f[u] < g[v] < f[u+1])\rangle.$

To make the quantifications identical, we observe that adding the condition for inclusion of $f[0]$ in g or $g[0]$ in f has no effect on the value of the predicate, because both of these predicates are *true*. Hence, we obtain

$$\langle \wedge\ u, v\ :\ 0 \leq u < N\ \wedge\ 0 \leq v < N\ ::$$
$$\neg(g[v] < f[u] < g[v+1])\ \wedge\ \neg(f[u] < g[v] < f[u+1])$$
$$\rangle.$$

Simplifying the expression in this predicate, we obtain

$$\langle \wedge\ u, v\ :\ 0 \leq u < N\ \wedge\ 0 \leq v < N\ ::$$
$$f[u] = g[v]\ \vee\ g[v] \geq f[u+1]\ \vee\ f[u] \geq g[v+1]$$
$$\rangle.$$

There are $O(N^2)$ conjuncts in the predicate; each conjunct is a disjunction of three terms. Hence the predicate can be evaluated in $O(\log N)$ time by $O(N^2)$ synchronous processors. In the following exercise we suggest a different algorithm that solves the problem in $O(\log N)$ time using $O(N)$ synchronous processors.

Exercise 6.6   It is easy to compare two ascending sequences when neither has duplicates: check whether the sequences are identical; it takes $O(\log N)$ time using $O(N)$ synchronous processors to carry out this computation. The purpose of this exercise is to create new arrays from f, g, removing duplicates from each one, in order to carry out the comparison. We show how to create such an array X from f. This is done in three steps: (1) identify all distinct elements of f, (2) compute the position in X for each distinct element of f, and (3) assign elements to their proper positions in X.

1. Identify all distinct elements of f. Let $e[i]$, $0 \leq i \leq N$, be *true* if and only if $f[i]$ does not appear to the left of i, i.e.,

$$\langle \|\ i\ :\ 0 \leq i \leq N\ ::$$
$$e[i] = true \quad \text{if}\quad i = 0\ \sim\ (f[i] \neq f[i-1]) \quad \text{if}\quad i > 0$$
$$\rangle.$$

   Show that e can be computed in $O(1)$ time by $O(N)$ processors.

2. Compute positions. The position in X of $f[i]$, for which $e[i]$ holds, is determined in this step. Let $r[i]$ be this position. It is clear that $r[i]$ is the number of indices to the left of i for which $e[i]$ holds, i.e.,

$$\langle \|\ i\ :\ 0 \leq i \leq N\ \wedge\ e[i]\ ::\ r[i] = \langle +\ j\ :\ 0 \leq j < i\ \wedge\ e[j]\ ::\ 1\rangle\rangle.$$

Show how to compute the entire array r in $O(\log N)$ time using $O(N)$ processors.

Hint: Use the prefix computation scheme of Ladner and Fischer [1980]; see Section 4.2.3 for a discussion.

3. Compute X.   Equate $f[i]$ for which $e[i]$ holds to $X[r[i]]$, i.e.,

$$\langle \| \; i \; : \; 0 \leq i \leq N \; \wedge \; e[i] \;\; :: \;\; X[r[i]] = f[i] \rangle.$$

Array X can be computed in $O(1)$ time using $O(N)$ processors.

Write a complete UNITY program consisting of these equations, similar equations for g, and the equations necessary to define the result of comparison.

$\triangledown$

6.7   Computing the Maximum of a Set of Numbers

Let $A[0..N-1]$ be an array of integers. It is required to compute m satisfying

$$m = \langle \max \; i \; : \; 0 \leq i < N \;\; :: \;\; A[i] \rangle.$$

The preferred way to achieve this goal in UNITY is to define m by the preceding equation. In this section we show how to implement the computation of m—and the computation of any quantified expression—on both sequential and parallel architectures. The computation can be carried out in $O(N)$ time on a sequential architecture or $O(\log N)$ time using $O(N)$ parallel synchronous processors, as shown in Chapter 4. Here we describe these algorithms in UNITY notation.

6.7.1 Sequential Architectures

The specification of m can be decomposed into the following invariant and fixed-point conditions:

invariant $m \leq \langle \max \; i \; : \; 0 \leq i < N \;\; :: \;\; A[i] \rangle$

$FP \quad \equiv \quad m \geq \langle \max \; i \; : \; 0 \leq i < N \;\; :: \;\; A[i] \rangle$

The latter condition may be written equivalently:

$FP \quad \equiv \quad \langle \wedge \; i \; : \; 0 \leq i < N \;\; :: \;\; m \geq A[i] \rangle$

or

$FP \quad \equiv \quad \langle \wedge \; i \; : \; 0 \leq i < N \;\; :: \;\; m = \max(m, A[i]) \rangle$

The next program is obtained by replacing each equality in the preceding condition by an assignment.

Program *Maximum1* {**sequential version**}

   initially $m = -\infty$ {the unit element of max}

   assign $\langle \| \; i \; : \; 0 \le i < N \; :: \; m \; := \; \max(m, A[i]) \rangle$

end {*Maximum1*}

Exercise 6.7   Show that $m \le \langle \max \; i \; : \; 0 \le i < N \; :: \; A[i] \rangle$ is an invariant of the program *Maximum1*. Also show that m increases with each state change. Since m is bounded from above (from the invariant), fixed point is reached.

$\triangledown$

For any j, $0 \le j < N$, multiple executions of

$m \; := \; \max(m, A[j])$

have the same effect as a single execution; m is not affected by subsequent executions of this statement. Hence we can achieve some efficiency by requiring that a statement assigns value to m no more than once during the execution. Also, if the goal is to compute the sum or product of an array of integers, for instance, multiple executions of such statements *must* be avoided. There are two useful heuristics to avoid any state change with multiple executions of statements. Call a statement execution *effective* if it leads to a state change.

1. Execute the statements effectively in some fixed order. This is the heuristic normally employed for sequential architectures. Statements are ordered based on an index i. This amounts to having only one statement in the program:

   $m, i \; := \; \max(m, A[i]), \; i + 1 \qquad \text{if} \quad i < N$

   where i is initially 0.

2. Associate a boolean variable with each statement. The boolean variable is *true* if the statement has never been executed. Letting $e[i]$ be the boolean variable for the ith statement, we propose the following assign-section:

   $\langle \| \; i \; : \; 0 \le i < N \; :: \; m, e[i] \; := \; \max(m, A[i]), \; false \qquad \text{if} \quad e[i] \rangle,$

   in which $e[i]$s are all *true* initially. Fixed point is reached when all $e[i]$s are *false*.

6.7.2 Parallel Architectures

Let the elements of A be placed at the leaf nodes of a tree. Define the value at any internal node to be the maximum of the values at its sons. Then the root node has the maximum value. The set of equations that defines this scheme is proper because a tree has no cycles. Also, computation of values for all nodes at one level of the tree may proceed in parallel. Hence, in a parallel synchronous architecture, it is possible to compute the value at the root in a number of steps proportional to the height of the tree.

We use the idea of a heap (see Chapter 19) to store the tree in an array. Then the height of the tree is $O(\log N)$. In the following program, array $X[1..(2 \times N - 1)]$ should be thought of as a tree where the sons of internal node i, $1 \leq i < N$, have indices $2.i$ and $2.i + 1$. Initially the elements $A[0..N - 1]$ are stored in the leaf nodes, i.e., in $X[N..(2 \times N - 1)]$.

Program *Maximum2*

     declare X : array$[1..(2 \times N - 1)]$ of integer

     always

          $\langle \| \; i \; : \; 0 \leq i < N \quad :: \quad X[N + i] = A[i] \rangle$

       $\| \; \langle \| \; i \; : \; 1 \leq i < N \quad :: \quad X[i] = \max(X[2.i], X[2.i + 1]) \rangle$

end {*Maximum2*}

We leave it to the reader to show that

$$X[1] = \langle \max \; i \; : \; 0 \leq i < N \quad :: \quad A[i] \rangle.$$

Program *Maximum2* uses about double the storage of array A. We can improve upon this as follows. If we are allowed to modify A, we can construct the heap entirely within A. Then every node, internal or leaf, contains some data item initially. In each step *every* internal node is assigned the maximum of the values of its sons. The number of steps for the maximum to propagate to the root of the tree is the height of the tree.

One difficulty with this solution is that the value at the root node is overwritten in each step (by the maximum of the values of its sons). If the root has the maximum value initially, for instance, this value will be overwritten after the first step, and the final result will be erroneous. Fortunately, this difficulty does not arise because: The index of the root is 0, and hence the root is one of its own sons. Therefore a larger value at the root is never overwritten by a smaller value. (Note that we do not have a tree structure.) The following program incorporates this idea.

Let M be such that $N = 2.M$. (If N is odd, a small element can be added to A in order to satisfy this condition without affecting the value of the maximum.)

Program *Maximum3* {**synchronous computation of maximum**}

  assign $\langle \| \ i \ : \ 0 \le i < M \ \ :: \ \ A[i] \ := \ \max(A[2.i], A[2.i + 1]) \rangle$

end {*Maximum3*}

To prove properties of this program—that it computes the maximum in $A[0]$ in $O(\log N)$ steps—we introduce an auxiliary integer variable t, with initial value N, that is set to $\lceil t/2 \rceil$ in each step ($\lceil x \rceil$ is the smallest integer greater than or equal to x). The reader may show that the following is an invariant, where $A^0[i]$ is the initial value of $A[i]$.

invariant $\langle \max i \ : \ 0 \le i < t \ \ :: \ \ A[i] \rangle = \langle \max i \ : \ 0 \le i < N \ \ :: \ \ A^0[i] \rangle$

It follows from this invariant that when $t = 1$,

  $A[0] = \langle \max i \ : \ 0 \le i < N \ \ :: \ \ A^0[i] \rangle.$

Note that t is set to $\lceil t/2 \rceil$ in each step and that the initial value of t is N. Hence it takes $O(\log N)$ steps for t to become 1. It is easy to see that *Maximum3* is then at fixed point.

  The implementation of *Maximum3* on a parallel synchronous architecture is obvious. In Chapter 4 we discussed how a single-statement program can be implemented on parallel asynchronous and distributed architectures.

Exercise 6.8   Let $B[0..N-1]$ be a boolean array. Modify program *Maximum3* to compute the value of the following expression:

  $\langle \max i \ : \ 0 \le i < N \ \wedge \ B[i] \ \ :: \ \ A[i] \rangle.$ ▽

Exercise 6.9   The following modification of *Maximum3* avoids needless assignments to internal nodes. Prove its correctness. (Hint: Use the previous invariant.) As before, assume that N is even.

Program *Maximum4*

  declare t : integer

  initially $t = N$

  assign

     $\langle \| \ i \ : \ 0 \le i < \lceil t/2 \rceil \ \ :: \ \ A[i] \ := \ \max(A[2.i], A[2.i + 1]) \rangle$
     $\| \ t \ := \ \lceil t/2 \rceil$

end {*Maximum4*}   ▽

6.8   Simulating a Petri Net

Petri nets are elegant mechanisms for the study of synchronization in concurrent systems. Here we show how the synchronizations encoded in a Petri net can be coded directly as a UNITY program fragment. To illustrate, we show the encoding in the context of a specific example: task sequencing in a program.

It is required to compare two arrays to determine whether they have the same set of elements. Program *Compare* (see Section 6.6) is not directly applicable since the arrays may not be ascending. Therefore a programming strategy is to sort each array into ascending order and then apply program *Compare*. The two arrays may be sorted in parallel; comparison can start only after both are sorted. The Petri net diagram in Fig. 6.1 captures the sequencing constraints among the tasks; labels assigned to the circles are used later in this section.

Each circle is a *place*, and each outgoing edge from a place points to a *transition*. A place may contain zero or more *markers*. In Fig. 6.1, places u, v initially hold one marker each; no other place holds a marker. A transition *fires*, i.e., the task corresponding to the transition is executed, only if all

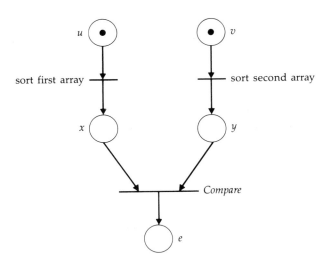

Figure 6.1 A Petri net diagram depicting sequencing constraints among three tasks. Initially, markers are at places u, v.

input places of the transition contain at least one marker. The firing of a transition has the effect of removing one marker from each of its input places and depositing one marker in each of its output places. Any transition that meets the preceding constraint may fire. A transition fires eventually if its input places continue to hold markers forever.

A Petri net can be represented directly in UNITY. Each place is represented by an integer-valued variable whose value is the number of markers in that place. A transition is modeled by a statement that reduces each of the variables corresponding to its input places by 1 (provided they are all nonzero) and increases the variables corresponding to its output places by 1. The program fragment corresponding to the Petri net in Fig. 6.1 is given next (the variable corresponding to a place is the label of the place in the diagram).

Program *Petri-net*

  initially $u, v, x, y, e = 1, 1, 0, 0, 0$
  assign

   u, x $:= u - 1, x + 1$ if $u > 0$ {sort first array}

  ▯ v, y $:= v - 1, y + 1$ if $v > 0$ {sort second array}

  ▯ $x, y, e := x - 1, y - 1, e + 1$ if $x > 0 \land y > 0$ {compare}

end {*Petri-net*}

Observe that multiple assignment is the appropriate mechanism for representing simultaneous modifications of all places incident on a transition, and that nondeterministic statement selection is the appropriate mechanism for modeling the arbitrary choice of a transition to fire.

Note: If a place is both an input and an output place of a transition, then the corresponding variable is simply assigned to itself in the statement corresponding to the transition.   ▽

A UNITY program corresponding to a Petri net increments a variable in at most one statement and decrements it in at most one statement. All variables are incremented or decremented by 1, and all are guaranteed to be nonnegative. Because of these restrictions, Petri nets enjoy several important properties—decidability of the reachability problem, for instance—that do not hold for arbitrary UNITY programs.

6.9   An Addition Circuit

It is required to design a circuit that adds two numbers represented in binary positional notation. The purpose of this example is to emphasize yet again the importance of invariants in designing and understanding programs (circuits).

Let $A[0..N-1]$ and $B[0..N-1]$ be two arrays, in which each array element is either 0 or 1; each array represents one of the numbers to be added; $A[0]$, $B[0]$ represent the lowest (rightmost) bits and $A[N-1]$, $B[N-1]$ the highest (leftmost) bits of the numbers. Instead of computing the sum, we compute the carry bits, from which the sum is readily computed. The carry into the ith bit, $C[i]$, is defined as follows:

$$C[0] = 0$$

$$\wedge \; \langle \forall \, i \; : \; 0 \leq i < N \quad :: $$

$$
\begin{array}{lll}
C[i+1] = 0 & \text{if} & A[i] + B[i] + C[i] \leq 1 \quad \sim \\
\quad\quad\quad 1 & \text{if} & A[i] + B[i] + C[i] > 1
\end{array}
$$

$$\rangle .$$

It is straightforward to compute the $C[i]$s from the preceding (proper) equations. The number of steps for such a computation is $O(N)$, because $C[i+1]$ can be computed only after computing $C[i]$. We propose an algorithm that requires $O(\log N)$ steps using $O(N)$ parallel synchronous processors. First we give an alternative characterization of the carry bits.

Theorem 6.1

$$\langle \forall \, i \; : \; 0 \leq i < N \quad :: $$

$$
\begin{array}{lll}
C[i+1] = A[i] & \text{if} & A[i] = B[i] \quad \sim \\
\quad\quad\quad C[i] & \text{if} & A[i] \neq B[i]
\end{array}
$$

$$\rangle$$

Proof: By analysis of the three cases $A[i] = B[i] = 0$, $A[i] = B[i] = 1$, and $A[i] \neq B[i]$. We sketch a proof for the last case.

$$
\begin{array}{ll}
A[i] \neq B[i] \;\; \Rightarrow \;\; A[i] + B[i] = 1 & \\
A[i] + B[i] + C[i] \leq 1 \;\; \equiv \;\; C[i] = 0 & \text{, given } A[i] \neq B[i] \\
C[i+1] = C[i] & \text{, from the definition} \quad \nabla
\end{array}
$$

By applying induction on Theorem 6.1, we conclude that for any i, $i > 0$, $C[i] = A[j]$, where j is the first index to the right of i such that $A[j] = B[j]$; if there is no such index $C[i] = C[0] = 0$. This observation can be used as the basis of an efficient parallel program. In the following program, we use a variable t, $t > 0$, and variable $d[i]$, for $0 \leq i \leq N$, which equals $C[i]$ at fixed point. Each $d[i]$ can take on *three* possible values, 0, 1, or U—the former two denoting that $d[i] = C[i]$ and the latter, for $i \geq t$, denoting that there is no j within t positions to the right of i where $A[j] = B[j]$, i.e., $\langle \forall\, j \; : \; i - t \leq j < i \; :: \; A[j] \neq B[j] \rangle$. Formally, we have the following invariant:

invariant

$$t > 0 \quad \wedge \quad \langle \forall\, i \; : \; 0 \leq i < t \; \wedge \; i \leq N \; :: \; d[i] = C[i] \rangle \; \wedge$$

$$\langle \forall\, i \; : \; t \leq i \leq N \; ::$$

$$\begin{array}{lll} d[i] = C[i] & \text{if} & \langle \exists\, j \; : \; i - t \leq j < i \; :: \; A[j] = B[j] \rangle \quad \sim \\ \qquad U & \text{if} & \langle \forall\, j \; : \; i - t \leq j < i \; :: \; A[j] \neq B[j] \rangle \end{array}$$

$$\rangle$$

The crucial observation is that t can be doubled and that all $d[i]$s can be recomputed in one assignment: $d[i]$ is assigned $d[i - t]$ if $d[i] = U$. We leave it to the reader to show that the following program (containing this assignment) satisfies the preceding invariant.

Program *Carry*

  declare

    d : array $[0..N]$ of $(0, 1, U)$,

    t : integer

  initially

    $t = 1 \; \| \; d[0] = 0 \; \|$

    $\langle \| \; i \; : \; 0 \leq i < N \; ::$

        $d[i + 1] \;\; = \;\; A[i] \quad \text{if} \quad A[i] = B[i] \;\; \sim \;\; U \quad \text{if} \quad A[i] \neq B[i]$

    $\rangle$

  assign

    $\langle \| \; i \; : \; t \leq i \leq N \; :: \; d[i] \; := \; d[i - t] \quad \text{if} \quad d[i] = U \rangle$

    $\| \qquad t \; := \; 2 \times t \qquad\qquad \text{if} \quad t \leq N$

end $\{Carry\}$

It is easily seen that

$$FP \quad \Rightarrow \quad t > N.$$

The correctness of the program is established from the invariant and this fixed-point condition. Since t is doubled in each step, the number of steps is $O(\log N)$. Each step can be executed in constant time by $O(N)$ synchronous processors. Hence this program can be executed in $O(\log N)$ steps by $O(N)$ parallel synchronous processors.

In Fig. 6.2, we show the carry computation circuit for $N = 8$ schematically. Each column denotes a bit position and each row corresponds to a step in the computation. The value of t doubles in successive rows. For $0 \leq i < N$, a line connects column i of the topmost row to column $i+1$ of the row labeled $t = 1$; this denotes that $d[i+1]$ is computed initially from the ith bits of inputs $A[i]$ and $B[i]$. For other rows, a line connecting column i in one row to column j in the next lower row ($j = i + t$, where t is the value associated with the lower row) denotes that if its value is U, $d[j]$ is to be assigned the previous value of $d[i]$ in this step.

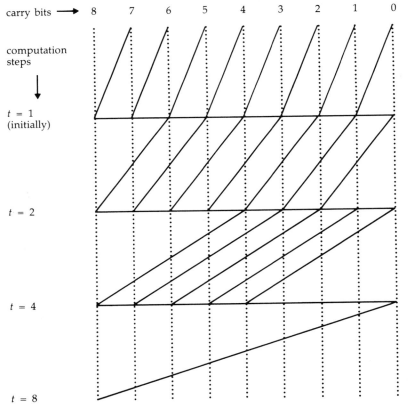

Figure 6.2 Schematic diagram of carry computation for $N = 8$. Rows correspond to computation steps, columns to bit positions, and lines to data paths.

6.10   Readers-Writers Problem

We are given a program, *user*, in which there are two integer variables nr, nw that satisfy:

invariant $0 \le nr \le N$ $\wedge$ $0 \le nw \le N$ (1)

for some given constant N. Initially, $nr = nw = 0$. The variables nr, nw are changed only in the following kinds of statements in *user*; we have attached a name to each kind of statement for easy reference.

$$\{startread\} \quad nr \quad := \quad nr + 1$$
$$\{endread\} \quad nr \quad := \quad nr - 1$$
$$\{startwrite\} \quad nw \quad := \quad nw + 1$$
$$\{endwrite\} \quad nw \quad := \quad nw - 1$$

These statements may change other variables and may have conditions (if-clauses) associated with them. Also, *user* may have other statements and variables. For our purposes, however, we need not know anything more about *user*.

It is required to modify the statements of *user* to guarantee an additional invariant:

invariant $nw \le 1$ $\wedge$ $(nr = 0 \ \vee \ nw = 0)$ (2)

This problem is known as the *readers-writers* problem. Variables nr, nw denote, respectively, the number of processes that are reading and writing into a common file at any time: A read operation is started by executing a startread statement and ended by executing an endread statement; similarly, startwrite and endwrite are executed at the initiation and completion of writing. The number of processes in the system is N, and hence invariant (1). Invariant (2) arises from the peculiarities of reads and writes: Any number of reads can proceed concurrently, but a write cannot be executed concurrently with a read or another write.

6.10.1 A Solution

Given,

$$0 \le nr \le N \quad \wedge \quad 0 \le nw \le N,$$

it is easy to see that

$$[nw \le 1 \ \wedge \ (nr = 0 \ \vee \ nw = 0)] \quad \equiv \quad [(nr + N \times nw) \le N].$$

Hence we will implement the invariant $nr + N \times nw \le N$ instead of invariant (2). Programming is simplified by introducing a variable t,

$$t = N - (nr + N \times nw),$$

and requiring that t satisfy

invariant $t \geq 0$ \hfill (3)

Reducing nr or nw increases t, and therefore endread and endwrite statements preserve $t \geq 0$. A startread statement increases nr by 1, thereby decreasing t by 1; hence a startread statement can execute only if $t \geq 1$ is a precondition. By similar reasoning, a startwrite statement can execute provided $t \geq N$.

This scheme can be interpreted in terms of a "pool of tokens"; t denotes the number of tokens in the pool. A reader acquires one token to startread and a writer N tokens to startwrite; both readers and writers release their tokens upon completion of the corresponding operations. Starting with a pool of N tokens, these requirements guarantee that a write cannot proceed concurrently with a read or another write, whereas an arbitrary number (up to N) reads can proceed concurrently.

Modifications to Program *user*

    declare t : integer

    always $t = N - (nr + N \times nw)$

    assign

        $\{startread\}$ $nr := nr + 1$ if $t \geq 1$

       ⫼ $\{endread\}$ $nr := nr - 1$

       ⫼ $\{startwrite\}$ $nw := nw + 1$ if $t \geq N$

       ⫼ $\{endwrite\}$ $nw := nw - 1$

end {**Modifications to Program** *user*}

6.10.2 Guaranteeing Progress for Writers

The proposed solution does not guarantee progress for either readers or writers. Since there is no requirement that read or write operations complete, it is not possible to claim that another read or write will eventually start. Now we impose the requirement that all reads complete in finite time. Then we modify the proposed solution such that readers do not overtake the writers forever.

Using only the variables nr, nw, there is no formal way to state that all reads complete in finite time. This is because we can make no statement about individual reads or writes. We represent the finiteness of read operations by assuming the following property for any modified program:

$$nr = k \ \wedge \ k > 0 \ \longmapsto \ nr \neq k. \tag{4}$$

Let nq denote the number of waiting writers (whenever a process waits to write, nq is incremented by 1, and whenever a process starts writing, nq is decremented by 1). Clearly $nq \geq 0$ is an invariant. Our goal is to modify *user* so as to guarantee that the previous invariants (1,3) hold and that the following progress property also holds:

$$nq > 0 \quad \longmapsto \quad nw = 1. \tag{5}$$

One solution strategy is to prevent any new read operation from starting if there is a process waiting to write. This solution, however, is very strict: A distributed implementation would require that a process waiting to write communicate its status to all potential readers and that every startread have a precondition, $nq > 0$. We propose a less strict strategy: Eventually, prevent startreads from executing if $nq > 0$. We do this by introducing a boolean variable b, where (1) b holds only if there is a process waiting to write, (2) if there is a process waiting to write, a write operation will start or b will hold, (3) once b holds, b continues to hold until eventually a write operation starts, and (4) no read operation is allowed to start if b holds. This strategy is implemented in the following program. In this program we do not show the statements incrementing nq because those statements are not modified.

Modifications to Program *user* {**ensuring progress for writers**}

> **declare** t : integer, b : boolean
>
> **always** $t = N - (nr + N \times nw)$
>
> **initially** $b = false$
>
> **assign**
>
> | | {*startread*} | nr | $:= nr + 1$ | if $t \geq 1 \wedge \neg b$ |
> | $\|$ | {*endread*} | nr | $:= nr - 1$ | |
> | $\|$ | {*startwrite*} | nw, nq, b | $:= nw + 1, nq - 1, false$ | if $t \geq N \wedge nq > 0$ |
> | $\|$ | {*endwrite*} | nw | $:= nw - 1$ | |
> | $\|$ | {*set-b*} | b | $:= nq > 0$ | |

end {**Modifications to Program** *user*}

The correctness of this solution—i.e., progress property (5)—follows from (4,6,7,8,9). Properties (6–9), given next, were stated informally earlier; their proofs are left to the human reader.

$$
\begin{aligned}
&b \;\Rightarrow\; nq > 0 && \text{\{used only in proofs of (8,9)\}} && (6)\\
&nq > 0 \;\; ensures \;\; nw = 1 \;\vee\; b && && (7)\\
&b \,\wedge\, nr = 0 \;\; ensures \;\; nw = 1 && && (8)\\
&b \,\wedge\, nr = k \,\wedge\, k > 0 \;\; unless \;\; b \,\wedge\, nr < k && && (9)
\end{aligned}
$$

Now we show that $nq > 0 \;\longmapsto\; nw = 1$:

$$b \;\wedge\; nr = k \;\wedge\; k > 0 \;\longmapsto\; b \wedge nr < k$$
, using the PSP theorem on (4,9)

$$b \;\longmapsto\; b \wedge nr = 0$$
, applying induction on the above

$$b \;\longmapsto\; nw = 1$$
, transitivity on the above and (8)

$$nq > 0 \;\longmapsto\; nw = 1$$
, cancellation on (7) and the above.

Exercise 6.10   Given that both read and write operations complete, write a modification to *user* to prevent infinite overtaking of readers by writers or of writers by readers.   ▽

6.11   Boolean Matrix Multiplication

Let $A[0..M-1, 0..N-1]$ and $B[0..N-1, 0..R-1]$ be two matrices with boolean elements. It is required to compute their product $C[0..M-1, 0..R-1]$, where element $C[i, k]$ is given by

$$C[i, k] = \langle \vee \; j \; : \; 0 \le j < N \;\; :: \;\; A[i,j] \;\wedge\; B[j,k] \rangle.$$

This definition leads to a straightforward program that can be executed in $O(M \times N \times R)$ time on one processor or in $O(\log N)$ time on $O(M \times N \times R)$ synchronous processors. However, it is possible to do considerably better; two boolean matrices of size $M \times M$ each can be multiplied in $O(M^3/\log M)$ steps on one processor. Next we develop such a program.

The major observation behind this program is that any row of the product matrix C is an *"or"* of some subset of rows of B. Let $B[i]$ denote the ith row of B (similarly, $A[i]$, $C[i]$). Let $(B[i]$ *or* $B[j])$ denote a row formed by applying $\vee$ to corresponding elements of $B[i]$, $B[j]$; that is, the kth element of $(B[i]$ *or* $B[j])$ is $B[i,k] \vee B[j,k]$. The generalization of *or* applied to a set of rows is obvious. Then

$$C[i] = \langle \; or \; j \; : \; 0 \le j < N \;\; \wedge \;\; A[i,j] \;\; :: \;\; B[j] \rangle. \qquad (10)$$

This equation can be understood as follows. Every $C[i]$ is an *or* of some subset of rows of B; the particular subset depends on $A[i]$: $B[j]$ is in the subset provided that $A[i, j]$ holds. A strategy to compute C, using equation (10), is first to compute a matrix D whose rows are the *ors* of all possible subsets of rows of B. Then select $C[i]$, based on $A[i]$, from D.

Since B has N rows, D has 2^N rows—each row of D is an *or* of some subset of the rows of B. We let the index of a row of D determine the rows of B from which it is constructed—i.e., for any r, $0 \le r < 2^N$,

$D[r] =$
$\langle$ _or_ j : $0 \leq j < N \wedge j^{th}$ bit in r's binary expansion is 1 :: $B[j]\rangle$ (11)

(In a binary expansion, bits are numbered starting from 0 for the lowest-order bit.) For any row $A[i]$ of A, let $\overline{A}[i]$ denote the number whose j^{th} bit in the binary expansion is 1 if and only if $A[i, j]$ holds—i.e., we interpret a _false_ as 0 and a _true_ as 1 in $A[i]$ to get the binary expansion of $\overline{A}[i]$. Then

$$D[\overline{A}[i]] = \langle \ or \ j \ : \ 0 \leq j < N \ \wedge \ A[i,j] \ :: \ B[j]\rangle \qquad \text{, from (11)}$$
$$= C[i] \qquad\qquad\qquad\qquad\qquad\qquad \text{, from (10)}.$$

The program follows.

Program {boolean matrix multiplication} _B1_

> **declare** D : $\text{array}[0..2^N - 1, 0..R - 1]$ of boolean
>
> **always**
>
> > $\langle\| \ r \ : \ 0 \leq r < 2^N \ ::$
> >
> > > $D[r] = \langle \ or \ j \ : \ 0 \leq j < N \ \wedge \ j^{th} \ \text{bit of } r \text{ is } 1 \ :: \ B[j]\rangle$
> >
> > $\rangle$
> >
> > $\|\ \langle\| \ i \ : \ 0 \leq i < M \ :: \ C[i] = D[\overline{A}[i]]\rangle$

end $\{B1\}$

6.11.1 Refinement of _B1_

Program _B1_ defines rows of D in terms of rows of B only. It is possible to perform a more efficient computation by defining rows of D in terms of other rows of D and rows of B. We next develop such a program.

For integers u, v let u _or_ v denote the number obtained by taking the _or_ of the binary expansions of u, v—i.e., the jth bit of u _or_ v is 1 if and only if the jth bit of u is 1 or the jth bit of v is 1. We have

$D[u \ or \ v] = D[u] \ or \ D[v]$.

A unique way to express any row index r as u _or_ v is based on the fact that $r = 2^j + k$ for some j, k, where $0 \leq j < N$ and $0 \leq k < 2^j$; the highest bit position where r has 1 is j, and k is the number corresponding to the remaining bits. Then $D[2^j + k] = B[j] \ or \ D[k]$. Using this, we obtain program _B2_.

Program {boolean matrix multiplication} B2

> **declare** D : array$[0..2^N - 1, 0..R - 1]$ of boolean
>
> **always**
>
>> $D[0] = \overline{0}$ {$\overline{0}$ is a row of all zeroes}
>>
>> $[\!]$ $\langle [\!]$ j, k : $0 \le j < N$ $\wedge$ $0 \le k < 2^j$ :: $D[2^j + k] = B[j]$ or $D[k] \rangle$
>>
>> $[\!]$ $\langle [\!]$ i : $0 \le i < M$ :: $C[i] = D[\overline{A}[i]] \rangle$

end {$B2$}

Exercise 6.11   Show that the equations in program $B2$ are proper. ∇

To count the number of *or* operations in $B2$, observe that for every value of j, variable k takes on 2^j different values. Since $0 \le j < N$, the number of *or* operations is proportional to $\langle + j : 0 \le j < N :: 2^j \rangle = O(2^N)$. The number of assignments to rows of C is $O(M)$. Hence the total number of row operations is $O(2^N + M)$. If N is $O(\log M)$, then boolean matrix multiplication can be done in $O(M)$ row operations or in $O(M \times R)$ time on a sequential architecture. Two boolean matrices of size $M \times M$ each can be multiplied by first partitioning the left matrix into $(M/\log M)$ submatrices of size $M \times \log M$, partitioning the right matrix into the same number of submatrices of size $\log M \times M$, and multiplying corresponding pairs each in $O(M^2)$ time on a sequential machine. The entire product matrix can be computed by taking elementwise disjunction of all the product submatrices. Therefore boolean matrix multiplication takes $O(M^3/\log M)$ time on a sequential architecture, an improvement over $O(M^3)$.

6.11.2 Boolean Matrix Multiplication on Parallel Architectures

Both programs $B1$ and $B2$ are in the equational schema. In Chapter 4 we showed how to implement such programs on asynchronous shared-variable or distributed architectures. Next we show a refinement of $B1$ that is suitable for implementation on parallel synchronous architectures.

Computation of each row of D requires $O(N)$ *or* operations on rows of B. Hence a row of D can be computed in $O(\log N)$ time using $O(N \times R)$ processors. (R is the number of elements in a row.) All the rows of D can be computed in parallel; hence matrix D can be computed in $O(\log N)$ time using $O(2^N \times N \times R)$ processors. Computation of C takes $O(1)$ time using $O(M \times R)$ processors.

Next we use the idea of program $B2$—forming the *or* of two rows to compute a row of D—to obtain a better parallel program, one that executes in $O(\log N)$ time using only $O(2^N \times R)$ processors. We use the fact that $D[r] = D[u]$ *or* $D[v]$, where $r = u$ *or* v. We can choose u, v so that they each have roughly half as many 1s in their binary expansions as r. Formally, let $|r|$ denote the number of 1s in the binary expansion of r. If $t < |r| \leq 2 \times t$, it is possible to find u, v such that $r = u$ *or* v and $|u| \leq t$ and $|v| \leq t$. Choose u, v as follows: u has 1s in its binary expansion exactly in t lower-order positions where r has 1s; v has 1s in the remaining positions where r has 1s. Therefore all rows of D whose indices have $2 \times t$ or fewer 1s in their binary expansions can be computed in one parallel step from the rows of D having t or fewer 1s in the expansions of their indices. A row index of D has at most N 1s in its binary expansion. Hence all rows of D can be computed in $O(\log N)$ steps. Computation of a row requires applying *or* to two rows, each of length R; hence $O(R)$ processors are required for this operation. Therefore $O(2^N \times R)$ processors are required for each synchronous step. This program is given next.

Program {boolean matrix multiplication} $B3$

    declare D : array$[0..2^N - 1, 0..R - 1]$ of boolean

    always

            $D[0] = \overline{0}$ $\{\overline{0}$ is a row of all zeroes$\}$

    $[\!]$ $\langle\| \; j \; : \; 0 \leq j < N \;\; :: \;\; D[2^j] = B[j]\rangle$

    $[\!]$ $\langle[\!] \; t \; : \; 1 \leq t < N \; \wedge \; t$ is a power of 2 ::

            $\{$compute $D[r]$, for all r, where r has more than t 1s and at most $2 \times t$ 1s in its binary expansion$\}$

            $\langle\| \; r \; : \; t < |r| \leq 2 \times t \; \wedge \; 1 \leq r < 2^N \;\; ::$

            $\{r_u$ has 1s in t lower-order positions where r has 1s;

            r_v has 1s in the remaining positions where r has 1s$\}$

              $D[r] = D[r_u]$ *or* $D[r_v]$

            $\rangle$

        $\rangle$

    $[\!]$ $\langle\| \; i \; : \; 0 \leq i < M \;\; :: \;\; C[i] = D[\overline{A}[i]]\rangle$

end $\{B3\}$

6.12   Nondeterministic Gaussian Elimination

We consider the Gaussian elimination scheme for solving a set of linear equations,

$$A.X = B,$$

where $A[0..N-1, 0..N-1]$ and $B[0..N-1]$ are given and the solution is to be stored in $X[0..N-1]$. Gaussian elimination is presented typically as a sequence of N pivot steps. We describe this scheme by a UNITY program that allows nondeterministic choices in the selections of the pivot rows.

6.12.1 A Solution

We give a quick introduction to Gaussian elimination. Let $M(A; B)$ (or M for short) denote a matrix with N rows and $N+1$ columns, where the first N columns are from A and the last column is from B. In the Gaussian elimination $M(A; B)$ is modified to $M(A'; B')$ by certain operations such that

$$A.X = B$$

and

$$A'.X = B'$$

have the same solutions for X. The goal of the algorithm is to apply a sequence of these operations to convert $M(A; B)$ to $M(I_N; X_F)$, where I_N is an identity matrix; then X_F is the desired solution vector. This goal can be realized if the rank of A is N, which we assume to be the case.

The following operations on M keep the solution vector invariant: (1) exchange two rows, (2) multiply all elements of a row of M by the same number, and (3) add a row, element by element, to another row of M (and replace the latter row with the result). The *pivot* operation in the Gaussian elimination combines the last two operations. To pivot the matrix with respect to a row u, where $M[u, u] \neq 0$, every element $M[v, j]$ in another row v is replaced by $M[v, j] - M[v, u] \times M[u, j]/M[u, u]$, and every element $M[u, j]$ in row u is replaced by $M[u, j]/M[u, u]$.

The program, given next, consists of two kinds of statements: (1) Pivot with row u, provided that $M[u, u] \neq 0$; this has the effect of setting $M[u, u]$ to 1 and $M[v, u]$ to 0, for all v, $v \neq u$. (2) Exchange two rows u, v, provided that both $M[u, u]$ and $M[v, v]$ are zero and at least one of $M[u, v]$, $M[v, u]$ is nonzero; this has the effect of replacing a zero diagonal element with a nonzero diagonal element.

Program *Gauss*

$\{u, v$ are quantified over $0..N$ and j over $0..N + 1\}$

assign

$\{$pivot with a row u if $M[u, u] \neq 0\}$

$\langle\!\![\ u\ ::$

$\langle\!\!\|\ v, j\ :\ v \neq u\ ::$

$\qquad M[v, j]\ :=\ M[v, j] - M[v, u] \times M[u, j]/M[u, u]\quad$ if $M[u, u] \neq 0$

$\rangle$

$\|\ \langle\!\!\|\ j\ ::$

$\qquad M[u, j]\ :=\ M[u, j]/M[u, u]\qquad\qquad\qquad\qquad$ if $\ M[u, u] \neq 0$

$\rangle$

$\rangle$

$[\!\!]$ $\{$exchange two rows if both have zero diagonal elements and the exchange results in at least one of these elements being set nonzero$\}$

$\langle\!\![\ u, v\ :\ u \neq v\ ::$

$\langle\!\!\|\ j\ ::\ M[u, j], M[v, j]\ :=\ M[v, j], M[u, j]$

$\qquad$if $\ M[u, u] = 0\ \wedge\ M[v, v] = 0\ \wedge\ (M[u, v] \neq 0\ \vee\ M[v, u] \neq 0)$

$\rangle$

$\rangle$

end $\{Gauss\}$

6.12.2 Correctness

Let M^0 denote the initial M matrix. Since each statement in the program modifies M such that the solutions to the given linear equations are preserved, we have

invariant M^0, M have the same solutions

In the following, A refers to the $N \times N$ matrix in the left part of M, and B, to the last column of M. Now we show that program *Gauss* reaches a fixed point and that at any fixed point, A is an identity matrix. Then, from the invariant, B is the desired solution vector. In the following, a *unit column* is a column in which the diagonal element is 1 and all other elements are 0. That is, column u is a unit column means that

$\qquad M[v, u] = 0\quad$ if $\ u \neq v\ \sim\ 1\quad$ if $\ u = v.$

To show that a fixed point is reached, we prove that the pair (m, n) increases lexicographically with every state change, where

m = number of unit columns in A

and,

n = number of nonzero diagonal elements in A.

We consider each statement in turn. Pivoting with row u, where column u is a unit column, causes no state change. This is seen as follows. Since column u is a unit column $M[u, u] = 1$, and hence all elements of the uth row are unchanged as a result of dividing by $M[u, u]$. An element $M[v, j]$, $u \neq v$, is set to $M[v, j] - M[v, u] \times M[u, j]/M[u, u]$. Since column u is a unit column and $u \neq v$, $M[v, u] = 0$. Hence $M[v, j]$ is unchanged. Therefore a state change results from a pivot operation with row u only if column u is not a unit column; the effect of the pivot operation is to set u to a unit column, thus increasing m. Two rows, u and v, are exchanged only when $M[u, u] = 0 \land M[v, v] = 0 \land (M[u, v] \neq 0 \lor M[v, u] \neq 0)$. Hence neither of the columns, u or v, is a unit column. The exchange preserves all the unit columns, also preserving m. In addition, at least one diagonal element, $M[u, u]$ or $M[v, v]$, is set to nonzero. Since both of these elements were previously zero, n increases. Therefore every state change in program *Gauss* increases (m, n) lexicographically. Since each of m, n is bounded from above by N, *Gauss* reaches a fixed point.

Now we show that A is an identity matrix at any fixed point. The proof is as follows. We prove in Lemma 6.1 that if any diagonal element $M[u, u]$ is nonzero at a fixed point, u is a unit column. In Lemma 6.2 we prove that if some diagonal element is zero at a fixed point, all elements in that row are zero. This contradicts our assumption that the determinant of A is nonzero. (Note that execution of any statement in *Gauss* preserves the determinant.) Therefore every diagonal element is nonzero and, using Lemma 6.1, A is an identity matrix. Now we prove Lemmas 6.1 and 6.2.

Lemma 6.1   At any fixed point of program *Gauss*,

$M[u, u] \neq 0 \implies u$ is a unit column.

Proof: Consider the statement for a pivot corresponding to row u. At any fixed point, given that $M[u, u] \neq 0$, we conclude that for any j, and $v \neq u$,

$$M[v, j] = M[v, j] - M[v, u] \times M[u, j]/M[u, u]$$

and

$$M[u, j] = M[u, j]/M[u, u].$$

In particular, with $j = u$,

$$M[v, u] = M[v, u] - M[v, u] \times M[u, u]/M[u, u] = 0$$

and

$$M[u, u] = M[u, u]/M[u, u] = 1.$$

Therefore u is a unit column. $\triangledown$

Lemma 6.2   At any fixed point of program *Gauss*,

$$M[u, u] = 0 \quad \Rightarrow \quad M[u, v] = 0$$

Proof: The result is trivial for $u = v$. Hence assume that $u \neq v$. Consider two cases: $M[v, v] = 0$ and $M[v, v] \neq 0$.

1. $M[v, v] = 0$.   Consider the exchange statement for rows u, v. At a fixed point, given that $M[u, u] = 0 \ \wedge \ M[v, v] = 0$, we have

$$(M[u, v] = 0 \ \wedge \ M[v, u] = 0) \ \vee \ \langle \wedge \ j \ :: \ M[u, j] = M[v, j] \rangle.$$

   Consider the particular case, $j = v$. Then,

$$(M[u, v] = 0 \ \wedge \ M[v, u] = 0) \ \vee \ (M[u, v] = M[v, v]).$$

   Using the fact that $M[v, v] = 0$, we conclude that

$$M[u, v] = 0.$$

2. $M[v, v] \neq 0$.   From Lemma 6.1, $M[u, v] = 0$. $\triangledown$

6.12.3   Discussion

Program *Gauss* can be implemented in a variety of ways on different architectures. For a sequential machine, it may be more efficient to choose the pivot rows in a particular order. The correctness of this scheme is obvious from our proof because it is obtained from the given program by restricting the nondeterministic choices in statement executions. For an asynchronous shared-memory or distributed architecture, the given program admits several possible implementations; the simplest one is to assign a process to a row. To facilitate the exchange operation, we allow the row number at a process to change. Two rows can then be exchanged simply by exchanging their row numbers; the rendezvous mechanism of CSP is particularly appropriate for implementation of this operation on a distributed architecture. A parallel synchronous architecture with $O(N)$ processors can complete each exchange operation in constant time and each pivot in $O(N)$ steps; with $O(N^2)$ processors, a pivot operation takes constant time.

The reader should note that we have ignored the very important issue of numerical stability—a gross omission of which we are guilty throughout this book.

6.13   Fast Fourier Transform

The discrete Fourier transform (or simply transform) of a vector of N complex numbers, $x[0..N-1]$, is a vector of N complex numbers, $u[0..N-1]$, defined as follows: For all i, $0 \le i < N$,

$$u[i] = \langle + j \ : \ 0 \le j < N \ :: \ x[j] \times r^{(i \times j)} \rangle,$$

where r is the Nth principal root of 1; $+, \times$, when applied to complex operands denote their sum and multiplication, respectively; and superscript denotes exponentiation.

Remark:

$r^N = 1$.

For any k, $1 \le k < N \ :: \ r^k \ne 1$. ∇

Henceforth we assume that N is a power of 2. We also adopt the following notational conventions for this example: We use juxtaposition to denote multiplication (in addition to . and $\times$), as in ij, when there can be no confusion.

The obvious algorithm for computing the transform of N elements requires $O(N^2)$ operations. The *fast Fourier transform* (FFT) algorithm reduces the number of operations to $O(N \log N)$. Also, this algorithm is readily implementable on a parallel architecture: $O(N)$ parallel synchronous processors can compute the transform in $O(\log N)$ steps.

6.13.1 Recursive Computation

First we show how to compute the transform of a vector x by "merging" the transforms of two component vectors of x, each having half the elements of x. Merging two transforms of size N each can be performed in $O(N)$ time sequentially or in $O(1)$ time by $O(N)$ parallel processors. Recursive application of merging gives us the fast Fourier transform. Later we describe an efficient iterative implementation of the recursive scheme.

Let $N = 2 \times M$ and let $y[0..M-1]$, $z[0..M-1]$ be a partition of the elements of x; it turns out that the most suitable way to partition for the transform is to place elements of x alternately in y and z. That is, for all i, $0 \le i < M$,

$$y[i] = x[2.i]$$

and

$$z[i] = x[2.i + 1].$$

Let $v[0..M-1]$ and $w[0..M-1]$ be the transforms of y, z, respectively. That is, for all i, $0 \le i < M$,

$$v[i] = \langle + j \; : \; 0 \leq j < M \; :: \; y[j] \times (r^2)^{ij} \rangle$$

and

$$w[i] = \langle + j \; : \; 0 \leq j < M \; :: \; z[j] \times (r^2)^{ij} \rangle.$$

Note that r^2, the Mth principal root of 1, is to be used in the transforms v, w. Now we express u in terms of v, w. For all i, $0 \leq i < N$,

$$\begin{aligned}
u[i] &= \langle + j \; : \; 0 \leq j < N \; :: \; x[j] \times r^{ij} \rangle \\
&= \langle + j \; : \; 0 \leq j < M \; :: \; x[2.j] \times r^{i(2j)} \rangle \; + \\
&\quad \langle + j \; : \; 0 \leq j < M \; :: \; x[2.j + 1] \times r^{i(2j+1)} \rangle.
\end{aligned}$$

For all i, $0 \leq i < M$,

$$\begin{aligned}
u[i] &= \langle + j \; : \; 0 \leq j < M \; :: \; y[j] \times (r^2)^{ij} \rangle \; + \\
&\quad \langle + j \; : \; 0 \leq j < M \; :: \; z[j] \times r^i \times (r^2)^{ij} \rangle \\
&= v[i] + r^i \times w[i]
\end{aligned} \tag{12}$$

Similarly, for all i, $0 \leq i < M$ (using the fact that $r^M = -1$),

$$u[M + i] = v[i] - r^i \times w[i]. \tag{13}$$

Equations (12) and (13) give us a recursive method for computing the transform of $2 \times M$ elements from two transforms of M elements, each using only M multiplications and $2 \times M$ additions. Each recursive application can be done in $O(1)$ time by $O(N)$ parallel synchronous processors or in $O(N)$ time on a sequential machine. Therefore the complete transform can be computed in $O(\log N)$ time by $O(N)$ parallel synchronous processors, or in $O(N \log N)$ time on a sequential machine.

6.13.2 Iterative Implementation

We observe another property of equations (12) and (13) that lets us compute the transform iteratively, from the bottom up, rather than recursively, from the top down. The elements $v[i]$, $w[i]$ are used only to compute $u[i]$, $u[M + i]$; conversely, $u[i]$, $u[M + i]$ can be computed from $v[i]$, $w[i]$. In Fig. 6.3 we depict this dependency relationship among the variables in computing the transform $u[0..3]$ of $x[0..3]$.

The advantage of iterative computation is that the storage locations that hold the original data points, x, can also be used to compute the transform. In the iterative scheme, elements of this diagram are computed level by level, from the top level to the bottom level. There are $n + 1$ levels in the diagram, where $N = 2^n$. Number the levels consecutively from 0 to n, starting at 0 for the top level; number the elements in a level from left to right starting at 0. At level 0, the elements are obtained by a simple permutation of x;

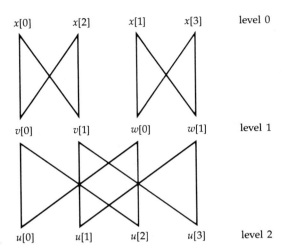

Figure 6.3 Data dependency in computing the Fourier transform of $x[0..3]$ in $u[0..3]$. An element can be computed from the values of elements above it to which it is connected.

the ith element of level 0 is $x[\bar{i}]$, where $\bar{i}$ is the number obtained by reversing the binary representation of i (see Fig. 6.3). At the nth level the sequence of elements is the desired Fourier transform. The elements of level $\ell + 1$ can be computed from the elements of level ℓ, $0 \le \ell < n$, as follows. Elements i, j of level $\ell + 1$, where i, j differ only in the ℓth bit of their binary expansions—bits in a binary expansion are numbered starting at 0 for the lowest order bit— and the ℓth bit of i is 0 (and hence $j = 2^\ell + 1$), can be computed from their previous values by the following assignment ($x[i], x[j]$ denote the values of the elements numbered i, j, respectively, in a level):

$$x[i], x[j] \;\; := \;\; x[i] + r^i \times x[j], x[i] - r^i \times x[j].$$

In the preceding assignment r is the $(2^{\ell+1})^{th}$ principal root of 1. The program follows.

Program *FFT*

    declare

        r : complex number, ℓ : $0..n$ $\{n$ is given by $N = 2^n\}$

    always $r = (2^{\ell+1})^{th}$ principal root of 1

    initially

        $\ell = 0 \;\; \| \;\; \langle \| \; i \; : \; 0 \le i < N \;\; :: \;\; x[i] = x[\bar{i}] \rangle$

assign

$\langle\| \ i,j \ : \ 0 \leq i < N \ \wedge \ \ell < n \ \wedge \ \ell^{th}$ bit of i is 0 $\wedge \ j = 2^\ell + i \ ::$

$\qquad x[i], x[j] \ := \ x[i] + r^i \times x[j], x[i] - r^i \times x[j]$

$\rangle$

$\qquad \| \ \ell \ := \ \ell + 1 \qquad$ if $\ \ell < n$

end $\{FFT\}$

This program consists of a single statement, and hence it can be implemented on a variety of architectures by using the implementation schemes described in Chapter 4. The number of statements executed to reach fixed point is n, i.e., $O(\log N)$. Each statement execution involves $O(N)$ parallel operations.

Summary

Several kinds of problems were studied in this chapter. Traditionally, their solutions are expressed using a variety of programming constructs: sequential programming constructs for the amortization schedule problem, synchronization constructs for the readers-writers problem, and synchronous parallel programming constructs for the circuit design problems, for instance. We have attempted to demonstrate the central thesis of UNITY in this chapter: a foundation based on assignments (and equations), nondeterminism, and their associated mathematics is adequate for designing and analyzing solutions of problems from diverse areas.

Bibliographic Notes

We give no references for the simpler problems treated in this chapter. A comprehensive treatment of Petri nets can be found in J. L. Peterson [1981]. The decidability of the reachability problem for Petri nets is in Kosaraju [1982] and Mayr [1984]. The readers-writers problem was first described in Courtois, Heymans, and Parnas [1971]. The boolean matrix multiplication scheme is from Arlazarov et al. [1970]. Gaussian elimination appears in every standard book on linear algebra; see, for example, Young and Gregory [1973]. The fast Fourier transform is due to Cooley and Tukey [1965].

CHAPTER 7

Program Structuring

7.1   Introduction

Experience in software engineering suggests that a large program should consist of a number of smaller component programs, where each component is developed and understood by itself. There are many different ways to compose a program from a set of components. In this chapter we consider some particularly simple ways to compose UNITY programs. We show how to deduce properties of a composite program from the properties of its components. We do not address the methodological issues of program design by composition/decomposition in this chapter; this topic is discussed briefly in Chapter 8. Examples of program structuring are given in Chapters 12 through 17.

We consider two different kinds of compositions in this chapter. *Union* of two programs is the same as appending their codes together. This form of composition is appropriate for building asynchronous shared-memory systems, and networks of communicating processes. Union is a commutative, associative operation on programs. Unlike union, *superposition*, the other type of composition treated here, describes modifications of a given program. The program is modified by adding new variables and assignments, but not altering the assignments to the original variables. Thus superposition preserves all the properties of the original program. Superposition is useful in building programs in layers; variables of one layer are defined only in terms of the variables of that layer and lower ones.

We have already seen a simple kind of composition: an always-section specifies a set of new variables, called transparent variables, and specifies the values to be assigned to these variables. A program that has an always-section can be transformed into an equivalent program in which there is no always-section; statements of the former program are augmented with assignments to the transparent variables to obtain an equivalent program. The reason for introducing an always-section is that it often simplifies writing and reasoning about programs. This is the only goal of program composition.

7.2   Program Composition by Union

The union of programs F,G is written as $F \parallel G$, where F,G are *component* programs and $F \parallel G$ is the *composite* program. Programs F,G can name common variables. The composite program is equivalent to the program obtained by appending the corresponding sections of the two component programs together. (We assume that there are no inconsistencies in definitions of variables, always-sections, or initializations in the two programs F,G. For instance, a variable should not be declared differently in F,G, nor should it be initialized to different values.) We study the effect of appending the assign-sections together. The basis for the study is the union theorem, given next.

Terminology and Convention: We write, Q in G, to denote that Q is a property of program G. We write, FP of G, for the fixed point predicate of program G.

7.2.1 The Union Theorem
Theorem 7.1

1. p *unless* q in $F \parallel G = (p$ *unless* q in $F \wedge p$ *unless* q in $G)$

2. p *ensures* q in $F \parallel G =$

   $[p$ *ensures* q in $F \wedge p$ *unless* q in $G]$ $\vee$
   $[p$ *ensures* q in $G \wedge p$ *unless* q in $F]$

3. $(FP$ of $F \parallel G)= (FP$ of $F) \wedge (FP$ of $G)$

Proof:

1. p *unless* q in $F \parallel G$

   $= \langle \forall s \; : \; s$ in $F \parallel G \; :: \; \{p \wedge \neg q\} \; s \; \{p \vee q\} \rangle$

   $= \langle \forall s \; : \; s$ in $F \; :: \; \{p \wedge \neg q\} \; s \; \{p \vee q\} \rangle \; \wedge$
   $\langle \forall s \; : \; s$ in $G \; :: \; \{p \wedge \neg q\} \; s \; \{p \vee q\} \rangle$

   $= p$ *unless* q in $F \wedge p$ *unless* q in G

2. p *ensures* q in $F \parallel G$

   $= p$ *unless* q in $F \parallel G \wedge \langle \exists s \; : \; s$ in $F \parallel G \; :: \; \{p \wedge \neg q\} \; s \; \{q\} \rangle$

   $= p$ *unless* q in $F \parallel G \wedge$
   $[\langle \exists s \; : \; s$ in $F \; :: \; \{p \wedge \neg q\} \; s \; \{q\} \rangle \; \vee$
   $\langle \exists s \; : \; s$ in $G \; :: \; \{p \wedge \neg q\} \; s \; \{q\} \rangle]$

   $= [p$ *unless* q in $F \parallel G \wedge \langle \exists s \; : \; s$ in $F \; :: \; \{p \wedge \neg q\} \; s \; \{q\} \rangle] \; \vee$
   $[p$ *unless* q in $F \parallel G \wedge \langle \exists s \; : \; s$ in $G \; :: \; \{p \wedge \neg q\} \; s \; \{q\} \rangle]$

$$= [p \ unless \ q \ \text{in} \ F \land p \ unless \ q \ \text{in} \ G \ \land$$
$$\langle \exists \ s \ : \ s \ \text{in} \ F \ :: \ \{p \land \neg q\} \ s \ \{q\}\rangle] \ \lor$$
$$[p \ unless \ q \ \text{in} \ F \land p \ unless \ q \ \text{in} \ G \ \land$$
$$\langle \exists \ s \ : \ s \ \text{in} \ G \ :: \ \{p \land \neg q\} \ s \ \{q\}\rangle]$$

$$= [p \ ensures \ q \ \text{in} \ F \land p \ unless \ q \ \text{in} \ G] \ \lor$$
$$[p \ ensures \ q \ \text{in} \ G \land p \ unless \ q \ \text{in} \ F]$$

3. $(FP \ \text{of} \ F \ [\!] \ G) = (FP \ \text{of} \ F) \land (FP \ \text{of} \ G)$ from the definition of FP.   ▽

This theorem says that in order to establish a property of the form $p \ unless \ q$ in $F \ [\!] \ G$, the property must be established in both F and G. Conversely, if a property of this form is established in both F and G, it holds for $F \ [\!] \ G$ as well. A property of the form $p \ ensures \ q$ can be established in $F \ [\!] \ G$ if and only if $p \ ensures \ q$ holds in at least one component and $p \ unless \ q$ holds in the other component. Finally, FP of any program is merely a conjunction of its component FPs.

Corollaries

1. p is stable in $F \ [\!] \ G = (p$ is stable in $F \ \land \ p$ is stable in $G)$

2. $$\frac{p \ unless \ q \ \text{in} \ F \ , \ p \ \text{is stable in} \ G}{p \ unless \ q \ \text{in} \ F \ [\!] \ G}$$

3. $$\frac{p \ \text{is invariant in} \ F \ , \ p \ \text{is stable in} \ G}{p \ \text{is invariant in} \ F \ [\!] \ G}$$

4. $$\frac{p \ ensures \ q \ \text{in} \ F \ , \ p \ \text{is stable in} \ G}{p \ ensures \ q \ \text{in} \ F \ [\!] \ G}$$ ▽

We derive an important corollary of the union theorem by considering the variables that programs F,G read and write. A *local predicate* of F mentions only variables that can be modified by program F alone. Clearly, a local predicate p of F cannot be falsified by any statement outside F—i.e., p is stable in G, for any G, $G \neq F$. (Syntactic mechanisms can be introduced into the programming notation to denote that a variable is *private* to one program, i.e., it cannot be modified by any other program. In this book we do not address many language-related issues, including such syntactic mechanisms.)

The next corollary follows from the union theorem.

Corollary (Locality)

If any of the following properties holds in F, where p is a local predicate of F, then it also holds in $F \parallel G$, for any G: p *unless* q, p *ensures* q, p is invariant.

$\triangledown$

Exercise 7.1   Show that, for any G and any predicate p,

$$\frac{p \;\; ensures \;\; \neg p \;\; \text{in} \;\; F}{p \;\; ensures \;\; \neg p \;\; \text{in} \;\; F \parallel G}$$

$\triangledown$

Exercise 7.2   Show counterexamples to the following claims.

1.
$$\frac{p \;\mapsto\; q \;\text{in}\; F \;,\; p \;\text{is stable in}\; G}{p \;\mapsto\; q \;\text{in}\; F \parallel G}$$

2.
$$\frac{p \;\mapsto\; q \;\text{in}\; F \;,\; p \;\mapsto\; q \;\text{in}\; G}{p \;\mapsto\; q \;\text{in}\; F \parallel G}$$

$\triangledown$

7.2.2 Specifications that Compose

A limitation of union is that a property of the form $p \;\mapsto\; q$ cannot be asserted in $F \parallel G$ even though the property holds in both F and G. This is a serious limitation since most useful progress properties are of this form. Fortunately, the union theorem tells us how to derive some properties of $F \parallel G$ from properties of F and G; based on this result, we propose a general mechanism for deriving properties of a program from properties of its components.

Conditional Property

Each program property seen so far is expressed using one or more predicates, the relations *unless*, *ensures* or *leads-to*, and *invariant*; these properties are called *unconditional properties*. A *conditional property* has two parts, a *hypothesis* and a *conclusion*, each of which is a set of unconditional properties. In a conditional property of F, both hypothesis and conclusion may be properties of F, G or $F \parallel G$, where G is a generic program. The meaning of such a property is as follows: Given the hypothesis as a premise, the conclusion can be proven from (the text or specification of) F.

Example 7.1

Consider the following program, F, in which x is not modified outside F and y is a variable that can be modified by other programs.

Program F

    declare x : integer

    assign

        $y := -y$ if $x \leq 0 \wedge y > 0$

    $[\!]$ $x := x - 1$

end $\{F\}$

The following unconditional properties can be proven from the text of F:

$y < 0$ is stable in F,
$y = 0$ is stable in F,
$y \neq 0$ is stable in F.

We prove the following conditional property of F in Section 7.2.3:

Hypothesis: $y \neq 0$ is stable in $F [\!] G$
Conclusion: $y > 0 \;\mapsto\; y < 0$ in $F [\!] G$

Here G refers to any program that shares only variable y with F. Observe that, using program F, a strong conclusion about a composite program can be drawn from a weak hypothesis. ∇

The use of conditional properties in program specification allows us to deduce more general properties of a composite program from its components than would be possible from the union theorem alone. In particular, it is possible to deduce general progress properties, of the form $p \;\mapsto\; q$, for a composite program. Next we show how conditional properties are proven for a program and how composite program properties are deduced from component program properties.

A Note on Quantification

Consistent with our convention (see Chapter 3), any free variable appearing in a conditional property is quantified universally, over the hypothesis and conclusion together. For instance,

Hypothesis: $y \geq k$ is stable in G
Conclusion: $y = k \;\mapsto\; y > k$ in $F [\!] G$

is to be understood as

$\langle \forall k \;::$

    Hypothesis: $y \geq k$ is stable in G

Conclusion: $y = k \;\mapsto\; y > k$ in $F \parallel G$

$\rangle$.

Proving with Conditional Properties

We consider the problem of proving a set of properties Q from a set of properties P, where P, Q may include both unconditional and conditional properties. If P, Q include unconditional properties only, then we take each property in P to be a premise; we repeatedly apply the inference rules (given in Chapter 3) and the union theorem to derive all properties in Q. When P or Q includes a conditional property we will use the following rules to convert the problem to a derivation problem with unconditional properties. Each application of a rule reduces the total number of conditional properties in P, Q.

- Treat any conditional property in P as an inference rule.

- Remove any conditional property from Q; add its hypothesis to P and its conclusion to Q.

We sketch some consequences of these rules. To prove that a program text meets its specification, we regard all properties derivable from the text as P and the specification as Q. To prove that one specification is a refinement of another, we regard the latter as Q and the former as P. To prove the specification of a composite program from specifications of its components, regard the latter specification as P and the former as Q. (Note that the free variables in P, Q are universally quantified across both P and Q. Moving the hypothesis of a conditional property from Q to P leaves the scope of quantification unchanged for any free variable named in that hypothesis. Usual renaming precautions should be taken to avoid name clashes among variables.)

Next we give a few simple examples to illustrate the proof strategy; Chapters 12, 13, and 14 contain detailed examples.

7.2.3 Examples of Proofs with Conditional Properties

Proving a Conditional Property from a Program Text

Consider program F of Example 7.1, for which the following conditional property was proposed:

Hypothesis: $y \neq 0$ is stable in $F \parallel G$
Conclusion: $y > 0 \;\mapsto\; y < 0$ in $F \parallel G$

To prove this property we have to establish the conclusion from the program text and the hypothesis. We give the proof in extreme detail, justifying each proof step with appeal to some inference rule. We will prove that:

$$true \;\mapsto\; x \le 0 \qquad\qquad \text{in } F [\![G \qquad\qquad (1)$$

$$x \le 0 \;\wedge\; y \ne 0 \;\mapsto\; y < 0 \quad \text{in } F [\![G \qquad\qquad (2)$$

From (1), and the fact that $y \ne 0$ is stable in $F [\![G$ (from the hypothesis), we deduce, using the PSP theorem:

$$y \ne 0 \;\mapsto\; (x \le 0 \;\wedge\; y \ne 0) \text{ in } F [\![G$$

$y \ne 0 \;\mapsto\; y < 0 \qquad\qquad$ in $F [\![G$, applying transitivity on
the above and (2)

$y > 0 \;\mapsto\; y < 0 \qquad\qquad$ in $F [\![G$, from the above and
$y > 0 \;\Rightarrow\; y \ne 0$

Proof: (1) $true \;\mapsto\; x \le 0$ in $F [\![G$

$x = k \;\; ensures \;\; x < k \qquad$ in $F \qquad\qquad$, from the text of F

$x = k \;\; ensures \;\; x < k \qquad$ in $F [\![G \qquad$, from the locality corollary

$true \;\mapsto\; x \le 0 \qquad\qquad$ in $F [\![G \qquad$, using induction on the above

Proof: (2) $x \le 0 \;\wedge\; y \ne 0 \;\mapsto\; y < 0$ in $F [\![G$

$x \le 0 \;\wedge\; y \ne 0$ is stable $\qquad$ in $F [\![G \qquad$, proven below $\qquad\qquad$ (3)

$x \le 0 \;\wedge\; y \ne 0 \;\; ensures \;\; y < 0 \quad$ in $F \qquad$, from the text of F

$x \le 0 \;\wedge\; y \ne 0 \;\; ensures \;\; y < 0 \quad$ in $F [\![G \quad$, union theorem on the
above two

$x \le 0 \;\wedge\; y \ne 0 \;\mapsto\; y < 0 \qquad$ in $F [\![G \quad$, from the above

Proof: (3) $x \le 0 \;\wedge\; y \ne 0$ is stable in $F [\![G$

$x \le 0$ is stable $\qquad\qquad$ in $F \qquad$, from the text of F

$x \le 0$ is stable $\qquad\qquad$ in $F [\![G \quad$, from the locality corollary

$y \ne 0$ is stable $\qquad\qquad$ in $F [\![G \quad$, from the hypothesis

$x \le 0 \;\wedge\; y \ne 0$ is stable in $F [\![G \quad$, conjunction on the above two

Deducing a Conditional Property from Other Properties

It is required to prove the following conditional property for program F of Example 7.1:

Hypothesis: $\;\; y > 0 \;\;$ is stable in G,
$\qquad\qquad\;\; y < 0 \;\;$ is stable in G
Conclusion: $\;\; y > 0 \;\mapsto\; y < 0$ in $F [\![G$,
$\qquad\qquad\;\; y < 0 \;\;$ is stable in $F [\![G$

We can prove this property directly from the text of F, employing a proof similar to that in the last example. Instead we use the properties proven in the last example and derive this property.

We have as premise the following unconditional properties of F, stated earlier:

$y < 0$ is stable in F $\hspace{8cm}$ (4)

$y = 0$ is stable in F $\hspace{8cm}$ (5)

$y \neq 0$ is stable in F $\hspace{8cm}$ (6)

We also have as premise the hypothesis of the conditional property to be proven:

$y > 0$ is stable in G $\hspace{8cm}$ (7)

$y < 0$ is stable in G $\hspace{8cm}$ (8)

We have the conditional property proven earlier for F, as an inference rule:

$$\frac{y \neq 0 \text{ is stable in } F \parallel G}{y > 0 \mapsto y < 0 \text{ in } F \parallel G} \hspace{3cm} (9)$$

The goal is to prove the conclusions (10, 11) of the given conditional property from (4–9):

$y > 0 \mapsto y < 0$ in $F \parallel G$ $\hspace{6cm}$ (10)

$y < 0$ is stable in $F \parallel G$ $\hspace{6cm}$ (11)

Proof: (10) $y > 0 \mapsto y < 0$ in $F \parallel G$

$\quad y \neq 0$ is stable in G $\hspace{2.5cm}$, from (7,8) using disjunction

$\quad y \neq 0$ is stable in $F \parallel G$ $\hspace{2cm}$, union theorem on the above and (6)

$\quad y > 0 \mapsto y < 0$ in $F \parallel G$ $\hspace{1.5cm}$, from the above and (9) $\triangledown$

Proof: (11) $y < 0$ is stable in $F \parallel G$

$\quad y < 0$ is stable in $F \parallel G$, union theorem on (4,8) $\triangledown$

Deducing Properties of a Composite Program from Its Components

Consider the specification of program F from Example 7.1. Let H be a program with the following specification:

Unconditional properties of H:

$\quad y = 0 \quad$ is stable in H,

$\quad y \neq 0 \quad$ is stable in H

Conditional property of H: For any G,

Hypothesis: $y > 0 \;\mapsto\; y < 0$ in $G \parallel H$
Conclusion: $y = k \;\mapsto\; y > k$ in $G \parallel H$

We derive some properties of $F \parallel H$:

$y = 0$ is stable	in $F \parallel H$	, from the unconditionals of F and H
$y \neq 0$ is stable	in $F \parallel H$	, from the unconditionals of F and H
$y > 0 \;\mapsto\; y < 0$	in $F \parallel H$	, from the above and the property (9) of F
$y = k \;\mapsto\; y > k$	in $F \parallel H$	, from the above and the conditional of H
$true \;\mapsto\; y > n$	in $F \parallel H$	, applying induction on the above

Exercise 7.3 (see Exercise 5.4) Consider program $P1$ of Chapter 5. Construct program G by adding the following statements to $P1$:

$$\langle \parallel i, j \;::\; d[i, j] \;:=\; \min(d[i, j], W[i, j]) \rangle.$$

Let F be any program that shares only matrix W with G. Prove the following conditional property of G:

Hypothesis: $W[i, j] \leq k$ is stable in F
Conclusion: $d[i, j] \geq D[i, j]$ is invariant in $G \parallel F$,
              $(D[i, j] \leq \ell) \;\mapsto\; (d[i, j] \leq \ell)$ in $G \parallel F$

Hint: In order to prove the progress property in the conclusion, apply induction on the number of edges on paths from i to j.   ▽

7.2.4 On the Substitution Axiom

In Chapter 3 we postulated that an invariant can be viewed as a theorem— that is, $I \equiv true$, where I is any invariant of the program. Some care must be exercised when applying this rule in proofs of programs that are composed with other programs. *An invariant can be viewed as a theorem only if it is an invariant of the composite program.* This general rule reduces to the rule given in Chapter 3 if we are dealing with a program having only one component.

To see the implication of the general rule, consider the following situation in program $F \parallel G$. Let predicate p name variables shared between F, G and let predicate q be local to F. Suppose that p is invariant in F and $p \Rightarrow q$. Then it may be claimed that since q is invariant in F and stable in G (from the locality of q), q is invariant in $F \parallel G$. This argument is invalid: The invariance of q depends on the invariance of p in $F \parallel G$, not in F alone. If p is falsified in G, for instance, p is not invariant, and q may not be invariant in $F \parallel G$. In this case, we can claim only the following conditional property of F: Under the hypothesis that p is stable in G, the conclusion is that q is invariant in $F \parallel G$.

7.2.5 Hierarchical Program Structures

A UNITY program can be the union of several component programs, some of which are themselves unions of other programs. Programs with hierarchical structures of arbitrary depth can be constructed by employing the union operator.

Conventionally, hierarchical program structures are used for two purposes: (1) as a form of abstraction—a program is described by its externally observable properties, and its implementation is hidden, and (2) as a means of disciplining the control flow—the locus of control is determined by the hierarchical structure. Since there is no notion of control flow in UNITY, the only reason for hierarchical program construction in UNITY is the power achieved by abstraction, and the consequent simplicity of program design.

In UNITY the set of statements of a hierarchically structured program consists of all statements of all component programs, irrespective of their depth in the hierarchy. All statements are treated alike in an execution: Each statement is executed infinitely often. The goal of modularity is hiding variables, making it possible to apply the locality corollary of the union theorem.

7.2.6 Discussion

The union theorem is fundamental for understanding the operation of union. Using this theorem, we showed that some simple kinds of properties are preserved under union. However, progress properties of the form $p \mapsto q$ for arbitrary p, q are not preserved under union. We therefore introduced the notion of conditional property.

The hypothesis in a conditional property for program F can be regarded as the specification of a system in which F can be embedded. The conclusion describes the effect of embedding F in the system. Different conditional properties for program F describe different kinds of systems in which F is expected to be embedded, and the results of doing such embeddings.

7.3   Superposition

A program development strategy is to structure a program as a set of "layers." Each layer implements a set of concerns; a layer can draw on the services provided by its lower layers. For instance, an application program can be viewed as a higher layer that calls on the operating system routines. However, an operating system—the lower layer—never calls on an application program. Similarly, the operating system itself can be structured as a set of layers: The lower layers implement functions closer to the hardware—clock and device management functions, for instance—while the upper layers provide services closer to the application programs—communication services and database facilities, for instance.

The structuring mechanism of union, described in Section 7.2, is symmetric in the program components; $F \parallel G$ is the same as $G \parallel F$. Layering, on the other hand, is asymmetric; a higher layer is allowed to access the variables of lower layers, while a lower layer cannot access the variables of higher layers. Therefore we introduce a new structuring mechanism, *superposition*, to help us with layered program development.

We view the task of layering as follows. We are given a program, called the *underlying program*, variables of which are *underlying variables*. It is required to transform the underlying program such that all its properties are preserved; furthermore, the *transformed program* is required to have some additional specified properties. The transformation proceeds by introducing new variables, called *superposed variables*, and then transforming the underlying program such that the assignments to underlying variables remain unaffected, though assignments to superposed variables may use the values of underlying variables. This process of transformation is called *superposition*. We will show that superposition preserves all the properties of the underlying program.

7.3.1 Rules of Superposition

A superposition is described by giving the initial values of superposed variables, and the transformations on the underlying program, by applying the following two rules.

1. Augmentation rule.   A statement s in the underlying program may be transformed into a statement $s \parallel r$, where r does not assign to the underlying variables.

2. Restricted Union rule.   A statement r may be added to the underlying program provided that r does not assign to the underlying variables.

The description of a superposition will be given in the following format.

Program name

    initially   initializations of superposed variables

    transform

        for each statement s in the underlying program a description
        of the transformation of s to a statement $s \parallel r$ in the transformed
        program (where r does not assign to the underlying variables).

add

> statements (which do not assign to the underlying variables)
> to be added to the underlying program.

end {name}

7.3.2 The Superposition Theorem

The next theorem shows that every property of the underlying program—unconditional and conditional—is inherited by the transformed program. This result is not too surprising since the underlying variables are not modified, yet it is nontrivial to see that all progress properties are preserved. Note that fixed point predicates are not necessarily preserved under superposition.

Theorem 7.2 Every property of the underlying program is a property of the transformed program.

Proof: We show that both rules of superposition—augmentation and restricted union—preserve properties of the underlying program.

1. Augmentation. If $\{p\}\ s\ \{q\}$ holds for some statement s of the underlying program, then $\{p\}\ s\ \|\ r\ \{q\}$ also holds, where s is augmented with r. This is because p, q name no variables that are assigned in r. Furthermore, the initial condition of the underlying program is unaffected by superposition. Since any proof is a collection of such assertions plus the initial conditions, the proofs are preserved under augmentation.

2. Restricted Union. Added statements do not write into underlying variables. From the locality corollary of the union theorem and the fact that the underlying program does not mention any superposed variable in its proof, every property of the underlying program is also a property of the transformed program that is obtained through restricted union. $\triangledown$

7.3.3 An Example of Superposition

In Chapter 3 we introduced the following relation, *detects*, for a given program:

$$p\ detects\ q\ \equiv\ (p\ \Rightarrow\ q)\ \wedge\ (q\ \mapsto\ p).$$

Thus p *detects* q means that p holds within a finite time of q holding, and if p holds, then so does q.

The detection problem is as follows. We are given an underlying program and a predicate q on its variables. It is required to transform this program, applying superposition, such that p *detects* q is a property of the transformed program, where p names only superposed variables.

An interesting example of q is as follows: "The underlying computation has reached a fixed point." General versions of the detection problem are treated in Chapters 9 and 11. Here we consider detection of a property W, defined as follows:

W $\equiv$ the number of statement executions in the underlying program exceeds 10.

We prove in the transformed program that *claim detects* W, where *claim* is a superposed boolean variable. We employ another superposed variable, *count*, where *count* is the number of statements executed in the underlying program. A solution for this detection problem, using only the augmentation rule, follows:

Program {using only augmentation} *Detection0*

   initially   *count, claim* $= 0$, *false*

   transform

      each statement s in the underlying program to
      $s \parallel count, claim := count + 1, count \geq 10$

end {*Detection0*}

This program has the following properties, proofs of which are straight-forward.

invariant   *count* = number of statements executed in the underlying program

invariant   *claim* $\equiv$ (*count* > 10)

Hence *claim detects W*.

Now we give a program for the same problem to illustrate both augmentation and restricted union.

Program {using augmentation and restricted union} *Detection1*

   initially   *count, claim* $= 0$, *false*

   transform

      each statement s in the underlying program to
      $s \parallel count := count + 1$

   add   *claim* $:= count > 10$

end {*Detection1*}

This program can be proven in a similar manner.

Exercise 7.4   Transform program *P4* of Section 5.4, using superposition, to additionally compute the number of edges on a path from i to j whose length is $d[i, j]$, for all i, j. $\bigtriangledown$

7.3.4 Discussion

Both union and superposition are methods for structuring programs. The union operation applies to two programs to yield a composite program. Unlike union, a transformed program resulting from superposition cannot be described in terms of two component programs, one of which is the underlying program. The absence of such a decomposition limits the algebraic treatment of superposition. Furthermore, a description of augmentation seems to require an intimate knowledge of the statements in the underlying program. Appropriate syntactic mechanisms should be developed to solve some of these problems.

In many cases of superposition, only the restricted union rule is applied. Program development in layers often has this flavor. This form of superposition is particularly attractive because it is both a union and a superposition. Hence the transformed program can be treated as a composite of two components, one being the underlying program. Also, all properties of the underlying program are preserved and the additional properties resulting from restricted union can be deduced by using the methods of Section 7.2.

7.4   A Format for Design Specification

It is often required to transform a given program F to a program H through successive applications of union and superposition, such that H has certain desirable properties. (In this book, we limit ourselves to these two types of program transformations.) Observe that any number of superpositions and unions can be described by a single application each of superposition and union, in either order—i.e., H is $F' \parallel G$, where F' is obtained from F through superposition.

The task of designing H from F can be specified by giving the specifications of F and H. For the specifications in this book, we find it convenient to adopt a particular format, consisting of three parts, and certain conventions.

1. Specification of F.   The program name, F, is dropped from all unconditional properties in the specification. The hypothesis and the conclusion in a conditional property are always properties of the composite program, H; hence the name H is also dropped in writing a conditional property in

the specification. Names of shared variables and the way they are modified outside F is a legitimate part of any hypothesis in a conditional property of F. However, we find it more convenient to specify these separately, in (3).

2. Specification of H.   In all cases in this book, the specification of H consists of a set of unconditional properties. The program name, H, is dropped from these properties.

3. Constraints.   This part specifies the variables of F that can be accessed outside F and the way they can be modified. For instance, we may specify that a boolean variable b of F can be modified in G, but that b cannot be set *true* in G. We state this formally as $\neg b$ is stable in G.

We next illustrate the specification scheme using the mutual exclusion problem as an example. This problem is treated in detail in Chapter 15; a generalization of it—the dining philosophers problem—appears in Chapter 12.

7.4.1 An Example of Specification

We are given a program, *user*, in which there is a variable $u.dine$ for each u in a given set. Variable $u.dine$ can take one of three possible values: t, h, or e. Informally, u denotes a philosopher and $u.dine = t$, $u.dine = h$, $u.dine = e$ denote that philosopher u is thinking, hungry, eating, respectively. We will use the abbreviations $u.t, u.h, u.e$ to denote the predicates $u.dine = t$, $u.dine = h$, $u.dine = e$, respectively. (In traditional terms, u is a process, $u.t$ denotes that u is executing code outside its critical section, $u.h$ denotes that u is waiting to execute code in its critical section, and $u.e$ denotes that u is executing code in its critical section.) It is given that every process completes eating in finite time. It is required to construct a composite program, *mutex*, applying superposition and union to program *user*, such that the following properties hold in *mutex*: At most one philosopher eats at a time, and every hungry philosopher eats eventually.

Now we specify the problem formally. In the following, *mutex* is *user'* ∥ G, where *user'* is obtained from *user* through superposition. The problem specification is given in the format described earlier: Specification of program *user* (i.e., what we may assume), specification of the composite program *mutex* (i.e., what we are required to establish), and the constraints (i.e., variables of program *user* that we are allowed to read in *user'* and the way we may write into them in G). In the following, u, v are universally quantified over all philosophers.

Specification of Program *user*

$u.t$ *unless* $u.h$

stable $u.h$

$u.e$ *unless* $u.t$

Conditional Property

Hypothesis: $\langle \forall\, u, v\ :\ u \neq v\ ::\ \neg(u.e \,\wedge\, v.e)\rangle$
Conclusion: $\langle \forall\, u\ ::\ u.e\ \longmapsto\ u.t\rangle$

Specification of Program *mutex*

invariant $\neg(u.e \,\wedge\, v.e \,\wedge\, u \neq v)$

$u.h\ \longmapsto\ u.e$

Constraints

The only variables of *user* that may be named outside *user* (i.e., in the assignment-components which have been added to *user* by the augmentation rule, or in G) are $u.dine$. Also, $u.t$ is constant (i.e., $u.t, \neg u.t$ are both stable), and $u.e$ is stable in G, for every u.

7.4.2 Deriving Properties from Specification of Mutual Exclusion

We derive some properties of programs *user* and *mutex* from the given specifications.

1. $\neg u.e$ is stable in *user*

Proof:

$u.t$ *unless* $u.h$ in *user*	, from the specification of *user*
$u.h$ is stable in *user*	, from the specification of *user*
$u.t \,\vee\, u.h$ *unless* *false* in *user*	, applying cancellation to the above two
$(u.t \,\vee\, u.h)\ \equiv\ \neg u.e$	, $u.dine$ has three possible values
$\neg u.e$ is stable in *user*	, from the above two $\triangledown$

2. $u.t$ *unless* $u.h$ in *mutex*

Proof:

$u.t$ *unless* $u.h$ in *user*	, from the specification of *user*
$u.t$ *unless* $u.h$ in *user′*	, applying the superposition theorem
$u.t$ is stable in G	, from the constraints
$u.t$ *unless* $u.h$ in *mutex*	, union theorem on the above two $\triangledown$

3. *u.h* *unless* *u.e* in *mutex*

Proof:

$u.h$ is stable in *user*	, from the specification of *user*
$u.h$ is stable in *user'*	, applying the superposition theorem (12)
$\neg u.t$ is stable in G	, from constraints
$\neg u.t \equiv (u.h \lor u.e)$	, $u.dine$ has three possible values
$u.h \lor u.e$ is stable in G	, from the above two
$u.h$ *unless* $\neg u.h$ in G	, from the antireflexivity of *unless*
$u.h$ *unless* $u.e$ in G	, conjunction on the above two
$u.h$ *unless* $u.e$ in *mutex*	, union theorem on the above and (12) $\triangledown$

4. *u.e* *unless* *u.t* in *mutex*

Proof:

$u.e$ *unless* $u.t$ in *user*	, from the specification of *user*
$u.e$ *unless* $u.t$ in *user'*	, applying the superposition theorem
$u.e$ is stable in G	, from the constraints
$u.e$ *unless* $u.t$ in *mutex*	, union theorem on the above two $\triangledown$

Summary

We have introduced union and superposition as program structuring schemes in this chapter. We studied how program properties are preserved (in the case of superposition) or modified (in the case of union) under these structuring schemes. Clearly, a variety of structuring schemes can be proposed for UNITY programs. The two structuring schemes described in this chapter have proven adequate for the problems treated in this book.

Bibliographic Notes

A pioneering paper on program structuring is Dijkstra [1972]. One of the first comprehensive theories of program structuring is found in Hoare [1984]. A technique for proving concurrent programs is presented in Owicki and Gries [1976]. Proof techniques for programs structured as networks of processes are discussed in Misra and Chandy [1981], Hoare [1984], Lamport and Schneider [1984], and Jonsson [1987]. Methods for specifying and proving modular programs are described in Lamport [1983b], Barringer, Kuiper, and Pnueli [1984], Gannon, Hamlet, and Mills [1987], and Lynch and Tuttle [1987]. Bouge and Francez [1987] and Katz [1987] propose other views of superposition. The idea of conditional properties, proposed in this chapter, is motivated by the concept of closed and open specifications described in Pnueli [1987].

CHAPTER 8

Communicating Processes

8.1   Introduction

Processing a stream of input data items to produce a stream of output data items is an important programming paradigm. Traditionally a *process* is employed for this purpose. A process can receive messages along channels connected to its input ports, carry out computations locally, and send messages along channels connected to its output ports. Many programs can be structured as networks of message-communicating processes. One advantage of the process-network view of a program is that such a program can be implemented efficiently on an asynchronous message-passing network of computers. Perhaps a more important advantage is that the interface between a pair of processes is the message sequence they communicate. This interface is quite narrow—narrower than in asynchronous shared-memory systems, for instance. The narrow interface imposes a discipline of modular program construction that has been found useful, particularly in systems programming.

In developing a program, we can partition the problem specification into a set of concerns and implement each concern by a module. One way to partition a problem is based on the flow of data, which may lead to structuring the program around message-communicating processes. But there are other kinds of concerns. The algorithms for termination detection (Chapter 9), dining philosophers (Chapter 12), drinking philosophers (Chapter 13), committee coordination (Chapter 14), and garbage collection (Chapter 16), for instance, are developed without considering communication or process boundaries explicitly. Eventually we may implement some of these solutions by networks of message-communicating processes. In developing a solution, however, our only requirement is that interfaces among modules be narrow, limited to the sharing of a few variables or based on a small number of assumptions about the shared variables.

A program structured as a set of modules can be partitioned into processes that do not correspond to the modules, for implementation on a message-communicating system. As an example, consider the schematic diagram in Fig. 8.1, which displays a communication protocol structured as a hierarchy of three modules: bit communication, data transfer, and connection management. Each module implements a concern related to the communication-protocol design, yet none corresponds to a process. In fact, each module is partitioned between the sender and the receiver processes. The overall communication protocol is understood better module by module, not process by process. Partitioning a program into processes should be an issue later on in the implementation.

In this chapter we discuss the structuring of UNITY programs by means of message-communicating processes. UNITY has no special provision for stream processing or for defining message-communicating processes. Stream processing, however, is especially convenient in our notation. Each process

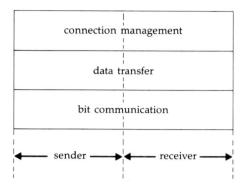

Figure 8.1 A communication protocol structured as a set of modules.

is a program; variables shared among programs are sequences. A process network is a program consisting of a set of processes composed through union. We give a number of examples of such programs in Sections 8.2 and 8.3. In Section 8.4, we show that variables shared among processes need not be sequences; arbitrary shared variables can be implemented by message communications provided that they satisfy certain conditions. This result is particularly important because it lets us reason about a program at a higher level, without explicitly mentioning message communication or channels, and yet leaves open a range of options for efficient implementation of the program on message-passing systems.

8.2 Message-Communicating Processes

In this section we consider two kinds of communication, asynchronous and synchronous.

8.2.1 Asynchronous Point-to-Point Communication

First we describe the rudiments of asynchronous point-to-point message communication (see Chapter 4). Then we show how such communications can be represented in UNITY.

In asynchronous point-to-point communication a process sends a message to another process by depositing the message in a channel, directed from the former to the latter. A message can be deposited in a channel provided there is some empty buffer space in the channel to hold the message. In the *unbounded buffer model*, we assume that each channel has an unbounded amount of buffer space; hence no sender is prevented from sending a message due to lack of buffer space. Of course, any implementation of this scheme requires that the physical constraint on the amount of buffer space in any channel is never violated. In the *bounded buffer model*, explicit bounds on the amount of buffer space for each channel are given; a sender may have to wait to send if the buffer is full. In both cases, a receiver can receive a message only if the channel has a message; a message is removed from the channel after it is received. Also in both cases, channels are assumed to be error free and first-in-first-out (FIFO).

In UNITY a channel is represented by a sequence. In the bounded buffer model, a message can be appended to the sequence, provided the sequence length is smaller than the amount of buffer space in the corresponding channel.

Notation and Convention: For sequence x, $\bar{x}$ denotes the whole sequence of all items ever appended to x; $|\bar{x}|$ denotes the length of $\bar{x}$. For sequences x, y, $x \sqsubseteq y$ denotes that x is a prefix of y. A sequence that has no items is denoted by *null*. We denote a sequence of items by enclosing it within $\ll$ and $\gg$. A sequence shared between two processes is assumed to be declared and initialized to *null*, outside these processes.

8.2.2 Proving Properties of Processes and Networks

The specification and verification techniques described in Chapter 7 for programs composed through union also applies to processes and process networks. However, because of the syntactic constraints on the ways in which processes interact, in many cases, from the process alone, it is possible to derive properties of *any* network in which that process is embedded. We make two observations about process networks that simplify their specifications and analysis in this manner.

First, if x is a shared variable—a sequence—then $\bar{x}$ never gets shorter. That is, for any constant sequence y,

stable $y \sqsubseteq \bar{x}$

is a property in any network. This property can be assumed, as a hypothesis, in proving conclusions in a process (about any network in which the process is embedded). A generalization of this observation is that any predicate that names $\bar{x}$ only, and remains *true* if $\bar{x}$ is extended, is a stable predicate of the network.

The second observation leads to a simplification of the locality corollary (Section 7.2.1) for process networks. Previously we defined p to be a local predicate of a program if no variable named in p can be modified by any other program. Applied to process networks, p is a local predicate of a process if it names only private variables of the process and sequence variables, $\bar{x}$, corresponding to *outgoing channels*, x, of the process. Then p is stable in

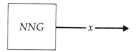

Figure 8.2 Program *NNG* outputs into sequence x.

every other process. (Note, however, that p may not be stable in the entire network because the process to which p is local may falsify it.)

These two observations, based on simple syntactic features of a program, nevertheless play a major role in simplifying specifications of processes and networks.

8.2.3 Examples of Message-Communicating Processes

In the following examples, the properties in the specifications are properties of any network in which this process is a component.

Natural Number Generator (*NNG*)

Program *NNG* outputs the sequence of natural numbers into x. A diagram of *NNG* is shown in Fig. 8.2. The specification of *NNG* (where $\aleph$ is the sequence of all natural numbers) is as follows:

invariant $\overline{x} \sqsubseteq \aleph$

$|\overline{x}| = k \quad \mapsto \quad |\overline{x}| > k$

The text of *NNG* is

Program *NNG*

   declare i : integer

   initially $i = 0$

   assign $x, i \;\; := \;\; (x; i) \;, \;\; i + 1$

end {*NNG*}

Fork

Program *Fork* receives input items from sequence x and outputs each item along either sequence y or sequence z. The schematic diagram of *Fork* appears

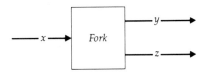

Figure 8.3 Program *Fork* receives inputs from x and outputs to y, z.

in Fig. 8.3. For the specification we employ a predicate, *split*, which has three argument sequences, formally stating that the first argument is a merge of the other two:

$split(null, null, null),$

$split(u, v, w) \Rightarrow [split(u; a,\ v,\ w; a) \wedge split(u; a,\ v; a,\ w)]$

The specification of program *Fork* (where $\bar{x} - x$ is the prefix of $\bar{x}$ excluding x) is:

invariant $split(\bar{x} - x, \bar{y}, \bar{z})$

$(|\bar{y}| + |\bar{z}| = k) \wedge (|\bar{x}| > k) \mapsto |\bar{y}| + |\bar{z}| > k$

The text of program *Fork* is

Program *Fork*

assign

$\quad x, y := \text{tail}(x),\ y; \text{head}(x) \qquad \text{if} \quad x \neq null$

$\| \quad x, z := \text{tail}(x),\ z; \text{head}(x) \qquad \text{if} \quad x \neq null$

end $\{Fork\}$

Exercise 8.1 Show that in program *Fork*, a particular output sequence, say $\bar{y}$, may not increase in length even if input sequence $\bar{x}$ is increased indefinitely. Modify the specification and the text of *Fork* to guarantee that every output sequence increases indefinitely in length if the input sequence increases indefinitely. (Hint: Use conditional properties.) $\triangledown$

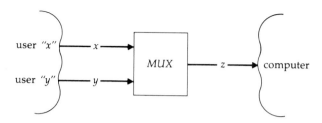

Figure 8.4 A multiplexor connected to two users and a computer.

Fair Merge

A set of users is connected to a computer via a multiplexor. Any character typed by a user is transmitted to the multiplexor over a channel linking the two. The multiplexor transmits a sequence of pairs to the computer, each pair consisting of a character received from a user and the user id. A schematic diagram of a multiplexor, MUX, with two users is shown in Fig. 8.4. The reader should note that MUX implements a fair merge of its input sequences.

   The specification of MUX, where zx, zy are the subsequences of z that consist of only the characters with id "x", "y", respectively, is

invariant $\overline{zx} \sqsubseteq \overline{x} \;\wedge\; \overline{zy} \sqsubseteq \overline{y}$

$|\overline{zx}| = k \;\wedge\; |\overline{x}| > k \;\;\longmapsto\;\; |\overline{zx}| > k$

$|\overline{zy}| = k \;\wedge\; |\overline{y}| > k \;\;\longmapsto\;\; |\overline{zy}| > k$

   The text of MUX is

Program MUX

  assign

      $x, z \;:= \text{tail}(x), \; z; (\text{``}x\text{''}, \text{head}(x))$ if $x \neq null$

    $\|\;\; y, z \;:= \text{tail}(y), \; z; (\text{``}y\text{''}, \text{head}(y))$ if $y \neq null$

end $\{MUX\}$

Exercise 8.2 (unfair merge)   Write the specification and code for a multiplexor that may ignore some user forever. (Unfair selection is discussed in Chapter 22.)

                                                                  $\triangledown$

Hamming's Problem

Problem Description   It is required to compute, in increasing order, the infinite sequence of integers of the form $2^i \times 3^j \times 5^k$, for all i, j, k, where $i \geq 0$, $j \geq 0$, $k \geq 0$. Let H denote this infinite sequence. Since only a finite portion of this infinite sequence can be computed at any time, we postulate computation of an ever-lengthening prefix of H as our goal. Specifically, we plan to compute a sequence G, where

invariant $\overline{G} \sqsubseteq H$

$$|\overline{G}| = k \quad \longmapsto \quad |\overline{G}| > k$$

Program Development   Consider the following equation, where F is an increasing sequence of natural numbers:

$$F = \;\ll 1 \gg;\; \mathrm{merge}(2 \times F, 3 \times F, 5 \times F). \tag{1}$$

Here $i \times F$ denotes the sequence obtained by multiplying each item of F by i, and the result of merge is an increasing sequence consisting of all elements, without duplicates, of the arguments. (The result of merging ascending infinite sequences is the limit of merging their finite prefixes; this limit exists and is unique.)

Exercise 8.3   Show that the unique solution for F in Eq. (1) is H.

Hint: Prove the following from (1), using induction on natural number n:

$$n \in F \;\equiv\; \langle \exists\, i, j, k \,:\, i \geq 0 \,\wedge\, j \geq 0 \,\wedge\, k \geq 0 \,::\, n = 2^i \times 3^j \times 5^k \rangle \quad \triangledown$$

Our problem is to compute the unique solution H of Eq. (1), or, more accurately, to compute ever-lengthening prefixes of H. From (1) we deduce the following invariant:

invariant $\overline{G} \sqsubseteq \mathrm{merge}(\ll 1 \gg;\; 2 \times H,\; \ll 1 \gg;\; 3 \times H,\; \ll 1 \gg;\; 5 \times H)$

Next we ask how $\overline{G}$ can be extended without violating this invariant. Since each argument sequence of merge in the invariant is an increasing sequence, the smallest number in each that does not appear in $\overline{G}$ can be compared, and the smallest of these can be appended to G. To carry out this computation efficiently, we introduce increasing sequences $v.2, v.3, v.5$, where $v.i$ consists of all items in $(\ll 1 \gg;\; i \times \overline{G})$ and not in $\overline{G}$. That is,

$$v.i = (\ll 1 \gg;\; i \times \overline{G}) - \overline{G}.$$

(For increasing sequences x, y, $x - y$ denotes the subsequence of x consisting of all items of x not in y.) We now restate the specification. Observe from the definition of $v.i$ that each $v.i$ is *nonnull* because $|\ll 1 \gg;\; i \times \overline{G}| > |\overline{G}|$.

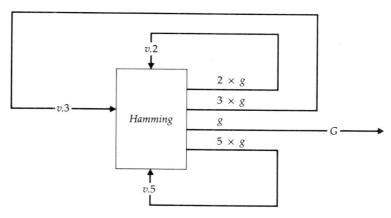

Figure 8.5 Stream processing in program *Hamming*.

invariant $\overline{G} \sqsubseteq H \;\; \wedge \;\; \langle \forall\, i \,:\, i \in \{2,3,5\} \;\; :: \;\; v.i = (\ll 1 \gg;\; i \times \overline{G}) - \overline{G}\,\rangle$
$|\overline{G}| = k \;\; \mapsto \;\; |\overline{G}| > k$

Let g denote $\langle \min\, i \,:\, i \in \{2,3,5\} \;\; :: \;\; head(v.i)\rangle$. Then $\overline{G}$ is extended by appending g to it. To preserve the invariant, each $v.i$ must be modified appropriately. The program follows.

Program *Hamming*

> **declare**
>
> > $G, \; v.2, \; v.3, \; v.5 \;$: sequence of integer,
> > $g \;$: integer
>
> **always** $g = \langle \min\, i \,:\, i \in \{2,3,5\} \;\; :: \;\; head(v.i)\rangle$
>
> **initially** $G = null \;\; \| \;\; \langle \| \, i \,:\, i \in \{2,3,5\} \;\; :: \;\; v.i = \ll 1 \gg\rangle$
>
> **assign**
>
> > $\langle \| \, i \,:\, i \in \{2,3,5\} \;\; ::$
> >
> > > > $v.i := tail(v.i);(i \times g)$ if $g = head(v.i)$ $\sim$
> > > > $\qquad\quad\; v.i \,;(i \times g)$ if $g \neq head(v.i)$
> >
> > $\rangle$
> >
> > $\|\qquad G := G; g$
>
> **end** {*Hamming*}

A schematic diagram of stream processing in program *Hamming* is given in Fig. 8.5.

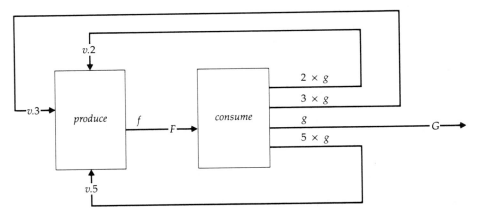

Figure 8.6 Stream processing in another solution to Hamming's problem.

The following exercise suggests a way to refine program *Hamming* into a pair of message-communicating processes.

Exercise 8.4 Split the single statement in program *Hamming* into two statements. One statement, *produce*, is for computing f, the smallest element in any of the sequences $v.2, v.3, v.5$; removing f from each sequence in which it occurs and appending f to F where F is shown in Fig. 8.6. The other statement, *consume*, removes an item, g, from F and appends appropriate elements to $v.2, v.3, v.5$, and G. Pay special attention to the fact that the sequences $v.2, v.3$, and $v.5$ may be *null*. The schematic diagram of stream processing is given in Fig. 8.6. $\triangledown$

Exercise 8.5 Further refine the solution proposed in the previous exercise as follows (see the schematic diagram in Fig. 8.7). Decompose program *produce* into four programs: One program each, for the sequences $v.2, v.3, v.5$, removes their head items and stores them in variables $h.2, h.3, h.5$, respectively, provided the corresponding variable is *empty* (*empty* is a special value of each variable); program *compare* computes $f = \min(h.2, h.3, h.5)$, when $h.2, h.3, h.5$ are all *nonempty*, sets $h.i$ to *empty*, for all i, where $h.i = f$, and appends f to F. Decompose program *consume* into four programs: Program *copy* removes the head item g of F and appends it to four different sequences as shown; the other three programs compute $2 \times g, 3 \times g, 5 \times g$, and append them to sequences $v.2, v.3, v.5$, respectively. $\triangledown$

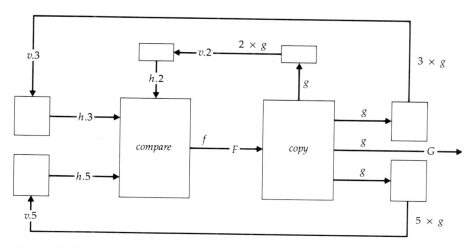

Figure 8.7 Refinement of the solution shown in Fig. 8.6.

Exercise 8.6 In the solution proposed in the preceding exercise, regroup the programs in various ways to create different process networks. Specifically, create processes for each of $v.2, v.3, v.5$ that append to and remove from these sequences. Thus sequences $v.2, v.3, v.5$ are private variables of these processes.

∇

8.2.4 Synchronous Communication

In synchronous communications between processes, as in CSP (see Hoare [1984]), one process is a sender and the others are receivers. A communication takes place only if all processes that can participate in the communication are waiting for the communication; this is termed a *rendezvous*. The effect of the communication is for all receivers to simultaneously receive the message sent. All processes may continue with their computations following a rendezvous.

We model such a communication in UNITY as follows. Let x be a variable of the sender whose value is the message to be sent; $x = empty$ means that the sender has no message to send (and consequently that the sender is not waiting to send). Let there be N receivers and $y[i]$, $0 \leq i < N$, be the variables into which the message value is to be received; $y[i] = empty$ means that the ith receiver is waiting to receive. The following statement captures the effect of synchronous communication.

$$\langle \| \ i \ : \ 0 \leq i < N \quad ::$$
$$\quad y[i] := x \qquad \text{if} \ \langle \wedge \ i \ : \ 0 \leq i < N \quad :: \quad y[i] = empty \rangle \ \wedge \ x \neq empty$$
$$\rangle$$

$$\| \ x \ := empty \quad \text{if} \ \langle \wedge \ i \ : \ 0 \leq i < N \quad :: \quad y[i] = empty \rangle \ \wedge \ x \neq empty$$

We show in Chapter 14 how such a statement can be implemented using asynchronous communications alone.

Now we consider synchronous point-to-point communication (i.e., between a sender and exactly one receiver), an important special case. Let x, y be variables of the sender and the receiver, respectively; $x \neq empty$ means that the sender is waiting to send, and $y = empty$ means that the receiver is waiting to receive. Synchronous communication is accomplished by executing the following statement:

$$x, y \; := \; empty, \; x \quad \text{if} \quad x \neq empty \; \wedge \; y = empty.$$

Synchronous communication can be used to simulate asynchronous communication. Consider, for instance, a program in which a sender and a receiver communicate asynchronously using a channel that has the buffer capacity to hold one message. The channel can be viewed as a process that communicates synchronously with the sender and the receiver. As before, let x, y denote the variables of the sender and the receiver, respectively. Let variable u denote the buffer on the channel; $u = empty$ means that all messages sent along the channel have been received, and $u \neq empty$ means that the value of u is the last message sent and it is yet to be received. Then, using only synchronous communications, we can implement the send and receive operations by the following statements.

$$x, u \; := \; empty, \; x \quad \text{if} \quad x \neq empty \; \wedge \; u = empty \quad \{send\}$$
$$\| \; u, y \; := \; empty, \; u \quad \text{if} \quad u \neq empty \; \wedge \; y = empty \quad \{receive\}$$

Exercise 8.7   Generalize the preceding scheme when the buffer capacity of the channel is arbitrary, though bounded. Also, show a scheme for unbounded buffer capacity. $\triangledown$

8.2.5 Discussion

We have briefly discussed synchronous and asynchronous communications and their representations in UNITY. Synchronous communications can be simulated by asynchronous communications, and asynchronous communications by synchronous communications. Therefore the choice of a communication mechanism for a problem should take into account the simplicity of expressing a solution with the given mechanism and the cost of implementing a mechanism in the given hardware. At higher levels of program design we choose the type of communication that best expresses the solution structure; at lower levels, we can refine the communication mechanism to best exploit the available hardware.

8.3   Process Networks

In Section 8.2 we gave a few examples of process specification and process implementation using UNITY. Networks of processes can be constructed by applying the union operation on the component processes (see Chapter 7). Connections among processes are implicit, via the sequences (or variables) they share.

In this section we first give an example of a process network that is a solution to a problem posed in Conway [1963]. This problem has become the standard benchmark problem on which all structuring mechanisms for process networks have to prove their worthiness; we develop a solution ignoring process boundaries at early stages of design. In the latter part of this section we describe pipelined networks, a simple and useful form of process network.

8.3.1 Conway's Problem

Problem Description

A sequence of cards, each with 80 characters, is to be read from a card reader and printed as a sequence of lines, each line with 125 characters, on a line printer. As many characters as possible should be packed into a line. The end of input is denoted by a special character, *eof*, in a card column. The following constraints apply to printing:

1. An extra *blank* is to be inserted at the end of every card.

2. A pair of consecutive asterisks (**) appearing in a card is to be replaced by a single *uparrow*. (A precise formulation of this requirement is as follows: a run of $2 \times k$ consecutive asterisks in a card are replaced by k uparrows and a run of $2 \times k + 1$ consecutive asterisks in a card are replaced by k uparrows followed by a single asterisk.)

3. The *eof* character is not to be printed.

4. The last output line is padded with extra blanks, if necessary, to fill the line.

A Specification

The desired program is a union of three program components: *Reader* (to read the next card), *Conway* (to produce line images from card images, implementing the preceding constraints), and *Printer* (to print a line image).

We specify program *Conway* only. The following variables are shared between *Conway* and the other programs:

$card[0..80]$, an array of characters {in which the current card image is stored; the dimensions of *card* are explained below},

i , an integer {for $i \leq 80$, i is the number of characters already scanned from the current card image},

$line[0..124]$, an array of characters {where the next line image is stored},

j , an integer {the length of the current line image}

We assume that program *Reader* stores the next card image in $card[0..79]$ and sets i to 0 whenever $i > 80$, and program *Printer* prints the next line image and sets j to 0 whenever $j = 125$.

Let *tca* be an abbreviation for "the next two input characters are asterisks":

$$tca \;\equiv\; i < 79 \;\wedge\; card[i] = asterisk \;\wedge\; card[i+1] = asterisk$$

Program *Conway* implements the following:
{the next input character is stored as the next output character if this character is not *eof* and *tca* is *false*}

$$i = i' \;\wedge\; j = j' \;\wedge\; i < 80 \;\wedge\; j < 125 \;\wedge\; card[i] \neq eof \;\wedge\; \neg tca \;\longmapsto$$
$$i = i' + 1 \;\wedge\; j = j' + 1 \;\wedge\; line[j'] = card[i'] \tag{2}$$

{an *uparrow* is stored as the next output character and two input characters are skipped if *tca* is *true*}

$$i = i' \;\wedge\; j = j' \;\wedge\; j < 125 \;\wedge\; tca \;\longmapsto$$
$$i = i' + 2 \;\wedge\; j = j' + 1 \;\wedge\; line[j'] = uparrow \tag{3}$$

{a *blank* is stored as the next output character if the current card image has been completely scanned}

$$j = j' \;\wedge\; i = 80 \;\wedge\; j < 125 \;\longmapsto\; i = 81 \;\wedge\; j = j' + 1 \;\wedge\; line[j'] = blank \tag{4}$$

{the current line is padded with blanks if $card[i] = eof$}

$$j = j' \;\wedge\; i < 80 \;\wedge\; 0 < j < 125 \;\wedge\; card[i] = eof \;\longmapsto$$
$$j = 125 \;\wedge\; \langle \forall k \,:\, j' \leq k < 125 \;::\; line[k] = blank \rangle \tag{5}$$

Condition (4) is a special case of (2) if we replace "$i < 80$" in (2) by "$i \leq 80$" and if we have

invariant $card[80] = blank$ (6)

Note: We have not explicitly stated the safety properties of *Conway*: The variables $i, j, card, line$ are not modified in any way other than as given in

(2,3,4,5). Also, to simplify matters, we require that input characters received after the *eof* symbol be ignored.   ▽

Note: We take *tca* to be *false* if $i \geq 79$, even though $card[i+1]$ may not be defined.   ▽

A Solution

The following program is derived in a straightforward manner from the specification. We implement invariant (6) by having $card[80] = blank$ in the always-section; the three progress conditions give rise to three different alternatives in assignments to $line[j], i, j$.

Program *Conway1*

>   **declare** i, j : integer , *tca* : boolean
>
>   **always**
>
>> $card[80] = blank$ {a permanent blank}
>>   ∥ $tca = (i < 79 \; \wedge \; card[i] = asterisk \; \wedge \; card[i+1] = asterisk)$
>
>   **initially**
>
>> $i = 81$ {to read the next card}   ∥ $j = 0$ {current line is empty}
>
>   **assign**
>
>> $line[j]$, i , j :=
>> $card[i]$, $i+1$, $j+1$ if $i \leq 80 \; \wedge \; j < 125 \; \wedge \; card[i] \neq eof \; \wedge$
>> $\neg tca$ ∼
>> $uparrow$, $i+2$, $j+1$ if $j < 125 \; \wedge \; tca$ ∼
>> $blank$, i , $j+1$ if $i < 80 \; \wedge \; 0 < j < 125 \; \wedge \; card[i] = eof$
>
> **end** {*Conway1*}

It is easy to see that program *Conway1* meets conditions (2,3,4,6) in the specification. We leave the proof of condition (5) to the reader.

Program *Conway1* displays little parallelism. We can introduce some parallelism by observing that we can decouple assignment to *line* and j from assignment to i: We store into a sequence y the characters to be appended to *line*. We now have two statements, one for producing into y and incrementing i, the other for consuming from y, storing into $line[j]$, and incrementing j. The test, $0 < j$, can be performed only in the second statement. Therefore we also transmit the *eof* character in y. The reader can formalize this argument to construct a proof of program *Conway2*, given next.

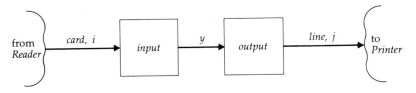

Figure 8.8 Data flow in *Conway2*.

Program *Conway2*

  declare

      i, j : integer , tca : boolean,

      y : sequence of character

  always

      $card[80] = blank$ {a permanent blank}

    ▯ $tca = (i < 79 \ \wedge \ card[i] = asterisk \ \wedge \ card[i+1] = asterisk)$

  initially $i = 81$ ▯ $j = 0$ ▯ $y = null$

  assign

      y , i $:=$

      $y; card[i]$, $i + 1$ if $i \leq 80 \ \wedge \ \neg tca$ $\sim$

      $y; uparrow$, $i + 2$ if tca

  ▯ $line[j]$, j , y $:=$

      $head(y)$, $j + 1$, tail(y) if $j < 125 \ \wedge \ y \neq null \ \wedge$
                                head$(y) \neq eof$ $\sim$

      $blank$, $j + 1$, y if $0 < j < 125 \ \wedge \ y \neq null \ \wedge$
                                 head$(y) = eof$

end {*Conway2*}

It is instructive to think of *Conway2* as consisting of two communicating processes, *input* and *output*. The *input* process executes the first statement, and the *output* process, the second statement. A schematic diagram of data flow between them is given in Fig. 8.8.

The next refinement results from observing that only two consecutive characters, $card[i]$ and $card[i+1]$, are required to determine the next character of y; the value of i itself is not necessary in this computation. Therefore the input characters can be accessed as a sequence rather than through the index i. We introduce two variables: d, a character, and x, a sequence of characters, where the input sequence $d; x$ is yet to be scanned. Again we leave the proof of this program to the reader.

Program *Conway3*

declare

   i, j : integer,

   x, y : sequence of character,

   d : character

always $card[80] = blank$

initially $i = 81$ ‖ $j = 0$ ‖ $x = null$ ‖ $d = empty$ ‖ $y = null$

assign

$$x, \ i \ := \ x; card[i], \ i + 1 \qquad \text{if} \quad i \leq 80$$

‖ $d, \ x \ := \text{head}(x), \text{tail}(x) \qquad \text{if} \quad x \neq null \ \wedge \ d = empty$

‖ $y \qquad , d \qquad , x \qquad :=$

   $y; d \qquad , empty , x \qquad$ if $\ d \neq empty \ \wedge \ (d \neq asterisk \ \vee$
   $\qquad\qquad\qquad\qquad\qquad\qquad (x \neq null \ \wedge \ \text{head}(x) \neq asterisk)) \ \sim$

   $y; uparrow \ , empty \ , \text{tail}(x) \quad$ if $\ d = asterisk \ \wedge \ x \neq null \ \wedge$
   $\qquad\qquad\qquad\qquad\qquad\qquad \text{head}(x) = asterisk$

‖ $line[j] \qquad , j \qquad , y \qquad :=$

   $\text{head}(y) \quad , j + 1 , \text{tail}(y) \quad$ if $\ j < 125 \ \wedge \ y \neq null \ \wedge$
   $\qquad\qquad\qquad\qquad\qquad\qquad \text{head}(y) \neq eof \ \sim$

   $blank \qquad , j + 1 , y \qquad$ if $\ 0 < j < 125 \ \wedge \ y \neq null \ \wedge$
   $\qquad\qquad\qquad\qquad\qquad\qquad \text{head}(y) = eof$

end {*Conway3*}

The statements in *Conway3* can be divided into three groups, each executing asynchronously: The first group, which we name *squasher*, consists of the first statement; the second group, *disassembler*, consists of the next two statements; the third group, *assembler*, consists of the last statement. This process network is similar to that appearing in the literature. We show the schematic of data flow in Fig. 8.9.

Remarks on the Solutions to Conway's Problem

Program *Conway1* is simple and can be implemented efficiently on a sequential computer. We refined this solution to a process network in *Conway2* and *Conway3*, which are better suited for distributed architectures. This example

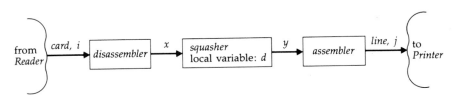

Figure 8.9 Data flow in *Conway3*.

illustrates that a process network need not be designed starting with processes; processes and channels can be introduced in later stages.

8.3.2 Pipelined Networks

A *pipelined network* is a special kind of process network. It consists of processes arranged in a linear fashion; data input at one end of the network is processed by the first process, which may then produce input for the next process in sequence, and so on. Programs *Conway2* and *Conway3* are examples of pipelined networks. It is possible to develop simple theories for such networks because of their simple structure. More general kinds of acyclic networks are studied in Chapter 21, which deals with systolic arrays.

We consider a simple problem. Let $D = \ll d_0, d_1, \ldots, d_M \gg$ be a sequence of data items and $F = \ll f_0, f_1, \ldots, f_N \gg$ be a sequence of functions. Let $f^i(x)$ denote $f_i(f_{i-1}(\ldots f_0(x)\ldots))$; we assume that $f^i(x)$ is defined for all i, $0 \le i \le N$ and all x in D. It is required to compute the sequence $f^N(D)$ where $f^N(D) = \ll f^N(d_0), \ldots, f^N(d_M) \gg$.

The straightforward sequential scheme is to compute $f^N(d_k)$ in increasing order of k. This problem admits of many parallel solutions. Observe that the computation of $f^{i+1}(d_j)$ can be initiated any time after the computation of $f^i(d_j)$ is completed. This is the only sequencing restriction implied by the problem. Therefore multiple processors can be employed to compute $f^i(d_j)$, for various values of i, j, in parallel.

Let $f^i(d_j)$, for all i, j, be computed at a processor indexed j. The jth processor applies the functions from F in the proper sequence to d_j. All the function codes can be initially available to all processors, or they can be pipelined among the processors. A schematic diagram of function pipelining is shown in Fig. 8.10. At fixed point, the desired sequence is available, element by element, at the sequence of processors from left to right.

If D is a long sequence or unknown in advance, then it may be preferable to pipeline the data items and hold the functions in place. The ith processor

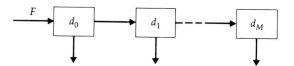

Figure 8.10 Functions are pipelined; data are held by processors.

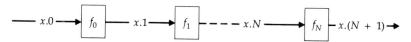

Figure 8.11 Schematic of data flow in a pipelined computation.

receives $f^{i-1}(d_j)$, for all j, from processor $(i-1)$ in sequence, computes $f^i(d_j)$, and transmits these values to processor $i+1$. A schematic diagram of data flow appears in Fig. 8.11.

In this figure the sequence $\overline{x.0}$ is the sequence D. The desired results are available at fixed point in the sequence $\overline{x.(N+1)}$. The following program captures the operation of the network in Fig. 8.11.

Program *Pipeline*

   initially

      $\langle \| \; i \; : \; 0 < i \leq N+1 \; :: \; x.i = null \rangle$
      $\| \; x.0 = D$

   assign

      $\langle \| \; i \; : \; 0 \leq i \leq N \; ::$
         $x.i, \; x.(i+1) \; := \; \text{tail}(x.i), \; (x.(i+1); \; f_i(\text{head}(x.i))) \quad \text{if} \quad x.i \neq null$
      $\rangle$

end {*Pipeline*}

For $d = \ll d_0, d_1 \ldots \gg$, let $f_i(d)$ denote the sequence $\ll f_i(d_0), f_i(d_1) \ldots \gg$. In the following, $\overline{x.i} - x.i$ denotes the prefix of $\overline{x.i}$ excluding $x.i$ (that is, the portion of $\overline{x.i}$ consumed by f_{i+1}). We have, for program *Pipeline*,

invariant $\langle \forall \; i \; : \; 0 \leq i \leq N \; :: \; \overline{x.(i+1)} = f_i(\overline{x.i} - x.i) \rangle$

$FP \quad \equiv \qquad \langle \forall \; i \; : \; 0 \leq i \leq N \; :: \; x.i = null \rangle$

Hence, at fixed point,

$$\langle \forall i \; : \; 0 \leq i \leq N \quad :: \quad \overline{x.(i+1)} = f_i(\overline{x.i}) \rangle$$
$$\Rightarrow \quad \overline{x.(N+1)} = f^N(\overline{x.0})$$
$$\Rightarrow \quad \overline{x.(N+1)} = f^N(D).$$

A fixed point is reached because the following sequence of numbers decreases lexicographically with each state change: $\ll |x.0| \, , \, |x.1|, \, \ldots, \, |x.N| \gg$.

Exercise 8.8   Modify program *Pipeline* such that for all i, $0 < i \leq N$, $|x.i| \leq 1$ is invariant. $\triangledown$

It is possible to pipeline both functions and data, computing $f^i(d_j)$ at processor $i - j$, for instance. More complex problems can also be solved using pipelining: The sequence of data items D, functions F, or both, may not be known in advance and the pipeline may not have a simple linear structure (see Chapter 21). In the following exercise, the functions are not known a priori; they are computed as the program execution proceeds.

Exercise 8.9   (prime number sieve; see also Section 6.5) It is required to compute the first N primes in an array $X[1..N]$; $X[i]$ will hold the ith prime. We employ the standard sieve technique, which is based on the observation that the $(k+1)^{th}$ prime, $k \geq 1$, is the smallest integer exceeding the kth prime that is not divisible by the first k primes. The first prime is 2. The sequential algorithm, given in Section 6.5, generates odd integers in sequence and tests every generated number for divisibility by all smaller primes. If the number is divisible by some prime, it is discarded; otherwise it is recognized to be the next prime and is added to the list. This problem fits the pipeline paradigm: Instead of checking a single number against all primes, the numbers can be pipelined and checked against the primes stored at the processors. The only difference from the previous pipeline scheme is that the functions—the primes by which numbers have to be sieved—are not known beforehand.
     Design a pipeline solution for this problem. Do not allow the source, i.e., the leftmost process, to generate an unending sequence of numbers. $\triangledown$

8.4   Program Transformations for Asynchronous Communication

At higher levels of design of a UNITY program, we normally ignore process boundaries. When such a design is to be implemented on a distributed architecture, we are faced with the problem of implementing shared variables by message communications. One way to solve this problem is to introduce processes to manage shared variables; to read or write a shared variable, a message is sent to the appropriate process (see Chapter 4 for details). Another possible solution is to use the dining philosopher (Chapter 12) or the drinking philosopher (Chapter 13) algorithms. (A process can be viewed as a dining philosopher, and is allowed to access a shared variable only when it is eating. To allow for simultaneous accesses to different shared variables by different processes, we can generalize this solution by regarding processes as drinking philosophers and shared variables as beverages. Then a solution to the drinking philosophers problem guarantees that accesses to shared variables are mutually exclusive, and yet different processes can simultaneously access different shared variables.)

These proposed solutions require elaborate mechanisms to implement arbitrary shared variables by message communications. However, if we know more about the shared variables—the way they are accessed and updated by various processes—we may be able to implement them efficiently without resorting to these elaborate schemes. As a simple example, consider an integer variable m that is incremented by 1 in a process u, and decremented by 1 in a process v only if it is positive. The variable m may represent a *semaphore*, for instance. Specifically, the statements in u, v that name m are of the following form (only the component of the assignment that names m is shown):

statement in u :: $m := m + 1$ if bu $\| \ldots$

statement in v :: $vs, m := vs', m - 1$ if $m > 0 \ \wedge \ bv$ $\| \ldots$

Here vs denotes some variables of process v, and vs' some expression that does not name m; bu, bv are boolean-valued functions of local variables, of u, v, respectively. We can implement m by message communication as follows. Replace variable m by c, a variable of type sequence, such that $|c| = m$ (c is a unary representation of m). The values of data items in c are irrelevant; for definiteness, assume that c is a sequence of zeroes. Then the statements in u, v can be transformed as follows:

statement in u :: $c := c;\ '0'$ if bu $\| \ldots$

statement in v :: $vs, c := vs', \text{tail}(c)$ if $c \neq null \ \wedge \ bv$ $\| \ldots$

Clearly, the shared variable c can be implemented by message communication. Thus we have implemented an integer that is accessed in a particular manner by message communications.

In this section we first show certain kinds of shared variables that can be implemented by message communication. Then we give a sufficient condition, called the *asynchrony condition*, such that any variable satisfying it can be implemented by message communications. Program development for a distributed architecture can stop at a point at which the shared variables satisfy these conditions; explicit communications using sequence variables are unnecessary. Obviously, the higher-level programs are easier to develop, understand, and prove.

8.4.1 Some Simple Transformations

The salient features of a bounded buffer model of communication are as follows. Let c be a variable, of type sequence, that is shared between processes u, v. Process u can name c in its statements in the following manner: (1) Test whether $|c| < L$, where L is a constant; (2) Append an item to c provided that $|c| < L$. Process v can name c in its statements as follows: (1) Test whether $|c| > 0$; (2) Remove the head item of c and assign it to a variable, provided that $|c| > 0$.

Implementation of c by a channel with buffer capacity L is well understood. We next show a number of cases in which a shared variable can be implemented using variable c, and hence such a variable can be implemented by message communication over bounded buffer channels.

Character

Let *char* be a variable whose value is either a character or a special value *empty*. Variable *char* is shared between processes u, v. Process u names *char* in its statements in the following manner: (1) Test whether *char* = *empty*; (2) Store a character in *char* if it is *empty*. Process v names *char* in its statements as follows: (1) Test whether *char* $\neq$ *empty*; (2) Assign *char* to a local variable and set *char* to *empty*, if *char* $\neq$ *empty*.

The variable *char* can be implemented by a variable c, of type sequence, as follows. The maximum length of c is 1, and the relationship between c and *char* is given by

$$(|c| = 0 \quad \equiv \quad char = empty) \quad \wedge$$
$$(|c| = 1 \quad \equiv \quad char = \text{head}(c)).$$

Then the statements in u, v can be modified to use c instead of *char*. The reader can verify that the accesses to c are of the form prescribed for communication with bounded buffer of capacity 1.

Boolean

Let b be a boolean variable shared between processes u, v. Statements in processes u, v manipulate b as follows: Process u sets b only to *true* and tests b for falsity, and process v sets b only to *false* and tests b for truth.

It is straightforward to implement variable b by a character, $char$, where $b \equiv (char \neq empty)$; the actual value of $char$, when it differs from $empty$, is irrelevant. It is also straightforward to show that accesses to $char$ satisfy the constraints on it for implementation by message communication. Therefore a shared boolean variable of the kind just described can be implemented by message communication over bounded buffer channels.

Bounded Integer

Let x be an integer variable shared between processes u, v. Process u names x in its statements in the following manner: (1) Test whether $x < L$, for some constant L; (2) Increase x by d, for some $d > 0$, if $x \leq L - d$. Process v names x in its statements in the following manner: (1) Test whether $x > 0$; (2) Decrease x by e, for some $e > 0$, if $x \geq e$. At the beginning of this section, we showed how to implement x by a sequence variable c when $d = 1$ and $e = 1$. For the general case, a similar transformation can be applied: Adding d to x amounts to appending d items to c, while subtracting e from x amounts to removing e items from c.

8.4.2 Toward a Theory of Transformations

Note: This section may be skipped on a first reading.

We give a sufficient condition for a shared variable to be implementable by asynchronous communication using unbounded buffers in channels. Informally, this condition is as follows:

1. Monotonicity.   Any part of the value of a shared variable read by a process (the head item of a nonnull sequence read by the receiver, for instance) is not changed by the actions of the other process (the sender adding items to the tail of a nonnull sequence, for instance).

2. Commutativity.   The value of a shared variable does not depend on the order in which the two processes update the variable (for a nonnull sequence, removing its head and adding to its tail may be done in either order).

We show a program transformation to implement such a variable by message communication.

Terminology: A statement executes *effectively* in a given program state if its execution changes the state.
                                                                    ▽

Consider a program F whose statements have been partitioned into processes. Let x be a variable that is shared between two processes u, v.

Variable x appears in two statements, se and re (corresponding to send and receive), belonging to processes u, v, respectively, as follows.

Program F: partial description

{only the statements naming x are shown}

$\quad \{se\} \quad x := x \oplus d \qquad\qquad$ if $\quad bu \quad \| \ldots \quad \{\oplus$ is a binary operator$\}$

$\| \quad \{re\} \quad vs, x := f(vs, x), g(x) \quad$ if $\quad b(x) \ \wedge \ bv \quad \| \ldots$

end {F: **partial description**}

Here vs denotes other variables (local or shared) of v and bu, bv are predicates that do not name x. Thus process u cannot test the value of x, nor can it use x in assigning a value to a variable other than x. Process v can read as well as alter x.

From the form of statements se, re, it is clear that after every execution of one of these statements, the new value of x must be communicated to and received by the other process before it can execute a statement naming x. We investigate the *asynchrony condition*, under which it is possible for both processes to execute their statements with old values of x and later update x to its proper value. If the asynchrony condition is met, process u can deposit the value of d in a channel to v whenever it executes se; then u, v can continue their computations—perhaps u will deposit more values in the channel and v will still use an old value of x in its computations—and v can update x appropriately whenever it receives a message along the channel from u.

Asynchrony Condition

In the following, x, d, vs are universally quantified over all values that these variables may take in the program.

$\quad b(x) \quad \Rightarrow$

$\quad ([b(x \oplus d) \ \wedge \ f(vs, x \oplus d) = f(vs, x)] \qquad$ {monotonicity} $\quad \wedge$

$\quad [g(x \oplus d) = g(x) \oplus d] \qquad\qquad$ {commutativity} $\quad)$

Monotonicity guarantees that values of b and f remain unchanged by execution of se; thus, if re executes effectively with some value of vs and x, then it would execute effectively and assign the same values to vs irrespective of whether se is executed. Commutativity guarantees that the value of x is independent of the order in which se and re execute. We can compute the value of x given the sequence of d-values and the number of executions of the statement re, by arbitrarily interleaving their executions. Before showing how to implement x by message communication, we consider a few examples.

Example 8.1

1. **Unbounded sequence.** Let x be a sequence variable. $\oplus$ is concatenation (;), functions f, g are head and tail, respectively, applied to a sequence, and $b(x)$ is $x \neq null$. Then we have for any d

$$x \neq null \;\Rightarrow\; ([x; d \neq null \wedge \text{head}(x; d) = \text{head}(x)] \quad \{\text{monotonicity}\} \;\wedge$$
$$[\text{tail}(x; d) = \text{tail}(x); d] \qquad\qquad \{\text{commutativity}\} \,).$$

   Therefore an unbounded sequence accessed in this manner may be implemented by message communication, no big surprise.

2. **Integer.** Let x be an integer variable. $\oplus$ is subtraction $(-)$, d is always a positive integer, f is independent of x, $g(x)$ is $x + e$, for some e (e may be positive or negative), and $b(x)$ is $x < 0$. We have

$$x < 0 \;\Rightarrow\; ([x - d < 0 \;\wedge\; f(vs) = f(vs)] \quad \{\text{monotonocity}\} \;\wedge$$
$$[(x - d) + e = x + e - d] \qquad \{\text{commutativity}\} \,).$$

3. **Integer.** Consider part (2) of this example, with the difference that $b(x)$ is $x = 0$. The monotonicity condition is violated.

4. **Set.** Let x be a set of elements. $x \oplus d$ is the union of element d with x, f is independent of x, and for some e, $g(x), b(x)$ are, respectively, $x - \{e\}$, $e \in x$. We have, for all x, d, e, vs, where $d \neq e$,

$$e \in x \;\Rightarrow\; ([e \in (x \cup \{d\}) \;\wedge\; f(vs) = f(vs)] \quad \{\text{monotonicity}\} \;\wedge$$
$$[(x \cup \{d\}) - \{e\} = (x - \{e\}) \cup \{d\}] \; \{\text{commutativity}\} \,)$$

5. **Set.** Same as part (4) of this example, except that d may be the same as e. Then the commutativity condition is violated. $\qquad\qquad \triangledown$

Observe, from part (2) of this example, that $\oplus$ need not be an associative operator to satisfy the asynchrony condition.

A Program Transformation

If the asynchrony condition is met, program F can be transformed to another program, G, as follows. A sequence variable c and a variable y, local to v, are introduced. Variable c denotes the channel from u to v by which u transmits its updates of x; variable y is v's local, possibly out of date copy of x. Initially c is $null$ and $y = x$. Assigning $x \oplus d$ to x in statement se is replaced by appending d to c. All occurrences of x in statement re are replaced by y. A new statement, ch, is added to process v to receive from sequence c and modify y appropriately. Specifically, we have the following program G.

Program G {modification of F}

initially $y = x$ ‖ $c = null$

assign

   {all statements and statement components of F that do not name x
   are included, without change, in G}

   {se} c $:= c; d$ if bu ‖ $\ldots$

   ‖ {re} $vs, y := f(vs, y),\ g(y)$ if $b(y)$ ∧ bv ‖ $\ldots$

   ‖ {ch} y, c $:= y \oplus \text{head}(c),\ \text{tail}(c)$ if $c \neq null$

end {G}

We write $F.se$, $F.re$ to distinguish the corresponding statements of F from those of G.

Correctness of the Transformation

Now we show that if the asynchrony condition is met, program G "does what program F does." Since x is not a variable of G, the predicates that describe properties of F cannot be directly interpreted in G because they may name x. We show that any property of F (except properties with *ensures*) is also a property of G, with x replaced by $y \oplus c$ (this notation is explained below). In particular, any property of F not naming x is also a property of G. First we prove a simple fact about $\oplus$.

Definition: For any x, and any sequence c, define

   $x \oplus c =$ x if $c = null$ $\sim$ $[x \oplus \text{head}(c)] \oplus \text{tail}(c)$ if $c \neq null$.

Lemma 8.1   For a given x and any $d \in D$, suppose that $g(x \oplus d) = g(x) \oplus d$. Then, for any sequence of values c from D, $g(x \oplus c) = g(x) \oplus c$.

Proof: By induction on $|c|$.

   $|c| = 0$: $g(x \oplus null) = g(x)$
                             $= g(x) \oplus null$

   $|c| > 0$: $g(x) \oplus c$

               $= [g(x) \oplus \text{head}(c)] \oplus \text{tail}(c)$, from the definition
               $= g(x \oplus \text{head}(c)) \oplus \text{tail}(c)$, from the condition in the lemma
               $= g[(x \oplus \text{head}(c)) \oplus \text{tail}(c)]$, from the induction hypothesis
               $= g(x \oplus c)$, from the definition of $x \oplus c$.   ▽

We will find it convenient to prove facts about program G in two steps. In the first step, we transform program F to a program H in which we retain

x while introducing c, y. In the next step, we eliminate x from H and obtain G. Program H follows; all statements of F that do not mention x are also included in H, though these statements are not shown.

Program H: partial description

{only modifications to F are shown}

initially $y = x$ [] $c = null$

assign

$\{se\}$ $x, c := x \oplus d, \; c; d$	if bu [] ...
[] $\{re\}$ $vs, x, y := f(vs, y), \; g(x), \; g(y)$	if $b(y)$ $\wedge$ bv [] ...
[] $\{ch\}$ $y, c := y \oplus \mathrm{head}(c), \; \mathrm{tail}(c)$	if $c \neq null$

end {H: partial description}

Observe that x appears only in assignments to itself, i.e., it is an auxiliary variable in H. Hence it is easy to eliminate x from H to obtain G. We work with H because it is easier to reason about it.

Theorem 8.1   If the asynchrony condition is met, $x = y \oplus c$ is an invariant of program H.

Proof: Initially, $x = x \oplus null$. All statements in H other than se, re, ch preserve the invariant because x, y, c are not named in other statements. To show that the statement $H.se$ preserves the invariant, a simple proof by induction establishes that

$$(y \oplus c) \oplus d = y \oplus (c; d).$$

Therefore

$$[x = y \oplus c] \quad \Rightarrow \quad [x \oplus d = y \oplus (c; d)].$$

To see that the statement $H.re$ preserves the invariant, it is sufficient to show that:

$$[b(y) \quad \wedge \quad x = y \oplus c] \quad \Rightarrow \quad [g(x) = g(y) \oplus c].$$

From $x = y \oplus c$, we have $g(x) = g(y \oplus c)$. From $b(y)$ and the commutativity condition, $g(y \oplus d) = g(y) \oplus d$, for any d in c. Therefore, from Lemma 8.1, $g(y \oplus c) = g(y) \oplus c$.

Statement $H.ch$ preserves the invariant because, from the definition of $\oplus$,

$$c \neq null \quad \Rightarrow \quad y \oplus c = [y \oplus \mathrm{head}(c)] \oplus \mathrm{tail}(c) \; . \qquad \triangledown$$

Next we show that all safety properties of program F are also safety properties of program H.

Theorem 8.2   (p *unless* q in F) $\Rightarrow$ (p *unless* q in H).

Proof: Since all statements in H other than $H.se$, $H.re$, $H.ch$ are also in F, it suffices to show that for these three statements $p \lor q$ is a postcondition, given $p \land \neg q$ as a precondition. It is sufficient to consider effective executions of these statements only because otherwise $p \lor q$ is implied by $p \land \neg q$.

   $H.se$: Assignment to x is as in $F.se$, and p, q do not name c.

$$H.re : b(y) \quad\Rightarrow\quad b(y \oplus c) \qquad\qquad \text{, from monotonicity}$$
$$\qquad b(y \oplus c) = \quad b(x) \qquad\qquad \text{, from Theorem 8.1.}$$

Hence effective executions of $F.re$, $H.re$ result in the same assignment to x. Also,

$$b(y) \quad\Rightarrow\quad [f(vs, y) = f(vs, y \oplus c)] \quad \text{, from monotonicity}$$
$$b(y) \quad\Rightarrow\quad [f(vs, y) = f(vs, x)] \qquad \text{, from the above and Theorem 8.1}$$

Hence assignment to vs is unaffected.

$H.ch$: The value of x does not change, and hence p (which does not name c or y) remains *true*. ∇

Corollary: Any invariant of F is also an invariant of H.

Proof: From Theorem 8.2, if p is a stable property of F (i.e., p *unless false* in F), then p is a stable property of H. Initial values of all variables of F are the same in H. Therefore all invariants of F are also invariants of H. ∇

   Next we show that any progress property of F is also a progress property of H.

Theorem 8.3   ($p \;\mapsto\; q$ in F) $\Rightarrow$ ($p \;\mapsto\; q$ in H).

Proof: We show that if (p *ensures* q in F) then ($p \mapsto q$ in H). Then the theorem follows by using induction on the structure of the proof of ($p \mapsto q$ in F).

From the definition, p *ensures* q in F means that

   p *unless* q in F

and that there is a statement $F.t$ in F:

   $\{p \land \neg q\}\; F.t\; \{q\}$.

From Theorem 8.2,

   p *unless* q in $F \Rightarrow p$ *unless* q in H.

Now consider two cases, $F.t$ is different from $F.re$, and $F.t$ is $F.re$. If $F.t$ differs from $F.re$, its corresponding statement, $H.t$ in H, assigns identical values to all variables other than y and c, and hence

   $\{p \land \neg q\}\; H.t\; \{q\}$.

This establishes p *ensures* q in H, and hence $p \mapsto q$ in H. Therefore we restrict attention to the case where $F.t$ is $F.re$, i.e., we assume

for all statements $F.s$ in F, $F.s \neq F.re$: $\{p \wedge \neg q\}$ $F.s$ $\{p \vee q\}$

for $F.re$: $\{p \wedge \neg q\}$ $F.re$ $\{q\}$

Since all statements of H except $H.re$ assign identical values to all variables of F as the corresponding statements of F, and $H.ch$ does not assign to any variable of F, we have

for all statements $H.s$ in H, $H.s \neq H.re$: $\{p \wedge \neg q\}$ $H.s$ $\{p \vee q\}$

Also,

$\{p \wedge \neg q \wedge b(y)\}$ $H.re$ $\{q\}$

because of the following:

- $F.re$ executes effectively with $p \wedge \neg q$ as a precondition since $\neg q$ is *true* before and q is *true* after execution of $F.re$.
- Hence $p \wedge \neg q \Rightarrow bv \wedge b(x)$.
- Given $p \wedge \neg q \wedge b(y)$, $H.re$ executes effectively, and it assigns identical values to all variables as $F.re$. (Using induction on $|c|$, show that in H, $b(y) \Rightarrow [f(vs, y) = f(vs, y \oplus c)]$; hence $b(y) \Rightarrow [f(vs, y) = f(vs, x)]$.)

Unfortunately $F.re$ may execute effectively in a program state though $H.re$ may not, because $b(y)$ may be *false*. We will show that, in H

$p \wedge \neg q \mapsto (p \wedge \neg q \wedge b(y)) \vee q$

$p \wedge \neg q \wedge b(y) \mapsto q$.

Then $p \mapsto q$, from the above two.

Sublemma 8.1 $p \wedge \neg q \mapsto (p \wedge \neg q \wedge b(y)) \vee q$ in H.

Proof:

$p \wedge \neg q \Rightarrow b(x)$, shown above

$b(x) = b(y \oplus c)$, from Theorem 8.1

When c has at least k items, let c^k, $k \geq 0$, be the prefix of c of length k. Thus $c^0 = null$ and $c^{|c|} = c$. Consequently,

$p \wedge \neg q \Rightarrow \langle \exists k : k \geq 0 :: b(y \oplus c^k) \rangle$, from the above, taking $k = |c|$

We claim that in H,

$p \wedge \neg q \wedge \neg b(y) \wedge b(y \oplus c^k)$ *ensures* $(p \wedge \neg q \wedge b(y \oplus c^{k-1})) \vee q$ (7)

(Observe that the left side of (7) is *false* for $k = 0$, and hence (7) is trivially established in this case.)

All statements in H except $H.ch$ preserve the left side of (7) or establish q, because of the following:

- $H.re$ does not execute effectively with $\neg b(y)$ as a precondition.

- Any statement other than $H.ch$ and $H.re$ preserves $p \wedge \neg q$ and it does not assign to y or to c, or else it establishes q.

Given the condition on the left side of (7), $H.ch$ executes effectively because

$$\neg b(y) \ \wedge \ b(y \oplus c^k) \ \Rightarrow \ k > 0 \ \Rightarrow \ c \neq null.$$

It is clear that effective execution of $H.ch$ establishes the first disjunct on the right side of (7). Applying induction on k in (7), in H,

$$p \wedge \neg q \wedge \neg b(y) \ \mapsto \ (p \wedge \neg q \wedge b(y)) \vee q \quad \{\text{observe that } b(y \oplus c^0) = b(y)\}$$
$$p \wedge \neg q \wedge b(y) \ \mapsto \ p \wedge \neg q \wedge b(y) \quad \text{, trivially}$$
$$p \wedge \neg q \ \mapsto \ (p \wedge \neg q \wedge b(y)) \vee q \quad \text{, disjunction on the above two.}$$

Sublemma 8.2 $\quad p \wedge \neg q \wedge b(y) \ \mapsto \ q \quad$ in H.

Proof: We know that $\{p \ \wedge \ \neg q \ \wedge \ b(y)\}$ $H.re$ $\{q\}$. Here we show that all statements in H, except $H.re$, preserve $p \ \wedge \ \neg q \ \wedge \ b(y)$ or establish q. All such statements preserve $p \ \wedge \ \neg q$ or establish q; all statements other than $H.ch$ preserve $b(y)$ because they do not assign to y, and the statement $H.ch$ preserves $b(y)$, because, from monotonicity, for any item d in c, $b(y) \ \Rightarrow \ b(y \oplus d)$. Theorem 8.3 follows from Sublemmas 8.1 and 8.2. $\hfill \triangledown$

In program H, variable x is auxiliary. Removing this variable gives us program G. Every property of F (except properties with *ensures*) is also a property of G, provided that x is replaced by $y \oplus c$ in predicates. In particular, all such properties of F that do not name x are also properties of G.

Exercise 8.10   We have restricted the shared variable x to appear in only two statements, one in process u and the other in process v. Propose an asynchrony condition for the case in which these restrictions do not apply. In particular, investigate the case in which a variable is shared between more than two processes. $\hfill \triangledown$

Exercise 8.11   In a program F, let t be a statement of the form

$$A \quad \text{if} \quad p$$

In this exercise, we explore the conditions under which p can be replaced by another predicate q without affecting the properties of the program. Suppose that

$$q \ \Rightarrow \ p,$$
$$q \ \textit{unless} \ \neg p,$$

and

$$p \ \mapsto \ q \text{ in program } F \text{ with statement } t \text{ deleted.}$$

Show that all the properties of F (except those with *ensures*) hold if p is replaced by q in statement t. $\triangledown$

Summary

Stream processing is an important programming paradigm. Programmers appreciate the elegance and economy of solutions that use it. In this chapter we have tried to demonstrate that a process that consumes streams of input and produces streams of output can be conveniently coded as a program in UNITY; its interface variables with other programs are of type sequence, representing the streams. We have shown that variables of other types can serve as interfaces among programs, provided that they are accessed in a somewhat constrained manner.

Bibliographic Notes

A definitive treatment of communicating sequential processes is found in Hoare [1984]. Milner [1983] contains a theory of distributed systems based on synchrony and asynchrony. Lamport [1983c] clearly explains that processes and modules are orthogonal concepts. Kahn [1974] defines a network of "deterministic" processes as the least fixed point of the equations defining those processes. Hamming's problem is described in Dijkstra [1976]. Conway's problem appears in Conway [1963]; our final solution closely follows Hoare [1978]. Lynch and Fischer [1983] describe a technique for transforming programs into forms suitable for execution on distributed architectures.

CHAPTER 9

Termination
Detection

9.1   Introduction

This chapter deals with a class of *reactive* programs. A reactive program is one that interacts with its environment on an ongoing basis. An operating system is an example of a reactive program; its environment is the collection of user programs. Many reactive programs do not terminate.

Sometimes it is argued that since reactive programs are tightly coupled to their environments, the structure of the environment—sequential, shared memory, distributed—dictates the structure of the reactive program; therefore concerns about the architecture (i.e., the structure of the environment) should not be postponed to later stages of design. For instance, in designing a distributed operating system to manage processes at many locations, the distributed nature of the problem should be considered at the outset (so the argument goes), and the focus of attention should be on what each location knows and needs to know.

We offer a different viewpoint: The structure of a reactive system need not mirror the structure of the environment with which it reacts. For instance, an operating system to manage processes at distant locations could be a centralized program (though this solution may be inefficient). The structure of a reactive system is a design choice. This choice is best made at the later stages of design after the problem has been understood. Efficiency is a key factor affecting this choice. Even for reactive systems, designs are simplified by getting a handle on the problem first, and only later considering architectures and efficiency. In this chapter, we attempt to demonstrate by means of examples that our viewpoint is sound.

The method we use to design reactive programs is first to propose a general solution strategy, next to describe the strategy formally in terms of its properties, and then to prove that the strategy solves the problem. We then derive simple programs (i.e., programs with simple proofs) from the specifications of the strategy. These simple solutions help achieve an initial grasp of the problem. Often these solutions are inefficient because they employ global data structures—structures that use data from several processes. Such structures may be bottlenecks because they are accessed by many processes. In these cases, making the program more efficient means distributing global structures, i.e., designing distributed structures that achieve the same goals. The invariants used in the simple program can be retained in the refined, more distributed version, or they can be weakened, and progress conditions strengthened. More often than not, the invariants describing global structures in initial designs are not retained in later, more distributed designs. The selection of a weaker invariant is a critical design decision, to which we pay a great deal of attention.

This chapter discusses an important problem—detection—the means by which a superposed computation detects stable properties (such as termination and deadlock) of the underlying computation. Section 9.2 contains a specification of the general detection problem: Detect a stable property W of the underlying computation. Later sections and chapters deal with specific instances of property W, such as termination and deadlock. Section 9.3 presents heuristics that are useful in solving detection problems, illustrating the heuristics and design strategy by simple problems. The remaining sections are concerned with the specific problem of termination detection. Section 9.4 contains a specification of the termination-detection problem. A simple solution is derived in Section 9.5. This solution is efficient for sequential machines but inefficient for distributed architectures. In Section 9.6, a weakened invariant and stronger progress condition are proposed, and a program suitable for an asynchronous multiprocessor shared-memory architecture is derived. Heuristics for handling channels are used in Section 9.7 to develop a distributed program. Memory-efficient termination-detection programs, suitable for garbage collection, are described in Section 9.8. These programs are derived from those developed in previous sections. Section 9.9 discusses termination detection of diffusing computations.

Notational Convention: To simplify exposition, we often omit the range of quantifications in programs and proofs. In this chapter, u, v range over processes. Thus

$$W \quad \mapsto \quad u.\mathit{flag}$$

is to be understood as

$$\langle \forall\, u\ :\ u \text{ is a process }\ ::\ W \quad \mapsto \quad u.\mathit{flag} \rangle.$$

9.2   The Generic Detection Problem: A Review

For convenience, the *detection problem* is repeated here from Section 7.3.3: For a given program F, define a relation *detects* between predicates p, q as follows:

p *detects* q in F $\equiv$

p $\Rightarrow$ q is an invariant of F $\wedge$

q $\mapsto$ p in F

Thus p *detects* q means that p holds within a finite time of q holding, and if p holds, so does q.

The generic detection problem is as follows: Given an underlying program and a stable property W of this program, apply superposition, introducing a superposed boolean variable *claim*, such that

  claim detects W.

A detection problem is considered in Section 9.4, where $W \equiv$ the underlying computation has terminated. To motivate some of the heuristics for program development, we work with a simpler example in this section; the example is from Section 7.3.3. It is required to detect W where

  $W \equiv$ the number of statement executions in the underlying program exceeds 10.

We employ an additional superposed variable *count* of type integer, where *count* is the number of statement executions in the underlying program. A solution, taken from Section 7.3.3, is as follows:

Program {superposition} *P1*

  initially $count = 0 \ [\!] \ claim = false$

  transform

    each statement s in the underlying program to:

      $s \ \| \ count := count + 1$

  add $claim := (count > 10)$

end {*P1*}

The program has the following properties:

invariant

count is the number of statement executions in the underlying program

claim detects $(count > 10)$

The proof is straightforward.

  This example is used in the next section to illustrate the heuristics.

9.3 Heuristics for Detection

The heuristics given in this section are useful for designing reactive programs; they are presented and illustrated by simple examples here, and are used repeatedly in this and later chapters. These heuristics may be used to develop programs by successive refinements.

9.3.1 Designing Detection Programs

Direct Implementation of Detection

We propose a method for implementing x *detects* e, where x is a superposed boolean variable and e is a stable predicate of the underlying program. The method has the nice property that x is also stable. Initially x is *false*. Exactly one statement is added to obtain the transformed program:

$x := e$.

We show, for the transformed program, that

invariant $x \Rightarrow e$

$e \longmapsto x$

The invariant holds initially because $\neg x$ holds. The invariant, $x \Rightarrow e$, can be falsified only by statement executions that (1) change e from *true* to *false* or (2) change x from *false* to *true*. Since e is a stable predicate, the first case does not arise. The second case may arise with the execution of $x := e$; the postcondition of this statement execution is $x = e$, and hence $x \Rightarrow e$.

The proof of progress is trivial since e is stable and e *ensures* x. Also observe that the implementation guarantees that x is stable.

This heuristic was used in program *P1* to implement *claim detects* ($count > 10$). (Observe that $count > 10$ is stable in *P1*.) Initially *claim* = *false*, and the only assignment to *claim* in *P1* is *claim* := ($count > 10$).

Next we propose a similar method for implementing

$(x \geq k)$ *detects* $(e \geq k)$,

where x is a superposed integer variable and e is a monotone nondecreasing integer expression. The specification is equivalent to

invariant $x \leq e$

$(e = k)$ $\longmapsto$ $(x \geq k)$

The implementation proposed for this specification is as follows. The initial value of x is chosen to ensure the invariant; this can be achieved by setting x to the initial value of e. Exactly one statement is added to obtain the transformed program:

$x := e$

The proof of correctness of this implementation is similar to that for the case in which x and e are boolean. The implementation has the nice property that x is itself monotone nondecreasing. The implementation also has a simple operational interpretation: From time to time, the superposition records the value of expression e in superposed variable x, and the precise times at which the recordings take place are not specified.

Heuristic for Program Refinement: Using the Transitivity of Detects

The next heuristic is based on weakening the invariant so that a centralized inefficient solution can be refined to a more distributed efficient one.

The relation *detects* is transitive:

$$(p \ detects \ q) \ \wedge \ (q \ detects \ r) \ \Rightarrow \ (p \ detects \ r).$$

To implement

$$claim \ detects \ W,$$

where it is inefficient to detect W directly on a target architecture, propose a more conveniently detectable predicate p, and design the program so that

$$(claim \ detects \ p) \ \wedge \ (p \ detects \ W).$$

The invariant describing p is usually weaker than that describing W. This is illustrated in Section 9.3.2.

9.3.2 Example of an Application of the Heuristics

Consider the last example, where $W \ \equiv$ the number of statement executions in the underlying program exceeds 10. The previous solution employed a superposed variable *count*, where each statement s in the underlying program is transformed to

$$s \ \| \ count \ := \ count + 1.$$

Suppose that the statements of the underlying program have been partitioned for execution on a set of asynchronous processors. Then the variable *count* is a bottleneck; it is modified by each processor in each statement execution, hence enforcing a sequential execution of the program. Therefore we refine our detection strategy as follows.

The Solution: Informal Description

We implement *count* in a distributed manner: We propose a superposed integer variable $u.m$ for each process u, where $u.m$ denotes the number of statement executions in process u; *count* is the sum of $u.m$, over all u. This means that *count* is an *auxiliary variable*—a variable that is used in reasoning about the program but that does not appear in the program itself. To reduce the bottleneck in the previous program, a nondecreasing superposed variable n is employed, where $(n > k)$ detects $(count > k)$, and *claim detects* $(n > 10)$. Since *count* is nondecreasing, the heuristic of Section 9.3.1 is used to guarantee that $(n > k)$ *detects* $(count > k)$—i.e., the only assignment to n is $n := \langle + u :: u.m \rangle$, which is equivalent to $n := count$. Unlike *count* in the previous program, in the proposed program n is *not* modified in parallel with the execution of every statement; this is an improvement because a bottleneck is removed.

The heuristic of Section 9.3.1 is employed again to guarantee that *claim detects* $(n > 10)$. Since n is nondecreasing, $(n > 10)$ is stable; therefore the only assignment to *claim* is *claim* $:= (n > 10)$, and initially *claim* is *false*.

The Solution Strategy: Formal Description

invariant $u.m$ = number of statement executions in process u

$(n > k)$ *detects* $(\langle + u \;\; :: \;\; u.m \rangle > k)$

claim   detects $(n > 10)$

Proof of Correctness of the Solution Strategy

From the transitivity of *detects*,

$\qquad$ *claim   detects $(count > 10)$*,

where $count = \langle + u \;\; :: \;\; u.m \rangle$.

Derivation of a Program from the Specification of the Solution Strategy

Next we propose a program to implement this solution strategy. The program is obtained directly from the heuristics.

Program {superposition} *P2*

> **initially** $n = 0$ $\;[\![\;$ *claim* = *false* $\;[\![\;$ $\langle [\![\; u \;\; :: \;\; u.m = 0 \rangle$
>
> **transform**
>
> $\qquad$ for each process u, transform each statement s in process u to
>
> $\qquad\qquad$ $s \;\;[\![\;\; u.m \;:=\; u.m + 1$
>
> **add**
>
> $\qquad$ $n \;:=\; \langle + u \;\; :: \;\; u.m \rangle$
>
> $\qquad [\![$ *claim* $:= (n > 10)$
>
> **end** {*P2*}

The proof that program *P2* satisfies the solution strategy is left to the reader.

Efficiency

Next we investigate whether program *P2* is more efficient than the previous program. Let variables $u.m$ be local to process u and let variables *claim* and n be local to some process that we call the *detecting* process. The detecting process may be one of the processes of the underlying computation or a process used exclusively for detection; it does not make any difference. The only statement that names variables of more than one process is

$$n := \langle + u \ :: \ u.m \rangle$$

No statement can be executed concurrently with this one because every other statement either modifies $u.m$ for some u or names n. Except for this statement, the superposition does not inhibit concurrency in the underlying computation. This is an improvement over program *P1*.

Another Example of the Application of the Heuristic

We apply the heuristic to program *P2*, once again using the transitivity of *detects*. The statement

$$n := \langle + u \ :: \ u.m \rangle$$

names variables in all processes. We shall refine the program to obtain a more asynchronous version in which a statement names variables from at most two processes.

The Solution: Informal Description

We propose a superposed integer variable $u.r$ for each process u, where $u.r$ is local to the detecting process, and

$$(u.r > k) \ \ detects \ \ (u.m > k).$$

Since $u.m$ is nondecreasing, the heuristic of Section 9.3.1 is employed: The only assignment to $u.r$ is $u.r := u.m$, and initially $u.r = u.m = 0$. The assignment $u.r := u.m$ names variables from two processes, u and the detector. We propose that $(n > k) \ detects \ (\langle + u \ :: \ u.r \rangle > k)$, and since $u.r$ is nondecreasing this is achieved by having only one assignment to n, i.e., $n := \langle + u \ :: \ u.r \rangle$. All variables in this assignment are local to the detector process. As in the previous program, *claim detects* $(n > 10)$, and since $n > 10$ is stable, this property is implemented in the usual way: Initially *claim* = *false* and the only assignment to *claim* is *claim* := $(n > 10)$. From the transitivity of *detects*, it follows that *claim detects* (*count* > 10), where *count* is defined as before.

The Solution Strategy: Formal Description

invariant $u.m$ = number of statement executions in process u

$(u.r > k)$ *detects* $(u.m > k)$

$(n > k)$ *detects* $(\langle + u :: u.r \rangle > k)$

claim   *detects* $(n > 10)$

We leave it to the reader to show from the first *detects* property that

$$(\langle + u :: u.r \rangle > k) \; detects \; (\langle + u :: u.m \rangle > k).$$

The correctness of this strategy is then straightforward from the transitivity of *detects*.

Derivation of a Program from the Specification of the Solution Strategy

A program is derived from the preceding specification by employing the heuristics of Section 9.3.1. It is instructive to compare the program with its specification.

Program {superposition} *P3*

initially $n = 0 \; \| \; claim = false \; \| \; \langle \| u :: u.m, u.r = 0, 0 \rangle$

transform

for each process u, transform each statement s in process u to

$s \; \| \; u.m := u.m + 1$

add

$\langle \| u :: u.r := u.m \rangle$
$\| \; n := \langle + u :: u.r \rangle$
$\| \; claim := n > 10$

end {*P3*}

Efficiency

The only statements that name variables from more than one process are, for each u,

$u.r := u.m$

This statement is executed by the detecting process, the only process that assigns values to $u.r$. This program is in the read-only schema. Program *P3* is efficient; it hardly interferes with the underlying computation.

Summary of Refinements for the Example Problem

For the example problem, the initial simple solution employed variable *count*. Though this solution is terribly inefficient, it gives us a handle on the problem. To obtain a more efficient solution we proposed a variable n that has an efficient distributed implementation and where

$$(n > k) \quad detects \quad (count > k).$$

This gives a more efficient solution, but one that is still not quite satisfactory. Nevertheless this intermediate solution indicates the bottleneck—the assignment

$$n := \langle + u \quad :: \quad u.m \rangle$$

This assignment names variables in all processes. To overcome this bottleneck, it is replaced by the assignment

$$n := \langle + u \quad :: \quad u.r \rangle$$

where $u.r$ is local to the detecting process and where

$$(u.r > k) \quad detects \quad (u.m > k).$$

Repeated application of the heuristic using the transitivity of *detects* is helpful in going from the initial solution to a suitably efficient one.

The development of the detection program illustrates stepwise refinement. In attempting to implement *claim detects W* in the first step, we postulate a stable predicate p and implement *claim detects p* and *p detects W*. These refinements continue until each of the detection properties is implemented directly into the program text by employing a simple heuristic.

9.3.3 Incremental Updating

This heuristic is illustrated by means of the simple example given earlier.

The Solution: Informal Description

For the example problem, we propose a program similar to program *P2* except that instead of employing monotone nondecreasing variable $u.m$, process u increments n at intervals and each process u maintains a variable $u.delta$, the number of statements executed by process u since process u last incremented n. Therefore the program has the property that the sum over all u of $u.delta$ is the difference between *count*—the total number of statement executions—and n. Therefore n is a lower bound on the total number of statement executions. Furthermore, because process u increments n at intervals, if *count* exceeds k then eventually n exceeds k. Hence n exceeds k detects that *count* exceeds k.

As in the previous program, *claim* detects that n exceeds 10. Next we describe the strategy in terms of invariant and progress conditions.

The Solution Strategy: Formal Description

Let *count* be the total number of statement executions.

invariant $n + \langle + u \;\;::\;\; u.delta \rangle = count$

invariant $u.delta \geq 0$

stable $n \geq k$

$count = k \;\;\mapsto\;\; n \geq k$

claim detects $(n > 10)$

Proof of Correctness of the Solution Strategy

$\qquad n \leq count$, from the invariants

$\qquad (n \geq k) \; detects \; (count \geq k)$, from the above and the progress property

$\qquad claim \; detects \; (count > 10)$, from the transitivity of *detects*

Derivation of a Program from the Specification of the Solution Strategy

The program follows from the meaning of *u.delta* and n given by the invariant. The familiar heuristic is employed to implement *claim detects* $(n > 10)$.

Program {superposition} *P4*

   initially $n = 0$ $\|$ $claim = false$ $\|$ $\langle \| u \;\;::\;\; u.delta = 0 \rangle$

   transform

      transform each statement s, where s is in process u, to

         $s \; \| \; u.delta \;:=\; u.delta + 1$

   add

         $\langle \| u \;\;::\;\; n \;:=\; n + u.delta \; \| \; u.delta \;:=\; 0 \rangle$

      $\|$ $claim \;:=\; n > 10$

end $\{P4\}$

The proof that this program satisfies the specification of the solution strategy is left to the reader.

Efficiency

Since $u.delta$ is local to process u, statement

$$s \; \| \; u.delta \; := \; u.delta + 1$$

is local to process u. The only statements that name variables from more than one process are those that modify n and $u.delta$ concurrently. These statements do not inhibit concurrency in the underlying program because they do not name underlying variables. Therefore this program is more efficient than $P1$.

9.3.4 Implementing Shared Variables by Tokens

A question in implementing program $P4$ is, how is variable n to be implemented on a distributed architecture? Program $P3$ suggests a method: Implement n by employing variables $u.r$. The shared-variable schema, given in Chapter 4, describes one method. Another method is to employ a *token*, an indestructible object that is passed from process to process; n and *claim* are fields of the token. Process u increments n and sets $u.delta$ to 0 only when it holds the token. In this scheme there is no permanent detecting process; rather, the token plays the role of the detecting process.

We shall not describe the many different ways to implement a variable to which many processes desire exclusive access; conflict-resolution algorithms (Chapter 12) and mutual-exclusion algorithms (Chapter 15) are relevant for such implementations. Next, we sketch one possible implementation of such a variable.

In $P4$, we employed the following set of statements:

$$\langle \| \; u \; :: \; n \; := \; n + u.delta \; \| \; u.delta \; := \; 0 \rangle$$

$$\| \; claim \; := \; n > 10$$

In a later stage of design, we replace these statements by other statements that are more efficient on a given architecture. If one set of statements is replaced by another, the programmer is obliged to prove that the resulting program is correct. If we limit ourselves to certain restricted program transformations, however, the proof of the transformed program is straightforward. We give one such transformation next.

This transformation is similar to superposition though it modifies the statements of the underlying program. A statement t is replaced by

$$t \quad \text{if} \quad b \; \| \; r \quad \text{if} \quad b$$

where b names only superposed variables and r assigns values only to superposed variables. Also, in the transformed program

$$true \; \longmapsto \; b$$

and the truth of b is maintained by all statements except the statement:
t if $b \parallel r$ if b. Hence once b holds it continues to hold until t if $b \parallel r$ if b
is executed. Since $true \mapsto b$, t is executed eventually. This transformation
preserves all properties of the underlying program except *ensures* properties.

An Example of the Transformation

First observe that in $P4$ the added statements can be combined into a multiple-
assignment statement for each process u, as follows:

$$\langle\!\mid u :: n := n + u.delta \parallel u.delta := 0 \parallel claim := (n + u.delta) > 10 \rangle$$

Now we employ a token in a token ring to implement n and *claim*. Let tok be
a superposed variable that takes on values $0..M - 1$, where M is the number of
processes. Let the processes be indexed by u, where $0 \leq u < M$. The predicate
$tok = u$ denotes that the token is at process u. The token travels in a circular
fashion, visiting process $(u + 1) \bmod M$ after visiting process u. Variables
n, *claim* are modified by process u only if u holds the token. Therefore the
statements in the transformed program are

$$\langle\!\mid u ::$$
$$n , u.delta , claim , tok :=$$
$$n + u.delta , 0 , (n + u.delta) > 10 , (u + 1) \bmod M \quad \text{if} \quad tok = u$$
$$\rangle$$

We are obliged to prove that, for all u,

$$true \mapsto tok = u,$$

and that $tok = u$ is preserved by all statements other than the one in which
it appears as an if-clause. This proof is straightforward.

9.3.5 On Detecting the States of Channels

Consider a channel c (represented by a sequence of messages) from a process
u to a process v. Process u appends messages to the tail of c and process
v removes messages from its head. One way in which processes u and v
can cooperate to determine information about the state (i.e., the value) of
c is for process v to reply to each message received along c by sending an
acknowledgment to process u; the state of c is a suffix of the sequence of
messages sent by process u along c for which process u has not received
acknowledgments. (A suffix of a sequence x is any subsequence of x consisting
of its last k elements, for some k, $k \geq 0$.) This cooperation between u and v
does not determine the precise value of c but only an upper bound. This is the
basic method of detecting a channel state, and it has several variations. For

instance, in some cases v acknowledges some, but not all, messages received along c. Even in this case, the state of c is a suffix of the sequence of messages sent, following the last message for which u has received an acknowledgment. If v does not acknowledge messages at all in the underlying computation, then the superposed program is designed so that v acknowledges messages sent to it in the superposed computation. Usually such messages are sent in the superposed computation to obtain information about the state of a channel; these messages are called *markers*. Markers are sent along the same channels employed by the underlying computation. The state of channel c is a suffix of the sequence of messages sent along it following the last marker for which u has received an acknowledgment.

The intent here is to demonstrate that there are ways by which processes can determine an upper bound on the state of channels. Therefore, in the initial stages of design, we do not concern ourselves with how channel states are to be determined; we choose an appropriate scheme at a later stage in the design.

9.3.6 Heuristics Employed for Detection: A Summary

The following heuristics have been discussed.

- The detection of stable properties is implemented in a straightforward way by assignments.
- To design a program to detect a predicate p, it may help to design it to detect a more convenient predicate q, where q *detects* p. Of course, proposing the "right" q is an important aspect of design, which is not always easy.
- One way to achieve a greater degree of asynchrony in a program is to partition statements that modify several variables into a sequence of statements that modify only a few variables.
- We do not concern ourselves with how variables are to be implemented on parallel architectures until the later stages of a design. Use of tokens, for example, is a useful way to implement such variables. (This is a general heuristic and is not restricted to detection programs.)
- In the initial design stages, we postpone consideration of how information about a channel state is to be obtained. The solution to a detection problem for an asynchronous shared-memory architecture, coupled with simple methods for obtaining information about channel states, often suggest a solution for a distributed architecture.

These heuristics and others are applied to another detection problem, termination detection, in the next few sections of this chapter.

9.4   Termination Detection: Problem Specification

The underlying program is represented by a directed graph $G = (V, E)$, where the (fixed) set V of vertices represents processes; the meaning of the (fixed) set E of edges is given later. Hereafter u, v represent vertices and (u, v) represents an edge. Associated with vertex u is a predicate $u.idle$. The structure of the underlying program is given next, followed by an explanation.

Program {structure of the underlying program} *R0*

   assign

$$\langle \, [\!] \; u, v \; : \; (u, v) \; \in \; E \; :: \; v.idle \; := \; u.idle \, \wedge \, v.idle \rangle$$

$$[\!] \quad \langle [\!] \; u \; : \; u \in V \; :: \; u.idle \; := \; true \rangle$$

end {*R0*}

Explanation: A process u for which $u.idle$ holds at a point in the computation is said to be *idle* at that point. A process that is not idle is said to be *active*. An active process u can make an idle process v become active if edge (u, v) exists; this is represented by the statement

$$v.idle \; := \; u.idle \, \wedge \, v.idle$$

If $\neg u.idle$ holds prior to execution of this statement, $\neg v.idle$ holds afterward. Hence if u is active before execution of the statement, v is active after execution of the statement. Also, if v is active, it remains active after the execution of this statement.

   An active process may become idle at any time; this is represented by the statement

$$u.idle \; := \; true$$

The initial state of each process—idle or active—is arbitrary. $\triangledown$

   Program *R0* is an abstraction of a class of programs. Process v is idle represents that v is at a fixed point, i.e., the equation obtained from each statement in v is satisfied in the given program state. Process u makes a process v active represents that u changes the value of a variable it shares with v, thus changing the state of v to a state that is not a fixed-point state of v.

   Let W be defined as follows:

$$W \; \equiv \; \langle \wedge u \; : \; u \in V \; :: \; u.idle \rangle.$$

The proof that W is a stable predicate of the underlying program is left to the reader. The problem is to transform the underlying program and introduce a superposed variable *claim* such that

> *claim detects W*.

The W employed here is called the *termination condition*. Note that if the termination condition holds then all processes are idle and will remain idle.

Exercise 9.1   The model of the underlying computation is somewhat simplistic because no process remains permanently active. Modify the program to allow for this possibility. Then observe that, if (u, v) is an edge, a permanently active process u makes an idle process v become active eventually. Refine the model so that a permanently active process u may or may not make v active. (Employ unfair nondeterminism; see Chapter 22.)   ▽

9.5   Sequential Architectures

The superposition is so simple (see the heuristic of Section 9.3.1) that it is given without an explanation or proof.

Program {superposition on R0} R1

> **initially**   *claim* = *false*
>
> **add**   *claim* := $\langle \wedge \, u \; :: \; u.idle \rangle$

end {R1}

This program is appropriate for a sequential machine. It is inefficient for an asynchronous shared-memory system because the added statement names variables from all processes; therefore its implementation requires some overhead, such as locking variables.

9.6   Asynchronous Shared-Memory Architectures

We shall derive a program by a sequence of refinements. Each refinement step is first motivated and then described in terms of a solution strategy.

9.6.1 Refinement Step: Inspecting Processes One at a Time

The difficulty with program $R1$ is that all the processes have to be inspected concurrently to determine if they are all idle. We attempt to overcome this difficulty.

The Solution: Informal Description

We seek a program in which each statement names variables from at most two processes. As a first step we propose a variable d, defined as the set of idle processes. From the meaning of d it follows that an idle process is removed from d when it becomes active, and an active process is added to d when it becomes idle. The superposed variable *claim* detects that d is the set of *all* processes; thus *claim* detects that all processes are idle. Next this strategy is couched in more formal terms.

The Solution Strategy: Formal Description

invariant $d \;=\; \{\, u \mid u.idle \,\}$

claim detects $(d = V)$

Proof of Correctness of the Solution Strategy

The correctness of the strategy follows from $W \;\equiv\; (d = V)$.

Derivation of a Program from the Specification of the Solution Strategy

The removal of a process v from d when it is made active by an active process u is carried out by transforming the statement

$v.idle \;:=\; u.idle \,\wedge\, v.idle$

in the underlying program to

$v.idle \;:=\; u.idle \,\wedge\, v.idle$

$\| \; d \;:=\; d - \{v\}$ if $\neg u.idle.$

Note: If v is not in d, then $d - \{v\} = d$ $\triangledown$

The addition of a process u to d when it becomes active is carried out by transforming the statement

$u.idle \;:=\; true$

in the underlying program to

$$u.idle := true$$
$$\| d := d \cup \{u\}$$

Note: If u is in d, then $d \cup \{u\} = d$. $\triangledown$

Since the predicate $(d = V)$ is stable, the progress condition can be implemented by the heuristic of Section 9.3.1.

Program {the transformed program} $R2$

initially $claim = false$ $\|$ $d = \{u \mid u.idle\}$

assign

$\langle \| (u, v) \quad :: \quad v.idle := u.idle \wedge v.idle$
$\| d := d - \{v\}$ if $\neg u.idle$
$\rangle$

$\| \langle \| u \quad :: \quad u.idle := true$
$\| d := d \cup \{u\}$
$\rangle$

$\| \quad claim := (d = V)$

end $\{R2\}$

The proof that the program satisfies the solution strategy is straightforward.

9.6.2 Refinement Step: A More Asynchronous Program

The last program is inefficient because d is a bottleneck variable; it is modified in every statement. This limits asynchrony. To achieve more asynchrony, we next attempt to decouple the modifications to d from the underlying computation.

The Solution: Informal Description

We propose that d be a *subset* of the idle processes. The weakening of the invariant regarding d is coupled with a progress condition that d becomes the set of all processes within finite time after all processes become idle. A process is not added to d *when* it becomes idle; instead, idle processes are added to d asynchronously. The heuristic is to break up a statement in which d and u are modified concurrently, into two statements: One statement makes $u.idle$ become *true* and the other statement adds u to d if $u.idle$ holds.

The Solution Strategy: Formal Description

invariant $d \subseteq \{u \mid u.idle\}$

$W \longmapsto (d = V)$

$claim \;\; detects \;\; (d = V)$

Proof of Correctness of the Solution Strategy

$(d = V) \;\Rightarrow\; W$, from the invariant

$(d = V) \;\; detects \;\; W$, from the above and the progress condition

$claim \;\; detects \;\; W$, from the transitivity of *detects*

Derivation of a Program from the Specification of the Solution Strategy

The multiple assignment

$\qquad u.idle \;:=\; true$

$\| \;\;\; d \;:=\; d \cup \{u\}$

in program *R2* is decoupled into two separate statements:

$\qquad u.idle \;:=\; true$

$\| \;\; d \;:=\; d \cup \{u\} \qquad$ **if** $u.idle.$

With this decoupling, the transformed program becomes

Program *R2′*

　initially

$\qquad claim = false \;\|\; d = empty \quad$ {initially d satisfies the invariant}

　assign

$\qquad \langle \| \; (u,v) \;\; :: \;\; v.idle \;:=\; u.idle \land v.idle$

$\qquad \| \; d \;:=\; d - \{v\} \qquad\qquad$ **if** $\neg u.idle$

$\qquad \rangle$

$\quad \| \; \langle \| \; u \;\; :: \;\; u.idle \;:=\; true$

$\qquad \| \; d \;:=\; d \cup \{u\} \qquad\qquad$ **if** $u.idle$

$\qquad \rangle$

$\quad \| \;\;\; claim \;:=\; (d = V)$

end {*R2′*}

The proof that the transformed program fits the solution strategy is left to the reader. It is instructive to compare programs *R2* and *R2′*.

9.6.3 Refinement Step: Further Decoupling of the Underlying and Superposed Computations

The Solution: Informal Description

The decoupling has not gone far enough. The transformed program inhibits parallelism in the underlying program in the statements

$$v.idle := u.idle \wedge v.idle$$
$$\| \quad d := d - \{v\} \qquad\qquad \text{if} \quad \neg u.idle$$

These statements modify the bottleneck variable d synchronously with the execution of the underlying program. Therefore the decoupling heuristic is applied again. The application of the heuristic is almost exactly the same as that employed in going from *P1* to *P4* in Section 9.3.3. (It will be helpful to skim through Section 9.3.3 again at this point.) The bottleneck variable d is replaced by a variable b—a set of processes—that satisfies a weaker invariant (given later) and where

$$(b = V) \quad detects \quad (d = V)$$

Replacing d by b is analogous to replacing *count* by n in Section 9.3.3. The statement in which $v.idle$ and d are modified synchronously is replaced by

$$v.idle := u.idle \wedge v.idle$$
$$\| \quad u.delta := u.delta \cup \{v\} \qquad\qquad \text{if} \quad \neg u.idle$$

where $u.delta$ is a set of processes, and $u.delta$ is local to process u. This is analogous to replacing

$$s \quad \| \quad count := count + 1$$

by

$$s \quad \| \quad u.delta := u.delta + 1$$

in Section 9.3.3. Variable b is modified asynchronously with executions of underlying statements; the modification is carried out by

$$b, u.delta := b \cup \{u\} - u.delta, \quad empty \qquad \text{if} \quad u.idle$$

This is analogous to the following assignment in Section 9.3.3:

$$n, u.delta := n + u.delta, 0$$

Thus $u.delta$ is the set of processes that u has activated since u last modified b.

A process is added to b only if it is idle. How can a process become active after it is added to b? Suppose there is an active process in b. Consider the first process to become active in b. This process became activated by an active process that is *outside* b. Once a process in b becomes active it may activate other processes. Therefore, if there is an active process v in b, there was a chain of activations: Some process u that is *not in* b activated some process x in b that, in turn, activated some process y in b that ... that activated v. Next we define chains formally. We also couch the strategy and our understanding of how it works in more formal terms.

The Solution Strategy: Formal Description

Define a relation *chain* between processes at a point in the computation as

u *chain* v $\equiv$ there exists a path in the underlying graph G from u to v
such that, for each edge (u', v') in the path, $v' \in u'.delta$.

invariant

$v \in b$ $\Rightarrow$ $[(v.delta = empty) \land v.idle] \lor \langle \exists u : u \notin b :: u$ *chain* $v \rangle$

stable $b = V$

W $\mapsto$ $(b = V)$

claim detects $(b = V)$

Proof of Correctness of the Solution Strategy

$(b = V)$ $\Rightarrow$ W , from the invariant because the second disjunct in the invariant does not apply.

$(b = V)$ *detects* W , from the above and the progress condition

claim detects W , from the transitivity of *detects*

Derivation of a Program from the Specification of the Solution Strategy

A program follows directly from the heuristics of Section 9.3. For example, *claim detects* $(b = V)$ is implemented by assigning $(b = V)$ to *claim* because $(b = V)$ is stable.

Program {asynchronous shared-memory} *R3*

   initially   *claim* $=$ *false* ‖ $b = empty$ ‖ $\langle ‖ u :: u.delta = empty \rangle$

   assign

     $\langle ‖ (u, v) :: v.idle := u.idle \land v.idle$

     ‖ $u.delta := u.delta \cup \{v\}$ **if** $\neg u.idle$

     $\rangle$

   ‖ $\langle ‖ u :: u.idle := true \rangle$

   ‖ $\langle ‖ u :: b, u.delta := b \cup \{u\} - u.delta, empty$ **if** $u.idle \rangle$

   ‖   *claim* $:= (b = V)$

end {*R3*}

Precondition	Postcondition
1. $v \notin b$	$v \in b$
2. $v.delta = empty \wedge v.idle$	$v.delta \neq empty$
3. $v.delta = empty \wedge v.idle$	$\neg v.idle$
4. $\langle \exists u : u \notin b :: u \ chain \ v \rangle$	$\langle \forall u : u \notin b :: \neg(u \ chain \ v) \rangle$

Table 9.1 Transitions that must be considered in proving the invariant.

Proof of Correctness of the Program

To prove that I is an invariant of a program we prove that I holds initially and that I is stable. The given invariant holds initially because b is *empty*. To prove that I is stable we demonstrate $\{I\} \ s \ \{I\}$ for all statements s of the program. Instead of proving $\{I\} \ s \ \{I\}$ for each statement s, it is sometimes helpful to identify what changes in values of variables can falsify I, and then show that these changes do not occur. This approach is helpful if the predicate I is an expression that has implications or disjunctions. For example, if the predicateis of the form $p \Rightarrow (q \vee r)$, then the predicate can be falsified only by (1) changing the value of p from *false* to *true*, (2) changing the value of q from *true* to *false*, or (3) changing the value of r from *true* to *false*. We demonstrate that all statements that change p to *true* or q to *false* or r to *false* preserve the predicate. Applying this approach to prove the invariant of program *R3*, we identify the changes in variables by which the invariant can be falsified; the pre- and postconditions of these transitions, i.e., the statements that can cause these changes, are listed in Table 9.1.

The types of transitions are numbered for convenience. The first type of transition occurs only upon execution of the statement

$$b, v.delta := b \cup \{v\} - v.delta, empty \qquad \text{if} \quad v.idle$$

If $v.idle$ holds before the statement is executed,

$$(v.delta = empty) \wedge v.idle$$

holds after the statement is executed, thus maintaining the invariant. If $\neg v.idle$ holds before the statement is executed, the state is not changed by the execution of the statement and the invariant is preserved.

The second type of transition occurs only if the following statement is executed for some u:

$$
\begin{aligned}
& u.idle && := && v.idle \wedge u.idle \\
\| \ & v.delta && := && v.delta \cup \{u\} \qquad \text{if} \quad \neg v.idle
\end{aligned}
$$

From the precondition of this type of transition, $v.idle$ holds; hence the execution of the statement does not change the state of the program and the invariant is maintained.

The third type of transition occurs only if the following statement is executed for some u:

$$v.idle := u.idle \wedge v.idle$$
$$\| \quad u.delta := u.delta \cup \{v\} \qquad \text{if} \quad \neg u.idle$$

If $u.idle$ holds before executing this statement, the execution of the statement leaves the state unchanged, thus maintaining the invariant. If $\neg u.idle$ holds prior to executing the statement, and since the invariant holds, the following predicate holds prior to executing the statement:

$$(u \notin b) \quad \vee \quad \langle \exists\, u' \,:\, u' \notin b \;::\; u' \ chain\ u \rangle.$$

That is, u is not in b or there is a chain from a vertex u' that is not in b to u, prior to executing the statement. After executing the statement the following condition holds:

$$[(u \notin b) \wedge (v \in u.delta)] \quad \vee$$
$$[\langle \exists\, u' \,:\, u' \notin b \;::\; u' \ chain\ u \rangle \wedge (v \in u.delta)],$$

which implies

$$[(u \notin b) \wedge (u \ chain\ v)] \quad \vee \quad \langle \exists\, u' \,:\, u' \notin b \;::\; u' \ chain\ v \rangle,$$

which implies   (allowing u to be u')

$$\langle \exists\, u' \,:\, u' \notin b \;::\; u' \ chain\ v \rangle.$$

Therefore the invariant is preserved.

The fourth type of transition occurs only if one of the following two situations occurs.

1. Before the transition there is a chain from a vertex u to v, where $u \notin b$, and this chain has a link (x, y); after the transition, link (x, y) is broken, thus breaking the chain from u to v. (Vertices u and x may be the same; vertices y and v also may be the same.)

2. Before the transition there is a chain from a vertex u, not in b, to v; after the transition, u is included in b.

Consider the first case:

Before Transition: $(u \ chain\ x) \wedge (y \in x.delta) \wedge (y \ chain\ v)$

After Transition: $y \notin x.delta$

This transition occurs only if the following statement is executed:

$$b, \ x.delta \ := \ b \ \cup \ \{x\} - x.delta, \ empty \qquad\qquad \text{if} \quad x.idle$$

After the statement is executed, $y \notin b$. The invariant is preserved because the following predicates hold after the transition:

$$y \neq v \ \Rightarrow \ (y \notin b) \wedge (y \ chain \ v)$$

$$y = v \ \Rightarrow \ v \notin b.$$

A similar argument, with $x = u$, applies to the second case (where u is not in b before the statement execution and u is in b after the statement execution). This completes a sketch of the proof of the invariant.

The following steps are helpful in constructing the proof of progress.

$$W \ \mapsto \ v.delta = empty$$

$$W \ \wedge \ (v.delta = empty) \ \text{is stable}$$

$$W \ \wedge \ \langle \wedge v \ :: \ v.delta = empty \rangle \ \mapsto \ u \in b$$

$$W \ \wedge \ \langle \wedge v \ :: \ v.delta = empty \rangle \ \wedge \ (u \in b) \ \text{is stable}$$

$$W \ \mapsto \ (b = V)$$

There is not much memory contention in program $R3$. The only statement that introduces contention is the one that modifies b and $u.delta$, but the degree of contention is not high. Contention can be reduced even further, as shown in the distributed programs that follow.

Employing a Token Instead of a Detecting Process

The next solution uses a variable tok, a token, that is passed from process to process; $tok = u$ means that the token is at u. Initially, the token is at some arbitrary process. The solution given here employs the heuristic presented in Section 9.3.4. To guarantee that the token can travel to all processes, we assume that the underlying graph G is completely connected. Variables b, $claim$ are fields of the token; a process u accesses b or $claim$ only if $tok = u$. To reduce the rate at which the token is passed, a process u passes the token to another process v only if u is idle, u is in b, $u.delta$ is $empty$, and v is not in b. The statements modifying b, $claim$, or tok are

> {process u modifies b and $u.delta$ only if u holds the token}
>
> $\langle \| u \ :: $
>
> $\qquad b, u.delta \ := \ b \ \cup \ \{u\} - u.delta, \ empty \qquad$ if $\quad u.idle \wedge (tok = u)$
>
> $\rangle$
>
> $\|$ {process u modifies $claim$ only if u holds the token}
>
> $\langle \| u \ :: \ claim \ := \ (b = V) \qquad$ if $\quad tok = u \rangle$

⟦ {process u sends the token to a process v only if u holds the token and is idle and has $u.delta$ $empty$ and is in b and v is not in b}

⟨⟦ (u,v) :: $tok := v$

    if $(tok = u)$ $\wedge$ $u.idle$ $\wedge$ $(u.delta = empty)$ $\wedge$ $(u \in b)$ $\wedge$ $(v \notin b)$

⟩

The proof of this program is very similar to that of *R3*. Progress conditions necessary for the proof in addition to those given for *R3* include the following:

$$W \wedge (b \neq V) \;\longmapsto\; \langle \exists v : v \notin b :: (tok = v) \rangle$$

$$W \wedge (tok = u) \;\longmapsto\; (u \in b) \wedge (u.delta = empty).$$

In this program a variable is modified by at most one process at a time. The only contention is for *tok*; one process may attempt to modify it while other processes attempt to read its value.

9.7   Distributed Architectures

9.7.1 Problem Description

The model of the underlying program in a distributed system is similar to that of the shared-memory system given in Section 9.3. The edges of graph G represent directed channels. An idle process becomes active only upon receiving a message. Idle processes do not send messages. The condition to be detected is as follows: All processes are idle and all channels are empty.

    The model of the underlying computation is given next. (Compare it with the model of shared-memory systems.) A channel from u to v is represented by the variable $(u,v).c$, which is of type sequence. The contents of messages in the underlying computation play no role in the superposed computation. Therefore, to minimize notation, all messages in the underlying computation are represented by m. (The reader should bear in mind that there are many different kinds of messages m.) For convenience, the structure of the underlying program for the shared-memory case is repeated:

Program {**underlying program structure—shared-memory**} *R0*

  assign

    ⟨⟦ u,v :: $v.idle := u.idle \wedge v.idle$⟩

  ⟦ ⟨⟦ u :: $u.idle := true$ ⟩

end {*R0*}

Program {**underlying program structure—distributed systems**} *ds*

   assign

       {u sends message m along channel $(u,v).c$ if u is active}

    ⟨▯ (u,v) :: $(u,v).c := (u,v).c; m$ if $\neg u.idle$⟩

       {v becomes active after receiving a message along channel (u,v)}

   ▯ ⟨▯ (u,v) :: $v.idle, m, (u,v).c := false,\ \mathrm{head}((u,v).c),\ \mathrm{tail}((u,v).c)$

                                if $(u,v).c \neq null$⟩

   ▯ ⟨▯ u :: $u.idle := true$⟩

end {ds}

Exercise 9.2 This model is simplistic because no process remains permanently active. Modify the program to allow for this possibility. Then observe that a permanently active process u eventually sends a message along each outgoing channel $(u,v).c$. Modify the model so that a permanently active process u may or may not send a message on an outgoing channel. (Employ unfair nondeterminism; see Chapter 22.)   ▽

9.7.2 Superposition in Distributed Architectures

The rules of superposition, described in Chapter 7, guarantee that the underlying variables are not modified by the transformations. This restriction was imposed in order to guarantee that all properties of the underlying program are properties of the transformed program. For an underlying program that can be directly mapped to a distributed architecture, it is often useful to employ the same channels for transmissions of both underlying and superposed messages. Thus the underlying variables corresponding to the channels may be modified by the transformations. The sending and receiving of superposed messages do not affect the underlying computation. For instance, in termination detection, an idle process can send superposed messages but not messages in the underlying computation; similarly, an idle process remains idle upon receiving a superposed message but becomes active upon receiving a message in the underlying computation.

    The restrictions on the transformations are as follows: Each message carries with it its type, underlying or superposed. The underlying computation takes no action on superposed messages. A proof is required that if there is an underlying message in a channel, then eventually an underlying message gets to the head of the channel. This ensures that the underlying computation is not blocked by the superposed computation.

9.7.3 A Solution to the Distributed Termination-Detection Problem

A heuristic in transforming shared-variable programs to distributed programs is to treat a process in the shared-variable program as being analogous to a process *and its outgoing channels* in a distributed system. The shared-memory solution is also a solution for distributed systems, where an idle process in the shared-memory case corresponds to a process that is idle *and has all its outgoing channels empty*. As discussed in Section 9.3.5, there are several ways in which a process can determine whether one of its outgoing channels is empty; the basic idea is that if a process has received acknowledgments for all messages it sent along a channel, the channel is empty. If messages are not acknowledged in the underlying computation, another strategy is used; a process sends superposed messages called *markers* that are acknowledged in the superposed computation: If a process has received acknowledgments for all markers it sent along a channel and has sent no messages along the channel since sending the last marker along that channel, the channel is empty.

We propose boolean variable $u.e$, local to u, where $u.e$ detects that all the outgoing channels of u are empty, i.e.,

$$u.e \quad detects \quad \langle \wedge\, v \;:\; (u, v) \in E \;\; :: \;\; (u, v).c = null \rangle.$$

We leave the task of implementing $u.e$ on a distributed system to the reader.

The following program is similar in structure to program $P4$. We propose, as in program $R3$ for shared-memory systems, that when u sends an underlying message to v along channel (u, v), process v is added to $u.delta$; the statements for assigning to b and *claim* are similar to those in $R3$.

Program $R4$
> {distributed termination detection—transformed program}

initially $claim = false$ $\|$ $b = empty$ $\|$ $\langle \| \, u \;\; :: \;\; u.delta = empty \rangle$

assign

> {u sends message m along channel $(u, v).c$ if u is active, and $u.delta$ is updated}

$\langle \| \, (u, v) \;\; :: $

> $(u, v).c,\; u.delta \;:=\; (u, v).c; m,\;\; u.delta\; \cup\; \{v\}$ if $\neg u.idle$

$\rangle$

> {v receives a message along channel (u, v) after which it becomes active}

$\| \, \langle \| \, (u, v) \;\; ::$

> $v.idle,\; m,\; (u, v).c \;:=\; false,\, \mathrm{head}((u, v).c),\, \mathrm{tail}((u, v).c)$
>> if $(u, v).c \neq null$

$\rangle$

$\|\ \langle\|\ u\ ::\ u.idle\ :=\ true\rangle$

{**added statements**}

$\|\ \langle\|\ u\ ::\ b,\ u.delta\ :=\ b\ \cup\ \{u\} - u.delta,\ empty\qquad$ if $\ u.idle\ \wedge\ u.e\rangle$

$\|\ claim\ :=\ (b = V)$

end{*R4*}

The meaning of b is given by the invariant, using the *chain* relations defined in Section 9.6.3:

invariant $\quad v \in b \ \Rightarrow\ ([[(v.delta = empty) \ \wedge\ v.idle \ \wedge\ v.e]\ \vee$
$\qquad\qquad\qquad\qquad\qquad \langle\exists\ u\ :\ u \notin b\ ::\ u\ chain\ v\rangle)$

The proof of this program is similar to that of program *R3* for the shared-memory case.

Exercise 9.3   Modify this solution by employing a token as for the shared-memory case. Only the process holding the token modifies b and *claim*. To reduce the rate at which the token is passed from one process to another, a process u sends the token to a process v if

$$u.idle \ \wedge\ u.e \ \wedge\ (u.delta = empty) \ \wedge\ (u \in b) \ \wedge\ (v \notin b).$$

This solution assumes that graph G is completely connected. What problems arise if G is not completely connected, and how can these be solved? ∇

9.8   Memory-Efficient Termination-Detection Programs

Some of the programs in Sections 9.6 and 9.7 require that each process u maintain a set $u.delta$ of processes. In some situations this is infeasible because of insufficient memory. Therefore we investigate programs in which the amount of memory used is substantially smaller than the number of processes in the system. Garbage collection, treated in Chapter 16, is an example of a problem in which memory-efficient programs are desirable.

9.8.1 Initial Design

The Solution: Informal Description

We postulate a set of detecting processes, J, where J is distinct from the set V of underlying processes. We introduce boolean variables $j.flag$ for all j in

J. The size of J does not matter provided that J is *nonempty*. The larger J is, the more memory is required to store $j.flag$, for all j, but a larger J results in less contention among the underlying processes for access to variables $j.flag$. The set V of underlying processes is partitioned among the members of J; each member of J is responsible for a subset of V. A function g that maps V to J is employed, where $g(v)$ is the member in J responsible for v.

Let us attempt to modify program $R3$ of Section 9.6 by employing $j.flag$ in place of $u.delta$. We propose that if $j.flag$ holds for all j, all processes in b are idle: This is the key invariant of our program. To establish this invariant, initially b is *empty*, and whenever a process u makes any process become active, $g(u).flag$ is set to *false*. Also to guarantee this invariant, when the value of a flag is changed from *false* to *true*, the set b is made *empty*. Furthermore, a process is added to b only if it is idle.

For progress, we propose that within finite time of W holding, $j.flag$ becomes *true* for all j; this progress condition is guaranteed by setting a *false* $j.flag$ to *true* (and concurrently setting b to *empty*) from time to time. We also propose that if W holds and $j.flag$ holds, $j.flag$ continues to hold thereafter; this stability property is guaranteed because $j.flag$ is set to *false* only when a process becomes active, and if W holds a process never becomes active. Therefore, within finite time of W holding, $j.flag$ holds for all j, and this situation continues to hold thereafter. We also propose that within finite time of W holding, an underlying process v that is not in b is added to b; this progress condition is achieved by adding idle processes to b. Therefore, within finite time of W holding, all underlying processes are in b (i.e., $b = V$), and all flags hold. From the invariant, if all flags hold then all processes in b are idle, and if $b = V$ then all processes are idle. Boolean variable *claim* detects that all flags hold and that $b = V$.

The Solution Strategy: Formal Description

In the following, variable j ranges over J.

invariant $\langle \wedge j \ :: \ j.flag \rangle \ \Rightarrow \ \langle \wedge v : v \in b \ :: \ v.idle \rangle$

$W \ \longmapsto \ W \wedge j.flag$

stable $W \wedge j.flag$

$W \wedge \langle \wedge j \ :: \ j.flag \rangle \ \longmapsto \ W \wedge \langle \wedge j \ :: \ j.flag \rangle \wedge (v \in b)$

stable $W \wedge \langle \wedge j \ :: \ j.flag \rangle \wedge (v \in b) \cdot$

claim detects $((b = V) \wedge \langle \wedge j \ :: \ j.flag \rangle)$

Proof of Correctness of the Solution Strategy

From the first pair of progress and stability conditions it follows that

$$W \;\mapsto\; W \;\wedge\; \langle \wedge\, j \; :: \; j.flag\rangle.$$

From the second pair of progress and stability conditions it follows that

$$W \;\wedge\; \langle \wedge\, j \; :: \; j.flag\rangle \;\mapsto\; W \;\wedge\; \langle \wedge\, j \; :: \; j.flag\rangle \;\wedge\; (b = V).$$

Therefore

$$W \;\mapsto\; (b = V) \;\wedge\; (\wedge\, j \; :: \; j.flag).$$

From the invariant,

$$(b = V) \;\wedge\; \langle \wedge\, j \; :: \; j.flag\rangle \;\Rightarrow\; W.$$

Hence from the above two properties

$$((b = V) \;\wedge\; \langle \wedge\, j \; :: \; j.flag\rangle) \;\; detects \;\; W.$$

From the above and the last property in the solution strategy, using the transitivity of *detects*,

$$claim \;\; detects \;\; W.$$

This completes the proof. From the arguments of the proof it follows (though not trivially) that

stable $(b = V) \;\wedge\; \langle \wedge\, j \; :: \; j.flag\rangle$

Hence the heuristic of section 9.3.1 can be used to implement

$$claim \;\; detects \;\; ((b = V) \;\wedge\; \langle \wedge\, j \; :: \; j.flag\rangle).$$

Derivation of a Program from the Specification of the Solution Strategy

Next we propose a program that fits the solution strategy. The proof that the program satisfies the specification of the solution strategy is straightforward.

Program {memory efficient} $R5$

   initially $claim = false \; \| \; b = empty$ $\{j.flag$ is arbitrary$\}$

   assign

$$\langle\| \; (u, v) \; :: \; v.idle := u.idle \wedge v.idle$$
$$\| \; g(u).flag := g(u).flag \wedge u.idle$$
$$\rangle$$
$$\| \; \langle\| \; u \; :: \; u.idle := true\rangle$$
$$\| \; \langle\| \; j \; :: \; b, j.flag := empty, true \qquad \text{if} \quad \neg j.flag\rangle$$
$$\| \; \langle\| \; u \; :: \; b := b \cup \{u\} \qquad\qquad\quad \text{if} \quad u.idle\rangle$$
$$\| \quad claim := [(b = V) \wedge \langle \wedge\, j \; :: \; j.flag\rangle]$$

end $\{R5\}$

A memory-efficient implementation of b is as follows. Processes are ordered in some total order, and a process is added to b only if it is the next process higher than the highest process in b. (When b is *empty* only the lowest process may be added to it.) Therefore b can be represented by its highest process; all lower processes in the ordering are also in b. Thus b can be implemented using $O(\log N)$ bits, where N is the number of processes in V.

9.8.2 Refinement Step: A More Asynchronous Program

Program $R5$ is not quite satisfactory because the statement that assigns values to *claim* names variable $j.flag$, local to detecting process j, for all j. Next this statement is broken down into statements each of which names b, a variable F, described next, and *at most one* variable local to a detecting process.

The Solution: Informal Description

We propose a set F, $F \subseteq J$, such that if $j.flag$ holds for all j not in F, then $j.flag$ also holds for all j in F. Thus, if $j.flag$ holds for all j not in F, all processes in b are idle, from the invariant of program $R5$.

Also we propose the invariant: If F is *nonempty* then $b = V$. It then follows that, if $F = J$, $j.flag$ holds for all j not in F (because there is no such j). Hence all processes in b are idle, and since F is *nonempty*, $b = V$, and it follows that all processes are idle.

The progress condition is as follows: If $b = V$ and all flags hold (in which case W holds), then in finite time a detecting process i is added to set F. Furthermore, if $b = V$ and all flags hold and i is in F, then i remains in F forever thereafter. Hence eventually all j are in F. Boolean variable *claim* detects that all j are in F.

Next we turn our attention to implementing the invariants and progress conditions just proposed. Consider the expression on the right side of the statement in $R5$ that assigns values to *claim*. We propose that this expression should be evaluated sequentially. First determine if $b = V$, and only then check the flags. Variable F is the set of all detecting processes whose flags have been checked. Initially F is *empty*. A process j is added to F only if $j.flag$ holds and $(b = V)$. If some $j.flag$ is found to be *false*, then F and b are both made *empty*, and concurrently $j.flag$ is set to *true*.

The Solution Strategy: Formal Description

The specification of the previous solution strategy carries over, and in addition there are a few invariants and progress conditions dealing with F; these are given next. In the following, i ranges over members of J.

invariant $[F \subseteq J] \wedge [(F = empty) \vee (b = V)]$

invariant $\langle \wedge\, j\, :\, j \notin F\, ::\, j.flag \rangle \;\Rightarrow\; \langle \wedge\, j\, :\, j \in F\, ::\, j.flag \rangle$

$(b = V) \wedge \langle \wedge\, j\, ::\, j.flag \rangle \;\longmapsto\; (i \in F)$

stable $(b = V) \wedge \langle \wedge\, j\, ::\, j.flag \rangle \wedge (i \in F)$

The *detects* condition in the previous specification is replaced by

$claim\ \ detects\ \ (F = J).$

Proof of Correctness of the Solution Strategy

From the pair of progress and stability conditions,

$(b = V) \wedge \langle \wedge\, j\, ::\, j.flag \rangle \;\longmapsto\; (F = J).$

From the second invariant,

$(F = J) \;\Rightarrow\; \langle \wedge\, j\, ::\, j.flag \rangle.$

From the first invariant,

$(F = J) \;\Rightarrow\; (b = V).$

Hence

$(F = J) \;\Rightarrow\; (b = V) \wedge \langle \wedge\, j\, ::\, j.flag \rangle.$

Combining with the first progress property proven,

$(F = J)\ detects\ [(b = V) \wedge \langle \wedge\, j\, ::\, j.flag \rangle].$

From the proof of the previous solution strategy,

$(b = V) \wedge \langle \wedge\, j\, ::\, j.flag \rangle\ detects\ W.$

From the transitivity of *detects*, and since *claim detects* $(F = J)$,

$claim\ \ detects\ \ W.$

This completes the proof of correctness of the solution strategy.

It follows from this proof that $F = J$ is stable. Therefore the heuristic of Section 9.3.1 can be employed to implement

$claim\ \ detects\ \ (F = J).$

Derivation of a Program from the Specification of the Solution Strategy

Next we propose a program that fits the solution strategy. As in most examples in this book, the proof that a program satisfies a solution strategy is straightforward because the solution strategy is described formally and in some detail. The proof of this particular program is not trivial. The reader should prove that the program satisfies the specification of program $R5$ and then verify the additional invariants, the stable property, and the progress condition proposed in this refinement step.

Program {memory efficient} $R5'$

initially

$$claim = false \quad \| \quad b = empty \quad \{j.flag \text{ is arbitrary}\} \quad \| \quad F = empty$$

assign

$$\langle\| \ (u,v) \ :: \ v.idle \ := \ u.idle \ \wedge \ v.idle$$
$$\| \ g(u).flag \ := \ g(u).flag \ \wedge \ u.idle$$
$$\rangle$$

$$\| \ \langle\| \ u \ :: \ u.idle \ := \ true\rangle$$

$$\| \ \langle\| \ j \ :: \ F, \ b, \ j.flag \ := \ empty, \ empty, \ true \quad \text{if} \ \neg j.flag\rangle$$

$$\| \ \langle\| \ u \ :: \ b \ := \ b \ \cup \ \{u\} \quad\quad\quad\quad\quad\quad \text{if} \ u.idle\rangle$$

$$\| \ \langle\| \ j \ :: \ F \ := \ F \ \cup \ \{j\} \quad\quad\quad\quad\quad\quad \text{if} \ j.flag \ \wedge \ (b = V)\rangle$$

$$\| \quad\quad claim \ := \ (F = J)$$

end $\{R5'\}$

9.9   Termination Detection of Diffusing Computations

9.9.1 What Is a Diffusing Computation?

In this section we restrict attention to an underlying computation called a *diffusing computation*. A diffusing computation is a special case of the underlying program $R0$ in Section 9.4. The initial condition in $R0$ is unspecified; a process may be either idle or active initially. In a diffusing computation the initial condition is specified: Initially, all processes are idle except a special process, called *init*.

Thus the structure of the underlying computation is as follows.

Program {underlying diffusing computation} dc

    initially $\langle \| \ u \quad :: \quad u.idle = (u \neq init) \rangle$

    assign

        $\langle \| \ (u,v) \quad :: \quad v.idle := u.idle \ \wedge \ v.idle \rangle$

    $\| \ \langle \| \ u \quad :: \quad u.idle := true \rangle$

end $\{dc\}$

Specification of the Termination-Detection Problem for Diffusing Computation

The problem, as before, is to apply superposition to dc, using superposed variable *claim*, such that

    claim detects W,

where

    $W \equiv \langle \wedge u \quad :: \quad u.idle \rangle$.

9.9.2 Initial Design

The steps of program development for termination detection of diffusing computations are the same as in the general case (Sections 9.4, 9.5, and 9.6). Rather than describe each refinement step in detail, the similarities between program development for the general case and the specific case of diffusing computations are outlined.

In Section 9.4, variable d was proposed, where d is the set of idle processes and $(d = V)$ *detects* W. Then a more convenient set b of processes was proposed where $(b = V)$ *detects* $(d = V)$ and where operations on b are not concurrent with the underlying computation. A dual approach is employed here. Let d' be the set of active (i.e., nonidle) processes. Hence $(d' = empty)$ *detects* W. A program based on d' is inefficient because operations on d' are synchronized with the underlying computation: When a process becomes active it is added to d', and when it becomes idle it is removed from d'. Therefore a set b' of processes is proposed where operations on b' are less tightly synchronized with the underlying computation: b' is implemented as a distributed structure (more about this later), $d' \subseteq b'$, and $(b' = empty)$ *detects* W.

The Solution: Informal Description

A set b' of processes is employed, where all active processes are in b'. (Set b' may contain idle processes as well.) Therefore, when a process that is not in

b' becomes active, it is added to b'. Within finite time of termination of the diffusing computation, b' shrinks to the empty set. Since all active processes are in b', it follows that if b' is *empty* then all processes are idle (and therefore computation has terminated). Variable *claim* detects that b' is *empty*. Applying the heuristic of Section 9.3.1, *claim* is initially *false*, and it is set to *true* if b' is *empty*.

Next the informal description of the strategy is couched in more formal terms.

The Solution Strategy: Formal Description

invariant $u \in b' \ \lor \ u.idle$ $\hspace{6cm}$ (1)

$W \ \mapsto \ b' = empty$ $\hspace{6cm}$ (2)

stable $W \land (b' = empty)$ $\hspace{5cm}$ (3)

claim detects $(b' = empty)$ $\hspace{5cm}$ (4)

Proof of Correctness of the Solution Strategy

$\hspace{1cm} (b' = empty) \ \Rightarrow \ W \hspace{2cm}$, from (1)

$\hspace{1cm} (b' = empty) \ detects \ W \hspace{1cm}$, from the above and (2)

$\hspace{1cm} claim \ detects \ W \hspace{2.5cm}$, from the transitivity of *detects* and (4)

This completes the proof of the strategy.

From the proof and the stability condition (3) in the specification, it follows that $(b' = empty)$ is stable. Hence the heuristic of Section 9.3.1 can be used in implementing

$\hspace{1cm} claim \ detects \ (b' = empty).$

Derivation of a Program from the Specification of the Solution Strategy

Next we propose a program that implements the solution strategy. The initial conditions are derived, as usual, from the invariants. Initially only *init* is in b' to satisfy invariant (1). Also initially *claim* has value *false* because of (4). We show the transformed program:

Program {termination detection of diffusing computations—
$\hspace{1cm}$ transformed program} *Q0*

$\hspace{1cm}$ **initially** $\langle [\![\ u \ :: \ u.idle = (u \neq init) \rangle \ [\![\ claim = false \ [\![\ b' = \{init\}$

$\hspace{1cm}$ **assign**

$\hspace{2cm}$ {to maintain invariant (1), when an active process u activates a process v in the underlying computation, add v to b'}

$\langle[\![\ (u, v)\ \ ::$
$\quad v.idle\ :=\ u.idle\ \wedge\ v.idle\ \|\ b'\ :=\ b'\ \cup\ \{v\}\qquad \text{if}\quad \neg u.idle$
$\rangle$

$[\![\ \{\text{a process } u \text{ becomes idle in the underlying computation}\}$
$\quad \langle[\![\ u\ \ ::\ u.idle\ :=\ true\rangle$

$[\![\ \{\text{to implement progress condition (2), remove an idle process } u \text{ from } b'\}$
$\quad \langle[\![\ u\ \ ::\ b'\ :=\ b'\ -\ \{u\}\qquad \text{if}\quad u.idle\rangle$

$[\![\ \{\text{implement condition (4) by the following assignment}\}$
$\quad claim\ :=\ (b'\ =\ empty)$

end $\{Q0\}$

The proof that program $Q0$ satisfies the solution strategy is simple.

9.9.3 Refinement Step: Distributing Data Structures

Next we propose a refinement of the solution strategy because in program $Q0$ the superposition is too tightly coupled to the underlying program by b'.

The Solution: Informal Description

The basic idea in the next program is to implement set b' as a distributed structure. This means that (1) b' is an auxiliary variable (there is an invariant relating b' to local variables of processes) and (2) all operations access local variables of at most two processes. This allows some operations that modify b' to be executed concurrently.

What distributed structure is appropriate for implementing b'? Since the underlying computation is implemented as a graph, a subgraph with vertex set b' is an appropriate structure. The invariant implies that when a process that is not included in the structure becomes active, the structure grows to include the process. The progress condition states that if W holds, the structure shrinks and eventually vanishes. A graph structure that supports growing and shrinking operations is a rooted tree. A tree grows by adding leaves. Once W holds, the tree does not grow and it shrinks by dropping leaves. Therefore a tree is employed to implement b', where the only operations on the tree are as follows:

1. When an idle process u that is not included in the tree becomes active, the tree grows to include u, by making u a leaf.

2. An idle process that is a leaf is deleted from the tree.

The Solution Strategy: Formal Description

The tree is implemented by variables $u.father$, local to process u, for all processes u. For all u, where $u \neq init$:

$$u.father = \text{the process that is } u\text{'s father in the tree} \quad \text{if} \quad u \in b' \quad \sim$$

$$nil \quad \text{if} \quad u \notin b',$$

where nil is a special symbol. For ease of exposition, another special symbol ext (for external) is proposed, where

$$init.father = ext \quad \text{if} \quad init \in b' \quad \sim$$
$$nil \quad \text{if} \quad init \notin b'.$$

Symbol ext does not represent a process; it is used merely for convenience in reasoning. No process other than $init$ has ext for a father.

The relationship between program $Q0$ and its refinement is given by $b' = \{u \mid u.father \neq nil\}$. We postulate that the set of processes whose fathers are *non-nil* form a rooted tree: The father of u in this tree is $u.father$ and $init$ is the root of the tree, if the tree is nonempty. Next we introduce boolean variable $u.leaf$, where $u.leaf$ holds if and only if u is a leaf of the tree, i.e., u is in the tree and u has no sons:

$$u.leaf \quad \equiv \quad u.father \neq nil \ \wedge \ \langle \wedge v \ :: \ v.father \neq u \rangle$$

The specification of the program employing the tree is given next; a discussion of the specification is given later.

invariant   The set of processes u, where $u.father \neq nil$, form a tree where the father of u in the tree is $u.father$ and, if the tree is nonempty, the root of the tree is $init$. (5)

invariant $u.father \neq nil \ \vee \ u.idle$ (6)

stable $W \ \wedge \ (u.father = nil)$ (7)

$W \ \wedge \ u.leaf \ \longmapsto \ u.father = nil$ (8)

$claim \ \ detects \ \ init.father \doteq nil$ (9)

Condition (6) says that all active processes are on the tree. Condition (7) says that once W holds, the tree stops growing: If W holds and u is not in the tree, then u is not in the tree thereafter. Progress condition (8) states that if W holds, leaves of the tree drop off in finite time. Condition (9) says that *claim* detects that the tree has vanished.

Proof of Correctness of the Solution Strategy

We show that conditions (5–9) imply conditions (1–4), where

$$u \in b' \;\equiv\; u.father \neq nil. \tag{10}$$

The proof of invariant (1) is trivial from (6) and (10). We prove progress condition (2) next.

for all values B' of b':

$W \;\wedge\; (b' = B')$ *unless* $W \;\wedge\; (b' \subset B')$
, from (7)

$(b' \neq empty) \;\Rightarrow\; \langle \exists\, u \;::\; u.leaf \rangle$
, from (10), (5), and the fact that a nonempty tree has a leaf

$W \;\wedge\; (b' = B') \;\wedge\; (b' \neq empty) \;\mapsto\; W \;\wedge\; (b' \subset B')$
, from the above two properties and (8)

$W \;\mapsto\; W \;\wedge\; (b' = empty)$
, by induction on the cardinality of b'

$W \;\mapsto\; b' = empty$
, by weakening the right side of the above

Stability condition (3) follows directly from (7) and (10). To prove (4), we show that

$$(init.father = nil) \;\equiv\; (b' = empty).$$

From invariant (5), $(init.father = nil)$ means that the tree is empty and hence no u has $u.father \neq nil$. Therefore

$(init.father = nil) \;\equiv\; \langle \wedge\, u \;::\; u.father = nil \rangle$, from (5)

$\equiv\; \langle \wedge\, u \;::\; u \notin b' \rangle$, from (10)

$\equiv\; (b' = empty)$

Property (4) now follows from (9).

Derivation of a Program from the Specification of the Solution Strategy

Initially, to guarantee invariants (5) and (6), the only process in the tree is *init* because it is the only active process. Also to guarantee these invariants, when an active process u activates a process v, the father of process v is set to u if v is not in the tree, thus making v a leaf. This is done by

$v.idle \;:=\; u.idle \;\wedge\; v.idle$
$\|\; v.father \;:=\; u$ if $v.father = nil \;\wedge\; \neg u.idle$

Idle leaves fall off the tree, thus guaranteeing progress condition (8), by

$$v.father := nil \qquad \text{if} \quad v.leaf \land v.idle$$

Since $init.father = nil$ is stable, we implement $claim$ $detects$ $(init.father = nil)$ by employing the familiar heuristic of Section 9.3.1, using the assignment

$$claim := (init.father = nil)$$

These arguments lead to the following program.

Program {termination detection of diffusing computations} $Q1$

> **always** {definition of leaf}
>
> $\langle [\![u \quad :: \quad u.leaf = (u.father \neq nil) \land \langle \land v \quad :: \quad v.father \neq u \rangle \rangle$
>
> **initially**
>
> $\langle [\![u \quad :: \quad u.idle = (u \neq init)$
>
> $[\![\qquad u.father = nil \qquad \text{if} \quad u \neq init \quad \sim \quad ext \qquad \text{if} \quad u = init$
>
> $\rangle$
>
> $[\![\qquad claim = false$
>
> **assign**
>
> $\langle [\![(u, v) \quad :: \quad v.idle := u.idle \land v.idle$
>
> $|| \qquad\qquad v.father := u \qquad \text{if} \quad v.father = nil \land \lnot u.idle$
>
> $\rangle$
>
> $[\![\ \langle [\![u \quad :: \quad u.idle := true \rangle$
>
> $[\![\ \langle [\![v \quad :: \quad v.father := nil \qquad \text{if} \quad v.leaf \land v.idle \rangle$
>
> $[\![\quad claim := (init.father = nil)$

end $\{Q1\}$

The proof that the program fits the solution strategy (i.e., the proof that the program satisfies (5–9)) is straightforward.

9.9.4 Refinement Step: Detecting that a Process Is a Leaf

Program $Q1$ is almost satisfactory. The problem arises in the implementation of $u.leaf$. The definition of $u.leaf$ names all processes. For reasons of efficiency we prefer statements that name variables from at most two processes; we propose a further refinement to implement this constraint.

The Solution: Informal Description

Instead of employing $u.leaf$ we employ an integer variable $u.n$: the number of sons of u. When a process v is added to the tree by making u the father of v, the value of $u.n$ is increased by one. When a process v is deleted from the tree, $v.father.n$ is decreased by one. A process u is a leaf if it has no sons (i.e., if $u.n = 0$) and its father is not nil.

The Solution Strategy: Formal Description

The specifications from the previous step carry over with one modification. In addition there is a new invariant defining $u.n$. The invariant and the modification are given next.

invariant $u.n = \langle + v : v.father = u :: 1 \rangle$ (11)

Hence

$$u.leaf \equiv (u.father \neq nil) \wedge (u.n = 0).$$

Progress condition (8) is replaced by

$$W \wedge u.n = 0 \longmapsto u.father = nil \tag{12}$$

Proof of Correctness of the Solution Strategy

Progress condition (8) follows from the definition of $u.leaf$ derived from (11), and from (12). Since all the specifications other than (8) carry over from the previous step, the correctness of the proposed strategy follows.

Derivation of a Program from the Specification of the Solution Strategy

The program follows from invariant (11) and program $Q1$.

Program {termination detection of diffusing computations} $Q2$

   initially

$$\langle [\!] \; u \;\; :: \;\; u.idle = (u \neq init) \;\; [\!] \;\; u.n = 0$$
$$[\!] \qquad u.father = nil \quad \text{if} \quad u \neq init \; \sim \; ext \quad \text{if} \quad u = init$$
$$\rangle$$
$$[\!] \qquad claim = false$$

   assign

$$\langle [\!] \; (u,v) \;\; ::$$
$$v.idle := u.idle \wedge v.idle$$
$$\| \quad v.father, u.n := u, u.n + 1 \quad \text{if} \quad v.father = nil \wedge \neg u.idle \rangle$$

$\llbracket \ \langle \llbracket \ u \ \ :: \ \ u.idle := true \rangle$

$\llbracket \ \langle \llbracket \ v \ \ ::$

$\qquad\qquad v.father, \ (v.father).n \ := \ nil, \ (v.father).n - 1$

$\qquad\qquad\quad if \ \ v.father \neq nil \ \wedge \ v.n = 0 \ \wedge \ v.idle \rangle$

$\llbracket \quad claim := (init.father = nil)$

end $\{Q2\}$

The proof of this program is left to the reader.

Efficiency

There is little synchronization across processes in this program: A statement names variables from at most two processes. An even more asynchronous program for distributed systems is developed next.

9.9.5 Refinement Step: Distributed Implementation

In $Q2$ a statement names variables local to at most two processes, whereas in the distributed program developed next, a statement names only variables local to one process and channels incident on that process. A study of the statements in $Q2$ that name local variables of two processes suggests changes in the design to obtain a more asynchronous program. The statements in $Q2$ corresponding to the addition of v as a child of u modifies $v.father$ and $u.n$, and the statement corresponding to the removal of leaf v from the tree modifies $v.father$ and $(v.father).n$. This suggests that $u.father$ or $u.n$ could be dispensed with and replaced by a variable that is defined by a weaker invariant. One solution is to dispense with $u.n$, the number of sons of u, and in its place use $u.\ell$, an *upper bound* on the number of sons of u. (The definition of $u.\ell$ is given later by invariant (15).) Progress condition (8), repeated next, is replaced by progress conditions (13) and (14).

$$W \ \wedge \ u.leaf \quad \longmapsto \quad u.father = nil \tag{8}$$

$$W \ \wedge \ u.leaf \quad \longmapsto \quad u.\ell = 0 \tag{13}$$

$$W \ \wedge \ u.\ell = 0 \quad \longmapsto \quad u.father = nil \tag{14}$$

The heuristic employed in replacing $u.n$ by $u.\ell$ is that of replacing an invariant and a progress condition by a weaker invariant and a sequence of progress conditions (see Section 9.3.3). In particular, a statement of $Q2$ that names local variables of two processes is replaced by a set of statements, each of which names variables local to *one* process and channels incident on it. For instance, the statement in $Q2$ in which $v.father$ is set to u, and $u.n$ is incremented, is replaced by two statements: The first increments $u.\ell$

(and modifies channel $(u, v).c$), and the second sets $v.father$ to u (and also modifies $(u, v).c$). Since $u.\ell$ is an upper bound on the number of u's sons, it is permissible to increment $u.\ell$ before $v.father$ is set to u. If $u.n$ is used, however, the operations of incrementing $u.n$ and setting $v.father$ to u must be concurrent.

As in Section 9.7.3, when transforming a shared-memory program into a distributed program, an idle process in the shared-memory program is considered equivalent to a process in the distributed system that is both idle *and has all its outgoing channels empty*. For instance, invariants (5) and (6) in the shared-memory program—all active processes are in the tree—is replaced in the distributed program by the following: All processes that are active *or have nonempty outgoing channels* are in the tree. This heuristic—treating a process in a shared-memory program as being similar to a process and its outgoing channels in a distributed system—is helpful in guiding the development of distributed programs from shared-memory programs.

As in the program discussed earlier, acknowledgments are used to determine whether a channel is empty. If u has received acknowledgments from v for all messages sent along $(u, v).c$, then $(u, v).c$ is empty. A clever optimization is to use the acknowledgments in a dual role: (1) determine that outgoing channels are empty and (2) determine that a process is a leaf. We assume that for each channel $(u, v).c$ along which messages are sent there is a channel $(v, u).c$ along which acknowledgments are sent.

The Solution: Informal Description

We require that $u.\ell$ be an upper bound on the number of sons of u. We design our program so that $u.\ell$ is the number of messages that u has sent for which u has yet to receive acknowledgments, and every son of u has received a message from u that it has not acknowledged. Therefore $u.\ell$ is at least the number of sons of u.

All messages received by processes in the tree are acknowledged immediately. However, if a process v that is not in the tree (i.e., $v.father = nil$) receives a message from a process u, then v is connected to the tree (i.e., $v.father := u$), and v does not acknowledge the message received from u until v is deleted from the tree.

The Solution Strategy: Formal Description

The dual role of acknowledgments is a consequence of the following important invariant:

invariant

$u.\ell = \langle + \ v \ :: \ $ number of messages in $(u,v).c$

$\qquad + $ number of acknowledgments in $(v,u).c$

$\qquad + 1 \quad$ if $\quad v.father = u \quad \sim \quad 0 \quad$ if $\quad v.father \neq u$

$\rangle$ (15)

Explanation of Invariant (15):   The value of $u.\ell$ is the number of messages u has sent minus the number of acknowledgments u has received.

Hence $u.\ell$ is the number of messages in u's outgoing channels (because these messages have not been acknowledged) plus the number of acknowledgments in u's incoming channels (because these acknowledgments have not yet been received by u) plus the number of u's sons (because every son of u has precisely one message from its father that it has not acknowledged).

Hence

$$(u.\ell = 0) \quad \Rightarrow \quad \langle \wedge \ v \ :: \ (u,v).c = null \ \wedge \ v.father \neq u \rangle \qquad \triangledown$$

We have the previous invariant (5):

invariant   The set of processes u, where $u.father \neq nil$, form a tree where the father of u in the tree is $u.father$ and, if the tree is nonempty, the root of the tree is $init$. (5)

Also,

invariant $(u.father \neq nil) \ \vee \ (u.idle \wedge \langle \wedge \ v \ :: \ (u,v).c = null \rangle)$ (16)

stable $W \ \wedge \ (u.father = nil)$ (17)

The following progress conditions were suggested earlier:

$$W \ \wedge \ u.leaf \quad \longmapsto \quad u.\ell = 0 \tag{13}$$

$$W \ \wedge \ u.\ell = 0 \quad \longmapsto \quad u.father = nil \tag{14}$$

$$claim \ \ detects \ \ (init.father = nil) \tag{9}$$

Proof of Correctness of the Solution Strategy

The proof is similar to the proofs of correctness at earlier steps in the refinement. The outline of the proof is given next.

$(init.father = nil) \quad \Rightarrow \quad W \qquad$, from (5,16)

$W \quad \longmapsto \quad (init.father = nil) \qquad$, from (13,14,17) and the stability of W

$(init.father = nil) \ \ detects \ \ W \qquad$, from the above two

$claim \ \ detects \ \ W \qquad\qquad\qquad$, from (9) and the above

Derivation of a Program from the Specification of the Solution Strategy

Invariant (15) indicates how $u.\ell$ is to be modified. The other actions are as in the previous program.

For convenience, the underlying distributed program is repeated. This program is the same as program ds in Section 9.7.1 except that initial conditions have been added.

Program {underlying distributed diffusing computation} ddc

   initially $\langle [\![\ u\ ::\ u.idle = (u \neq init)\rangle\ [\![\ \langle [\![\ (u,v)\ ::\ (u,v).c = null\rangle$

   assign

   $\langle [\![\ (u,v)\ ::\ (u,v).c\ :=\ (u,v).c\ ;m$ if $\neg u.idle$

   $[\![\ v.idle,\ m,\ (u,v).c\ :=\ false,\ \text{head}((u,v).c),\ \text{tail}((u,v).c)$

                                            if $(u,v).c \neq null$

   $\rangle$

   $[\![\ \langle [\![\ u\ ::\ u.idle\ :=\ true\rangle$

end {ddc}

In the following transformed program, a generic received message in the underlying program is denoted by msg, and a generic superposed message is denoted by ack (for acknowledgment).

Program {termination detection of a diffusing computation:
        transformed program} $Q3$

   initially

   $\langle [\![\ u\ ::\ u.idle = (u \neq init)\ [\![\ u.\ell = 0$

   $[\![$ $u.father = nil$ if $u \neq init$ $\sim$ ext if $u = init$

   $\rangle$

   $[\![$ $claim = false$ $[\![\ \langle [\![\ (u,v)\ ::\ (u,v).c = null\rangle$

   assign

   $\langle [\![\ (u,v)\ ::\ \{\text{statements about channels } (u,v)\}$

   {when an active process u sends a message m to a process v,
     it increments $u.\ell$ to maintain (15)}

   $(u,v).c,\ u.\ell\ :=\ (u,v).c\ ;m,\ u.\ell + 1$ if $\neg u.idle$

   {when v receives a message m from u it becomes active, and if v
     is not on the tree prior to receiving the message, it attaches itself

to the tree by making u its father, thus preserving (5) and (16); if v is on the tree when it receives the message, it replies to u with an acknowledgment to maintain (15)}

$\llbracket\ v.idle,\ m,\ (u,v).c\ :=\ false,\ \text{head}((u,v).c),\ \text{tail}((u,v).c)$
$\qquad\qquad\qquad\quad$ if $\ \text{head}((u,v).c) = msg$

$\Vert\ v.father\ :=\ u\qquad\qquad$ if $\ v.father = nil \land \text{head}((u,v).c) = msg$

$\Vert\ (v,u).c\ :=\ (v,u).c;\ ack$ if $\ v.father \neq nil \land \text{head}((u,v).c) = msg$

{when u receives an acknowledgment from v it decrements $u.\ell$ to maintain (15)}

$\quad\llbracket\ u.\ell,(v,u).c\ :=\ u.\ell - 1,\ \text{tail}((v,u).c)\qquad$ if $\ \text{head}(v,u).c = ack$
$\rangle$

$\llbracket\ \langle\llbracket\ u\ ::\ \{\text{statements about process } u\}$

{a process u becomes idle in the underlying computation}
$\quad u.idle\ :=\ true$

{If u's father is not nil and $u.\ell = 0$, then u is a leaf of the tree and it has no message in its outgoing channels; delete such a u from the tree by setting u's father to nil and concurrently replying to u's father with an acknowledgment; this maintains invariants (5,15,16) and guarantees progress conditions (13) and (14)}

$\quad\llbracket\ u.father, (u, u.father).c\ :=\ nil,\ (u, u.father).c;\ ack$
$\qquad\qquad$ if $\ (u.father \neq nil) \land (u.\ell = 0) \land u.idle$
$\quad\rangle$

$\llbracket\ \{\text{to implement (20)}\}$
$\quad claim\ :=\ (init.father = nil)$

end $\{Q3\}$

The proof of the program is along the lines described earlier. The proof of progress requires that all acknowledgments sent be received eventually.

Exercise 9.4 Complete the development of a distributed program from $R4$ for a system with buffered channels. Consider the statement

$\quad b, u.delta\ :=\ b\ \cup\ \{u\} - u.delta, empty$
$\qquad\qquad$ if $\ u.idle \land u$'s outgoing channels are empty.

The strategy is to employ a token with b and $claim$ as fields of the token. A process u modifies b and $u.delta$ only if u holds the token. To minimize the rate at which the token is transferred between processes, a process u sends the token to a process v only if u is in b, u is idle and its outgoing channels are empty, and v is not in b. A disadvantage of this program is that the token contains b, and it requires N bits to store b, where N is the number of processes in the system. In most practical situations, the size of N is not a problem because messages (and the token is sent as a message) can be quite large without imposing substantial overhead. However, derive a program in which the token contains $O(\log N)$ bits.

Hint: Number the processes with distinct numbers from 0 to $N - 1$. The token travels in a ring visiting process $(i + 1)$ mod N after visiting process i. Employ an index k, where $0 \leq k < N$, and define b as the set of processes between k and the current position of the token (in the direction in which the token travels around the ring). The index k requires $O(\log N)$ bits. (See Chandy and Misra [1986a] for a solution.)   ▽

Exercise 9.5 This exercise deals with the use of hierarchies in reactive programs. The underlying computation is carried out by two sets of processes, in which each set is tightly coupled in the sense that there are channels from each process in the set to most of the other processes in the set, and processes within each set communicate with one another frequently until termination. The two sets are loosely coupled to each other. Assume that there are precisely two channels between the two sets, one in each direction. Use a hierarchy of detecting processes to detect termination. For each set, one detecting process detects termination of computation within that set. A third detecting process detects termination of the entire system; the other two detecting processes communicate with it. Design a program along these lines. Extend the design to handle arbitrary numbers of sets of tightly coupled processes, where the coupling between sets is loose. (Such systems occur in practice when workstations in a given region are tightly coupled and there is much less communication between regions.)   ▽

Exercise 9.6 In the diffusing computation program, initially there is only one active process: *init*. Extend the program that detects termination of diffusing computations to the case where initially there are an arbitrary number of active processes. The set of processes that are active initially is given.   ▽

Exercise 9.7 Extend the program that detects termination of diffusing computations to allow *init* to determine the state of each process at termination. To make matters simple, assume that each process u has a local variable $u.state$ that represents its state. The state of a process does not change while the process is idle. Therefore the state of a process does not change after

W holds. The problem is for *init* to detect W and to determine the value of *u.state* when W holds, for each u. Three approaches are outlined next; design programs for each one.

1. After *init* detects W, it initiates a (superposed) diffusing computation to collect the value of *u.state* for each u.

2. A process u sends *u.state* with its acknowledgment to *u.father*, in the operation that deletes u from the tree. Since a process may be added to, and deleted from, a tree several times, a process u may send *u.state* to *u.father* several times; therefore it is necessary to be able to recognize the most recent value of *u.state*. Process u keeps a count *u.count* of the number of times u has sent *u.state* to *u.father*; the message u sends to *u.father* is the triple $(u, u.state, u.count)$, thus allowing later values of *u.state* to be recognized. Each process maintains a set of triples $(u, u.state, u.count)$ with at most one triple for each u. Upon receiving a triple $(u, u.state, u.count)$, a process retains only the triple containing the latest value of *u.state*. When a process removes itself from the tree, it sends its set of triples and its own triple to its father. The set of triples that *init* has when *init* detects W gives the final values of *u.state* for each u.

3. The program is essentially that just outlined in (2). The only difference is in the way that later values of *u.state* are recognized. Instead of a set of triples, a process v uses two bags *v.pos* and *v.neg* of pairs $(u, u.state)$. The bag *v.neg* contains "old" states, and *v.pos* contains states that may be old as well as states that may be current. Each process u has a local variable *u.old*, where *u.old* is the value of *u.state* when u was last deleted from the tree. When u deletes itself from the tree it adds $(u, u.old)$ to *u.neg*, $(u, u.state)$ to *u.pos*, sends *u.neg* and *u.pos* to *u.father*, sets *u.neg* and *u.pos* to *empty*, and updates *u.old*. A process v on receiving bags *u.neg*, *u.pos*, adds *u.neg* to *v.neg*, and *u.pos* to *v.pos*. The final states are contained in *init.pos* − *init.neg* when *init* detects W.

Give invariants that define *u.neg* and *u.pos*. Suppose *u.state* is a number; show that in this case a process v can employ a pair $(u, u.k)$, for each u, instead of bags *v.neg* and *v.pos*, where *u.k* is the sum of the values of *u.state* in *v.pos* − the sum of the values of *u.state* in *v.neg*.

Compare the efficiency of each of the methods in two cases: (1) computation proceeds for a long time, and processes are added to and deleted from the tree several times before termination, and (2) computation proceeds for a short time, and processes are added to and deleted from the tree very few times before termination. (See Misra and Chandy [1982].)   ▽

Summary

The intent of this chapter is to describe an approach to the design of reactive programs. The design heuristics are illustrated first by means of a simple example—detecting that the number of statement executions in an underlying program exceeds 10—and later by means of an important problem: termination detection. Separation of concerns is crucial to the design of these programs. In the initial stages of design an obvious program is proposed. The decoupling heuristic is applied repeatedly to decouple synchronous modifications of superposed bottleneck variables from the underlying computation. In the early design stages, little attention is paid to the target architectures. Later, a method for implementing shared variables by means of tokens is employed to derive an asynchronous shared-memory program. This program is modified, in an obvious way, to obtain a distributed program.

Programs are derived by stepwise refinement. At each step, the specification proposed in the previous step is refined. The proof obligation is to show that the specification proposed at each step implies the specification in the previous step. Much of the work in proving the correctness of UNITY programs lies in proving the correctness of specifications; program derivation from refined specifications is usually straightforward.

In this chapter, as in all others, we have attempted to illustrate the unity of the program design task. We have applied the same methodology of program construction to reactive systems as we did for nonreactive systems in the earlier chapters. Furthermore, we found it useful to ignore the target architecture in the early stages of design.

Bibliographic Notes

The notion of reactive programs is from Pnueli [1987]. The relation *detects* is a generalization of the *probe* primitive for communication introduced in Martin [1985]. The first design of a termination-detection program in this chapter is from Chandy and Misra [1986a]. Termination detection algorithms for diffusing computations are proposed in Dijkstra and Scholten [1980] and Chang [1982]; the material in this chapter on diffusing computations is based on the former paper. The memory-efficient programs in this chapter are motivated by van de Snepscheut [1987]. There is an immense body of work on termination detection; Francez [1980] is one of the earlier works, and Apt [1986] includes a review of correctness proofs of termination-detection programs.

CHAPTER 10

Global Snapshots

10.1   Introduction

The problem treated in this chapter is how to record the state of a given underlying computation. Recording the state of a program is called "taking a global snapshot." State recording is useful for checkpointing and for detecting stable properties. The goal in checkpointing is to record a state in which the underlying computation can be restarted should a hardware malfunction be detected. One way to detect a stable property of an underlying computation is to record its state: If the recorded state has the required property, the current state also has that property, because the property is stable. This approach can be used to detect termination, deadlock, or any other stable property. This chapter presents methods of recording global states of programs executing on asynchronous architectures.

The problem of recording the state of an underlying computation is a fundamental problem in asynchronous systems. It arises in different guises in a variety of situations. Luckily, the problem is simple and admits several straightforward solutions. Specifying the problem formally is one of its more difficult aspects.

Recording the state of a sequential program is straightforward: The underlying program is interrupted (i.e., temporarily halted), its state is recorded, and then the program is resumed. Recording the state of a synchronous, shared-memory, parallel program is also straightforward: At a predetermined time each processor records the portion of memory for which it is responsible. The problem is not trivial in the case of asynchronous parallel programs because there is no common clock; therefore all processes cannot record their states at the same time. The problem is more interesting in the case of distributed systems because the state of a channel (i.e., the sequence of messages in transit along it) cannot be read by a single process—the state is determined by the cooperation of all processes that employ the channel.

The following simple example demonstrates some of the difficulties associated with recording the state of an asynchronous parallel program.

Example 10.1

Consider the following program.

Program EG

    declare x, y, z : integer

    initially $x, y, z = 0, 0, 0$

    assign $x := z + 1 \ \| \ y := x \ \| \ z := y$

end $\{EG\}$

A state of this program is a triple of values, of x, y, and z, respectively. A little thought shows that the program admits only the sequence of states

$$(0,0,0) \rightarrow (1,0,0) \rightarrow (1,1,0) \rightarrow (1,1,1) \rightarrow (2,1,1) \rightarrow \ldots$$

The program satisfies

invariant $(x \geq y) \wedge (y \geq z) \wedge (z+1 \geq x)$.

If the value of x is recorded in state $(0,0,0)$, and the values of y and z are recorded in state $(1,1,0)$, then the recorded state is $(0,1,0)$; this state does not arise in any computation. Therefore some care should be taken in recording values of variables in such cases. $\triangledown$

10.1.1 Structure of the Chapter

The problem of recording global states is specified in Section 10.2. All the solutions to the problem are based on a single idea, described in Section 10.3. Section 10.4 contains simple programs derived from the central idea. More efficient programs are developed in Section 10.5. Methods for recording sequences of states by employing logical clocks are discussed in Section 10.6.

10.2   Specification

To simplify exposition, we treat the problem of recording a state of a program precisely once. Extending the recording algorithm for repeated execution is trivial.

It is required to transform a given underlying program (using superposition) such that the transformed program records a state of the underlying computation. The recorded state is one that can arise in the execution of the underlying program between the points at which recording is initiated and completed. Some notation is introduced next to formalize the specification.

Recording is initiated when a superposed boolean variable, *begun*, is set *true*. Variable *begun* is stable; once it holds, it continues to hold thereafter. It is required that the recording complete within finite time of *begun* being *true*. How, when, or even whether *begun* is set *true* is not a concern here.

In the following, *state* means state of the underlying program. The notation $[s0]\ \mathbf{v}\ [s1]$, where $s0$ and $s1$ are states and $\mathbf{v}$ is a finite sequence of statements of the underlying program, means that starting in state $s0$ execution of the sequence of statements $\mathbf{v}$ results in state $s1$. We use a **bold** lower-case letter to denote a sequence of statements.

Let *init* be the state in which recording is initiated, i.e., *init* is the state in which *begun* is set *true*. Let *rec* be a state recorded by the transformed program. We require that there exist sequences $\mathbf{u}$ and $\mathbf{v}$ such that, for any state *cur* that occurs during execution after the recording is complete,

$[init]$ **u** $[rec]$ $\wedge$ $[rec]$ **v** $[cur]$.

In other words, there exists a computation **u** of the underlying program that takes it from its initial state, *init*, to the recorded state, *rec*, and there exists a computation **v** that takes the underlying program from the recorded state, *rec*, to the current state, *cur*.

Associated with each variable x of the underlying program is a superposed boolean variable $x.done$, where $x.done$ holds if and only if a value of x has been recorded by the superposed program; thus $\neg x.done$ holds before x is recorded and $x.done$ holds after x is recorded. The recording is complete if and only if $x.done$ holds for all underlying variables x. Since a state is recorded only once, we require that $x.done$ be stable.

A value of x is recorded in a superposed variable $x.rec$ for each x. The state *rec* is given by the values of $x.rec$, for all x. The current state, *cur*, is given by the current values of x, for all x. The complete specification appears in Section 10.2.1, next.

10.2.1 Specification of Recording

invariant $\langle \wedge\, x \; :: \; x.done \rangle$ $\Rightarrow$ $\langle \exists\, \mathbf{u,v} \; :: \; [init]\; \mathbf{u}\; [rec] \;\wedge\; [rec]\; \mathbf{v}\; [cur] \rangle$

$begun$ $\mapsto$ $\langle \wedge\, x \; :: \; x.done \rangle$

Informal Explanation

The progress condition states that the recording algorithm terminates within finite time of its initiation. The invariant states that the recorded state is one that occurs in *some* computation after *init* and before the current state. The invariant *does not* state that the recorded state occurred between *init* and *cur*; it merely states that the recorded state *could* occur between *init* and *cur* as a result of some execution sequence. In terms of a state-transition system, there exists a path from the initial state to the current state via the recorded state.

10.2.2 A Simple Recording Program

An obvious program to implement the specification in Section 10.2.1 is to copy the value of x into $x.rec$, for all x, in a single assignment statement.

Program {transformation of the underlying computation} *P1*

  initially $\langle \| \; x \; :: \; x.done = \mathit{false} \rangle$

  add $\langle \| \; x \; :: \; x.rec, x.done := x, \mathit{true} \quad \text{if} \quad begun \wedge \neg x.done \rangle$

end {*P1*}

The proof of correctness of *P1* is trivial.

This program is suitable for sequential machines but is inappropriate for parallel asynchronous systems because the added statement (which records values of all variables) names all variables in the underlying program. Next we propose a stronger specification from which we can derive programs for asynchronous recording of variable values.

10.2.3 A Refinement of the Specification for Recording

At any point during execution of the transformed program, define a possible state, *partial*, of the underlying program as follows. For an underlying variable x, define $x.partial$, the value of x in state *partial*:

$$x.partial = x.rec \qquad \text{if} \quad \neg x.done$$
$$\qquad\qquad x \qquad\qquad \text{if} \quad x.done \quad \sim$$

A refinement of the previous specification, using *partial*, is given next.

invariant

$$begun \quad \Rightarrow \quad \langle \exists \ \mathbf{u,v} : \mathbf{v} \text{ names only recorded variables } ::$$
$$[init] \ \mathbf{u} \ [partial] \ \wedge \ [partial] \ \mathbf{v} \ [cur] \rangle$$
$$begun \quad \mapsto \quad \langle \wedge \ x \quad :: \quad x.done \rangle$$

Informal Explanation

The state *partial* is a combination of the two states *rec* and *cur*; the value of a recorded variable x—i.e., one for which $x.done$ holds—is the same in *partial* and *rec*; the value of an unrecorded variable is the same in *partial* and *cur*. When recording is initiated, *partial* and *init* are identical. When all variables are recorded, *partial* and *rec* are identical. Therefore this specification implies the specification in Section 10.2.1.

It is important to note that recording the value of a variable does not change *partial*. To see this, consider the recording of a variable x. Prior to the recording, $\neg x.done$ holds, and hence $x.partial = x$. After the recording, which sets $x.rec$ to x, $x.done$ holds, and hence $x.partial = x.rec$. Therefore recording x leaves $x.partial$ unchanged. Also note that in the specification, the sequence $\mathbf{v}$ names only recorded variables, i.e., for all variables x named in $\mathbf{v}$, $x.done$ holds. Thus execution of $\mathbf{v}$ leaves unrecorded variables unchanged. Therefore execution of $\mathbf{v}$ leaves *partial* unchanged.

Example 10.2

Table 10.1 shows an execution sequence interspersed with recordings for program *EG* of Example 10.1. As an exercise, determine the values of sequences $\mathbf{u,v}$ at every step in the example.

Events: Recording/ State Transition	State	Recorded Variables	partial	x.rec	y.rec	z.rec
Initially	0,0,0	none	0,0,0	—	—	—
State transition	1,0,0	none	1,0,0	—	—	—
Record x	1,0,0	x	1,0,0	1	—	—
Record y	1,0,0	x, y	1,0,0	1	0	—
State transition	1,1,0	x, y	1,0,0	1	0	—
Record z	1,1,0	x, y, z	1,0,0	1	0	0
State transition	1,1,1	x, y, z	1,0,0	1	0	0

Table 10.1 A scenario of state recording.

10.3   The Central Idea in Recording

The central idea in global state recording is rule R (where R stands for Recording), given next. It is no exaggeration to say that rule R is the foundation of most global snapshot programs. All programs in this chapter implement this rule.

10.3.1 Rule R

When a statement in the underlying program is executed, either

- all variables named in the statement are recorded, or

- all variables named in the statement are unrecorded.

To implement rule R, we require that no statement of the underlying program be executed in which some variables have been recorded and others have not been recorded. Rule R specifies an interval in which the value of a variable can be recorded: The value of x can be recorded any time after the recording is initiated and before the execution of a statement that names x and some other recorded variable. Recording programs differ in the selection of the point in the interval at which a value is recorded. The reader may construct different recording programs in which the value recorded for x is the value of x at the beginning, middle, or end of the interval. The central result is that any program that implements rule R satisfies the invariant of Section 10.2.3.

Next we outline the proof of this result, later presenting a complete proof. The invariant holds when recording is initiated with **u**,**v** as *null* sequences. We show that the invariant is maintained by the execution of a statement t in the underlying computation in which (1) all variables named in t are unrecorded or (2) all variables named in t are recorded. In the former case, since **v** names only recorded variables, **v** and t have no variables in common. Statements with no variables in common can be executed in arbitrary order without affecting the state that obtains after they are executed. Therefore the invariant is maintained, with **u** becoming **u**;t and **v** remaining unchanged. In the latter case, *partial* is unchanged and hence the invariant is maintained, with **u** remaining unchanged and **v** becoming **v**;t. Next the complete proof is presented.

10.3.2 Proof of Correctness of Rule R

At the point at which recording is initiated (i.e., *begun* is set *true*):

$init = cur \quad \wedge \quad partial = cur.$

Hence the invariant is satisfied with **u** and **v** as *null* sequences. Suppose that the invariant holds at a point in computation with some values of **u**,**v**. We consider three cases that could possibly change *partial* or *cur*. Note that *init* remains unchanged by program execution once *begun* has become *true*.

1. Value of an unrecorded variable is recorded. As shown in Section 10.2.3, recording a variable value leaves *partial* unchanged. Clearly, *cur* is unaffected by a recording. Hence the invariant holds with the same values of **u**,**v**.

    In the following two cases we consider execution of some statement t of the underlying program. Let cur' denote the program state before execution of t and cur denote the state after execution of t. Let $partial'$, $partial$ be obtained from cur', cur, respectively, using the definition in Section 10.2.3. From the invariant,

    $[init] \quad \mathbf{u} \quad [partial'] \quad \wedge \quad [partial'] \quad \mathbf{v} \quad [cur'].$

    Because cur results from cur' by execution of t, we have

    $[cur'] \quad t \quad [cur]$

    To show that the invariant holds, we will show $\mathbf{u}'$, $\mathbf{v}'$ such that

    $[init] \quad \mathbf{u}' \quad [partial] \quad \wedge \quad [partial] \quad \mathbf{v}' \quad [cur].$

    The execution of t does not affect the values of $x.done$ or $x.rec$.

2. Statement t names no recorded variable. For this case, we first prove that

    $[partial'] \quad t \quad [partial].$

That is, executing t in state $partial'$ results in state $partial$. Consider a variable x. If $x.done$ holds in the transformed program execution prior to execution of t, then t does not name x (from the assumption for this case); therefore the execution of t starting in $partial'$ leaves the value of x unchanged—i.e., $x = x.partial'$ both before and after the execution of t. If $\neg x.done$ holds in the transformed program prior to execution of t, then $x.partial' = x.cur'$; execution of t results in the value of x being set to $x.cur$. Therefore the value of x resulting from execution of t in state $partial'$

$$= x.partial' \quad \text{if } x.done \quad \sim \quad x.cur \quad \text{if } \neg x.done$$

$$= x.rec \quad \text{if } x.done \quad \sim \quad x.cur \quad \text{if } \neg x.done \qquad \text{, definition of } partial'$$

$$= x.partial \qquad \qquad \qquad \qquad \qquad \qquad \qquad \text{, definition of } partial$$

Hence

$[partial'] \; t \; [partial]$.

Now, from

$[init] \;\; \mathbf{u} \;\; [partial'] \quad$ and $\quad [partial'] \; t \; [partial]$,

we obtain

$[init] \;\; \mathbf{u};t \;\; [partial]$.

Next we show that $[partial] \; \mathbf{v'} \; [cur]$, for some $\mathbf{v'}$ that names only recorded variables. We have

$([partial'] \;\; \mathbf{v} \;\; [cur']) \;\; \wedge \;\; ([cur'] \; t \; [cur])$.

Hence

$[partial'] \;\; \mathbf{v};t \;\; [cur]$.

Since $\mathbf{v}$ names only recorded variables (from the invariant) and t names only unrecorded variables (from the assumption for this case), there is no variable common to $\mathbf{v}$ and t. Therefore execution of $\mathbf{v};t$ has the same effect as $t;\mathbf{v}$. Hence

$[partial'] \;\; t;\mathbf{v} \;\; [cur]$.

That is,

$([partial'] \;\; t \;\; [partial]) \;\; \wedge \;\; ([partial] \;\; \mathbf{v} \;\; [cur])$.

Thus we have shown $[partial] \; \mathbf{v} \; [cur]$. Since $\mathbf{v}$ names only recorded variables in $partial'$ and every recorded variable in $partial'$ is also recorded in $partial$, $\mathbf{v}$ names only recorded variables in $partial$.

3. Statement t names some recorded variable. From the definitions of $partial$, $partial'$, cur, cur', and rec:

$$x.partial = x.rec \qquad \text{if} \quad x.done \quad \sim \quad x.cur \qquad \text{if} \quad \neg x.done$$

$$x.partial' = x.rec \qquad \text{if} \quad x.done \quad \sim \quad x.cur' \qquad \text{if} \quad \neg x.done$$

Hence if $x.done$ holds, then $x.partial' = x.partial$. Now, from rule R, t names only recorded variables. Therefore if $\neg x.done$, then $x.cur = x.cur'$, and hence $x.partial' = x.partial$. Therefore in all cases,

$$x.partial' = x.partial$$

or

$$partial' = partial.$$

Hence we deduce $[init]$ **u** $[partial]$ from $[init]$ **u** $[partial']$. Also from $[partial']$ **v** $[cur']$ t $[cur]$ we have $[partial]$ **v**;t $[cur]$. Note that the recorded variables in $partial'$ and $partial$ are the same and that **v**;t names only recorded variables. This completes the proof for this case and completes the proof of the theorem.   ▽

To prove that a recording program is correct it is sufficient to prove that it implements rule R, and that all variables are recorded within finite time of the initiation of recording.

For a structured variable such as an array, a record, or a sequence, any consistent definition of "variable" can be used in interpreting rule R. For instance, consider a statement $B[3] := D[2]$. If each element of arrays B and D is treated as a "variable" in interpreting rule R, then either both $B[3]$ and $D[2]$ must be recorded before the statement is executed, or both $B[3]$ and $D[2]$ must be unrecorded before the statement is executed, independent of whether other elements of B and D are recorded. On the other hand, if the entire array is treated as a variable in interpreting R, either the entire arrays B and D are recorded before the execution of the statement or the entire arrays are unrecorded before the execution of the statement. In designing global snapshot algorithms for distributed systems it is helpful to treat all variables local to a process as part of a single structured variable that is entirely recorded or entirely unrecorded. Also, we can treat each message as a distinct variable. The smaller the size of the variable in our interpretation, the more the amount of memory required to store the variable $x.done$; however, it is usually easier to record a small amount of memory in an atomic action than a large amount.

Exercise 10.1   Is R$'$, the following alternative proposal to rule R, correct? Prove or give a counterexample.

Rule R$'$:   When a statement in the underlying program is executed, either all variables named in the right side of the statement (and all subscripts) are recorded, or all such variables are unrecorded.

What if "right side" in rule R$'$ is replaced by "left side"?   ▽

10.4   Simple Programs for State Recording

10.4.1 Asynchronous Shared-Memory Architectures

Recording in asynchronous shared-memory systems can be accomplished as follows: Processes are halted temporarily at *arbitrary* times. A process, once halted, remains halted until the global system state has been recorded. When all processes are halted, their states are recorded. After all process states have been recorded, the processes are restarted at *arbitrary* times. The program trivially satisfies rule R.

10.4.2 Distributed Architectures

We employ a process, called the *central* process, for recording global states. To record a state the following program is used.

1. The central process sends a message to each process requesting it to halt execution of the underlying computation.

2. After receiving the message, a process halts and sends an acknowledgment to the central process indicating that it has suspended the underlying computation.

3. After receiving acknowledgments from all processes, the central process sends a message to each process requesting it to record its state.

4. After receiving the message, a process records its state and sends the recorded state to the central process.

5. After receiving recorded process states from all processes, the central process sends a message to each process instructing it to resume execution of the underlying computation.

6. After receiving the message, a process resumes execution of the underlying computation and sends an acknowledgment to the central process.

7. After receiving acknowledgments from all processes, the central process is ready to initiate another recording.

A total of six messages per process is employed in this program. It is evident that the program satisfies rule R.

In this discussion a critical aspect of recording distributed system states has been ignored: How are channel states to be recorded? A process cannot read a channel state directly. However, the state of a channel can be computed from the sequences of messages sent and received along the channel: A channel state is the sequence of messages sent and not received along that channel (assuming that channels are empty initially). To compute the states of channels, when the state of a process is recorded, the sequences of messages that the process has sent and received along all its incident channels can be recorded in the usual manner. The recorded channel state is *computed* as the recorded sequence of messages sent along the channel excluding the recorded sequence of messages received along the channel. More formally, the state of a channel c, *c.state*, is a sequence of messages that satisfies

$$c.sent = c.received;\ c.state$$

where *c.sent* and *c.received* are the sequences of messages sent along channel c and received along channel c, respectively. For purposes of computation, we write *c.state* as a function of *c.sent* and *c.received*:

$$c.state = c.sent \ominus c.received$$

where $\ominus$ indicates deletion of a prefix.

Variable *c.sent* is local to the process that sends messages along channel c, and variable *c.received* is local to the process that receives messages along channel c. The recorded state of c is *defined* as a function of the recorded values of local variables *c.sent* and *c.received*:

$$c.state.rec = c.sent.rec \ominus c.received.rec$$

where, as before, *x.rec* represents the recorded value of x.

A disadvantage of recording *c.sent* and *c.received* is that a great deal of memory may be required to store these variables. Since only the "difference" between *c.sent* and *c.received* must be computed, it is not necessary to store entire sequences. We propose a more efficient scheme. Each process sends a special message, called a *marker*, on each outgoing channel after the process halts its underlying computation and before it records its state. Thus *c.sent.rec* is the sequence of messages sent along c before the marker. From the definition, *c.received.rec* is the sequence of messages received along c before the receiving process along c records its state. Therefore *c.sent.rec* $\ominus$ *c.received.rec* is the sequence of messages received by the process along channel c after recording its state and before receiving the marker along c. This difference can be computed by the process that receives the marker from c.

Efficiency

The program of Section 10.2.2 is efficient for sequential machines. The adaptation of this program for parallel asynchronous systems is somewhat inefficient because there are two synchronization points at which no process is executing the underlying computation: One point at which all processes have stopped and no process has recorded its state, and a later point at which all processes have stopped and all processes have recorded their states. The requirement that all processes communicate with the central process in the distributed program may appear unacceptable for some distributed architectures because the cost of establishing channels between a central process and every other process is high. It is not necessary, however, for all processes to communicate directly with the central process; a diffusing computation (see Section 9.9) in which each process relays messages to its neighbors can be employed. In certain architectures there is a bus from a central processor to all other processors, and this bus can be used effectively to record states.

10.5   Efficient Programs for State Recording

10.5.1 Asynchronous Shared-Memory Architectures

Rule R requires that when a statement t is executed, either all variables named in t are unrecorded or all variables named in t have been recorded. Suppose that a variable y named in statement t has been recorded—i.e., $y.done$ holds— and suppose that another variable x named in t has not been recorded—i.e., $\neg x.done$ holds. Then rule R tells us that x should be recorded before t is executed. If x is recorded concurrently with the execution of t, however, the recorded value of x is the value before the execution of t, thus satisfying rule R. This observation leads to the following transformation of each statement t in the underlying program where "t names x" denotes that variable x appears in statement t:

$$\langle \| \; x \; : \; t \text{ names } x \; \wedge \; \neg x.done \; :: \; x.rec, x.done := x, true$$
$$\text{if} \; \langle \exists \, y \; : \; t \text{ names } y \; :: \; y.done \rangle$$
$$\rangle$$
$$\| \; t$$

Next we turn our attention to progress: Every variable is to be recorded within finite time of *begun* being set *true*. Suppose that recording is initiated by recording one specific variable, *first*. The recording of *first* is done by executing

$$first.rec, \; first.done \; := \; first, \; true \quad \text{if} \quad begun \; \wedge \; \neg first.done$$

Now consider a variable x that is named with *first* in some statement t. Since t is executed eventually, it follows that x is recorded within finite time of *first* being recorded. By the same argument, all variables named in a statement are recorded within finite time of the recording of any variable named in that statement. Define a reflexive, symmetric binary relation *appears-with* for a given program as follows:

$$x \; appears\text{-}with \; y \; \equiv$$
$$\langle \exists \text{ a statement } t \text{ in the program} :: (t \text{ names } x) \wedge (t \text{ names } y) \rangle.$$

Then, formalizing the previous argument, it can be shown that

$$x.done \ \land \ x \ appears\text{-}with \ y \ \longmapsto \ y.done \ .$$

Define *appears-with** as the transitive closure of *appears-with*. Then it follows from the preceding progress condition that

$$x.done \ \land \ x \ appears\text{-}with^* \ y \ \longmapsto \ y.done \ .$$

Thus within finite time of *first* being recorded, all variables x, for which *first appears-with** x, are recorded. If, for a variable y, $\neg(first \ appears\text{-}with^* \ y)$, then *first* and y belong to two disjoint subsets of variables; each statement names variables from one subset only. Such a program can be considered as consisting of independent programs; state recording can be applied independently to each program.

    The complete transformed program follows.

Program {**transformation of underlying program**} *P2*
    initially $\langle \| \ x \ \ :: \ \ x.done = false \rangle$
    transform
        each statement t in the underlying program to
        $\langle \| \ x \ : \ t$ names $x \ \ \land \ \ \neg x.done \ \ :: \ \ x.rec, x.done \ := \ x, true$
                       if $\langle \exists \ y \ : \ t$ names $y \ \ :: \ \ y.done \rangle$
        $\rangle$
        $\| \ t$
    add
        $\|$ $first.rec, \ first.done \ := \ first, \ true$ if $begun \ \land \ \neg first.done$
end {*P2*}

10.5.2 Distributed Architectures

The only problem with employing program *P2* in a distributed system is that the state of a channel cannot be read directly by a process. The technique for recording channel states, described earlier, is employed again; define the recorded state of a channel as the difference between the recorded sequence of messages sent along the channel and the recorded sequence of messages received along the channel:

$$c.state.rec = c.sent.rec \ominus c.received.rec$$

Markers can be used, as described earlier: The recorded state of a channel c is the sequence of messages received on the channel after the receiving process records its state and before a marker is received on the channel. The outline of the program employing markers is as follows:

1. Let *initiator* be a process that initiates the recording by recording its own state and sending markers on all outgoing channels.

2. A process that has not recorded its state, on receiving a marker, records its state and sends a marker on each of its outgoing channels.

3. The state of a channel is recorded by the process receiving messages along the channel—it is the sequence of messages received after the receiver's state is recorded and before the marker is received along that channel.

It can be shown, using similar arguments as for *P2*, that this scheme records a state of the processes and channels that are reachable from the *initiator* process (via a sequence of directed channels starting at *initiator*).

10.6   Logical Clocks

We introduce the notion of *logical clocks* and show how they may be used in state recording. We limit our discussion to distributed systems.

Let **E** be a finite sequence of statement executions of a distributed program. We associate a nonnegative integer $e.m$ with each statement execution e in **E**; we call $e.m$ the *logical time* of e. The logical times satisfy the following constraints:

1. For any two statement executions e, f in **E** where e, f are on the same process, $e.m < f.m$ if and only if e precedes f in **E**.

2. For any two statement executions e, f in **E** where the effect of e is to send a message and the effect of f is to receive that message, $e.m < f.m$.

Note: If e precedes f in **E** it may not be the case that $e.m < f.m$.   ▽

Now we show that statement executions in **E** performed in any order of ascending logical times result in the same system state. More formally, let the initial state of the system be $S0$. Let **z** be any permutation of **E** in which the logical times are nondecreasing (i.e., if e precedes f in **z** then $e.m \leq f.m$). Let *cur* be the system state that results by executing **E** starting in state $S0$. Then

$$[S0] \quad \mathbf{z} \quad [cur].$$

The proof of this claim is very similar to the proof of case (2) for rule R (see Section 10.3). For empty sequence **E**, $\mathbf{z} = \mathbf{E}$ and $cur = S0$. Now consider a sequence $(\mathbf{E}; e)$. Let **z** be a permutation of **E** and $\mathbf{z}'$ be a permutation of $(\mathbf{E}; e)$ where the logical times are ascending in both $\mathbf{z}, \mathbf{z}'$. Using induction it can be shown that the states obtained after executions of **E** and **z** are the same, and hence the states obtained after $(\mathbf{E}; e)$ and $(\mathbf{z}; e)$ are the same. We leave it to the reader to show that the same state is produced by $(\mathbf{z}; e)$ and $\mathbf{z}'$.

We next describe how logical time can be implemented in a distributed manner. Associated with each process u is a nonnegative integer variable $u.m$, called the logical clock of u; $u.m$ is initially 0. To satisfy the constraints on logical times the following rules are employed to modify $u.m$:

1. $u.m$ is increased concurrently with the execution of each statement in u. The logical time assigned to a statement execution is the value assigned to $u.m$ concurrently with that statement execution.

2. A message sent by u is tagged (i.e., timestamped) with the value that is assigned to $u.m$ concurrently with sending the message.

3. Concurrently with v receiving a message with timestamp k, $v.m$ is assigned a value that is greater than k.

Note: In rule 1 $u.m$ can be increased by an arbitrary amount; in rule 3 $v.m$ can be assigned any value greater than k. $\triangledown$

10.6.1 Applications of Logical Clocks

An obvious application of logical clocks is in global state recording. Each process u records its state when $u.m = K$, where K is some constant. A message is recorded as being in a channel if the logical time at which the message is sent is at or before K and the logical time at which the message is received is after K.

Some algorithms rely on a total order of statement executions. Logical time is a way to obtain a total order of all statement executions—ties between statement executions with the same logical times are broken by employing process indices. An example of an algorithm that relies on a total ordering of all statement executions is a mutual exclusion program that guarantees that processes enter critical sections in the order (of logical times) in which they start to wait.

Exercise 10.2   Explore algorithms for global snapshots in distributed systems where each process has access to a common global clock, paying particular attention to the determination of channel states. $\triangledown$

Exercise 10.3   Consider a distributed system consisting of two processes u, v, connected only by a directed channel from u to v. Given two global snapshots, determine conditions under which the states of u and of the channel in the first snapshot, composed with the state of v in the second snapshot, constitute a global snapshot. Investigate in general the possibility of obtaining global snapshots from asynchronous snapshots of subsystems. $\triangledown$

Summary

Rule R is the basis of programs to record global states. This rule applies regardless of architecture. The generality of the rule suggests the potential of a unified approach to programming, independent of architectural considerations. It is preferable to propose a general rule and then to develop minor variations in programs necessitated by architectural idiosyncrasies and efficiency, rather than to develop new programs for each kind of architecture.

Global state recording plays a key role in detecting stable properties; this issue is discussed further in the next chapter.

Bibliographic Notes

The marker algorithm for taking global snapshots of distributed systems is from Chandy and Lamport [1985]. A clear exposition of the marker algorithm is given in Dijkstra [1985]. The problem of recording global states of transaction-based distributed system is formulated and solved in Fischer, Griffeth, and Lynch [1982]. In Lamport [1978], the notion of logical clocks is introduced and its importance in the study of distributed systems is illustrated; in that paper, the use of timestamps to order operations is attributed to Paul Johnson and Robert Thomas. The use of timestamps in solving the mutual exclusion problem is in Lamport [1978] and Ricart and Agrawala [1981].

CHAPTER 11

Stability Detection

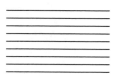

11.1   Introduction

The primary goal of this chapter is to present a methodology for the design of programs to detect stable properties. A secondary goal is to discuss two important deadlock problems: database deadlock and communication deadlock.

Detection problems become simpler when two concerns are separated. The first concern is common to all detection problems: The superposed program is required to detect a property of an *ongoing* underlying computation. It is more difficult to determine properties of a *dynamic* system than of a *static* system. A brute-force approach is to halt the underlying computation, thus dealing only with static systems, but such a solution is often inefficient. The second concern is specific to a given detection problem: How to develop an efficient program to determine whether the specified stable property holds for a given state of the underlying program. Here we are dealing with a given state—which is static—and the concern is to exploit the given stable property to derive efficient programs.

The global snapshot technique of Chapter 10 suggests how to separate the concerns. First record a global state of the underlying computation and then determine whether the *static* recorded state has the specified property. The global snapshot program takes care of the first concern; this chapter focuses on the second one.

A general detection strategy is proposed and proved in Section 11.2. Section 11.3 describes solutions to determine reachability in static graphs; these solutions form the basis for determining whether a recorded state is deadlocked. Database deadlock is described in Section 11.4, and communication deadlock in Section 11.5.

11.2   A General Detection Strategy

For convenience, we repeat the generic detection problem described in Chapters 7 and 9. Apply superposition to an underlying program with a (superposed) boolean variable *claim*, where *claim* detects a given stable property W of the underlying computation, i.e.,

>   *claim   detects   W.*

Recall that this is equivalent to the following invariant and progress condition:

invariant   *claim* $\Rightarrow$ W
W $\mapsto$ *claim*

We propose a detection strategy employing a superposed variable *rec* that is used to store recorded states of the underlying computation. The value of W in a state s is denoted by $W(s)$. Define *claim* as follows:

> *claim* $\equiv$ $W(rec)$.

The initial value of *rec* is such that $\neg W(rec)$ holds. The solution strategy is

> *rec* := a global state of the underlying computation   if $\neg W(rec)$.

In operational terms, the strategy is to record the global state of the underlying computation in *rec* from time to time, until $W(rec)$ holds.

11.2.1 Proof of Correctness of the Solution Strategy

We shall prove that $W(rec)$ *detects* W by first proving the invariant, $W(rec) \Rightarrow W$, and then proving the progress condition $W \mapsto W(rec)$.

Proof of the Invariant

From the specification of the recording algorithm, for all states *st* that occur after recording is complete, *st* is reachable from *rec* (i.e., there exists a sequence **v** of statement executions in the underlying computation such that $[rec]$ **v** $[st]$; see Chapter 10).

Since W is stable, for all states $s0, s1$ where $s1$ is reachable from $s0$,

> $W(s0)$ $\Rightarrow$ $W(s1)$

Hence, for all states s that occur after recording is complete,

> $W(rec)$ $\Rightarrow$ $W(s)$.

Proof of Progress

From the specifications of recording, the recorded state is reachable from the state in which recording is initiated. Therefore, if recording is initiated when W holds, then since W is stable, W holds in the recorded state as well. We observe that

> W *ensures* $W(rec)$,

because

> $\{W \ \wedge \ \neg W(rec)\}$
>   *rec* := a global state of the underlying computation   if $\neg W(rec)$
> $\{W(rec)\}$.

11.2.2 Application of the Detection Strategy

The general detection strategy applies to all detection problems considered in this book. However, detection programs are often tailored to exploit special features of W, the property to be detected. In particular, it is possible in some cases to employ some of the steps in state recording to compute $W(rec)$ as well. The next few sections explore such optimizations for two well-known problems: detection of database deadlock and detection of communication deadlock. The development of these detection programs starts from the general solution strategy.

In the next section we review diffusing computations in the context of the reachability problem in graphs. Diffusing computation forms the basis of deadlock detection. The general form of diffusing computation was introduced in Section 9.9.

This chapter is somewhat different from the others because the problems considered here have straightforward solutions, namely, record the global state and then apply diffusing computations to determine properties of the recorded state. All that remain are optimizations such as reducing the number of messages.

11.3   Deadlock as Reachability in Graphs

In this section we provide examples of diffusing computations that are employed in deadlock detection. The underlying problem in much of deadlock detection is computing reachability in graphs. A solution to this problem appears in Section 6.4. The reachability problem can also be solved by the programs developed for computing all-points shortest paths, presented in Chapter 5. This problem appears again in Chapter 16 in the context of garbage collection.

11.3.1 Identifying All Vertices Reachable from a Given Vertex

Let G be a static finite directed graph. Variables u, v, w represent vertices in G, and (v, w) represents an edge from v to w. Unless otherwise specified, universal quantification over all edges in G is to be assumed where the symbol (v, w) appears, and universal quantification over all vertices in G is to be assumed where the symbol u, v, or w appears. Let R be the reachability matrix of the graph, i.e., $R[v, w]$ is a boolean constant where $R[v, w]$ holds if and only if $v = w$ or there is a directed path from v to w.

One vertex in G is called *root*. Associated with each vertex v is a boolean variable *v.reachable*. The problem is to design a diffusing computation such that

$$v.reachable \quad detects \quad R[root, v].$$

Furthermore, the diffusing computation must terminate (i.e., reach a fixed point).

The Solution Strategy: Informal Description

The obvious marking algorithm is used. The program is built around the invariant—only reachable vertices are marked—and progress condition—every reachable vertex is eventually marked. Initially only *root* is marked; then for every edge (v, w), if v is marked, w is eventually marked. When no more vertices can be marked, all vertices reachable from *root* are marked; vertices not reachable from *root* are unmarked.

We propose a distributed program in which each process represents a vertex of G. Each edge in G corresponds to a directed channel in the process network. The solution employs a message called *msg*, where a vertex receives *msg* only if it is reachable from *root*. Initially *root.reachable* holds and there is a message *msg* in all outgoing channels from *root*; for all vertices v other than *root*, $\neg v.reachable$ holds and all outgoing channels from v are empty. A vertex v, upon receiving a message *msg*, sets *v.reachable* to *true* and sends one *msg* message to each vertex w to which v has an outgoing edge, if v has not done so previously. Thus if there is a path from *root* to v, precisely one *msg* message traverses channels corresponding to each edge in the path.

The Solution Strategy: Formal Description

Let $nmsg[v, w]$ be the number of messages in transit in the channel from v to w. The only variables used in the program are $nmsg[v, w]$ and *v.reachable*, for all v, w. We propose the properties (MA1–MA7) for the marking algorithm, suggested in the informal discussion.

invariant	$root.reachable$	(MA1)
invariant	$v.reachable \;\Rightarrow\; R[root, v]$	(MA2)
invariant	$(nmsg[v, w] > 0) \;\Rightarrow\; v.reachable$	(MA3)
invariant	$\langle \forall\, (v, w) \;:\; v.reachable \;::\; nmsg[v, w] > 0 \;\lor\; w.reachable \rangle$	(MA4)
invariant	$0 \leq nmsg[v, w] \leq 1$	(MA5)
stable	$v.reachable \;\land\; (nmsg[v, w] \leq k)$	(MA6)
$true \;\mapsto\; nmsg[v, w] = 0$		(MA7)

Proof of Correctness of the Solution Strategy

$\langle \forall (v, w) :: v.reachable \mapsto w.reachable \rangle$
, from (MA4,MA6,MA7)

$\langle \forall v, w : R[v, w] :: v.reachable \mapsto w.reachable \rangle$
, by induction on the above

$R[root, v] \mapsto v.reachable$
, from (MA1) and the above

$v.reachable \ detects \ R[root, v]$
, from (MA2) and the above

$true \mapsto (v.reachable \equiv R[root, v])$
, from the above (see Exercise 11.1)

We leave it to the reader, in Exercise 11.2, to show that the following predicate, *final*, is stable, and $true \mapsto final$.

$final \equiv$
$\langle \forall v :: v.reachable \equiv R[root, v] \rangle \land \langle \forall (v, w) :: nmsg[v, w] = 0 \rangle$

Since $v.reachable$ and $nmsg[v, w]$, for all v, w, are the only variables of the program, it follows that a fixed point is eventually reached.

Exercise 11.1 Given $p \ detects \ q$ show that

$true \mapsto (p \equiv q)$.

Hint: Observe from $p \Rightarrow q$ that

$p \Rightarrow (p \equiv q)$

and

$\neg q \Rightarrow (p \equiv q)$.

Then show from $p \ detects \ q$ that

$q \mapsto (p \equiv q),$
$\neg q \mapsto (p \equiv q).$ ▽

Exercise 11.2 Prove that the predicate *final*, defined previously, is stable and that $true \mapsto final$.

Hint: Use (MA2,MA3,MA5,MA6) to prove stability. Use (MA7) and that $true \mapsto (v.reachable \equiv R[root, v])$ to prove progress. ▽

Derivation of a Program from the Specification of the Solution Strategy

We derive a program from the strategy just specified. The initial conditions are obtained from the invariants. The statements in the program are derived to guarantee the progress condition and to maintain the invariants. The derivation of the program from properties (MA1–MA7) is almost mechanical. For this problem, as in many others, most of the work is in proposing and proving properties of programs.

Program {**diffusing computation for**} *Reachability*

  initially

  $\langle \| \ v \ :: \ v.reachable = (v = root) \rangle$

  $\| \ \langle \| \ (v,w) \ :: \ nmsg[v,w] = 0 \quad \text{if} \quad v \neq root \ \sim \ 1 \quad \text{if} \quad v = root \rangle$

  assign

  $\langle \| \ (v,w) \ :: \ \{\text{action taken by } w \text{ on receiving } msg \text{ from } v\}$

   {receive the message and set $w.reachable$ to *true*}
   $nmsg[v,w], w.reachable \ := \ nmsg[v,w] - 1, true$
       if $nmsg[v,w] > 0$

  $\|$ {send messages if $w.reachable$ changes value from *false* to *true*}

   $\langle \| \ (w,x) \ ::$
   $nmsg[w,x] \ := \ nmsg[w,x] + 1$
       if $\neg w.reachable \ \wedge \ nmsg[v,w] > 0$

   $\rangle$

  $\rangle$

end {*Reachability*}

This program can be implemented on a distributed system in the obvious way. The shared variable $nmsg[v,w]$ is incremented only by process v and decremented only by process w; further, process w tests $nmsg[v,w]$ only to determine whether it is positive, and process v does not test this value at all. Therefore incrementing $nmsg[v,w]$ is accomplished by v sending a message along the channel from v to w; decrementing $nmsg[v,w]$ is accomplished by w removing a message from the channel.

11.3.2 Finding Cycles in Graphs

This problem occurs in deadlock detection in distributed databases. Given a finite graph G, the problem is to detect whether there is a cycle in the graph from some vertex *root* to itself. For this purpose, the diffusing computation program *Reachability* can be employed. In *Reachability*, a vertex receives an *msg* message only if there is a path (of at least one edge) from *root* to that vertex; in particular, *root* receives an *msg* message only if *root* is in a cycle. Conversely, a vertex receives an *msg* message eventually if there is a path from *root* to that vertex. In particular, *root* receives an *msg* message eventually if *root* is in a cycle.

11.3.3 Determining the Existence of Reachable Black Vertices

This problem arises in deadlock detection of communication systems. We are given a finite graph, where associated with each vertex v is a boolean constant $v.black$. The problem is to determine whether there exists a black vertex (i.e., a vertex v such that $v.black$ holds) that is reachable from a given vertex $root$. Boolean variables $claim$ and $finished$ are employed, where

invariant $finished \Rightarrow (claim \equiv \langle \exists\, v :: v.black \wedge v.reachable \rangle)$

$true \mapsto finished$

The Solution: Informal Description

The obvious solution is to employ program $Reachability$, which guarantees that

$$v.reachable \equiv R[root, v].$$

Then employ another computation to determine whether there is a vertex v such that $v.reachable \wedge v.black$ holds. We consider these two phases of the solution in more detail.

We propose an optimization for program $Reachability$: Since the goal of this computation is to determine whether there exists a reachable black vertex, there is no point in continuing the computation after a black vertex is known to be reachable. Therefore the program $Reachability$ can be modified so that no black vertex sends an msg message, and furthermore, if $root$ is black, all its outgoing channels are initially empty. It is easy to see that even with this modification, at fixed point $v.reachable \wedge v.black$ holds for some vertex v if and only if there is a black vertex reachable from $root$.

Now we deal with how we determine that there exists a vertex v such that $v.reachable \wedge v.black$ holds. We assume that termination detection of $Reachability$ is done by employing superposition (see Section 9.9). We apply superposition yet again, this time on the termination detection program, to determine the existence of reachable black vertices.

The termination detection program (program $Q3$ in Section 9.9.5) employs ack (acknowledgment) messages. We propose a superposition that employs a boolean field $dark$ with each ack; this field is not used for termination detection. An ack for which $dark$ holds is called a "dark ack," and one for which $\neg dark$ holds is called a "light ack."

A dark ack denotes that the sender or one of its descendants in the diffusing computation tree is black. The solution strategy is to propagate these dark acks from each vertex in the diffusing computation tree to its father, thus propagating dark acks all the way up to $root$. Thus if $root$ receives one or more dark acks, there is a black vertex reachable from $root$. On the other hand, if $root$ receives only light acks for all the messages it sent, there is no black vertex reachable from $root$.

To implement this strategy, a black vertex sends only dark acks, and a nonblack vertex sends only light acks until it receives its first dark ack, after which it sends only dark acks. For a process v, we propose superposed boolean variable $v.someblack$, where $v.someblack$ holds for black vertices, $\neg v.someblack$ holds for a nonblack vertex until it receives a dark ack, and $v.someblack$ holds after it receives a dark ack. Thus a vertex v sends dark acks if and only if $v.someblack$ holds. There exists a black vertex reachable from $root$ if and only if, when $root$ detects termination (i.e., the fixed point of the diffusing computation), $root.someblack$ holds.

The Solution Strategy: Formal Description

As required for termination detection according to program $Q3$ (of Section 9.9.5), we assume that for every edge (u, v) in the graph, there is a channel (v, u) in the process network that carries ack messages. Let $ndark[v, w]$ be the number of dark acks in the channel from v to w. We propose the following invariant.

invariant

$$\langle \exists\, x \;\; :: \;\; x.black \;\wedge\; R[root, x]\rangle \;\; \equiv$$
$$[\; root.someblack \;\vee$$
$$\quad \langle \exists\, (v, w) \;:\; w.father \neq nil \;\;::\;\; ndark[v, w] > 0\rangle \;\vee$$
$$\quad \langle \exists\, w, x \;:\; w.father \neq nil \;\;::\;\; R[w, x] \;\wedge\; x.black\rangle \qquad \text{(BL1)}$$
$$]$$

The above invariant says that a reachable black vertex exists in the graph if and only if $root.someblack$ holds, or a channel to a vertex in the diffusing computation tree has a dark ack, or there is a black vertex that is reachable from some vertex w in the tree.

Proof of Correctness of the Solution Strategy

Since the tree vanishes when $root$ is deleted from it,

invariant $(root.father = nil) \;\Rightarrow\; \langle \forall\, w \;\;::\;\; w.father = nil\rangle$ (BL2)

Hence, from (BL1,BL2),

invariant

$$(root.father = nil) \;\Rightarrow$$
$$[root.someblack \;\equiv\; \langle \exists\, x \;\;::\;\; x.black \;\wedge\; R[root, x]\rangle]$$

Therefore a black vertex is reachable from $root$ if and only if $root.someblack$ holds when $root.father$ is nil. From the arguments given for program $Q3$,

$$true \;\longmapsto\; (root.father = nil).$$

Hence the solution strategy satisfies the problem specification with

$$finished \;\equiv\; (root.father = nil),$$

and

$$claim \equiv root.someblack.$$

Derivation of a Program from the Specification of the Solution Strategy

We sketch the transformations of the termination detection program, $Q3$, of Section 9.9.5 and the program *Reachability* of Section 10.3.1. Initially $root.father \neq nil$ and hence (BL1) is satisfied by

initially $\langle \parallel v \; :: \; v.someblack = v.black \rangle.$

The statements in $Q3$ are transformed as follows:

1. When an *ack* is sent in the underlying computation by a vertex v, its *dark* field is set by

$$ack.dark := v.someblack.$$

2. When a dark *ack* is received by a vertex w, *w.someblack* is set to *true* by executing

$$w.someblack := w.someblack \lor ack.dark.$$

The statements in *Reachability* are transformed as follows:

3. Upon receiving an *msg* message, vertex v sends *msg* messages only if $\neg v.someblack$ holds.

Observe that variable *ndark* is an auxiliary variable, used only in the proof.

11.4   Database Deadlock

11.4.1 Problem Definition

Here only the bare essentials of the database deadlock detection problem are given. Details about the context in which the problem arises are given later.

A distributed database consists of a set of processes. At any point during computation, associated with each process u is a set of processes, *u.blocks*, where

$$[(u \in v.blocks) \land (v \in w.blocks)] \; unless$$
$$[(u \in v.blocks) \land (v \notin w.blocks)]$$

Equivalently, for all statements t and all processes u, v, w,

$$\{(u \in v.blocks) \land (v \in w.blocks)\} \; t \; \{u \in v.blocks\}.$$

Hence, if u is a member of $v.blocks$, and v is a member of $w.blocks$, then u can cease to be a member of $v.blocks$ only *after* v ceases to be a member of $w.blocks$.

In the database context, $u \in v.blocks$ means that v has a lock on a file that u needs to continue execution; thus u is "blocked" by v. A blocked process does not release the locks it holds. Therefore, if u is blocked by v, and v is blocked by w, then u can obtain the file it needs from v only after v becomes unblocked; hence u can become unblocked only after v becomes unblocked.

A process does not block itself:

$$u \notin u.blocks$$

Considering *blocks* as a binary relation over processes, let *blocks** be the transitive closure of *blocks*—i.e., $x.blocks^*$, for all processes x, are the smallest sets satisfying

$$u \in v.blocks^* \ \equiv$$
$$u \in v.blocks \ \lor \ \langle \exists w \ :: \ (u \in w.blocks) \ \land \ (w \in v.blocks^*) \rangle.$$

That is, $u \in v.blocks^*$ holds if and only if there is a nonempty sequence of processes from u to v where each process in the sequence is blocked by the next process in the sequence.

It can be shown from these properties (see Exercise 11.3) that

$$[(u \in v.blocks^*) \ \land \ (v \in w.blocks^*)] \ unless$$
$$[(u \in v.blocks^*) \ \land \ (v \notin w.blocks^*)]$$

Substituting u for both v and w in the preceding property,

$$(u \in u.blocks^*) \ \ unless \ \ false.$$

Therefore $u \in u.blocks^*$ is stable.

Define u is *deadlocked* as $u \in u.blocks^*$. Process u is deadlocked means that there is a cycle of processes, including u, where each process in the cycle is blocked by the next. The problem is to detect whether u is deadlocked. The problem specification is as follows: Transform the given program using a superposed boolean variable $u.claim$ for each u such that

$$u.claim \ \ detects \ \ (u \in u.blocks^*).$$

Exercise 11.3 Prove that

$$\frac{\langle \forall \ i \ : \ 0 \le i < N \ :: \ p_i \ \land \ p_{i+1} \ \ unless \ \ p_i \ \land \ \neg p_{i+1} \rangle}{\langle \land \ i \ : \ 0 \le i \le N \ :: \ p_i \rangle \ \ unless \ \ \langle \land \ i \ : \ 0 \le i < N \ :: \ p_i \rangle \ \land \ \neg p_N}$$

Hint: Use the conjunction rule for *unless* and apply induction on N. $\quad\triangledown$

11.4.2 Application of the General Detection Strategy

For simplicity in exposition we restrict attention to the problem of detecting whether a specific process u is deadlocked. Later we consider the general problem of detecting whether *any* process is deadlocked. For the remainder of this section, u refers to a specific process; u is not quantified over all processes.

The general detection strategy is as follows: First record a global state, then determine whether u is deadlocked in the recorded state. Specifically, first record $v.blocks$ for all v using a state recording program and then compute $v.blocks^*$ using the recorded values of $v.blocks$. Deadlock is detected if $u \in u.blocks^*$.

Separating concerns in this way helps. First we note that the underlying state is changing, which is why we record a state (the recorded state does not change with underlying computation). Second we apply an algorithm to determine whether W holds for the recorded state. In the case of database deadlock, the problem reduces to the trivial one of determining whether there is a cycle in a (static) graph. This problem was solved in Section 11.3.2.

11.4.3 Optimization

Now we propose an optimization to the solution just suggested. The general detection strategy gives a two-phase solution. In the first phase a global state is recorded. In the second phase a cycle containing u, in a static graph, is detected. The algorithms in both phases are quite similar. In the first phase a process sends a marker on each of its outgoing channels after it records its state, and in the second phase a process sends an *msg* message on each of its outgoing edges. An obvious optimization in distributed systems is to employ the *same* message as both the marker of the state-recording program and as the *msg* message of the cycle-detection program. Before carrying out the optimization, the database environment in which the problem arises is described in more detail—the environment offers other opportunities for optimization. Readers not particularly concerned with distributed databases may skip the remainder of Section 11.4; they should solve as an exercise the problem of treating a single message as both marker and *msg*.

11.4.4 Details about Distributed Databases

Details about databases are introduced in steps. Here we present just enough detail to develop a deadlock detection program in its entirety. In a later step the problem is presented in all its wealth of complexity.

A process is either *active* or *idle*. An idle process is waiting for a set of files. When a process transits from active to idle it sends requests to the processes that hold the files for which it is waiting. Let $v.waits$ be the set of processes for which process v is waiting—$v.waits$ is the set of processes to which v has sent requests and from which v has yet to receive replies (granting access to the requested files). Process v is active if and only if $v.waits$ is *empty*. A request spends an arbitrary time in a channel, as does the reply to a request. Associated with each process w is a set $w.blocks$ of processes, where $w.blocks$ is the set of processes from which w has received requests and to which w has yet to reply. Therefore, when w receives a request from v, it adds v to $w.blocks$, and when it replies to the request it removes v from $w.blocks$. Hence if $v \in w.blocks$, then $w \in v.waits$.

This discussion suggests the following optimization step: Since the goal of the recording algorithm is restricted to recording values of $v.blocks$, it is not necessary for a process w to send markers on *all* its outgoing channels; it is sufficient that w send markers to all processes in $w.waits$.

11.4.5 Derivation of an Optimized Program

Next consider the optimization of employing the same message as both marker and *msg*. In the state-recording program, a process, on receiving a marker, records its state and sends a marker on each outgoing channel if it has not already done so. In the program to detect a cycle in a static graph, a process, on receiving an *msg* message, sends an *msg* message on each outgoing edge if it has not already done so. In the context of the deadlock detection problem, recording a state of a process v reduces to that of recording $v.blocks$ and $v.waits$. These facts suggest the following program.

Let *marmsg* be the superposed message that represents both *marker* and *msg*. Associated with each v is a boolean variable $v.flag$, where $v.flag$ holds after v sends message *marmsg*, and $\neg v.flag$ holds before. The program to detect whether u is deadlocked is initiated by u, which sends *marmsg* to each process v in $u.waits$ and sets $u.flag$ to *true*. It is not necessary for u to record $u.blocks$ or $u.waits$. A process w, upon receiving a message *marmsg* from a process x in $w.blocks$, sends *marmsg* to all processes in $w.waits$ and sets $w.flag$ to *true* if $\neg w.flag$ holds. It is not necessary for w to record the values of $w.blocks$ and $w.waits$ because it employs these values only once. Observe that if $w.waits$ is *empty* then w does not propagate *marmsg*. Process u is deadlocked if it receives a *marmsg* from a process w in $u.blocks$. In the following program, $c[u, v]$ represents the channel from u to v.

**Program {deadlock detection in distributed databases:
    transformed Program}** *DD*

> **initially** $u.claim = false$ ‖ $\langle \| v \ :: \ v.flag = false \rangle$
> **add**   {the following statements to the underlying program}
>
>> {u initiates a detection computation by sending *marmsg* to all
>> processes v in $u.waits$ and setting $u.flag$ to *true* to indicate that
>> deadlock detection has been initiated}

$\langle\|\ v\ :\ v\ \in\ u.waits\ ::$

$\quad c[u,v]\ :=\ c[u,v]; marmsg \qquad \text{if}\quad \neg u.flag$

$\rangle$

$\|\ u.flag\ :=\ true$

▯ {w propagates $marmsg$ to all processes v in $w.waits$ on receiving $marmsg$ from a process x in $w.blocks$, if it has not sent a $marmsg$ earlier}

$\langle▯\ (x,w)\ ::$

$\quad\langle\|\ v\ :\ v\ \in\ w.waits\ ::$

$\qquad c[w,v]\ :=\ c[w,v]; marmsg$

$\qquad\qquad \text{if}\quad \neg w.flag \wedge \text{head}(c[x,w]) = marmsg\ \wedge\ x \in w.blocks$

$\quad\rangle$

$\|\ c[x,w]\ :=\ \text{tail}(c[x,w])\ \text{if head}(c[x,w]) = marmsg$

$\|\ w.flag\ :=\ true \qquad \text{if head}(c[x,w]) = marmsg\ \wedge\ (x \in w.blocks)$

$\rangle$

▯ {u is deadlocked if u receives a $marmsg$ from a process w in $u.blocks$}

$\langle▯\ (w,u)\ ::$
$\quad u.claim\ :=\ true \qquad \text{if}\quad \text{head}(c[w,u]) = marmsg\ \wedge\ w \in u.blocks$

$\|\ c[w,u]\ :=\ \text{tail}(c[w,u])\ \text{if}\quad \text{head}(c[w,u]) = marmsg$

$\rangle$

end {DD}

The following invariant can be used in establishing the correctness of program DD:

invariant

$\langle\forall\ (x,w)\ :\ x \neq u\ \wedge\ c[x,w] \text{ contains a } marmsg\ ::$

$\quad$ (there is a request ahead of the $marmsg$ in $c[x,w]\ \vee\ x\ \in\ w.blocks$)
$\qquad \Rightarrow\ u \in x.blocks^{*}$

$\rangle$

We leave it to the reader to prove the invariance of this predicate. (It is necessary to consider the following cases: Sending of a $marmsg$ by u or by x, $x \neq u$; receiving of a $marmsg$ by u; sending and receiving of requests and replies.) If u receives a *marmsg* from some w where $w \in u.blocks$ then—using w for x and u for w in the invariant—before receiving this message, $c[w, u]$ contains a *marmsg*, $w \neq u$, and there is no request ahead of this *marmsg* in $c[w, u]$. Therefore, from the invariant, $u \in u.blocks^*$.

The progress property of *DD*, that u detects it is deadlocked (i.e., *u.claim* is set *true*) if u is deadlocked at the initiation of the algorithm, can be proved from the progress property of the program that detects cycles in a static graph.

We may want the detection program to run more than once during an execution. Then it is necessary to distinguish between different executions of the program. There are two common ways of doing this. The first way is to initiate a detection computation only after the previous one has terminated; this requires a superposition of termination detection on the deadlock detection computation. Since the deadlock detection computation is a diffusing computation, termination detection is straightforward. An alternative, perhaps less satisfactory way, is to tag each computation with its sequence number: All variables and messages in the ith computation are tagged with i, thus keeping the computations distinct. Similarly different processes may initiate deadlock detection computations, and the different computations can be kept distinct by appending the initiator's index to each variable and message in that computation.

Exercise 11.4 Sometimes the definition of deadlocked is extended. Define "process is stuck" as follows. The set of stuck processes is the smallest set satisfying these two rules:

- [v is deadlocked $\Rightarrow$ v is stuck].
- [$(v \in w.blocks) \wedge w$ is stuck $\Rightarrow$ v is stuck].

With this definition it is not necessary that v be in $v.blocks^*$ for v to be stuck. Extend the deadlock detection program such that every stuck process detects that it is stuck. $\triangledown$

Exercise 11.5 Suppose that a process v initiates a deadlock detection when it is idle (i.e., $v.waits$ is not *empty*), but that v is not deadlocked. Suppose that v remains idle, becoming deadlocked after the detection program terminates. For instance, v is waiting for w (i.e., $w \in v.waits$) but w is not waiting for v when the deadlock detection program is initiated and when it terminates; *after* it terminates, however, w starts waiting for v, causing both v and w to become deadlocked. Is it necessary for v to start another detection program to determine whether it is deadlocked? The answer is no; it is sufficient if a process initiates a detection program *once* each time it becomes idle. Develop a program by which the *last* process to transit from active to idle in a cycle of waiting processes detects deadlock and then informs the others. $\triangledown$

11.4.6 More Implementation Details about Distributed Databases

The discussion of deadlock detection in distributed databases is complete. In the next few paragraphs we provide additional background information about the problem. In particular, we answer this question: How does a process determine the processes to which it should send requests? For example, if process u needs a file F, it sends a request to the process, say v, holding F; how is u to determine that v holds F? These questions are not directly relevant to deadlock detection, but they are discussed here for completeness. (We refer the reader to Menasce and Muntz [1979] for details.)

A distributed database has a set of processors with one *database manager* per processor. Communication between database managers is by means of messages. A *transaction* consists of a set of processes with one process per database manager. A process and its manager share memory. A process is indexed (t, m), where t is the transaction to which the process belongs and m is the manager that manages the process. At certain points in its computation a transaction may need locks on a set of files. All locks are exclusive—that is, at most one transaction holds the lock on a given file. Files are partitioned (statically) among database managers; each manager is responsible for granting locks on its set of files. A transaction may hold locks on several files, and these files may have different managers.

When a process (t, m) needs a file managed by m', where $m' \neq m$, the process sends a request to (t, m')—the process belonging to the same transaction t but managed by m'. A process (t, m') that needs a file managed by m' requests m' directly. A manager keeps a list indicating the process (if any) that holds a lock on each file. Thus, if (t, m') requests a file F managed by m' that is held by transaction t', then manager m' sets

$$(t', m').blocks := (t', m').blocks \ \cup \ \{(t, m')\}$$
$$\| \ \ (t, m').waits \ := (t, m').waits \ \cup \ \{(t', m')\}$$

Since processes with a common manager share memory, parallel operations on their variables are permitted. If file F is released by transaction t' and is then allocated to another transaction t''—while transaction t continues to wait for it—then manager m' sets

$$(t', m').blocks \ := (t', m').blocks - \{(t, m')\}$$
$$\| \ \ (t'', m').blocks := (t'', m').blocks \ \cup \ \{(t, m')\}$$
$$\| \ \ (t, m').waits \ := (t, m').waits \ \cup \ \{(t'', m')\} - \{(t', m')\}$$

So the answer to the question of how process (t, m') determines that process (t', m') holds file F is that it does not determine this. Rather, manager m' determines the waiting relationships between processes that it manages. Therefore the waiting relationships between processes in distributed systems has the following structure: A process can wait for a process in the same transaction or for a process with the same manager. A process does not wait for a process in a different transaction *and* with a different manager. A process (t, m) waits for a process (t, m') if the former process needs a file managed by m'. A process (t, m') waits for a process (t', m') if the former process needs a file held by the latter; this waiting relationship is maintained by m'. The definition of deadlock and the detection program are the same in the simple model described previously, as well as in the actual complex situation. It is easier to solve the simpler problem and then adapt the solution to the more complex situation.

Next we describe a different kind of deadlock, employing the same general detection strategy to solve it.

11.5   Communication Deadlock

A very terse definition of the communication deadlock problem is given first; it is then explained in detail. The definition is given in terms of shared-variable systems. (The term *communication* deadlock, a misnomer, is indicative of its origin in distributed systems. The problem is equally valid for shared-memory systems.)

We are given an asynchronous program in which associated with each process u is a set $u.waits$ of processes and a boolean variable $u.idle$ satisfying

$$u.idle \quad unless \quad u.idle \wedge \langle \exists v : v \in u.waits :: \neg v.idle \rangle. \tag{CD1}$$

For all possible values B of $u.waits$,

$$(u.waits = B) \quad unless \quad \neg u.idle \tag{CD2}$$

Define $waits^*$ as the reflexive, transitive closure of $waits$—i.e., $u.waits^*$ is the smallest set of processes such that

$$v \in u.waits^* \quad \equiv$$
$$(v = u) \quad \vee \quad \langle \exists w :: (v \in w.waits) \wedge (w \in u.waits^*) \rangle.$$

Define $u.dead$ as

$$u.dead \quad \equiv \quad \langle \wedge v : v \in u.waits^* :: v.idle \rangle.$$

Define u to be deadlocked if and only if $u.dead$ holds. The problem is to detect $u.dead$ for a given process u.

Explanation: Process u is said to be *idle* if $u.idle$ holds. A process that is not idle is said to be *active*. Process u is waiting for v means v is a member of $u.waits$. An idle process may become active only if it is waiting for an active process. Equivalently, an idle process remains idle as long as it is waiting only for idle processes. The meaning of $v \in u.waits^*$ is that there is a sequence of processes from u to v such that each process in the sequence (except the last one) is waiting for the next; if there is such a sequence and v is active, the possibility that u will become active cannot be ruled out: Each process in the sequence, starting with v, could make the previous process in the sequence become active.

An idle process does not change the set of processes that it is waiting for while it remains idle; therefore an idle process that is waiting for a set B of processes continues waiting for B or becomes active.   ▽

If all processes in $u.waits^*$ are idle, then they remain idle and $u.waits^*$ remains unchanged. The reason for this is as follows.

For a process v in $u.waits^*$ to become active, from (CD1), some w in $v.waits$ must be first active. But $w \in u.waits^*$. Hence there is no first process that can become active. Next we formalize these arguments to show that $u.dead$ is stable.

Proof: $u.dead$ is stable

  $u.idle$ *unless* $u.idle$ $\wedge$ $\langle \exists v : v \in u.waits :: \neg v.idle \rangle$
   , repeating (CD1)

  $u.idle$ *unless* $u.idle$ $\wedge$ $\langle \exists v : v \in u.waits^* :: \neg v.idle \rangle$
   , weakening the right side of the above

  $w.idle$ *unless* $w.idle$ $\wedge$ $\langle \exists y : y \in w.waits^* :: \neg y.idle \rangle$
   , using w for u, and y for v in the above

Apply the conjunction rule for *unless* to the above two where $w \in u.waits^*$. Note that $w \in u.waits^* \Rightarrow w.waits^* \subseteq u.waits^*$, from the definition of $waits^*$.

  $(u.idle \wedge w.idle)$ *unless*
  $(u.idle \wedge w.idle \wedge \langle \exists v : v \in u.waits^* :: \neg v.idle \rangle)$.

Apply the conjunction rule to the preceding, for all w in $u.waits^*$. Note that u is in $u.waits^*$:

  $\langle \forall v : v \in u.waits^* :: v.idle \rangle$ *unless*
  $\langle \forall v : v \in u.waits^* :: v.idle \rangle \wedge \langle \exists v : v \in u.waits^* :: \neg v.idle \rangle$
  $\langle \forall v : v \in u.waits^* :: v.idle \rangle$ *unless false*   , from the above
  $u.dead$ *unless false*   , from the definition of $u.dead$ ▽

11.5.1 Specification

The problem is to transform the given program according to the rules of superposition such that

> $u.claim$ detects $u.dead$,

where, for each u, $u.claim$ is a superposed boolean variable.

We again apply the general detection strategy to detect whether $u.dead$ holds: First record a global state and then analyze this (static) recorded state. The recording algorithm records $v.waits$ and $v.idle$ for all v. A program to determine whether a given process u is deadlocked, in the recorded state, is the same as one to determine whether there is a black vertex reachable from vertex u (this problem was solved in Section 11.3.3). To see this, construct a graph as follows. There is one vertex in the graph for each process. There is an edge (v, w) in the graph if and only if v is waiting for w—i.e., if $w \in v.waits$. Active processes are black and idle ones are nonblack. The problem is to determine whether all vertices reachable from vertex u are nonblack, or, equivalently, whether there is a black vertex reachable from vertex u. Process u is deadlocked if and only if all processes reachable from u are nonblack. Observe that the graph is static since it is constructed from the recorded state.

All that remains is to optimize the program by combining the recording algorithm with the diffusing computation algorithm of Section 11.3.3; this is left to the reader. The optimization is much the same as that employed in database deadlock. The same message is employed in a dual role: as a message in both the global snapshot program and the diffusing computation (see Exercise 11.6).

Exercise 11.6   Employ the msg message in the diffusing computation for a dual purpose: Make it also play the role of $marker$ in the global state-recording algorithm. You can think of it as "piggybacking" a marker on a msg message.

$\triangledown$

Exercise 11.7   A more subtle optimization is to employ $acks$ in the diffusing computation in a dual role: Make them play the role of marker as well. Develop this idea into a formal specification and derive a program. $\triangledown$

Exercise 11.8   Show that if every process initiates a deadlock detection computation when it becomes idle, then the very *last* process to become idle in a deadlocked set will detect that it is deadlocked. How can this process inform the others? $\triangledown$

The answers to these exercises can be obtained from Chandy, Misra, and Haas [1983].

Summary

The central idea in this chapter is that a general technique for implementing *claim detects* W, where W is a stable property, is to record global states from time to time until W holds for the recorded state. Thus the problem of determining whether a *dynamic* system has property W reduces to that of determining whether a *static* recorded state *rec* has property W.

This idea is applied to the detection of two stable properties: database deadlock and communication deadlock. Diffusing computation is found to be helpful in computing $W(rec)$. Programs are optimized by combining the global state recording and diffusing computation programs.

Bibliographic Notes

The generic solution to detecting stable properties by employing global snapshots is from Chandy and Lamport [1985]. Termination-detection algorithms for diffusing computations are found in Dijkstra and Scholten [1980] and Chang [1982]. The database deadlock detection problem is described in Menasce and Muntz [1979]. Most of the material about deadlock detection in this chapter is from Chandy, Misra, and Haas [1983]. A great deal of work has been carried out on detection problems; the use of global states for detection appears in Bracha and Toueg [1984] and Gafni [1986].

CHAPTER 12

Dining
Philosophers

12.1   Introduction

This chapter has two goals: to demonstrate stepwise refinement and modular design of reactive systems, and to derive programs to resolve conflicts among processes in asynchronous systems.

12.1.1 Conflicts

Conflicts can arise in asynchronous systems because there are actions in the system that can be carried out by only one process at a time—for example, obtaining exclusive access to a file. Conflicts arise when more than one process attempts to carry out such an action. The problem is to design a program to adjudicate conflicts: Only one of the conflicting processes is allowed to carry out the action while the others wait.

In this chapter, we study a representation of conflict resolution called the *dining philosophers* problem, or the *diners* problem for short. The next chapter presents programs for a generalization of the diners problem called the *drinking philosophers* problem, or the *drinkers* problem for short. The drinkers problem better represents conflicts that arise from file access. Mutual exclusion, a special case of the diners problem, is considered in Chapter 15.

12.1.2 The Central Idea in Conflict Resolution

The resolution of a conflict requires the selection of one process—the winner—from a set of conflicting processes. If all conflicting processes are identical and are in the same state, there is no nonprobabilistic basis for selecting the winner. The central idea in conflict resolution is the imposition of an asymmetry on processes that allows an adjudicator to select a winner. To guarantee that the adjudicator does not permanently discriminate against a process, the asymmetry must be dynamic and fair over time.

12.1.3 The Specification Structure

In the design of reactive systems it is sometimes not clear what is given and what the designer is expected to produce. To avoid this confusion, our specifications have the form described in Chapter 7. We are required to design a program *os* (for *o*perating system, which represents the adjudicator) given the following:

1. the specification of a program *user* (which represents the program for the conflicting processes);

2. the specification of a program that is the union of *user* and *os*; and

3. the specification of the protocol by which *os* is allowed to modify the variables shared with *user*.

This specification structure may seem strange. Why not give the designer a specification for *os* directly, without mentioning *user* or *user* ∥ *os*? Because it is often easier to specify the composite system, *user* ∥ *os*, and leave it to the designer to develop a program *os* so that the composite program behaves as specified.

The same specification structure is employed in Chapters 13–15.

12.1.4 The Design Structure

The first step in our design is to propose a specification for *os*. We are then obliged to prove that our specification is correct: We show that the composite program, *user* ∥ *os*, satisfies its specification, and that the protocol by which *os* modifies shared variables satisfies its specification.

Programs are derived by stepwise refinement in this chapter. Each refinement step is described in four parts: (1) an informal description of the solution, (2) a formal description of the proposed solution strategy, i.e., a specification of *os*, (3) a proof of correctness of the specification—a proof that the proposed specification is indeed a refinement of the specification proposed in the previous step, and (4) the motivation for the next refinement step.

The goal in stepwise refinement is to produce a specification from which a program can be derived easily. A further refinement is called for when it is not clear how to implement some aspect of the specification proposed in the current refinement. A refinement consists of replacing some proposed property by others from which programs can be derived easily. The proof of correctness of the refinement is a demonstration that the refined specification implies the property that is replaced.

Most of this chapter deals with specifications—proposed properties of programs—rather than with programs themselves. A program is derived only after the last refinement step.

12.1.5 The Chapter Structure

The specifications for *user*, the composite program, and the protocol by which *os* accesses shared variables are given in Section 12.2. A specification for *os* is proposed and proved correct in Section 12.3. Sections 12.4–12.7 propose stepwise refinements of the specification for *os*. To help the reader keep track of the refinements, a summary of the refinements is given in Section 12.8. A program is derived in Section 12.9.

Each section begins with an informal description, and the last subsection in Sections 12.3–12.6 is a motivation for the next refinement step. A basic understanding of the design can be obtained by reading the informal descriptions and the motivation for each refinement.

12.2   Problem Specification

The specification of the mutual exclusion problem, a special case of the diners problem, is given in Chapter 7. The specifications of the two problems are similar.

12.2.1 Notation

We are given a static, finite, undirected and connected graph G. The vertices of G represent processes. Traditionally the processes are called philosophers. Symbols u, v, w represent vertices (or processes). An edge between u and v is denoted by (u, v), or equivalently by (v, u). For convenience, the graph is also represented by the constant boolean incidence matrix E, where $E[u, v]$ holds if and only if there is an edge between u and v in G. Since G is undirected, $E[u, v] = E[v, u]$. There is no edge in G from a vertex to itself: $\neg E[u, u]$, for all u. Two vertices are said to be *neighbors* if and only if there is an edge between them. Universal quantification over vertices, and over edges, is to be assumed unless the quantification is explicit.

Associated with each u is a variable $u.dine$ that takes on values t, h, e. For convenience, we also employ boolean variables $u.t, u.h, u.e$, defined as

$$u.t \equiv (u.dine = t),$$
$$u.h \equiv (u.dine = h),$$
$$u.e \equiv (u.dine = e).$$

The meaning of these variables is given next.

12.2.2 Informal Description of the Problem

Each process u is in one of three states: *thinking, hungry, eating*. The value of $u.dine$ is t, h, or e if u is thinking, hungry, or eating, respectively. The only transitions are from thinking to hungry, from hungry to eating, and from eating to thinking. Transitions from thinking to hungry, and from eating to thinking, are only in the given program, *user*. Transitions from hungry to eating are only in *os*. We are required to design *os* so that in the composite program, *user* [] *os*, neighbors do not eat simultaneously and hungry processes eat eventually, given that no process eats forever.

Note: This problem formulation includes the classical dining philosophers problem—five philosophers seated in a circle so that every philosopher has two neighbors—as a special case; the underlying graph G is a simple cycle with five vertices. Also, mutual exclusion among N processes can be represented by a completely connected graph of N vertices.   ▽

12.2.3 Specification of *user*

The only transitions in *user* are from thinking to hungry (udn1) and from eating to thinking (udn3); there are no transitions from a hungry state, in *user* (udn2).

Any composite program containing *user* has the property that no process eats forever in that program if neighbors do not eat simultaneously (udn4).

u.t unless u.h	in *user*		(udn1)
stable *u.h*	in *user*		(udn2)
u.e unless u.t	in *user*		(udn3)
Conditional Property			(udn4)

Hypothesis: $\langle \forall\ (u,v)\ ::\ \neg(u.e \wedge v.e)\rangle$
Conclusion: $\langle \forall u\ ::\ u.e \mapsto \neg u.e\rangle$

Derived Properties of *user*

It follows by applying the disjunction rule to (udn1) and (udn2), as shown in Chapter 7, that there are no transitions to eating in *user*, i.e.,
stable $\neg u.e$ in *user*

12.2.4 Specification of the Composite Program

Neighbors do not eat simultaneously (dn1), and hungry processes eat eventually (dn2).

invariant $\neg(u.e \wedge v.e \wedge E[u,v])$	in *user* [] *os*	(dn1)
$u.h \mapsto u.e$ in *user* [] *os*		(dn2)

12.2.5 Constraints on *os*

The only variables shared between *user* and *os* are *u.dine*, for all *u*. There are no transitions in *os* from eating (odn2), from thinking (odn1), or to thinking (odn1).

constant	*u.t*	in *os* {value of *u.t* is not changed by *os*}	(odn1)
stable	*u.e*	in *os*	(odn2)

Derived Properties of *os*

From (odn1) and (odn2) it follows that there are no transitions to hungry in *os*, and that the only transition in *os* from hungry is to eating:

stable $\neg u.h$ in os

$u.h$ $unless$ $u.e$ in os

12.2.6 Derived Properties of the Composite Program

From (udn1–udn3) in the specification of *user* and the constraints (odn1,odn2) on os, it follows (as in Chapter 7) that the only transitions in the composite program are from thinking to hungry (dn3), from hungry to eating (dn4), and from eating to thinking (dn5):

$$u.t \ unless \ u.h \qquad \text{in } user \ \| \ os \qquad\qquad (\text{dn3})$$
$$u.h \ unless \ u.e \qquad \text{in } user \ \| \ os \qquad\qquad (\text{dn4})$$
$$u.e \ unless \ u.t \qquad \text{in } user \ \| \ os \qquad\qquad (\text{dn5})$$

Notational Convention: All the specifications in this chapter are about properties of os. The program name, os, will not be shown explicitly with these properties, from now on. ∇

12.3   A Preliminary Design

12.3.1 The Solution: Informal Description

We propose a particularly simple specification of os which guarantees that the composite program has the specified properties (dn1,dn2) and that os satisfies the specified constraints (odn1,odn2).

It is fairly obvious that the specification of os should include constraints (odn1,odn2). This also allows us to conclude that the only transitions in the composite program are thinking to hungry to eating to thinking (dn3–dn5). How shall we guarantee (dn1), that neighbors are not eating simultaneously in the composite program? We specify that neighbors are not eating simultaneously as an invariant of os. This invariant is maintained by *user*, which has no transitions from noneating to eating. Therefore the invariant holds for the composite program as well.

Since we have the invariant—neighbors are not eating—in the composite program, the hypothesis of (udn4) is satisfied, and therefore we conclude that no process eats forever in the composite program ($u.e \ \mapsto \ \neg u.e$).

How shall we guarantee the only remaining requirement (dn2), hungry processes eat eventually, in the composite program? We design os to guarantee that in the composite program hungry processes eat eventually provided that no process eats forever (and also provided that various safety conditions hold). Since no process eats forever in the composite program from the arguments given earlier, hungry processes eat eventually.

12.3.2 The Solution Strategy: Formal Description

In this section we propose a specification *spec1* of *os*.

spec1   [(odn1,odn2) plus (odn3,odn4) given next]

{neighbors are not eating simultaneously}

invariant $\neg(u.e \land v.e \land E[u,v])$ (odn3)

Conditional Property   (odn4)

{if the only transitions are from thinking to hungry to eating to thinking and neighbors do not eat simultaneously, and no process eats forever in the composite program, then a hungry process eats eventually}

Hypothesis: (dn1,dn3–dn5), $\langle \forall\ u\ ::\ u.e\ \mapsto\ \neg u.e \rangle$
Conclusion: $\langle \forall\ u\ ::\ u.h\ \mapsto\ u.e \rangle$

12.3.3 Proof of Correctness of the Solution Strategy

The proof obligation is to show that the composite program, *user* ⫿ *os*, has the specified properties (dn1,dn2) and that *os* satisfies the specified constraints (odn1,odn2). Properties of the composite program are deduced from the specifications of *user* and *os* as described in Section 7.2.3.

(dn3–dn5)   hold in the composite program because (odn1,odn2) hold in *os* and (udn1–udn3) hold in *user*

$\neg(u.e \land v.e \land E[u,v])$ is stable in *user* because $\neg u.e$ and $\neg v.e$ are stable in *user* and $E[u,v]$ is constant

(dn1)   holds in the composite program from the above and because it holds in *os* (odn3)

$\langle \forall\ u\ ::\ u.e\ \mapsto\ \neg u.e \rangle$ holds in the composite program because it is the conclusion of (udn4), and the hypothesis of (udn4)–(dn1) holds in the composite program

$\langle \forall\ u\ ::\ u.h\ \mapsto\ u.e \rangle$ holds in the composite program because it is the conclusion of (odn4), and the hypothesis of (odn4) holds in the composite program

(dn2)   holds in the composite program from the above   ▽

12.3.4 Motivation for the Next Refinement

Let us attempt to derive a program from *spec1*. An obvious algorithm is this: A hungry process eats if its neighbors are not eating. This algorithm satisfies the invariant (odn3) that neighbors are not eating simultaneously.

Unfortunately, the progress condition (odn4)—hungry processes will eat—may not hold. This is because a process may repeatedly cycle through the states: thinking, hungry, eating, thinking, ..., and thus starve its neighbors. We need some mechanism to guarantee that a process does not forever repeat the cycle thinking $\rightarrow$ hungry $\rightarrow$ eating $\rightarrow$ thinking while it has a hungry neighbor. The next refinement step proposes such a mechanism.

The goal of the next refinement step is to replace the progress property (odn4)—hungry processes will eat—by properties that can be implemented more readily.

12.4 Refinement Step: Introduction of a Partial Ordering

12.4.1 The Solution: Informal Description

How shall we design *os* to guarantee that hungry processes will eat? The central idea is to impose an asymmetry on processes, allowing *os* to select a single winner from a set of conflicting processes. The asymmetry we propose is a partial ordering on processes. A hungry process eats or it rises in the ordering until it reaches the top. A hungry process at the top of the ordering eats eventually. Therefore every hungry process eats eventually.

The partial ordering is represented by a directed acyclic graph G', obtained from the given undirected graph G by giving directions to edges in G. The edge between neighbors u,v is directed from u to v in G' if and only if u is higher in the ordering than v.

The ordering is dynamic and the directions of edges in G' change to reflect changes in the ordering. It is more efficient to make local changes than massive global changes. Therefore the direction of an edge is changed only when a process, on which the edge is incident, changes state. The central design issue is as follows: How can directions of edges in G' be changed so that (1) G' remains acyclic, (2) hungry processes never become lower in the ordering because of changes in edge direction, and (3) a process that remains hungry rises in the ordering until it reaches the top? The answer is trivial but nevertheless important in understanding the dining philosophers program.

The Key Idea: Rules for Changing Edge Direction in G'

1. The direction of an edge is changed *only* when a process on which the edge is incident changes state from hungry to eating.

2. All edges incident on an eating process are directed toward it; equivalently, an eating process is lower in the ordering than all its neighbors.

These rules exploit the following property of directed graphs: If all edges incident on a vertex u are directed toward u, then there is no path through u (i.e., u is not an intermediate vertex on any path). Therefore directing all incident edges of u toward u does not create a path from w to v, for any w and $v \neq u$.

It follows that redirecting edges according to the rules does not create cycles; therefore the acyclicity of G' is preserved. Also, while a vertex v remains hungry, no new paths to v are created; therefore v does not drop in the ordering while it remains hungry.

Next we give rules that guarantee that a hungry process eats or rises in the ordering. We propose that the following condition does not last forever: A process u is hungry and is higher in the ordering than all its hungry neighbors. In this case, u eats eventually or some thinking neighbor of u that is higher than u in the ordering, becomes hungry. From the given rules, when a hungry process eats it sinks to the bottom of the ordering, and lower processes rise. This guarantees that a hungry process eventually eats, or rises in the ordering until it reaches the top, at which point it is guaranteed to eat.

12.4.2 The Solution Strategy: Formal Description

To give a formal specification of *os*, we introduce a few variables. For every pair of neighbors u,v, we introduce a variable $prior[u,v]$ that has value u or v; $prior[u,v] = u$ if and only if the edge between u and v in G' is directed from u to v. Of course, $prior[u,v] = prior[v,u]$. We say that u has priority over v if and only if $prior[u,v] = u$.

For each u we introduce a boolean variable $u.top$ where $u.top$ holds if and only if u has higher priority than all its hungry neighbors:

$$u.top \;\equiv\; \langle \forall\, v \;:\; E[u,v] \,\wedge\, v.h \;::\; prior[u,v] = u \rangle .$$

In specification *spec2* of *os* proposed in this refinement step, properties (odn1–odn3) of *spec1* are retained, but (odn4) is replaced by (odn5–odn8). These properties are as follows. All edges incident on an eating process are directed toward it or, equivalently, an eating process has lower priority than its neighbors (odn5). An edge directed from v to u in G' does not change direction until v eats, or, equivalently, a process yields priority only when it eats (odn6). Graph G' is acyclic (odn7). The hypothesis of the conditional property (odn8) is stronger than in (odn4) of *spec1* because it also includes the safety properties (odn5–odn7). The conclusion of (odn8) is that a topmost hungry process ceases to be the topmost process or ceases to be hungry.

spec2   [(odn1–odn3) plus (odn5–odn8), given next]

invariant $u.e \wedge E[u,v] \Rightarrow (prior[u,v] = v)$ (odn5)

$(prior[u,v] = v)$ *unless* $v.e$ (odn6)

invariant G' is acyclic   (odn7)

Conditional Property   (odn8)

Hypothesis: (dn1,dn3–dn5), (odn5–odn7), $\langle \forall u :: u.e \mapsto \neg u.e \rangle$
Conclusion: $\langle \forall u :: u.h \wedge u.top \mapsto \neg(u.h \wedge u.top) \rangle$

12.4.3 Proof of Correctness of the Solution Strategy

We prove that the property that is replaced, (odn4), is implied by the refined specification, *spec2*.

Properties (odn5–odn7) are maintained in *user* because $\neg u.e$ is stable in *user*, *prior* is local to *os*, and E is constant. Therefore (odn5–odn7) are properties of the composite program.

We assume that the hypothesis of (odn4) holds; we prove its conclusion from *spec2*. From the hypothesis of (odn4) and since (odn5–odn7) are invariants of the composite program, the hypothesis of (odn8) holds. Therefore the conclusion of (odn8) holds in the composite program.

In the remainder of the proof, all the properties are properties of the composite program; the program name is not shown explicitly with the properties. Let $R[u,v]$ denote that there is a directed path from u to v in G'. For any u, define sets $u.ab$ (for *above* u) and $u.tab$ (for *thinking* and *above* u) and a metric $u.m$, as follows:

$$u.ab = \{v \mid R[v, u]\}$$
$$u.tab = \{v \mid R[v, u] \wedge v.t\}$$
$$u.m = \text{size of } u.ab + \text{size of } u.tab$$

We show, from the hypothesis of (odn4), that $u.m$ does not increase unless u eats, and if $u.h$ holds, eventually $u.e$ holds or $u.m$ decreases. Therefore every hungry process eats eventually.

First we show a simple result concerning any set d: Given that no element can be added to d unless p holds, $d = D$ continues to hold for any constant set D unless d shrinks or p holds. That is, from

$$x \notin d \quad unless \quad p,$$

where p does not name x, we deduce

$$d = D \quad unless \quad (d \subset D) \vee p, \tag{1}$$

where D is any constant set.

Proof:

$x \notin d \;\; unless \;\; p$
   {where p does not name x} , given
$\langle \wedge \; x \; : \; x \notin D \; :: \; x \notin d \rangle \;\; unless \;\; p$
   , simple conjunction on all $x, x \notin D$
$d \subseteq D \;\; unless \;\; p$
   , the left side of above is $d \subseteq D$
$d = D \;\; unless \;\; d \neq D$
   , trivially from $q \;\; unless \;\; \neg q$
$d = D \;\; unless \;\; (d \subset D) \vee p$
   , conjunction on the above two $\triangledown$

Now we show that neither $u.ab$ nor $u.tab$ decreases unless u eats.

Proof: $u.ab = u.AB \;\; unless \;\; u.e \vee (u.ab \subset u.AB)$ (2)

$\neg R[v, u] \;\; unless \;\; u.e$, see Exercise 12.1
$v \notin u.ab \;\; unless \;\; u.e$, from the definition of $u.ab$

The result follows by applying (1) to the above. $\triangledown$

Proof: $u.tab = u.TAB \;\; unless \;\; u.e \vee (u.tab \subset u.TAB)$ (3)

$\neg v.t \;\; unless \;\; v.e$, from $\neg v.t \;\equiv\; (v.h \vee v.e)$ and
                                                $v.h \;\; unless \;\; v.e$
$\neg v.t \;\; unless \;\; \neg R[v, u]$, from the above using $v.e \;\Rightarrow\; \neg R[v, u]$
$\neg R[v, u] \;\; unless \;\; u.e$, see Exercise 12.1
$v \notin u.tab \;\; unless \;\; u.e$, using cancellation on the above two

The result follows by applying (1) to the above. $\triangledown$

We now show that every hungry process eats eventually.

Proof: $u.h \;\mapsto\; u.e$

$u.ab = u.AB \;\wedge\; u.tab = u.TAB \;\; unless \;\; u.e \vee$
$(u.ab = u.AB \;\wedge\; u.tab \subset u.TAB) \vee (u.ab \subset u.AB \;\wedge\; u.tab = u.TAB)$
   , conjunction of (2,3)

$u.m = k \;\; unless \;\; u.e \vee u.m < k$
   , from the above using the definition of $u.m$

We leave the proofs of the following two properties, (4,5), to the reader.

$$v \in u.ab \ \wedge \ v.m = j \ \wedge \ u.m = k \ \ unless \ \ u.e \ \vee \ u.m < k \tag{4}$$

$$u.top \ \wedge \ u.m = k \ \ unless \ \ u.e \ \vee \ u.m < k \tag{5}$$

$u.h \ \ unless \ \ u.e$
, from (dn4) $\tag{6}$

$u.h \ \wedge \ v \in u.ab \ \wedge \ v.m = j \ \wedge \ u.m = k \ \ unless \ \ u.e \ \vee \ u.m < k$
, simple conjunction of (4,6) $\tag{7}$

$u.h \ \wedge \ u.top \ \wedge \ u.m = k \ \ unless \ \ u.e \ \vee \ u.m < k$
, simple conjunction of (5,6)

$u.h \ \wedge \ u.top \ \mapsto \ \neg(u.h \ \wedge \ u.top)$
, conclusion of (odn8)

$u.h \ \wedge \ u.top \ \wedge \ u.m = k \ \mapsto \ u.e \ \vee \ u.m < k$
, PSP theorem on the above two $\tag{8}$

$v.h \ \wedge \ v.top \ \wedge \ v.m = j \ \mapsto \ v.e \ \vee \ v.m < j$
, from (8) substituting v for u and j for k

$u.h \ \wedge \ v \in u.ab \ \wedge \ v.m = j \ \wedge \ u.m = k \ \wedge \ v.h \ \wedge \ v.top \ \mapsto$
   $u.e \ \vee \ u.m < k$
   , PSP theorem on the above and (7), and $v \in u.ab \ \Rightarrow \ \neg v.e$

$\neg u.top \ \Rightarrow \ \langle \exists \ v \ :: \ v.h \ \wedge \ v \in u.ab \ \wedge \ v.top \rangle$
, from the definition of $u.top$ and graph theory

$u.h \ \wedge \ \neg u.top \ \wedge \ u.m = k \ \mapsto \ u.e \ \vee \ u.m < k$
, from the above two using transitivity

$u.h \ \wedge \ u.m = k \ \mapsto \ u.e \ \vee \ u.m < k$
, disjunction on the above and (8)

$u.h \ \wedge \ u.m = k \ \mapsto \ u.e \ \vee \ (u.h \ \wedge \ u.m < k)$
, PSP theorem on the above and (6)

$u.h \ \mapsto \ u.e$
, induction on the above $\qquad \triangledown$

Exercise 12.1   Show from *spec2* that $\neg R[v, u] \ \ unless \ \ u.e$.

Hint: Apply induction on the length of the path from v to u. For the base case:

$(prior[v, u] = u) \ \ unless \ \ u.e$, from (odn6) $\qquad \triangledown$

Exercise 12.2   Is the following derivable from *spec2*?

$R[v, u] \ \ unless \ \ u.e$ $\qquad \triangledown$

12.4.4 Motivation for the Next Refinement

Next we attempt to derive a program from *spec2*. The specification suggests a program consisting of a single rule: A hungry process u transits to eating if $u.top$ holds and if no neighbor of u is eating, and when u begins to eat, $prior[u,v]$ becomes v for all neighbors v of u.

The proposed program is unsuitable for a distributed architecture because a hungry process has to determine that its neighbors are not eating before it transits to eating. How is a process to determine that its neighbors are not eating? The next refinement answers this question.

12.5   Refinement Step: How a Process Determines that Its Neighbors Are Not Eating

The goal of this refinement step is to replace the invariant (odn3)—neighbors do not eat simultaneously—by properties that are implementable more obviously on distributed architectures.

12.5.1 The Solution: Informal Description

For each pair of neighbors a token, called a *fork*, is introduced. The fork shared by neighbors u and v is held either by u or by v; the fork cannot be simultaneously held by both u and v. The key invariant about forks is as follows: A process eats only if it holds all forks that it shares with its neighbors.

Neighbors u and v cannot eat at the same time because both of them cannot simultaneously hold the same fork. Therefore (odn3) is guaranteed by the refined specification.

12.5.2 The Solution Strategy: Formal Description

For each pair of neighbors u,v, a variable $fork[u,v]$ is introduced that takes on one of the values, u or v.
spec3

[(odn1,odn2,odn5–odn8), plus (odn9) that replaces (odn3), as shown next]

invariant $\neg(u.e \land v.e \land E[u,v])$ (odn3)

is replaced by

invariant $u.e \land E[u,v] \Rightarrow (fork[u,v] = u)$ (odn9)

12.5.3 Proof of Correctness of the Solution Strategy

To show that (odn3) follows from (odn9):

$$u.e \land v.e \land E[u,v] \Rightarrow (u = v) \land E[u,v] \quad , \text{from (odn9)}$$

$\neg((u = v) \ \wedge \ E[u,v])$, because $\neg E[u, u]$

$\neg(u.e \ \wedge \ v.e \ \wedge \ E[u,v])$, from the above two

12.5.4 Motivation for the Next Refinement

Specification *spec3* suggests the following program. The program consists of two statements, one for the acquisition of forks and the other for the transition from hungry to eating.

1. A noneating process u sends the fork that it shares with a hungry neighbor v, to v, if v has higher priority than u or if u is thinking.

2. A hungry process u eats if it holds all forks that it shares and for each neighbor v : u has priority over v, or v is thinking.

A difficulty with implementing this program on a distributed architecture is that a process has to determine whether it has priority over its neighbor, and the priority between a pair of neighbors is changed by both neighbors. How is a process to determine whether it has priority over a neighbor? The next refinement suggests a way to answer this question.

12.6   Refinement Step: Distributed Implementation of Priority

In this refinement step we replace properties (odn5,odn6), dealing with priority by properties that can be implemented more easily on distributed architectures. The properties we wish to refine are as follows: (1) an eating process has lower priority than its neighbors (odn5), and (2) a process yields priority only when it eats (odn6). We propose a distributed implementation of priority that satisfies these properties.

12.6.1 The Solution: Informal Description

We associate an attribute *clean/dirty* with each fork: A fork is either clean or dirty. We define priority as follows: A process u has priority over a neighbor v if and only if the fork they share is (1) at u and clean, or (2) at v and dirty.

The properties regarding the attributes clean and dirty are as follows; these properties are described formally in Section 12.6.2 (by odn10–odn13):

An eating process holds all forks that it shares and all such forks are dirty.
{suggested by(odn5)}   (see odn10)

A process holding a clean fork continues to hold it, and the fork remains clean until the process eats. {suggested by (odn6)}   (see odn11)

A dirty fork remains dirty until it is sent from one process to another, and when it is sent it is cleaned. {suggested by (odn6)}   (see odn12)

Clean forks are held only by hungry processes.   (see odn13)

(This strategy is called a "hygienic solution" to the dining philosophers problem because forks are cleaned when sent by a process to a neighbor.)

It is obvious from these rules that eating processes have lower priority than their neighbors, and that a process yields priority only when it eats.

Why do we propose that clean forks be held only by hungry processes? Suppose that a thinking process holds a clean fork. A process yields a fork only when it is dirty. Therefore a thinking process holding a clean fork continues to hold the fork while it is thinking. But it may think forever, and therefore hold the fork forever, thus starving a neighbor.

12.6.2 The Solution Strategy: Formal Description

A boolean variable $clean[u,v]$ is introduced for each pair of neighbors u,v. (The fork shared by u,v is said to be clean if $clean[u,v]$ holds and is said to be dirty otherwise.)

Define $prior[u,v]$ as

$$(prior[u,v] = u) \quad \equiv \quad ([fork[u,v] = u] = clean[u,v]).$$

spec4   [(odn1,odn2,odn7,odn8) plus (odn10–odn13), which are given next]

Replace (odn5,odn9) by (odn10):

invariant $u.e \ \wedge \ E[u,v] \ \Rightarrow \ (prior[u,v] = v)$ (odn5)

invariant $u.e \ \wedge \ E[u,v] \ \Rightarrow \ (fork[u,v] = u)$ (odn9)

invariant $u.e \ \wedge \ E[u,v] \ \Rightarrow \ (fork[u,v] = u \ \wedge \ \neg clean[u,v])$ (odn10)

Replace (odn6) by (odn11,odn12):

$(prior[u,v] = v) \ \ unless \ \ v.e$ (odn6)

$(fork[u,v] = v) \ \wedge \ clean[u,v] \ \ unless \ \ v.e$ (odn11)

$(fork[u,v] = u) \ \wedge \ \neg clean[u,v] \ \ unless \ (fork[u,v] = v) \ \wedge \ clean[u,v]$ (odn12)

Add (odn13):

invariant $(fork[u,v] = u) \ \wedge \ clean[u,v] \ \Rightarrow \ u.h$ (odn13)

Note: Part of (odn10), that an eating process holds only dirty forks, follows from (odn13). We have stated (odn10) in this manner to show its relationship to (odn5,odn9) which it replaces.   ▽

12.6.3 Proof of Correctness of the Solution Strategy

Since $\neg u.e, u.h$ are stable in *user*, and *fork*, *clean* are local to *os*, it follows that (odn10–odn13) are properties of the composite program. We show that the properties that are replaced (odn5,odn9,odn6) are implied by *spec4*.

(odn5): Follows from (odn10), and the definition of *prior* in terms of *fork* and *clean*.

(odn9): Follows from (odn10).

(odn6): Follows from (odn11,odn12) by applying the disjunction rule, weakening the right side and employing the definition of *prior*.

Note: (odn13) is suggested by the progress condition (odn8). Strictly speaking, we need not introduce (odn13) in this refinement step. We would have to introduce it, however, when we study implementations of (odn8), and it is more convenient to introduce all properties dealing with cleanliness in the same refinement.   ▽

12.6.4 Motivation for the Next Refinement

Let us derive a program from *spec4*. The program consists of two rules, one for sending forks and the other for transitions from eating to hungry.

1. A noneating process u sends the fork that it shares with a hungry neighbor v, to v, if the fork is dirty.

2. A hungry process u eats if it holds all forks that it shares, and if, for each neighbor v, the fork u shares with v is clean or v is thinking. Furthermore, when a process eats, it dirties all forks.

This program is not quite suitable for distributed implementation because a process u sends the fork that it shares with a neighbor v, to v, only if v is hungry. How is u to determine whether v is hungry? The next refinement proposes a mechanism by which v informs u that v is hungry.

12.7   Refinement Step: How a Process Informs a Neighbor that It Is Hungry

The goal of this refinement step is to replace the progress property (odn8) by properties from which a program can be derived easily.

12.7.1 The Solution: Informal Description

The motivation for this refinement step is this question: How is a process to determine whether its neighbor is hungry and hence needs the fork they share? To answer this question, we employ a token called a *request-token* for each pair of neighbors. A request-token shared by u and v is either at u or at v. The key invariant is this: If u holds both the fork and the request-token shared with v then v is hungry (see odn14).

The invariant and the motivation for this refinement step (see Section 12.6.4) suggest the following rules.

1. Sending request-tokens (see odn15,odn16). A process u sends the request-token that it shares with v, to v, if (1) u holds the request-token, (2) u does not hold the fork that it shares with v, and (3) u is hungry.

2. Sending forks (see odn17,odn18). A process u sends the fork that it shares with v, to v, if (1) u holds both the fork and the request-token that it shares with v, (2) the fork is dirty, and (3) u is not eating. When the fork is sent it is cleaned (see odn12).

3. Transition from hungry to eating (see odn19). A hungry process u eats if it holds all forks that it shares with its neighbors, and, for each neighbor v, the fork u and v share is clean, or u does not hold the request-token shared with v. When u eats, all forks it holds are dirtied (see odn10).

First we show that if $u.top$ holds, i.e., if u has no higher-priority hungry neighbor, then, for every higher priority neighbor v of u, u holds the fork but not the request-token shared with v. If v holds the fork that it shares with u, the fork is clean (because v has priority over u). But clean forks are held only by hungry processes. If $u.top$ holds, u has no higher-priority hungry neighbor. Therefore, if $u.top$ holds, u holds the fork shared with a higher priority neighbor v. Now u holds the request-token as well as the fork only if v is hungry. Since a higher-priority neighbor v is not hungry, u does not hold the request-token shared with v.

Next we show that a hungry process u eventually holds the (clean) fork that it shares with a lower-priority neighbor v. If u does not hold the fork, from the rule for sending request-tokens, v receives the request-token from u. Since eating periods are finite, v eventually stops eating if it is eating. A hungry process v does not start eating if it holds a dirty fork and the corresponding request-token (see the rule for transition from hungry to eating), and it eventually sends the fork (see the rule for sending forks).

From the arguments of the last two paragraphs, if $u.h \wedge u.top$ holds and continues to hold, then eventually the condition for the transition of u from hungry to eating is satisfied.

12.7.2 The Solution Strategy: Formal Description

For each pair u,v of neighbors, a variable $rf[u,v]$ is introduced, where $rf[u,v]$ takes on one of the values, u or v. We say that the request-token shared by u and v is at u if and only if $rf[u,v] = u$. (The letters rf stand for request fork.)

We introduce abbreviations $u.mayeat$ (the condition under which a hungry u may eat), $sendreq[u,v]$ (the condition under which u sends a request-token to v) and $sendfork[u,v]$ (the condition under which u sends a fork to v), defined as follows:

$$u.mayeat \equiv \langle \forall v : E[u,v] :: (fork[u,v] = u) \land (clean[u,v] \lor (rf[u,v] = v))\rangle,$$
$$sendreq[u,v] \equiv (fork[u,v] = v) \land (rf[u,v] = u) \land u.h,$$
$$sendfork[u,v] \equiv (fork[u,v] = u) \land \neg clean[u,v] \land (rf[u,v] = u) \land \neg u.e \,.$$

We propose specification *spec5*, obtained from *spec4*, by replacing (odn8) with (odn14–odn19).

spec5   [odn1,odn2,odn7,odn10–19]

invariant $(fork[u,v] = u) \land (rf[u,v] = u) \Rightarrow v.h$	(odn14)
$rf[u,v] = u$ *unless* $sendreq[u,v]$	(odn15)
$sendreq[u,v]$ *ensures* $rf[u,v] = v$	(odn16)
$fork[u,v] = u$ *unless* $sendfork[u,v]$	(odn17)
$sendfork[u,v]$ *ensures* $fork[u,v] = v$	(odn18)
$(u.h \land u.mayeat)$ *ensures* $\neg(u.h \land u.mayeat)$	(odn19)

12.7.3 Proof of Correctness of the Solution Strategy

Properties (odn14–odn19) hold for the composite program because $u.h$ and $\neg u.e$ are stable in *user*, and *fork*, *rf* are local to *os*. Now we are obliged to prove from the hypothesis of (odn8) and the specifications of the refined program that the conclusion of (odn8) holds. All properties in the following proof refer to the composite program.

The proof is based on the two properties (prf1,prf2), proofs of which are sketched later. We introduce the abbreviation $u.tmh$, for u is a *topmost hungry* process:

$$u.tmh \equiv u.h \land u.top$$

$u.tmh \ \mapsto\ (fork[u,v] = u) \land (clean[u,v] \lor (rf[u,v] = v))$	(prf1)
$(fork[u,v] = u) \land (clean[u,v] \lor (rf[u,v] = v))$ *unless* $\neg u.tmh$	(prf2)

Proof: the conclusion of (odn8), $u.h \land u.top \ \mapsto\ \neg(u.h \land u.top)$

$u.tmh \ \mapsto\ u.mayeat \lor \neg u.tmh$

, using the completion theorem over all neighbors v of u in (prf1,prf2)

$u.tmh \;\longmapsto\; (u.tmh \wedge u.mayeat) \vee \neg u.tmh$
, trivially from the above $\hspace{6cm}$ (prf3)

$u.mayeat \;\; unless \;\; \neg u.tmh$
, apply simple conjunction to (prf2) for all neighbors v of u

$u.h \wedge u.mayeat \;\; ensures \;\; \neg(u.h \wedge u.mayeat)$
, from (odn19)

$u.h \wedge u.mayeat \;\; \longmapsto \;\; \neg u.tmh$
, applying the PSP theorem to the above two and
observing that $\neg u.h \Rightarrow \neg u.tmh$

$u.tmh \wedge u.mayeat \;\; \longmapsto \;\; \neg u.tmh$
, from the above and $u.tmh \Rightarrow u.h$

$u.tmh \;\; \longmapsto \;\; \neg u.tmh$
, cancellation on the above and (prf3)

$u.h \wedge u.top \;\; \longmapsto \;\; \neg(u.h \wedge u.top)$
, from the above and the definition of $u.tmh$ $\hspace{3cm}$ ▽

Proof: (prf1) $u.tmh \;\longmapsto\; (fork[u,v] = u) \wedge (clean[u,v] \vee (rf[u,v] = v))$

We show (prf1) from (prf4,prf5). The proofs of (prf4,prf5) are left to the reader.

$u.top \wedge (prior[u,v] = v) \;\Rightarrow\; (fork[u,v] = u) \wedge (rf[u,v] = v)$ $\hspace{1.5cm}$ (prf4)

$u.h \wedge (prior[u,v] = u) \;\longmapsto\; (fork[u,v] = u) \wedge clean[u,v]$ $\hspace{1.5cm}$ (prf5)

Strengthening the left sides of (prf4,prf5), and replacing $\Rightarrow$ by $\longmapsto$, gives

$u.tmh \wedge (prior[u,v] = v) \;\longmapsto\; (fork[u,v] = u) \wedge (rf[u,v] = v)$

$u.tmh \wedge (prior[u,v] = u) \;\longmapsto\; (fork[u,v] = u) \wedge clean[u,v].$

Applying disjunction to the above two properties gives (prf1). $\hspace{2cm}$ ▽

Proof: (prf2) $(fork[u,v] = u) \wedge (clean[u,v] \vee (rf[u,v] = v)) \;\; unless \;\; \neg u.tmh$

We show (prf2) by applying the simple disjunction rule to the following two properties. The proof of (prf6) is left to the reader; see Exercise 12.3.

$(fork[u,v] = u) \wedge \neg clean[u,v] \wedge (rf[u,v] = v) \;\; unless \;\; \neg u.top$ $\hspace{1cm}$ (prf6)

$(fork[u,v] = u) \wedge clean[u,v] \;\; unless \;\; \neg u.h$
, from (odn11) and $u.e \Rightarrow \neg u.h$ $\hspace{3cm}$ ▽

Exercise 12.3   Prove (prf6).

Hint: Apply conjunction to (odn12,odn17) and then to (odn15 with u,v interchanged). This gives

$$(fork[u,v] = u) \;\wedge\; \neg clean[u,v] \;\wedge\; (rf[u,v] = v) \;\; unless$$

$$(fork[u,v] = u) \;\wedge\; \neg clean[u,v] \;\wedge\; sendreq[v,u]$$

The right side of the above *unless* implies $\neg u.top$. $\triangledown$

12.8   A Review of the Refinement Steps

A summary of the stepwise refinements is given next. First we state all the properties proposed for *os*. Then we summarize the refinement steps and the resulting specification in each step.

12.8.1 Properties of *os* Proposed in Stepwise Refinement

constant $u.t$ (odn1)

stable $u.e$ (odn2)

invariant $\neg(u.e \wedge v.e \wedge E[u,v])$ (odn3)

Conditional Property   (odn4)

Hypothesis: (dn1,dn3-dn5), $\langle \forall u \;::\; u.e \;\mapsto\; \neg u.e \rangle$
Conclusion: $\langle \forall u \;::\; u.h \;\mapsto\; u.e \rangle$

invariant $u.e \wedge E[u,v] \;\Rightarrow\; (prior[u,v] = v)$ (odn5)

$(prior[u,v] = v) \;\; unless \;\; v.e$ (odn6)

invariant G' is acyclic   (odn7)

Conditional Property   (odn8)

Hypothesis: (dn1,dn3–dn5), (odn5–odn7), $\langle \forall u \;::\; u.e \;\mapsto\; \neg u.e \rangle$
Conclusion: $\langle \forall u \;::\; u.h \wedge u.top \;\mapsto\; \neg(u.h \wedge u.top) \rangle$

invariant $u.e \wedge E[u,v] \;\Rightarrow\; (fork[u,v] = u)$ (odn9)

invariant $u.e \wedge E[u,v] \;\Rightarrow\; (fork[u,v] = u \wedge \neg clean[u,v])$ (odn10)

$(fork[u,v] = v) \;\wedge\; clean[u,v] \;\; unless \;\; v.e$ (odn11)

$(fork[u,v] = u) \;\wedge\; \neg clean[u,v] \; unless \; (fork[u,v] = v) \;\wedge\; clean[u,v]$ (odn12)

invariant $(fork[u,v] = u) \;\wedge\; clean[u,v] \;\Rightarrow\; u.h$ (odn13)

invariant $(fork[u,v] = u) \; \land \; (rf[u,v] = u) \;\; \Rightarrow \;\; v.h$ (odn14)

$rf[u,v] = u \;\; unless \;\; sendreq[u,v]$ (odn15)

$sendreq[u,v] \;\; ensures \;\; rf[u,v] = v$ (odn16)

$fork[u,v] = u \;\; unless \;\; sendfork[u,v]$ (odn17)

$sendfork[u,v] \;\; ensures \;\; fork[u,v] = v$ (odn18)

$(u.h \; \land \; u.mayeat) \;\; ensures \;\; \neg(u.h \; \land \; u.mayeat)$ (odn19)

12.8.2 Summary of Specifications Proposed in Stepwise Refinements

spec1: Preliminary design (odn1–odn4)

spec2: Introduction of a partial ordering, *prior* (odn1–odn3,odn5–odn8)

spec3: Guaranteeing that neighbors do not eat simultaneously—the introduction of forks (odn1,odn2,odn5–odn9)

spec4: Distributed implementation of priority—the introduction of clean/dirty attributes of forks (odn1,odn2,odn7,odn8, odn10–odn13)

spec5: Guaranteeing progress—the introduction of request-tokens (odn1, odn2, odn7, odn10–odn19)

12.9   Derivation of a Program from the Specification of the Solution Strategy

In this section we derive a program satisfying the refined specification *spec5* of *os*.

First consider the initial conditions. The invariants of *os* are as follows: G' is acyclic (i.e., *prior* is a partial ordering), an eating process holds all forks corresponding to its incident edges, clean forks are held only by hungry processes, and a process holds both a fork and its corresponding request token only if its neighbor is hungry. To simplify matters, we assume that processes are initially thinking (we include this initialization in the next program, though the initial process states are determined by *user* rather than by *os*).

Now the invariants suggest that all forks are dirty, that a fork and its corresponding request-token are at different processes, and that forks are arranged to guarantee the acyclicity of G'. For convenience in implementing the initial condition we assume that the process indices are numbers (or that there is a total ordering among processes). So as to guarantee that G' is acyclic initially, a fork shared by two processes is placed at the process with the lower index. Therefore initially (since all forks are dirty) a process has higher priority if and only if it has a higher index. Of course, there are many initial conditions that satisfy the invariant; we are proposing an obvious one.

Next we derive the statements of the assign-section. The progress condition (odn19)—a hungry process u for which $u.mayeat$ continues to hold transits from hungry state, or $u.mayeat$ is falsified—and the invariant that all forks held by eating processes are dirty, (odn10), suggest that

> {u changes state from hungry to eating if $u.mayeat$ holds}
>
> $u.dine := e$ if $u.h \land u.mayeat$
>
> {and all forks held by u are dirtied}
>
> $\|\ \langle\| \ v \ : \ E[u,v] \ :: \ clean[u,v] := false$ if $u.h \land u.mayeat\rangle$

The progress condition (odn16)—a hungry process u sends a request-token to a neighbor v if u does not hold the corresponding fork—suggests that

> $rf[u,v] := v$ if $sendreq[u,v]$

The progress condition (odn18) (a noneating process u holding both a dirty fork and the corresponding request-token for edge (u,v) sends the fork to v) and the requirement (odn12) (a fork is cleaned when it is sent) suggest that:

> $fork[u,v], \ clean[u,v] := v, \ true$ if $sendfork[u,v]$

The complete program follows.

Program {distributed dining philosophers} *os*

always

> $\langle\| \ u \ :: \ u.mayeat =$
> $\quad \langle \land \ v \ : \ E[u,v] \ ::$
> $\qquad (fork[u,v] = u) \ \land \ (clean[u,v] \ \lor \ (rf[u,v] = v))\rangle$
> $\rangle$
>
> $\| \ \langle\| \ u,v \ : \ E[u,v] \ ::$
> $\qquad sendreq[u,v] = ((fork[u,v] = v) \ \land \ (rf[u,v] = u) \ \land \ u.h)$
> $\quad \| \quad sendfork[u,v] =$
> $\qquad\qquad ((fork[u,v] = u) \ \land \ \neg clean[u,v] \ \land \ (rf[u,v] = u) \ \land \ \neg u.e)$
> $\rangle$

initially

> $\langle\| \ u \ :: \ u.dine = t\rangle$ {all processes are thinking}

⫿ ⟨⫿ (u,v) :: $clean[u,v] = false$⟩   {all forks are dirty}
⫿ {a fork and the corresponding request token
    are at different processes}
    ⟨⫿ (u,v) : $u < v$ :: $fork[u,v]$, $rf[u,v] = u,v$⟩

assign

⟨⫿ u :: $u.dine := e$ if $u.h \wedge u.mayeat$
    ∥⟨∥ v : $E[u,v]$ :: $clean[u,v] := false$ if $u.h \wedge u.mayeat$⟩
⟩

⫿ ⟨⫿ (u,v) ::
        $rf[u,v] := v$ if $sendreq[u,v]$
    ⫿ $fork[u,v], clean[u,v] := v, true$ if $sendfork[u,v]$
⟩

end {os}

12.9.1 Distributed Implementation of os

The reader may replace the shared variables $fork[u,v]$, $clean[u,v]$, and $rf[u,v]$ in program os by variables local to processes u,v and channels, in both directions, between u and v. Implement $fork[u,v]$ and $rf[u,v]$ as tokens that are at the processes or in the channels between them. Implement $clean[u,v]$ as an attribute of the token $fork[u,v]$.

Exercise 12.4   Given that all thinking periods are of finite duration, investigate simplifications in the specification and design.   ▽

Exercise 12.5   Does the solution given in this chapter extend to the case in which *hungry* to *thinking* transitions are permissible in program *user*?   ▽

Exercise 12.6   Given graph G' and the states of all processes (including the locations of forks and request-tokens), determine the minimum number of messages that must be transmitted between processes before a given hungry process u eats.   ▽

Summary

A summary of the design is given in Section 12.8.2. The design of the dining philosophers program in UNITY has more to do with refining of specifications than with producing UNITY code. At each refinement step, some program properties proposed in previous steps are replaced by other, more detailed properties. Of course, the motivation for a stepwise refinement (see Sections 12.3.4, 12.4.4, 12.5.4, and 12.6.4) is an operational view of a computer; we propose certain refinements rather than others because we hope to derive efficient programs for some target architecture. Therefore at certain stages in design we focus on the operational view, but when it comes to specifications and proofs it is easier to deal with properties of programs rather than with programs themselves.

A traditional view of program design by stepwise refinement is to propose a program skeleton, and to flesh out a part of the skeleton at each refinement step. This approach has the advantage of making the structure of the program apparent at the earliest stages of design. The approach to program design employed in this chapter is different; the derivation of a program is postponed to the very last stage of design, and indeed program derivation is the least inventive part of the design.

Bibliographic Notes

The distributed dining philosophers problem is described in Dijkstra [1978]. The program derived in this chapter is based on Chandy and Misra [1984].

CHAPTER 13

Drinking Philosophers

13.1   Introduction

The goal of this chapter is to demonstrate an application of the theory of program composition (see Chapter 7) and to solve an important problem in conflict resolution called the *drinking philosophers*, or the *drinkers* problem for short.

13.1.1 The Problem: Informal Description

The drinkers problem is a generalization of the diners problem of Chapter 12. A process in the drinkers problem is in one of three states, *tranquil*, *thirsty*, or *drinking*, by analogy to the thinking, hungry, or eating states of the diners problem. The only state transitions are tranquil → thirsty → drinking → tranquil. There is a nonempty set of *beverages* associated with each thirsty or drinking process. The set of beverages associated with a process remains unchanged while the process is nontranquil. When a tranquil process becomes thirsty, a set of beverages becomes associated with the process. It is not our concern here how the set of beverages is chosen. Different sets of beverages may be chosen for the same process on different transitions from tranquil to thirsty. The problem is to design a program that guarantees that (1) neighbors do not drink at the same time if they have a beverage in common, and (2) every thirsty process drinks eventually, assuming that no process drinks forever.

The drinkers problem reduces to the diners problem if there is only one beverage because in this case neighboring processes cannot drink at the same time, and therefore drinking and eating are equivalent.

Example 13.1

Figure 13.1 shows a possible snapshot of the processes in the drinkers problem. Sue cannot drink while her neighbor Jim is drinking because Sue and Jim share a common beverage: tonic. Also, Jim and Tom can both be drinking the same beverage, gin, because they are not neighbors. Neighbors Jim and Bob can both be drinking because they are not drinking a common beverage.   ▽

13.1.2 An Application

An application of the drinking philosophers problem is in the management of conflicts for access to files. Each file is represented by a beverage. A process that is computing without access to shared files is tranquil. A process that has halted its computation, and is waiting for access rights to certain files so that it can resume computation, is thirsty; the set of files for which the process is waiting is the set of beverages associated with that process. A process that is computing while it holds access rights to files is drinking; the set of files

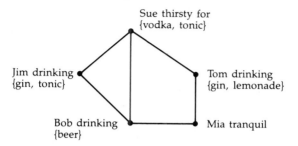

Figure 13.1 A snapshot in a drinkers problem.

to which the process has access rights is the set of beverages associated with that process. Two processes are neighbors if at least one of them writes into a file that they share; two processes that only read common files need not be neighbors. A process does not read or write a file while another process is writing it because neighbors do not drink the same beverage at the same time.

13.1.3 The Central Idea of the Solution

It is tempting to try to solve the drinkers problem the same way we solved the diners problem, but the approach does not work, as illustrated by the following example. Consider a situation in which neighboring processes v and w are both drinking, where v is drinking gin and w is drinking tonic. Now suppose that v and w both become tranquil and then become thirsty for both gin and tonic. Should v yield to w or w to v? The situation is symmetric unless we give priority to the process that last drank gin over the process that last drank tonic—or vice versa. In this chapter, we choose not to rank beverages. The resolution of a conflict requires some basis for discrimination among processes: The conflict is resolved in favor of one process and against others. For symmetric conflicts, how can we decide which process to favor?

The central idea in this chapter, elaborated next, is the use of the diners solution to introduce fair asymmetry into the drinkers problem.

Resolving Drinking Conflicts through Asymmetry Introduced by Dining

Each process executes both dining cycles, i.e., thinking $\rightarrow$ hungry $\rightarrow$ eating $\rightarrow$ thinking $\rightarrow$ ..., and drinking cycles, i.e., tranquil $\rightarrow$ thirsty $\rightarrow$ drinking $\rightarrow$ tranquil $\rightarrow$ .... Thus the state of a process is the pair (dining-state, drinking-state). The following transitions of the drinking-state are not under our control, but are determined by the given program for the drinkers problem: $(x,$ tranquil$) \rightarrow (x,$ thirsty$)$, and $(x,$ drinking$) \rightarrow (x,$ tranquil$)$, where x denotes any

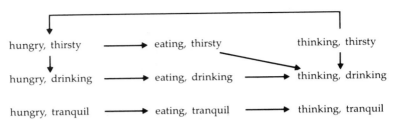

Figure 13.2 State transitions in the solution.

dining state. We propose that the other state transitions satisfy the following rules.

1. A thinking-thirsty process becomes hungry or drinking.

2. Hungry processes eat eventually provided that no process eats forever. (This rule is implemented by the diners solution.)

3. An eating-thirsty process becomes thinking-drinking. An eating-nonthirsty process becomes thinking or thirsty.

The key idea in implementing these conditions is that drinking conflicts are resolved in favor of eating processes. Therefore an eating-thirsty process eventually wins its drinking conflict with its neighbors and becomes drinking.

The state transitions in our proposed solution are shown in Fig. 13.2.

Now we argue informally that these progress conditions guarantee that a thirsty process will drink. We first show that all eating periods are finite, and hence, from the dining philosophers solution, every hungry process becomes eating: Rule 3 guarantees that an eating process becomes thinking because an eating-nonthirsty process either becomes eating-thirsty or thinking, and an eating-thirsty process becomes thinking. We now show that a thirsty process is guaranteed to drink. A thinking-thirsty process becomes hungry-thirsty or drinking (rule 1); a hungry-thirsty process becomes eating-thirsty or drinking (rule 2); and an eating-thirsty process becomes thinking-drinking (rule 3). Therefore a thirsty process (which is either eating, hungry, or thinking) drinks eventually.

Exercise 13.1   An obvious solution is that a thirsty process drinks only if it is eating. What is inefficient about this solution?   ▽

13.1.4 Structure of the Solution

The specification structure and design structure employed in this chapter are identical to those used in the previous one. We are required to design a program *osdrink* given the specifications of (1) a program *userdrink*, (2)

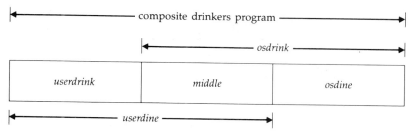

Figure 13.3 Composite drinkers program: *userdrink* ‖ *middle* ‖ *osdine*.

the composite program *userdrink* ‖ *osdrink*, and (3) the protocol by which *osdrink* modifies variables shared with *userdrink*. Section 13.1.3 suggests that we design *osdrink* as the union of two programs: *osdine*, the solution for the diners problem designed in Chapter 12, and a program *middle*, designed in this chapter. (Note: We use *osdine* for the name of the program in the diners problem, rather than *os* as in the last chapter, because we want to identify the diners and drinkers components clearly.) Figure 13.3 shows the structure of the composite drinkers problem.

We are required to design program *middle* so that

1. *userdrink* ‖ *middle* satisfies the specifications of *userdine* because the program *userdrink* ‖ *middle* interfaces with *osdine*,

2. *userdrink* ‖ *middle* ‖ *osdine* satisfies the specifications for the composite program for the drinkers problem, and

3. *middle* satisfies the specifications for *osdrink* on modifying variables that it shares with *userdrink*.

Designing *osdrink* as a composition of two program components simplifies the design task because one of the components, *osdine*, has already been designed; this is the essential advantage of modularity.

The problem is specified in Section 13.2. An initial design for *middle* is proposed in Section 13.3. Sections 13.4 and 13.5 describe stepwise refinements of the design of *middle*. A program is derived in Section 13.6.

The sections of this chapter on design and stepwise refinements have the following structure. The first subsection is an informal description of the solution; the second subsection is a formal description of the solution in terms of the properties that we want our program to have; the third subsection is a proof that the proposed solution is correct; the last subsection includes an informal description of a program with the proposed properties and presents motivations for further refinements. (After the very last refinement step, we do not present motivations for further refinements, nor do we describe programs informally.) An overview of the design can be obtained from the informal discussions in each section.

13.2   Problem Specification

13.2.1 Notation

As in the previous chapter, we are given a static finite undirected graph G. Associated with each vertex (i.e., process) u is a variable $u.imbibe$ that takes on values $tranquil$, $thirsty$, $drinking$. For convenience, we also employ boolean variables $u.tranquil$, $u.thirsty$, $u.drinking$, defined as $u.tranquil \equiv (u.imbibe = tranquil)$, $u.thirsty \equiv (u.imbibe = thirsty)$, and $u.drinking \equiv (u.imbibe = drinking)$. Also associated with each u is a variable $u.bev$, where $u.bev$ is a subset of a given constant set of beverages.

To avoid confusion between the drinkers and diners problems, we use $thinking$, $hungry$, $eating$ in place of t, h, e as the states of the diner.

As in Chapter 12, we do not explicitly show the program names with the properties; the name of the program is clear from the context.

13.2.2 Specification of *userdrink*

The only transition in *userdrink* from tranquil is to thirsty (udr1). There are no transitions from thirsty in *userdrink* (udr2). The only transition from drinking is to tranquil (udr3). The value of $u.bev$ remains unchanged while u is nontranquil (udr4). For simplicity in exposition, we assume that $u.bev$ is $empty$ if and only if u is tranquil (udr5). Drinking periods are of finite duration in any program with which *userdrink* is composed (udr6).

$u.tranquil \quad unless \quad u.thirsty$ (udr1)

stable $\quad u.thirsty$ (udr2)

$u.drinking \quad unless \quad u.tranquil$ (udr3)

For any constant subset B of beverages:

$(u.bev = B) \quad unless \quad u.tranquil$ (udr4)

invariant $\quad (u.bev = empty) \quad \equiv \quad u.tranquil$ (udr5)

Conditional Property (udr6)

Hypothesis: $\quad true$
Conclusion: $\quad \langle \forall u \quad :: \quad u.drinking \; \mapsto \; \neg u.drinking \rangle$

The hypothesis and the conclusion of (udr6) are properties of the composite program. Since the hypothesis is $true$, it follows that the conclusion holds for any program of which *userdrink* is a component.

Derived Properties of *userdrink*

It follows, by applying the disjunction rule to (udr1,udr2), that there are no transitions to drinking in *userdrink*, i.e.,

stable $\neg u.drinking$ (udr7)

13.2.3 Specification of the Composite Program

Neighbors do not drink the same beverage at the same time (dr1), and thirsty processes drink eventually (dr2).

invariant

$\neg(u.drinking \land v.drinking \land (u.bev \cap v.bev \neq empty) \land E[u,v])$ (dr1)

$u.thirsty \longmapsto u.drinking$ (dr2)

13.2.4 Constraints on *osdrink*

The only variables that are shared between *userdrink* and *osdrink* are $u.bev$ and $u.imbibe$, for all u. There are no transitions in *osdrink* from drinking (odr2), from tranquil (odr1), or to tranquil (odr1). Also, $u.bev$ is not modified by *osdrink*, i.e., for any constant subset of beverages B, $u.bev = B$ remains unchanged in value (odr1).

constant $u.tranquil, u.bev = B$ (odr1)

stable $u.drinking$ (odr2)

Derived Properties of *osdrink*

From (odr1,odr2) it follows that there are no transitions to thirsty in *osdrink* (odr3), and that the only transition from thirsty in *osdrink* is to drinking (odr4).

stable $\neg u.thirsty$ (odr3)

$u.thirsty \; unless \; u.drinking$ (odr4)

13.2.5 Derived Properties of the Composite Program

From the specification of *userdrink* and the constraints (odr1,odr2) on *osdrink*, it follows that the only transitions in the composite program, *userdrink* [*osdrink*, are from tranquil to thirsty (dr3), from thirsty to drinking (dr4), and from drinking to tranquil (dr5). Also, the properties about $u.bev$ in *userdrink* hold for the composite program because $u.bev$ is not modified in *osdrink* and $u.tranquil$ is constant (dr6,dr7). Drinking periods are finite (dr8), from (udr6).

$u.tranquil \; unless \; u.thirsty$ (dr3)

$u.thirsty \; unless \; u.drinking$ (dr4)

$u.drinking \; unless \; u.tranquil$ (dr5)

	userdrink	*middle*	*osdine*
drinking transitions	tranquil ➙ thirsty drinking ➙ tranquil	thirsty ➙ drinking	
eating transitions		thinking ➙ hungry eating ➙ thinking	hungry ➙ eating

Figure 13.4 Transitions in the different programs.

For any constant subset B of beverages:

$$(u.bev = B) \quad unless \quad u.tranquil \tag{dr6}$$

$$\textbf{invariant} \quad (u.bev = empty) \quad \equiv \quad u.tranquil \tag{dr7}$$

$$u.drinking \quad \longmapsto \quad \neg u.drinking \tag{dr8}$$

13.3   Preliminary Design

13.3.1 The Solution: Informal Description

As proposed in Section 13.1.4, program *osdrink* is a union of *osdine*, the operating system program of the diners problem, and *middle*, a program designed in this chapter. (The structure of the composite program is shown in Fig. 13.3.) The only variables shared by *userdrink* and *middle* are *u.imbibe* and *u.bev*, for all *u*. These variables are not named in *osdine*.

The transitions for which each of the three programs—*userdrink*, *middle*, and *osdine*—is responsible are shown in Fig. 13.4.

The reader is referred to Section 13.1.3 for an informal description of the central idea of the solution.

13.3.2 The Solution Strategy: Formal Description

This section proposes a specification for *middle*.

The constraints (odr1,odr2) on *osdrink* regarding the modification of variables shared with *userdrink* are adopted in *middle* (see mdr1,mdr2). The properties of *userdine* (udn1–udn3), given in the specification in Section 12.2.3, are adopted in *middle* (see mdr3–mdr5) because *userdrink* [] *middle* is required to have the properties of *userdine*. We propose that the invariant (dr1) of the composite program is also an invariant of *middle* (see mdr6). From Section 13.1.3 (see Fig. 13.2), we propose that thinking-thirsty processes and eating-nonthirsty processes change state (see mdr7,mdr8). Finally, *middle* is designed so that an eating-thirsty process eventually becomes thinking-drinking in any composite program that has *middle* as one of its components, provided that drinking periods are finite in the composite program (see mdr9).

Specification of *middle*   [(mdr1–mdr9)]

The only variables shared between *middle* and *userdrink* are *u.imbibe* and *u.bev*, for all *u*. In (mdr1) B is any constant subset of beverages.

constant $u.tranquil, u.bev = B$ (mdr1)

stable $u.drinking$ (mdr2)

$u.thinking$ *unless* $u.hungry$ (mdr3)

stable $u.hungry$ (mdr4)

$u.eating$ *unless* $u.thinking$ (mdr5)

invariant

$\neg(u.drinking \land v.drinking \land (u.bev \cap v.bev \neq empty) \land E[u,v])$ (mdr6)

$(u.thinking \land u.thirsty)$ *ensures* $\neg(u.thinking \land u.thirsty)$ (mdr7)

$(u.eating \land \neg u.thirsty)$ *ensures* $\neg(u.eating \land \neg u.thirsty)$ (mdr8)

Conditional Property   (mdr9)

Hypothesis: (dr3-dr7), and (dr8): $\langle \forall u \ :: \ u.drinking \ \mapsto \ \neg u.drinking \rangle$
Conclusion: $\langle \forall u \ :: \ u.eating \land u.thirsty \ \mapsto \ u.thinking \land u.drinking \rangle$

13.3.3 Proof of Correctness of the Solution Strategy

Our obligation is to prove that

1. *middle* satisfies the constraints on *osdrink*,

2. *userdrink* ∥ *middle* satisfies the specification of *userdine*, and

3. *userdrink* ∥ *middle* ∥ *osdine* satisfies the specification of the composite program for the drinkers problem.

Constraints on *osdrink* are met

Program *middle* satisfies the specifications regarding modification of variables shared with *userdrink* because (mdr1,mdr2) are the same as (odr1,odr2). Therefore (dr3–dr8) hold for the composite drinkers program. Hence the conclusion of (mdr9) holds for the composite program as well.

Specification of *userdine* is met

Now we prove that *userdrink* ‖ *middle* satisfies the specification of *userdine*. (See Section 12.2.3 for the specification of *userdine*.)

The properties (udn1–udn3) are the same as (mdr3–mdr5); these are properties of *userdrink* ‖ *middle* because they are properties of *middle*, and *u.dine* is not modified in *userdrink* (from the constraints on the interface between *userdrink* and *osdrink*; see Section 13.2.4).

Next we prove the conditional property (udn4) of *userdine*: Eating periods are finite, given that neighbors are not eating simultaneously. Here we prove the stronger result that *userdrink* ‖ *middle* guarantees the conclusion of (udn4) for any program of which it is a component, without employing the hypothesis of (udn4).

The following properties refer to the composite drinkers program:

$(u.eating \ \wedge \ \neg u.thirsty) \ \ unless \ \ \neg(u.eating \ \wedge \ \neg u.thirsty)$
, $p \ unless \ \neg p$ holds in any program

$(u.eating \ \wedge \ \neg u.thirsty) \ \ ensures \ \ \neg(u.eating \ \wedge \ \neg u.thirsty)$
, union theorem on the above and (mdr8)

$u.eating \ \wedge \ \neg u.thirsty \ \mapsto \ \ \neg u.eating \ \vee \ (u.eating \ \wedge \ u.thirsty)$ (1)
, from the above rewriting its right side

hypothesis of (mdr9) holds
, because (dr3–dr8) have been proven

$u.eating \ \wedge \ u.thirsty \ \mapsto \ \ u.thinking \ \wedge \ u.drinking$
, conclusion of (mdr9) using the above

$u.eating \ \mapsto \ \ \neg u.eating \ \vee \ (u.thinking \ \wedge \ u.drinking)$
, from the above and (1) by cancellation and disjunction

$u.eating \ \mapsto \ \ \neg u.eating$
, from the above because $u.thinking \ \Rightarrow \ \neg u.eating$

Hence specifications (udn1–udn4) of *userdine* are met. Therefore the composite program, *userdrink* ‖ *middle* ‖ *osdine*, satisfies the specifications for the composite program of the diners problem. From the specification of the composite diners program, we conclude (see condition (dn2) in Section 12.2.4) that the following holds in the composite drinkers program:

$u.hungry \ \mapsto \ \ u.eating$ (dr9)

Specification of Composite Drinkers Program Is Met

Proof: (dr1)

Property (mdr6) is stable in *userdrink* because $\neg u.drinking$ is stable in *userdrink*, $u.bev$ remains unchanged while $u.drinking$ holds, and $E[u,v]$

is constant. The property is also stable in *osdine* because *osdine* does not modify the variables named in the property. Hence (mdr6) is invariant in the composite program. This proves (dr1). $\triangledown$

Proof: (dr2),   *u.thirsty* $\mapsto$ *u.drinking*

In the following proof, all properties are for the composite program.

(*u.thinking* $\wedge$ *u.thirsty*) *unless* $\neg$(*u.thinking* $\wedge$ *u.thirsty*)
   , *p unless* $\neg p$ holds in any program

(*u.thinking* $\wedge$ *u.thirsty*) $\mapsto$ $\neg$(*u.thinking* $\wedge$ *u.thirsty*)
   , union theorem on the above and (mdr7); replacing *ensures* by $\mapsto$

u.thinking $\wedge$ *u.thirsty* $\mapsto$ $\neg$*u.thirsty* $\vee$ *u.hungry*
   , PSP theorem on (mdr3) and the above; weakening the right side

u.thinking $\wedge$ *u.thirsty* $\mapsto$ $\neg$*u.thirsty* $\vee$ (*u.hungry* $\wedge$ *u.thirsty*)
   , from the above using predicate calculus

u.hungry $\wedge$ *u.thirsty* $\mapsto$ $\neg$*u.thirsty* $\vee$ (*u.eating* $\wedge$ *u.thirsty*)
   , from (dr9), *u.hungry* $\mapsto$ *u.eating*, strengthening the left side and weakening the right side

u.eating $\wedge$ *u.thirsty* $\mapsto$ $\neg$*u.thirsty*
   , from the conclusion of (mdr9)—since its hypothesis has been proven—by weakening its right side

u.thirsty $\mapsto$ $\neg$*u.thirsty*
   , from the above three by cancellation and disjunction

u.thirsty $\mapsto$ *u.drinking*
   , PSP theorem on the above and (dr4) $\triangledown$

13.3.4 Motivation for the Next Refinement

A rule for the thirsty to drinking transition, suggested by the specification, is as follows:

A thirsty process *u* drinks if, for all its neighbors *v*, (1) *u* is eating and *v* is not drinking a beverage that *u* needs, or (2) there is no conflict for a common beverage between *u* and *v*.

A difficulty in implementing this rule is that *u* must determine that a neighbor *v* is not drinking a beverage in *u.bev*. In the next refinement step we propose a mechanism by which this determination can be made asynchronously by *u*, without reading the state of *v*.

13.4   Refinement Step: The Introduction of Bottles

13.4.1 The Solution: Informal Description

For each beverage b and for each pair of neighbors u,v, a token called a *bottle* is introduced, where the bottle is held by u or by v (but not by both u and v simultaneously). Bottles are analogous to forks. The key invariant about bottles is the following:

> If process u is drinking then, for all beverages b in $u.bev$, process u holds all bottles of b that u shares.

Neighbors do not drink the same beverage at the same time because they do not hold the same bottle at the same time.

13.4.2 The Solution Strategy: Formal Description

Here we propose a refinement of the specification given in Section 13.3.2.

Specification of *middle*   [(mdr1–mdr5,mdr7–mdr9) and (mdr10)]

The bottle of beverage b shared by neighbors u,v is implemented by a variable $bot[u,v,b]$ that takes on values u,v, where $bot[u,v,b] = u$ means that the bottle is held by u. In this refinement step, invariant (mdr6) is replaced by the following:

invariant

$$u.drinking \quad \Rightarrow \quad \langle \forall\, b,v\; :\; (b \in u.bev)\; \wedge\; E[u,v]\; ::\; bot[u,v,b] = u \rangle \qquad \text{(mdr10)}$$

13.4.3 Proof of Correctness of the Solution Strategy

The proof obligation is to show that the refined specification implies (mdr6), the property that has been replaced.

$$u.drinking \;\wedge\; v.drinking \;\wedge\; (b \in u.bev) \;\wedge\; (b \in v.bev) \;\wedge\; E[u,v]$$
$$\Rightarrow \quad (bot[u,v,b] = u) \;\wedge\; (bot[u,v,b] = v) \;\wedge\; E[u,v] \quad \text{, from (mdr10)}$$
$$\Rightarrow \quad \textit{false} \qquad\qquad\qquad\qquad \text{, because } E[u,v] \;\Rightarrow\; (u \neq v)$$

Hence (mdr6) follows.

13.4.4 Motivation for the Next Refinement

A program suggested by the last specification is as follows:

- Transfer of bottles.   A thirsty process u acquires the bottle of beverage b that it shares with a neighbor v if (1) v does not need b (i.e., $b \notin v.bev$) or (2) u is eating and v is not drinking.

- Thirsty to drinking transition.   A thirsty process u drinks if, for all b in $u.bev$ and all neighbors v, the bottle of beverage b is held by u, and it is not the case that v is both eating and needs b for drinking.

A difficulty with asynchronous implementation of this program is that a process u has to determine that a neighbor v is not eating. Another difficulty is that process u has to determine that b is not in $v.bev$. In the next section we propose methods for overcoming these difficulties.

13.5   Refinement Step: How Drinking Conflicts Are Resolved in Favor of Eating Processes

In this refinement step, (mdr9) is replaced by properties that can be implemented directly.

13.5.1 The Solution: Informal Description

For each bottle, we introduce a *request-token* by which a process informs its neighbor that it needs the bottle. In order to guarantee that drinking conflicts are resolved in favor of eating processes, we propose that a conflict between neighbors u,v be resolved in favor of the *process holding the fork* that u,v share. Since an eating process holds all forks that it shares, all conflicts between an eating process and its neighbors are resolved in favor of the eating process. These arguments suggest the following rules.

1. Thinking to hungry (as in Section 13.1.3). A thinking-thirsty process does not remain thinking-thirsty forever; it becomes hungry or it drinks (see mdr7).

2. An eating-nonthirsty process does not remain eating-nonthirsty forever; it becomes thinking or thirsty (see mdr8). Furthermore the only transition from eating-thirsty is to thinking-drinking (see mdr11).

3. Thirsty to drinking: A thirsty process u drinks, if for all beverages b in $u.bev$ and for all neighbors v:

   u holds the bottle of beverage b that it shares with v, and

   u holds the fork that it shares with v or u does not hold the request-token for the bottle (see mdr12,mdr13).

4. Sending a bottle: A process u sends the bottle of beverage b that it shares with a neighbor v, to v, if u holds both the bottle and the request-token for the bottle and

   u does not need the bottle $(b \notin u.bev)$, or

   u is not drinking and u does not hold the fork that it shares with v (see mdr14,mdr15).

5. Sending a request-token for a bottle: A process u sends the request-token for a bottle of beverage b that it shares with v, to v, if u holds the request-token but not the bottle, and u is thirsty for beverage b (see mdr16,mdr17).

Our proof obligation is to show from the preceding rules that an eating-thirsty process becomes thinking-drinking (which is the conclusion of (mdr9)). The outline of the proof is as follows. The only transition possible from eating-thirsty is to thinking-drinking; therefore an eating-thirsty process either remains eating-thirsty forever or becomes thinking-drinking. We shall show that a process does not remain eating-thirsty forever.

An eating-thirsty process u sends request-tokens to its neighbors for bottles it needs and does not hold. Consider a neighbor v of u. If v is not drinking and v holds a bottle that u needs, then v sends the bottle to u, according to the rule for sending bottles—because v does not hold the fork that u and v share, since u is eating. If v is drinking a beverage that u needs, then eventually v stops drinking—because drinking periods are finite (dr8)—and then v sends the requested bottle to u. Therefore u holds a bottle it needs and shares with v or eventually v sends the bottle to u.

An eating-thirsty process holds onto bottles it needs until it becomes thinking-drinking, according to the rule for sending bottles. Therefore eventually an eating-thirsty process holds all the bottles it needs. According to the rule for transitions from thirsty to drinking, an eating-thirsty process that holds all bottles it needs becomes a drinking process.

13.5.2 The Solution Strategy: Formal Description

In this section we propose a refinement of the specification given in Section 13.4.2.

The request-token for a bottle of beverage b shared by neighbors u,v is implemented by a variable $rb[u,v,b]$ that takes on values u,v, where $rb[u,v,b] = u$ means that the request-token is at u.

For ease of exposition, the following abbreviations are introduced:

$u.maydrink \equiv$
$\langle \forall\, b,v \;:\; b \in u.bev \;\wedge\; E[u,v] \;::$
$\quad bot[u,v,b] = u \;\wedge\; (rb[u,v,b] = v \;\vee\; fork[u,v] = u) \rangle$

$sendbot[u,v,b]$ $\equiv$
$bot[u,v,b] = u$ $\wedge$ $rb[u,v,b] = u$ $\wedge$
$\quad [b \notin u.bev$ $\vee$ $(fork[u,v] = v$ $\wedge$ $\neg u.drinking)]$

$sendreq[u,v,b]$ $\equiv$ $(rb[u,v,b] = u$ $\wedge$ $bot[u,v,b] = v$ $\wedge$ $b \in u.bev)$,

where $u.maydrink$ is the condition under which a thirsty process u may drink, $sendbot[u,v,b]$ is the condition under which process u sends the bottle of beverage b to a neighbor v, and $sendreq[u,v,b]$ is the condition under which a thirsty process u sends the request-token for beverage b to its neighbor v.

The specification proposed in this step is to replace (mdr9) in the specification of Section 13.4.2 by (mdr11–mdr17).

Specification of *middle*   [mdr1–mdr5,mdr7,mdr8,mdr10–mdr17]

$(u.eating \wedge u.thirsty)$ unless $(u.thinking \wedge u.drinking)$	(mdr11)
$u.thirsty$ unless $u.thirsty \wedge u.maydrink$	(mdr12)
$(u.thirsty \wedge u.maydrink)$ ensures $\neg(u.thirsty \wedge u.maydrink)$	(mdr13)
$bot[u,v,b] = u$ unless $sendbot[u,v,b]$	(mdr14)
$sendbot[u,v,b]$ ensures $\neg sendbot[u,v,b]$	(mdr15)
$rb[u,v,b] = u$ unless $sendreq[u,v,b]$	(mdr16)
$sendreq[u,v,b]$ ensures $\neg sendreq[u,v,b]$	(mdr17)

13.5.3 Proof of Correctness of the Solution Strategy

The proof obligation is to show from the refined specifications and the hypothesis of (mdr9) that its conclusion holds as well. Properties (mdr11–mdr17) hold for the composite program for the following reasons.

1. (mdr11,mdr12) hold because $u.eating$ is stable in *osdine*, $u.thirsty$ is stable in *userdrink*, $u.eating$ is not modified in *userdrink*, and $u.thirsty$ is not named in *osdine*.

2. (mdr13,mdr15,mdr17) hold because p unless $\neg p$ holds for all p in all programs, including *userdrink* and *osdine*.

3. (mdr14,mdr16) hold because bot and rb are local to *middle*.

We next prove the conclusion of (mdr9):

$$u.eating \wedge u.thirsty \;\mapsto\; u.thinking \wedge u.drinking$$

Hereafter we refer only to properties of the composite program. In the remainder of the proof we consider a specific process u; v represents any neighbor of u, B is any given nonempty set of beverages, and b is any beverage in B.

For brevity, the following abbreviations are employed in the proof:

$uetB$: $u.eating \wedge u.thirsty \wedge u.bev = B$

utd : $u.thinking \wedge u.drinking$

uhb : $bot[u,v,b] = u$ $\{uhb$ stands for u holds bottle$\}$

uhr : $rb[u,v,b] = u$ $\{uhr$ stands for u holds request-token$\}$

The proof is based on the following lemma.

Lemma 13.1 $uetB \quad \longmapsto \quad uetB \wedge uhb$

We defer proof of this lemma; we use it to prove the conclusion of (mdr9).

Proof: the conclusion of (mdr9), $uetB \quad \longmapsto \quad utd$

$uetB \quad unless \quad utd$
: , applying conjunction on (mdr11) and (dr6) and then weakening the right side

$uetB \wedge uhb \quad unless \quad utd$
: , conjunction on the above and (mdr14); then weaken the right side   (prf1)

$uetB \quad \longmapsto \quad (uetB \wedge uhb) \vee utd$
: , from Lemma 13.1, by weakening its right side

$uetB \quad \longmapsto \quad (uetB \wedge \langle \forall b,v \quad :: \quad bot[u,v,b] = u \rangle) \vee utd$
: , completion theorem on the above two for all b,v (recall $b \in B$)   (prf2)

$uetB \wedge \langle \forall b,v \quad :: \quad bot[u,v,b] = u \rangle \quad unless \quad utd$
: , simple conjunction on (prf1) over all b (prf3)

$uetB \wedge \langle \forall b,v \quad :: \quad bot[u,v,b] = u \rangle \quad \Rightarrow \quad u.thirsty \wedge u.maydrink$
: , from definitions of $uetB, u.maydrink$ (prf4)

$uetB \wedge \langle \forall b,v \quad :: \quad bot[u,b,v] = u \rangle \quad \longmapsto \quad utd$
: , PSP theorem on (prf3,mdr13), and using (prf4)

$uetB \quad \longmapsto \quad utd$
: , from the above and (prf2), by cancellation $\triangledown$

Proof: Lemma 13.1: $uetB \quad \longmapsto \quad uetB \wedge uhb$

$uetB \quad unless \quad uetB \wedge u.maydrink$
: , conjunction on (mdr12,dr6,mdr11)

$uetB \quad unless \quad uetB \wedge uhb$
: , weakening the right side of the above   (prf5)

$uetB \ \wedge \ \neg uhb \ \wedge \ uhr \ \longmapsto \ uetB \ \wedge \ (uhb \ \vee \ \neg uhr)$
, PSP theorem on the above and (mdr17)

$uetB \ \wedge \ (uhb \ \vee \ \neg uhr) \ \longmapsto \ uetB \ \wedge \ (uhb \ \vee \ \neg uhr)$
, $p \ \longmapsto \ p$ for all p

$uetB \ \longmapsto \ uetB \ \wedge \ (uhb \ \vee \ \neg uhr)$
, disjunction on the above two

$uetB \ \longmapsto \ (uetB \ \wedge \ uhb) \ \vee \ (uetB \ \wedge \ \neg uhb \ \wedge \ \neg uhr)$
, predicate calculus on the above   (prf6)

$uetB \ \wedge \ \neg uhb \ \ unless \ \ uetB \ \wedge \ uhb$
, from (prf5) because $(p \ \ unless \ \ q) \ \equiv \ (p \ \wedge \ \neg q \ \ unless \ \ q)$

$uetB \ \wedge \ \neg uhb \ \wedge \ \neg uhr \ \ unless \ \ uetB \ \wedge \ uhb$
, conjunction on the above and (mdr16, with u,v interchanged);
weaken the right side   (prf7)

$uetB \ \wedge \ \neg uhb \ \wedge \ \neg uhr \ \wedge \ v.drinking \ \longmapsto$
$(uetB \ \wedge \ \neg uhb \ \wedge \ \neg uhr \ \wedge \ \neg v.drinking) \ \vee \ (uetB \ \wedge \ uhb)$
, PSP theorem on (prf7) and (dr8, using v for u)   (prf8)

$\neg v.drinking \ \ unless \ \ v.maydrink$
, cancellation on (udr1,mdr12); weaken the right side

$uetB \ \wedge \ \neg uhb \ \wedge \ \neg uhr \ \wedge \ \neg v.drinking \ \ unless \ \ uetB \ \wedge \ uhb$
, conjunction on (prf7) and the above

$uetB \ \wedge \ \neg uhb \ \wedge \ \neg uhr \ \wedge \ \neg v.drinking \ \longmapsto \ uetB \ \wedge \ uhb$
, PSP theorem on the above and (mdr15 with u,v interchanged)

$uetB \ \wedge \ \neg uhb \ \wedge \ \neg uhr \ \longmapsto \ uetB \ \wedge \ uhb$
, from the above and (prf8) using cancellation and disjunction

$uetB \ \longmapsto \ uetB \ \wedge \ uhb$
, cancellation on the above and (prf6) $\triangledown$

13.6 Derivation of a Program from the Specification of the Solution Strategy

Next we derive a program from the specification proposed in Section 13.5.2; this derivation is almost mechanical. The resulting program is an implementation of the five rules proposed in Section 13.5.1.

The condition (mdr7),

$(u.thinking \ \wedge \ u.thirsty) \ \ ensures \ \ \neg(u.thinking \ \wedge \ u.thirsty),$

suggests that

$u.dine := hungry$ if $u.thinking \wedge u.thirsty$

The condition (mdr8),

$(u.eating \wedge \neg u.thirsty)$ $ensures$ $\neg(u.eating \wedge \neg u.thirsty),$

suggests that

$u.dine := thinking$ if $u.eating \wedge \neg u.thirsty$

The condition (mdr13),

$(u.thirsty \wedge u.maydrink)$ $ensures$ $\neg(u.thirsty \wedge u.maydrink),$

suggests that

$u.imbibe := drinking$ if $u.thirsty \wedge u.maydrink$

The condition (mdr11) states that the only transition from eating-thirsty is to thinking-drinking. To guarantee that the eating to thinking transition takes place when the thirsty to drinking transition occurs, the last statement is modified as follows:

$u.imbibe := drinking$ if $u.thirsty \wedge u.maydrink$

$\|$ $u.dine := thinking$ if $u.thirsty \wedge u.maydrink \wedge u.eating$

The conditions (mdr14,mdr15) suggest that

$bot[u,v,b] = v$ if $sendbot[u,v,b]$

The conditions (mdr16,mdr17) suggest that

$rb[u,v,b] = v$ if $sendreq[u,v,b]$

We propose that initially all processes are thinking-tranquil. This is consistent with the initial conditions of the diners solution.

Program *middle*

always

$$\langle \| \ u \ ::$$
$$u.maydrink = \langle \forall \ b, v \ : \ b \in u.bev \ \wedge \ E[u,v] \ ::$$
$$bot[u,v,b] = u \ \wedge \ (rb[u,v,b] = v \ \vee \ fork[u,v] = u) \rangle$$
$$\rangle$$
$$\| \ \langle \| \ u,v,b \ : \ E[u,v] \ ::$$
$$sendbot[u,v,b] = (bot[u,v,b] = u \ \wedge \ rb[u,v,b] = u \ \wedge$$
$$[b \notin u.bev \ \vee \ (fork[u,v] = v \ \wedge \ \neg u.drinking)])$$
$$\| \ sendreq[u,v,b] = (rb[u,v,b] = u \ \wedge \ bot[u,v,b] = v \ \wedge \ b \in u.bev)$$
$$\rangle$$

initially $\langle \llbracket u \; :: \; u.dine, u.imbibe = thinking, tranquil \rangle$

assign

$\langle \llbracket u \; ::$
  $\quad u.dine := hungry \qquad$ if $u.thinking \wedge u.thirsty \quad \sim$
  $\qquad\qquad\quad thinking \qquad$ if $u.eating \wedge \neg u.thirsty$
$\rangle$

$\llbracket \; \langle \llbracket u \; ::$
  $\quad u.imbibe := drinking \qquad$ if $u.thirsty \wedge u.maydrink$
  $\quad \| \; u.dine \quad := thinking \qquad$ if $u.thirsty \wedge u.maydrink \wedge u.eating$
$\rangle$

$\llbracket \; \langle \llbracket u,v,b \; : \; E[u,v] \quad ::$
  $\quad bot[u,v,b] := v \qquad$ if $sendbot[u,v,b]$
  $\quad \| \; rb[u,v,b] \; := v \qquad$ if $sendreq[u,v,b]$
$\rangle$

end $\{middle\}$

The proof that the program fits the specification in Section 13.5.2 is straightforward and is left to the reader.

Exercise 13.2   Explore alternative approaches to the drinkers problem in which there is a total order among the beverages. A thirsty process acquires "locks" on beverages that it needs in the specified order. Introduce a separate diners problem for each beverage to resolve conflicts for that beverage. $\triangledown$

Exercise 13.3   Explore alternative approaches to the drinkers problem for the case in which *all* pairs of (distinct) vertices are neighbors. Assume that you are given total orders over processes and over beverages. A thirsty process sends a request for the set of beverages it needs to all other processes. Associated with each request is a *priority* based on the number of times the process has drunk, and the id of the process. $\triangledown$

Exercise 13.4   Will the following approach work for the drinkers problem? A partial ordering among processes is implemented by means of a token on each edge: A process has a higher priority than a neighbor if and only if it holds the token they share. A conflict between neighbors for a bottle is resolved in favor of the process holding the token that they share. The only change to priority is as follows: When a thirsty process that holds *all* tokens it shares becomes a drinking process, it sends a token to each of its neighbors. Prove that your solution is correct or propose a counterexample. $\triangledown$

Summary

The solution to the drinkers problem exploits the power of program composition. We proposed that the program be composed of two programs—*middle* and *osdine*. Program *osdine* had been designed earlier, and this reduced our design effort. Stepwise refinement of the specification of *middle* was carried out until a straightforward implementation of the specification was possible. As in the previous chapter, most of the design in this chapter deals with properties of programs (i.e., their specifications) rather than with the programs themselves.

Bibliographic Notes

The drinking philosophers problem was introduced and solved in Chandy and Misra [1984]. More efficient solutions for this problem have been proposed recently in Lynch and Welch [1987]. Examples of resource management in distributed systems are in Brinch-Hansen [1977] and Peterson and Silberschatz [1983].

CHAPTER 14

Committee Coordination

14.1   Introduction

The following story captures the essence of synchronization in many asynchronous systems. Professors in a certain university have organized themselves into committees. Each committee has an unchanging membership roster of one or more professors. From time to time, a professor may decide to attend a committee meeting (presumably, when it has no more publishable ideas); it starts waiting and remains waiting until a meeting of a committee of which it is a member is started. The restrictions on meetings are as follows: (1) a committee meeting may be started only if *all* members of that committee are waiting, and (2) no two committees may meet simultaneously if they have a common member. Given that all meetings terminate in finite time, the problem is to devise a protocol, satisfying these restrictions, that also guarantees that if all members of a committee are waiting, then at least one of them will attend some meeting. (Note: We do not require that if all members of a committee are waiting, then the committee meets. Such a requirement may be impossible to satisfy if, for instance, all members of two different committees are waiting and these committees have a common member. Suppose that after one of the committees meets, its members never wait again. Then the other committee can never meet.)

In the context of asynchronous systems, a professor represents a *process*; a committee, a *synchronization*; and a committee meeting, a *synchronization event*. A waiting professor represents a process that is waiting for any one of a set of synchronization events to occur. A committee membership roster is the set of processes that participate in each occurrence of that synchronization. The problem is to guarantee that if all processes required for a synchronization event are waiting to participate in it, then at least one of these processes participates in some synchronization event.

The committee-coordination problem arises in implementing rendezvous-based communication—as in ADA, CSP, or RADDLE—on a distributed architecture. For two-process communication, each committee consists of two members—a sender and a receiver—and the effect of a meeting is a message transfer. Note that this formulation treats the sender and the receiver in a symmetric manner.

The specification of the committee-coordination problem, given in Section 14.2, includes aspects of both synchronization and exclusion: A committee meeting is started only if *all* its members are waiting simultaneously (synchronization), and two committees that have a common member cannot meet simultaneously (exclusion). An obvious solution is derived from the specification in Section 14.3. We considered exclusion problems in Chapters 12 and 13. In Section 14.4, we solve the exclusion requirement by mapping this problem to a dining philosophers problem: Philosophers are committees, neighboring philosophers have a common member, and a meeting is held only when the corresponding philosopher is eating. This guarantees that the exclusion aspect of the problem will be met. Then, in Sections 14.5 and 14.6, we propose two strategies to solve the synchronization issue.

This chapter illustrates once again the effectiveness of modularity in reducing the design effort. As in Chapter 13, we compose two programs, one of which was designed earlier (the solution to the diners problem) in constructing our solution.

Remark: We assume throughout this chapter that a waiting professor may attend a meeting of *any* committee of which it is a member. A generalization is as follows: A professor chooses to wait for a subset of the committees of which it is a member; the subset may be different each time it waits. A solution to this general problem can be obtained by minor modifications to the solution proposed in this chapter; see Exercise 14.9 at the end of this chapter.   ▽

14.2   Problem Specification

Symbol u denotes a professor and x, y denote committees. Associated with committee x is a constant set of professors $x.mem$, $x.mem \neq empty$, denoting the nonempty membership roster of committee x. For professor u, boolean variable $u.g$ is *true* if and only if u is waiting. For committee x, boolean variable $x.co$ is *true* if and only if a meeting of x is *convened*: Informally, $x.co$ holds means that a meeting of x has started and has not yet terminated.

Define committees x, y to be *neighbors* if $x \neq y$ and $(x.mem \cap y.mem) \neq empty$. We write $E[x, y]$ to denote that x, y are neighbors.

Notation: We write $x.g$ to denote that all members of x are waiting and $x^*.co$ to denote that $x.co$ holds or $y.co$ holds for some neighbor y of x:

$$x.g \;\equiv\; \langle \forall u \;:\; u \in x.mem \;::\; u.g \rangle$$
$$x^*.co \;\equiv\; x.co \;\vee\; \langle \exists y \;:\; E[x, y] \;::\; y.co \rangle. \qquad\qquad ▽$$

We are given a program *prof* (*prof*essor). We are required to design a program *coord* (*coord*inator). The union of these two programs, *prof* ∥ *coord*, is denoted by *sync* (*sync*hronization). The formal specifications of *prof*, *sync*, and the constraints on *coord*, are given next.

14.2.1 Specification of *prof*

$$u.g \;\; unless \;\; \langle \exists x \;:\; u \in x.mem \;::\; x.co \rangle \qquad\qquad\qquad \text{(pr1)}$$

stable $\neg x.co$ (pr2)

Conditional Property   (pr3)

Hypothesis: *true*

Conclusion: $\langle \forall\ x\ ::\ x.co\ \mapsto\ \neg x.co \rangle$

Condition (pr1) states that a waiting professor remains waiting until some committee of which it is a member meets. Condition (pr2) guarantees that meetings are not started in program *prof*. The conditional property, (pr3), states that any program of which *prof* is a component has the property that every meeting terminates.

Derived Properties of *prof*

We derive a property of program *prof* from this specification:

$$x.g\ \ unless\ \ x^*.co\ \ in\ prof \tag{pr4}$$

To see this, apply the simple conjunction rule for *unless* to (pr1) for all u in $x.mem$:

$$\langle \wedge\ u\ :\ u \in x.mem\ ::\ u.g \rangle\ \ unless$$
$$\langle \vee\ u\ :\ u \in x.mem\ ::\ \langle \exists\ y\ :\ u \in y.mem\ ::\ y.co \rangle \rangle\ \ in\ prof$$

$$x.g\ \ unless\ \ \langle \exists\ y\ :\ E[x,y]\ ::\ y.co \rangle\ \vee\ x.co\ \ in\ prof$$
, from the definition of $x.g$ and simplifying the right side

$$x.g\ \ unless\ \ x^*.co\ \ in\ prof$$
, from the definition of $x^*.co$

14.2.2 Specification of *sync*

$$\neg x.co\ \ unless\ \ x.g \tag{sy1}$$

$$\textbf{invariant}\ \ \ \neg(x.co\ \wedge\ y.co\ \wedge\ E[x,y]) \tag{sy2}$$

$$x.g\ \ \mapsto\ \ x^*.co \tag{sy3}$$

Condition (sy1) is a statement about synchronization: A meeting is not started unless all its members are waiting. Condition (sy2) is a statement about exclusion: No two committees meet simultaneously if they have a common member. The progress condition (sy3) guarantees that if all members of committee x are waiting, some committee whose membership includes a member of x has a meeting.

14.2.3 Constraints on *coord*

Shared variables between *prof* and *coord* are $u.g$ and $x.co$ (cd1)

$\textbf{constant}$ $u.g$ in *coord* $\{u.g, \neg u.g$ are both stable in *coord*$\}$ (cd2)

$\textbf{stable}$ $x.co$ in *coord*   (cd3)

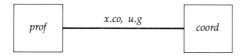

Figure 14.1 The program *sync* is *prof* ‖ *coord*.

Conditions (cd1,cd2) imply that program *coord* can read but cannot alter the waiting status of professors. Condition (cd3) states that a meeting cannot be terminated by program *coord*.

The structure of program *sync*—with component programs *prof* and *coord* and the variables shared between the components—is given schematically in Fig. 14.1.

Exercise 14.1   Prove that $x.g$ *unless* $x^*.co$ in *sync*.   ▽

14.2.4 Discussion

The specification of the committee-coordination problem is quite general. The specification of program *prof* does not say how, or whether, a professor changes state from waiting to nonwaiting. It is entirely possible that a professor remains waiting even though a committee of which it is a member meets. Also, no assumption is made about when, or whether, a professor attends or leaves a meeting. In particular, the following scenario is possible: A meeting of committee x begins, professor u participates in the meeting, then u ceases to wait, carries out some computation, begins to wait, and then rejoins the meeting of x that is still in progress. Also, the purpose of a meeting is of no concern in this problem. A meeting may result in the transfer of a message from a sender to a receiver, or it may involve processing a complex transaction involving many processes. A meeting is terminated by program *prof*; it is not our concern how the termination is done. One reason for specifying as little as possible is to encompass a variety of situations.

14.3   A Trivial Solution

We propose a very simple—in fact trivial—design of program *coord*. The idea is to set $x.co$ to *true* provided that (1) all members of x are waiting and (2) no neighbor of x is meeting. It is straightforward to see that the safety specifications of *sync* are satisfied by this program; the proof of progress is not entirely trivial.

14.3.1 A Program

Program *coord1*

  always

$$\langle \| x \quad :: \quad x.g = \langle \forall u : u \in x.mem \quad :: \quad u.g \rangle$$
$$\| \qquad x^*.co = x.co \vee \langle \exists y : E[x,y] \quad :: \quad y.co \rangle$$
$$\rangle$$

  initially $\langle \| x \quad :: \quad x.co = \textit{false} \rangle$

  assign $\langle \| x \quad :: \quad x.co := \textit{true} \quad$ if $\quad x.g \wedge \neg x^*.co \rangle$

end {*coord1*}

14.3.2 Proofs

First observe that constraints (cd1–cd3) are met by *coord1*: No variable other than $u.g$ or $x.co$ is mentioned (cd1), $u.g$ is constant (cd2), and $x.co$ is stable (cd3).

    Next we show that the union of *coord1* and any program *prof* that has the properties (pr1–pr3) satisfies the specification of *sync*.

Proof: (sy1) $\neg x.co$ *unless* $x.g$ in *sync*

    $\neg x.co$ *unless* $x.g$ in *coord1*   , from the text of *coord1*

    $\neg x.co$ is stable in *prof*   , from (pr2)

    $\neg x.co$ *unless* $x.g$ in *sync*   , applying the union theorem $\triangledown$

Proof: (sy2) $\neg(x.co \wedge y.co \wedge E[x,y])$ in *sync*

    $\neg(x.co \wedge y.co \wedge E[x,y])$ in *coord1*   , from the text of *coord1*.

    $\neg(x.co \wedge y.co \wedge E[x,y])$ is stable in *prof*   , from(pr2)

    The result follows by applying the union theorem. $\triangledown$

Proof: (sy3) $x.g \mapsto x^*.co$ in *sync*

    $x.g$ *ensures* $x^*.co$ in *coord1*   , from the text of *coord1*

    $x.g$ *unless* $x^*.co$ in *prof*   , from derived property (pr4)

    $x.g$ *ensures* $x^*.co$ in *sync*   , applying the union theorem $\triangledown$

    The assumption that meetings terminate—condition (pr3)—is not required for the correctness proof of *coord1*.

14.3.3 Discussion

Program *coord1* is an acceptable solution if all decisions about meetings are to be centralized. Then the statement that sets $x.co$ to *true* can be implemented by (1) checking $y.co$ for all neighbors y and $x.co$ (in order to compute $\neg x^*.co$), and (2) computing $x.g$ by polling all members of x.

It is difficult to implement program *coord1* directly in a distributed manner. The computation of $x.g$ is the crux of implementing synchronization (check that all members of x are waiting *simultaneously*), and the computation of $\neg x^*.co$ is the essence of exclusion (check that no neighbor of x, or x is meeting). Next we show how to address both these issues. We first consider the question of exclusion, and then show how, once the exclusion problem is solved, synchronization can be implemented in a straightforward manner.

14.4   Addressing the Exclusion Question

As we remarked in the introduction, the requirement that neighboring committees do not meet simultaneously can be likened to the requirement in the dining philosophers problem (Chapter 12) that neighboring philosophers do not eat simultaneously. This suggests that we regard a committee as a philosopher (and neighboring committees as neighboring philosophers), and that conflicts be resolved in favor of eating processes, i.e., only an eating committee can convene a meeting. Therefore committees meet only if the corresponding philosophers are eating—i.e., we postulate the invariant $x.co \Rightarrow x.e$ (where $x.e$ denotes that x is eating).

Recall that the dining philosopher program has two component programs: *user*, the given program, and *os*, the solution. We solve the committee-coordination problem in a manner similar to the drinking philosophers problem (Chapter 13): We design a program, *middle*, that acts as an interface between programs *prof* and *os*, where the union of *prof* and *middle* behaves like *user* in the diners problem. The transitions to hungry and to thinking states are in program *middle*. In the present problem, we transform the *os* component of the dining philosophers solution to *os1*, using superposition; the setting of $x.co$ is done in *os1*. The design of *middle* and *os1* are such that the union of all three components, *prof* ⫾ *middle* ⫾ *os1*, meets the specification of *sync*. The union of *middle* and *os1* is the desired program *coord*. Relationships between the various components and the variables shared between them are shown in Figure 14.2.

For convenience, we repeat the specification of *user* from Section 12.2.3. Here committees x, y have the same role as philosophers in Chapter 12; hence the specification is given using x, y. Recall that $x.dine$ denotes the state of philosopher x. Possible values of $x.dine$ are t, h, e (denoting *thinking, hungry,*

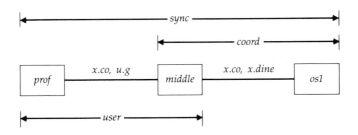

Figure 14.2 *sync* = *prof* ∥ *middle* ∥ *os1*.
prof ∥ *middle* meets the specification of *user*.
middle ∥ *os1* is the desired program *coord*.

and *eating*, respectively). We use $x.t, x.h$ and $x.e$ as shorthand for $x.dine = t, x.dine = h$ and $x.dine = e$, respectively.

14.4.1 Specification of *user*   {from Section 12.2.3}

$x.t$ *unless* $x.h$ (udn1)

stable $x.h$ (udn2)

$x.e$ *unless* $x.t$ (udn3)

Conditional Property   (udn4)

Hypothesis: $\langle \forall\ x, y\ :\ E[x, y]\ \ ::\ \ \neg(x.e\ \wedge\ y.e) \rangle$
Conclusion: $\langle \forall\ x\ \ ::\ \ x.e\ \ \mapsto\ \ \neg x.e \rangle$

We have the constraint on *os* that it shares only $x.dine$ with *user*; $x.t$ is constant and $x.e$ is stable in *os*.

14.4.2 A Program

In designing program *middle*, we have to devise the conditions for (1) the thinking to hungry transition and (2) the eating to thinking transition. (Setting $x.co$ to *true* is done in *os1*.) Since the purpose of eating is to start a committee meeting (if possible), we postulate that a thinking committee becomes hungry only if all members of the committee are waiting. Once a committee becomes hungry it will eat, eventually, from the dining philosopher solution (assuming that our design of *middle* and the specification of *prof* meets the specification of *user*). Some members of a committee x may not be waiting when x starts eating. This is because a neighboring committee y may have met during the interval between x becoming hungry and x starting to eat; therefore some common members of x and y may have stopped waiting in this interval. Hence variable $x.co$ is set *true* in *os1*, along with the hungry to eating transition, only if all members of x are waiting when x begins to eat. Finally, from our postulated invariant, $x.co \Rightarrow x.e$, committee x can stop eating only when $x.co$ is *false*. In order to meet the specification of *user*—that all eating periods be finite—we set $x.dine$ to t within a finite time after $x.co$ becomes *false*.

Program *middle1*

> **always** $\langle \| \ x \ :: \ x.g = \langle \forall \ u \ : \ u \ \in \ x.mem \ :: \ u.g \rangle \rangle$
>
> **initially** $\langle \| \ x \ :: \ x.co = false \rangle$
>
> **assign**
>
> $\langle \| \ x \ ::$
> > $x.dine \ := \ h$ if $x.t \ \wedge \ x.g$
> > $\| \ x.dine \ := \ t$ if $x.e \ \wedge \ \neg x.co$
>
> $\rangle$

end $\{middle1\}$

Program *os1* $\{$transformation of program *os*$\}$

> **transform**
>
> the statements in program *os* so that the following assignment is performed whenever $x.dine$ changes value from h to e :
>
> $x.co \ := x.g$

end $\{os1\}$

14.4.3 Proofs

A key invariant of *sync1* is $x.co \ \Rightarrow \ x.e$ (see Lemma 14.1). All safety properties are based on this invariant; in particular, neighboring committees do not meet simultaneously because they do not eat simultaneously. There are two main progress proofs: (1) eating periods are finite (to establish that the specification of *user* is met) and (2) if all members of a committee are waiting, then that committee or one of its neighbors meets (to establish property (sy3)). The key ideas in the first progress proof are as follows. If $x.co$ is *true*, it will be set *false*, eventually, from the specification of *prof*; hence eventually $\neg x.co$ holds. Then, from the text of *middle1*, x will transit to thinking if it is eating. The main points in the second progress proof are as follows. From the specification of *prof*, $x.g$ is falsified only if $x^*.co$ holds; hence consider the situation where $x.g$ remains *true*. If x is eating it transits to thinking; if x is thinking (and $x.g$

continues to hold), then x becomes hungry, from the text of *middle1*. If x is hungry it starts eating, from the dining philosopher solution, at which point $x.co$ is set *true* if $x.g$ holds. Therefore $x.co$ holds eventually if $x.g$ remains *true*.

We have three proof obligations. We must show that

1. *middle1* ‖ *os1* meets the constraints on *coord*, (cd1–cd3),

2. *prof* ‖ *middle1* meets the specification of *user*, and

3. *prof* ‖ *middle1* ‖ *os1* meets the specification of *sync*.

In the following, we refer to *prof* ‖ *middle1* ‖ *os1* as *sync1*.

Constraints on *coord* Are Met

It is easy to see that *middle1* ‖ *os1* meets the constraints on *coord*, (cd1–cd2). Constraint (cd3) is met because $\neg x.e \Rightarrow \neg x.co$ (for a proof see Lemma 14.1), and hence, in *os1*, $x.co$ is not falsified.

Terminology: In many proof steps, a predicate is asserted to be stable in a program (or union of program components) because the terms in it are local to other programs, or because there are constraints on how this program can change variable values. We write *locality* as the justification for such a proof step.   ▽

Lemma 14.1 $x.co \Rightarrow x.e$ in *sync1*

Initially $x.co$ is *false* and hence $x.co \Rightarrow x.e$ holds. To prove the stability of $x.co \Rightarrow x.e$ (or, equivalently, $\neg x.co \lor x.e$) we show below that $\neg x.co \lor x.e$ is stable in each of *prof*, *middle1*, and *os1*. The result then follows by applying the union theorem.

$\neg x.co$ is stable in *prof*	, rewriting (pr2)
$x.e$ is stable in *prof*	, from locality
$\neg x.co \lor x.e$ is stable in *prof*	, simple disjunction on the above two
$\neg x.co \lor x.e$ is stable in *middle1*	, from the text of *middle1*
$\neg x.co$ *unless* $x.e$ in *os1*	, from the text of *os1*
$x.e$ is stable in *os1*	, from constraints (see Section 12.2.5)
$\neg x.co \lor x.e$ is stable in *os1*	, cancellation on the above two ▽

Specification of *user* Is Met

Properties (udn1–udn3) hold in *prof* ‖ *middle1* because each property holds in *middle1* and program *prof* does not modify $x.dine$. Next we prove the conclusion of (udn4): Eating periods are finite in *sync1*.

Proof: The conclusion of (udn4), $x.e \mapsto \neg x.e$ in *sync1*

$x.co \mapsto \neg x.co$ in *sync1*
  , from (pr3)
$x.e \wedge x.co \mapsto \neg x.e \vee (x.e \wedge \neg x.co)$ in *sync1*
  , strengthening the left side and weakening the right side of the above
$x.e \wedge \neg x.co \mapsto \neg x.e$ in *sync1*
  , proven below
$x.e \mapsto \neg x.e$ in *sync1*
  , cancellation and disjunction on the above two $\triangledown$

Proof: $x.e \wedge \neg x.co \mapsto \neg x.e$ in *sync1* (used in the proof of (udn4)):

$x.e \wedge \neg x.co$ *ensures* $\neg x.e$ in *middle1*	, from the text of *middle1*
$x.e \wedge \neg x.co$ is stable in *prof*	, from (pr2) and locality
$x.e \wedge \neg x.co$ is stable in *os1*	, from text of *os1* and locality
$x.e \wedge \neg x.co \mapsto \neg x.e$ in *sync1*	, from the union theorem $\triangledown$

Specification of *sync* Is Met

First we observe some properties of *sync1*. Since *prof* ‖ *middle1* meets the specification of *user*, *sync1* meets the specification of the composite program in the dining philosophers problem. In particular, in *sync1* neighbors do not eat simultaneously (sy4). Also, every hungry process eats eventually, and from the text of superposition, $x.co$ is set to $x.g$ when x starts to eat (sy5). Property (sy6) is the conclusion of (udn4) that has been proven already.

$$\langle \forall\, x, y\ :\ E[x, y]\ \ ::\ \ \neg(x.e \wedge y.e) \rangle \text{ in } sync1 \tag{sy4}$$

$$x.h \mapsto x.e \wedge (x.co = x.g) \text{ in } sync1 \tag{sy5}$$

$$x.e \mapsto \neg x.e \text{ in } sync1 \tag{sy6}$$

Now we prove that *sync1* has properties (sy1–sy3).

Proof: (sy1) $\neg x.co$ *unless* $x.g$ in *sync1*

$\neg x.co$ is stable in *prof*	, from (pr2)
$\neg x.co$ is stable in *middle1*	, from the text of *middle1*
$\neg x.co$ *unless* $x.g$ in *os1*	, from the text of superposition in *os1*
$\neg x.co$ *unless* $x.g$ in *sync1*	, union theorem on the above three $\triangledown$

Proof: (sy2) $\neg(x.co \wedge y.co \wedge E[x,y])$ in *sync1*

$\qquad x.co \wedge y.co \;\Rightarrow\; x.e \wedge y.e$ in *sync1*   , from Lemma 14.1

$\qquad x.e \wedge y.e \;\Rightarrow\; \neg E[x,y]$ in *sync1*   , from (sy4) $\triangledown$

Proof: (sy3) $x.g \;\mapsto\; x^*.co$ in *sync1*

$\qquad x.e \;\mapsto\; x.t$ in *sync1*
$\qquad$, PSP theorem on (sy6,udn3)

$\qquad x.g \wedge x.e \;\mapsto\; \neg x.g \vee (x.g \wedge x.t)$ in *sync1*
$\qquad$, strengthen the left side and weaken the right side of the above

$\qquad x.g \wedge x.t \;\mapsto\; \neg x.g \vee (x.g \wedge x.h)$ in *sync1*
$\qquad$, proven below

$\qquad x.g \wedge x.h \;\mapsto\; x.co = x.g$ in *sync1*
$\qquad$, strengthening the left and weakening the right side of (sy5)

$\qquad x.g \;\mapsto\; \neg x.g \vee (x.co = x.g)$ in *sync1*
$\qquad$, cancellation and disjunction on the above three

$\qquad x.g$ *unless* $x^*.co$ in *sync1*
$\qquad$, from (pr4,cd2)

$\qquad x.g \;\mapsto\; x^*.co$ in *sync1*
$\qquad$, PSP theorem on the above two $\triangledown$

Proof: $x.g \wedge x.t \;\mapsto\; \neg x.g \vee (x.g \wedge x.h)$ in *sync1*
$\qquad$ (used in the proof of (sy3))

$\qquad x.g$ *unless* $\neg x.g$ in *prof* $\|$ *os1*
$\qquad$, trivially

$\qquad x.t$ is stable in *prof* $\|$ *os1*
$\qquad$, from locality

$\qquad x.g \wedge x.t$ *unless* $\neg x.g$ in *prof* $\|$ *os1*
$\qquad$, simple conjunction on the above two

$\qquad x.g \wedge x.t$ *unless* $\neg x.g \vee x.h$ in *prof* $\|$ *os1*
$\qquad$, weakening the right side of the above

$\qquad x.g \wedge x.t$ *ensures* $\neg x.g \vee x.h$ in *middle1*
$\qquad$, from the text of *middle1*

$\qquad x.g \wedge x.t$ *ensures* $\neg x.g \vee x.h$ in *sync1*
$\qquad$, union theorem on the above two $\triangledown$

Note: In the preceding proof, we used the fact that

$\qquad x.g \wedge x.t$ *ensures* $\neg x.g \vee x.h$ in *middle1*

instead of the stronger

$\qquad x.g \wedge x.t$ *ensures* $x.h$ in *middle1*.

This is because we plan to use this proof for programs obtained in subsequent
refinement steps. $\triangledown$

Exercise 14.2   Is the hypothesis of (udn4) required in the proof of *sync1*? ▽

14.4.4 Discussion

Program *middle1* assumes that $x.g$ can be computed in one atomic operation. Our next task is to implement the computation of $x.g$ by an asynchronous scheme.

14.5   Addressing the Synchronization Question: Polling

In *middle1*, $x.g$ appears in the thinking to hungry transition for x. The term $x.g$ can be dropped from this condition because the only property that we require (in the proof of (sy3)) is $x.g \wedge x.t \mapsto x.h$.

In *os1*, $x.g$ appears only in assignment to $x.co$. We show that for this assignment the value of $x.g$ can be computed by all members of x in an asynchronous fashion. The assignment to $x.co$ is synchronous with the hungry to eating transition of x; therefore a precondition of this assignment is that neither x nor any of its neighbors is eating—i.e., $\neg x^*.e$ holds (the definition of $x^*.e$ is analogous to that of $x^*.co$). As long as $\neg x^*.e$ holds, no member of x can change state from waiting to nonwaiting. That is, for any u and x where $u \in x.mem$,

> $u.g$ *unless* $x^*.e$ in *sync1*.

This is because

> $u.g$ *unless* $x^*.co$ in *sync1*
>   , from (pr1,cd2)
> $u.g$ *unless* $x^*.e$ in *sync1*
>   , weakening the consequence using Lemma 14.1

Hence $x.g$ can be evaluated by asynchronous inspection (polling) of all $u.g$, $u \in x.mem$, when the condition for a hungry to eating transition for x holds.

To implement polling, introduce a boolean variable $x.prp$ to denote the partial result of polling: $x.prp$ is *true* if and only if $u.g$ is *true* for all members u polled so far. Polling can be terminated if $x.prp$ is *false* or if all members have been polled. Variables $x.co$ and $x.dine$ are set to $x.prp$ and e, respectively, upon completion of polling. The actual details of polling are straightforward: Members of a committee may be polled in some fixed order (based on seniority of professors, say), or the order may be random; we leave the implementation details of polling to the reader.

14.6   Addressing the Synchronization Question: Tokens

The polling scheme of Section 14.5 requires committees to send messages to their members to determine their status. In this section we propose an alternative scheme: Professors communicate their status to all committees of which they are members, while they are waiting. We consider changes to *middle1* that are necessary to implement this strategy.

As we have seen for dining and drinking philosophers problems, programming and proofs dealing with message communication are simplified by introducing *tokens*. As before, tokens are not created, destroyed, or divided. Every token *belongs* to some professor: The number of tokens belonging to professor u is the number of committees of which it is a member; denote this number by $u.N$. A professor *holds* only its tokens. Let $u.n$ denote the number of tokens held by u; then $0 \leq u.n \leq u.N$. A committee x holds at most one token from a member u. For each x and u define a boolean variable $x.tok[u]$ as follows: $x.tok[u]$ is *true* if and only if x holds a token from u. We have the invariant for token conservation: For any u, $u.n$ plus the number of x for which $x.tok[u]$ is *true* equals $u.N$.

In order to manipulate tokens, we find it necessary to distinguish between the following two cases when x is eating: (1) $x.co$ was set *true* when x started eating, and (2) $x.co$ remained *false* when x started eating. To this end, we introduce a boolean variable $x.on$, for each committee x, where $x.on$ is *true* if and only if x is eating and $x.co$ was set *true* in the last hungry to eating transition of x. Variable $x.on$ is initially *false*; it is set *true* whenever $x.co$ is set *true*, and *false* whenever $x.e$ is set *false*. Therefore we have the following generalization of Lemma 14.1:

$$x.co \quad \Rightarrow \quad x.on \quad \Rightarrow \quad x.e \ .$$

For assignment to $x.co$ in *os1*, we have to determine whether $x.g$ is *true* based on the tokens that x holds. We propose that at the time of the hungry to eating transition of x, if x holds a token of u, then u is waiting. Hence $x.g$ is *true* if x holds a token from each member when it transits to eating. This proposal can be implemented by using the following invariant for every u: (1) $y.on$ is *true* for some committee y of which u is a member, or (2) u holds all its tokens, or (3) u is waiting. To see that this invariant actually implements the proposal, consider some x and one of its members u: A precondition of the hungry to eating transition of x is that neither x nor any neighbor of x is eating, and hence the first disjunct of the invariant is *false* (because $\neg y.e \Rightarrow \neg y.on$); if x holds a token from u, then the second disjunct is *false*; therefore u is waiting. Next we show how this invariant can be established initially and then maintained.

Initially the invariant can be established by having every professor hold all its tokens. Now consider how each of the disjuncts in the invariant can be falsified. The disjunct that u is waiting is falsified only if $y.co$, for some y of which u is a member, is *true*—from the problem specification—and hence $y.on$ is *true*. The disjunct that u holds all its tokens can only be falsified by a token transmission from u to some x; we postulate that such a transmission takes place only if u is waiting (thus the purpose of this token transmission is to inform x that u is waiting). The falsification of the first disjunct, by setting of some $x.on$ to *false*, must be accompanied by a guarantee that $u.g$ is *true* or that u holds all its tokens. Since we are not allowed to modify $u.g$, our only choice is to guarantee that all members of x hold all their tokens whenever $x.on$ is set *false*; this is implemented by having x and all its neighbors return the tokens they hold to the members of x, synchronously.

14.6.1 A Program

The following program, *middle2*, manipulates tokens in the manner described earlier. Token transmission from a waiting professor to all its committees is done synchronously—this simplifies the program and the proof. Later we show how the synchronous communication can be implemented by asynchronous communication.

Notation: We use $x.has$ as an abbreviation for the expression "x holds a token from each member." $\triangledown$

Program *middle2*

    always

        {token conservation}

        $\langle\!\lbrack\ u\ \ ::\ \ u.n = u.N - \langle + x\ :\ x.tok[u]\ \ ::\ \ 1\ \rangle\rangle$

    $\lbrack\ \langle\!\lbrack\ x\ \ ::\ \ x.has = \langle \forall\ u\ :\ u \in x.mem\ \ ::\ \ x.tok[u]\rangle\rangle$

    initially

        $\langle\!\lbrack\ x\ \ ::\ \ x.co, x.on = \textit{false}, \textit{false}\rangle$

    $\lbrack\ \langle\!\lbrack\ x, u\ \ ::\ \ x.tok[u] = \textit{false}\rangle$

    assign

        {token transmissions from waiting professors to committees}

        $\langle\!\lbrack\ u\ \ ::$

            $\langle\| \ x\ :\ u \in x.mem\ \ ::\ \ x.tok[u]\ :=\ \textit{true}\ \ \textbf{if}\ \ u.g \wedge u.n = u.N\rangle$

        $\rangle$

⫿ {assignments to $x.dine, x.on$}

⟨⫿ x ::

$x.dine := h$	if $x.t \wedge x.has$
⫿ $x.dine, x.on := t, false$	if $x.e \wedge \neg x.co$

⫿ ⟨⫿ $u, y : u \in (x.mem \cap y.mem)$ ::

$y.tok[u] := false$	if $x.on \wedge \neg x.co$

⟩

⟩

end {$middle2$}

Program $os2$ {**transformation of program** os}

transform

the statements in program os so that the following assignment is performed whenever $x.dine$ changes value from h to e:

$x.co, \ x.on := x.has, \ x.has$

end {$os2$}

14.6.2 Proofs

As before, our proof obligation is to show that

1. $middle2 \, ⫿ \, os2$ meets the constraints on $coord$,

2. $prof \, ⫿ \, middle2$ meets the specification of $user$, and

3. $prof \, ⫿ \, middle2 \, ⫿ \, os2$ meets the specification of $sync$.

We leave the proof that $middle2 \, ⫿ \, os2$ meets the constraints on $coord$, (cd1–cd3) to the reader.

In the following, we refer to $prof \, ⫿ \, middle2 \, ⫿ \, os2$ as $sync2$. A number of results from $sync1$ carry over for $sync2$. Most of the remaining proof deals with manipulations of tokens. Analogous to the definition of $x^*.co$, we define

$$x^*.on \equiv x.on \vee \langle \exists y : E[x,y] :: y.on \rangle$$
$$x^*.e \equiv x.e \vee \langle \exists y : E[x,y] :: y.e \rangle.$$

Specification of *user* Is Met

It is easy to see that $prof \, ⫿ \, middle2$ satisfies properties (udn1–udn3) of $user$. The proof of (udn4) is the same as for $sync1$. Therefore properties (sy4,sy6) hold for $sync2$, and corresponding to (sy5) we have

$$x.h \;\; \mapsto \;\; x.e \;\wedge\; (x.co = x.has) \;\wedge\; (x.on = x.has) \text{ in } sync2. \qquad (\text{sy}5')$$

Specification of *sync* Is Met

First we prove four lemmas about *sync2*.

Lemma 14.1′   (generalization of Lemma 14.1)

$$x.co \;\; \Rightarrow \;\; x.on \;\; \Rightarrow \;\; x.e \text{ in } sync2$$

Proof: Similar to the proof of Lemma 14.1.   ▽

Lemma 14.2 $(u.n = 0 \;\vee\; u.n = u.N)$ in *sync2*

Proof: From the text of *middle2*, and the fact that these variables are not modified in *prof* or *os2*.   ▽

Lemma 14.3 $x.on \;\Rightarrow\; x.has$ in *sync2*

Proof: Initially $x.on$ is *false*, and hence the invariant holds. Variable $x.on$ is set *true* only by being set to $x.has$. Whenever $x.has$ is falsified either $x.on$, or $y.on$ for some neighbor y of x, is falsified. Therefore, following falsification of $x.has$, from Lemma 14.1′, $\neg x^*.on$ holds, and hence $\neg x.on$ holds.   ▽

Lemma 14.4

For any u, $\langle \exists\, x \;:\; u \in x.mem \;\; :: \;\; x.on \rangle \;\vee\; u.n = u.N \;\vee\; u.g$ in *sync2*.

Proof: This predicate is initially *true* because $u.n = u.N$. To prove the stability of the predicate we will show that no disjunct in it can be falsified unless another disjunct holds.

$\langle \exists\, x \;:\; u \in x.mem \;\; :: \;\; x.on \rangle$ *unless* $u.n = u.N$ in *sync2*
, because this property holds in *middle2* (from the text of *middle2*) and $\langle \exists\, x \;:\; u \in x.mem \;\; :: \;\; x.on \rangle$ is stable in *prof* ∥ *os2* (from the locality and text of *os2*)

$u.n = u.N$ *unless* $u.g$ in *sync2*
, from the text of *middle2* and locality

$u.g$ *unless* $\langle \exists\, x \;:\; u \in x.mem \;\; :: \;\; x.on \rangle$ in *sync2*
, from (pr1), Lemma 14.1′, and (cd2)

Hence (see Exercise 14.3)

$\langle \exists\, x \;:\; u \in x.mem \;\; :: \;\; x.on \rangle \;\vee\; u.n = u.N \;\vee\; u.g$ *unless*
$\langle \exists\, x \;:\; u \in x.mem \;\; :: \;\; x.on \rangle \;\wedge\; u.n = u.N \;\wedge\; u.g$ in *sync2*.

The right side of *unless* in the above property is *false* because for any x, where $u \in x.mem$,

$$x.on \quad \Rightarrow \quad x.tok[u] \qquad \text{, from Lemma 14.3}$$
$$x.tok[u] \Rightarrow \quad u.n \neq u.N \quad \text{, from token conservation}$$

This completes the proof.   ▽

Exercise 14.3 Variable i is quantified $0 \leq i < N$ in the following, and $\oplus$ denotes addition modulo N. Show that

$$\frac{\langle \forall\, i \quad :: \quad p_i \quad unless \quad p_{i\oplus 1} \rangle}{\langle \vee\, i \quad :: \quad p_i \rangle \quad unless \quad \langle \wedge\, i \quad :: \quad p_i \rangle}$$

Hint: First establish from the premise that, for any j, $0 \leq j < N$,

$$\langle \vee\, i \quad :: \quad p_i \rangle \quad unless \quad p_j .$$

Then apply the disjunction rule for *unless* to all these properties.   ▽

Now we show that properties (sy1–sy3) hold in *sync2*.

Proof: (sy1) $\neg x.co \;\; unless \;\; x.g$ in *sync2*

$\neg x.co \;\; unless \;\; \neg x^*.e \;\wedge\; x.has$ in *os2*
    , from the text of *os2*

$\neg x.co \;\; unless \;\; \neg x^*.on \;\wedge\; x.has$ in *os2*
    , Lemma 14.1′ applied to the above   (1)

$x.has \;\; \Rightarrow \;\; \langle \forall\, u : u \in x.mem \;\; :: \;\; u.n \neq u.N \rangle$ in *sync2*
    , from token conservation

$\neg x^*.on \;\wedge\; x.has \;\; \Rightarrow \;\; x.g$ in *sync2*
    , from Lemma 14.4 and the above

$\neg x.co \;\; unless \;\; x.g$ in *os2*
    , from (1) and the above

$\neg x.co$ is stable in *prof* $\|$ *middle2*
    , from (pr2) and the text of *middle2*

$\neg x.co \;\; unless \;\; x.g$ in *sync2*
    , union theorem on the above two   ▽

Proof: (sy2) $\neg(x.co \;\wedge\; y.co \;\wedge\; E[x,y])$ in *sync2*

This follows from Lemma 14.1′ and (sy4)   ▽

Proof: (sy3) $x.g \;\; \mapsto \;\; x^*.co$ in *sync2*

For any x, u, where $u \in x.mem$, we show that

$$u.g \;\; \mapsto \;\; x.tok[u] \;\vee\; x^*.on \text{ in } sync2 \tag{sy7}$$
$$x.tok[u] \;\; unless \;\; x^*.on \text{ in } sync2 \tag{sy8}$$

$x.has \quad \mapsto \quad x^*.on$ in *sync2* $\hfill$ (sy9)

$x^*.on \quad \mapsto \quad \neg x^*.on$ in *sync2* $\hfill$ (sy10)

$\neg x^*.on \quad unless \quad x^*.co$ in *sync2* $\hfill$ (sy11)

The proof of (sy3) from (sy7–sy11) is as follows:

$x.g \quad \mapsto \quad x.has \ \lor \ x^*.on$ in *sync2*
   , completion theorem on (sy7,sy8)

$x.g \quad \mapsto \quad x^*.on$ in *sync2*
   , cancellation on the above and (sy9) $\hfill$ (2)

$x.g \quad \mapsto \quad \neg x^*.on$ in *sync2*
   , transitivity on the above and (sy10)

$x.g \ unless \ x^*.co$ in *sync2*
   , from (pr4,cd2)

$x.g \quad \mapsto \quad (x.g \ \land \ \neg x^*.on) \ \lor \ x^*.co$ in *sync2*
   , PSP theorem on the above two

$x.g \ \land \ \neg x^*.on \quad \mapsto \quad x^*.co$ in *sync2*
   , PSP theorem on (2) and (sy11)

$x.g \quad \mapsto \quad x^*.co$ in *sync2*
   , from the above two by cancellation $\hfill \triangledown$

Property (sy10) follows from Lemma 14.1′ and the fact that eating periods are finite (sy6). Proof of (sy11) is straightforward using the text of *os2*. Next we prove (sy7–sy9).

Proof: (sy7) $u.g \quad \mapsto \quad x.tok[u] \ \lor \ x^*.on$ in *sync2*

$u.g \ unless \ \langle \exists \, y \, : \, u \, \in \, y.mem \, :: \, y.co \rangle$ in *prof*
   , rewriting (pr1)

$u.g \ unless \ x^*.on$ in *prof*
   , using Lemma 14.1′ on the above

$u.g$ is stable in *os2*
   , from locality

$u.g \ ensures \ x.tok[u] \ \lor \ x^*.on$ in *middle2*
   , from Lemma 14.2 and the text of *middle2*

$u.g \ ensures \ x.tok[u] \ \lor \ x^*.on$ in *sync2*
   , union theorem on the above three $\hfill \triangledown$

Note: In the preceding proof, we showed that

$u.g \ ensures \ x.tok[u] \ \lor \ x^*.on$ in *middle2*

instead of the stronger

$u.g \ ensures \ x.tok[u]$ in *middle2*.

This is because we plan to use this proof for programs obtained in subsequent refinement steps. $\triangledown$

Proof: (sy8) $x.tok[u]$ *unless* $x^*.on$ in *sync2*

   $x.tok[u]$ is stable in *prof* $\llbracket$ *os2*   , from locality

   $x.tok[u]$ *unless* $x^*.on$ in *middle2*   , from the text of *middle2*

   $x.tok[u]$ *unless* $x^*.on$ in *sync2*   , union theorem on the above two $\triangledown$

Proof: (sy9) $x.has$ $\mapsto$ $x^*.on$ in *sync2*

   Use the proof of (sy3) in Section 14.4.3—$x.g$ $\mapsto$ $x^*.co$ in *sync1*—with $x.g, x.co$ replaced by $x.has$, $x.on$, respectively. The reference to (sy5) should be replaced by (sy5$'$) in that proof, and the additional fact needed (corresponding to $x.g$ *unless* $x^*.co$) is

   $x.has$ *unless* $x^*.on$ in *sync2*
      , from the text of *middle2* and locality $\triangledown$

Exercise 14.4   Modify the code and the proof of *middle2* for asynchronous transmissions of tokens from professors to committees. $\triangledown$

14.6.3 Introducing More Asynchrony

We have introduced a good deal of asynchrony in the computation of $x.g$ in going from *middle1* to *middle2*. Next we show how synchronous actions in *middle2* can be implemented asynchronously. Program *middle2* has two synchronous actions: (1) tokens are transmitted from a professor to all its committees synchronously, and (2) an eating to thinking transition of x is accompanied by synchronous transmissions of tokens from x and its neighbors to the members of x. First we consider case (2); case (1) is considered in Section 14.6.4.

Token Transmissions from Committees to Professors

Token transmission from committees to professors is broken up into a sequence of actions as follows. First committee x acquires all tokens of all its members while $x.on$ is *true*. Then $x.on$ is set *false*, at which point tokens are transmitted from x to all its members. Finally x ceases eating.

   To see how x acquires all tokens of all its members, observe, from Lemma 14.3, that while $x.on$ is *true*, committee x holds a token from each of its members. Therefore, from token conservation and Lemma 14.2, no member of x holds any token—i.e., all tokens of all members are with the committees. Hence x can acquire the tokens by receiving them from its neighbors. Since

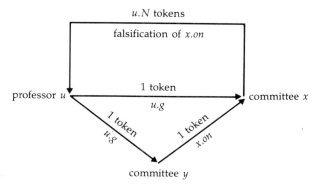

Figure 14.3 Token transmissions between one professor and two committees. Number of tokens transmitted and the condition under which transmission takes place, is shown on each edge.

the acquisition takes place when $x.on$ is *true*, there is no contention in token acquisition because $y.on$ is *false* for every neighbor y (from Lemma 14.1′). The flow of tokens is shown schematically in Fig. 14.3, for one professor and two committees.

We introduce integer variables $x.num[u]$ to denote the number of tokens of u that x holds. We define $x.tok[u]$ by $x.tok[u] \equiv (x.num[u] \geq 1)$ and eliminate $x.tok[u]$ from the program. The statements for token acquisition by x are

$$\langle [\!| \ x,y,u \ : \ E[x,y] \ \wedge \ u \ \in \ (x.mem \ \cap \ y.mem) \ :: $$
$$\quad x.num[u], y.num[u] \ := \ x.num[u] + y.num[u], 0 \qquad \text{if} \quad x.on$$
$$\rangle$$

Next we propose that $x.on$ be set *false* some time after $x.co$ becomes *false* and x acquires all its tokens. This preserves the condition in Lemmas 14.1′, 14.2, and 14.3; in order to preserve the condition in Lemma 14.4, the setting of $x.on$ to *false* is accompanied by transmissions of all tokens to members of x. In the following, $x.all$ is an abbreviation for x holds all tokens of all its members: $\langle \wedge \ u \ : \ u \ \text{in} \ x.mem \ :: \ x.num[u] = u.N \rangle$. The statement for setting $x.on$ and transmitting tokens is

$$x.on \ := \ false \qquad\qquad\qquad \text{if} \quad \neg x.co \ \wedge \ x.on \ \wedge \ x.all$$
$$\| \ \langle [\!| \ u \ : \ u \ \in \ x.mem \ :: \ x.num[u] \ := \ 0 \quad \text{if} \quad \neg x.co \ \wedge \ x.on \ \wedge \ x.all\rangle$$

Finally, the eating to thinking transition of x is accomplished by

$$x.dine \ := \ t \quad \text{if} \quad x.e \ \wedge \ \neg x.on$$

The complete program for the next refinement, *sync3*, is *prof* ∥ *middle3* ∥ *os2*, where *middle3* is given below.

Program *middle3*

always

$$\langle [\![\ x \ \ ::$$
$$x.has = \langle \wedge \ u \ : \ u \ \in \ x.mem \ \ :: \ \ x.num[u] \geq 1 \rangle$$
$$[\![\ x.all = \langle \wedge \ u \ : \ u \ \in \ x.mem \ \ :: \ \ x.num[u] = u.N \rangle$$
$$\rangle$$
$$[\![\ \langle [\![\ u \ \ :: \ \ u.n = u.N - \langle + \ x \ \ :: \ \ x.num[u] \rangle \rangle$$

initially

$$\langle [\![\ x \ \ :: \ \ x.co, x.on = \textit{false}, \textit{false} \rangle$$
$$[\![\ \langle [\![\ x, u \ \ :: \ \ x.num[u] = 0 \rangle$$

assign

{token transmissions from professors to committees}

$$\langle [\![\ u \ ::$$
$$\langle \| \ x \ : \ u \in x.mem \ \ :: \ \ x.num[u] := 1 \ \ \text{if} \ \ u.g \wedge u.n = u.N \rangle$$
$$\rangle$$

$$[\![\ \{\text{assignments to } x.dine, x.on\}$$

$$\langle [\![\ x \ ::$$
$$x.dine := h \qquad \qquad \text{if} \quad x.t \wedge x.has$$

$$[\![\ x.on := \textit{false} \qquad \text{if} \quad \neg x.co \wedge x.on \wedge x.all$$
$$\| \ \langle \| \ u \ : \ u \in x.mem \ ::$$
$$x.num[u] := 0 \quad \text{if} \quad \neg x.co \wedge x.on \wedge x.all$$
$$\rangle$$

$$[\![\ x.dine := t \qquad \qquad \text{if} \quad x.e \wedge \neg x.on$$
$$\rangle$$

$$[\![\ \{\text{token acquisition}\}$$
$$\langle [\![\ x, y, u \ : \ E[x, y] \wedge u \in (x.mem \cap y.mem) \ ::$$
$$x.num[u], y.num[u] := x.num[u] + y.num[u], 0 \qquad \text{if} \quad x.on$$
$$\rangle$$

end {*middle3*}

Proof of *sync3*

Almost all the proofs in *sync2* apply to *sync3*, with $x.tok[u]$ replaced by $(x.num[u] \geq 1)$. The places where proofs of *sync2* must to be modified are as follows. A stronger version of Lemma 14.3 (Lemma 14.3′, given next) is needed in proving the following fact that arises in the proof of (sy7):

$u.g$ *ensures* $x.num[u] \geq 1 \lor x^*.on$ in *middle3*.

A more elaborate version is also needed in the proof of (udn4): That eating is finite.

Lemma 14.3′

$(x.on \Rightarrow x.has) \land (\neg x.on \Rightarrow \langle \land u :: x.num[u] \leq 1 \rangle)$ in *sync3*

Proof: Similar to the proof of Lemma 14.3.   ▽

The proof that eating is finite goes as follows. If $\neg x.on$ is *true*, then $x.e$ becomes *false*. Also $x.co$ becomes *false* and stays *false* until $x.e$ becomes *false*. Therefore consider the case where $(x.on \land \neg x.co)$ is *true*. We show that x will hold all tokens of all its members eventually, and hence $(x.on \land \neg x.co \land x.all)$ will become *true*, after which $x.on$ will become *false*. Formally:

Proof: the conclusion of (udn4), $x.e \mapsto \neg x.e$ in *sync3*

> $x.on \land \neg x.co \mapsto \neg x.on$ in *sync3*
> , proven below
>
> $\neg x.on \mapsto \neg x.e$ in *sync3*
> , from the text of *middle3* and locality
>
> $\neg x.co \mapsto \neg x.e$ in *sync3*
> , using transitivity and disjunction on the above two
>
> $x.co \mapsto \neg x.co$ in *sync3*
> , from (pr3)
>
> $true \mapsto \neg x.e$ in *sync3*
> , cancellation and disjunction on the above two   ▽

Proof: $x.on \land \neg x.co \mapsto \neg x.on$ in *sync3*
     (used in the preceding proof of (udn4))

> $x.on \land (\langle + u :: x.num[u] \rangle = k) \land \neg x.all$ *ensures*
> $x.on \land (\langle + u :: x.num[u] \rangle > k)$ in *sync3*
> , from Lemmas 14.2 and 14.3′, the text of *middle3*, and locality
>
> $x.on \mapsto x.on \land x.all$ in *sync3*
> , using induction on the above and the definition of $x.all$
>
> $x.on \land \neg x.co$ *unless* $x.on \land \neg x.co \land x.all$ in *sync3*
> , from the text of *middle3* and locality

$x.on \ \wedge \ \neg x.co \ \mapsto \ x.on \ \wedge \ \neg x.co \ \wedge \ x.all$ in $sync3$
    , PSP theorem on the above two
$x.on \ \wedge \ \neg x.co \ \wedge \ x.all \ \ ensures \ \ \neg x.on$ in $sync3$
    , from the text of $middle3$ and locality
$x.on \ \wedge \ \neg x.co \ \mapsto \ \ \neg x.on$ in $sync3$
    , from the above two $\triangledown$

Exercise 14.5 Where is the hypothesis of (udn4) required in the proof of $sync3$? $\triangledown$

Exercise 14.6 In the statement in $middle3$ in which tokens are returned to members, can $x.on$ be removed from the condition? Does not $x.all$ imply $x.on$, using Lemma 14.3'? $\triangledown$

14.6.4 Distributed Implementation

Program $middle3$ can be implemented by message communication. We partition $middle3$ into a set of processes as follows: The statement for token transmission from u is in process u, and statements for assignments to $x.dine, x.on$ are in process x (statements for token acquisition are considered in the next paragraph). The shared variables between these processes are $x.tok[u]$ and $u.n$, for all x and u. These variables are related by the token-conservation invariant. The variable $x.tok[u]$ is set $true$ by process u and $false$ by committees; furthermore, the value of this variable is never tested by u, and it is tested for a $true$ value by the committees. Hence this variable meets the conditions for implementation by message transmission (see Chapter 8). We propose to have $x.tok[u], u.n$ be local to x and u, respectively. The setting of $x.tok[u]$ to $true$ is accomplished by u sending a message to the committees and decrementing $u.n$ to zero. The setting of $x.tok[u]$ to $false$ is accompanied by committee x sending a message to u, upon receipt of which u increments $u.n$ to $u.N$.

The only remaining synchrony is in assignments to $x.num[u]$, $y.num[u]$ when x acquires a token from y. The precondition for this assignment is $x.on$, which remains $true$ as long as $y.num[u] > 0$. Therefore, fortunately, synchronous assignments to $x.num[u], y.num[u]$ can be implemented by message communication: x sends a message if $x.on$ is $true$ and y responds by returning all tokens for the common members to x. If y does not hold a token for every common member, which is possible when token transmissions from professors to committees are not instantaneous, y has to wait to send the tokens (our solution guarantees that y will hold those tokens eventually).

14.6.5 Discussion

It is possible to optimize program *middle3* slightly by using Lemma 14.3': We show that $x.num[u]$ can be replaced by boolean variable $x.tok[u]$, and only the sum of $x.num[u]$ over all u need to be stored for each x. From Lemma 14.3', if a committee holds at least as many tokens as the number of its members, it holds at least one token from each member; the converse of this statement is also true trivially. Hence $x.has$ can be defined as $x.num \geq x.M$, where $x.num$ is the total number of tokens held by x and $x.M$ is the number of members of x. Similarly, $x.all$ can be defined as $x.num = x.N$, where $x.N$ is the sum of $u.N$, over all members u of x. The only statement requiring an explicit value of $x.num[u]$, $y.num[u]$ is the one for token acquisition; in this case, $y.num[u]$ is either 0 or 1 (from Lemma 14.3', because $y.on$ is *false*), and hence a single bit suffices to encode this value; incrementation of $x.num[u]$ is replaced by incrementation of $x.num$.

Program *sync3* admits of a number of scenarios that are not intuitively obvious. We sketch two such scenarios here. These scenarios and the following exercises illustrate the need for formal proofs; there are simply too many possibilities, and informal arguments might miss some of them.

The specification of *prof* does not require a professor to ever change state from waiting to nonwaiting. Consider two professors u, v and three committees x, y, z, whose members are $\{u, v\}$, $\{u\}$, $\{v\}$, respectively. It is possible that u, v are permanently waiting and yet that $x.co$ is permanently *false*. Similarly, it is possible that $x.has$ is *true* infinitely often though $x.co$ never becomes *true*.

Exercise 14.7   Construct examples of the preceding scenarios. $\triangledown$

Exercise 14.8   Suppose that all members of committee x cease to wait exactly when $x.co$ changes from *true* to *false*. Modify the problem specification to include this as a condition. Does the solution become simpler given this additional condition? $\triangledown$

Exercise 14.9   Generalize the problem specification and solution to allow professors to wait for an arbitrary number of committees of which they are members, rather than all committees.

Hint: Let a professor send colored tokens to the committees for which it is waiting, and uncolored tokens to the other committees of which it is a member. $\triangledown$

Summary

The committee-coordination problem is not trivial; it embodies both synchronization and exclusion aspects. Therefore the solution was derived in stages. First the synchronization problem was ignored, and the exclusion problem was solved assuming that the waiting status of all members of a committee can be checked synchronously. It was possible to solve this simpler problem using the dining philosophers solution. Next we showed how the synchronization issue can be addressed.

The stepwise refinement of the solution was *not* based on refining a process into a set of communicating processes. Program development would have been complicated greatly had we concentrated on what each committee does and on the messages it sends and receives. It was helpful to partition the program around the issues of exclusion and synchronization, not around data flow (i.e., message communication). We showed in the final stages of the design that our solution can be implemented on a message-based architecture.

Bibliographic Notes

The importance of multiway synchronization was brought to our attention by Forman [1986]. A description of a programming language, RADDLE, that employs multiway synchronization is found in Forman [1987]. Other languages that use communication synchronization include CSP (see Hoare [1984]) and ADA (see Gehani [1983]). A solution to the committee-coordination problem is proposed in Bagrodia [1987], which also includes a detailed study of the efficiency of coordination algorithms.

CHAPTER 15

Mutual Exclusion

15.1   Introduction

We consider a special case of the dining philosophers problem (Chapter 12) in this chapter: All processes are neighbors of each other. From the specification of the dining philosophers problem, it follows that at most one process may eat at any time. This special case, known as the *mutual exclusion problem*, was one of the first problems posed in connection with concurrent programming, and remains to this date a source of further research.

The problem is defined formally in Section 15.2. A simple solution for mutual exclusion between two processes appropriate for a shared-memory architecture is given in Section 15.3. The generalization of any two-process mutual exclusion algorithm to N processes, $N > 2$, is straightforward: Recursively, apply the algorithm to two nonempty subsets into which the processes are partitioned, and then resolve the conflict between the subsets using a two-process exclusion algorithm. We sketch such an N-process algorithm in Section 15.4. In Sections 15.5 and 15.6, we present two versions of another algorithm, known as the bakery algorithm, for this problem.

The diners program, given in Chapter 12, has been shown to be asymptotically optimal for distributed architectures. The mutual-exclusion problem is a special case of the diners problem.

Next we describe a simple method, known as the token-passing scheme, to provide some insight into the problem. Imagine that the processes are arranged in a unidirectional circular ring. There is a single token in the system. A process holds the token while eating. Since there is only one token, at most one process may eat at any time. To guarantee that every hungry process eats, we require that every process send the token to the next process in the ring within finite time of its receipt. This requirement is met if upon receipt of the token, (1) a thinking process immediately sends the token, and (2) a hungry process starts eating and sends the token upon completion of eating.

Unlike the dining philosophers algorithm of Chapter 12, in the token-passing scheme, a hungry process need not initiate any action such as requesting forks. Therefore this scheme is efficient during periods of heavy contention—i.e., when several processes are hungry simultaneously. On the other hand, in this scheme the overhead of message transmission may be substantial compared with the amount of underlying computation during periods of low contention. In this chapter we describe programs that are more complex than the token-passing scheme, but that are more efficient during periods of low contention.

Exercise 15.1   Encode the token-passing scheme in UNITY and prove its correctness.

Hint: First ignore channels. ∇

15.2   Problem Specification

The mutual-exclusion problem was used to illustrate program specification in Section 7.4.1. We repeat that specification next.

A given program, *user*, has variables *u.dine*, for all philosophers *u*. Variable *u.dine* can take one of three possible values: t, h, or e, corresponding to *thinking*, *hungry*, or *eating*, respectively.

We use the abbreviations $u.t, u.h$, and $u.e$ for $u.dine = t$, $u.dine = h$, and $u.dine = e$, respectively. It is required to transform the program *user* to a program *mutex*, where $mutex = user' \,[\!]\, G$. Program *user'* is obtained from *user* by superposition only; G denotes the program component that is composed with *user'* by the union operation.

15.2.1 Specification of Program *user*

$u.t$ *unless* $u.h$

stable $u.h$

$u.e$ *unless* $u.t$

Conditional Property

Hypothesis: $\langle \forall\, u, v\ :\ u \neq v\ ::\ \neg(u.e \wedge v.e) \rangle$
Conclusion: $\langle \forall\, u\ ::\ u.e\ \longmapsto\ u.t \rangle$

15.2.2 Specification of Program *mutex*

invariant $\neg(u.e\ \wedge\ v.e\ \wedge\ u \neq v)$ (MX1)

$u.h\ \longmapsto\ u.e$ (MX2)

15.2.3 Constraints

The only variables of *user* that can be named outside *user* (i.e., named in the assignment-components which have been added to *user* by the augmentation rule, or in G) are *u.dine*. Also, $u.t$ is constant (i.e., $u.t, \neg u.t$ are both stable), and $u.e$ is stable in G, for every u.

The reader should observe the resemblance between this specification and the specification of the dining philosophers problem (Chapter 12). The difference is that in constructing the solution to the latter, we employed only union of program components. In this chapter we employ superposition as well as union in solving the mutual-exclusion problem.

15.2.4 Derived Properties

The following properties were derived in Section 7.4.2 from the specification. For all u,

$\neg u.e$ is stable in *user*

$u.t$ *unless* $u.h$ in *mutex*

$u.h$ *unless* $u.e$ in *mutex*

$u.e$ *unless* $u.t$ in *mutex*

Exercise 15.2   Write a mutual-exclusion program given that any number of variables (local to any number of processes) can be accessed in one statement. Pay special attention to progress. $\triangledown$

15.3   Two-Process Mutual Exclusion

15.3.1 A Program

In a shared-memory system it is typical to assume that a memory reference is an atomic operation. This leads to an easy mechanism for arbitration: If several processes write into a variable, then the writings will be in some arbitrary order, thereby inducing asymmetry among the processes. Hence a simple strategy for mutual exclusion is to allow eating in the same order in which processes write into a shared variable. In the following algorithm, a shared variable, *turn*, is employed for this purpose.

The algorithm is given for two processes, x, y. In the following discussion and the program texts, u refers to either process, x or y, and $\hat{u}$ refers to the process other than u. For each u, we propose a boolean variable $u.b$ that is set *true* when u writes into *turn* and is set *false* when u transits to thinking. A hungry process u eats provided that $u.b$ holds, and either $\hat{u}.b$ is *false* or u wrote into *turn* before $\hat{u}$ did. We assume that initially both processes are thinking.

Program {transformation of *user*} *mutex2*

     declare $turn$: (x, y) {*turn* takes one of the two values, x or y}

     initially $\langle\, [\!]\ u$ :: $u.dine, u.b = t, false\rangle$

     transform   {to *user'*}

         statements in program *user* so that the following assignment is performed whenever $u.dine$ is set to t:

         $u.b$:= *false*

add {program G}

$\langle [\!| \; u \; :: $
$\quad u.b, turn \; := \; true, u \qquad \text{if} \quad \neg u.b \;\wedge\; u.h$
$\quad [\!| \; u.dine \; := \; e \qquad\qquad \text{if} \quad u.b \;\wedge\; \neg(\hat{u}.b \;\wedge\; turn = u)$
$\rangle$

end {$mutex2$}

15.3.2 Correctness of *mutex2*

It is easy to see that the constraints of Section 15.2.3 are met by program *mutex2*. The remaining obligation is to prove (MX1,MX2) for *mutex2*.

Proof of Mutual Exclusion, (MX1)

We first prove an invariant from which (MX1) is proven easily.

invariant $\quad u.e \;\Rightarrow\; [u.b \;\wedge\; \neg(\hat{u}.b \;\wedge\; turn = u)]$ in *mutex2* $\hfill$ (I1)

Initially (I1) holds because $u.e$ is *false*. We next show that this predicate is stable in *mutex2*. The proof consists of showing that the predicate is stable in both *user'* and G (recall that *user'* is obtained from *user* by augmentation and *mutex2* = *user'* $[\!|$ G) and then applying the union theorem.

Proof: $\quad u.e \;\Rightarrow\; [u.b \;\wedge\; \neg(\hat{u}.b \;\wedge\; turn = u)]$ is stable in *user'*

$\neg\hat{u}.b$ is stable in *user'*
$\quad$, from the text of *user'*

$turn = \hat{u}$ is stable in *user'*
$\quad$, *turn* is not accessed in *user'*

$\neg\hat{u}.b \;\vee\; turn = \hat{u}$ is stable in *user'*
$\quad$, disjunction on the above two

$u.b$ *unless* $\neg u.e$ in *user'*
$\quad$, from the text of *user'*

$u.b \;\wedge\; (\neg\hat{u}.b \;\vee\; turn = \hat{u})$ *unless* $\neg u.e \;\wedge\; (\neg\hat{u}.b \;\vee\; turn = \hat{u})$ in *user*
$\quad$, conjunction on the above two

$\neg u.e$ is stable in *user'*
$\quad$, from the derived property of *user* (see Section 15.2.4) and
$\quad\quad$ then applying the superposition theorem

$\neg u.e \;\vee\; [u.b \;\wedge\; (\neg\hat{u}.b \;\vee\; turn = \hat{u})]$ is stable in *user'*
$\quad$, disjunction on the above two

$u.e \;\Rightarrow\; [u.b \;\wedge\; \neg(\hat{u}.b \;\wedge\; turn = u)]$ is stable in *user'*
$\quad$, rewriting the above predicate $\hfill \triangledown$

Proof: $u.e \Rightarrow [u.b \land \neg(\hat{u}.b \land turn = u)]$ is stable in G

This follows from the text of G. $\triangledown$

We next prove (MX1) for the case of two processes, u and $\hat{u}$.

Proof: (MX1) $\neg(u.e \land \hat{u}.e)$ in $mutex2$

$\qquad u.e \Rightarrow u.b$ in $mutex2$
$\qquad\quad$, from (I1)

$\qquad u.e \land \hat{u}.e \equiv (u.e \land u.b) \land (\hat{u}.e \land \hat{u}.b)$ in $mutex2$
$\qquad\quad$, from the above

$\qquad u.e \land \hat{u}.e \equiv (u.e \land \hat{u}.b) \land (\hat{u}.e \land u.b)$ in $mutex2$
$\qquad\quad$, rewriting the above

$\qquad u.e \land \hat{u}.b \Rightarrow turn = \hat{u}$ in $mutex2$
$\qquad\quad$, from (I1)

$\qquad u.e \land \hat{u}.e \Rightarrow turn = \hat{u} \land turn = u$ in $mutex2$
$\qquad\quad$, from the above two

$\qquad u.e \land \hat{u}.e \Rightarrow false$ in $mutex2$
$\qquad\quad$, from the above $\triangledown$

Proof of Progress, (MX2)

We show that if u is hungry $u.b$ will be set *true*. If $\neg(\hat{u}.b \land turn = u)$ also holds at that time, u has the priority and hence u will eat. Otherwise, $(\hat{u}.b \land turn = u)$ holds and hence $\hat{u}$ has priority; $\hat{u}$ will eat, and upon completion of eating $\hat{u}.b$ will be set *false*, thereby giving priority to u.

Proof: (MX2) $u.h \mapsto u.e$ in $mutex2$

$\qquad u.h \mapsto u.h \land u.b$ in $mutex2$
$\qquad\quad$, proven below   (1)

$\qquad u.h \land u.b \land \neg(\hat{u}.b \land turn = u) \mapsto u.e$ in $mutex2$
$\qquad\quad$, proven below   (2)

$\qquad u.h \land u.b \land \hat{u}.b \land turn = u \mapsto u.e$ in $mutex2$
$\qquad\quad$, proven below   (3)

$\qquad u.h \land u.b \mapsto u.e$ in $mutex2$
$\qquad\quad$, disjunction on (2,3)

$\qquad u.h \mapsto u.e$ in $mutex2$
$\qquad\quad$, transitivity on (1) and the above $\triangledown$

Proof: (1) $u.h \mapsto u.h \land u.b$ in $mutex2$

u.h ensures u.h $\wedge$ *u.b* in *G*
: , from the text of *G*

u.h is stable in *user′*
: , from the specification of *user* (see Section 15.2.1) and then applying the superposition theorem

u.h ensures u.h $\wedge$ *u.b* in *mutex2*
: , union theorem on the above two

u.h $\longmapsto$ *u.h* $\wedge$ *u.b* in *mutex2*
: , from the above $\triangledown$

Proof: (2) *u.h* $\wedge$ *u.b* $\wedge$ $\neg(\hat{u}.b$ $\wedge$ *turn* $= u)$ $\longmapsto$ *u.e* in *mutex2*

$\neg\hat{u}.b$ is stable in *user′*
: , from the text of *user′*

turn $\neq u$ is stable in *user′*
: , *turn* is not accessed in *user′*

$\neg(\hat{u}.b$ $\wedge$ *turn* $= u)$ is stable in *user′*
: , disjunction on the above two

u.h $\wedge$ *u.b* is stable in *user′*
: , from the text of *user′*

u.h $\wedge$ *u.b* $\wedge$ $\neg(\hat{u}.b$ $\wedge$ *turn* $= u)$ is stable in *user′*
: , conjunction on the above two

u.h $\wedge$ *u.b* $\wedge$ $\neg(\hat{u}.b$ $\wedge$ *turn* $= u)$ *ensures u.e* in *G*
: , from the text of *G*

u.h $\wedge$ *u.b* $\wedge$ $\neg(\hat{u}.b$ $\wedge$ *turn* $= u)$ $\longmapsto$ *u.e* in *mutex2*
: , union theorem on the above two, then replacing *ensures* by $\longmapsto$ $\triangledown$

Proof: (3) *u.h* $\wedge$ *u.b* $\wedge$ $\hat{u}.b$ $\wedge$ *turn* $= u$ $\longmapsto$ *u.e* in *mutex2*

Hypothesis of the conditional property of *user* holds
: , (MX1) has been proven

$\hat{u}.e$ $\longmapsto$ $\hat{u}.t$ in *mutex2*
: , from the conclusion of the conditional property of *user* (see Section 15.2.1) using the above

$\hat{u}.t$ $\Rightarrow$ $\neg\hat{u}.b$ in *mutex2*
: , left to the reader

$\neg\hat{u}.h$ $\longmapsto$ $\neg\hat{u}.b$ in *mutex2*
: , from the above two using transitivity and disjunction

$\hat{u}.h$ $\wedge$ $\hat{u}.b$ $\wedge$ *turn* $= u$ $\longmapsto$ $\neg\hat{u}.b$ in *mutex2*
: , from (2) substituting $\hat{u}$ for *u* and then strengthening the left side and using $\hat{u}.e$ $\longmapsto$ $\neg\hat{u}.b$ for the right side

$\hat{u}.b \ \wedge \ turn = u \ \longmapsto \ \neg \hat{u}.b$ in *mutex2*
    , disjunction on the above two; strengthening the left side

$(u.h \ \wedge \ u.b) \ unless \ u.e$ in *mutex2*
    , from the program text

$u.h \ \wedge \ u.b \ \wedge \ \hat{u}.b \ \wedge \ turn = u \ \longmapsto$
    $(u.h \ \wedge \ u.b \ \wedge \ \neg \hat{u}.b) \ \vee \ u.e$ in *mutex2*
    , PSP theorem on the above two

$u.h \ \wedge \ u.b \ \wedge \ \neg \hat{u}.b \ \longmapsto \ u.e$ in *mutex2*
    , from (2) by strengthening the left side

$u.h \ \wedge \ u.b \ \wedge \ \hat{u}.b \ \wedge \ turn = u \ \longmapsto \ u.e$ in *mutex2*
    , cancellation on the above two $\triangledown$

15.3.3 Introducing Asynchrony in *mutex2*

In program *mutex2*, synchronous assignments to $u.b$ and $turn$ can be decoupled
provided that $turn$ is set to u only after $u.b$ is set *true*. We introduce a local
boolean variable $u.r$ of u—$u.r$ holds if $u.b$ has been set *true* and $turn$ is yet to
be set to u—to perform these two assignments in order. The resulting program
is shown next.

Program {transformation of program *user*} *mutex2′*

    initially $\langle [\![\ u \ :: \ u.dine, u.b, u.r = t, false, false \rangle$

    transform

        statements in program *user* so that the following assignment is
        performed whenever $u.dine$ is set to t:

        $u.b \ := \ false$

    add

        $\langle [\![\ u \ ::$
          $u.b, u.r \ := \ true, true \ \ \text{if} \ \ \neg u.b \ \wedge \ u.h$
        $[\![\ u.r, turn \ := \ false, u \ \ \text{if} \ \ u.r$
        $[\![\ u.dine \ := \ e \ \ \ \ \ \ \ \text{if} \ \ u.b \ \wedge \ \neg u.r \ \wedge \ \neg(\hat{u}.b \ \wedge \ \neg \hat{u}.r \ \wedge \ turn = u)$
        $\rangle$

end {*mutex2′*}

The proof of this program is similar to the previous one. Now $u.r$ must
appear in the invariant and the progress proof. The invariant corresponding
to (I1) is

$$u.e \ \Rightarrow \ u.b \ \wedge \ \neg u.r \ \wedge \ \neg(\hat{u}.b \ \wedge \ \neg \hat{u}.r \ \wedge \ turn = u) \ \text{in } mutex2'. \qquad (\text{I1}')$$

We need the additional invariant

$$u.r \quad \Rightarrow \quad u.b \text{ in } mutex2'. \qquad (12')$$

The structure of the progress proof is similar to the previous one; $u.h \mapsto u.e$ in $mutex2'$ is easily proven from the following properties.

$$u.h \quad \mapsto \quad u.h \wedge u.b \wedge u.r \text{ in } mutex2'$$
$$u.h \wedge u.b \wedge u.r \quad \mapsto \quad u.h \wedge u.b \wedge \neg u.r \text{ in } mutex2'$$
$$u.h \wedge u.b \wedge \neg u.r \wedge \neg(\hat{u}.b \wedge \neg \hat{u}.r \wedge turn = u) \quad \mapsto \quad u.e \text{ in } mutex2'$$
$$u.h \wedge u.b \wedge \neg u.r \wedge \hat{u}.b \wedge \neg \hat{u}.r \wedge turn = u \quad \mapsto \quad u.e \text{ in } mutex2'$$

In the following exercise, we propose some other modifications to $mutex2$ and $mutex2'$ to make them even more asynchronous.

Exercise 15.3 In $mutex2$, the precondition for the transition of u to eating is $u.b \wedge \neg(\hat{u}.b \wedge turn = u)$. We show that this predicate can be evaluated term by term, asynchronously. We introduce a boolean variable $u.check$ for the evaluation of the second conjunct; this conjunct can be written as ($\neg \hat{u}.b \vee turn \neq u$). The following statements are added instead of the statements shown in $mutex2$. (We do not show modifications to program $user$, nor do we show the initially-section, both of which are exactly as in $mutex2$.)

add

$$\langle\!\!\!| \; u \quad ::$$
$$\quad u.b, u.check, turn \; := \; true, false, u \quad \text{if} \quad \neg u.b \wedge u.h$$
$$\quad |\!| \; u.check \; := \; u.check \vee \neg \hat{u}.b$$
$$\quad |\!| \; u.check \; := \; u.check \vee turn \neq u$$
$$\quad |\!| \; u.dine \; := \; e \qquad\qquad\qquad \text{if} \quad u.b \wedge u.check$$
$$\rangle$$

Prove the correctness of this program. Use the invariants

$$u.e \quad \Rightarrow \quad u.b \wedge u.check$$

and

$$\neg u.check \vee \neg u.b \vee \neg \hat{u}.b \vee turn \neq u.$$

Apply similar modifications to $mutex2'$ and prove correctness. ∇

15.4   *N*-Process Mutual Exclusion

In this section we show, informally, how to construct an *N*-process mutual-exclusion algorithm for any N, $N \geq 1$. For $N = 1$, the problem is easily solved:

The code consists of a single statement for a hungry process to transit to eating. For $N = 2$, we saw some two-process mutual-exclusion algorithms in Section 15.3. For $N > 2$, partition the processes into two nonempty subsets A, B. The program consists of code for mutual exclusion in A and in B (these codes are obtained by recursive applications of this strategy), and the code for two-process mutual exclusion for a process in A and a process in B. We illustrate this procedure for a system of four processes, w, x, y, z.

Divide the processes into two subsets, $A = \{w, x\}$ and $B = \{y, z\}$. Consider the steps by which a hungry process, say w, transits to eating. First w competes with x, the other member of A. This competition determines which member of A will eat next. For the mutual-exclusion problem in A, we introduce boolean variables $u.h1$, $u.e1$ with every u in A. Variable $u.h1$ holds if and only if u is a contender in A: It is hungry and has not yet won the competition in A. Variable $u.e1$ holds if u has won the competition in A. The variables $u.h1$, $u.e1$ can be likened to $u.h, u.e$; the latter denote that u is hungry or eating with respect to all processes, whereas the former denote that u is hungry or eating with respect to processes in A. Then we have the following code for mutual exclusion in $\{w, x\}$; this is obtained by suitably modifying the code of program $mutex2$.

initially

$$\langle \|\ u\ :\ u\ \in\ \{w, x\}\quad ::\quad u.dine, u.b, u.e1 = t, \textit{false}, \textit{false} \rangle$$

always

$$\langle \|\ u\ :\ u\ \in \{w, x\}\quad ::\quad u.h1 = u.h\ \wedge\ \neg u.e1 \rangle$$

add

$$\langle \|\ u\ :\ u\ \in\ \{w, x\}\quad ::$$
$$u.b1, turn\ :=\ true, u \qquad\quad \text{if}\quad \neg u.b1\ \wedge\ u.h1$$
$$\|\ u.e1\ :=\ true \qquad\qquad\quad \text{if}\quad u.b1\ \wedge\ \neg(\hat{u}.b1\ \wedge\ turn = u)$$
$$\rangle$$

A similar set of statements is included in the code for mutual exclusion in the set $\{y, z\}$. (The variable $turn$ used for $\{w, x\}$ is different from the $turn$ used for $\{y, z\}$.)

Next we add the code for two-process mutual exclusion between a process from $\{w, x\}$ and a process from $\{y, z\}$; for any such contending process u, $u.e1$ holds. Now, for every u in $\{w, x, y, z\}$, we introduce boolean variables $u.h2$, $u.e2$. Variable $u.e2$ holds only if u has won the competition in the set $\{w, x, y, z\}$. Therefore $u.dine$ can be set to e if $u.e2$ holds. Variable $u.h2$ holds if and only if u is competing in the set $\{w, x, y, z\}$ after having won the competition in its two-member set; thus $u.h2$ is the same as $u.e1\ \wedge\ \neg u.e2$. The code for this exclusion problem is again obtained from $mutex2$.

initially

$\langle \llbracket\ u\ :\ u\ \in\ \{w,x,y,z\}\ \ ::\ \ u.b2, u.e2 = \textit{false}, \textit{false} \rangle$

always

$\langle \llbracket\ u\ :\ u\ \in\ \{w,x,y,z\}\ \ ::\ \ u.h2 = u.e1\ \wedge\ \neg u.e2 \rangle$

add

$\langle \llbracket\ u\ :\ u\ \in\ \{w,x,y,z\}\ \ ::$

$u.b2, turn\ :=\ true, u$	if $\neg u.b2\ \wedge\ u.h2$
$\llbracket\ u.e2\ :=\ true$	if $u.b2\ \wedge\ \neg(\hat{u}.b2\ \wedge\ turn = u)$
$\llbracket\ u.dine\ :=\ e$	if $u.e2$

$\rangle$

The variables $u.b1$, $u.b2$, $u.e1$, $u.e2$ are to be set *false* when $u.dine$ is set to t in the program *user*.

In the preceding code, $\hat{u}$ denotes the identity of the process with which u contends. Since this identity may change with time—w or x is the contender from $\{w,x\}$, and similarly for $\{y,z\}$—additional variables must be employed to identify the contenders from the two subsets. Also note that the variable *turn*, employed for exclusion in $\{w,x,y,z\}$, is different from the other *turns*.

The algorithm imposes a static binary tree structure on the processes. All thinking processes are at the leaves of the tree. For each internal node, a mutual-exclusion algorithm is run between the sons of that node, and the winner proceeds to its father's position in the tree. If the tree is balanced, then a process must participate in about $\log_2 N$ algorithms for two-process mutual exclusion in order to eat, where N is the number of processes.

15.5   A Simple Bakery Program

15.5.1 A Program

A simple version of the bakery algorithm uses the arbitration mechanism for serving customers in a bakery. Any customer entering the bakery obtains a number from a machine, which dispenses distinct numbers. Let variable *issue* show the next number to be dispensed. Variable *serve* shows the number currently receiving service or the next number to receive service if no customer is currently receiving service. An eating process can be likened to a customer receiving service, and a hungry process to a customer not receiving service; thinking processes are outside the bakery. If *issue* is increased by 1 each time a number is dispensed, and *serve* is increased by 1 each time service to a customer is completed, then each customer receives service eventually (assuming that initially $issue = serve$). Furthermore, mutual exclusion in service is guaranteed because a customer receiving service holds a number equal to $serve$, and distinct customers hold distinct numbers.

In the following algorithm, we use $issue$ and $serve$ with the meanings just given. If there are at most N customers, then it is possible to work with only the numbers between 0 and $N - 1$ (inclusive), and all arithmetic on $issue$ and $serve$ can be done modulo N. We use $\oplus$, $\ominus$ to denote addition, subtraction modulo N, respectively. A program simulating the operation of the simple bakery just described is given next. The value of variable $u.num$ is the number held by customer u; if u is outside the bakery (u is thinking), then $u.num = N$.

Program {transformation of program $user$**}** $Simple\text{-}Bakery$

declare

$\quad\quad issue, serve \ : \ 0..N - 1,$

$\quad\quad num \ : \text{array[processes] of } 0..N$

initially

$\quad\quad issue, serve = 0, 0$

$\quad \| \ \langle\| \ u \ :: \ u.num, u.dine = N, t\rangle$

transform

$\quad\quad$ statements in program $user$ so that the following assignment is performed whenever $u.dine$ is set to t:

$\quad\quad u.num, serve \ := \ N, serve \oplus 1$

add

$\quad\quad \langle\| \ u \ ::$

$\quad\quad\quad u.num, issue \ := \ issue, issue \oplus 1 \quad\quad \text{if} \quad u.num = N \ \wedge \ u.h$

$\quad\quad\quad \| \ u.dine \ := \ e \quad\quad\quad\quad\quad\quad\quad\quad\quad \text{if} \quad u.num = serve$

$\quad\quad \rangle$

end {$Simple\text{-}Bakery$}

15.5.2 Correctness

One would expect the proof of this program to be trivial; after all, bakeries have been operating for centuries without serious breakdowns in customer service. Unfortunately, the proof has to make explicit a number of facts that one assumes implicitly about real bakeries. For instance, our program operates correctly only if every customer enering the bakery leaves only after receiving service—i.e., we do not allow hungry to thinking transitions. A real bakery would use a time-out mechanism to ignore customers whose numbers are called but who fail to show up for service.

We will consider a far more refined version of this program in the next section. Thus here we merely sketch a proof of the program *Simple-Bakery*. In the following, $\ll$ *serve..issue* $\gg$ denotes the sequence of successive numbers modulo N, from *serve* up to, but not including, *issue*. Thus $\ll$ $k..k$ $\gg$ is the *null* sequence, for any k, $0 \leq k < N$. In the following, u, v are quantified over all processes. In the proof all properties are for the composite program, *Simple-Bakery*; the program name is not shown explicitly.

invariant

> {a thinking process holds number N, a hungry process either N or some number in $\ll$ *serve..issue* $\gg$, and an eating process holds *serve*}
>
> $[(u.t \;\Rightarrow\; u.num = N)\; \wedge$
>
> $(u.h \;\Rightarrow\; u.num \in \ll serve..issue \gg \;\vee\; u.num = N)\; \wedge$
>
> $(u.e \;\Rightarrow\; u.num = serve)$
>
> $]$ (I2)

invariant

> {numbers held by processes, if different from N, are distinct}
>
> $(u.num = v.num) \;\Rightarrow\; (u = v \;\vee\; u.num = N)$ (I3)

invariant

> {every number in $\ll$ *serve..issue* $\gg$ is held by some process}
>
> $\{x \mid x \in \ll serve..issue \gg\} = \{u.num \mid u.num \neq N\}$ (I4)

We leave to the reader the proof of these invariants, and the proof that constraints on variable access are met.

Proof: mutual exclusion (MX1) $u.e \;\wedge\; v.e \;\Rightarrow\; u = v$

> $u.e \;\wedge\; v.e \;\Rightarrow\; u.num = serve \;\wedge\; v.num = serve$
>
>   , from (I2)
>
> $(u.num = v.num) \;\wedge\; (u.num < N)$
>
>   , from the above and $serve < N$
>
> $u = v$
>
>   , from the above and (I3) $\triangledown$

Proof: progress (MX2) $u.h \;\longmapsto\; u.e$

$u.h$ *ensures* $u.num \neq N$	, from the program text and $issue < N$
$u.h \;\longmapsto\; u.num \neq N$	, from the above
$u.num \neq N \;\longmapsto\; u.e$	, proof sketched below
$u.h \;\longmapsto\; u.e$	, transitivity on the above two $\triangledown$

Proof: sketch of $u.num \neq N \; \mapsto \; u.e$

We show that

$$u.num \neq N \; \mapsto \; u.num = serve$$

and

$$(u.num = serve) \; ensures \; u.e$$

The second property follows from the program text. The first property can be deduced by using induction on the following, which says that the server gets closer to serving each customer eventually.

$$(u.num \neq N \; \wedge \; (u.num \ominus serve) = k)$$
$$\mapsto \; ([u.num = serve] \; \vee \; [u.num \neq N \; \wedge \; (u.num \ominus serve) < k])$$

The proof of the preceding property is similar to one we prove in the next section; therefore we do not present it here. The idea is that if $u.num \ominus serve > 0$, there is some v for which $v.num = serve$; eventually v eats, and when v transits to thinking $serve$ is increased, thus decreasing $u.num \ominus serve$. $\triangledown$

15.6 A Sophisticated Bakery Program

15.6.1 A Program

The program *Simple-Bakery* uses variables *issue* and *serve*, which are assigned synchronously with a process acquiring a number and completing service, respectively. We propose a finer-grain solution in this section: Every variable is local to a process, and a variable can be written only by the process to which it is local. We have $u.num$ of the previous section with the following difference: $u.num = 0$ if u is thinking; this convention makes it easier to write the next program. The major new idea is to introduce a *rank* for a process: $u.rank$ is the number of processes whose *num* values are zero, plus the number of processes v for which $(u.num, u)$ is lexicographically less than or equal to $(v.num, v)$. (We assume that process ids are integers, and hence they can be compared.) The higher the rank, the closer a process to receiving service. A hungry process u sets $u.num$ to nonzero by increasing it beyond every $v.num$, thus acquiring a rank lower than every other hungry process. It can be shown that for distinct u, v, if $u.num \neq 0$ and $v.num \neq 0$, then the ranks are distinct. If process u is hungry and $u.num \neq 0$ and $u.rank = N$, then u may transit to eating. From the distinctness of ranks, mutual exclusion is guaranteed. Progress is guaranteed because the rank of a process u never decreases as long as $u.num \neq 0$; the rank increases if any other process completes eating.

Notation: $u \leq v$ denotes that $(u.num, u)$ is lexicographically less than or equal to $(v.num, v)$. Note that $\leq$ is a total ordering on the given pairs. $\triangledown$

Program *Bakery*

always $\langle [\![\ u\ ::\ u.rank = \langle +\ v\ :\ v.num = 0\ \vee\ u \leq v\ ::\ 1 \rangle\ \rangle$

initially $\langle [\![\ u\ ::\ u.num, u.dine = 0, t \rangle$

transform

statements in program *user* so that the following assignment is performed whenever *u.dine* is set to *t*:

$u.num\ :=\ 0$

add

$\langle [\![\ u\ ::$

$\quad u.num\ :=\ \langle \max\ v\ ::\ v.num \rangle + 1 \quad$ if $\ u.h\ \wedge\ u.num = 0$

$\quad [\![\ u.dine\ :=\ e \quad$ if $\ u.h\ \wedge\ u.num \neq 0\ \wedge\ u.rank = N$

$\rangle$

end {*Bakery*}

15.6.2 Correctness

Proofs are based on the following facts:

1. For distinct u, v, if $u.num \neq 0$ and $v.num \neq 0$, then the ranks are distinct.

2. $u.rank$ does not decrease as long as $u.num \neq 0$ and increases if some other process completes eating.

3. Process u eats eventually if $(u.num \neq 0\ \wedge\ u.rank = N)$.

These ideas are formalized next. All properties in the following proof are of the program *Bakery*; program name is not shown explicitly.

Lemma 15.1   The following are invariants.

$u.t\ \Rightarrow\ u.num = 0,$

$u.e\ \Rightarrow\ u.num \neq 0,$

$u.rank \leq N.$

Proof: From the program text.   ▽

Note: Based on this lemma, it is possible to drop the term $u.h$ in the precondition for hungry to eating transition for u. To see this, observe that the term $u.num \neq 0$ appears in that precondition and, from the lemma, that $u.num \neq 0\ \Rightarrow\ \neg u.t\ \Rightarrow\ u.h \vee u.e$. If $u.e$ holds, executing the statement causes no state change.   ▽

Lemma 15.2

invariant $(u.num \neq 0 \ \wedge \ v.num \neq 0 \ \wedge \ u.rank = v.rank) \ \Rightarrow \ (u = v)$

Proof: From the definition,

$$u.rank = \langle + \ w \ : \ w.num = 0 \ \vee \ u \leq w \ :: \ 1 \rangle.$$

If $u.num \neq 0$ then, for any w,

$$\neg(w.num = 0 \ \wedge \ u \leq w).$$

Hence, given that $u.num \neq 0$, we have

$$u.rank = \langle + \ w \ : \ w.num = 0 \ :: \ 1 \rangle + \langle + \ w \ : \ u \leq w \ :: \ 1 \rangle.$$

Similarly, from $v.num \neq 0$, we have

$$v.rank = \langle + \ w \ : \ w.num = 0 \ :: \ 1 \rangle + \langle + \ w \ : \ v \leq w \ :: \ 1 \rangle.$$

Hence

$$u.num \neq 0 \ \wedge \ v.num \neq 0 \ \wedge \ u.rank = v.rank$$
$$\Rightarrow \quad \langle + \ w \ : \ u \leq w \ :: \ 1 \rangle = \langle + \ w \ : \ v \leq w \ :: \ 1 \rangle$$
$$\Rightarrow \qquad u = v \qquad\qquad \text{, from properties of finite total orderings} \quad \triangledown$$

Lemma 15.3 $(u.num \neq 0 \ \wedge \ u.rank \geq k) \ unless \ u.t$

Proof: We deduce this from the program text as follows. For any v (v need not be distinct from u),

1. Setting $v.num$ to nonzero establishes $u \leq v$ (because, since $u.num \neq 0$, we have $u \neq v$ and hence $v.num$ is set to a value larger than $u.num$), thereby preserving the antecedent of *unless*.

2. Transition of v from hungry to eating preserves the antecedent of *unless*.

3. Transition of v from eating to thinking is as follows: If $u = v$, then the consequent of the *unless* is established; if $u \neq v$, the antecedent is preserved ($u.rank$ may increase). $\triangledown$

Lemma 15.4

invariant $\neg u.e \ \vee \ u.rank = N$

Proof: From the program text. $\triangledown$

Lemma 15.5   (mutual exclusion), (MX1)

  invariant $u.e \ \wedge \ v.e \ \Rightarrow \ u = v$

Proof:

$$u.e \ \wedge \ v.e$$

$\Rightarrow \quad u.num \neq 0 \ \wedge \ u.rank = N \ \wedge \ v.num \neq 0 \ \wedge \ v.rank = N$
 , from Lemmas 15.1 and 15.4

$\Rightarrow \quad u = v$
 , from Lemma 15.2 $\triangledown$

Lemma 15.6 $u.h \ \mapsto \ u.e$

Proof:

$u.h \ ensures \ u.num \neq 0$
 , from the program text

$u.num \neq 0 \ \wedge \ u.rank = N \ ensures \ u.e$
 , from the program text   (4)

$u.num \neq 0 \ \wedge \ u.rank < N \ \mapsto \ u.num \neq 0 \ \wedge \ u.rank = N$
 , proven below   (5)

$u.num \neq 0 \ \wedge \ u.rank \leq N \ \mapsto \ u.e$
 , from (4,5), replacing *ensures* by $\mapsto$ in (4) and
 using transitivity and disjunction

$u.num \neq 0 \ \mapsto \ u.e$
 , using the substitution axiom since $u.rank \leq N$ is
 invariant (Lemma 15.1)

$u.h \ \mapsto \ u.e$
 , transitivity on the first property (replacing *ensures* by $\mapsto$) and
 the above

Next we prove (5). If $u.rank < N$, then from the definition of rank, there is a v such that $v.num \neq 0 \ \wedge \ u < v$. Clearly $v.rank > u.rank$. By a simple induction, we deduce that

$$u.num \neq 0 \ \wedge \ u.rank < N \ \Rightarrow$$
$$\langle \exists \ w \ :: \ w.num \neq 0 \ \wedge \ w.rank = N \rangle. \tag{6}$$

We show that w will eat and that upon completion of eating, $u.rank$ will increase. We use the following properties, whose proofs are straightforward from the program text. For any $x, y, x \neq y$,

$$x.num \neq 0 \ \wedge \ x.rank \geq k \ unless \ x.num \neq 0 \ \wedge \ x.rank = N \tag{7}$$
$$x.num \neq 0 \ \wedge \ x.rank \geq k \ \wedge \ y.e \ ensures \ x.num \neq 0 \ \wedge \ x.rank > k \tag{8}$$

Now we prove (5) from (4,6–8). Consider the given u, w.
From (4), replacing u by w,

$$w.num \neq 0 \ \wedge \ w.rank = N \ \mapsto \ w.e \tag{9}$$

Using the PSP theorem on (7,9), where x is replaced by u in (7), and simplifying,

$$u.num \neq 0 \ \wedge \ u.rank \geq k \ \wedge \ w.num \neq 0 \ \wedge \ w.rank = N \ \mapsto$$

$$(u.num \neq 0 \;\wedge\; u.rank \geq k \;\wedge\; w.e) \quad \vee \quad (u.num \neq 0 \;\wedge\; u.rank = N) \qquad (10)$$

From (8) replacing x by u and y by w,

$$u.num \neq 0 \;\wedge\; u.rank \geq k \;\wedge\; w.e \;\mapsto\; u.num \neq 0 \;\wedge\; u.rank > k \qquad (11)$$

Using cancellation on (10,11) and then using (6) it follows that

$$u.num \neq 0 \;\wedge\; k = u.rank \;\wedge\; k < N \;\mapsto\; u.num \neq 0 \;\wedge\; u.rank > k \qquad (12)$$

Applying induction on (12), we obtain (5). $\triangledown$

15.6.3 Introducing More Asynchrony

The computation of $u.rank$ in Program *Bakery* requires the values of all $v.num$ simultaneously. Similarly, assigning a value to $u.num$ requires simultaneous access to all $v.num$. The program was written in this manner because it allows a simpler proof. Now we sketch a modification that allows ranks to be computed in an asynchronous manner. We also suggest how to compute $u.num$ in a series of assignments by comparing it with one other $v.num$ in each step.

The previous program uses the predicate $u.num \neq 0 \;\wedge\; u.rank = N$. No other value of $u.rank$ appears explicitly in the program. Therefore we introduce a boolean variable, $u.highest$, which equals $u.num \neq 0 \;\wedge\; u.rank = N$. The precondition for a hungry to eating transition is $u.highest$. From Lemma 15.3, once $u.highest$ becomes *true* it remains *true* until u completes eating—i.e., $u.highest$ *unless* $u.t$. The following statement can be used to compute $u.highest$:

$$u.highest \;:=\; \langle \wedge v \;::\; v.num = 0 \;\vee\; u \leq v \rangle \;\wedge\; u.num \neq 0.$$

Also, $u.highest$ is to be set *false* whenever u transits from eating to thinking.

The introduction of $u.highest$ gets rid of $u.rank$ but retains the problem of simultaneous access to $v.num$ in computing $u.highest$. This can be solved as follows. Introduce boolean variables $u.higher(v)$ and the assignments

$$u.higher(v) \;:=\; (v.num = 0 \;\vee\; u \leq v) \;\wedge\; u.num \neq 0$$

and

$$u.highest \;:=\; \langle \wedge v \;:\; u \neq v \;::\; u.higher(v) \rangle$$

Observe that $u.higher(v)$ *unless* $u.t$. Again $u.higher(v)$, for all v, should be set *false* whenever u transits from eating to thinking.

The computation of $u.num$ by comparing it with one other $v.num$ in each step can be accomplished as follows: Introduce boolean variables $u.set(v)$ to denote that $u.num$ has been set in comparison with $v.num$. To assign to $u.num$, introduce the following statement for each v, $u \neq v$:

$$u.num, u.set(v) \;:=\; \max(u.num, v.num + 1), true \quad \text{if} \;\; \neg u.set(v) \;\wedge\; u.h$$

As before, $u.set(v)$ is to be set *false* when u transits from eating to thinking. We rewrite the assignment to $u.higher(v)$ by replacing the predicate, $v.num = 0$

by $\neg v.set(u)$ and $u.num \neq 0$ by $\langle \wedge\ w\ :\ u \neq w\ ::\ u.set(w)\rangle$. The complete program is given next.

Program {transformation of Program *user*} *Bakery-with-Asynchrony*

initially

$\langle \| \ u,v \ :\ u \neq v \ ::\ u.set(v), u.higher(v) = false, false\rangle$

$\|\ \langle \| \ u \ ::\ u.num, u.highest, u.dine = 0, false, t\rangle$

transform

statements in program *user* so that the following assignment is performed whenever *u.dine* is set to *t*:

$u.num, u.highest \ :=\ 0, false$

$\|\ \langle \| \ v \ :\ u \neq v \ ::\ u.set(v), u.higher(v) \ :=\ false, false\rangle$

add

$\langle \| \ u,v \ :\ u \neq v \ ::$

    $u.num, u.set(v) \ :=$

        $\max(u.num, v.num + 1), true \quad \text{if} \quad \neg u.set(v) \ \wedge\ u.h$

    $\|\ u.higher(v) \ :=$

        $(\neg v.set(u)\ \vee\ u \leq v)\ \wedge\ \langle \wedge\ w\ :\ u \neq w\ ::\ u.set(w)\rangle$

$\rangle$

$\|\ \langle \| \ u \ ::$

    $u.highest \ :=\ \langle \wedge\ v\ :\ u \neq v\ ::\ u.higher(v)\rangle$

    $\|\ u.dine \ :=\ e \quad \text{if} \quad u.highest$

$\rangle$

end {*Bakery-with-Asynchrony*}

15.6.4 Correctness of the Asynchronous Solution

The proof of correctness of this program is almost identical to the previous proof. We merely state the lemmas that need to be proven. The correspondence between the (primed) lemmas given next and the (unprimed) ones in the previous proof should be noted.

Lemma 15.1′

$u.highest \ \Rightarrow\ \langle \wedge\ v\ :\ u \neq v\ ::\ u.higher(v)\rangle$

and for $u \neq v$

$u.higher(v) \ \Rightarrow\ (\neg v.set(u)\ \vee\ u \leq v)\ \wedge\ \langle \wedge\ w\ :\ u \neq w\ ::\ u.set(w)\rangle$

Lemma 15.2′   For $u \neq v$, $\neg[u.higher(v)\ \wedge\ v.higher(u)]$

Lemma 15.3$'$ $u.higher(v)$ *unless* $u.t$

Lemma 15.4$'$ $\neg u.e \;\lor\; u.highest$

Lemma 15.5$'$ (mutual exclusion) $[u.e \;\land\; v.e] \;\Rightarrow\; [u = v]$

Lemma 15.6$'$ $u.h \;\mapsto\; u.e$

For the proofs—especially of Lemma 15.6$'$—define $u.rank$ as the number of v's for which $u.higher(v)$ holds (assume $u.higher(u)$ holds). Then a proof of Lemma 15.6 is also a proof of Lemma 15.6$'$.

We leave it to the reader to introduce further asynchrony into program *Bakery-with-Asynchrony*. In particular, to compute $u.higher(v)$, variables $v.set(u)$ and $v.num$ can be read asynchronously at arbitrary times after $\langle \land\; w \;:\; u \neq w \;::\; u.set(w) \rangle$ holds. Also, $\langle \land\; w \;:\; u \neq w \;::\; u.set(w) \rangle$ can be computed asynchronously term by term.

Summary

The literature contains a large number of solutions to the mutual-exclusion problem and its variants. We have sketched two solutions—a two-process mutual-exclusion algorithm and the bakery algorithm—merely to illustrate how they may be expressed, proved, and refined within UNITY. The heuristic used in this chapter starts with a synchronous solution and then introduces greater degrees of asynchrony, similar to the approach in Chapter 9. The UNITY model proved helpful in stating several solutions with varying degrees of synchrony.

Bibliographic Notes

The problem of mutual exclusion and a solution are described in Dijkstra [1968]. The two-process mutual-exclusion algorithm is in G. L. Peterson [1981], and a pleasant exposition of the algorithm appears in Feijen and Bijlsma [1985]. The bakery algorithms are discussed in Lamport [1974]. Ben-Ari [1982] contains developments of several mutual-exclusion algorithms. A distributed mutual-exclusion algorithm in which time stamps and process ids are used to resolve conflicts is presented in Ricart and Agrawala [1981]. The asymptotic optimality of the number of message communications in the dining philosophers solution is shown in Chandy and Misra [1986c].

CHAPTER 16

Parallel Garbage Collection

16.1   Introduction

The primary goal of this chapter is to present an example that shows how superposition (described in Chapter 7) is employed in program design. Another goal of this chapter is to study garbage collection, an important problem in memory management.

Superposition, also employed in Chapters 9, 11, 14, and 15, is a transformation of a given program in which the transformed program inherits the properties of the given program. Designing programs as a sequence of superpositions simplifies the design task because each superposition deals with a small set of concerns.

The garbage collection problem is specified in Section 16.2: We are given an underlying program, *mutator*, and specification of a program *marker*. We are required to transform *mutator*, according to the rules of superposition, so that the transformed program satisfies the specification of *marker*. Properties of *mutator* are derived in Section 16.3. A design structure—a sequence of superpositions—is proposed and proved correct in Section 16.4. In Section 16.5 we design the first superposition, which deals with marking nongarbage memory cells. In Section 16.6 we design the second superposition, which deals with detecting that marking has terminated. The program obtained after the second superposition is shown to satisfy the specification of *marker*. An optimization is proposed in Section 16.7 to reduce memory requirements by imposing restrictions on the order in which nongarbage cells are marked. Each section has an informal description followed by a formal description. An overview of the design can be obtained from the informal parts.

16.2   Specification

16.2.1 Informal Description

The problem studied here is an abstraction of the memory-management problem. It is first presented as a graph problem; its relationship to memory management is described later.

We are given a program called *mutator* and a graph with a fixed set of vertices; edges in the graph can be added or deleted by *mutator*. One of the vertices is called *root*. All vertices reachable from *root* are called *food* vertices, and all nonfood vertices are called *garbage* vertices. Vertices that are garbage when *mutator* is initiated are called *manure* vertices.

Program *mutator* obeys the following rules for adding and deleting edges:

1. An edge from u to v is added if a certain condition $add[u,v]$ holds; we are given that $add[u,v]$ implies that v is a food vertex.

2. An edge from u to v is deleted only if a certain condition $del[u,v]$ holds.

The conditions add and del are of no concern to us; all we need to know about them is that $add[u,v]$ implies that v is a food vertex.

The problem is to transform $mutator$ to mark vertices so that, upon completion of marking, all food is marked and all manure is unmarked. Marking is indicated by a boolean variable $u.m$ for each vertex u, where $u.m$ holds if and only if u is marked. Vertices that become garbage after $mutator$ is initiated (i.e., nonmanure garbage) may be marked or unmarked. A superposed boolean variable $over$ is employed to signal whether marking has terminated. The specification of $marker$ is as follows: (1) if $over$ holds, then all food is marked and all manure is unmarked, and (2) eventually $over$ holds.

Origins of the Problem in Memory Management

A cell in memory is in one of three states: (1) on the free list, (2) in the data structure of a process, or (3) garbage. Cells can be taken from the free list and placed in a process data structure. All cells in a data structure are reachable (via a succession of pointers) from a special cell in the structure called its header. The free-list cells can also be reached from its header. Garbage cells are not reachable from any header. A data structure can be modified by the addition or deletion of pointers between cells in the structure or by the acquisition of cells from the free list. The deletion of pointers may cause a cell to become unreachable from any header, and thus become garbage. No pointer to a garbage vertex is ever created.

In the abstraction of the problem, vertices represent cells and edges represent pointers. For convenience, a special cell $root$ is proposed that has pointers to all headers, including the header of the free list. A manure vertex represents a cell that is garbage when the garbage collector starts execution.

The garbage collector is a program that moves garbage cells into the free list. Each execution of the garbage collector consists of an execution of a program called $marker$ followed by an execution of a program called $collector$. Program $marker$ marks all food cells; then program $collector$ places unmarked cells on the free list. The problem studied in this chapter is the design of $marker$.

Here we restrict attention to a single execution of the marking phase of the garbage collector.

16.2.2 Formal Description

Symbols u, v, w, x represent vertices. Universal quantification is assumed where these symbols appear, unless otherwise specified. The *mutator* program manipulates the incidence matrix E, where

$$E[u,v] \quad \equiv \quad \text{there is an edge from } u \text{ to } v \text{ in the graph.}$$

Reachability matrix R is defined to be the reflexive transitive closure of E:

$$R[u,v] \quad \equiv \quad (u = v) \lor \text{ there is a directed path from } u \text{ to } v \text{ in the graph.}$$

The behavior of the *mutator* is given by the following program.

Program *mutator*

   always

$$R = E^* \quad \{R \text{ is the reflexive, transitive closure of } E\}$$

$$[\!] \; \langle [\!] \; u \; :: \; u.food = R[root, u] \; [\!] \; u.garbage = \neg u.food \rangle$$

   initially $\quad \langle [\!] \; u \; :: \; u.manure = u.garbage \rangle$

   assign

$$\langle [\!] \; u,v \; ::$$
$$\quad E[u,v] \; := \; true \quad \text{if} \quad add[u,v]$$
$$\quad [\!] \; E[u,v] \; := \; false \quad \text{if} \quad del[u,v]$$
$$\rangle$$

end {*mutator*}

Observe that program *mutator* creates edges only to food vertices because $add[u,v] \Rightarrow v.food$.

Specification of the Transformed Program

We are required to transform *mutator*, according to the rules of superposition, where the transformed program employs superposed boolean variables $u.m$ and *over*, and satisfies the following specification:

invariant

$$over \quad \Rightarrow \quad \langle \forall u : u.manure :: \neg u.m \rangle \land \langle \forall u : u.food :: u.m \rangle \qquad \text{(sp1)}$$

$$true \quad \mapsto \quad over \qquad \text{(sp2)}$$

We are required to design the superposition so that it does not name $u.food$, $u.garbage$, $u.manure$, or R; only E, *add*, and *del* may be named.

16.3   Properties of *mutator*

16.3.1 Informal Description

We are interested in properties of the underlying program, *mutator*, because these properties are inherited by programs obtained by successive layers of superposition. Therefore we can exploit properties of the underlying program in proving the correctness of our solution.

Vertices reachable from *root* are food vertices, and nonfood is garbage. Therefore there are no paths from food to garbage: Food reaches only food, and hence garbage can be reached only from garbage.

No edge to a garbage vertex is created, and hence no new path to a garbage vertex is created. Therefore no path from root to garbage is created; hence garbage remains garbage.

Manure is (always) garbage because manure is garbage initially and garbage remains garbage. Therefore the set of vertices can be partitioned into three subsets: food, nonmanure garbage, and manure. The only change in the state of a vertex is from food to nonmanure garbage.

Next we show that manure is reachable only from manure. This is the case initially because manure is garbage initially, and garbage is reachable only from garbage. No paths are created to manure vertices because all manure is garbage, and no paths are created to garbage. Therefore manure remains reachable only from manure.

In summary, these are some of the properties of *mutator*:

- Food reaches only food; garbage is reachable only from garbage; see (mu4,mu5).

- No new path to a garbage vertex is created; see (mu6).

- Garbage remains garbage; see (mu7).

- Manure is garbage; see (mu8).

- Manure is reachable only from manure; see (mu9).

16.3.2 Formal Description

In this section we first state some properties of the *mutator* that are obtained directly from the program text.

Properties Proved Directly from the Program *mutator*

$$\neg E[u,v] \quad unless \quad \neg E[u,v] \ \wedge \ v.food \tag{mu1}$$

$$\textbf{initially} \quad u.manure = u.garbage \tag{mu2}$$

constant $u.manure$ (mu3)

Next we derive a few additional properties of *mutator* from (mu1–mu3).

Derived Properties

invariant $R[u,v] \;\wedge\; u.food \;\Rightarrow\; v.food$ (mu4)

invariant $R[u,v] \;\wedge\; v.garbage \;\Rightarrow\; u.garbage$ (mu5)

$\neg R[u,v] \;\; unless \;\; \neg R[u,v] \;\wedge\; v.food$ (mu6)

stable $v.garbage$ (mu7)

invariant $v.manure \;\Rightarrow\; v.garbage$ (mu8)

invariant $R[u,v] \;\wedge\; v.manure \;\Rightarrow\; u.manure$ (mu9)

Proofs of Derived Properties

Proof: (mu4,mu5)

From the definitions of R, *food*, and *garbage* in program *mutator*. $\triangledown$

Proof: (mu6) $\neg R[u,v] \;\; unless \;\; \neg R[u,v] \;\wedge\; v.food$

Define $R^{(k)}[u,v]$ for $k \geq 0$ as follows:

   $R^{(k)}[u,v] \;\equiv\;$ there exists a path with at most k edges from u to v.

Next we show, by induction on k, that

   $\neg R^{(k)}[u,v] \;\; unless \;\; \neg R^{(k)}[u,v] \;\wedge\; v.food$

The base case, $k = 0$, follows from $R^{(0)}[u,v] \;\equiv\; (u = v)$. For $k \geq 0$, from the induction hypothesis, substituting (v, w) for (u,v),

   $\neg R^{(k)}[v, w] \;\; unless \;\; \neg R^{(k)}[v, w] \;\wedge\; w.food$ (mu10)

   $R^{(k)}[v, w] \;\wedge\; v.food \;\Rightarrow\; w.food$
       , from (mu4) using $R^{(k)}[v, w] \;\Rightarrow\; R[v, w]$

Apply disjunction to (mu10) and (mu1), and weaken the right side of the resulting *unless* property by employing the preceding property to obtain:

   $(\neg E[u,v] \;\vee\; \neg R^{(k)}[v, w]) \;\; unless \;\; (\neg E[u,v] \;\vee\; \neg R^{(k)}[v, w]) \;\wedge\; w.food$
                                                                            (mu11)

From the definition of $R^{(k+1)}$,

   $R^{(k+1)}[u, w] = (\langle \exists v \;::\; E[u,v] \;\wedge\; R^{(k)}[v, w] \rangle \;\vee\; R^{(k)}[u, w])$.

   For predicates p, q, r: if (p *unless* $p \;\wedge\; r$) and (q *unless* $q \;\wedge\; r$), then ($p \;\wedge\; q$ *unless* $p \;\wedge\; q \;\wedge\; r$), by applying conjunction.

Using the preceding two facts, we apply conjunction over all v to (mu11) and then apply conjunction of this property to (mu10, with u substituted for v) to obtain

$$\neg R^{(k+1)}[u, w] \quad unless \quad \neg R^{(k+1)}[u, w] \;\wedge\; w.food$$

Property (mu6) follows because $R = R^{(N)}$, where N is the number of vertices.

$\triangledown$

Proof: (mu7) $v.garbage$ is stable

Substitute $root$ for u in (mu6), and use the definition of $garbage$, i.e.,

$$v.garbage \quad \equiv \quad \neg R[root, v],$$

and

$$v.food \quad \equiv \quad \neg v.garbage$$

$\triangledown$

Proof: (mu8) $v.manure \;\Rightarrow\; v.garbage$

$v.garbage \;\vee\; \neg v.manure$ is stable   , disjunction on (mu3,mu7)

$v.manure \;\Rightarrow\; v.garbage$, from the above and (mu2) $\triangledown$

Proof: (mu9) $R[u,v] \;\wedge\; v.manure \;\Rightarrow\; u.manure$

$\neg v.manure$ is stable
    , from (mu3)

$\neg R[u,v] \;\vee\; \neg v.manure$ is stable
    , disjunction on the above and (mu6) and using (mu8)

$\neg R[u,v] \;\vee\; \neg v.manure \;\vee\; u.manure$ is stable
    , from the above and (mu3)

The result follows from the above and (mu2,mu5). $\triangledown$

16.4   The Structure of the Design

16.4.1 Informal Description

The approach proposed in Chapter 11 for solving detection problems is to record the global state and then compute properties of the recorded state. This approach, applied to our problem, records E and then computes reachability from the (static) recorded value of E. Garbage collection programs are required to be parsimonious in their use of memory; therefore storing the entire array E is unacceptable. We shall design a program with memory requirement proportional to the number of vertices.

The program is designed in two layers of superposition. First *mutator* is transformed into a program called *propagator*, and then *propagator* is transformed into the desired program *marker*. The first transformation is concerned with propagating marks, and the second transformation is concerned with detecting that mark propagation has terminated. In *propagator* only the root is marked initially; *propagator* marks a vertex only if there is an edge to it from a marked vertex. Program *propagator* has the invariant that manure is unmarked. Program *marker* detects termination of marking. From the superposition theorem (Chapter 7), properties of *mutator* are inherited by *propagator*, and properties of *propagator* are inherited by *marker*.

The specification of *propagator* is as follows. Let predicate T denote that (1) *root* is marked and that (2) all vertices with edges from marked vertices are marked. Program *propagator* establishes T within finite time of initiation; see (pr3). It also has the invariant that manure is unmarked; see (pr1). To allow T to be detected by the next superposition, *propagator* is designed to guarantee that T is stable; see (pr2).

The specification of *marker* is

over detects T.

The proof of correctness of the design is straightforward. Our proof obligation is to show that the properties proposed for *propagator* and *marker* together with the properties of *mutator* satisfy specifications (sp1,sp2), given in Section 16.2.2. If *over* holds, then so does T (from the specification of *marker*), and if T holds then (from the definition of T) all food is marked and (from the invariant of *propagator*) manure is unmarked; this establishes (sp1). The proof of progress, (sp2), follows from the facts that: T is established within finite time (from the specification of *propagator*) and that *over* is established within finite time of T being established (because from the specification of *marker over detects T*).

16.4.2 Formal Description

Define T as

$$T \;\equiv\; root.m \;\wedge\; \langle \forall\, u,v \,:\, u.m \,\wedge\, E[u,v] \,::\, v.m \rangle.$$

Transform *mutator* into a program *propagator*, according to the rules of superposition, where *propagator* has the following specification.

Specification of *propagator*

invariant $v.manure \;\Rightarrow\; \neg v.m$ (pr1)

stable T (pr2)

$true \;\mapsto\; T$ (pr3)

Transform *propagator* into a program *marker*, according to the rules of superposition, where *marker* has the following specification.

Specification of *marker*

$$over \quad detects \quad T \tag{ma1}$$

16.4.3 Proof of Correctness of the Design

Our proof obligation is to show that *marker* satisfies (sp1,sp2). We employ the superposition theorem (see Chapter 7) that *marker* inherits all properties of *mutator* and *propagator*.

Proof: (sp1) $over \Rightarrow \langle \forall u : u.manure :: \neg u.m \rangle \land \langle \forall u : u.food :: u.m \rangle$

$T \equiv root.m \land \langle \forall u,v : u.m \land R[u,v] :: v.m \rangle$
, applying induction on the definition of T

$T \Rightarrow \langle \forall v : v.food :: v.m \rangle$
, substituting *root* for u in the above expression

$over \Rightarrow T$
, from (ma1)

The result follows from the preceding two properties and (pr1) $\triangledown$

Proof: (sp2) $true \mapsto over$

$true \mapsto T$, rewriting (pr3)

$T \mapsto over$, from (ma1)

$true \mapsto over$, transitivity on the above two $\triangledown$

16.5   Design of *propagator*

16.5.1 The Solution: Informal Description

Let us attempt to employ the reachability program from Section 6.4 to mark vertices. Initially only *root* is marked. The program consists of a statement for each ordered pair of vertices (u,v) to mark v if u is marked and there is an edge from u to v. It is a nice exercise to attempt a proof of correctness of the program.

Unfortunately, as doing the exercise shows, the proposed program is wrong. The program of Section 6.4 applies to a static graph, whereas in the present instance the graph is dynamic because edges are added and deleted. Therefore *mutator* may prevent a food vertex from ever being marked, as illustrated by the following example. Consider a computation that is a repetition of the following loop.

Loop

{initially u, v, w are food vertices; u, v are marked but w is unmarked, and there is an edge from v to w, but no edge from u to w}

- Pair(u, w) is checked, and w is left unmarked because there is no edge from u to w.

- *mutator* adds an edge from u to w.

- *mutator* deletes an edge from v to w.

- Pair(v, w) is checked, and w is left unmarked because there is no edge from v to w.

- *mutator* adds an edge from v to w.

- *mutator* deletes an edge from u to w.

end Loop

The example suggests a way out of our difficulty. We propose that when an edge from u to v is created, v is marked; doing so is safe because an edge to v is created only if v is food, and therefore this action does not mark manure. The properties we propose for *propagator* are next given informally; they are given formally as (pr4–pr8) in Section 16.5.2.

Properties of *propagator*

1. Adding edges; see (pr4). If an edge from u to v is added, v becomes marked.

2. Marking an unmarked vertex; see (pr5). An unmarked vertex v is marked only if v is a food vertex or if there is an edge from a marked vertex u to v.

3. Stability of marks; see (pr6). A marked vertex remains marked.

4. Progression of marks; see (pr7). If there is an edge from a marked vertex u to an unmarked vertex v, then eventually v becomes marked or the edge is removed; this guarantees progress.

5. Initial conditions; see (pr8). Initially only *root* is marked; this satisfies the desired invariant that manure is unmarked.

An Informal Proof of Correctness

Our obligation is to show that for program *propagator* (1) manure is unmarked, (2) T is stable, and (3) eventually T holds.

We first prove the invariant that manure is unmarked. Initially manure is unmarked because only root is marked. We next show that if manure is unmarked before an unmarked vertex v is marked, then v cannot be manure; therefore manure remains unmarked. The property for marking unmarked vertices states that an unmarked vertex v is marked only if v is a food vertex (in which case v is not manure) or if there is an edge from a marked vertex u to v (in which case u is not manure—from the hypothesis—and therefore v is not manure—because manure is reachable only from manure).

Next we show that T is stable. If T holds, then all food is marked; also, if there is an edge from a marked vertex u to v, then v is marked. Also, if T holds, then no edges are added to unmarked vertices because unmarked vertices are garbage and *mutator* does not add edges to garbage. Therefore, from the property for marking an unmarked vertex, if T holds, then no unmarked vertex becomes marked. From the stability of marks property, all marked vertices stay marked. Thus, once T holds, it continues to hold thereafter.

Next we show that eventually T does hold. Define c as the set of marked vertices and define d as the set of ordered pairs (u,v), where if u is marked and there is an edge from u to v then v is marked—i.e., $c = \{u \mid u.m\}$ and $d = \{(u,v) \mid u.m \wedge E[u,v] \Rightarrow v.m\}$. Since marked vertices remain marked, c does not shrink. The only way in which a pair (u,v) can be removed from d is if an unmarked vertex u becomes marked (and there is an edge from u to v where v is unmarked), or if an edge (u,v) is added from a marked vertex u to an unmarked vertex v. In either case an unmarked vertex becomes marked: In the former case u becomes marked, and in the latter case v becomes marked (see property (1) for adding edges). Therefore, if d shrinks, then c becomes larger.

Define a lexicographic metric as the pair (size of c, size of d). The metric does not decrease because c does not shrink, and c becomes larger if d shrinks. The metric is bounded from above because c is a subset of the set of all vertices, and d is a subset of the set of all vertex pairs. Next we show that if $\neg T$ holds, then the metric changes, guaranteeing that eventually T holds because the metric cannot increase indefinitely.

Let VV be the set of all ordered pairs of vertices. From the definition of T and since *root.m* is an invariant, it follows that $T \equiv (d = VV)$. To show that the metric changes if $\neg T$ holds, we show that d changes if $d \neq VV$. If d differs from VV then there is a pair of vertices (u,v) that is not in d. From the definition of d, u is marked, there is an edge from u to v, and v is unmarked. The progression of marks property tells us that eventually (u,v) will be added to d, thus changing d. Hence if $d \neq VV$, then d changes eventually.

The program derived from the properties consists of the following rules.

Rules for Program *propagator*

1. Initially only *root* is marked.

2. When *mutator* adds an edge (u,v), vertex v becomes marked.

3. If u is marked and there is an edge from u to v, then v becomes marked (or the edge is deleted by *mutator*).

16.5.2 The Solution Strategy: Formal Description

We propose the following specification (pr4–pr8) for *propagator* as a refinement of the previous specification (pr1–pr3).

$$\neg E[u,v] \quad unless \quad v.m \tag{pr4}$$

$$\neg v.m \quad unless \quad \neg v.m \ \wedge \ (v.food \ \vee \ \langle \exists \ u \ :: \ u.m \ \wedge \ E[u,v]\rangle) \tag{pr5}$$

$$\textbf{stable} \quad v.m \tag{pr6}$$

$$true \ \mapsto \quad (u.m \ \wedge \ E[u,v] \ \Rightarrow \ v.m) \tag{pr7}$$

$$\textbf{initially} \quad u.m = (u = root) \tag{pr8}$$

In addition to properties (pr4–pr8), *propagator* also inherits all properties of *mutator*.

16.5.3 Proof of Correctness of the Solution Strategy

Our proof obligation is to show that the proposed specification (pr4–pr8) of *propagator*, and the properties of *mutator*, imply the specification (pr1–pr3) of *propagator* in the previous refinement step.

Proof: (pr1) $v.manure \ \Rightarrow \ \neg v.m$

$\neg v.manure \ unless \ false$
, from (mu3)

$(\neg v.m \ \vee \ \neg v.manure) \ unless$
$\quad (\neg v.m \ \wedge \ v.manure \ \wedge \ \langle \exists \ u \ :: \ u.m \ \wedge \ E[u,v]\rangle) \tag{1}$
, disjunction on the above and (pr5) by employing (mu8)

$v.manure \ \wedge \ \langle \exists \ u \ :: \ u.m \ \wedge \ E[u,v]\rangle \ \Rightarrow \ \langle \exists \ u \ :: \ u.m \ \wedge \ u.manure\rangle$
, from (mu9)

$(\neg v.m \ \vee \ \neg v.manure) \ unless$
$\quad (\neg v.m \ \vee \ \neg v.manure) \ \wedge \ \langle \exists \ u \ :: \ u.m \ \wedge \ u.manure\rangle$
, weakening the right side of (1) and using the above fact

$\langle \forall v :: \neg v.m \lor \neg v.manure \rangle$ *unless false*
　　, apply conjunction over all v to the above property
　　{employ the result that if (p *unless* $p \land r$) and
　　(q *unless* $q \land r$) then ($p \land q$ *unless* $p \land q \land r$)}
(pr1) follows from (pr8) and the above property.　　　　　　　$\triangledown$

Proof:　(pr2)　T is stable

$\neg v.m \land v.food \implies \neg T$
　　, from $T \implies \langle \forall v : v.food :: v.m \rangle$

$\neg v.m \land \langle \exists u :: u.m \land E[u,v] \rangle \implies \neg T$
　　, from the definition of T

$\neg v.m$ *unless* $\neg v.m \land \neg T$
　　, weakening the right side of (pr5) by employing the
　　above two properties　　　　　　　　　　　　　　　　　(2)

$w.food \implies w.m \lor \neg T$
　　, from $T \implies \langle \forall v : v.food :: v.m \rangle$

$\neg E[v,w]$ *unless* $\neg E[v,w] \land (w.m \lor \neg T)$
　　, weakening the right side of (mu1) by employing the above property

Apply simple disjunction to the preceding property and (2), and then apply disjunction to $w.m$ *unless false* (see pr6) to obtain:

$\neg v.m \lor \neg E[v,w] \lor w.m$ *unless* $(\neg v.m \lor \neg E[v,w]) \land \neg T \land \neg w.m$

Weaken the right side of this property to $(\neg v.m \lor \neg E[v,w] \lor w.m) \land \neg T$ so that the property is of the form (p *unless* $p \land r$), where

$p \equiv \neg v.m \lor \neg E[v,w] \lor w.m$

and

$r \equiv \neg T.$

Then apply conjunction over all v, w and use the result—if (p *unless* $p \land r$) and (q *unless* $q \land r$) then ($p \land q$ *unless* $p \land q \land r$)—to obtain

$\langle \forall v,w : v.m \land E[v,w] :: w.m \rangle$ *unless*
$\langle \forall v,w : v.m \land E[v,w] :: w.m \rangle \land \neg T$

Apply conjunction to the preceding property and ($root.m$ *unless false*), which follows from (pr6), and use the definition of T to obtain (T *unless false*), from which (pr2) follows.　　　　　　　　　　　　　　$\triangledown$

Proof:　(pr3)　*true* $\longmapsto T$

Define sets c, d as

$c = \{ u \mid u.m \}$

and

$$d = \{(u,v) \mid u.m \ \wedge \ E[u,v] \ \Rightarrow \ v.m\}.$$

Define VV to be the set of all ordered pairs of vertices. We show that, for all values C, D of c, d (respectively),

$$c = C \ \wedge \ d = D \ \wedge \ d \neq VV \ \longmapsto \ (c \supset C) \ \vee \ (c = C \ \wedge \ d \supset D) \tag{3}$$

From (3) by induction on the lexicographic metric, (size of c, size of d), which is bounded from above,

$$true \ \longmapsto T \quad , \text{because } T \ \equiv \ (d = VV) \qquad\qquad \triangledown$$

Proof: (3) $c = C \ \wedge \ d = D \ \wedge \ d \neq VV \ \longmapsto \ (c \supset C) \ \vee \ (c = C \ \wedge \ d \supset D)$

$u \notin C$ is stable
    , because C is constant
$\neg u.m \ \wedge \ c = C \ \ unless \ \ u.m \ \vee \ c \neq C$
    , antireflexivity of $unless$
$u \notin C \ \wedge \ \neg u.m \ \wedge \ c = C \ \ unless \ \ u \notin C \ \wedge \ (u.m \ \vee \ c \neq C)$
    , conjunction on the above two
$\neg u.m \ \wedge \ c = C \ \ unless \ \ c \neq C$
    , using $u.m \ \equiv \ u \in c$ to simplify left and right sides of the above   (4)
$\neg E[u,v] \ \vee \ v.m \ \ unless \ \ false$
    , taking disjunction of (pr4,pr6)
$(\neg E[u,v] \ \vee \ v.m) \ \wedge \ (c = C) \ \ unless \ \ c \neq C$
    , simple conjunction of the above and $(c = C) \ \ unless \ \ (c \neq C)$
$(u,v) \ \in \ d \ \wedge \ c = C \ \ unless \ \ c \neq C$
    , disjunction of (4) and the above, and using the definition of d
$c = C \ \wedge \ d \supseteq D \ \ unless \ \ (c \neq C)$
    , from the above by simple conjunction over all pairs (u,v) in D
$c = C \ \wedge \ d = D \ \ unless \ \ (c \neq C) \ \vee \ (d \supset D)$
    , conjunction of the above with $d = D \ \ unless \ \ d \neq D$.
$c = C \ \ unless \ \ c \supset C$
    , because $u.m$ is stable; see (pr6)
$c = C \ \wedge \ d = D \ \ unless \ \ (c \supset C) \ \vee \ (c = C \ \wedge \ d \supset D)$
    , conjunction of the above two   (5)
$true \ \longmapsto \ (u, v) \ \in \ d$
    , rewriting (pr7) using definition of d
$d = D \ \wedge \ d \neq VV \ \wedge \ (u,v) \notin D \ \longmapsto \ (u,v) \ \in \ d$
    , strengthening the left side of the above
$(u,v) \ \notin \ D$ is stable
    , D is constant

$d = D \ \wedge \ d \neq VV \ \wedge \ (u,v) \notin D \ \longmapsto \ d \neq D$
, PSP theorem on the above two and then weakening the right side

$d = D \ \wedge \ d \neq VV \ \wedge \ \langle \exists \ (u,v) \ :: \ (u,v) \notin D \rangle \ \longmapsto \ d \neq D$
, disjunction on the above over all $(u,v) \notin D$

$d = D \ \wedge \ d \neq VV \ \longmapsto \ d \neq D$
, from the above because
$$d = D \ \wedge \ d \neq VV \ \Rightarrow \ \langle \exists \ (u,v) \ :: \ (u,v) \notin D \rangle$$

Property (3) follows by applying the PSP theorem on the preceding and (5). $\triangledown$

16.5.4 Derivation of a Program from the Specification of the Solution Strategy

Progress condition (pr7) and safety conditions (pr5,pr6) suggest that if v is marked, then it remains marked, and if v is unmarked, then it gets marked if there is an edge to v from a marked vertex u, by using the following assignment:

$v.m \ := \ v.m \ \vee \ (u.m \ \wedge \ E[u,v])$

To guarantee (pr4), whenever an edge (u,v) is created v is marked:

$E[u,v], v.m \ := \ true, true \qquad \text{if} \quad add[u,v]$

These are the only changes required to transform the underlying program *mutator* to program *propagator*. For convenience, the complete program is given next.

Program *propagator* {**transformation of** *mutator*}

always

$R = E^* \quad \{R \text{ is the reflexive, transitive closure of } E\}$

$\[\] \ \langle \[\] \ u \ :: \ u.food = R[root, u] \ \[\] \ u.garbage = \neg u.food \rangle$

initially $\langle \[\] \ u \ :: \ u.manure = u.garbage \ \[\] \ u.m = (u = root) \rangle$

assign

$\langle \[\] \ u,v \ ::$
$\qquad E[u,v], v.m \ := \ true, true \qquad \text{if} \quad add[u,v]$
$\qquad \[\] \ E[u,v] \ := \ false \qquad\qquad \text{if} \quad del[u,v]$
$\qquad \[\] \ v.m \ := \ v.m \ \vee \ (u.m \ \wedge \ E[u,v])$

$\rangle$

end {*propagator*}

16.6   Design of *marker*: Detecting Termination

Now the problem is to transform *propagator* to detect that marking has terminated. Since garbage collection programs are required to use a small amount of memory, the memory-efficient termination-detection program *R5* of Section 9.8.1 is employed.

In most chapters, a program is designed by first proposing a specification and proving its correctness, and then deriving a program. We do not carry out these design steps for the termination detection program in this chapter because we already did so in Chapter 9. Instead we repeat the key ideas of the program and then present it.

Our objective is to detect T, where

$$T \equiv root.m \wedge \langle \forall u,v :: u.m \wedge E[u,v] \Rightarrow v.m \rangle.$$

For this purpose we employ a set b of vertex pairs and two boolean variables *ma.flag* and *mu.flag* (for *m*arking and *mu*tator flags, respectively) with the following invariant:

invariant

$$ma.flag \wedge mu.flag \Rightarrow$$
$$\langle \forall u,v : (u,v) \in b :: u.m \wedge E[u,v] \Rightarrow v.m \rangle \qquad \text{(ma2)}$$

Since *root.m* is invariant, (from (pr6,pr8)), it follows from (ma2) that

$$ma.flag \wedge mu.flag \wedge (b = VV) \Rightarrow T.$$

Therefore we propose that

$$T \mapsto ma.flag \wedge mu.flag \wedge b = VV, \qquad \text{(ma3)}$$

from which,

$$(ma.flag \wedge mu.flag \wedge b = VV) \ detects \ T.$$

We also propose that

$$over \ detects \ (ma.flag \wedge mu.flag \wedge b = VV) \qquad \text{(ma4)}$$

From the transitivity of *detects* it follows that *over detects* T. Therefore (ma2–ma4) imply (ma1).

The proposed properties (ma2–ma4) are satisfied by a program with the following outline. (See Section 9.8.1 for a detailed discussion.)

1. Initially b is *empty* and *over* is *false*.

2. Add any pair (u,v) to b if $u.m \wedge E[u,v] \Rightarrow v.m$.

3. Make b *empty* and set both flags *true* if any flag is *false*.

4. Set any flag to *false* when an unmarked vertex is marked (because marking an unmarked u may falsify $u.m \land E[u,v] \Rightarrow v.m$).

5. Variable *over* is made *true* if both flags are *true* and $b = VV$.

Efficient implementations of b are considered in the next section. Program *marker* is given next. The proof that the program satisfies (ma2–ma4) is along the same lines as the proof of program $R5$ in Section 9.8.1.

Program *marker*

   always

$$R = E^* \quad \{R \text{ is the reflexive, transitive closure of } E\}$$

$\langle\!\!\!| \; \langle\!\!\!| \; u \;\; :: \;\; u.food = R[root, u] \;\; |\!\!\!\rangle \;\; u.garbage = \neg u.food \rangle$

   initially

$\langle\!\!\!| \; u \;\; :: \;\; u.manure = u.garbage \;\; |\!\!\!\rangle \;\; u.m = (u = root) \rangle$

$|\!\!\!\rangle \;\; b = empty \quad \{ma.flag, mu.flag \text{ have arbitrary values}\}$

   assign

$\langle\!\!\!| \; u,v \;\; ::$

     $E[u,v], v.m \;\; := \;\; true, true \qquad$ **if** $add[u,v]$

     $\| \;\; mu.flag \;\; := \;\; false \qquad$ **if** $add[u,v] \land \neg v.m$

    $|\!\!\!\rangle \;\; E[u,v] \;\; := \;\; false \qquad$ **if** $del[u,v]$

    $|\!\!\!\rangle \;\; v.m \;\; := \;\; v.m \lor (u.m \land E[u,v])$

     $\| \;\; ma.flag \;\; := \;\; false \qquad$ **if** $\neg v.m \land (u.m \land E[u,v])$

    $|\!\!\!\rangle \;\; b \;\; := \;\; b \cup \{(u,v)\} \qquad$ **if** $u.m \land E[u,v] \;\; \Rightarrow \;\; v.m$

$\rangle$

$|\!\!\!\rangle \;\; b, ma.flag, mu.flag \;\; := \;\; empty, true, true$ **if** $\neg ma.flag \lor \neg mu.flag$

$|\!\!\!\rangle \;\; over \;\; := \;\; (b = VV) \land ma.flag \land mu.flag$

   end $\{marker\}$

16.7   Optimizations

16.7.1 Memory-Efficient Implementation of a Set

The implementation of an arbitrary set b of vertex pairs requires $O(N^2)$ memory, where N is the number of vertices; this is unacceptably large for a garbage collection program. To obtain a more efficient implementation, we restrict b to contain only lexicographically consecutive vertex pairs. With this restriction, b can be represented by a pair (j, k), where b is the set of all pairs (u, v) that are lexicographically smaller than (j, k). The ranges of j, k are $0..N$ and $0..N - 1$, respectively.

In program *marker* of Section 16.6, an arbitrary pair (u, v) is added to b if $u.m \wedge E[u, v] \Rightarrow v.m$. In the modified program, pairs of vertices are inspected *sequentially* in the following increasing lexicographic order:

$$(0, 0), \ldots, (0, N - 1), (1, 0), \ldots (1, N - 1), \ldots, (N - 1, N - 1).$$

We replace

$$b := b \cup \{(u, v)\} \qquad \text{if} \quad u.m \wedge E[u, v] \quad \Rightarrow \quad v.m$$

of *marker*, in Section 16.6, by

$$(j, k) := (j, k) \oplus 1 \qquad \text{if} \quad (j.m \wedge E[j, k] \quad \Rightarrow \quad k.m) \wedge (j, k) \neq (N, 0)$$

where the addition, $\oplus$, is carried out modulo N except that

$$(N - 1, N - 1) \oplus 1 = (N, 0) .$$

The remaining modifications of *marker* are as follows:

$$\text{replace} \quad b = empty \quad \text{by} \quad (j, k) = (0, 0) ,$$

and

$$\text{replace} \quad b = VV \quad \text{by} \quad (j, k) = (N, 0) .$$

16.7.2 Optimizations Regarding Execution Time

If b is implemented as a pair (j, k), then another optimization suggests itself. In *marker*, a flag is made *false* when an unmarked vertex becomes marked in order to guarantee invariant (ma2); this is because marking an unmarked u may falsify the condition $u.m \wedge E[u, v] \Rightarrow v.m$, for a pair (u, v) in b. If, in the modified program, an unmarked u becomes marked where $u > j$, then it is *not* necessary to set a flag to *false* because there is no v such that (u, v) is in b. Thus (ma2) is preserved without a flag being set to *false*. We leave it to the reader to derive a program with this optimization.

16.7.3 Optimizations for Sequential Architectures

The detection and mark-propagation activities can be tightly coupled, with some additional efficiency, in a sequential machine. We proposed in Section 16.7.1 that (j, k) be incremented if $j.m \wedge E[j, k] \Rightarrow k.m$. Marking can be carried out at the same time: Mark k if $j.m \wedge E[j, k] \wedge \neg k.m$, and increment (j, k). Incorporating the optimization of Section 16.7.2, the statement for marking and for incrementing (j, k) is

$$k.m \ := \ k.m \ \lor \ (j.m \ \land \ E[j,k]) \qquad \text{if} \quad (j,k) \neq (N,0)$$
$$\|\quad (j,k) \ := \ (j,k) \oplus 1 \qquad\qquad\qquad \text{if} \quad (j,k) \neq (N,0)$$
$$\|\quad ma.flag \ := \ false$$
$$\qquad\qquad \text{if} \quad (k \leq j) \ \land \ (j.m \ \land \ E[j,k] \ \land \ \neg k.m) \ \land \ (j,k) \neq (N,0)$$

This single statement replaces two sets of statements in *marker*: the assignments to $v.m$ and $ma.flag$ (for all v), and the assignments to b. Also, replace $(b = empty)$ by $(j,k) = (0,0)$ and replace $(b = VV)$ by $(j,k) = (N,0)$.

Exercise 16.1 Improving efficiency: Redesign the detection program so that $ma.flag$ is not a "bottleneck" variable—in *marker*, $ma.flag$ is assigned a value synchronously with the assignment of values to $u.m$, for all u, and this limits parallelism in *propagator*. A possible design is suggested by the memory-efficient program $R5'$ in Section 9.8.2, where several flags are used.
$\triangledown$

Exercise 16.2 Greater concurrency: Develop a program with several muta-tors, each with its own $mu.flag$.
$\triangledown$

Exercise 16.3 Greater concurrency: Redesign the detection program so that b is replaced by two sets $b0$ and $b1$, as follows. Partition the set of all vertex pairs VV into two subsets $VV0$ and $VV1$, where

invariant $(b0 \subseteq VV0) \ \land \ (b1 \subseteq VV1) \ \land \ (b = b0 \cup b1)$

Is your redesigned program more suitable for execution on a shared-memory, multiprocessor system than the original program? Generalize your solution to arbitrary number of subsets of vertex pairs.
$\triangledown$

Exercise 16.4 Fine-grain atomicity: An assignment to $ma.flag$ in the program *marker* of Section 16.6 names four variables $ma.flag, u.m, E[u,v]$, and $v.m$. Develop a program in which an assignment names at most three variables. This may require that the *marker* first check $u.m$, then check $E[u,v]$, then check $v.m$, and finally assign to $ma.flag$, thus using four atomic operations. Also construct a program with the same fine-grain atomicity for assignment to $mu.flag$.
$\triangledown$

Summary

This chapter illustrates the use of superposition to separate concerns in program design. A program for the marking phase of a garbage collector was derived by first restricting attention to the propagation of marks and later concentrating on termination detection. The program was optimized for a target architecture only toward the end of the design.

The use of modularity in design allows us to use programs from other contexts. The program designed in this chapter incorporated the reachability computation program from Chapter 6. Also, a termination-detection program, $R5$, from Section 9.8.1 was used with little change.

Bibliographic Notes

One of the most intricate applications of concurrent programming is parallel garbage collection, as described in Dijkstra et al. [1978]. The material in this chapter is inspired by van de Snepscheut [1985a], which is based on Ben-Ari's algorithm [1984].

CHAPTER 17

Fault Tolerance: A Protocol for Communication over Faulty Channels

17.1   Introduction

The goal of this chapter is to study an example of fault-tolerant programming—a protocol that guarantees reliable communication from a sender to a receiver even though the communication channel linking them may be faulty. We propose a formal specification of a faulty channel and develop a protocol for communication over faulty channels.

Viewing a faulty channel as a program has several advantages. The specification of a faulty channel is a program specification, just like the specifications in previous chapters of this book. Designing a protocol for communication over faulty channels can be viewed as a problem in program composition: The union of the protocol program and the faulty-channel program is required to guarantee fault-free communication. Therefore the study of faults falls entirely within the domain of programming and specification techniques we have studied previously.

The protocol is specified in Section 17.2 without specifying faulty channels. In Section 17.3, we show a solution to the protocol design problem with a simplified specification of faulty channels. A complete specification of a faulty channel is given in Section 17.4. In Section 17.5, we refine the solution of Section 17.3 for communication over full-faulty channels, i.e., those that lose and/or duplicate messages (though loss or duplication does not continue indefinitely). The well-known *alternating bit protocol* is derived in Section 17.6 by a minor optimization of this solution.

17.2   Specification

A process called the *sender* has access to an infinite sequence of data, ms. Another process, *receiver*, is required to output a sequence, mr, satisfying the following specification:

invariant $mr \sqsubseteq ms$ {i.e., mr is a prefix of ms}

$|mr| = n \;\mapsto\; |mr| = n + 1$ {i.e., length of mr increases eventually}

If the sender and the receiver can communicate over an unbounded reliable FIFO channel c, the problem is solved easily by using the following statements:

$$c, ms := c;\text{head}(ms) \quad , \text{tail}(ms) \qquad\qquad \{\text{sender}\}$$
$$\parallel\; c, mr := \text{tail}(c) \qquad , mr;\text{head}(c) \;\; \text{if} \;\; c \neq null \;\; \{\text{receiver}\}$$

where initially both c and mr are *null*. (For the moment, we ignore the implementation problem of assigning an infinite sequence as a value.) In this chapter, we study an algorithm for solving this problem when c is faulty:

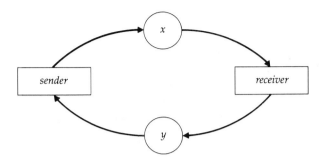

Figure 17.1 The sender and the receiver communicate through shared variables x,y.

Messages sent along c can be lost or duplicated (though only a finite number of messages can be lost consecutively and a message can be duplicated only a finite number of times).

17.3   Some Simplified Communication Problems

In this section we start with a trivial version of the problem, for which we propose a solution. Then we make the problem more realistic by removing some of the assumptions made in the problem statement, and derive a solution to the more realistic problem.

17.3.1 A Trivial Problem

We postulate that the sender and receiver communicate through shared variables, x,y: The sender writes into x and reads from y; the receiver reads from x and writes into y. A message sent by the sender to the receiver is lost if the sender writes into x before the receiver has read the last message written; a message is duplicated if the receiver reads from x consecutively without x being assigned a new value by the sender. Similarly, messages sent by the receiver to the sender via y may be lost and/or duplicated. A schematic diagram of message communication between the sender and the receiver is shown in Fig. 17.1.

Next we assume that the message sequence that the sender must send is the sequence of all positive integers . Let ks be the last number sent by the sender, and kr the last number received by the receiver. Initially $ks = 1$ and $kr = 0$. The specification for this simplified problem is as follows:

invariant $kr \leq ks$ {receiver receives only what has been sent}

$kr = n \quad \mapsto \quad kr = n + 1$ {receiver receives all positive integers}

The objective is to write a UNITY program satisfying this specification whose statements can be partitioned into two groups, for sender and receiver, such that (1) ks is accessed (read and written) only by the sender and kr is accessed only by the receiver, (2) x,y are the only variables that may appear in statements of both groups, and (3) x is assigned values only in sender's statements, and y only in receiver's statements.

17.3.2 A Solution to the Trivial Problem

We refine the progress condition as follows:

$$kr = n \quad \mapsto \quad ks = n + 1 \quad \mapsto \quad kr = n + 1$$

This progress condition can be implemented by the following statements:

$$ks := kr + 1$$
$$\| \quad kr := ks$$

However, these statements cannot be partitioned between the sender and the receiver under the requirement that ks, kr be accessed only by the sender and the receiver, respectively. Hence we further refine the progress condition, introducing variables x,y:

$$kr = n \quad \mapsto \quad y = n \quad \mapsto \quad ks = n + 1 \quad \mapsto \quad x = n + 1 \quad \mapsto \quad kr = n + 1 \, .$$

The following program is suggested immediately.

Program *P1* {protocol for communication over faulty channels—
first trivial version}

    declare x,y, ks, kr : integer

    initially $x,y, ks, kr = 1, 0, 1, 0$

    assign

       $y \ := kr$

    $\| \quad ks := y + 1$

    $\| \quad x \ := ks$

    $\| \quad kr := x$

end $\{P1\}$

Note: The first and last statements of *P1* are in the receiver process, and the remaining two statements are in the sender process.   ▽

What Program *P1* Represents

Variable x is the faulty channel along which the sender sends ks and the receiver reads kr. The receiver, in turn, sends acknowledgments using the faulty channel y. The sender sends a new message only upon receiving an acknowledgment for ks. This can be seen from invariant (I1) (see below): y equals $ks - 1$ or ks, and hence ks is increased only if $ks = y$.

Correctness of *P1*

For *P1*, we prove the following invariant.

invariant $y \leq kr \leq x \leq ks \leq y + 1$ (I1)

Clearly, (I1) holds initially. Every assignment in *P1* is of the form $a := b$, where a, b appear consecutively and $a \leq b$, in (I1). Hence execution of $a := b$ preserves $a \leq b$. Also observe that execution of $y := kr$ can only increase y, and hence preserves $ks \leq y + 1$. Therefore (I1) is an invariant for *P1*.

Now we prove the progress condition:

$$kr = n \quad \mapsto \quad y = n \quad \mapsto \quad ks = n + 1 \quad \mapsto \quad x = n + 1 \quad \mapsto \quad kr = n + 1 \ .$$

Each proof follows a similar pattern. We illustrate one.

Proof: $y = n \quad \mapsto \quad ks = n + 1$

$y = n \ \ ensures \ \ ks = n + 1$

follows from the following two facts:

$$y = n \ \wedge \ ks \neq n + 1 \quad \Rightarrow \quad y = kr = x = ks \qquad \text{, from invariant (I1)}$$
$$\{y = n\} \ \ ks := y + 1 \ \{ks = n + 1\}. \qquad\qquad\qquad \triangledown$$

17.3.3 A Refinement: Transmission of an Arbitrary Data Sequence

Next we modify *P1* to allow transmission of arbitrary data, not just consecutive positive integers. These data come from an infinite sequence ms local to the sender and are to be added to a sequence mr local to the receiver. Let $ms[j]$, $j > 0$ denote the jth item of ms. Now the sender writes a data item and its index as a pair into x. Let $x.dex$, $x.val$ denote the index and value parts, respectively, of x.

Our next program, *P2*, is very similar to *P1*, with the only changes that

1. x is assigned the pair $(ks, ms[ks])$, instead of just ks;

2. kr is assigned $x.dex$, instead of x;

3. $x.val$ is appended to mr provided that this is a new data item, i.e., provided that kr changes as a result of the assignment, $kr := x.dex$ and

4. initial conditions are appropriately modified.

Program $P2$ {protocol for communication over faulty channels— second trivial version}

declare

$\qquad x$: (integer, data item),

$\qquad y, ks, kr$: integer

initially $y, ks, kr = 0, 1, 0$ $\|$ $mr = null$ $\|$ $x = (1, ms[1])$

assign

$\qquad y \qquad := kr$

$\quad \| \quad ks \qquad := y + 1$

$\quad \| \quad x \qquad := (ks, ms[ks])$

$\quad \| \quad kr, mr := x.dex, mr; x.val \qquad$ if $\quad kr \neq x.dex$

end $\{P2\}$

Correctness of $P2$

We prove the specification given earlier:

invariant $mr \sqsubseteq ms$

$|mr| = n \quad \mapsto \quad |mr| = n + 1$

Observe that the invariant (I1), with x replaced by $x.dex$, is an invariant of $P2$ because

1. mr can be removed from program $P2$ because it appears only in assignments to itself;

2. the assignment to x in $P1$ is the same as the assignment to $x.dex$ in $P2$; and

3. the assignment

$\qquad kr := x.dex \qquad$ if $\quad kr \neq x.dex$

is equivalent to

$\qquad kr := x.dex$

Therefore program *P2* is the same as *P1* with x replaced by $x.dex$. Now we give an additional invariant for *P2*. (We write $x.val \in ms$ to denote that for some j, $x.val = ms[j]$.)

invariant $x.val \in ms \;\land\; mr \sqsubseteq ms \;\land\; |mr| = kr$ (I2)

Proof of this invariant is left to the reader. (Hint: From (I1), use the fact that $kr \neq x.dex \;\Rightarrow\; kr + 1 = x.dex$)

Proof of the progress condition is (almost) identical to that for *P1*.

Note: From invariant (I1), $kr \neq x.dex \;\Rightarrow\; kr + 1 = x.dex$. Hence

$\qquad kr \;:=\; x.dex \quad$ if $\quad kr \neq x.dex$

can be replaced by

$\qquad kr := kr + 1 \quad$ if $\quad kr \neq x.dex$

in the last statement of *P2*. Also, since $ks = y$ or $ks = y + 1$, from invariant (I1), the statement $ks := y + 1$ can be written, equivalently, as

$\qquad ks \;:=\; ks + 1 \quad$ if $\quad ks = y$

These changes appear in program *P3* in Section 17.5.1. $\triangledown$

Exercise 17.1   Show that in *P2* the items of ms are sequentially accessed in the order of increasing indices. $\triangledown$

17.4   Introducing Full Faulty Channels

In the previous section, each faulty channel was modeled by a variable. This model is incorrect because message loss and duplication were entirely under the control of the sender and the receiver: For instance, the sender can guarantee message delivery by never overwriting a message until it "knows" that the receiver has received the last message sent. In this section, we consider full faulty channels that may lose and/or duplicate messages, autonomously. We describe properties of a faulty channel informally and then propose a formal specification. Next we show a UNITY program that models the behavior of a faulty channel.

17.4.1 Specification of a Faulty Channel

Informal Description

A faulty channel exhibits the following behavior:

1. Any message sent along the channel can be lost. However, only a finite number of messages can be lost consecutively.

2. Any message sent along the channel can be duplicated. However, no message can be duplicated forever.

3. Messages are not permuted—i.e., the order of delivery is the order in which the messages are sent.

4. Messages are not corrupted.

Formal Description

Next we formalize this informal description of a channel behavior. A faulty channel from a sender to a receiver is modeled by two nonfaulty channels cs and cr, where the sender sends along cs and the receiver receives from cr, and a program that manipulates the contents of cs and cr.

We define a binary relation *loss* over finite sequences of messages as follows. Let u,v be finite sequences of messages and let m denote a message; u *loss* v denotes that v is a possible output sequence of a faulty channel given u as its input sequence. Formally,

$$null \ loss \ null,$$
$$(u \ loss \ v) \quad \Rightarrow \quad (u; m \ loss \ v),$$
$$(u; m \ loss \ v) \quad \Rightarrow \quad (u; m \ loss \ v; m).$$

The safety properties state that a faulty channel can only remove the head of cs or append to the rear of cr; furthermore, a faulty channel may lose messages from cs and/or duplicate messages in cr.

A progress specification of a faulty channel is that, if a message m is appended infinitely often to cs and no other message is appended to cs, then m appears in cr eventually. To allow for the transmission of a variety of messages, we specify a more general fact. We postulate the existence of a set of predicates, $p.m$, for message m; no message other than m can be appended to cs as long as $p.m$ holds. We assume that $p.m$ holds for at most one m at any point in the computation, and that once $p.m$ is *true*, eventually it is either set *false* or a message (message m) is appended to cs (i.e., the length of $\overline{cs}$ increases). Under these hypotheses, a faulty channel establishes that once $p.m$ is *true*, eventually it is either set *false* or m appears in cr. (Recall from Chapter 8 that for a sequence variable z, $\overline{z}$ denotes the sequence of all items appended to z.)

Specification of Faulty Channel

stable cs is a suffix of cs^0 {for any constant sequence cs^0}

stable cr^0 is a prefix of cr {for any constant sequence cr^0}

invariant $(\overline{cs} - cs)$ $loss$ $\overline{cr}$

$\qquad\qquad$ {$\overline{cs} - cs$ is the prefix of $\overline{cs}$ that excludes the suffix cs}

Conditional Property

Hypothesis:

$$p.m \ \wedge \ p.n \ \Rightarrow \ m = n$$

$$p.m \ \wedge \ cs \ = null \ \ unless \ \ \neg p.m \ \vee \ cs = \ \ll m \gg$$

$$p.m \ \wedge \ (cs^0 = cs) \ \wedge \ (cs \neq null) \ \ unless$$
$$\qquad \neg p.m \ \vee \ cs = \mathrm{tail}(cs^0) \ \vee \ cs = cs^0; \ m$$

$$p.m \ \wedge \ |\overline{cs}| = k \ \ \mapsto \ \ \neg p.m \ \vee \ |\overline{cs}| > k$$

Conclusion: $p.m \ \mapsto \ \neg p.m \ \vee \ (m \in cr)$

In Section 17.4.2 (which may be skipped), we show that a faulty channel can be represented by a UNITY program. This demonstration, however, is not necessary for the study of communication protocols; only the specification of a faulty channel—for instance, the specification given above—is required to develop and verify protocols.

Exercise 17.2   Specify a faulty channel that loses at most one copy of each message.   ▽

17.4.2 A Program that Simulates a Faulty Channel

Many programs satisfy the specification of a faulty-channel. In particular, a program for a nonfaulty channel—i.e., one in which every message in cs is transferred to cr—also meets the specification. Here we propose a program for which the converse is also true: Each possible behavior of a faulty channel corresponds to some execution sequence of this program.

A possible message loss is simulated by the statement

$$cs \ := \ \mathrm{tail}(cs) \qquad \mathrm{if} \quad cs \neq null$$

because a message removed from cs may not have been transferred to cr. A possible message duplication is simulated by the statement

$$cr \ := \ cr;\mathrm{head}(cs) \qquad \mathrm{if} \quad cs \neq null$$

because a message is appended to cr and is not removed from cs. A correct message transfer is simulated by the following statement:

$$cs, cr := \text{tail}(cs), \ cr;\text{head}(cs) \qquad \text{if} \quad cs \neq null$$

These statements, however, do not meet the given specification for a faulty channel. For instance, we can display an execution sequence in which an infinite number of consecutive messages are lost: Whenever $cs \neq null$, the statement corresponding to message loss is executed until $cs = null$, then the other two statements are executed, and only after that are messages added to cs (by the sender); this execution strategy is fair but it loses all messages. Therefore we have to modify these statements to guarantee that eventually there is a correct transfer of a message if an infinite number of messages are sent along cs. To do so, we introduce a boolean variable b to prevent any message loss or duplication as long as b is *true*. Variable b becomes *true* eventually and remains *true* until a message is correctly transferred from cs to cr. The following program incorporates this idea.

Program {Faulty Channel} FC

> **declare** b : boolean

> **initially**

>> $b = \textit{false}$ {initially, no statement is prevented from effective execution}

> **assign**

>> {loss}
>> $cs \qquad := \text{tail}(cs) \qquad \text{if} \quad cs \neq null \land \neg b$

>> {duplication}
>> $[\!] \quad cr \qquad := cr;\text{head}(cs) \qquad \text{if} \quad cs \neq null \land \neg b$

>> {correct transfer}
>> $[\!] \quad b, cs, cr := \textit{false},\text{tail}(cs), cr;\text{head}(cs) \qquad \text{if} \quad cs \neq null$

>> {to guarantee correct transfer eventually}
>> $[\!] \quad b \qquad := \textit{true}$

end $\{FC\}$

Exercise 17.3   Write a program to simulate a faulty channel that reorders messages as follows: Two messages that are apart by at most M in the sending order may be received out of order, though messages that are further apart in the sending order (i.e., more than M) must be received in the order in which they are sent.   ▽

Proof of *FC*

The following exercise shows that *FC* simulates all possible behaviors of a faulty channel.

Exercise 17.4 Given any two finite message sequences u,v, where u *loss* v holds, show a finite execution sequence of *FC* for which $\overline{cs} = u$ and $\overline{cr} = v$.

$\triangledown$

Next we show that *FC* meets the specification of a faulty channel. The proof that the safety properties are met is left to the reader. We show a somewhat simpler conditional property for *FC*: If message m is appended indefinitely to cs, then m appears eventually in cr; the proof of the more general conditional property given in the specification is along the same lines. Formally we prove the following conditional property for *FC*.

Hypothesis:

$$cs = null \quad unless \quad cs = \ll m \gg$$
$$(cs^0 = cs) \;\wedge\; (cs \neq null) \quad unless \quad cs = \mathrm{tail}(cs^0) \;\vee\; cs = cs^0; m$$
$$|\overline{cs}| = k \quad \mapsto \quad |\overline{cs}| > k \;\;.$$

Conclusion:

$$true \quad \mapsto \quad m \in cr \;.$$

The proof formalizes the following argument. Program *FC* eventually removes the head item of cs; from the hypothesis, only message m is appended to cs. Hence, eventually, cs consists of zero or more copies of message m; from then on, cs consists of nothing but message m. Variable b is set *true* some time after cs consists of copies of message m only. If $cs = null$ when b is set *true*, b remains *true* until cs becomes nonnull. If $b \wedge (cs \neq null)$, then $\mathrm{head}(cs) = m$; in this case, eventually message m will be appended to cr.

In the following, $\ll m^i, i \geq 0 \gg$ denotes a sequence consisting of zero or more copies of message m; the obvious notation is employed to denote a sequence of one or more copies of m. The meaning of $cs \in \ll m^i, i \geq 0 \gg$ is that cs is a sequence consisting of zero or more copies of m. The structure of the proof is as follows: We will show the following properties (a property written without a program name applies to any composite program of which *FC* is a component):

$$true \quad \mapsto \quad cs \in \ll m^i, i \geq 0 \gg \tag{1}$$
$$cs \in \ll m^i, i \geq 0 \gg \quad \mapsto \quad b \,\wedge\, cs \in \ll m^i, i \geq 0 \gg \tag{2}$$
$$b \,\wedge\, cs = null \quad \mapsto \quad b \,\wedge\, cs \in \ll m^i, i > 0 \gg \tag{3}$$
$$b \,\wedge\, cs \in \ll m^i, i > 0 \gg \quad \mapsto \quad m \in cr \;. \tag{4}$$

Using the properties of *leads-to*, it follows from (1–4) that $true \mapsto m \in cr$. We give a proof of (3); the remaining proofs are left to the reader.

Proof: (3) $b \wedge cs = null \quad \mapsto \quad b \wedge cs \in \ll m^i, i > 0 \gg$

Let H denote a program with which FC is composed where H satisfies the preceding hypothesis.

b is stable in H
    , from locality of b

$cs = null \quad unless \quad cs = \ll m \gg$ in H
    , H satisfies the hypothesis

$b \wedge cs = null \quad unless \quad b \wedge cs = \ll m \gg$ in H
    , conjunction on the above two

$b \wedge cs = null$ is stable in FC
    , from the text of FC

$b \wedge cs = null \quad unless \quad b \wedge cs = \ll m \gg$
    , union theorem on the above two

$cs = null \quad \mapsto \quad cs = \ll m \gg$
    , can be derived from the hypothesis

$b \wedge cs = null \quad \mapsto \quad b \wedge cs = \ll m \gg$
    , PSP theorem on the above two $\triangledown$

17.5   A Protocol for Communications over Faulty Channels

A communication protocol is a program that is to be composed with a program, such as FC, that meets the specification of a faulty channel. The composite program is required to satisfy the following specification (also given earlier):

invariant $mr \sqsubseteq ms$

$|mr| = n \quad \mapsto \quad |mr| = n + 1$

To develop such a communication protocol we start with program $P2$. The variable x is replaced by a pair of channels, cs and cr, where the sender adds messages to cs and the receiver receives from cr. The variable y is similarly replaced by a pair of channels, $acks$ and $ackr$, where the sender receives from $acks$ and the receiver adds to $ackr$. In Fig. 17.2 we show the communication topology schematically.

Program $P3$ is obtained from $P2$ by replacing assignment to x by appending appropriate messages to cs. Also each occurrence of x on the right side of a statement is replaced by head(cr), provided that cr is nonnull. Similarly, variable y is replaced appropriately. Program $P3$ incorporates these changes as well as the minor changes noted after program $P2$.

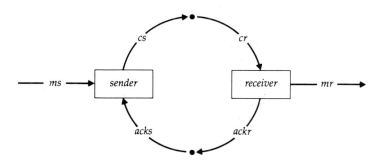

Figure 17.2 The sender and the receiver communicate through faulty channels modeled by (cs, cr) and $(ackr, acks)$.

17.5.1 A Protocol

Program {protocol for communication over faulty channels} *P3*

    declare ks, kr : integer

    initially

      $ks, kr = 1, 0 \ \| \ cs, cr, acks, ackr = null, null, null, null \ \| \ mr = null$

    assign

        $ackr$:= $ackr; kr$

  $\|$ ks := $ks + 1$ if $acks \neq null \ \wedge \ ks = \text{head}(acks)$

   $\|$ $acks$:= tail($acks$)   if $acks \neq null$

  $\|$ cs := $cs;\ (ks, ms[ks])$

  $\|$ kr, mr := $kr + 1, mr;\text{head}(cr).val$

                       if $cr \neq null \ \wedge \ kr \neq \text{head}(cr).dex$

   $\|$ cr := tail(cr)   if $cr \neq null$

end {*P3*}

As before, the first and the last statements are in the receiver process, and the other two are in the sender process.

17.5.2 Correctness of the Protocol

We use the same invariants, (I1, I2), that were proposed for program *P2*. We rewrite them as follows (with x replaced by $x.dex$ in (I1)), where we interpret x to mean any item of cs or cr, and y to mean any item of $acks$ or $ackr$:

invariant $y \leq kr \leq x.dex \leq ks \leq y + 1$ in $P3$ (I1)

invariant $x.val \in ms \land mr \sqsubseteq ms \land |mr| = kr$ in $P3$ (I2)

Note: The appropriate way to write (I1)—because x or y may be undefined if the corresponding channels are *null*—is as follows:

$$\langle \forall y : y \in acks \lor y \in ackr :: y \leq kr \land ks \leq y + 1 \rangle \land$$
$$\langle \forall x : x \in cs \lor x \in cr :: kr \leq x.dex \leq ks \rangle \qquad \land$$
$$kr \leq ks \leq kr + 1 .$$

Similar remarks apply to (I2). $\triangledown$

We need an additional invariant, (I3). In (I3), $cs.dex$ is the sequence of *dex* parts of messages in cs (and similarly $cr.dex$):

invariant

Each of the following is a sequence of nondecreasing integers in $P3$:

$cs.dex, cr.dex, acks, ackr$ (I3)

Invariants (I1,I2,I3) are stable in the program for a faulty channel. Proofs of these invariants in program $P3$ are left to the reader. Now we prove the progress condition (using kr for $|mr|$, from invariant (I2)):

Proof: $kr = n \longmapsto kr = n + 1$

$kr = n \longmapsto kr = n + 1 \lor (n \in acks)$
  , proven below   (5)

$n \in acks \longmapsto ks = n + 1$
  , proven below   (6)

$kr = n \longmapsto (kr = n + 1) \lor (ks = n + 1)$
  , cancellation on the above two

$ks = n + 1 \longmapsto kr = n + 1$
  , left to the reader

$kr = n \longmapsto kr = n + 1$
  , cancellation on the above two $\triangledown$

To prove (5), consider transmission from the receiver to the sender. The hypothesis in the conditional property of faulty channel (Section 17.4.1) is met by defining $p.m$ to be $kr = m$; the properties in the hypothesis follow from the text of program $P3$ and the safety properties of a faulty channel. Therefore we can assert the conclusion of that conditional property:

$kr = n \longmapsto kr \neq n \lor (n \in acks)$

$kr = n \; unless \; kr = n + 1$
  , from the text of $P3$ and locality

$kr = n \mapsto kr = n + 1 \lor (n \in acks)$
  , PSP theorem on the above two

The proof of (6), $n \in acks \mapsto ks = n + 1$, follows by using the property of a FIFO channel from the text of *P3*: Any item in the channel is eventually delivered if the head item is eventually removed.

17.6   Optimizations

17.6.1 Alternating Bit Protocol

From invariant (I1) for *P3*, if $cr \neq null$ then $kr \leq \text{head}(cr).dex \leq kr + 1$. Therefore

$(kr \neq \text{head}(cr).dex) \equiv (kr \bmod 2 \neq [\text{head}(cr).dex] \bmod 2),$

$(ks = \text{head}(acks)) \equiv (ks \bmod 2 = \text{head}(acks) \bmod 2).$

We exploit these two facts to simplify program *P3*. Variables kr, ks can be replaced by $kr \bmod 2$, $ks \bmod 2$, respectively—i.e., kr, ks need only be computed modulo 2. Therefore the *dex* parts of messages in cs, cr and the messages in $acks, ackr$ need only be 0 or 1. The correctness arguments for this modification are similar to those in Section 17.5.2. The name *alternating bit protocol* comes from the observation that the sequence of *dex* parts used in transmitting the different messages of *ms* is an alternating sequence of 0s and 1s.

17.6.2 Restricting Acknowledgments Sent by the Receiver

The execution of the statement $ackr := ackr; kr$ in program *P3* is the way in which the receiver acknowledges that it has received a message with index kr. It is sufficient to acknowledge a message only when it is received. Hence the following two statements for the receiver in *P3*,

$ackr \quad := ackr; kr$

$[\!|\quad kr, mr \quad := kr + 1 \quad , mr; \text{head}(cr).val$
$\qquad\qquad\qquad\qquad \text{if} \quad cr \neq null \land kr \neq \text{head}(cr).dex$

$\|\ cr \qquad := \text{tail}(cr) \qquad \text{if} \quad cr \neq null$

may be replaced by a single statement:

$kr, mr \quad := kr + 1 \quad , mr; \text{head}(cr).val$
$\qquad\qquad\qquad \text{if} \quad cr \neq null \land kr \neq \text{head}(cr).dex$

$$\| \; cr, ackr := \text{tail}(cr) \;, \; ackr;\text{head}(cr).dex$$
$$\text{if} \quad cr \neq null$$

We leave the proof of correctness to the reader.

Exercise 17.5   What changes to *P3*, and its proof, are necessary if *ms* is a finite sequence?   ▽

Exercise 17.6   Generalize *P3* so that the sender may send *W* different messages, where $W > 0$ is a system parameter, without receiving acknowledgments. This generalization forms the basis for the *Window protocol*.   ▽

Exercise 17.7   Propose a specification of a channel that can only duplicate, but not lose, messages. As before, a message can be duplicated only a finite number of times. Propose a protocol for transmission over such a channel. ▽

Summary

A communication protocol is a program; when a communication protocol is composed with a program that models a faulty channel, the composite program guarantees fault-free communication. A faulty channel is also a program; it has a specification similar in structure to program specifications given in earlier chapters; it can be modeled by a UNITY program. Program composition by union allows us to design a fault-tolerant program by viewing one of the components as being faulty. Program composition provides a unifying framework for treating faulty and nonfaulty programs alike. We have developed a protocol in a series of refinement steps to illustrate one simple idea: The sender sends a message repeatedly until it "knows" that the message is received.

Bibliographic Notes

The alternating bit protocol is described in Bartlett, Scantlebury, and Wilkinson [1969]. Many proofs of correctness have been proposed for this protocol. We have been most influenced by those found in Hailpern [1980] and Shankar and Lam [1987].

CHAPTER 18

Fault Tolerance: Byzantine Agreement

18.1   Introduction

In this chapter we study an important paradigm for fault tolerance in distributed systems, known as the *Byzantine agreement* problem. This problem can be described informally as follows. A message-communicating system has two kinds of processes, *reliable* and *unreliable*. There is a process, called *general*, that may or may not be reliable. Each process x has a local variable $byz[x]$. It is required to design an algorithm, to be followed by all reliable processes, such that every reliable process x eventually sets its local variable, $byz[x]$, to a common value. Furthermore, if *general* is reliable, this common value is $d^0[g]$, the initial value of one of *general*'s variables. The solution is complicated by the fact that unreliable processes send arbitrary messages. Since reliable processes cannot be distinguished from the unreliable ones, the straightforward algorithm—*general* transmits its initial value to all processes and every reliable process u assigns this value to $byz[u]$—does not work, because *general* itself may be unreliable, and hence may transmit different values to different processes.

Our approach to this problem is noteworthy because of the way we model faults. We propose that a program for this problem be a set of equations. Any equation that names a variable of an unreliable process is discarded. The resulting subset of equations must satisfy the problem specification. Because programmers do not know which processes are reliable, they do not know which equations will be discarded. They must design their programs to meet the specification no matter which equations are discarded. The design can rely only upon the fact that there are a limited number of unreliable processes. Discarding an equation that names a variable of an unreliable process models "malicious behavior" of that process. This is because the variable value can be changed arbitrarily by the process, and hence it cannot be guaranteed that this equation holds.

The reader should contrast this approach to programming a faulty system with the design of communication protocols for faulty channels (Chapter 17). A protocol designer constructs a program (i.e., a communication protocol) that, when composed with a program for a faulty channel, still guarantees fault-free communication. The effect of program union is to enlarge the set of execution sequences; the protocol designer must guarantee that the problem specification is met by each execution sequence in this enlarged set. The effect of discarding equations is similar—it enlarges the set of solutions to the equations—and the program designer must guarantee that all solutions in the enlarged set meet the problem specification.

We specify the problem in Section 18.2. The program for this problem is derived in stages, in Sections 18.3, 18.4, and 18.5, by successively refining the specification (and proving the correctness of each refinement). The final refined specification is in the form of equations, and hence a program is readily obtained from it. We show in Section 18.6 how these equations can be implemented on a distributed architecture. By eliminating the operational details of message communications among processes at higher levels of refinement, we have simplified the correctness proofs considerably.

18.2   Problem Specification

A system has two different kinds of processes: *reliable* and *unreliable*. There are t, $t \geq 0$, unreliable processes and more than $2.t$ reliable processes. (It is known that there is no algorithm for the Byzantine agreement problem unless the number of reliable processes is more than double the number of unreliable ones.) There is a distinguished process, called the *general*, denoted by g, that may or may not be reliable.

Notation: We use u, v, w to denote reliable processes and x, y, z to denote arbitrary processes, reliable or unreliable. All process symbols in propositions are universally quantified appropriately—u, v, w over all reliable processes and x, y, z over all processes—unless the quantification is explicit.   ▽

Every variable in the system is designated as *local* to exactly one process. We have, for all x, variable $byz[x]$ local to x. Our solution may introduce additional variables; as part of the solution, the processes to which these variables are local should be specified. A variable of a reliable process is called a *reliable variable*; *unreliable variables* are defined analogously.

A program is a set of equations. It is required that the subset of equations that name only reliable variables have a solution and that any such solution satisfy the following specification.

18.2.1 Specification, spec1

$byz[u] = byz[v]$

and

if g is reliable, then $byz[u] = d^0[g]$,

where $d^0[g]$ is the initial value of some variable of the general.

Observe that if g is reliable, the second requirement implies the first.

We impose one restriction on the equations to guarantee that they can be implemented on a distributed architecture: Each side, left and right, of an equation names local variables of exactly one process.

18.2.2 Discussion

Observe that it is sufficient to restrict attention to the case where $d^0[g]$ is boolean. If initially $d^0[g]$ can have one of 2^m possible values, $m > 0$, then this value can be encoded by m bits, and m different instances of the boolean algorithm can be run in parallel, one instance for each bit. Eventually all reliable processes agree on each individual bit, and if the *general* is reliable, each agreed-on bit value is the same as the corresponding bit value for $d^0[g]$.

To understand the implication of discarding equations, consider two equations,

$$d = f \ \| \ e = f,$$

where d, e are reliable variables and f is an unreliable variable. The programmer cannot assert that $d = e$ because both equations will be discarded. This models the fact that the processes to which d and e are local can be supplied with different values of f by f's process. Traditionally this is termed "malicious behavior by f's process."

As a consequence of discarding equations, the following equations do not solve the Byzantine agreement problem:

$$\langle \| \ x \ :: \ byz[x] = d^0[g] \rangle .$$

If g is unreliable, all equations will be discarded. This program models the strategy in which the general transmits its initial value to all processes, and each reliable process u assigns the value to $byz[u]$.

Exercise 18.1   Develop more efficient solutions for the case where $d^0[g]$ can take on 2^m, $m > 0$, possible values. (See Turpin and Coan [1984].) $\triangledown$

Exercise 18.2   Consider the following scheme for Byzantine agreement for the case where $t \leq 1$ and there are four processes in the system (including *general*). In the first round, *general* sends its value to all other processes. In the next round, all processes other than *general* send their values to all other processes excluding *general*. After the second round every process other than *general* has three values; the process picks their median as the final value. If *general* is reliable it assigns $d^0[g]$ to $byz[g]$.

Express this solution as a set of equations and prove its correctness. Attempt to extend your solution for higher values of g. (See Pease, Shostak, and Lamport [1980].) $\triangledown$

18.3   Refinement Step: Authenticated Broadcast

We introduce a variable *con* that is a sequence of matrices; the rows and columns of each matrix are indexed by processes, and we use a superscript r

to denote the rth matrix in the sequence. Thus $con^r[x, y]$ is the $(x, y)^{th}$ entry in the rth matrix in con. Variable $con^r[x, y]$ is boolean and is local to process x. We will prescribe values of $con^r[x, y]$ for all x, y and all r, $r \geq 0$. Later we show that only a finite number of these matrices need be computed. We also introduce variable $d^r[x]$, a local boolean variable of x, for all r, $r \geq 0$. (Variable $d^0[g]$ already appeared in the specification.)

A Note on Notation: This is one of the few instances in this book in which we use superscripts. The reason for introducing superscripts is that arithmetic operations are carried out on the superscript r but not on x, y, which are process indices.   ▽

In the following, $con^r[u, *]$ denotes the number of x for which $con^r[u, x]$ holds:

$$con^r[u, *] = \langle + \ x \ : \ con^r[u, x] \ :: \ 1 \rangle.$$

18.3.1 Refined Specification, spec2

The following specification is over all u, v, x and all r, $r \geq 1$, wherever the quantification is not shown explicitly.

$$\langle \wedge u \ : \ u \neq g \ :: \ \neg d^0[u] \rangle \ \wedge \ \langle \wedge u, x \ :: \ \neg con^0[u, x] \rangle \tag{B1}$$

$$con^r[u, v] = d^{r-1}[v] \tag{A1}$$

$$con^{r-1}[u, x] \ \Rightarrow \ con^r[v, x] \tag{A2}$$

$$d^r[u] = [d^{r-1}[u] \ \vee \ (con^r[u, *] \geq r \ \wedge \ con^r[u, g])] \tag{E1}$$

$$byz[u] = d^{t+1}[u] \tag{E2}$$

18.3.2 Discussion

The refined specification, *spec2*, can be viewed as a solution to the Byzantine agreement problem using "authenticated broadcast." Let r denote computation steps or "rounds." Predicate (A1) can be implemented if every reliable process, u, receives a value from another reliable process, v, correctly, within one round; this property is known as "correctness and unforgeability." Predicate (A2) can be implemented if every reliable process u relays its local variable value $con^r[u, x]$—if it is *true*—to every other reliable process within one round; this is known as the "relay property." Equations (B1,E1,E2) can be implemented by local computations at process u.

Byzantine agreement with authenticated broadcasts can tolerate any number of faulty processes; the fact that the number of reliable processes is more than double the number of unreliable ones is not used in the proof of correctness of this specification.

18.3.3 Correctness

We prove that *spec2* implies *spec1*—i.e., from (B1,A1,A2,E1,E2) we deduce that

$$byz[u] = byz[v]$$

and

if g is reliable, then $byz[u] = d^0[g]$.

(We do not show that there is a solution to *spec2*. We will show that our final specification is a proper set of equations, and hence has a solution.)

Theorem 18.1   If g is reliable, then

$$\langle \forall\, r\ :\ r \geq 1\ ::\ d^r[u] = d^0[g] \rangle.$$

Proof: By induction on r.

$r = 1$:

$$
\begin{aligned}
d^1[u] \quad &= \ [d^0[u]\ \vee\ (con^1[u,*] \geq 1\ \wedge\ con^1[u,g])] \\
&\qquad\qquad\qquad\qquad\qquad , \text{from (E1)} \\
con^1[u,g] &\Rightarrow (con^1[u,*] \geq 1) \qquad\quad , \text{from the definition of } con^1[u,*] \\
con^1[u,g] &= \ d^0[g] \qquad\qquad\qquad\qquad , \text{from (A1) and because} \\
&\qquad\qquad\qquad\qquad\qquad\quad\ g \text{ is reliable} \\
d^1[u] \quad &= \ (d^0[u]\ \vee\ d^0[g]) \qquad\qquad , \text{from the above three facts} \\
u = g\ :\ & d^1[u] = (d^0[g]\ \vee\ d^0[g]) = d^0[g]\ , \text{by simple substitution} \\
u \neq g\ :\ & d^1[u] = (false\ \vee\ d^0[g]) = d^0[g]\ , \text{from (B1)}
\end{aligned}
$$

$r > 1$:

$$
\begin{aligned}
d^r[u] \quad &= \ [d^{r-1}[u]\ \vee\ (con^r[u,*] \geq r\ \wedge\ con^r[u,g])] \\
&\qquad\qquad\qquad\qquad\qquad , \text{from (E1)} \\
d^{r-1}[u] &= \ d^0[g] \qquad\qquad\qquad , \text{from the induction hypothesis} \\
con^r[u,g] &= d^{r-1}[g] \qquad\qquad , \text{from (A1) and because } g \text{ is reliable} \\
d^{r-1}[g] &= \ d^0[g] \qquad\qquad\qquad , \text{from the induction hypothesis} \\
d^r[u] \quad &= \ [d^0[g]\ \vee\ (con^r[u,*] \geq r\ \wedge\ d^0[g])] \\
&\qquad\qquad\qquad\qquad\qquad , \text{from the above four facts} \\
d^r[u] \quad &= \ d^0[g] \qquad\qquad\qquad\quad , \text{trivially from the above} \qquad \triangledown
\end{aligned}
$$

Theorem 18.2 $d^{t+1}[u] = d^{t+1}[v]$

Proof: If g is reliable, this result follows from Theorem 18.1. Hence assume that g is unreliable.

Let r, if it exists, be the smallest natural number such that $d^r[u]$ holds for some u. If no such r exists, then $\neg d^{t+1}[v]$, for all v, which proves the theorem. Therefore assume that such r and u exist. We show that $r \leq t$ and $d^{r+1}[v]$ hold for all v.

From (B1), $\neg d^0[v]$ holds for all v (recall that g is unreliable and hence $v \neq g$). Therefore $r > 0$. Hence

$\neg d^{r-1}[u] \ \wedge \ d^r[u]$

$con^r[u, *] \geq r \ \wedge \ con^r[u, g]$, from (E1).

$con^r[u, x] \ \Rightarrow \ con^{r+1}[v, x]$, from (A2)

$\neg con^r[u, u]$, from $\neg d^{r-1}[u]$ and (A1)

$con^{r+1}[v, u]$, from $d^r[u]$ and (A1)

$con^{r+1}[v, *] > con^r[u, *]$, from the above three facts

$con^{r+1}[v, *] \geq r + 1$, from the above and $con^r[u, *] \geq r$

$con^{r+1}[v, g]$, from $con^r[u, g]$ and (A2)

$d^{r+1}[v]$, from the above two and (E1)

Next we show that $r \leq t$, and hence

$d^{r+1}[v] \ \Rightarrow \ d^{t+1}[v]$, using induction with (E1)

which proves the theorem.

From our choice of r as the smallest natural number for which $d^r[u]$ holds for some u, we have, for any w,

$\neg d^{r-1}[w]$

$\neg con^r[u, w]$, from (A1)

$con^r[u, *] \leq t$, from the above and because there are t unreliable processes

$r \leq t$, from $con^r[u, *] \geq r$ $\bigtriangledown$

It follows from Theorems 18.1 and 18.2 and from (E2) that *spec2* implies *spec1*.

Exercise 18.3 Explore the possibility of "early stopping"—i.e., under what condition can $byz[u]$ be set to $d^r[u]$, for some r, $r \leq t$? $\bigtriangledown$

18.4   Refinement Step: Unauthenticated Broadcast

Next we propose refinements to implement authenticated broadcasts—properties (A1,A2)—by unauthenticated message communications.

We introduce three new variables, *sum*, *obs*, and *val* each of which is a sequence of matrices like *con*. Variables $sum^r[x,y]$, $obs^r[x,y]$, and $val^r[x,y]$ are integer, boolean, and boolean, respectively, and each of these variables is local to x.

18.4.1 Refined Specification, spec3

We include (B1,E1,E2) from *spec2*. Additionally, for all u, v, x and r, $r \geq 0$,

$$\neg obs^0[u,x] \tag{B2}$$

$$0 \leq sum^r[u,x] - \langle + w \ : \ obs^r[w,x] \ :: \ 1 \rangle \leq t \tag{A3}$$

$$obs^{r+1}[u,x] = (obs^r[u,x] \ \vee \ sum^r[u,x] > t \ \vee \ val^r[u,x]) \tag{E3}$$

$$val^{\,r}[u,v] = d^r[v] \tag{E4}$$

$$con^r[u,x] = (sum^r[u,x] > 2.t) \tag{E5}$$

Note: The definition of $con^0[u,x]$, in (E5), does not conflict with its definition in (B1); it will be evident from the following proof that $con^0[u,x]$ is *false*. Because of (E5), specification of $con^0[u,x]$ may be removed from (B1). ▽

Note: From equation (E4), it is clear that all variables $d^r[v]$ (except $d^0[g]$) can be eliminated; each occurrence of $d^r[v]$ can be replaced by $val^r[v,v]$. Also, using equation (E5), we can eliminate the variables $con^r[u,x]$. ▽

18.4.2 Discussion

Variable $sum^r[u,x]$ is an estimate by u of the number of processes v for which $obs^r[v,x]$ holds (A3). Variable $val^r[u,x]$ is an estimate by u of the value of $d^r[x]$; it is exact if x is reliable (E4). Variable $obs^{r+1}[u,x]$ holds only if $obs^r[v,x]$ holds for some reliable process v ($obs^r[u,x] \ \vee \ sum^r[u,x] > t$), or if u estimates that $d^r[x]$ holds (E3). Similarly, $con^r[u,x]$ holds only if $obs^r[v,x]$ holds for more than t reliable processes, v (E5).

18.4.3 Correctness

We show that *spec3* implies *spec2*; it is sufficient to show that *spec3* implies (A1,A2). We note the following facts from (A3):

$$\langle \exists \ w \ :: \ obs^r[w,x] \rangle \ \vee \ sum^r[u,x] \leq t \tag{D1}$$

$$\langle \forall \ w \ :: \ obs^r[w,x] \rangle \ \Rightarrow \ sum^r[u,x] > 2.t \tag{D2}$$

$$sum^r[u,x] > 2.t \ \Rightarrow \ sum^r[v,x] > t \tag{D3}$$

Proof: (D1) $\langle \exists \, w \;\; :: \;\; obs^r[w,x] \rangle \;\; \vee \;\; sum^r[u,x] \leq t$

$\quad sum^r[u,x] > t \;\; \Rightarrow \;\; (\langle + \, w \; : \; obs^r[w,x] \;\; :: \;\; 1 \rangle > 0)$ $\qquad$, from (A3)

$\quad (\langle + \, w \; : \; obs^r[w,x] \;\; :: \;\; 1 \rangle > 0) \;\; \equiv \;\; \langle \exists \, w \;\; :: \;\; obs^r[w,x] \rangle$ $\quad$, trivially

(D1) follows from the above two facts. $\hfill \triangledown$

Proof: (D2) $\langle \forall \, w \;\; :: \;\; obs^r[w,x] \rangle \;\; \Rightarrow \;\; sum^r[u,x] > 2.t$

$\quad \langle \forall \, w \;\; :: \;\; obs^r[w,x] \rangle \;\; \Rightarrow \;\; (\langle + \, w \; : \; obs^r[w,x] \;\; :: \;\; 1 \rangle > 2.t)$

$\qquad$, there are more than $2.t$ reliable processes

$\quad \langle + \, w \; : \; obs^r[w,x] \;\; :: \;\; 1 \rangle \leq sum^r[u,x]$ $\qquad\qquad\qquad$, from (A3)

The result follows from these two facts. $\hfill \triangledown$

Proof: (D3) $sum^r[u,x] > 2.t \;\; \Rightarrow \;\; sum^r[v,x] > t$

$\quad sum^r[u,x] > 2.t \;\; \Rightarrow \;\; (\langle + \, w \; : \; obs^r[w,x] \;\; :: \;\; 1 \rangle > t)$, from (A3)

$\quad sum^r[v,x] \geq \langle + \, w \; : \; obs^r[w,x] \;\; :: \;\; 1 \rangle$ $\qquad\qquad\qquad$, from (A3)

The result follows from these two facts. $\hfill \triangledown$

Lemma 18.1 $\langle \forall \, r \; : \; r \geq 0 \;\; :: \;\; obs^{r+1}[u,v] = d^r[v] \rangle$

Proof: By induction on r.

$r = 0$:

$\quad obs^1[u,v] = (obs^0[u,v] \;\; \vee \;\; sum^0[u,v] > t \;\; \vee \;\; val^0[u,v])$

$\qquad\qquad\qquad\qquad\qquad$, from (E3) $\hfill (1)$

$\quad \langle \forall \, w \;\; :: \;\; \neg obs^0[w,v] \rangle$ $\qquad$, from (B2)

$\quad \neg obs^0[u,v] \;\; \wedge \;\; sum^0[u,v] \leq t$ $\quad$, from the above and (D1)

$\quad obs^1[u,v] = val^0[u,v]$ $\qquad\qquad$, from (1) and the above

$\quad obs^1[u,v] = d^0[v]$ $\qquad\qquad\quad$, from the above and (E4)

$r > 1$:

$\quad obs^{r+1}[u,v] = (obs^r[u,v] \;\; \vee \;\; sum^r[u,v] > t \;\; \vee \;\; val^r[u,v])$

$\qquad$, from (E3) $\hfill (2)$

$\quad sum^r[u,v] > t \;\; \Rightarrow \;\; \langle \exists \, w \;\; :: \;\; obs^r[w,v] \rangle$

$\qquad$, from (D1)

$\quad obs^r[u,v] \;\; \vee \;\; sum^r[u,v] > t \;\; \Rightarrow \;\; \langle \exists w \;\; :: \;\; obs^r[w,v] \rangle$

$\qquad$, from the above

$\quad \langle \exists \, w \;\; :: \;\; obs^r[w,v] \rangle \;\; \Rightarrow \;\; d^{r-1}[v]$

$\qquad$, from the induction hypothesis

$\quad d^{r-1}[v] \;\; \Rightarrow \;\; d^r[v]$

$\qquad$, from (E1)

$val^r[u, v] = d^r[v]$
    , from (E4)
$obs^{r+1}[u, v] = d^r[v]$
    , from (2) and the above four facts   ▽

Lemma 18.2 $\langle \forall\ r\ :\ r \geq 0\ ::\ con^r[u, v] = obs^r[u, v] \rangle$.

Proof: By induction on r.

$r = 0$:

$sum^0[u, v] \leq t$	, from (B2, D1)
$\neg con^0[u, v]$	, from the above and (E5)
$con^0[u, v] = obs^0[u, v]$	, from the above and (B2)

$r > 0$:

$obs^r[u, v] = d^{r-1}[v]$	, from Lemma 18.1
$\langle \forall\ w, w'\ ::\ obs^r[w, v] = obs^r[w', v] \rangle$	, from the above
$obs^r[u, v] = (sum^r[u, v] > 2.t)$	, from the above and (D1,D2)
$obs^r[u, v] = con^r[u, v]$	, from the above and (E5) ▽

Note that Lemma 18.2 does not say that $con^r[u, x] = obs^r[u, x]$ for all x. This equality may not apply if x is unreliable.

The following two theorems, 18.3 and 18.4, respectively, show that (A1) and (A2) are satisfied.

Theorem 18.3 $\langle \forall\ r\ :\ r \geq 1\ ::\ con^r[u, v] = d^{r-1}[v] \rangle$

Proof: From Lemmas 18.1 and 18.2.   ▽

Theorem 18.4 $\langle \forall\ r\ :\ r \geq 0\ ::\ con^r[u, x]\ \Rightarrow\ con^{r+1}[v, x] \rangle$

Proof:

$con^r[u, x]$	, assumed
$sum^r[u, x] > 2.t$	, from the above and (E5)
$\langle \forall\ w\ ::\ sum^r[w, x] > t \rangle$	, from the above and (D3)
$\langle \forall\ w\ ::\ obs^{r+1}[w, x] \rangle$	, from the above and (E3)
$sum^{r+1}[v, x] > 2.t$	, from the above and (D2)
$con^{r+1}[v, x]$	, from the above and (E5) ▽

18.5   Refinement Step: Shared-Variable Implementation

We have shown how to implement properties of authenticated broadcasts given by predicates (A1,A2) using unauthenticated broadcasts, given by predicates (B2,A3,E3–E5). It is easy to implement (B1,B2) by equations. (E1–E5) are already in the form of equations. Further refinement is aimed toward implementing inequality (A3) by equations and then implementing the equations by point-to-point message communications among processes. In this section we propose equations to implement (A3).

18.5.1 Refined Specification, spec4

We introduce variable $robs^r[u, z, x]$, a local variable of u, into which $obs^r[z, x]$ is read; $sum^r[u, x]$ is the number of z for which $robs^r[u, z, x]$ is $true$. The next specification consists of all predicates except (A3) from $spec3$, (B1,B2,E1–E5), plus the following, for all u, z, x, and r, $r \geq 0$:

$$robs^r[u, z, x] = obs^r[z, x] \qquad \text{(E6)}$$

$$sum^r[u, x] = \langle + \; z \; : \; robs^r[u, z, x] \; :: \; 1 \rangle \qquad \text{(E7)}$$

Note: Using equation (E7) we can eliminate variables $sum^r[u, x]$. $\triangledown$

18.5.2 Discussion

(E6,E7) implement (A3) as follows: A process u counts the number of processes z for which $obs^r[z, x]$ holds; $sum^r[u, x]$ is assigned this count. Since all reliable processes w for which $obs^r[w, x]$ holds will be counted, the lower bound on $sum^r[u, x]$ holds. Since there are t unreliable processes, the value of sum cannot exceed the value of $\langle + \; w \; : \; obs^r[w, x] \; :: \; 1 \rangle$ by more than t.

18.5.3 Correctness

We leave the proof—that (E6,E7) imply (A3)—to the reader; the proof is a formalization of the argument in Section 18.5.2.

18.6   Refinement Step: Distributed Implementation

All the predicates in $spec4$ are in the form of equations (predicates (B1,B2) can be easily stated as equations); this is our program for the Byzantine agreement problem. We show that these equations are proper and hence have a solution.

Furthermore, the left and right sides of any equation each name variables of one process only; hence we can implement these equations by point-to-point communications among processes. We sketch such an implementation and discuss its computational complexity.

As we noted after presenting *spec3* and *spec4*, variables $d^r[v]$, $con^r[u,x]$, and $sum^r[u,x]$ can be eliminated. In the following program, however, we have retained all the variables, as well as the equations proposed in all the refinements. The equations are now indexed over all processes—we have replaced u by y and v by x—though we know that all equations that name variables of unreliable processes will be discarded. Superscript r runs up to $t + 1$, in view of Theorem 18.2.

Program *Byzantine-Agreement*

  always

      {from (B1,B2)}

      $\langle\!\!\parallel y \; : \; y \neq g \;\; :: \;\; d^0[y] = \mathit{false}\rangle$ {B1}

  $\parallel$ $\langle\!\!\parallel y, x \;\; :: \;\; obs^0[y,x] = \mathit{false}\rangle$ {B2}

  $\parallel$ {from (E1, E2) of *spec2*}

      $\langle\!\!\parallel r, y \; : \; 1 \leq r \leq t+1 \;\; ::$

          {$con^r[y,*]$ is an abbreviation for $\langle+ \, z \; : \; con^r[y,z] \;\; :: \;\; 1\rangle$}

          $d^r[y] = [d^{r-1}[y] \; \lor \; (con^r[y,*] \geq r \; \land \; con^r[y,g])]$ {E1}

      $\rangle$

  $\parallel$ $\langle\!\!\parallel y \;\; :: \;\; byz[y] = d^{t+1}[y]\rangle$ {E2}

  $\parallel$ {from (E3,E4,E5) of *spec3*}

      $\langle\!\!\parallel r, y, x \; : \; 0 \leq r \leq t+1 \;\; ::$

          $obs^{r+1}[y,x] = (obs^r[y,x] \; \lor \; sum^r[y,x] > t \; \lor \; val^r[y,x])$ {E3}

      $\parallel$ $val^r[y,x] = d^r[x]$ {E4}

      $\parallel$ $con^r[y,x] = (sum^r[y,x] > 2.t)$ {E5}

      $\rangle$

  $\parallel$ {from (E6,E7) of *spec4*}

      $\langle\!\!\parallel r, y, z, x \; : \; 0 \leq r \leq t+1 \;\; :: \;\; robs^r[y,z,x] = obs^r[z,x]\rangle$ {E6}

  $\parallel$ $\langle\!\!\parallel r, y, x \; : \; 0 \leq r \leq t+1 \;\; ::$

      $sum^r[y,x] = \langle+ \, z \; : \; robs^r[y,z,x] \;\; :: \;\; 1\rangle$ {E7}

      $\rangle$

end {*Byzantine-Agreement*}

The proof that the equations in the preceding program are proper follow from ordering the equations in the following sequence: (E6), (E7), (E4), (E3), (E5), (E1), and finally (E2).

The implementation of this program requires communications among processes: Equation (E4) requires message transmission from x to y, $x \neq y$, for assignment to $val^r[y, x]$, and equation (E6) requires message transmission from z to y, $z \neq y$, for assignment to $robs^r[y, z, x]$. The remaining equations each name variables of only a single process and hence can be implemented by local computations at processes. From this discussion, we can derive the total amount of message traffic in bits. Let N be the number of processes. The computation of $val^r[y, x]$ requires transmission of one bit, namely, $d^r[x]$. Hence $O(N^2.t)$ bits in all are communicated to implement computations of $val^r[y, x]$, for $0 \leq r \leq t + 1$ and all values of y and x. Similarly, $O(N^3.t)$ bits are communicated for computations of $robs^r[y, z, x]$, for $0 \leq r \leq t + 1$ and all values of y, z, x. (This argument does not take into account that unreliable processes may transmit an arbitrary number of bits among themselves.)

Next consider implementation of the program by synchronizing the computations and communications. Suppose that all variables with superscript r have been computed. Then $obs^{r+1}[y, x]$ can be computed locally at process y, for all y and x. Next, $robs^{r+1}[y, z, x]$ can be computed for all y, z, x by one synchronized round of communication. After that, $sum^{r+1}[y, x]$, $con^{r+1}[y, x]$ and $d^{r+1}[y]$ can be computed locally at process y, for all y and x. Another synchronized round of communication is then required to compute $val^{r+1}[y, x]$ from $d^{r+1}[x]$, for all y, x. Hence two rounds of communication are required to compute all variables with superscript $r+1$ from those with superscript r. Since $0 \leq r \leq t + 1$, $(2t + 2)$ rounds of synchronized communication are required for the entire algorithm. Note that synchronous communication is unnecessary as long as it can be guaranteed that every process, including unreliable ones, sends all messages required of it. (If some process in an asynchronous system stops sending messages after some point in the computation, then it is known that remaining processes cannot agree on a common value. Therefore the requirement that all processes send all messages required of them is the weakest requirement under which a solution exists in an asynchronous system.) Synchronous communication has the advantage that a single storage location can be allocated for all variables of a process that only differ in the superscript: The values of variables are computed in the increasing order of the superscript, and once a variable with a higher superscript is computed, it overwrites any old value because no previous value is required for further computation.

Summary

During the refinement of specifications, we found it convenient to eliminate operational details of computations and communications. We used predicates and substitutions of equals for equals in expressions. Later we showed a distributed implementation of the proposed solution. Our experience with this problem (and several other problems in this book) suggests that programs should be proven at a level of abstraction that is different from the implementation level.

Bibliographic Notes

The problem of Byzantine agreement was first stated in Pease, Shostak, and Lamport [1980], where it is shown that the number of reliable processes must be more than double the number of unreliable ones for the existence of a solution. The paper also gives a solution using $(t + 1)$ rounds of synchronized communication. Dolev and Strong [1982] contains a solution using authenticated broadcasts, and Dolev et al. [1982] contains a solution without authentication. Our presentation is inspired by Srikanth and Toueg [1987], though we prefer to use predicates and equations rather than processes and messages in describing our solution. The impossibility result for consensus in asynchronous systems is in Fischer, Lynch, and Paterson [1985]; the proof is presented in a more axiomatic fashion in Chandy and Misra [1985]. A survey of the literature up to mid-1983 is in Fischer [1983]. A clever algorithm for extending binary Byzantine agreement to multivalued Byzantine agreement is found in Turpin and Coan [1984].

CHAPTER 19

Sorting

19.1   Introduction

In this chapter we develop sorting programs for a variety of architectures. The goal is to demonstrate how programs are developed in UNITY rather than to design new sorting programs. Therefore only a handful of algorithms are presented; important algorithms such as Batcher's sort and Quicksort are omitted.

Section 19.2 contains a specification of the problem. Two general solution strategies are proposed in Section 19.3. In Section 19.4 simple programs (i.e., programs with simple proofs) are derived from specifications by applying the solution strategies. In that section the only concern is simplicity; concerns about efficiency and architecture are postponed. Sequential programs are derived in Section 19.5, much of which deals with the development of the heapsort. Parallel synchronous architectures are considered in Section 19.6, and parallel asynchronous architectures in Section 19.7. Distributed architectures are considered in Section 19.8.

Systematic developments of sorting programs show that programs for different architectures are related. Indeed, we shall not develop programs for asynchronous shared-memory multiprocessors or distributed architectures because programs developed for other architectures can be employed.

19.2   Specification

Given: Positive integer N and an array $X[1..N]$ of distinct integers.

Obtain: Array $y[1..N]$, where y is a permutation of X and y is in increasing order.

Formally y is specified by the following:

y is a permutation of X $\land$

$$\langle \forall\, i\ :\ 1 \leq i < N\ \ ::\ \ y[i] < y[i+1] \rangle. \tag{1}$$

19.3   General Solution Strategies

The sorting programs developed here are *in situ* sorts: Initally y is X and then y is permuted in place. We propose two general strategies.

19.3.1 Reduce the Number of Out-of-Order Pairs

The basic operation in this strategy is as follows: Permute some elements of y so that the number of pairs of elements in y that are out of order is decreased. The strategy is broad: It does not specify the number of elements that are permuted at each step, nor does it specify the order in which permutations take place. In the following, Metric M is the number of out-of-order pairs in y—i.e., it is the number of pairs of indices (i, j), where $i < j$ and $y[i] > y[j]$:

$$M = \langle +\, i, j \; : \; 0 < i < j \leq N \; \wedge \; y[i] > y[j] \; :: \; 1 \rangle.$$

The strategy is described formally by the following invariant, fixed-point condition, and progress condition.

invariant y is a permutation of X (2)

$FP \quad \equiv \quad (M = 0)$ (3)

$\langle \forall\, k \; : \; k > 0 \; :: \; M = k \; \mapsto \; M < k \rangle$ (4)

Proof of Correctness

Our proof obligation is to show from (2,3,4) that $true \mapsto FP$, and that (1) holds at any fixed point.

Proof: $true \; \mapsto \; FP$

$\qquad true \; \mapsto \; (M \leq 0) \qquad$, using induction on (4)

$\qquad M \geq 0 \qquad\qquad\qquad$, from the definition of M

$\qquad true \; \mapsto \; FP \qquad\quad$, from the above two properties and (3) $\triangledown$

Proof: (1) holds at any fixed point

$\qquad (M = 0) \; \equiv \; \langle \forall\, i \; : \; 0 < i < N \; :: \; y[i] < y[i+1] \rangle$
$\qquad\qquad$, from the definition of M

$\qquad (M = 0)$ and (2) imply (1). $\triangledown$

19.3.2 Sort Part of the Array

This strategy employs an integer variable m, where $1 \leq m \leq N$ and at any point during program execution:

1. $y[m + 1..N]$ is sorted, i.e.,

$\qquad \langle \wedge\, i, j \; : \; m < i < j \leq N \; :: \; y[i] < y[j] \rangle$, and

2. all elements in $y[1..m]$ are less than all elements in $y[m + 1..N]$, i.e.,

$\qquad \langle \wedge\, i, j \; : \; 1 \leq i \leq m < j \leq N \; :: \; y[i] < y[j] \rangle$

Putting the two conditions together gives

$$\langle \wedge\ i, j\ :\ 1 \leq i < j \leq N\ \wedge\ m < j\ ::\ y[i] < y[j] \rangle.$$

Initially $m = N$ establishes this condition. To reduce m if m exceeds 1, permute elements of $y[1..m]$ so that for some integer k, where $1 < k \leq m$, $y[k..m]$ is sorted and the elements in $y[k..m]$ are greater than the elements in $y[1..k-1]$; set $m := k - 1$.

The strategy is described formally by the following invariant, fixed-point condition, and progress condition.

invariant

y is a permutation of $X\ \ \wedge\ \ 1 \leq m \leq N\ \ \wedge$

$\langle \wedge\ i, j\ :\ 1 \leq i < j \leq N\ \wedge\ m < j\ ::\ y[i] < y[j] \rangle$ (5)

$FP\ \equiv\ m \leq 1$ (6)

$\langle \forall\ k\ :\ k > 1\ ::\ m = k\ \mapsto\ m < k \rangle$ (7)

The proof of correctness of this strategy is as follows. Our proof obligation is to show from (5,6,7) that $true\ \mapsto\ FP$, and that (1) holds at any fixed point. From (6,7), $true\ \mapsto\ FP$. From (5) and (6) it follows that (1) holds at any fixed point.

19.4   Simple Solutions

Next we develop a couple of simple solutions to give concrete examples of the solution strategies. In these programs only the assign-section is given; in all cases initially y is x, i.e.,

initially $\langle \|\ i\ :\ 1 \leq i \leq N\ ::\ y[i] = X[i] \rangle$

19.4.1 Reduce the Number of Out-of-Order Pairs

Program *P1*

  assign

    $\langle \|\ i\ :\ 1 \leq i < N\ ::$

      $y[i]\ :=\ \min(y[i], y[i+1])\ \|\ y[i+1]\ :=\ \max(y[i], y[i+1])$

    $\rangle$

end *{P1}*

Program $P1$ consists of $N-1$ statements. A statement execution exchanges adjacent elements of y if they are out of order.

It is more convenient to write program $P1$ as

Program $P1'$

   assign $\langle \| \, i \; : \; 1 \leq i < N \quad :: \quad y[i], y[i+1] := \text{sort2}(y[i], y[i+1]) \rangle$

end $\{P1'\}$

Here sort2 is a function with two integer arguments that returns two values, the first of which is the smaller of the arguments, and the second the larger.

Proof of Correctness

Our proof obligation is to show that $P1'$ satisfies (2,3,4). The proof of invariant (2) is trivial.

Proof: (3) $FP \; \equiv \; (M = 0)$

From the definition of FP, for program $P1'$,

$$
\begin{aligned}
FP \; &\equiv \; \langle \wedge \, i \; : \; 1 \leq i < N \quad :: \quad y[i], y[i+1] = \text{sort2}(y[i], y[i+1]) \rangle \\
&\equiv \; \langle \wedge \, i \; : \; 1 \leq i < N \quad :: \quad y[i] < y[i+1] \rangle \qquad \text{, from the above} \\
&\equiv \; (M = 0) \qquad\qquad\qquad\qquad\qquad\qquad \text{, from the definition of } M \quad \triangledown
\end{aligned}
$$

Proof: (4) $\langle \forall \, k \; : \; k > 0 \quad :: \quad M = k \;\mapsto\; M < k \rangle$

   The proof has two parts: Show that the metric M does not increase—and this is straightforward—and show that if the metric is positive, there exists a statement, the execution of which reduces the metric. If $M > 0$ then—from the definition of M—there exists some j, where $1 \leq j < N$ and $y[j] > y[j+1]$; we leave it to the reader to show that interchanging $y[j]$ and $y[j+1]$ reduces the metric, i.e.,

$\{M = k \,\wedge\, y[j] > y[j+1]\} \;\; y[j], y[j+1] = \text{sort2}(y[j], y[j+1]) \;\; \{M < k\}$

$M = k \,\wedge\, y[j] > y[j+1] \;\; ensures \;\; M < k$
   , from the above and the program text

$M = k \,\wedge\, \langle \exists \, j \; : \; 1 \leq j < N \quad :: \quad y[j] > y[j+1] \rangle \;\mapsto\; M < k$
   , replacing $ensures$ by $\mapsto$ and taking disjunction

$M = k \,\wedge\, k > 0 \;\Rightarrow\; \langle \exists \, j \; : \; 1 \leq j < N \quad :: \quad y[j] > y[j+1] \rangle$
   , from the definition of M

$M = k \,\wedge\, k > 0 \;\mapsto\; M < k$
   , from the above two $\triangledown$

19.4.2 Sort Part of the Array

Next we derive a program from the second strategy. Let f be a function of y and m that returns the index of the largest element in $y[1..m]$. The program interchanges the elements with indices m and $f(y, m)$, and decrements m by one.

For notational simplicity, in the following program we employ an integer variable x, where x is always $f(y, m)$.

Program *P2*

declare	x : integer	
always	$x = f(y, m)$	{hence $y[x] \geq y[i]$ for all i, $1 \leq i \leq m$}
initially	$m = N$	
assign	$y[m], y[x], m := y[x], y[m], m - 1$	if $m > 1$

end {*P2*}

The proof that the program satisfies (5,6,7) is straightforward.

19.5   Sequential Architectures

Let us map program *P1* onto a sequential machine. The obvious schedule is to execute the $N - 1$ statements repeatedly in increasing order of i. We leave it as an exercise for the reader to show that a fixed point is reached after $O(N^2)$ steps. In particular, a fixed point is reached after each of the $N - 1$ statements has been executed $N - 1$ times. (Hint: After each of the $N - 1$ statements has been executed k times, where $k \geq 0$, $y[N + 1 - k..N]$ is sorted and all elements in $y[N + 1 - k..N]$ exceed all elements in $y[1..N - k]$.)

Next let us map program *P2* onto a sequential machine. A fixed point is reached after the statement has been executed $N - 1$ times. The computation of function f requires $O(m)$ time. Hence a fixed point is reached in $O(N^2)$ time.

The obvious mappings of the simple solutions *P1* and *P2* onto sequential architectures are not very efficient. Next we derive a particularly interesting program, heapsort, from the second strategy, sort part of the array. Execution of the heapsort requires $O(N \log N)$ time on a sequential architecture. The key difference between program *P2* and the heapsort is that the maximum element of $y[1..m]$ is computed in a clever way in the heapsort. The elements $y[1..m]$ are arranged in a heap (a data structure that is described later), and

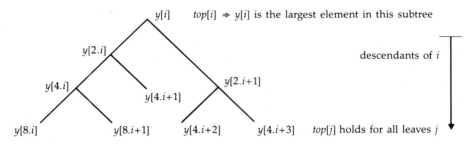

Figure 19.1 The heap data structure.

the maximum element of the heap is $y[1]$. The heapsort makes a heap of $y[1..m]$, and then interchanges $y[m]$ and $y[1]$ and decrements m by 1.

Program *skeleton-of-heapsort*

   declare m : integer

   initially $m = N$

   assign

      $y[m], y[1], m \; := \; y[1], y[m], m - 1$
            if $(y[1] = \langle \max j \; : \; 1 \le j \le m \; :: \; y[j] \rangle) \; \wedge \; (m > 1)$

   ⫿ statements to permute $y[1..m]$ so that $y[1]$ becomes
      the largest element in $y[1..m]$

end {*skeleton-of-heapsort*}

    The heap data structure is shown pictorially in Fig. 19.1. Our somewhat unconventional representation allows parallel operations to be performed on the structure. The heap is a binary tree implemented on a linear array. Every node of the tree is an array element: Sons of $y[i]$ are $y[2.i]$ and $y[2.i + 1]$. Define binary relations *son-of* and *descendant* between integers:

    j *son-of* $i \;\; \equiv \;\; (j = 2.i) \; \vee \; (j = 2.i + 1)$,

and *descendant* is the irreflexive transitive closure of *son-of*.

    A boolean array $top[1..N]$ is introduced, where $top[i]$ implies that $y[i]$ is larger than $y[j]$, where j is any descendant of i and $1 \le j \le m$, i.e.,

invariant

$$\langle \forall \, i, j \; : \; 1 \le i \le m \; \wedge \; j \le m \; \wedge \; j \; descendant \; i \; \wedge \; top[i] \; :: \; y[i] > y[j] \rangle \qquad (8)$$

Hence

$$top[1] \quad \Rightarrow \quad (y[1] = \langle \max\ j\ :\ 1 \le j \le m\ ::\ y[j] \rangle).$$

The program maintains the following "boundary conditions":

invariant $\langle \forall\ i\ :\ \frac{m}{2} < i \le N\ ::\ top[i] \rangle$ (9)

In other words, $top[i]$ holds for all leaves i of the heap as well as for the sorted portion of the array.

We assume that N is odd because it simplifies matters. In constructing the heap, the key idea is that if $top[2.i]$ and $top[2.i+1]$ hold, then $top[i]$ can be made to hold by setting $y[i]$ to the largest of $y[i], y[2.i]$ and $y[2.i+1]$.

In the following program, $\ell[i]$ denotes the index of the larger son of i; if i does not have a son, $\ell[i]$ is defined to be $2.i$.

Program {nondeterminstic heapsort} *P3*

    declare ℓ : array[1..N] of integer, top : array[1..N] of boolean

    always

        $\langle [\!]\ :\ 1 \le i \le N\ ::$

        $\ell[i] = 2.i + 1 \quad$ if $\quad (y[2.i+1]\ >\ y[2.i])\ \wedge\ (2.i+1 \le m)\ \sim$

        $\ 2.i \quad\quad$ if $\quad \neg((y[2.i+1]\ >\ y[2.i])\ \wedge\ (2.i+1 \le m))$

    $\rangle$

    initially

        $\langle [\!]\ i\ :\ 1 \le i \le N\ ::\ top[i] = (2.i > N)\ [\!]\ y[i] = X[i] \rangle$

        $[\!]\ \ m = N$

    assign

        {see first statement of skeleton program}

        $y[m],\ y[1],\ m\ :=\ y[1],\ y[m],\ m-1 \quad\quad$ if $\quad top[1]\ \wedge\ m > 1$

        $\|\ top[1],\ top[\lceil \frac{m}{2} \rceil]\ :=\ false, true \quad\quad$ if $\quad top[1]\ \wedge\ m > 2$

   $[\!]$ {order $y[\ell[i]]$ and $y[i]$ if $top[2.i]$ and $top[2.i+1]$ hold}

        $\langle [\!]\ i\ :\ 1 \le i \le \frac{N}{2}\ ::\ y[\ell[i]]\ ,\ y[i]\ ,\ top[i]\ ,\ top[\ell(i)]\ :=$

                                $\mathrm{sort2}(y[\ell(i)]\ ,\ y[i]),\ true\ ,\ (2 \times \ell(i) > m)$

        if $\quad (2.i \le m)\ \wedge\ \neg top[i]\ \wedge\ top[2.i]\ \wedge\ top[2.i+1]$

    $\rangle$

end {P3}

The first statement in the assign-section implements the first statement of the skeleton program; $y[1]$ and $y[m]$ are interchanged, and m is decremented if $y[1]$ is the largest element in $y[1..m]$. In parallel, $top[1]$ is set *false* if m

exceeds 2 (because interchanging $y[1]$ and $y[m]$ may result in $top[1]$ not being the largest element in $y[1..m-1]$). Also, in parallel $top[\lceil \frac{m}{2} \rceil]$ is set *true* to maintain invariant (9), presented before. The second set of statements builds and maintains the heap: $y[i]$ is set to the largest of $y[i]$ and the larger of its sons, and *top* is modified appropriately.

Now we sketch an outline of the proof. Our proof obligation is to show that *P3* satisfies (5,6,7). From the text of *P3*, invariants (5), (8), and (9) hold. Next we prove (7); later we prove (6).

Proof: (7) $\langle \forall k \; : \; k > 1 \; :: \; m = k \; \mapsto \; m < k \rangle$

We will show that

$$true \;\; \mapsto \;\; top[1] \tag{10}$$

$$m = k \;\; unless \;\; m < k \tag{11}$$

$$m = k \;\wedge\; k > 1 \;\wedge\; top[1] \;\; \mapsto \;\; m < k. \tag{12}$$

Then

$m = k \;\; \mapsto \;\; (m = k \;\wedge\; top[1]) \;\vee\; m < k$
     , PSP theorem on (10,11)

$m = k \;\wedge\; k > 1 \;\; \mapsto \;\; m < k$
     , from the above and (12)

This proves the required result. $\triangledown$

The proof of (11) is obtained directly from the program text; (12) is also proved directly (replace $\mapsto$ by *ensures*).

Proof: (10) $true \;\; \mapsto \;\; top[1]$

Introduce a metric d, defined as follows:

$d = \langle + \; i \; : \; top[i] \; :: $ number of nodes in the subtree rooted at $i \rangle$.

Execution of a statement that sets $top[i]$ to *true*, for any i, also increases the value of d because the size of the subtree rooted at i is larger than the size of the subtree rooted at any of its sons. Hence, from the program text, for any value D of d,

$d = D \;\; ensures \;\; top[1] \;\vee\; d > D$

The value of d is bounded from above. Hence, using induction,

$true \;\; \mapsto \;\; top[1]$ $\triangledown$

Proof: (6) $FP \;\equiv\; (m \leq 1)$

$m > 1 \;\; \mapsto \;\; m \leq 1$, from (7).

Given $p \;\mapsto\; q$, we can deduce $FP \;\Rightarrow\; (p \Rightarrow q)$ from the corollary in Section 3.6.4. Hence from $p \;\mapsto\; \neg p$ we deduce $FP \;\Rightarrow\; \neg p$. Letting p be $m > 1$ we obtain

$FP \;\Rightarrow\; m \leq 1$

$m \leq 1 \;\Rightarrow\; FP$, from the program text

Property (6) follows from the above two facts. $\qquad\qquad\qquad\qquad$ $\triangledown$

19.6   Parallel Synchronous Architectures

19.6.1 The Odd-Even Transposition Sort

A useful heuristic in deriving parallel programs is to transform programs—such as $P1'$—by gathering assignments that can be executed concurrently, into multiple-assignment statements. Which of the $N-1$ assignments in $P1'$ can be executed concurrently? It is possible to sort the pairs $(y[1], y[2])$, $(y[3], y[4])$, $(y[5], y[6]), \ldots$ concurrently, and it is also possible to sort the pairs $(y[2], y[3])$, $(y[4], y[5])$, $(y[6,], y[7]), \ldots$ concurrently. Therefore we transform $P1'$ into the following program:

Program {the odd-even transposition sort} $P4$

   assign

$$\langle \| \; i \;:\; 1 \leq i < N \;\wedge\; \text{even}(i) \;::\; y[i],\; y[i+1] \;:=\; \text{sort2}(y[i],\; y[i+1]) \rangle$$
$$[\!]\;\; \langle \| \; i \;:\; 1 \leq i < N \;\wedge\; \text{odd}(i) \;::\; y[i],\; y[i+1] \;:=\; \text{sort2}(y[i],\; y[i+1]) \rangle$$

end {$P4$}

The proof of $P4$ is the same as that of $P1'$.

    Program $P4$ consists of two statements, one of which sorts all pairs $(y[i],\; y[i+1])$, where i is odd; the other sorts all pairs $(y[i],\; y[i+1])$, where i is even. Consecutive repeated execution of a statement does not change values of variables because once a pair of elements is sorted, resorting it does not change its value. It can be shown that the program terminates within N executions of statements when no statement is executed twice in sequence. Each statement can be executed in constant time by $O(N)$ processors. Hence this sorting program can be executed in $O(N)$ time by $O(N)$ processors. The parallelism in the program is made more apparent by writing $P4$ using a variable k that counts the number of steps executed. It simplifies notation to assume that y is indexed $[0..N+1]$, with $y[0] = -\infty$, and $y[N+1] = +\infty$. In the following program, $P5$, the pairs $(y[2], y[3]), (y[4], y[5]), \ldots$ are sorted in even numbered steps (the first step is numbered 0), and the pairs $(y[1], y[2]), (y[3], y[4]), \ldots$ are sorted in odd numbered steps. Correctness of $P5$ follows in a straightforward manner from the proof of $P4$.

Program {odd-even transposition sort} *P5*

    declare k : integer

    initially $k = 0$ ▯ $y[0] = -\infty$ ▯ $y[N + 1] = \infty$

    assign

$$\langle \| \; i \; : \; 1 \leq i \leq N \;\; :: \;\; y[i] := \min(y[i], \; y[i + 1]) \quad \text{if} \quad (i = k \bmod 2) \; \sim$$
$$\max(y[i], \; y[i - 1]) \quad \text{if} \quad (i \neq k \bmod 2)$$
$$\rangle$$
$$\| \; k \; := \; k + 1 \qquad\qquad\qquad\qquad\quad\;\; \text{if} \quad k < N$$

end {*P5*}

19.6.2 The Rank Sort

Another useful heuristic in deriving parallel programs is to attempt to employ operations that are efficient on parallel architectures. In particular, operations that are associative and commutative (such as computing the sum) on sets of elements can be carried out efficiently on parallel synchronous architectures. This heuristic leads us to the following strategy. The rank of an element of X is the number of elements in X that are less or equal to it. (Recall that all elements of X are distinct.) Thus, for all k, the kth smallest element of X has rank k. The rank of an element tells us precisely where that element belongs in array y—an element with rank k occupies the kth position in y. Parallel processors can efficiently count the number of elements in an array that satisfy a certain property because counting is a special case of summing. Also, the rank of each element can be computed in parallel. The next sorting algorithm determines the rank of each element in parallel and places the element with rank k in $y[k]$. We employ a rank array r of the same dimension as X, where $r[i]$ is the rank of $X[i]$. These arguments lead to the following program.

Program {the rank sort} *P6*

    declare r : array$[1..N]$ of integer

    always

        {definition of rank array r}
$$\langle \| \; i \; : \; 1 \leq i \leq N \;\; :: \;\; r[i] = \langle + \; j \; : \; 1 \leq j \leq N \; \wedge \; X[j] \leq X[i] \;\; :: \;\; 1 \rangle \rangle$$
    ▯ {definition of sorted array y}
$$\langle \| \; i \; : \; 1 \leq i \leq N \;\; :: \;\; y[r[i]] = X[i] \rangle$$

end {*P6*}

Proof of Correctness

Proof: the equations are proper

All we need to show is that all $r[i]$s are distinct in the second equation (where $y[r[i]]$s are defined).

$$(r[j] < r[i]) \; \equiv \; (X[j] < X[i])$$
, from the definition of r $\hspace{5em}$ (13)

$$(r[j] = r[i]) \; \equiv \; (X[j] = X[i])$$
, from the above

$$(r[j] = r[i]) \; \equiv \; (j = i)$$
, from the above because the elements of X are distinct $\hspace{1em}$ (14) $\hspace{1em}\triangledown$

Proof: y is a permutation of X

$$1 \leq r[i] \leq N$$
, from the definition of r

r is a permutation of $1..N$
, from the above and (14)

y is a permutation of X
, from the above and the definition of y in $P6$ $\hspace{5em}\triangledown$

Proof: y is in increasing order

$$(y[r[j]] < y[r[i]]) \; \equiv \; (X[j] < X[i])$$
, from the definition of y in $P6$

$$(y[r[j]] < y[r[i]]) \; \equiv \; (r[j] < r[i])$$
, from the above and (13)

$$(y[j] < y[i]) \; \equiv \; (j < i)$$
, from the above

$$y[i] < y[i+1]$$
, from the above $\hspace{5em}\triangledown$

Efficiency

Consider the definition of $r[i]$. The comparison $X[j] \leq X[i]$ can be carried out for all j, in constant time by $O(N)$ processors, and hence the expression

$$\langle + \; j \; : \; 1 \leq j \leq N \; \wedge \; X[j] \leq X[i] \; :: \; 1 \rangle$$

can be evaluated in $O(\log N)$ time by $O(N)$ processors. Hence $r[i]$, for all i, can be computed in $O(\log N)$ time by $O(N^2)$ processors. The computation of y requires constant time with $O(N)$ processors. Hence the rank sort requires $O(\log N)$ time with $O(N^2)$ processors.

The rank sort is an efficient parallel sort. It is straightforward to show that the rank sort can be executed in $O(N)$ time by $O(N)$ processors because each element $r[i]$ of the rank array can be computed in $O(N)$ time by one processor, and hence the entire rank array can be computed in parallel in $O(N)$ time by $O(N)$ processors. Thus it is as good as the odd-even transposition sort when only $O(N)$ processors are available.

19.7   Parallel Asynchronous Architectures

19.7.1 The Odd-Even Transposition Sort

The odd-even transposition sort, program $P5$, can be mapped directly onto a parallel asynchronous machine because it is a single statement program (see Chapter 4). Given N processors, one element of y is assigned to each processor. Memory contention between processors is small because $y[i]$ is needed only in the computation of $y[i-1]$ and $y[i+1]$. (If there are fewer than N processors, then consecutive elements of y are assigned to a processor, thus reducing memory contention.)

19.7.2 The Rank Sort

The rank sort, program $P6$, can be mapped onto an asynchronous machine because the program is a set of equations (see Chapter 4). Given N processors, the ith processor is made responsible for computing the $r[i]^{th}$ element of y. All elements of X, the array to be sorted, are placed in each processor i, which asynchronously and independently computes $r[i]$ and then writes $y[r[i]]$. There is no memory contention.

19.8   Distributed Architectures

The odd-even transposition sort and the rank sort can be executed on distributed architectures because single-statement programs and programs consisting of equations can be executed on them (see Chapter 4).

The odd-even transposition sort ($P5$) can be executed on a distributed system consisting of N processors, each responsible for computing an element of y. The processor-interconnection structure is linear: There are channels between the processors responsible for computing $y[i]$ and $y[i+1]$. On its kth step, processor i compares values with processor $i+1$ if $i = k \bmod 2$, and with processor $i-1$ if $i \neq k \bmod 2$.

The rank sort can be implemented efficiently in distributed systems. Given N processors, each of which has the entire array X initially, the ith processor computes $r[i]$ and then sends a message containing $X[i]$ and $r[i]$ to output.

Exercise 19.1 Explore algorithms for creating a heap that is suitable for parallel synchronous computers, and evaluate the computational complexity of your solution.   ▽

Exercise 19.2 Extend the rank sort given in this chapter to apply to arrays whose elements are not necessarily distinct.   ▽

Exercise 19.3 (set partitioning) We are given a distributed system consisting of two processes u, v with a channel between them in each direction. Associated with u, v are variables su, sv, respectively, where these variables are sets of integers. Let SU, SV be the initial values of su, sv, respectively. Propose a program that reaches a fixed point and at any fixed point the following predicate holds:

$$(su \ \cup \ sv = SU \ \cup \ SV) \ \wedge$$
$$|su| = |SU| \ \wedge \ |sv| = |SV| \ \wedge$$
$$\langle \forall \ x, y \ : \ (x \ \in \ su) \ \wedge \ (y \ \in \ sv) \ :: \ x \le y \rangle.$$

Hint: It simplifies program development to ignore the distributed nature of the target architecture.   ▽

Summary

Two aspects of the development of sorting programs are worth pointing out. First, proposing a general solution strategy in the beginning does help in the development of programs for target architectures. Second, it is not necessary to consider the details of an architecture when programming; it is sufficient to write the program in a schema that maps into the target architectures. For example, the odd-even transposition sort is in the single-statement schema, and so it maps onto synchronous parallel processors, asynchronous shared-memory multiprocessors, and distributed systems.

Bibliographic Notes

An extensive treatment of various aspects of sorting, including references to original sources, can be found in Knuth [1973].

CHAPTER 20

Combinatorial
Search

20.1   Introduction

In this chapter we consider a few combinatorial search techniques, such as backtrack search, and path-finding in graphs using breadth-first and depth-first search. We give an example of dynamic programming, a technique in which an exhaustive search of a solution space is replaced by a more limited search. We do not develop the most general formulations of these search strategies; instead we introduce the ideas through suitably chosen examples.

We do not propose new algorithms, but present and prove a few important algorithms in UNITY. A goal of this chapter is to demonstrate that even sequential algorithms have succinct representations in UNITY.

20.2   Backtrack Search

Backtrack search and many of its variations (branch and bound, alpha-beta pruning) are used extensively in many areas of computer science and operations research. Here we introduce backtrack search in the context of a specific problem, the subset-sums problem.

20.2.1 Specification

Let $A[0..N-1]$, $N > 0$, be an array of positive integers, and let M be a positive integer. It is required to determine whether any subset of integers in A sum to M.

20.2.2 A Program

Any subset of elements from A can be represented by array indices of the elements; a unique representation is a sequence of increasing indices. An exhaustive search procedure for solving this problem is to generate all subsets—that is, all increasing sequences of indices—and check each one to see whether it is a solution. A systematic method for generating all such sequences is in lexicographic order. However, we can do better than an exhaustive search for this problem: Observe that for a sequence of indices seq, if the sum of the corresponding elements exceeds M, no solution includes *all* the elements whose indices are in seq. Hence we backtrack by removing the last index in seq and generating the next lexicographically larger sequence for consideration. To simplify matters, we assume that no element of A exceeds M and that A is sorted in ascending order: $A[i] \leq A[i+1]$, for all i, $0 \leq i < N-1$.

Let v be the next index under consideration that can be appended to seq, and let sum denote the sum of elements whose indices are in seq plus $A[v]$.

Index v is appended to seq provided that $sum < M$. If $sum = M$, we have found a solution. If $sum > M$, however, then neither v nor any index larger than v is eligible for appending. We backtrack by removing top(seq), the last element of seq (provided that $seq \neq null$), and we start the search for the next index to be appended to seq, from top(seq) + 1. To simplify programming, we add an artificial element, $A[N]$, where $A[N] = M$; then there is always a subset of A, namely $A[N]$, that sums to M. Therefore our problem is to determine whether there is a subset of elements of A, not including $A[N]$, that sums to M.

In the following program, when seq is nonnull, pop(seq) denotes the sequence obtained by removing the last element of seq and top(seq) denotes the last element of seq.

Program *Subset-Sum*

    declare sum, v : integer , seq : sequence of integer

    always $sum = \langle + \ i \ : \ i \ \in \ seq \ :: \ A[i]\rangle + A[v]$

    initially $seq, v = null, 0$

    assign

        seq , v :=

        $seq; v$, $v + 1$ if $sum < M$ {extend sequence by v} $\sim$

        pop(seq), top(seq) + 1   if $sum > M$ {backtrack}

end {*Subset-Sum*}

20.2.3 Proof of Correctness

We show that the program *Subset-Sum* reaches a fixed point and at any fixed point,

    $(v \neq N)$ $\equiv$ some subset of $A[0..N-1]$ sums to M.

Proof of the following invariant is left to the reader.

invariant

    ($seq; v$) is an increasing sequence of indices drawn from $0..N$ $\wedge$
    no sequence that is lexicographically smaller than ($seq; v$) is a solution

To show that the program reaches a fixed point, observe that ($seq; v$) increases lexicographically with each state change, and, from the invariant, that ($seq; v$) does not exceed $\ll N \gg$ lexicographically.

    From the program text, the fixed-point condition is

$$FP \;\equiv\; (sum = M)$$
$$\equiv\; (\langle + \, i \; : \; i \, \in \, seq \;\; :: \;\; A[i]\rangle + A[v] = M).$$

If $v \neq N$ at fixed point, then $(seq; v)$ is a solution. If $v = N$ at fixed point, then, since $A[N] = M$ and all elements of A are positive, $seq = null$. From the invariant, the problem has no solution lexicographically smaller than $(seq; v) = \ll N \gg$, which means there is no solution.

Program *Subset-Sum* is appropriate for implementation on a sequential architecture; there is relatively little parallelism in this program. Note that the sequential behavior of the program could be expressed concisely without explicitly defining the sequence of program steps.

The problem of subset-sum belongs to the notoriously difficult class of *NP*-complete problems for which polynomial algorithms are not known; in the worst case, the given program requires $O(2^N)$ steps on a sequential machine to reach a fixed point.

Exercise 20.1 The "eight-queens problem" asks for a placement of eight queens on a chessboard so that no queen captures another. Propose a backtrack search strategy to find such a placement. Observe that exactly one queen is placed in each row and in each column, and that at most one queen is placed in each diagonal. $\triangledown$

20.3   Dynamic Programming

Dynamic programming is a problem-solving technique based on the observation that solutions to many problems can be expressed as functions of solutions to their subproblems. The subproblems are of smaller sizes than the original problem and usually have the same structure as the original problem. Therefore a top-down approach to the problem solution can be employed: Start with the original problem and decompose (sub)problems successively until the resulting (sub)problems can be solved trivially; then their solutions can be used to build solutions to successively larger problems until the original problem is solved. Alternatively, a bottom-up approach can be employed, where subproblems are solved in some order (and their solutions stored), such that whenever a subproblem is to be solved all subproblems necessary for its solution have already been solved. This latter type of solution procedure is known as dynamic programming.

Dynamic programming solutions are especially easy to express in UNITY because the solution is usually expressed as a proper set of equations. We introduce dynamic programming in the context of a specific problem, optimal order of multiplication of a sequence of matrices.

20.3.1 Specification

It is required to multiply a sequence of matrices, $M_1, M_2, \ldots, M_N$, $N \geq 1$. Since matrix multiplication is associative, there are several different sequences in which N matrices may be multiplied; for instance, with $N = 3$, there are two possible multiplication sequences, $(M_1 \times M_2) \times M_3$ and $M_1 \times (M_2 \times M_3)$. We assume that multiplication of two matrices with dimensions u, v and v, w requires $u \times v \times w$ scalar operations. The number of scalar operations for different multiplication sequences may be different. It is required to find the optimal sequence of multiplication—i.e., the sequence requiring the smallest number of scalar operations, given the dimensions of all matrices to be multiplied.

20.3.2 A Solution Strategy

The brute-force approach to solving this problem requires enumeration of all possible multiplication sequences, a task that takes an exponential number of steps in N. We can do much better using the following strategy.

For $N = 1$, the solution is trivial; the number of scalar operations is 0. For $N > 1$, the last matrix multiplication is between matrices A, B, where, for some k, $1 \leq k < N$: A is the result of multiplying $M_1, \ldots, M_k$ and B is the result of multiplying $M_{k+1}, \ldots, M_N$. Let matrix M_i have $r[i-1]$ rows and $r[i]$ columns, $1 \leq i \leq N$. Then the dimensions of A are $r[0], r[k]$, and those of B are $r[k], r[N]$. Hence the total number of scalar operations in computing the entire matrix product is the number of operations in computing A plus the number of operations in computing B plus $r[0] \times r[k] \times r[N]$. Since an optimal solution is desired, the number of operations in computing each of A, B must be optimal. Furthermore, since computation of the result requires multiplication of some A, B pair (there are $N - 1$ such pairs, one for each value of k in the range $1..N - 1$), it follows that if optimal solutions to all such subproblems are known, then the optimal solution to the original problem can be deduced by taking the minimum of the preceding expression over all such A, B pairs. The same arguments can be employed in computing the optimal number of scalar multiplications for any subsequence of matrices, $M_i, \ldots, M_j$, $i < j$.

Formally, let $g[i, j]$, for all i, j, $1 \leq i \leq j \leq N$, be the minimum number of operations required to multiply $M_i, \ldots, M_j$. The dynamic programming formulation of the solution can be expressed by the following program:

Program *DP1* {sequential version}

   always

      $\langle [\![\, i \ : \ 1 \leq i \leq N \ \ :: \ \ g[i, i] = 0 \rangle$

$$\| \quad \langle \| \ i,j \ : \ 1 \le i < j \le N \quad ::$$
$$\quad g[i,j] =$$
$$\quad\quad \langle \min \ k \ : \ i \le k < j \quad :: \quad g[i,k] + g[k+1,j] + r[i-1] \times r[k] \times r[j] \rangle$$
$$\rangle$$

end {*DP1*}

The set of equations in *DP1* is proper. In fact, all (discrete, finite-horizon) dynamic programming solutions can be expressed as proper sets of equations. The computation of the right-hand side for each $g[i,j]$ takes $O(N)$ steps on a sequential machine. Hence the running time of this program is $O(N^3)$ on a sequential machine.

20.3.3 Parallel Synchronous Architectures

We now propose a strategy for reducing the execution time of the preceding program using more processors. We apply a standard heuristic: In one equation, define all $g[i,j]$s that can be computed simultaneously. In program *DP1*, computation of $g[u,v]$ needs the value of $g[x,y]$ only if $(v - u) > (y - x)$. Hence we define $g[u,v]$, $g[x,y]$ in one equation if $v - u = y - x$, i.e., for any t, $g[i, i + t]$, for all i, are defined in one equation.

Program *DP2*   {**parallel version**}

  always

$$\quad \langle \| \ i \ : \ 1 \le i \le N \quad :: \quad g[i,i] = 0 \rangle$$

$$\| \quad \langle \| \ t \ : \ 1 \le t < N \quad :: \quad \{\text{define } g[i, i+t], \text{ for all } i\}$$
$$\quad\quad \langle \| \ i,j \ : \ 1 \le i \ \wedge \ j = i+t \ \wedge \ j \le N \quad ::$$
$$\quad\quad g[i,j] =$$
$$\quad\quad\quad \langle \min \ k \ : \ i \le k < j \quad :: \quad g[i,k] + g[k+1,j] + r[i-1] \times r[k] \times r[j] \rangle$$
$$\quad\quad \rangle$$
$$\rangle$$

end {*DP2*}

For each value of t, at most $O(N)$ variables are defined in an equation in *DP2*; the computation of each variable requires taking the minimum over $O(N)$ elements. Hence computation for each equation takes $O(\log N)$ time using $O(N^2)$ processors. Since there are $O(N)$ equations in the whole program, $O(N \log N)$ time is required with $O(N^2)$ processors. We leave it to the reader to observe that program *DP2* can be executed in $O(N^2)$ time by $O(N)$ processors.

Exercise 20.2 Using superposition, transform program *DP2* so that the optimal sequence of multiplications (not just the number of scalar operations in the optimal multiplication sequence) can be determined. ▽

20.4 Search Strategies in Graphs

In this section, we consider two classical algorithms—breadth-first search and depth-first search—for finding a path, if one exists, between designated vertices of a directed graph. We also give an algorithm for finding the shortest paths from a given vertex to all other vertices in a directed graph whose edges have positive weight; this algorithm is a generalization of breadth-first search.

20.4.1 Breadth-first Search

Let the vertices of a given directed graph be numbered 0 through N, $N \geq 0$. The connectivity matrix is E—i.e., $E[u, v]$ is *true* if and only if there is an edge from vertex u to vertex v. Define *distance* of a vertex u, $dist(u)$, to be the minimum number of edges on any path from 0 to u, if a path exists; if no path exists from 0 to u, the distance of u is ∞. Clearly $dist(0) = 0$. It is required to find distances of all vertices. We show how to compute all the distances using breadth-first search.

The idea behind breadth-first search is that any vertex at distance $(k + 1)$, $k \geq 0$, has a predecessor at distance k. Hence, given all vertices with distances k or less, all vertices with distances $(k + 1)$ or less can be identified: Each vertex in the latter set, other than vertex 0, is a direct successor of some vertex in the former set.

In the following program, the value of $d[v]$ at fixed point is the distance of vertex v. Variable k denotes the number of steps executed in the program.

Program {breadth-first search} *BFS*

declare

    k : integer,

    d : array$[0..N]$ of integer

initially

    $k = 0 \ \parallel \ d[0] = 0$

  $\parallel \ \langle \parallel v \ : \ 0 < v \leq N \ :: \ d[v] = \infty \rangle$

assign

$\langle \| \ v \ : \ 0 < v \leq N \quad :: $

$\qquad d[v] \ := \ \min(d[v], k+1)$

$\qquad\qquad \text{if} \quad \langle \exists \ u \ : \ 0 \leq u \leq N \quad \wedge \quad E[u,v] \quad :: \quad d[u] = k\rangle$

$\rangle$

$\quad \| \ k \ := \ k + 1 \qquad \text{if} \quad k < N$

end $\{BFS\}$

Proof of Correctness of BFS

We have, for program BFS,

invariant

$[0 \leq k \leq N] \quad \wedge$

$[dist(v) \leq k \quad \Rightarrow \quad d[v] = dist(v)] \quad \wedge$

$[dist(v) > k \quad \Rightarrow \quad d[v] = \infty]$

The proof of the invariant is left to the reader.

It is easily seen from the program text and the invariant that at any fixed point, $k = N$. From graph theory,

there exists a path to $v \ \equiv \ dist(v) \leq N$.

Hence, from the invariant and the fixed-point condition, $d[v] = dist(v)$ at any fixed point.

Execution of program BFS may take as long as $O(N^3)$ time on one processor and $O(N \log N)$ time on $O(N^2)$ processors. To see the latter claim, observe that each statement execution assigns to $O(N)$ variables and each assignment to a variable requires computing a set of $O(N)$ boolean terms and then taking their disjunction. Therefore each statement execution can be completed in $O(\log N)$ steps on $O(N^2)$ processors. There are N statement executions. The program BFS is inefficient because with one processor it is possible to complete a breadth-first search in $O(N^2)$ time; next we develop such a program. (See Chapter 5 for other shortest-path algorithms.)

20.4.2 Single-Source Shortest Path

A generalization of breadth-first search can be employed for computing shortest paths from a single vertex (vertex 0) to all other vertices in a directed graph, where each edge (x, y) has a positive length $\ell(x, y)$. Assume that $\ell(x, y) = \infty$ if edge (x, y) does not exist and that $\ell(x, x) = \infty$, for all x. The length of a path is the sum of lengths of edges on the path, and the distance of a vertex, $dist(v)$ for vertex v, is the minimum length of any path to that vertex from vertex 0 and $dist(0) = 0$. If all edge lengths are 1, then the problem is the same as in Section 20.4.1. We describe an elegant algorithm whose performance for this general problem is superior to that of *BFS*; it requires $O(N^2)$ steps with one processor, or $O(N \log N)$ steps with $O(N)$ processors.

The idea behind the algorithm is to divide the set of vertices into two sets, *known* and *unknown*, with the following property:

> The distance of any vertex in *known* is less than or equal to that of any vertex in *unknown*.

To increase the size of *known*, some vertex u has to be moved from *unknown* to *known*. In order to meet the preceding constraint, vertex u must satisfy the following:

$$\langle \forall\, v : v \in unknown \quad :: \quad dist(u) \leq dist(v) \rangle. \tag{1}$$

Since $dist(v)$ for $v \in unknown$ may not be readily available, we express (1) differently. We observe that, for any y, $y \neq 0$,

$$
\begin{aligned}
dist(y) &= \langle \min\ x \quad :: \quad dist(x) + \ell[x, y] \rangle \\
&= \min(\langle \min\ x : x \in known \quad :: \quad dist(x) + \ell[x, y] \rangle, \\
&\qquad\quad \langle \min\ x : x \in unknown \quad :: \quad dist(x) + \ell[x, y] \rangle)
\end{aligned} \tag{2}
$$

$$
\begin{aligned}
dist(u) &= \langle \min\ x : x \in known \quad :: \quad dist(x) + \ell(x, u) \rangle \\
&\quad , \text{from (1) and } \ell(x, u) > 0 \text{ provided} \\
&\quad known \text{ is nonempty}
\end{aligned} \tag{3}
$$

Define $d[0] = 0$, and for any y, $y \neq 0$,

$$d[y] = \langle \min\ x : x \in known \quad :: \quad dist(x) + \ell[x, y] \rangle \tag{4}$$

Then

$$
\begin{aligned}
dist(u) &= d[u] \qquad\quad \text{, from (3,4)} \\
dist(v) &\leq d[v] \qquad\quad \text{, from (2,4)}
\end{aligned}
$$

Hence

$$\langle \forall\, v : v \in unknown \quad :: \quad d[u] \leq d[v] \rangle \tag{5}$$

Using (5), we can identify u and then move it to *known*; also $dist(u) = d[u]$ is then trivially computed. For any $v \in unknown$, $d[v]$ is recomputed to maintain (4) (after u is moved to *known*) by setting it to the minimum of $d[v]$ and $d[u] + \ell[u, v]$.

In the following program, *unknown* is a boolean array where $unknown[v]$ means that v is in *unknown*. Variable u in the program satisfies (1) and du denotes $d[u]$. We define the pair (du, u) in the always-section as the lexicographic minimum (lexmin) of the pairs $(d[v], v)$, over all v in *unknown*. To guarantee that these variables are always defined, i.e., *unknown* is never *empty*, we introduce a vertex, numbered N, which remains in *unknown* forever. Vertex N is not connected to any other vertex, i.e., $dist(N) = \infty$; hence (∞, N) is the largest possible value of the pair (du, u). Also, to guarantee that *known* is nonempty, vertex 0 is initially in *known*.

Program *single-source-shortest-path*

declare

du, u : integer,

$unknown$: array$[0..N]$ of boolean,

d : array$[0..N]$ of integer

always $(du, u) = \langle \text{lexmin } v \ : \ 0 \leq v \leq N \ \wedge \ unknown[v] \ :: \ (d[v], v) \rangle$

initially

$d[0] = 0$

$\| \ \langle \| \ v \ : \ 0 < v \leq N \ :: \ d[v] = \ell[0, v] \rangle$

$\| \ \langle \| \ v \ : \ 0 \leq v \leq N \ :: \ unknown[v] = (v \neq 0) \ \| \ \ell[v, N] = \infty \rangle$

assign

$\langle \| \ v \ : \ 0 < v < N \ \wedge \ unknown[v] \ :: \ d[v] \ := \ \min(d[v], du + \ell[u, v]) \rangle$

$\| \ unknown[u] \ := \ (u = N)$

end {*single-source-shortest-path*}

Proof of Correctness of *Single-Source-Shortest-Path*

We leave the proof of the following invariant to the reader.

invariant

$unknown[N] \ \wedge \ unknown[u] \ \wedge \ d[N] = \infty$ $\qquad\qquad\qquad \wedge$

$dist(u) = du = d[u]$ $\qquad\qquad\qquad\qquad\qquad\qquad\qquad\quad \wedge$

$\langle \forall \ v \ : \ 0 \leq v < N \ \wedge \ \neg unknown[v] \ :: \ d[v] = dist(v) \leq du \rangle \ \wedge$

$\langle \forall \ v \ : \ 0 \leq v < N \ \wedge \ \ \ unknown[v] \ :: \ du \leq dist(v)$ $\qquad\quad \wedge$

$\qquad d[v] = \langle \min \ x \ : \ 0 \leq x < N \ \ \wedge \ \ \neg unknown[x] \ :: \ d[x] + \ell[x, v] \rangle$

$\rangle$

From the program text and the invariant, at any fixed point, $unknown[u] = (u = N)$. Hence, at any fixed point,

$u = N$

, from the invariant $unknown[u]$ holds

$du = \infty$

, from the invariant $du = d[N] = \infty$

$unknown[v] \ \Rightarrow \ (\infty, N) \leq (d[v], v)$

, from the definition of (du, u)

$\langle \forall\, v\ :\ 0 \leq v < N\quad ::\quad \neg unknown[v] \rangle$
   , from the above

$\langle \forall\, v\ :\ 0 \leq v < N\quad ::\quad d[v] = dist(v) \rangle$
   , from the invariant.

A fixed point is reached because the metric, the number of $unknown[v]$s that are *true*, decreases with each state change. This also shows that the number of state changes is at most N.

This program can be executed in $O(N^2)$ steps on a sequential machine because each statement execution and computation of (du, u) takes $O(N)$ steps and there are at most N effective statement executions. Similar arguments can be employed to show that $O(N)$ synchronous processors can complete execution of this program in $O(N \log N)$ steps.

Exercise 20.3 Compute all-points shortest paths by applying the *single-source-shortest-path* program N times, each time starting at a different source vertex. Show how these N computations can proceed asynchronously. Can you use the results of one computation in another computation?   ▽

20.4.3 Depth-first Search

Consider the problem of finding a path from a specific vertex, say vertex 0, to another vertex, *dest*, in a directed graph. Depth-first search attempts to build a path by adding one edge at a time to a partially constructed path. Initially the path contains only vertex 0. The current path is extended using an edge from u, the last vertex on the path, to some vertex outside the path. If $u \neq dest$ and no such edge exists, it can be asserted that there is a path from 0 to *dest* if and only if there is a path from 0 to *dest* avoiding u. Therefore u is removed from the path and is never considered again. The algorithm is one of backtrack search, and hence has the same structure as program *Subset-Sum* (Section 20.2). The only difference is that a vertex once removed from the path is never added to the path again.

Let the vertices in the graph be numbered $0..N-1$, and let $E[u, v]$ be *true* if and only if there is a directed edge from u to v; we assume that $E[u, u]$ is *false* for all u. We find it convenient to have for each vertex a successor that is permanently outside the path. To this end, we introduce a vertex N such that every vertex has an outgoing edge to N. We use an array p with the following meaning; for any vertex x, $0 \leq x \leq N$,

$(p[x] < 0\ \Rightarrow\ x$ has never been added to the path) $\wedge$

$(0 \leq p[x] < N\ \Rightarrow\ x$ is on the path and
         if $x \neq 0$, $p[x]$ is x's predecessor on the path) $\wedge$

$(p[x] \geq N\ \Rightarrow\ x$ has been removed from the path).

In the following program, u is the last vertex on the path and v is a successor of u that has never been added to the path; such a successor always exists because of vertex N.

Program *DFS*

  declare

        u, v : integer,

        p : array$[0..N]$ of integer

  always $v = \langle \min\ j\ :\ 0 \le j \le N\ \wedge\ E[u, j]\ \wedge\ p[j] < 0\ ::\ j \rangle$

  initially

      {vertex N is a successor of all other vertices}

      $\langle \| \ j\ :\ 0 \le j < N\ ::\ E[j, N] = \textit{true} \rangle$

      $\| \ u = 0 \ \| \ p[0] = 1$ {for $N > 1$ vertex 0 is on the path}

      $\| \ \langle \| \ j\ :\ 0 < j \le N\ ::\ p[j] = -1 \rangle$ {no other vertex is on the path}

  assign

      $u, p[v] = v, u$ if $v \ne N\ \wedge\ u \ne \textit{dest}$ {extend path}

      $\| \ u, p[u] = p[u], N$ if $v = N\ \wedge\ u \ne 0\ \wedge\ u \ne \textit{dest}$ {backtrack}

end {*DFS*}

Proof of Correctness of *DFS*

We show that there is a path from 0 to *dest* if and only if $u = \textit{dest}$ at fixed point of *DFS*. The reader should show that the following invariant is satisfied by program *DFS*:

invariant

      $0 \le u < N\ \ \wedge\ \ p[u] \ne u$ $\wedge$

      there is a simple path from 0 to u in which the predecessor of any vertex x on the path, $x \ne 0$, is $p[x]$, and $p[x] < N$ $\wedge$

      $0 \le p[x] < N\ \ \Rightarrow\ \ x$ is on the path $\wedge$

      there is a path from 0 to *dest* if and only if there is a path from 0 to *dest* in which for every vertex x, $p[x] < N$.

The meanings of the first three conjuncts should be obvious. The last conjunct states that a path from 0 to *dest* exists only if a path can be constructed out of vertices that are on the current path or that have never been added to the path. This conjunct allows us to ignore all vertices that have been removed from the path.

The fixed-point condition for program DFS is

$FP \equiv$

$\quad (v = N \ \vee \ u = dest \ \vee \ (u = v \ \wedge \ p[v] = u)) \ \wedge$

$\quad (v \neq N \ \vee \ u = 0 \ \vee \ u = dest \ \vee \ (u = p[u] \ \wedge \ p[u] = N)).$

Since $p[u] \neq u$, from the invariant, we have at any fixed point

$\quad (v = N \ \vee \ u = dest) \ \wedge \ (v \neq N \ \vee \ u = 0 \ \vee \ u = dest)$

$\equiv \ u = dest \ \vee \ (v = N \ \wedge \ u = 0).$

If $u = dest$ then, from the invariant, there is a path from 0 to $dest$. If $u \neq dest$, then $v = N \ \wedge \ u = 0$. From the definition of v in the always-section, no successor w of 0, $w < N$, has $p[w] < 0$. Since the current path includes 0 as the only vertex, all successors w of 0 have $p[w] \geq N$. Therefore, from the last conjunct in the invariant, there is no path from 0 to $dest$.

To show that a fixed point is reached, we show that the following metric decreases with each state change: $m - n$, where

$\quad m =$ number of vertices w for which $p[w] < 0$

$\quad n =$ number of vertices w for which $p[w] \geq N$.

Extending the path decreases m while keeping n unchanged; backtracking increases n and keeps m unchanged. Since $-N \leq m - n \leq N$, the number of state changes is $O(N)$. Computation of v can be performed in $O(N)$ time on one processor, or in $O(\log N)$ time on $O(N)$ processors. Therefore the total execution time is $O(N^2)$ on one processor or $O(N \log N)$ on $O(N)$ processors. More efficient algorithms are obtained by using linked lists instead of the matrix E to represent the graph; computation time on a sequential machine can then be made proportional to the number of edges in the graph.

Summary

A few combinatorial search techniques have been described in this chapter. We have shown how to represent traditional sequential algorithms for these problems in UNITY.

Bibliographic Notes

References for the algorithms given in this chapter can be found in Aho, Hopcroft, and Ullman [1983]. An extensive treatment of data structures employed for network algorithms is found in Tarjan [1983].

CHAPTER 21

Systolic Arrays
as Programs

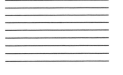

21.1   Introduction

A systolic algorithm is a special kind of parallel synchronous program. A systolic algorithm is designed to be executed on a systolic array—a collection of synchronous processors connected in a regular pattern. A computation step consists of each processor reading data from its input lines, performing some computation, and writing new data values into the output lines. This form of computation can be represented by a multiple assignment statement in UNITY: Each line is represented by a variable; the value assigned to (the variable corresponding to) an output line of a processor is a function of the values of input lines of the processor; synchrony in a systolic computation is represented by synchronous assignments. It is convenient to derive programs in equational schemas and then transform them to multiple assignment statements.

In this chapter we study two matrix problems—matrix multiplication and *L-U* decomposition—and a sorting program. The matrix problems provide interesting variations in solutions when the number of processors or the topology of the processor interconnection is altered. For instance, matrix multiplication is easily solved when any piece of data can be accessed by an arbitrary number of processors in a step (see Section 21.2). Restricting data access to one processor per data item in each step, as appropriate for pipelined and systolic networks, leads to entirely new algorithms, given in Section 21.3. An *L-U* decomposition algorithm, inspired by the systolic algorithms of Section 21.3, is given in Section 21.4. Several sorting programs were given in Chapter 19; in Section 21.5, we propose a systolic sorting program that is appropriate for bubble-memory architectures.

21.2   Matrix Multiplication: An Introduction

Let $A[0..M-1, 0..N-1]$ and $B[0..N-1, 0..R-1]$ be two matrices of numbers. It is required to compute their product $C[0..M-1, 0..R-1]$, where element $C[i, k]$ is given by

$$C[i, k] = \langle + j : 0 \le j < N :: A[i, j] \times B[j, k] \rangle.$$

This definition leads to an equational schema program:

Program {matrix multiplication} *P1*

   $\{i, j, k$ are quantified: $0 \le i < M, \ 0 \le j < N, \ 0 \le k < R\}$

always

$$\langle \| \ i, k \ :: \ C[i,k] = \langle + \ j \ :: \ A[i,j] \times B[j,k] \rangle \rangle$$

end $\{P1\}$

Program $P1$ can be executed in $O(M \times N \times R)$ time on one processor or in $O(\log N)$ time on $O(M \times N \times R)$ processors, where N processors may be employed for computing each $C[i,k]$. With fewer processors, say $O(M \times R)$, one processor may be assigned to compute one $C[i,k]$, and hence the execution time is $O(N)$.

21.3   Data Pipelining in Matrix Multiplication

Program $P1$ can be implemented efficiently on parallel processors, provided that each element of A and of B can be accessed by an arbitrary number of processors in a step. The requirement for simultaneous data access is manifested in the form of equations in $P1$: $A[i,j]$ appears in M expressions in the right sides of equations of program $P1$, and hence M different processors may require access to this data value in a step. The purpose of this section is to show how this access requirement can be relaxed. Ultimately we will require that a data item be accessed by at most one processor in a step—i.e., a variable may appear at most once in the right side of any statement. This constraint is appropriate for pipelined and systolic architectures in which a processor has connections to a small number of neighbors with whom it can communicate data values.

Define $d[j,i,k]$, for all i, j, k, $0 \le i < M$, $0 \le j \le N$, and $0 \le k < R$, to be the sum of the first j terms in the expression for $C[i,k]$—i.e.,

$$d[j,i,k] = \langle + \ r \ : \ 0 \le r < j \ :: \ A[i,r] \times B[r,k] \rangle.$$

A program for matrix multiplication, using d, is given next. The correctness of this program follows from the definition of $d[j,i,k]$.

Program $P2$

$\{i,j,k \text{ are quantified: } \ 0 \le i < M, \ 0 \le j < N, \ 0 \le k < R\}$

always

$$\langle \| \ i,k \ :: \ d[0,i,k] = 0 \rangle$$
$$\| \ \langle \| \ j \ :: \ \langle \| \ i,k \ :: \ d[j+1,i,k] = d[j,i,k] + A[i,j] \times B[j,k] \rangle \rangle$$
$$\| \ \langle \| \ i,k \ :: \ C[i,k] = d[N,i,k] \rangle$$

end $\{P2\}$

Each $A[i,j]$ appears in the right-side of assignment to $d[j+1,i,k]$, for all k (similarly for $B[j,k]$). Therefore a synchronous computation in which one processor is assigned to compute $d[j,i,k]$, for every i,k, has the same problem of data access as previously.

One way to overcome the data-access problem is to replace $\parallel$ by $[\!]$ in an equational schema program. Converting an equation in this manner does not affect correctness of the program. Programs obtained this way are better suited for asynchronous architectures. We apply this strategy to *P2* to obtain a program suitable for asynchronous execution. Then we recombine the equations (in a different manner) to obtain a program suitable for synchronous execution that also meets the data-access constraint.

21.3.1 Asynchronous Architectures

We postulate that $d[j,i,k]$ be computed at a processor indexed (j,k), for all values of i. (Other choices of a processor index are possible: We have already considered (i,k), and index (i,j) leads to a program symmetric to the one we develop.) To emphasize the processor index (j,k) we rename the variables used by this processor as follows; in the renaming, the first two indices are the processor index. For all i,j,k,

$$V[j,k,i] = d[j,i,k]$$
$$H[j,k,i] = A[i,j] \ .$$

Then the equation

$$d[j+1,i,k] = d[j,i,k] + A[i,j] \times B[j,k]$$

can be rewritten

$$V[j+1,k,i] = V[j,k,i] + H[j,k,i] \times B[j,k] \ .$$

Also, we have, for all i,j,k ::

$$H[j,k+1,i] \ \ \{= A[i,j]\} = H[j,k,i] \ .$$

We rewrite program *P2* using these equations.

Program {asynchronous matrix multiplication} *P3*

  declare

   V : array$[0..N, 0..R-1, 0..M-1]$ of integer,
   H : array$[0..N-1, 0..R, 0..M-1]$ of integer

  always

   $\{i,j,k$ are quantified, $0 \le i < M, \ 0 \le j < N, 0 \le k < R\}$
   $\langle [\!] \ i,k \ :: \ V[0,k,i] = 0 \rangle$

⟦ ⟨⟦ i, j :: $H[j, 0, i] = A[i, j]$⟩

⟦ ⟨⟦ i, j, k ::

$V[j + 1, k, i] = V[j, k, i] + H[j, k, i] \times B[j, k]$

‖ $H[j, k + 1, i] = H[j, k, i]$

⟩

⟦ ⟨⟦ i, k :: $C[i, k] = V[N, k, i]$⟩

end {P3}

Program P3 can be implemented on a grid of $N \times R$ asynchronous processors. The data item $B[j, k]$ is local to processor (j, k). At the beginning of its ith step, processor (j, k) has $V[j, k, i]$, $H[j, k, i]$, and $B[j, k]$; in the ith step, it computes $V[j, k, i] + H[j, k, i] \times B[j, k]$ and assigns it to $V[j + 1, k, i]$, and it also assigns $H[j, k, i]$ to $H[j, k + 1, i]$. The data flow from processor (j, k) to its neighboring processors is shown in Fig. 21.1.

In program P3, $V[0, k, i] = 0$, and hence the $(0, k)^{th}$ processor (a processor on the topmost row) receives a stream of M zeros, one for each i, $0 \le i < M$. Similarly, $H[j, 0, k] = A[i, j]$, for all i, j, and hence the $(j, 0)^{th}$ processor (a processor in the leftmost column) receives $A[i, j]$ at the beginning of its ith step. Processor (j, k) may discard $V[j, k, i]$, $H[j, k, i]$ upon completion of its ith

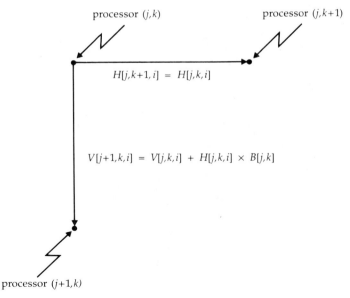

Figure 21.1 Data flow in horizontal and vertical directions for matrix multiplication on a grid of processors.

step since these are never needed in a later step. The product matrix elements, $C[i, k]$s, are available from the $(N, k)^{th}$ processors, those on the bottommost row. We leave implementations of program *P3* on distributed architectures to the reader; this implementation is straightforward because the program is in equational schema.

21.3.2 Synchronous Architectures

Next we combine equations of program *P3* into equations more suitable for parallel synchronous execution. To ensure that the resulting set of equations is proper, we employ the following strategy. Associate an integer value with each variable such that variables on the left side of any assignment have higher associated values than those on the right. Then all variables with the same associated value can be defined in one equation; it is easily seen that the resulting equations are proper. Let $t(j, k, i)$ be the value associated with $V[j, k, i]$ and $H[j, k, i]$ (we associate the same value with both because they appear together in the right sides of equations). Intuitively, $t(j, k, i)$ is the (synchronous) step number at which $V[j, k, i]$ and $H[j, k, i]$ are to be computed.

$$t(j + 1, k, i) > t(j, k, i) \quad \text{, from defining equation for } V[j + 1, k, i]$$
$$t(j, k + 1, i) > t(j, k, i) \quad \text{, from defining equation for } H[j, k + 1, i]$$

We postulate, as in the asynchronous implementation, that $V[j, k, i + 1]$ is computed after $V[j, k, i]$ (at processor (j, k)). Hence

$$t(j, k, i + 1) > t(j, k, i).$$

We choose $t(i, j, k) = i + j + k$, which satisfies these inequalities. Arbitrary negative t-values are associated with all $A[i, j]$s and $B[j, k]$s, and $C[i, k]$ has the associated value $N + i + k + 1$. In the following program, all variables with the same associated value, t, are defined in one equation. Note that the maximum value associated with any variable is $M + N + R - 1$ (for $C[M - 1, R - 1]$) and hence t takes on values from 0 to $M + N + R - 1$.

Program *P4*

$\{i, j, k \text{ are quantified:} \quad 0 \leq i < M, \ 0 \leq j < N, \ 0 \leq k < R\}$

always

$\langle \| \ t \ : \ 0 \leq t < M + N + R \ :: $

$\quad \langle \| \ i, k \ : \ t = i + k \ :: \ V[0, k, i] = 0 \rangle$

$\quad \| \ \langle \| \ i, j \ : \ t = i + j \ :: \ H[j, 0, i] = A[i, j] \rangle$

$\quad \| \ \langle \| \ i, j, k \ : \ t = i + j + k + 1 \ :: $

$\qquad V[j + 1, k, i], H[j, k + 1, i] = V[j, k, i] + H[j, k, i] \times B[j, k], \ H[j, k, i]$

$\rangle$

$$\| \ \langle\| \ i, k \ : \ t = N + i + k + 1 \ \ :: \ \ C[i, k] = V[N, k, i]\rangle$$
$$\rangle$$

end {*P4*}

Program *P4* has $M + N + R$ equations, one equation for each value of t in the range $0 \leq t < M + N + R$. It may be helpful to imagine that the tth equation, $0 \leq t < M + N + R$, is satisfied in the tth step by a parallel synchronous architecture, each of whose processors satisfy appropriate parts of the tth equation. However, program *P4* is better understood purely as a set of equations. The operational behavior of processors in a synchronous architecture is better captured in program *P5*, given next. Program *P5*, a "dual" of *P4*, is structured around processors; it describes what each processor does at the tth step. We use variables $V[j, k], H[j, k]$, local to processor (j, k), whose i^{th} values are the same as $V[j, k, i], H[j, k, i]$, respectively, of program *P4*.

Program *P5*

    declare t : integer

    initially $t = 0$

    assign

      $\{i, j, k$ are quantified: $0 \leq i < M, \ 0 \leq j < N, \ 0 \leq k < R\}$

      $\langle\| \ i, k \ : \ t = i + k \ \ :: \ \ V[0, k] \ := \ 0\rangle$

    $\| \ \langle\| \ i, j \ : \ t = i + j \ \ :: \ \ H[j, 0] \ := \ A[i, j]\rangle$

    $\| \ \langle\| \ i, j, k \ : \ t = i + j + k + 1 \ \ ::$

          $V[j + 1, k], \ H[j, k + 1] \ := \ V[j, k] + H[j, k] \times B[j, k], \ H[j, k]$

      $\rangle$

    $\| \ \langle\| \ i, k \ : \ t = N + i + k + 1 \ \ :: \ \ C[i, k] \ := \ V[N, k]\rangle$

    $\| \ \ \ \ t \ := \ t + 1 \ \ \text{if} \ \ t < M + N + R$

end {*P5*}

Exercise 21.1   Show that program *P5* reaches a fixed point.   ▽

Program *P5* can be executed in $O(M + N + R)$ time on $O(M \times R)$ parallel synchronous processors (see Fig. 21.1). It also meets the limited data access constraint: A variable with index (j, k) is read by processor (j, k) only. In Fig. 21.1, data is pipelined in both horizontal and vertical directions.

The transformation of program *P4* to *P5* is almost mechanical. Henceforth, we will not show this transformation; we will stop at a program written in equational schema, as in *P4*.

21.3.3 Pipelining All Three Matrices

Programs $P4$ and $P5$ pipeline matrices A and C, whereas elements of matrix B remain fixed at specific processors. We investigate the possibility of pipelining all three matrices in this section. One advantage of such a scheme is that data are not loaded into processors initially, and hence the same network of processors can be used to form a sequence of matrix products without interruptions for initializations.

As in program $P2$, variables $A[i,j]$, $B[j,k]$ are to be multiplied and added to $d[j,i,k]$. Suppose that this multiplication is carried out by some processor (u,v) at a step w; u,v,w are yet to be determined. We introduce local variables $x[u,v,w], y[u,v,w], z[u,v,w]$ of processor (u,v), which have the following relationships to A, B, d:

$$x[u,v,w] = A[i,j]$$
$$y[u,v,w] = B[j,k]$$
$$z[u,v,w] = d[j,i,k].$$

Instead of pipelining rows or columns, as in $P4$ and $P5$, we pipeline diagonal elements of A, B. Since elements $A[i,j]$, $B[j,k]$ are in the $(i-j)^{th}$ and $(j-k)^{th}$ diagonals of the respective matrices, we propose that

$$u = i - j, \; v = j - k \; .$$

Step w is taken from program $P4$ to be $i+j+k$. Now we write a proper set of equations defining elements of x, y, z. In the following discussion i, j, k are quantified $0 \le i < M$, $0 \le j < N$, $0 \le k < R$.

Consider any i, j, and $w = i + j + k = 0$. Then $k = -(i+j)$. Hence $(u,v,w) = (i-j, i+2.j, 0)$. Also $x[u,v,w] = A[i,j]$. Hence

$$x[i-j, i+2.j, 0] = A[i,j].$$

By similar reasoning, for any j, k,

$$y[-2.j - k, \; j - k, \; 0] = B[j,k].$$

For any i, k, and $w = i + j + k = 0$, we have

$$(u,v,w) = (2.i + k, -i - 2.k, 0)$$

and

$$z[u,v,w] = d[j,i,k] = 0$$

because $j \le 0$, given $i + j + k = 0$, $i \ge 0$, and $k \ge 0$.

Hence

$$z[2.i + k, \; -i - 2.k, \; 0] = 0.$$

These equations establish the values of some elements of x, y, z when the last index is 0. Next we obtain some equations for elements with a nonzero last index.

Since

$$A[i,j] = x[u,v,w] \text{ and } A[i,j] = x[u,v-1,w+1],$$

we have

$$x[u,v-1,w+1] = x[u,v,w].$$

Similarly,

$$y[u+1,v,w+1] \ \{= B[j,k]\} = y[u,v,w]$$

and

$$z[u-1,v+1,w+1] \ \{= d[j+1,i,k] = d[j,i,k] + A[i,j] \times B[j,k]\}$$
$$= z[u,v,w] + x[u,v,w] \times y[u,v,w].$$

Also,

$$C[i,k] \ \{= d[N,i,k]\} = z[i-N, N-k, i+k+N].$$

These equations are proper because the w-index for variable on the left side of any equation is higher than those on the right (assume that $C[i,k]$ has a w-index of $i+k+N+1$). Program $P6$, given next, is derived from these equations. The flow of data in a processor network implementing $P6$ is shown in Fig. 21.2.

Program {pipelining all three matrices} $P6$

$\quad$ {declarations of arrays x, y, z is left to Exercise 21.3}

$\quad$ {i, j, k are quantified: $\ \ 0 \le i < M, \ 0 \le j < N, \ 0 \le k < R$}

$\quad$ **always**

$$\langle \| \ i,j \ \ :: \ \ x[i-j, i+2.j, \ 0] = A[i,j]\rangle$$
$$\| \ \langle \| \ j,k \ \ :: \ \ y[-2.j-k, j-k, 0] = B[j,k]\rangle$$
$$\| \ \langle \| \ i,k \ \ :: \ \ z[2.i+k, \ -i-2.k, \ 0] = 0\rangle$$

$$\llbracket \ \ \langle \llbracket \ w \ : \ 0 \le w < M+N+R-1 \ \ ::$$
$$\langle \| \ i,j,k,u,v \ : \ u = i-j \ \ \wedge \ \ v = j-k \ \ \wedge \ \ w = i+j+k \ \ ::$$
$$x[u,v-1,w+1] \ , \ y[u+1,v,w+1] \ , \ z[u-1,v+1,w+1] =$$
$$x[u,v,w] \ , \ y[u,v,w] \ , \ z[u,v,w] + x[u,v,w] \times y[u,v,w]$$
$$\rangle$$
$$\| \ \ \langle \| \ i,k \ : \ w = i+k+N \ \ :: \ \ C[i,k] = z[i-N, N-k, i+k+N]\rangle$$
$$\rangle$$

end {$P6$}

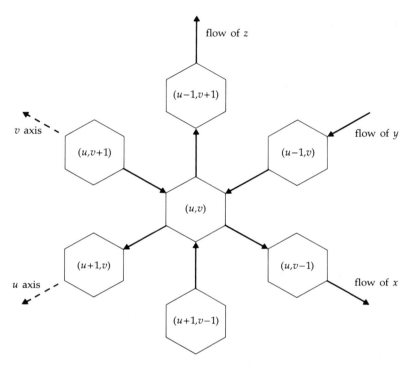

Figure 21.2 Flow of data in program *P6*.

Exercise 21.2   Rewrite program *P6* eliminating variables i, j, k.   ▽

Exercise 21.3   Determine the dimensions of arrays x, y, z in program *P6*.   ▽

21.4   *L-U* Decomposition

We describe a parallel synchronous algorithm, with similar constraints on data access as for matrix multiplication, to compute the *L-U* decomposition of a given matrix.   Let $A[0..M - 1, 0..M - 1]$ be a matrix that has an *L-U* decomposition: *L* is a lower triangular matrix with 1s on its diagonals and *U* is an upper trangular matrix. Both *L* and *U* satisfy the following equations. In this section, i, j, k are quantified $0 \leq i < M, \; 0 \leq j < M, \; 0 \leq k < M$.

$$A^0[i, k] \quad = A[i, k]$$

$$A^{j+1}[i, k] \; = \; A^j[i, k] - L[i, j] \times U[j, k]$$

$$L[i,j] = 0 \qquad\qquad \text{if} \quad i < j \quad \sim$$
$$1 \qquad\qquad\quad \text{if} \quad i = j \quad \sim$$
$$A^j[i,j]/U[j,j] \qquad \text{if} \quad i > j$$

$$U[j,k] = 0 \qquad\qquad\quad \text{if} \quad j > k \quad \sim$$
$$A^j[j,k] \qquad\qquad \text{if} \quad j \leq k$$

In this section we consider A to be a band matrix; let BA, TA be such that $A[i,j] = 0$ unless $BA \leq i - j \leq TA$. It can be shown that

$$A^{j+1}[i,k] = A[i,k] \qquad\qquad \text{if} \ (i - j > TA) \vee (j - k < BA) \quad \sim$$
$$A^j[i,k] - L[i,j] \times U[j,k] \ \ \text{if} \ (i - j \leq TA) \wedge (j - k \geq BA) \ .$$

The form of computation of A suggests matrix multiplication. Hence we attempt to use the same strategy as for matrix multiplication, pipelining all three matrices. As before, let $u = i - j$, $v = j - k$, and $w = i + j + k$. We postulate

$$i \leq j \ \wedge \ k > j \ \Rightarrow \ L[i,j] \ = x[u,v,w],$$
$$i > j \ \wedge \ k \geq j \ \Rightarrow \ U[j,k] \ = y[u,v,w],$$
$$i \geq j \ \wedge \ k \geq j \ \Rightarrow \ A^j[i,k] = z[u,v,w].$$

We restrict ourselves to $u \geq 0$ $(i \geq j)$ and $v \leq 0$ $(k \geq j)$ in the following discussion.

The major difference between this problem and matrix multiplication is that matrices L, U are not available; they must be computed. Proceeding in the same manner as for matrix multiplication, we derive

$$\langle \| \ i, k \ : \ z[2.i + k, \ -i - 2.k, 0] = A[i,k] \rangle$$

Next consider $x[u,v,w]$. If $v < 0$ (i.e., $k > j$), then $x[u,v,w] = L[i,j] = x[u, v - 1, w + 1]$. Therefore

$$x[u, v - 1, w + 1] = x[u,v,w] \quad \text{if} \quad v < 0$$

For $v = 0$,

$$x[u, v - 1, w + 1] = x[u, -1, w + 1] = L[i,j]$$
$$= A^j[i,j]/U[j,j] \qquad \text{if} \quad i > j \quad \sim \quad 1 \qquad \text{if} \quad i = j$$
$$= z[u,0,w]/y[u,0,w] \qquad \text{if} \quad u > 0 \quad \sim \quad 1 \qquad \text{if} \quad u = 0$$

Therefore we have

$$x[u, v - 1, w + 1] = x[u,v,w] \qquad\qquad\quad \text{if} \quad v < 0 \quad \sim$$
$$z[u,0,w]/y[u,0,w] \qquad \text{if} \quad u > 0 \ \wedge \ v = 0 \quad \sim$$
$$1 \qquad\qquad\qquad\qquad\ \text{if} \quad u = 0 \ \wedge \ v = 0$$

Similarly, we derive equations for y and z. Grouping all defining equations for variables with the same value of index w (the third index), we obtain the following program for L-U decomposition:

Program *L-U—Decomposition*

> **always**
>
> $\{i, j, k$ are quantified: $\ 0 \le i < M, \ 0 \le j < N, \ 0 \le k < R\}$
>
> $\langle \| \ i, k \ \ :: \ \ z[2.i + k, -i - 2.k, 0] = A[i, k] \rangle$
>
> $\| \ \langle \| \ w \ : \ 0 \le w < M + N + R \ \ :: $
>
> $\quad \langle \| \ i, j, k, u, v \ : $
>
> $\qquad u = i - j \ \wedge \ u \ge 0 \ \wedge \ v = j - k \ \wedge \ v \le 0 \ \wedge \ w = i + j + k \ \ :: $
>
> $\quad x[u, v - 1, w + 1] = x[u, v, w] \qquad\qquad\ \ \text{if} \ \ v < 0 \ \ \sim$
>
> $\qquad\qquad\qquad z[u, 0, w]/y[u, 0, w] \quad \text{if} \ \ u > 0 \ \wedge \ v = 0 \ \ \sim$
>
> $\qquad\qquad\qquad\qquad\qquad 1 \qquad\qquad \text{if} \ \ u = 0 \ \wedge \ v = 0$
>
> $\quad \| \ y[u + 1, v, w + 1] = y[u, v, w] \qquad\qquad\ \text{if} \ \ u > 0 \ \ \sim$
>
> $\qquad\qquad\qquad\qquad z[0, v, w] \qquad\quad \text{if} \ \ u = 0$
>
> $\quad \| \ z[u - 1, v + 1, w + 1] = z[u, v, w] - x[u, v, w] \times y[u, v, w]$
>
> $\qquad\qquad\qquad\qquad\qquad\qquad \text{if} \ \ u \le TA \ \wedge \ v \ge BA \ \ \sim$
>
> $\qquad\qquad\qquad z[u, v, w] \qquad\qquad \text{if} \ \ u > TA \ \vee \ v < BA$
>
> $\quad \rangle$
>
> $\rangle$

end $\{L\text{-}U\text{—}Decomposition\}$

21.5 Systolic Sorting for Bubble Memory

In this section we develop a systolic sorting program suitable for bubble memories and charge-coupled devices. The program is called the *rebound-sort*. The hardware structure on which the sort is carried out is called a *ladder*. We choose to think of ladders in terms of the operations that may be performed on them; these operations are described next. (The electronics of ladders is interesting; it is described at the end of this section. It is not necessary, however, to understand electronics to appreciate the problem or derive a solution.)

21.5.1 The Problem

A ladder of length N, where N is a positive integer, consists of an array $z[0..N - 1]$ of distinct integers. The following primitive operations can be performed on elements of a ladder:

1. A pair of adjacent elements of the array z can be exchanged. This is represented by an assignment of the following form, for some i, where $0 < i < N$:

$$z[i-1], \; z[i] \; := \; z[i], \; z[i-1].$$

2. A pair of adjacent elements of the array can be ordered in increasing or decreasing order. These operations are represented by assignments of the following form, where sort2 (from Section 19.4.1) is a function of two arguments that returns two values—i.e., its arguments in increasing order.

$$z[i-1], \; z[i] \; := \; \text{sort2}(z[i-1], \; z[i])$$

$$z[i], \; z[i-1] \; := \; \text{sort2}(z[i-1], \; z[i])$$

The former assignment sorts $z[i-1], z[i]$ in increasing order, and the latter assignment sorts them in decreasing order.

3. The element at one end of the array may be assigned a value or read out; these operations are represented by

$$z[N-1] \; := \; u \qquad \{\text{write from } u\}$$
$$v \; := \; z[N-1] \quad \{\text{read into } v\}$$

(An arbitrary choice is made to use $z[N-1]$, rather than $z[0]$, as the input-output port of the ladder.)

The ladder operates in a synchronous manner. An arbitrary number of basic operations can be performed in parallel at each step, provided that each element of the ladder participates in at most one operation. (An element $z[i]$ participates in an operation means that $z[i]$ appears on the left or right side of the assignment corresponding to this operation.) The array to be sorted is $X[0..N-1]$, and the output array is $y[0..N-1]$.

This completes the presentation of the problem. Next two solutions are presented, starting with an obvious one and going on to the rebound sort.

21.5.2 An Obvious Solution

An obvious solution, given the basic operations permitted on the ladder, is to copy X into z, then carry out the odd-even transposition sort (see Section 19.6.1) on z, and finally copy z into y. Since an element of the ladder participates in at most one basic operation on each step, an element of X can be copied into $z[N-1]$—the input port of the ladder—only on alternate steps because after each element of X is written into $z[N-1]$, one step is required to read the value out of $z[N-1]$. Note that $2 \times N$ steps are required to copy X into z, that N steps are required for the odd-even transposition sort, and that $2 \times N$ steps are required to copy z into y—a total of $5 \times N$ steps.

t	0	1	2	3	4	5	6	7
$z[3]$	?	$X[0]$	?	$X[1]$	?	$X[2]$	?	$X[3]$
$z[2]$	?	?	$X[0]$	?	$X[1]$	?	$X[2]$	*
$z[1]$	?	?	?	$X[0]$	?	$X[1]$	*	*
$z[0]$	?	?	?	?	$X[0]$	*	*	*

Table 21.1 Illustration of the invariant describing the copying of X into z.

21.5.3 The Rebound Sort

The rebound sort is a clever variation of the obvious solution given in Section 21.5.2; it accomplishes the sort in $4 \times N$ steps. The new idea is this: Carry out steps of the odd-even transposition sort in parallel with copying data into and out of z.

Steps of the transposition sort are carried out on the subarray $z[0..k]$ when the subarray contains data—i.e., when each element of $z[0..k]$ is an element of X. Initially all elements of z have arbitrary value. After $N + K$ steps, all elements in $z[0..k]$ are from X, and therefore the transposition sort is begun on this subarray.

The program is described in terms of three invariants (I1–I3): The first deals with copying X into z, the second with the transposition sort, and the third with copying z into y. The invariants are complex because at the same point in the algorithm different elements of z can participate in different phases of computation. Let t be the step number; initially $t = 0$ and t is incremented by 1 in each step.

Input Phase

The invariant describing the copying of X into z is as follows:

invariant

$$\langle \wedge \; i, j, t \; : \; (0 \leq i < N \; \wedge \; 0 \leq j < N) \; \wedge \; (N - i \leq t \leq N + i) \\ \wedge \; t = 2.j + N - i \; :: \; z[i] = X[j] \rangle \tag{I1}$$

The invariant is illustrated in Table 21.1, which shows the contents of a four-element ladder after t steps, $t \geq 0$. Each column of the table shows the contents of the ladder at a given step number. A row shows the contents of an element of z. Question marks ("?") represent arbitrary values, and the symbol * represents some element of X.

t	5	6	7	8	9	10	11
$z[3]$				$perm-of$			
$z[2]$			$perm-of$		$perm-of$		
$z[1]$		$perm-of$				$perm-of$	
$z[0]$	$perm-of$						$perm-of$
	$X[0..0]$	$X[0..1]$	$X[0..2]$	$X[0..3]$ $y[0..3]$	$y[1..3]$	$y[2..3]$	$y[3..3]$

Table 21.2 Illustration of the invariant for the sorting phase, $N = 4$.

t	5	6	7	8	9	10	11
$z[3]$				$\min z[0..3]$			
$z[2]$			$\min z[0..2]$		$\min z[0..2]$		
$z[1]$		$\min z[0..1]$		$\min z[0..1]$		$\min z[0..1]$	
$z[0]$	$\min z[0..0]$		$\min z[0..0]$		$\min z[0..0]$		$\min z[0..0]$

Table 21.3 Another illustration of the invariant for the sorting phase, $N = 4$.

Transposition-Sort Phase

The invariant describing the transposition-sort phase is as follows:

invariant

$$\langle \wedge\ i,t\ :\ (0 \leq i < N)\ \wedge\ (N + i < t < 3.N - i)\ ::$$
$$(t \leq 2.N\ \Rightarrow\ z[0..t - N - 1] \text{ is a permutation of } X[0..t - N - 1])\qquad \wedge$$
$$(t \geq 2.N\ \Rightarrow\ z[0..3.N - t - 1] \text{ is a permutation of } y[t - 2.N\ ..N - 1])\qquad \wedge$$
$$(odd(N + i - t)\ \Rightarrow\ z[i] = \min z[0..i])\qquad\qquad\qquad (I2)$$
$$\rangle$$

This invariant is illustrated in Tables 21.2 and 21.3; in Table 21.2 *perm-of* denotes that the set of the corresponding elements of z is a permutation of the given elements of X or y. Note the symmetry between X and y in Table 21.2.

Output Phase

The invariant describing the output phase is as follows:

t	8	9	10	11	12	13	14
$z[3]$	$y[0]$		$y[1]$		$y[2]$		$y[3]$
$z[2]$		$y[1]$		$y[2]$		$y[3]$	
$z[1]$			$y[2]$		$y[3]$		
$z[0]$				$y[3]$			

Table 21.4 Illustration of the invariant describing the output phase.

invariant

$$\langle \wedge\ i, j, t\ :$$
$$0 \leq i < N\ \wedge\ 0 \leq j < N\ \wedge\ (3.N - i - 1 \leq t \leq 3.N + i - 1)\ \wedge$$
$$t = N + 1 + i + 2.j\ \ ::\ \ z[i] = y[j]$$
$$\rangle \tag{I3}$$

This invariant is illustrated in Table 21.4.

Once the invariants are understood, the program development is straightforward. Next statements are developed to maintain each of the invariants. Finally the statements are put together to form a program.

Copying X into z is achieved by writing into $z[N - 1]$ and exchanging adjacent elements of z. The following statements maintain invariant (I1):

$$\langle \|\ i\ :\ 0 < i < N\ \ ::$$
$$z[i], z[i - 1]\ :=\ z[i - 1], z[i]\ \ \text{if even}(i + t - N)\ \wedge\ (N - i \leq t < N + i)$$
$$\rangle$$
$$\|\ z[N - 1]\ :=\ X[\tfrac{t}{2}]\ \ \ \ \ \ \ \ \ \text{if even}(t)\ \wedge\ t < 2.N$$
$$\|\ t\ :=\ t + 1$$

Statements that carry out the odd-even transposition sort and maintain invariant (I2) are

$$\langle \|\ i\ :\ 0 < i < N\ \ ::$$
$$z[i], z[i - 1]\ :=$$
$$\text{sort2}(z[i - 1],\ z[i])\ \ \ \ \text{if}\ \ \text{even}(i + t - N)\ \wedge\ (N + i \leq t < 3.N - i)$$
$$\rangle$$
$$\|\ t\ :=\ t + 1$$

Finally, copying z into y and maintaining invariant (I3) is accomplished by exchanging adjacent elements of z and reading values from $z[N - 1]$:

$$\langle \|\ i\ :\ 0 < i < N\ \ ::\ \ z[i], z[i - 1]\ :=\ z[i - 1], z[i]$$
$$\text{if}\ \ \text{even}(i + t - N)\ \wedge\ (3.N - i \leq t < 3.N + i)$$
$$\rangle$$

$\| \ y[\frac{t}{2} - N] \ := \ z[N-1]$
    if even$(t) \ \wedge \ 2.N \leq t < 4.N$
$\| \ t \ := \ t+1$

Putting these statements together gives the rebound sort. (The program is somewhat simplified by exchanging arbitrary values during the reading-in and writing-out phases. For instance, array z has arbitrary values initially, yet adjacent elements are exchanged in the program in order to make it simpler. Only the assign-section of the program is given, the declare and initially sections having been given earlier.

Program *rebound-sort*

  assign

    $\langle \| \ i \ : \ 0 < i < N \ \ :: $
       $z[i], z[i-1] \ :=$
         $z[i-1], z[i]$ if even$(i + t - N) \ \wedge \ \neg(N + i \leq t < 3.N - i)$ $\sim$
         sort2$(z[i-1], z[i])$ if even$(i + t - N) \ \wedge \ (N + i \leq t < 3N - i)$
    $\rangle$
    $\| \ z[N-1] := X[\frac{t}{2}]$ if even$(t) \ \wedge \ (t < 2.N)$
    $\| \ y[\frac{t}{2} - N] := z[N-1]$ if even$(t) \ \wedge \ (2.N \leq t < 4.N)$
    $\|$ $t := t+1$ if $t < 4.N$

end {*rebound-sort*}

Notes about Sorts on Ladders

A ladder can be employed to sort arrays repeatedly. While one array is being read out of a ladder, another array can be pumped in concurrently. By overlapping input and output in this manner, the effective number of steps per sort of N items can be reduced asymptotically to $2.N$.

If data can be fed into a ladder from both ends, then the obvious solution—read in, then do a transposition sort, and then write out the result— takes only $3.N$ steps because *two* items of data can be transferred between the ladder and the environment in each step.

Exercise 21.4 Design a sorting program for a ladder in which data can be transferred to the ladder from both ends. $\triangledown$

21.5.4 The Ladder Hardware

This subsection, which describes the ladder hardware, may be skipped because the hardware is not relevant to the remainder of the book.

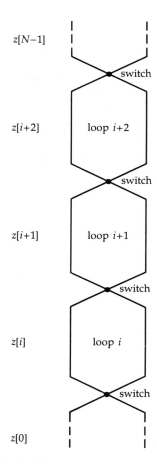

Figure 21.3 The structure of a ladder.

An N-element ladder consists of a sequence of N *loops*, each loop separated from the next by a *switch* (see Fig. 21.3).

Loop i contains $z[i]$. A loop has two sides—a left side and a right side. In odd steps of the program, the data in all loops are on the same side, say the left side, and in even steps the data in all loops are on the other side. The data item in a loop is traveling toward the switch at the top of the loop or toward the switch at the bottom of the loop; for a given switch, either data items in both adjacent loops are traveling toward it or both traveling away from it.

Figure 21.4 shows the data in loops $i + 1$ and $i + 2$ traveling toward each other (and the data in loops i and $i + 1$ traveling away from each other). A switch plays a role in a step only if data in adjacent loops are traveling

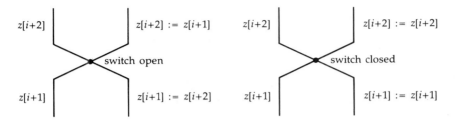

Figure 21.4 Data transmissions for open and closed positions of switches.

towards it. A switch has two positions. In the *open* position the data in the two loops on each side of the switch are exchanged, and in the *closed* position the data remain within each loop (see Fig. 21.4). The position of the switch is set by a logic circuit that compares the values in adjacent loops and reads the clock (the step number). This hardware gives rise to the basic operations described in the beginning of this section.

Summary

We have studied a few problems in connection with systolic arrays just to give a flavor of how UNITY might be applied toward developing their solutions. We find that it is useful to state the problem in terms of equations and then to manipulate these equations to meet additional constraints—such as efficient parallelization or data access. Manipulations of equations are not always entirely mechanical. For instance, in deriving the program for pipelining all three matrices, program *P6*, we had to postulate $u = i - j$, $v = j - k$, and $w = i + j + k$. These choices were justified on grounds of processor network topology. It is mechanical, however, to derive a program with assignments (as in program *P5*) from a program, e.g., *P4*, in the equational schema. We have studied the design of a bubble-memory ladder to illustrate how unconventional architectures are handled within UNITY.

Bibliographic Notes

Some of the early ideas of systolic computation, using cellular automata as the basis, are in Kosaraju [1969]. The seminal work of Kung and Leiserson [1978] firmly established this area of research; see IEEE [1987a] for a wide variety of systolic computer architectures, and Chen [1986] and Huang and

Lengauer [1987] for a few systolic algorithm designs. Representing systolic algorithms by assignment statements, where synchrony in execution is modeled by multiple assignment, is from Chandy and Misra [1986b]. A similar approach has been taken by van de Snepscheut and Swenker [1987] in designing a number of clever systolic algorithms. The asynchronous matrix multiplication algorithm, program *P4*, is from Hoare [1978]; in that paper the program was presented using the explicit message communication mechanism of CSP. Sections 21.3.3 and 21.4 are based on Kung and Leiserson [1978]. The rebound sort is from Chen, Lum, and Tung [1978].

CHAPTER 22

Alternative Programming Models

22.1   Introduction

In this chapter we compare programming in UNITY with other styles of programming such as functional, rule-based, imperative, and logic programming.

In preceding chapters we have emphasized the strengths of UNITY—its simple theory and computational model, and its expressive power in representing programs for a variety of architectures. Here most of our concern is with the weaknesses of UNITY, particularly in comparison with other styles of programming.

It is impossible to give a brief comprehensive description of a programming style to which an entire book can be devoted. Instead we give an overview of a few programming styles, point out their salient aspects, and compare them with UNITY.

22.2   Functional Programming

A functional program defines a set of functions. An execution of a functional program is an application of a function to a set of arguments: the input data. Therefore programs are problem oriented rather than machine oriented: They do not describe how to implement the function on the underlying machine. There is no notion of a program state, and hence no possibility of "side effect." As a consequence, concurrent evaluation of multiple functions is permitted. Functions that take infinite structures as arguments or return infinite structures are allowed; "lazy evaluation" is employed in computing values of such functions. Some functional languages employ "higher order functions," a useful abstraction mechanism.

Functional programming has an impressive mathematical foundation. The useful properties of a program are derived by manipulating its text algebraically rather than by reasoning about execution sequences and program states. "Referential transparency," or substitution of an expression for an equivalent expression, is a key feature of algebraic manipulation. A functional program that consists of only definitions (and no assignments) has this beautiful property. In a UNITY program only transparent variables, which can be replaced by their defining equations (in the always-section), exhibit referential transparency.

The representation of nondeterminism is difficult within functional programming. The fair merge of two sequences cannot be expressed as a function because functions are deterministic, while the fair merge is not. As a consequence, the behavior of a multiplexor (see Section 8.2.3)—which merges the inputs it receives from two channels in arbitrary order, never ignoring any channel forever—cannot be expressed by a functional program. Many nonterminating systems—such as communication protocols, operating systems, and data bases—are inherently nondeterministic in this sense and hence functional programming seems inadequate to represent them. We have chosen to work with states and assignments because we do not know any other way to represent nondeterministic state-transition systems.

One way to exploit the power of functional programming, while retaining some of the advantages of states and assignments, is to create a programming system that incorporates both, with a clean separation between the functional and the nonfunctional components. A UNITY program has both a functional component and a nondeterministic state-based component. Functions, perhaps written in a functional programming notation, and transparent variables can appear in the right sides of assignments and in the always-section. The mechanism for statement selection and assignments are used to model nondeterminism and state transitions, respectively.

A programmer can select the mix of functional and nonfunctional constructs in a program; a program can be entirely functional or can employ assignments. Mixing functional and nonfunctional components in the UNITY context poses no conceptual problem; the only requirement is that the right side of an assignment be computable in finite time. This requirement does not preclude the possibility of using functions that accept or return infinite structures. The following example illustrates this requirement.

Example 22.1

Let $\aleph$ be the (infinite) sequence of natural numbers in increasing order. A UNITY statement of the form

$\quad n \; := \; \text{head}(\aleph)$

can be executed in finite time, using lazy evaluation to compute the right side. This is a perfectly acceptable UNITY statement provided that head($\aleph$) is computable in finite time.

Now suppose we modify the program to assign $\aleph$ to a variable m in one statement and then assign head(m) to n in another statement. This is not an acceptable UNITY program because the computation of the right side in the assignment to m does not terminate. UNITY requires the evaluation of a right side to terminate in finite time. $\triangledown$

Both functional programming and UNITY are motivated by the desire to treat a program as a mathematical object. The approaches adopted, however, are radically different. UNITY advocates the use of assignments (in which functions may appear in the right side). The additional power of UNITY is bought at the price of new constructs: nondeterminism, states, and assignments.

22.3   Rule-based Programming

A rule-based program defines a set of data items and a set of rules. A rule is a guarded command of the form

$$b \;\; \rightarrow \;\; s$$

where guard b is a predicate and command s is a sequence of actions that creates new rules, creates new data items, or manipulates the values of existing data items. Computation proceeds by executing a rule that is selected nondeterministically. In this section, we explore the differences between UNITY and a rule-based language, OPS5. OPS5 was developed to facilitate knowledge representation and inferencing—goals that differ from those of UNITY. Therefore there are differences in the style of programming between UNITY and OPS5.

An OPS5 program has a set of objects that can be thought of as PASCAL-like records. During execution of an OPS5 program, objects can be added to a set, removed from a set, or changed in value. OPS5 permits (implicit) quantification over sets of objects. An example of a rule in an OPS5 program follows.

$$
\begin{array}{lll}
(\text{person} & \uparrow city\text{-}of\text{-}residence & \langle city1 \rangle) \\
- \; (city & \uparrow name & \langle city1 \rangle) \\
\rightarrow (\text{make } city & \uparrow name & \langle city1 \rangle)
\end{array}
$$

The effect of this statement is to add a data item $city1$ to the set $city$ if there is a person whose city-of-residence is $city1$, and $city1$ is not already in $city$. A translation of this into a UNITY-like notation follows. In this program segment, symbol $\cup$ denotes set union.

$$\langle [\!] \; p : \; p \text{ is a person} :: \; city \; := \; city \; \cup \; \{p.city\_of\_residence\} \rangle$$

As the example illustrates, OPS5 allows a programmer to extract any record that satisfies a predicate and then to manipulate its component values. To select a record from a static set of records in UNITY, we use a quantified statement (like the one just given), with quantification over all records, where the predicate in the quantification selects the desired record. If the set of records is dynamic, a different form of quantification is used, as in

$$city \; := \; \langle \cup \; p : \; p \text{ is a person} :: \; \{p.city\_of\_residence\} \rangle \cup \; city$$

Some rule-based languages allow self-modifying programs: A program may add new rules to itself during its execution. Self-modifying programs simulate "learning." In contrast, the set of statements in a UNITY program is static (Section 22.7.4 presents the reasons for this decision).

The next rule to be executed in an OPS5 program is determined by a complex selection strategy; UNITY's selection rule is straightforward. The power of the OPS5 rule-selection strategy allows programmers to control executions to achieve maximum efficiency. In UNITY, execution sequences are controlled by describing mappings that are external to the program.

In a nutshell, OPS5 has constructs that UNITY lacks. We have restricted UNITY to a small set of concepts for which we have been able to develop the necessary mathematics. For instance, with the ability to add rules, proving the progress of computation (of the form $p \mapsto q$) becomes far more difficult. It may well be the case that different measures of progress, and hence entirely different mathematical concepts, are appropriate for machine-learning systems.

22.4 Sequential Imperative Programming

Four decades of experience suggest that imperative programming can be made to work reasonably well, at least for sequential machines. Most programmers readily accept the imperative mode of programming with its strict locus of control. Even nonprogramming tasks, such as registering for courses at a university, are often described in terms of flow charts. There is little evidence that programmers will readily accept the UNITY model with its nondeterministic control.

Much has been said about the dangers of operational reasoning: It is safer to annotate a program than to reason about all its action sequences. Yet it must be admitted that many programmers do surprisingly well with operational arguments. It is much more difficult to use operational arguments to prove nondeterministic UNITY programs than to prove deterministic imperative programs. Thus UNITY suffers from the weakness that operational arguments, which work at least some of the time for deterministic imperative programs, work hardly at all for UNITY.

Unnecessary sequencing has been cited as a weakness of sequential programming. This weakness is a serious one for our purposes: the development of programs for a variety of architectures. If a solution is inherently sequential, however, it is more economical to represent it in an imperative language than in UNITY. In such a program, control flows sequentially from one statement to the next unless otherwise specified. To force control to flow in a prescribed manner in UNITY, variables are introduced to mimic the program counter; these variables are used to ensure that the execution of any statement, other than the next one in the prescribed sequence, does not change the program state. Introduction of such variables may appear unnecessary and bothersome. Indeed, if most problems admit only sequential solutions, there would be little advantage in using UNITY (and little point in writing this book).

It may appear that if one's goal is limited to developing a sequential program, an imperative language is preferable to UNITY. Even for this limited goal, however, UNITY has advantages—compare the UNITY solutions to the shortest-path problem for sequential architectures (Section 5.2) with a PASCAL solution.

22.5   Communicating Sequential Processes

A network of comunicating sequential processes is a form of imperative programming in which each process has its own locus of control. Processes communicate by messages. It is straightforward to implement a network of processes on a distributed architecture that supports concurrent processes and message passing.

A UNITY program differs from a network of processes in that it contains neither processes nor loci of control. To implement a UNITY program on a distributed architecture, the body of the program is partitioned into processes (i.e., subsets of statements), where variables common to two processes are accessed in a prescribed manner (see Chapter 4).

A disadvantage of UNITY for the development of distributed programs is that instructions for partitioning a UNITY program into processes are given outside the program. No such instructions are necessary for networks of processes. Furthermore, UNITY programmers are obliged to prove that their partitionings are correct: For instance, they must demonstrate that the variables shared by processes are sequences, that these variables are accessed in a specified manner, and that the lengths of these sequences do not exceeed the capacity of buffers used in the implementation.

There are two aspects to the development of a UNITY program for a target architecture: (1) the derivation of an "abstract" program, and (2) the design of a mapping of the abstract program to the architecture. Similarly, proofs of UNITY programs have two parts: (1) a proof of the abstract program, and (2) a proof of the mapping. The development of UNITY programs exhibits a clear separation of these concerns. There is, however, an advantage in not separating concerns: The use of a notation designed specifically to exploit the target architecture allows the programmer to avoid the second part of program development and proof.

These remarks apply equally well to processes that communicate through shared variables.

Object-oriented languages allow objects (we can think of objects as processes) to be created dynamically. One process can create another, and a process can send the address of one process to another. A process can send a message to any process for which it has an address. In contrast, UNITY is static. (It is possible to simulate creation of a bounded number of processes in UNITY by treating processes yet to be created as existing but idle.) We choose not to make use of the considerable power of dynamic object creation for two reasons. First, we wish to use a small number of constructs, and we choose to avoid additional power if we can do so without making our programs much larger. In addition, we have not as yet extended our theory to process creation and termination.

22.6   Logic Programming

An interesting view of logic programming, particularly relevant to a comparison of logic programming and UNITY, is given in Kowalski [1979]. An algorithm in a conventional notation expresses both the information used in solving a problem and the manner in which the information is employed in solving the problem; the information is called the logic component, and the manner of its use the control component of the algorithm. A logic program expresses only the logic component; the control component is either left implicit and is built into the executor of the logic program, or is specified separately, using a notation different from the logic program.

The execution strategy employed by a logic program executor can sometimes be inefficient. To obtain an efficient execution, the programmer provides instructions (external to the logic program) for the control component that constrain the executor to operate in an efficient manner. Thus efficient logic programs can be derived by stepwise refinement where a refinement step describes the control component in greater detail than before and leaves the logic component unchanged. Logic programming and UNITY share the goal of separating the concerns of logic and control. To a great extent, to postpone concerns about target architectures in UNITY is to postpone concerns about efficiency and control.

Although logic programming and UNITY share this important goal of separation of concerns, there are some significant differences. To help understand the differences, we describe a mapping from logic programs to UNITY programs. We begin by giving a very brief, incomplete description of logic programming; we refer the reader to Kowalski's pioneering book on the subject.

In the rest of this section, we restrict ourselves to the propositional fragment of logic programming.

22.6.1 Logic Programming: A Brief, Incomplete Description

A logic program is a set of logical implications. An execution of a logic program determines whether the implications are consistent.

To show that a conclusion C follows from a set S of implications, we execute a logic program consisting of S and the implication $C \Rightarrow false$. (Note: $C \Rightarrow false$ is equivalent to $\neg C$.) If the execution shows that the set of implications consisting of S and $C \Rightarrow false$ is inconsistent, then C follows from S.

We will show how to transform logic programs into UNITY. We first consider an example of a logic program.

Example 22.2

This example is taken from Kowalski* [1979].

Given:

- Mary is pretty.

- John is kind, handsome and strong.

- If John is rich or Mary likes John then John is happy.

- If John likes Mary and John is kind, or John is both handsome and strong, then Mary likes him.

- If Mary is pretty then John likes her.

Desired Conclusion: John is happy.

To describe the problem precisely, we write $b[x]$ to denote that x has attribute b, and $y[p, q]$ to denote that (p, q) is in relation y.

A logic program that captures the given facts is as follows.

Given:

$$
\begin{aligned}
true &\Rightarrow pretty[Mary] \\
true &\Rightarrow kind[John] \\
true &\Rightarrow handsome[John] \\
true &\Rightarrow strong[John] \\
rich[John] \lor likes\,[Mary, John] &\Rightarrow happy[John] \\
(likes[John, Mary] \land kind[John]) \lor (handsome[John] \land strong[John]) &\Rightarrow \\
likes[Mary, John] \\
pretty[Mary] &\Rightarrow likes[John, Mary]
\end{aligned}
$$

Desired Conclusion: $happy[John]$ ▽

---

*Permission to reprint as requested is granted by Elsevier Science Publishing Company, Inc., 52 Vanderbilt Avenue, New York, N.Y. 10017.

Note: The implications as just written do not follow the syntax of typical logic programming languages; in particular, the implications are not in the form of Horn clauses. $\triangledown$

22.6.2 Transformation of Logic Programs to UNITY

Each implication in a logic program is of the form

$$b \;\Rightarrow\; x,$$

where the consequent x is an atomic formula. We represent each consequent by a boolean variable. Observe that the preceding implication is the same as

$$x = x \;\vee\; b \, .$$

Hence each implication can be written as an equation, and the goal of logic programming is to find the strongest solution to this set of equations.

The strongest solution to a finite set of boolean equations can be obtained by using a UNITY program in which each equality is replaced by an assignment. Initially, all variable values are *false*. The strongest solution is given by the values of variables at a fixed point. (An implication of the form $b \;\Rightarrow\; false$ is not encoded in UNITY. The set of implications is declared inconsistent if b is *true* at a fixed point of the UNITY program.)

A fixed point is always reached in a UNITY version of a logic program in which there are a finite number of variables. Since

$$b \;\Rightarrow\; x$$

is encoded by

$$x \;:=\; x \;\vee\; b \, ,$$

once x is *true*, it remains *true*. Therefore each state change of the UNITY program is accompanied by a decrease in the number of variables whose value is *false*; since the number of variables is finite, a fixed point is reached.

The conclusion C holds at the fixed point of the UNITY program if and only if C follows from S. We now illustrate this transformation with the logic program of the previous example.

Example 22.3

We introduce boolean arrays *pretty, kind*, . . . with indices ranging over *John, Mary*, etc. Initially all variables are *false*. The assign-section of a UNITY program that simulates the preceding logical implications is as follows.

assign

$$pretty[Mary] \qquad := \quad true \quad \{\text{we replace } pretty[Mary] \lor true \text{ by } true\}$$

$[\![\quad kind[John] \qquad := \quad true$

$[\![\quad handsome[John] \quad := \quad true$

$[\![\quad strong[John] \qquad := \quad true$

$[\![\quad happy[John] \qquad := \quad happy[John] \lor rich[John] \lor likes[Mary, John]$

$[\![\quad likes[Mary, John] :=$

$\qquad (likes[Mary, John]) \lor$

$\qquad (likes[John, Mary] \land kind[John]) \lor$

$\qquad (handsome[John] \land strong[John])$

$[\![\quad likes[John, Mary] := likes[John, Mary] \lor pretty[Mary]$

Since *happy*[*John*] holds at the fixed point of this program, *happy*[*John*] follows from the implications of the logic program.

Observe that even though ¬*rich*[*John*] holds at the fixed point of the UNITY program, we cannot conclude that ¬*rich*[*John*] is deducible in the logic program. In other words, conclusions can be drawn only about variables, not their negations. ▽

22.6.3 Stopping the Program after the Conclusion Is Established

Since all variables in the UNITY version of a logic program are stable, once a conclusion is established there is no need to continue execution of the program. Therefore, to achieve greater efficiency, we transform an assignment $b \Rightarrow x$ in the logic program to the following assignment.

$$x := x \lor b \quad \text{if} \quad \neg C$$

where C is the conclusion to be established. Hence, if C holds, the program is at its fixed point.

22.6.4 Logic Programs with Infinite Search Spaces

The search spaces for the logic programs given earlier are finite. Hence, in such cases, the proof of termination of the corresponding UNITY program is straightforward: Any state change is accompanied by a variable being set *true*; hence the number of variables that have value *false* decreases. Now we consider logic programs with infinite search spaces. Typically these programs use functions or relations. They are transformed into UNITY programs in which each relation is represented by a set. (A function is treated as a special case of a relation.) Elements are added to, but never removed from, these sets. For instance, a tuple (x, y, z) is added to a set representing a relation R, provided that $R(x, y, z)$ holds. Next we illustrate the mapping of a logic program that uses relations to a UNITY program.

Example 22.4

Factorial computation is defined in an uncoventional manner in logic programs. Let f be a relation with two arguments, both natural numbers, where

$$f(x, y) = (x! = y)$$

Let t be a relation with three integer arguments, where

$$t(x, y, z) = (x \times y = z)$$

Factorial computation in a logic program uses the following implications:

$$true \quad \Rightarrow \quad f(0, 1)$$
$$f(x, v) \ \wedge \ t(x + 1, v, u) \quad \Rightarrow \quad f(x + 1, u)$$

To compute the factorial of n, the conclusion

$$f(n, m) \quad \Rightarrow \quad false$$

is added to the set. A refutation of the conclusion also displays a value of m for which $f(n, m)$ holds.

In UNITY, we use sets F, T to represent relations f, t; elements in these sets are pairs and triples of integer, respectively. All sets are initially empty. An implication

$$b \quad \Rightarrow \quad f(x, y)$$

is encoded in UNITY as

$$F \ := \ F \ \cup \ \{(x, y)\} \qquad \text{if} \quad b$$

An implication of the following form that is implicitly quantified over all x, y, z

$$b(x, y, z) \quad \Rightarrow \quad f(x, y)$$

is transformed into

$$F \ := \ \langle \cup \, x, y, z \ : \ (x, y, z) \ \in \ B \ :: \ (x, y) \rangle \ \cup \ F$$

where B is the set representing relation b.

The program can be terminated when a pair of the form (n, m), for any m, is in F. We introduce a transparent variable, *done*, to denote that such a pair is in F. A UNITY program corresponding to a logic program for computing factorial of n is given next. (The program does not define T.)

Program *factorial*

    declare   *done* : boolean

    always   *done* $= \langle \exists \, m \ :: \ (n, m) \ \in \ F \rangle$

    initially $F = \{(0, 1)\}$

assign

$$F := \langle \cup\ x, v, u\ :\ (x, v) \in F\ \wedge\ (x+1, v, u) \in T\ \ ::\ \ (x+1, u) \rangle\ \cup\ F$$
$$\text{if}\ \ \neg done$$

end {*factorial*}

Note: The example here merely illustrates a relationship between logic programming and UNITY; it is not the best way to compute factorials. The statement of choice for defining m, the factorial of n, in UNITY is

$$m = \langle \times\ i :\ 0 < i \leq n\ \ ::\ \ i \rangle \qquad\qquad \triangledown$$

There is no guarantee that the sets used to represent relations in a UNITY program are finite. Therefore the proof of termination of such programs is not always trivial. A logic program with an infinite search space has to employ a search strategy that guarantees termination. This search strategy can be mapped to the corresponding UNITY program by forcing (effective) executions of UNITY statements to follow prescribed sequences—the sequences corresponding to the search strategy.

22.6.5 A Comparison of Logic Programming with UNITY

Logic programming and UNITY share the goal of separating the concerns of logic and control. Sophisticated built-in search strategies, coupled with auxiliary control languages by which the programmer can guide the search, make logic-programming languages powerful tools for certain classes of problems. In contrast, the statement-scheduling strategy in UNITY is not designed specifically for searching. A search strategy must be built explicitly into the UNITY program to search infinite spaces. Therefore the generality of UNITY is also its limitation when applied to a specific class of problems. The simplicity of the mapping from propositional logic programs to UNITY shows that UNITY shares some concepts with logic programming.

22.7 The Rationale for Some Design Choices in UNITY

In this section we contrast a few features of UNITY with the alternatives proposed in the literature.

22.7.1 The Need for Fair Selection

Statement selection in UNITY is *fair*: Every statement is selected infinitely often in an infinite execution. The possible execution sequences of a program under the fair selection rule are fair merges of the sequences corresponding to an infinite number of executions of each program statement. The mathematics of fair selection is complicated by the fact that a fair merge of sequences is not a function. A function over binary sequences whose value is *true* if and only if the argument sequence is fair (i.e., finite or has an infinite number of 0s and 1s) is not continuous. In particular, the claim that a sequence is fair cannot be refuted by observing any of its finite prefixes, and induction cannot be applied on the prefixes to deduce properties of a fair sequence. Hence it is often argued that fair selection should be abolished from programming.

Unfortunately, weaker selection rules have more serious drawbacks. For instance, consider the following rule: A program execution is any infinite sequence of statement executions in which either a program is at a fixed point or the state changes eventually. (Note that this rule allows execution of a statement of the form $b := \neg b$, forever ignoring all other statements.) The part of the union theorem that deals with *ensures* does not hold under this weaker rule. To see the implication of this, consider any solution to the dining philosophers problem (Chapter 12) that has the property that every hungry philosopher eats eventually. The property no longer holds if another table with its own dining philosophers is introduced because an acceptable execution sequence may consist of activities on only one table. The class of properties broadly termed "absence of system-wide deadlock" can be guaranteed by the weaker selection rule, whereas absence of individual starvation seems to require a fairness rule of the type that we have adopted. For instance, our fairness rule guarantees that a message sent along a channel is delivered eventually, independent of communications along other channels—a property that is crucial in reasoning about distributed programs.

There are many other notions of fairness. We have chosen a selection rule which admits of a simple theory to reason about progress properties.

22.7.2 Simulating Unfair Selection Using Fair Selection

Unfair selection is useful in modeling situations in which a variable *may* take on a certain value. For example, a *thinking* philosopher in the dining philosophers problem (Chapter 12) *may* become *hungry*, or a link in a communication system *may* fail. These situations can be specified in our logic, or modeled as a UNITY program fragment using fair selection. In the following, we write a set of expressions separated by | on the right side of an assignment to denote that any one of the expressions may be selected for assignment, with no fairness constraint. (This notation is not used in the rest of the book.)

{the state of a philosopher u may change from thinking to hungry, i.e.,

to implement $u.dine = thinking$ *unless* $u.dine = hungry$}

$u.dine := thinking$ if $u.dine = thinking$ |
$\quad\quad\quad\quad hungry$ if $u.dine = thinking$

{a link may fail and then stays failed, i.e. *link-failed* is stable}

link-failed := *link-failed* | *true*

UNITY does not have an unfair selection mechanism because this can be simulated using fair selection. A statement

$x := 0 \mid 1$

can be simulated by the following program fragment, where boolean variable *b* has arbitrary initial value:

$x := 0$ if b ~   1   if $\neg b$

‖ $b := \neg b$

It is left for the reader to show that these programs are equivalent: For any execution sequence in one program, there exists an execution sequence in the other such that *x* takes on the same sequence of values in both.

22.7.3 Assignments versus Guarded Commands

There are syntactic and semantic differences between guarded commands, as defined in Dijkstra [1976], and UNITY. In this description of guarded commands, we restrict ourselves to a loop consisting of guarded commands each of which has a guard (a boolean expression) and a command that is an assignment statement.

The syntactic difference is mainly stylistic: whether to emphasize the conditions under which actions take place or the actions themselves. The answer is not clear-cut. We give some reasons for our choice and explain when guarded commands may be preferable.

We allow assignments that have several alternatives of the form

$x := u$ if $x < 0$ ~

$\quad\quad v$ if $x = 0$ ~

$\quad\quad w$ if $x > 0$

This follows traditional mathematical practice. It is easier to understand the assignment to *x* in this form, using a single statement, rather than guarded commands:

$x < 0$ → $x := u$

‖ $x = 0$ → $x := v$

‖ $x > 0$ → $x := w$

There are problems, such as command and control, where under certain conditions many actions take place. For instance, if an airplane gets too close to another: Sound a buzzer in the cockpit, send an emergency message to ground control, begin preparation for automatic evasive measures, etc. A guarded command representation may be more suitable in such situations; it may be easier to enumerate the actions to be taken under each condition rather than the set of (pre)conditions for each action.

The semantic differences between guarded commands and UNITY have to do with fairness. In the guarded command theory, a statement is selected for execution only if its guard is *true* (or "enabled"). If an arbitrary statement is selected for execution, it is possible that a statement whose guard is *false* is chosen forever—because there is no fairness constraint—and then there is no progress of computation in this case. Therefore the notion of a guard is crucial; only the statements with enabled guards are eligible for execution.

In UNITY, the fairness rule obviates the need for guards. A statement whose execution does not change the program state may be selected for execution; it can, however, be executed only a finite number of times. Therefore a statement whose execution changes program state—if such a statement exists—is selected eventually for execution. This is how progress of computation is guaranteed in UNITY. There is no notion of guards or enabling, and this has simplified the proof theory.

22.7.4 Why the Set of Statements in a UNITY Program Is Static

The set of statements in a UNITY program is fixed at "compile time." We do not allow statements of the form

$$\langle [\![\ i\ :\ 0 \le i < n\ ::\ statement(i)\rangle$$

where n is a variable whose value might change during program execution. It is difficult to define a fair execution rule for statements if the set of statements is dynamic. Should a statement that is part of the program infinitely often be executed infinitely often? Such a rule is difficult to implement and is difficult to reason about. Therefore we have chosen to work with a static set of statements.

22.7.5 On the Choice of Logic and the Proof System

Our proof system is based on Hoare-style assertions. We found it necessary to introduce existential and universal quantifications over program statements to apply to such assertions. The extended forms of assertions that we have introduced—$\langle \forall\ s\ ::\ \{p\}\ s\ \{q\}\rangle$, $\langle \exists\ s\ ::\ \{p\}\ s\ \{q\}\rangle$—are the nucleus of our proof system. It is convenient to employ additional concepts, such as *unless*, *ensures*, and *leads-to* in the proof system. These have been defined using universal and existential quantifications over program statements.

Our proof system is inappropriate for other languages because other languages have constructs in addition to assignment; also, quantifications over statements are of little use in programs with control flow. Proof by noninterference—showing that the execution of a statement does not falsify the preconditions of others—is a powerful technique for proving properties of programs consisting of sequential processes. Noninterference is inapplicable in UNITY, however, because UNITY does not have process as a construct.

Trace logic does not seem particularly appropriate for UNITY programs because the set of traces of a UNITY program is the set of fair statement execution sequences; hence this set has no interesting structure. There are some systems, however, that are best described in terms of their observable action sequence (e.g., a vending machine that accepts coins and dispenses chocolates), and there trace logic is most useful. For UNITY programs, all actions are assignments and all assignments are (assumed) observable. It appears more convenient to employ invariants to describe the admissible states in this case. The UNITY proof system is restricted to UNITY programs only, whereas trace logic can be applied to a wide range of discrete systems.

Summary

In this chapter a few other programming styles have been described and contrasted with UNITY. At higher levels of program design, UNITY shares the goal of separating the logic of a program from its implementation, as in functional and logic programming. However, a UNITY program can be refined to describe the implementation at any desired degree of detail, for a specific architecture or for a family of architectures. This flexibility is the strength of UNITY. A weakness of UNITY, compared with functional and logic programming, is that its central construct—the assignment statement—is outside the domain of traditional mathematics and logic, and therefore new logical operators must be introduced to reason about it.

Bibliographic Notes

Functional programming is described, among others, in Backus [1978], Turner [1985], and Hudak [1986]. The use of equational logic as a programming notation is found in O'Donnell [1985]. Logic programming is described in Kowalski [1979], which also contains the logic-programming examples studied in this chapter. A view of programs as predicates is advocated in Hehner [1984]. Milner [1983] and Hoare [1984] contain comprehensive mathematical treatments of communicating sequential processes. An expert system notation, OPS5, is described in Brownston et al. [1985]. The guarded command and the use of nondeterminacy in programming is introduced in Dijkstra [1976].

Trace logics and their use in distributed systems are in Hoare [1984], Rem [1985], and van de Snepscheut [1985b]. Some of the limitations of trace-based specifications have been explored in Keller [1978] and Brock and Ackerman [1981]. For different forms of fairness, see Francez [1986]. Mok [1987] extends UNITY notation to the design of real-time systems.

Thoughts on Programming

The Interplay between Formalism and Intuition

Program development is often inspired by flashes of intuition. The intuition may be difficult to articulate because it may be based on experience, analogy, and insight. Formalism complements, but does not supplant, intuition. For example, intuition may lead us to suggest the introduction of concepts such as forks, bottles, and tokens during program design. A role of formalism is to support intuition by representing these concepts in formal terms.

Although we expect formalism to support intuition, we do not expect intuition to support formalism. Once we have modeled our intuition in formal terms, such as *force = mass* × *acceleration*, we expect to use symbol manipulation to deduce that *acceleration = force/mass*; no intuitive support is required to justify this step. These manipulations are second nature to us. Similarly, employing the PSP theorem on $p \mapsto q$ and p' *unless* q' to deduce $p \wedge p' \mapsto (p' \wedge q) \vee q'$ becomes second nature, and we no longer need to justify this symbol manipulation on intuitive grounds. One of the attractive features of formalism is that long, elaborate intuitive arguments can often be replaced by short proofs. Formal reasoning is not merely intuitive argumentation couched in mathematical notation; indeed, formalisms allow us to take short cuts that may have no obvious counterpart in the informal argument.

On the one hand, we should not hesitate to rely on intuition to propose programs and theorems. On the other hand, we should not hesitate to dispense with intuition in proof steps.

One reason that intuitive arguments appear shorter and simpler than formal proofs is that intuitive arguments use contexts with which readers are already familiar. For example, it is obvious that philosophers do not eat forks—they eat *with* forks—and therefore the assumption that philosophers do not consume forks can be conveniently left unstated in an informal specification. A program, however, deals with variables, and programmers can do almost anything they please with variables. There is nothing, unfortunately, to prevent a programmer from designing a dining philosophers program in which philosophers eat forks. Therefore all assumptions in our formal proofs are stated explicitly, and the proofs employ only the rules given in Chapters 3 and 7; despite this, our experience suggests that formal proofs can be concise.

What Is Programming?

In the old days (the 1950s), programming was simply writing code for a given machine. Efficiency was king. Programmers had to go through whatever contortions were necessary to get programs to run efficiently on machines with millisecond cycle times and 16K 16-bit words of memory. A programmer's primary concern was a specific machine—model X of vendor Y. In the *very* old days, a programmer's concern was even more specific: e.g., the physical machine located in the basement of Taylor Hall. Later "transportability" became important. Programs written for 18-bit machines from one manufacturer were required to execute on 16-bit machines from another. Contortions to extract the last iota of efficiency from a given machine proved a hindrance to transportability. The programmer was no longer concerned with the specific machine in the basement or even with model X; transportability became a synonym for generalization.

Thus programmers gave a fresh answer to the question What is programming? It became the art of developing programs for a generic machine—a FORTRAN or COBOL machine. Programmers distanced themselves a little from their machine code; compilers stood in between. This distancing meant that the esoteric features of a machine could not always be exploited by programmers, but this price was worth paying in the interests of transportability.

The change in a programmer's primary concern, from a specific machine— i.e., one in Taylor Hall—to a generic machine—i.e., a FORTRAN machine— was the first in a series of steps toward increasing abstraction. The abstraction of using higher level languages was adequate for the computing community then dealing with the third generation of computers because the languages were effective in hiding the evolving hardware. Data processing managers rested assured that each succeeding generation of computer would be a variation of the previous one—cheaper and faster, but still a von Neumann machine. Their investments in programs were safe. But then computer architects began introducing strange machines. They demolished the comforting cocoon of conformity.

The UNITY response to the challenge of novel machines is to propose yet another answer to the question What is programming? Our answer is a logical progression to the answers given by our programming forebears. Once again we generalize our view of programming.

Programming is the art of making a series of stepwise refinements of specifications. We begin with a large space of potential solutions, each refinement rules out some solutions, and we end with a small number of "good" concrete solutions. We expect that the decisions we make early in our designs are appropriate for *all* architectures. As design proceeds and the target architectures are defined more narrowly, our decisions are appropriate for smaller sets of architectures. This approach is not unlike that made by programmers who, when opting for one PASCAL data structure rather than another, expect their decisions to be appropriate for *all* machines on which their programs run. In the final stages of design, programmers may code a few subroutines in assembly language to exploit features of a target machine. But programmers know that it is not cost effective to *begin* design by programming in the assembly languages of all machines on which their programs may be required to execute.

The core of programming is not concerned with a specific architecture, a specific operating system, or a specific programming language any more than it is concerned with the machine in the basement. The core of programming is a theory that allows programmers to make a series of design decisions. This book has attempted to present such a theory.

Bibliography

Agerwala, T., and Arvind, eds. [1982]. *IEEE Computer* (Special issue on data-flow machines), February 1982.

Aho, A. V., J. E. Hopcroft, and J. D. Ullman [1983]. *Data Structures and Algorithms*, Reading, Massachusetts: Addison-Wesley, 1983.

Alpern, B., and F. B. Schneider [1985]. "Defining Liveness," *Information Processing Letters*, **24**:4, October 1985, pp. 181–185.

Andrews, G. R., and F. B. Schneider [1983]. "Concepts and Notations for Concurrent Programming," *Computing Surveys*, **15**:1, March 1983, pp. 3–43.

Apt, K. R. [1986]. "Correctness Proofs of Distributed Termination Algorithms," *ACM TOPLAS*, **8**:3, July 1986, pp. 388–405.

Arlazarov, V. L., et al, [1970]. "On Economical Construction of the Transitive Closure of a Directed Graph," *Dokl. Akad. Nank SSSR*, **194**, pp. 487–488 (in Russian); also in *Soviet Math. Dokl.*, **11**:5, 1970, pp. 1209–1210 (in English).

Backus, J. [1978]. "Can Programming Be Liberated from the von Neumann Style? A Functional Style and Its Algebra of Programs," *C.ACM*, **21**:8, August 1978, pp. 613–641.

Bagrodia, R. [1987]. "An Environment for the Design and Performance Analysis of Distributed Systems," Ph.D. dissertation, The University of Texas at Austin, Austin, Texas, 1987.

Barringer, H., R. Kuiper, and A. Pnueli [1984]. "Now You May Compose Temporal Logic Specifications," *Proc. 16th ACM Symposium on Theory of Computing*, 1984, pp. 51–63.

Bartlett, K. A., R. A. Scantlebury, and P. T. Wilkinson [1969]. "A Note on Reliable Full-Duplex Transmissions over Half-Duplex Links," *C.ACM*, **12**:5, May 1969, pp. 260–261.

Ben-Ari, M. [1982]. *Principles of Concurrent Programming*, London: Prentice-Hall International, 1982.

Ben-Ari, M. [1984]. "Algorithms for On-the-Fly Garbage Collection," *ACM TOPLAS*, **6**:3, July 1984, pp. 333–344.

Bertsekas, D. P. [1982]. "Distributed Dynamic Programming," *IEEE Transactions on Automatic Control*, **AC-27**:3, June 1982, pp. 610–616.

Bouge, L., and N. Francez [1987]. "A Compositional Approach to Super-imposition" (unpublished manuscript), 1987.

Bracha, G., and S. Toueg [1984]. "A Distributed Algorithm for Generalized Deadlock Detection," *Proc. of the 3rd Annual ACM Symposium on Principles of Distributed Computing*, Vancouver, British Columbia, Canada, 1984, pp. 285–301.

Brinch-Hansen, P. [1977]. *The Architecture of Concurrent Programming*, Englewood-Cliffs, New Jersey: Prentice-Hall, 1977.

Brock, J. D., and W. B. Ackerman [1981]. "Scenarios: A Model of Non-determinate Computation," in *Formalization of Programming Concepts*, eds. J. Diaz and I. Ramos, *Lecture Notes in Computer Science*, **107**, New York: Springer-Verlag, 1981, pp. 252–259.

Brown, G. M. [1987]. "Self Stabilizing Distributed Resource Allocation," Ph.D. dissertation, The University of Texas at Austin, Austin, Texas, 1987.

Brownston, L., et al, [1985]. *Programming Expert Systems in OPS5*, Reading, Massachusetts: Addison-Wesley, 1985.

Chandra, A. K., L. J. Stockmeyer, and U. Vishkin [1982]. "A Complexity Theory for Unbounded Fan-in Parallelism," *Proc. 23rd IEEE Symposium on Foundations of Computer Science*, 1982, pp. 1–13.

Chandy, K. M. [1984]. "Concurrent Programming for the Masses," invited address, *3rd Annual ACM Symposium on Principles of Distributed Computing*, Vancouver, British Columbia, Canada, August 5–7, 1984. (The text appears in *Proc. of the 4th Annual ACM Symposium on Principles of Distributed Computing*, 1985, pp. 1–12.)

Chandy, K. M., and L. Lamport [1985]. "Distributed Snapshots: Determining Global States of Distributed Systems," *ACM TOCS*, **3**:1, February 1985, pp. 63–75.

Chandy, K. M., J. Misra, and L. Haas [1983]. "Distributed Deadlock Detection," *ACM TOCS*, **1**:2, May 1983, pp. 144–156.

Chandy, K. M., and J. Misra [1984]. "The Drinking Philosophers Problem," *ACM TOPLAS*, **6**:4, October 1984, pp. 632–646.

Chandy, K. M., and J. Misra [1985]. "On the Nonexistence of Robust Commit Protocol" (unpublished manuscript), Department of Computer Sciences, The University of Texas at Austin, Austin, November 1985.

Chandy, K. M., and J. Misra [1986a]. "An Example of Stepwise Refinement of Distributed Programs: Quiescence Detection," *ACM TOPLAS*, **8**:3, July 1986, pp. 326–343.

Chandy, K. M., and J. Misra [1986b]. "Systolic Algorithms as Programs," *Distributed Computing*, **1**, 1986, pp. 177–183.

Chandy, K. M., and J. Misra [1986c]. "How Processes Learn," *Distributed Computing*, **1**:1, 1986, pp. 40–52.

Chang, E. [1982]. "Echo Algorithms: Depth Parallel Operations on General Graphs," *IEEE Transaction on Software Engineering*, **SE-8**:4, July 1982, pp. 391–401.

Chen, M. C. [1986]. "A Parallel Language and Its Compilation to Multiple Processor Machines or VLSI," *Proc. of 13th Annual Symposium on Principles of Programming Languages*, January 1986, pp. 131–139.

Chen, T. C., V. Y. Lum, and C. Tung [1978]. "The Rebound Sorter: An Efficient Sort Engine for Large Files, in Very Large Data Bases," *Proc. of 4th IEEE International Conference on Very Large Data Bases*, West Berlin, September 13–15, 1978, pp. 312–318.

Clarke, E. M., E. A. Emerson, and A. P. Sistla [1986]. "Automatic Verification of Finite-State Concurrent Systems Using Temporal Logic Specifications," *ACM TOPLAS*, **8**:2, April 1986, pp. 244–263.

Cook, S. A. [1983]. "The Classification of Problems which Have Fast Parallel Algorithms," *Proc. of 24th IEEE Symposium on the Foundations of Computer Science*, 1983.

Conway, M. E. [1963]. "Design of a Separable Transition-Diagram Compiler," *C.ACM*, **6**:7, July 1963, pp. 396–408.

Cooley, J. M., and J. W. Tukey [1965]. "An Algorithm for the Machine Calculation of Complex Fourier Series," *Math. Comp.*, **19**, 1965, pp. 297–301.

Courtois, P. J., F. Heymans, and D. L. Parnas [1971]. "Concurrent Control with 'Readers' and 'Writers,' " *C. ACM*, **14**:10, October 1971, pp. 667–668.

Dijkstra, E. W. [1968]. "Cooperating Sequential Processes," in *Programming Languages*, ed. F. Genuys, New York: Academic Press, 1968, pp. 43–112.

Dijkstra, E. W. [1972]. "Notes on Structured Programming," in *Structured Programming*, eds. O. J. Dahl, E. W. Dijkstra, and C. A. R. Hoare, New York: Academic Press, 1972.

Dijkstra, E. W. [1976]. *A Discipline of Programming*, Englewood Cliffs, New Jersey: Prentice-Hall, 1976.

Dijkstra, E. W. [1978]. "Two Starvation Free Solutions to a General Exclusion Problem," EWD 625, Plataanstraat 5, 5671 Al Nuenen, The Netherlands.

Dijkstra, E. W., et al, [1978]. "On-the-Fly Garbage Collection: An Exercise in Cooperation," *C.ACM*, **21**:11, November 1978, pp. 966–975.

Dijkstra, E. W. [1985]. "The Distributed Snapshot of K. M. Chandy and L. Lamport," in *Control Flow and Data Flow*, ed. M. Broy, Berlin: Springer-Verlag, 1985, pp. 513–517.

Dijkstra, E. W., and C. S. Scholten [1980]. "Termination Detection for Diffusing Computations," *Information Processing Letters*, **11**:1, August 1980.

Dolev, D., and S. Strong [1982]. "Polynomial Algorithms for Multiple Processor Agreement," *Proc. of 14th ACM Symposium on Theory of Computing*, 1982, pp. 401–407.

Dolev, D., et al, [1982]. "An Efficient Byzantine Algorithm without Authentication," Technical Report RJ 3428, IBM, March 1982.

Feijen, W. H. J., and A. Bijlsma [1985]. "An Explanation of Peterson's Mutual Exclusion Algorithm," AB2/WF68, Technological University Eindhoven, 1985.

Fischer, M. J., N. D. Griffeth, and N. A. Lynch [1982]. "Global States of a Distributed System," *IEEE Transactions on Software Engineering*, **SE-8**:3, May 1982, pp. 198–202.

Fischer, M. J. [1983]. "The Consensus Problem in Unreliable Distributed Systems (a Brief Survey)," Yale University Department of Computer Science Technical Report 273, June 1983.

Fischer, M. J., N. A. Lynch, and M. S. Paterson [1985]. "Impossibility of Distributed Consensus with One Faulty Process," *J.ACM*, **32**:2, April 1985, pp. 374–382.

Floyd, R. W. [1962]. "Algorithm 97, Shortest Path," *C.ACM*, **5**, 1962, p. 345.

Forman, I. R. [1986]. Personal communication, 1986.

Forman, I. R. [1987]. "On the Design of Large Distributed Systems," STP-098-86 (Rev. 1.0), Microelectronics and Computer Technology Corp., Austin, Texas, January 1987. (Preliminary version in *Proc. of First International Conference on Computer Languages*, Miami, Florida, October 25–27, 1986.)

Francez, N. [1980]. "Distributed Termination," *ACM TOPLAS*, **2**:1, January 1980, pp. 42–55.

Francez, N. [1986]. *Fairness*, New York: Springer-Verlag, 1986.

Gafni, E. [1986]. "Perspectives on Distributed Network Protocols: A Case for Building Blocks," *Proc. of MILCOM '86*, Monterey, California, October 5–9, 1986.

Gannon, J. D., R. G. Hamlet, and H. D. Mills [1987]. "Theory of Modules," *IEEE Transactions on Software Engineering*, **SE-13**:7, July 1987, pp. 820–829.

Gehani, N. [1983]. *Ada: An Advanced Introduction*, Englewood-Cliffs, New Jersey: Prentice-Hall Software Series, 1983.

Goldschlager, L. M. [1977]. "Synchronous Parallel Computation," Ph.D. dissertation, University of Toronto, Toronto, Ontario, Canada (1977). (See also *Proc. of 10th ACM Symposium on the Theory of Computing*, 1978, pp. 89–94, and *J.ACM*, **29**:4, October 1982, pp. 1073–1086.)

Gries, D. [1981]. *The Science of Programming*, New York: Springer-Verlag, 1981.

Hailpern, B. T. [1980]. "Verifying Concurrent Processes Using Temporal Logic," Ph.D. dissertation, Stanford University, Stanford, California, 1980. (See also *Lecture Notes in Computer Science*, **129**, Berlin: Springer-Verlag, 1982.)

Hehner, E. C. R. [1984]. *The Logic of Programming*, London: Prentice-Hall International, 1984.

Hillis, W. D. [1985]. *The Connection Machine*, Cambridge, Massachusetts: The MIT Press, 1985.

Hoare, C. A. R. [1969]. "An Axiomatic Basis for Computer Programming," *C.ACM*, **12**, 1969, pp. 576–580.

Hoare, C. A. R. [1978]. "Communicating Sequential Processes," *C.ACM*, **21**:8, August 1978, pp. 666–677.

Hoare, C. A. R. [1984]. *Communicating Sequential Processes*, London: Prentice-Hall International, 1984.

Huang, C. H., and C. Lengauer [1987]. "An Implemented Method for Incremental Systolic Design," in *Parallel Architectures*, Vol. I, eds. J. W. deBakker, A. J. Nijman, and P. C. Treleaven, *Lecture Notes in Computer Science* **258**, Berlin: Springer-Verlag, 1987, pp. 160–177.

Hudak, P. [1986]. "Para-Functional Programming," *IEEE Computer*, August 1986, pp. 60–70.

IEEE [1987a]. *Computer*, **20**:6, Computer Society of the IEEE, June 1987.

IEEE [1987b]. *Computer*, **20**:7, Computer Society of the IEEE, July 1987.

Jonsson, B. [1987]. "Compositional Verification of Distributed Systems," Ph.D. dissertation, Uppsala University, Uppsala, Sweden, 1987.

Kahn, G. [1974]. "The Semantics of a Simple Language for Parallel Programming," *Proc. of IFIP Congress 74*, Amsterdam: North Holland, 1974.

Karp, R. M., and R. E. Miller [1969]. "Parallel Program Schemata," *J.Computer and System Sciences*, **3**, 1969, pp. 147–195.

Katz, S. [1987]. "A Superimposition Control Construct for Distributed Systems" (unpublished manuscript), The Technion, Israel, 1987.

Keller, R. M. [1978]. "Denotational Models for Parallel Programs with Indeterminate Operators," in *Formal Descriptions of Programming Concepts*, ed. E. J. Neuhold, Amsterdam: North-Holland, 1978, pp. 337–365.

Knuth, D. E. [1973]. *The Art of Computer Programming*, Vol. 3, *Sorting and Searching*, Reading, Massachusetts: Addison-Wesley, 1973.

Kosaraju, S. R. [1969]. "Computations on Iterative Automata," Ph.D. dissertation, University of Pennsylvania, Philadelphia, Pennsylvania, 1969.

Kosaraju, S. R. [1982]. "Decidability of Reachability in Vector Addition Systems," *Proc. 14th Annual ACM Symposium on the Theory of Computing*, 1982, pp. 267–280.

Kowalski, R. [1979]. *Logic for Problem Solving*, Amsterdam, North-Holland, 1979.

Kung, H. T., and C. E. Leiserson [1978]. "Systolic Arrays (for VLSI)," in *Sparse Matrix Proc.*, 1978, eds. I. S. Duff and G. W. Stewart, 1979, Philadelphia, Pennsylvania: SIAM, pp. 256–282.

Ladner, R. E., and M. J. Fischer [1980]. "Parallel Prefix Computation," *J.ACM*, **27**, 1980, pp. 831–838.

Lamport, L. [1974]. "A New Solution of Dijkstra's Concurrent Programming Problem," *C.ACM*, **17**:8, August 1974, pp. 453–455.

Lamport, L. [1977]. "Proving the Correctness of Multiprocess Programs," *IEEE, Trans. on Software Engineering* **SE-3**:2, March 1977, pp. 125–143.

Lamport, L. [1978]. "Time, Clocks, and the Ordering of Events in a Distributed System," *C.ACM*, **21**:7, July 1978, pp. 558–565.

Lamport, L. [1982]. "An Assertional Correctness Proof of a Distributed Algorithm," *Science of Computer Programming*, **2**, Amsterdam: North Holland, 1982, pp. 175–206.

Lamport, L. [1983a]. "Reasoning about Nonatomic Operations," *Proc. of the 10th Annual ACM Symposium on Principles of Programming Languages*, Austin, Texas, January 24–26, 1983, pp. 28–37.

Lamport, L. [1983b]. "Specifying Concurrent Program Modules," *ACM TOPLAS*, **6**:2, 1983, pp. 190–222.

Lamport, L. [1983c]. "Solved Problems, Unsolved Problems, and Non-Problems in Concurrency," invited address, *2nd Annual ACM Symposium on Principles of Distributed Computing*, Montreal, Canada, 1983. (The text appears in *Proc. of the 3rd Annual ACM Symposium on Principles of Distributed Computing*, 1984.)

Lamport, L., and F. B. Schneider [1984]. "The 'Hoare Logic' of CSP, and All That," *ACM TOPLAS*, **6**:2, April 1984, pp. 281–296.

Lehmann, D., A. Pnueli, and J. Stavi [1981]. "Impartiality, Justice and Fairness: The Ethics of Concurrent Termination," *Proc. of 8th ICALP*, Acre, Israel, July 1981. In: *LNCS 115* (eds. O. Kariv and S. Even), Springer-Verlag, 1981.

Lynch, N. A., and M. J. Fischer [1983]. "A Technique for Decomposing Algorithms which Use a Single Shared Variable," *Journal of Computer and System Sciences*, **27**:3, December 1983, pp. 350–377.

Lynch, N. A., and M. R. Tuttle [1987]. "Hierarchical Correctness Proofs for Distributed Algorithms," *Proc. of 6th Annual ACM Symposium on*

Principles of Distributed Computing, Vancouver, British Columbia, Canada, 1987.

Lynch, N. A., and J. L. Welch [1987]. "Synthesis of Efficient Drinking Philosopher Algorithms," unpublished manuscript, 1987.

Manna, Z., and A. Pnueli [1983]. "How to Cook a Temporal Proof System for Your Pet Language," *Proc. of the 10th Annual ACM Symposium on Principles of Programming Languages*, Austin, Texas, 1983.

Martin, A. J. [1985]. "The Probe: An Addition to Communication Primitives," *Information Processing Letters*, **20**, April 1985, pp. 125–130.

Martin, A. J. [1986]. "Compiling Communicating Processes into Delay-Insensitive VLSI Circuits," *Journal of Distributed Computing*, **1**:3, 1986.

Mayr, E. [1984]. "An Algorithm for the General Petri Net Reachability Problem," *SIAM Journal of Computing*, **13**:3, 1984, pp. 441–460.

Menasce, D. A., and R. R. Muntz [1979]. "Locking and Deadlock Detection in Distributed Data Bases," *IEEE Transactions on Software Engineering*, **SE-5**:3, May 1979, pp. 195–202.

Milner, R. [1983]. "Calculi for Synchrony and Asynchrony," *Theoretical Computer Science*, **25**, 1983, pp. 267–310.

Misra, J. [1986]. "Axioms for Memory Access in Asynchronous Hardware Systems," *ACM TOPLAS*, **8**:1, January 1986, pp. 142–153.

Misra, J., and K. M. Chandy [1981]. "Proofs of Networks of Processes," *IEEE Transaction on Software Engineering*, **SE-7**:4, July 1981.

Misra, J., and K. M. Chandy [1982]. "A Distributed Graph Algorithm: Knot Detection," *ACM TOPLAS*, **4**:4, October 1982, pp. 678–686.

Mok, A. [1987]. Personal communication, 1987.

O'Donnell, M. J. [1985]. *Equational Logic as a Programming Language*, Cambridge, Massachusetts: The MIT Press, 1985.

Owicki, S., and D. Gries [1976]. "An Axiomatic Proof Technique for Parallel Programs I," *Acta Informatica*, **6**:1, 1976, pp. 319–340.

Owicki, S., and L. Lamport [1982]. "Proving Liveness Properties of Concurrent Programs," *ACM TOPLAS*, **4**:3, July 1982, pp. 455–495.

Parker, R. A., et al, [1980]. "Abstract Interface Specifications for the A-7E Device Interface Module," U.S. Navy Research Laboratories Memorandum, Report 4385, November 1980.

Pease, M., R. Shostak, and L. Lamport [1980]. "Reaching Agreement in the Presence of Faults," *J.ACM*, **27**:2, April 1980, pp. 228–234.

Peterson, G. L. [1981]. "Myths about the Mutual Exclusion Problem," *Information Processing Letters*, **12**:3, June 1981, pp. 115–116.

Peterson, J. L. [1981]. *Petri Net Theory and Modeling of Systems*, Englewood Cliffs, New Jersey: Prentice-Hall, 1981.

Peterson, J. L., and A. Silberschatz [1983]. *Operating Systems Concepts*, Reading, Massachusetts: Addison-Wesley, 1983.

Pippenger, N. [1979]. "On Simultaneous Resource Bounds," *Proc. of 20th IEEE Symposium on Foundations of Computer Science*, 1979, pp. 307–311.

Pnueli, A. [1981]. "The Temporal Semantics of Concurrent Programs," *Theoretical Computer Science*, **13**, 1981, pp. 45–60.

Pnueli, A. [1987]. "Temporal Logic," in *Proceedings University of Texas Year of Programming*, Vol. I, *Concurrent Programming*, ed. C. A. R. Hoare, Reading, Massachusetts: Addison-Wesley, 1987.

Rem, M. [1985]. "Concurrent Computations and VLSI Circuits," in *Control Flow and Data Flow: Concepts of Distributed Programming*, ed. M. Broy, Berlin: Springer-Verlag, 1985.

Ricart, G., and A. Agrawala [1981]. "An Optimal Algorithm for Mutual Exclusion in Computer Networks," *C.ACM*, **24**:1, Janaury 1981, pp. 9–17.

Schwarz, J. T. [1980]. "Ultracomputers," *ACM TOPLAS*, **2**:4, 1980, pp. 484–521.

Seitz, C. [1980]. "System Timing," in *Introduction to VLSI Systems*, eds. C. Mead and L. Conway, Reading, Massachusetts: Addison-Wesley, 1980.

Seitz, C. [1984]. "Concurrent VLSI Architectures," *IEEE Transactions on Computers*, **C-33**:12, December 1984.

Seitz, C. [1985]. "The Cosmic Cube," *C.ACM*, **28**:1, January 1985, pp. 22–33.

Shankar, A. U., and S. S. Lam [1987]. "Time Dependent Distributed Systems: Proving Safety, Liveness and Real-Time Properties," *Distributed Computing*, **2**:2, August, 1987, pp. 61–79.

Singh, A. K., J. H. Anderson, and M. G. Gouda [1987]. "The Elusive Atomic Register," *Proc. of 6th Annual ACM Symposium on Principles of Distributed Computing*, Vancouver, British Columbia, Canada, 1987.

Srikanth, T. K., and S. Toueg [1987]. "Simulating Authenticated Broadcasts to Derive Simple Fault Tolerant Algorithms," *Distributed Computing*, **2**:2, August, 1987, pp. 80–94.

Tannenbaum, Andrew S. [1981]. *Computer Networks*, Englewood Cliffs, New Jersey: Prentice-Hall, 1981.

Tarjan, R. E. [1983]. *Data Structures and Network Algorithms*, Philadelphia, Pennsylvania: Society of Industrial and Applied Mathematics, 1983.

Turner, D. A. [1985]. "Functional Programs as Executable Specifications," in *Mathematical Logic and Programming Languages*, eds. C. A. R. Hoare and J. C. Shepherdson, Englewood Cliffs, New Jersey: Prentice-Hall, 1985.

Turpin, R., and B. A. Coan [1984]. "Extending Binary Byzantine Agreement to Multi-valued Byzantine Agreement," *Information Processing Letters*, **18**, 1984, pp. 73–76.

van de Snepscheut, J. L. A. [1985a]. "Algorithms for On-the Fly Garbage Collection Revisited," JAN 118, Groningen, The Netherlands: University of Groningen, 1985.

van de Snepscheut, J. L. A. [1985b]. "Trace Theory and VLSI Design," *Lecture Notes in Computer Sciences* **200**, Berlin: Springer-Verlag, 1985.

van de Snepscheut, J. L. A. [1986]. "Distributed Warshall's Algorithm," *Science of Computer Programming*, **7**, 1986, pp. 55–60.

van de Snepscheut, J. L. A. [1987]. Personal communication, 1987.

van de Snepscheut, J. L. A., and J. B. Swenker [1987]. "On the Design of Some Systolic Algorithms," JAN 131a, Groningen, The Netherlands: University of Groningen, 1987.

van Gasteren, A. J. M., and E. W. Dijkstra [1985]. "On Notation," AVG65/EWD 950, The University of Texas at Austin, Austin, Texas, 1985.

Van Scoy, F. L. [1980]. "The Parallel Recognition of Classes of Graphs," *IEEE Trans. on Computers*, **C-29**:7, July 1980, pp. 563–570.

Warshall, S. [1962]. "A Theorem on Boolean Matrices," *J.ACM*, **9**, 1962, pp. 11–12.

Wirth, N. [1971]. "The Programming Language Pascal," *Acta Informatica*, **1**, 1971, pp. 35–63.

Young, D. M., and R. T. Gregory [1973]. *A Survey of Numerical Mathematics*, Vol. II, Reading, Massachusetts: Addison-Wesley, 1973.

Index